International Investment Law: A Chinese Perspective

Increasing and intensified cross-border economic exchange such as trade and investment is an important feature of globalization. In the past, a distinction could be made between capital importing and exporting countries, or host and home countries for foreign direct investment ("FDI"). Due to globalization, FDI is presently made by and in both developed and developing countries. Differences in political, economic, and legal systems and culture are no longer obstacles for FDI, and to varying degrees the economic development of almost all countries is closely linked with the inflow of FDI.

This book conducts critical assessments of aspects of current international law on FDI, focusing on cases decided by the tribunals of the International Centre for Settlement of Investment Disputes ("ICSID") and other tribunals, as well as decisions of annulment and *ad hoc* Committees of the ICSID. In examining such cases, Guiguo Wang takes into account the Chinese culture and China's practice in the related areas. The book explores topics including: the development and trend of international investment law; unilateral, bilateral, and multilateral mechanisms for encouraging and protecting FDI; determination of qualified investors and investments and consent as conditions for protection; relative and absolute standards of treatment; determination of expropriation in practice; assessment of compensation for expropriation; difficulties in enforcing investment arbitral awards; and alternatives for improving the existing system.

The book will be of great use and interest to scholars, practitioners, and students of international investment law and international economic law, Asian law, and Chinese studies.

Guiguo Wang is Chair Professor of Chinese and Comparative Law and Director of the Centre for Judicial Education and Research at the City University of Hong Kong.

Routledge Research in International Economic Law

Available:

**Recognition and Regulation of
Safeguard Measures Under GATT/
WTO**
Sheela Rai

**The Interaction between WTO Law
and External International Law**
The Constrained Openness of WTO
Law
Ronnie R.F. Yearwood

**Human Rights, Natural Resource
and Investment Law in a
Globalised World**
Shades of Grey in the Shadow of the
Law
Lorenzo Cotula

**The Domestic Politics of Negotiating
International Trade**
Intellectual Property Rights in
US-Colombia and US-Peru Free Trade
Agreements
Johanna von Braun

**Foreign Investment and Dispute
Resolution Law and Practice in Asia**
Vivienne Bath and Luke Nottage (eds.)

**Improving International Investment
Agreements**
Armand De Mestral and Céline Lévesque (eds.)

**Public Health in International
Investment Law and Arbritration**
Valentina Vadi

The WTO and the Environment
Development of Competence beyond
Trade
James Watson

**Foreign Direct Investment and
Human Development**
The Law and Economics of International
Investment Agreements
*Olivier De Schutter, Johan Swinnen and Jan
Wouters*

Microtrade
A New System of International Trade
with Volunteerism Towards Poverty
Elimination
Yong-Shik Lee

**Science and Technology in
International Economic Law**
Balancing Competing Interests
Bryan Mercurio and Kuei-Jung Ni

**The WTO and Infant Industry
Promotion in Developing Countries**
Perspectives on the Chinese Large Civil
Aircraft
Juan He

Trade Remedies
A Development Perspective
Asif Qureshi

**International Investment Law: A
Chinese Perspective**
Guiguo Wang

Forthcoming:

**Culture and International Economic
Law**
Valentina Vadi and Bruno de Witte

**Equity and Equitable Principles in
the World Trade Organization**
Addressing Conflicts and Overlaps
between the WTO and Other Regimes
Anastasios Gourgourinis

International Investment Law: A Chinese Perspective

Guiguo Wang

Routledge
Taylor & Francis Group

LONDON AND NEW YORK

First published 2015
by Routledge
2 Park Square, Milton Park, Abingdon, Oxfordshire OX14 4RN

and by Routledge
711 Third Avenue, New York, NY 10017

First issued in paperback 2016

Routledge is an imprint of the Taylor & Francis Group, an informa business

British Library Cataloguing in Publication Data
A catalogue record for this book is available from the British Library

Library of Congress Cataloging-in-Publication Data
Wang, Guiguo, author.
A Chinese perspective on international law / Guiguo Wang.
pages cm. -- (Routledge research in international economic law)
Includes index.
ISBN 978-0-203-73868-9 (hbk) -- ISBN 978-0-415-50003-6 (ebk)
1. Investments, Foreign--Law and legislation--China. I. Title.
KNQ3202.W359 2014
346.51'092--dc23
2014007760

ISBN 13: 978-1-138-21524-5 (pbk)
ISBN 13: 978-0-415-50003-6 (hbk)

Typeset in 10/12 Baskerville MT by
Servis Filmsetting Ltd, Stockport, Cheshire

Contents

Foreword

Every legal arrangement is always under pressure for change. The content of each arrangement reflects the shared interests of those who have shaped it. As soon as an arrangement is installed, it begins to be tested and challenged—not only by those who never benefited from it, but even by actors within the entities and communities which established and participated in the arrangement if they come to believe that their own interests are insufficiently served or have changed and especially if those actors have since acquired more power. Thus law, for all its pretensions to being stable and unchanging, is actually a continuously dynamic dialectical process of agreement, challenge, adjustment, accommodation, new agreement, new challenges—*ad infinitum*.

This dialectic is particularly dramatic in contemporary international economic law. Thanks to the globalization of the world economy and the imperative compelling all governments to secure the economic development and enhancement of life opportunities for their constituents, we witness the creation of specialized international institutions, rapid developments in bilateral, regional, and multilateral conventional international law and the proliferation of publicly accessible third-party decisions.

Nowhere is this dynamic more pronounced than in international investment law. All states now vie for foreign investment and the reasons are hardly recondite. China, pre-1978, demonstrated, by example, the virtual impossibility of autochthonous economic development; China, post-1978, demonstrated, again by example, the contribution which direct foreign investment can make to rapid national economic development. But it is not only governments that are impelling the dynamism in this area of law: profit-maximizing entities worldwide are driven by their own economic imperatives to seek venues for foreign investment, whether for natural resources, more efficient venues for production or markets for their products. We are not speaking of a few actors. There are approximately 80,000 multinational enterprises, which are, by definition, foreign direct investors. In turn, these entities have some 100,000 affiliates. Add to that the almost 3000 bilateral and multilateral investment treaties and the hundreds of investment arbitrations each year and one can begin to appreciate the inter-stimulating factors propelling the velocity of change in this area of international law.

Inevitably, this has had consequences for the sociology of legal knowledge. In this new milieu, it is no longer useful for scholars to confine themselves to synthesizing and restating "the rules" in black-letter formulations. Treatises which are comprised of "snapshots" of the law at a particular moment are more and more time-bound and, for that reason, less and less reliable guides for behavior and decision. Such treatises must be replaced by more searching analyses of decision trends, their conditioning factors and projections of possible future decisions. In a context of relentless change, the task of the contemporary scholar must also include identifying and appraising the policies at play, their purported justifications, the conflicting claims with respect to them and, above all, proposing, *de lege ferenda*, arrangements that may better contribute to the common interests of the world community.

Dr Wang Guiguo's comprehensive treatise is an outstanding example of this form of scholarship. Long recognized as a world expert on international trade law, Dean Wang has here produced a comprehensive treatise on international investment law that will serve as the indispensable *vade mecum* for practitioners, scholars, and students in this area.

Notwithstanding its sub-title, this book is not so much a Chinese perspective on international investment law as a systematic examination and appraisal of trends in decisions in international investment law. In the short period since 1978, China has emerged as a major participant in the world economy and, in particular, in the importation *and* exportation of direct foreign investment. It has also become a full participant in the international law-making process to the point that referring to a "Chinese perspective" on international investment law is as anachronistic as viewing the author of this extraordinary book as a "Chinese" scholar, rather than as the world class international legal authority that he has, again and again, proved himself to be.

W. Michael Reisman
Yale Law School
New Haven, Connecticut

April 10, 2014

Preface

Seven years ago, Professor W. Michael Reisman of Yale Law School—my mentor—visited the School of Law, City University of Hong Kong. Out of his love for students and to support the School of Law, Professor Reisman agreed to co-teach with me a course on Selected Problems of International Investment Law. What an honor for me and what an opportunity for the students! Professor Reisman adopted the syllabus that he used in the Yale Law School as well as the teaching method he employed there—examination of arbitral awards by students. As Professor Reisman was unable to teach in person on a weekly basis in Hong Kong, part of the course was taught via video link facilities, which was a novel experience for all of us. This co-taught course was offered for six years in a row and was a complete success every time.

Students say that "Professor Reisman's class is like a feast for the mind." This is true for a number of reasons. In the first place, Professor Reisman always links the most up-to-date materials, including cases, with the history and evolution of the subject. Apart from acquiring contemporary knowledge, students have opportunities to review the development of any given issue. Second, students are always provided with plenty of opportunities to express themselves. Even if they say something incorrect, Professor Reisman still encourages them by patiently explaining the issues involved. Third, it is absolutely an enjoyable experience listening to Professor Reisman's scrutinization of cases and related issues. The approach that he takes, his penetrating, detailed, and comprehensive analysis and his foresightedness are not only forcefully convincing but also enlightening. This is, of course, nothing new for those who know Professor Reisman well. Last, but certainly not least, is Professor Reisman's humility. Before meeting him, students were naturally nervous, for they knew what a great jurist he is. Yet, in less than 30 minutes into his first class, students started actively to participate. This came about because Professor Reisman always treats students as his equals and listens to their views carefully, sometimes even taking out his small notebook to write down what students say. In such an environment, I learned a great deal myself—about investment law as well as the way that Professor Reisman conducts his class.

To have a great jurist as teacher is very fortunate. To have the opportunity to continue to receive education from one's teacher after school time has ended is fortuitous. Being just such a lucky person, I must do justice to this heaven-sent opportunity. The result is the current book, which has received the direct benefit of Professor Reisman's teachings, even though it may not accurately reflect their quality.

This book is designed as a brand new book, although I did an earlier book on international investment law (in the Chinese language) several years ago. Essentially based on the syllabus of the course on Selected Problems of International Investment Law, this book is divided into 11 chapters, namely: 1. International investment and law; 2. The control system pertinent to foreign direct investment; 3. Determination of foreign investors; 4. Determination of foreign investments; 5. Consent as a condition of jurisdiction; 6. The absolute standards of treatment; 7. The relative standards of treatment; 8. Expropriation; 9. Compensation for violation of obligations; 10. State responsibility and enforcement of obligations; and 11. Conclusions and alternatives. The first chapter serves as an introduction to the history of foreign direct investment and international investment law, whilst the second chapter outlines the mechanisms pertinent to foreign direct investment. The rest of the chapters—with the last one as an exception—deal with the substantive issues of international investment law. At the end of each chapter, there is a section particularly devoted to the Chinese practice in the subject area, which is followed by conclusions and alternatives. The last chapter addresses the general issues and offers some conclusions and alternatives for advancing the development of international investment law.

In writing the book, my intellectual indebtedness to Professor Michael Reisman is immeasurable. This author is also lucky to have the invaluable assistance of Mr James Boyce, who has, as senior research assistant, contributed to the book at all stages from the beginning to the completion of writing and in various forms. The School of Law of City University of Hong Kong has supported me all along. I am deeply grateful to all of them. I am of course solely and fully responsible for any errors and mistakes contained in the book.

Last but not the least, I must thank my wife Priscilla and my sons Hongxi and Chenxi for their unswerving support and generous tolerance, without which it would not have been possible to complete this book.

Guiguo Wang
February 8, 2014

Table of cases

ICSID Arbitrations

UNCITRAL Arbitrations

Iran–United States Claims Tribunal Arbitrations

Stockholm Chamber of Commerce Arbitrations

Other Arbitrations

Permanent Court of International Justice/International Court of Justice Cases

European Court of Human Rights Cases

South African Development Community Tribunal

National Courts
France

Hong Kong

United Kingdom

United States

1 International investment and law

Globalization is the principal trend of the contemporary world. It is irresistible and its impact exists in every corner of the world and touches everyone's life. An important feature of globalization is increasing and intensified cross-border economic exchanges, such as trade and investment. In the past, a distinction could be made between capital importing and exporting countries, or host and home countries for foreign direct investment ("FDI"). Nowadays, however, as a result of globalization, FDI is both imported and exported by developed and developing countries alike. Differences in political, economic, and legal systems, history, and culture are no longer obstacles to FDI. In fact, the economic development of almost all countries is closely linked with, if not heavily dependent upon, the inflow of FDI, even though the degree of dependence on it may differ from country to country. It is often the case that the very legitimacy and survival of a national government may depend on the performance of FDI.

Against the background of globalization, and thanks to the rapid advancement of science and technology—especially information technology, including the Internet and computers—the sources of FDI have now become very diversified. Not long ago, the making of international investments was an exclusive privilege of multinational corporations. Nowadays, small and medium-sized companies, as well as individuals are frequent international investors.

The legal regime regulating FDI has been constantly evolving hand-in-hand with the making of cross-border investments, although not at the same pace. Of course, no system is either perfect or without need for improvement, and that truism applies to both the national and international legal regimes governing FDI.

I. A brief history of international investment

Investment takes various forms, which can be categorized into domestic investment and international investment in geographic terms, and foreign direct investment and foreign indirect investment in terms of its nature. Traditionally, foreign direct investment mainly referred to controlling shares of the enterprise concerned, e.g. a national of one country investing in a corporation established in another country and exercising effective control over it. Effective control by a foreign investor of a corporation's management and decision-making was also considered as direct investment.[1] However, there are different views with regard to "effective" control. In the United States, for example, this means that the investor must own at least 10 percent of the total shares or effective control cannot be realized. The minimum share percentage for effective control is 5 percent in some countries, but it is 50 percent in some others.[2] Indirect investment may also take different forms, including the extension of loans, the provision of management services, technology licensing, equipment sales, and on-the-spot instruction, among others.

The history of international investment can be traced back at least to the initial phases of capitalism. Such early foreign investment vehicles as the East India Company, the Hudson's Bay Company, etc.[3] were established against specific historical and political backgrounds and to serve various purposes. For example, some were incorporated to acquire cheap labor and raw materials, while others aimed to enter into potential markets.

Modern international investment emerged mainly after World War II, especially after many former European colonies gained independence. Roughly speaking, international investment can be divided into four phases. The first phase comprises the period before the 1950s, when international investment was mainly made among the Western developed countries, especially from the United States to Europe and Canada, whilst European countries had to focus on their domestic economic reconstruction to recover from the War instead of making outward investment. Most international investors at that time were US and UK transnational companies ("TNCs") that invested mainly in overseas oil enterprises and raw material extraction projects.

The second phase extended from the late 1950s to the early 1970s, as two important regional economic blocs, namely the European Common Market and the European Free Trade Union, were established in 1958 and 1960, respectively. They significantly expanded the regional market and attracted massive foreign investment inflows. Moreover, some Western European countries, and Japan, loosened their domestic restrictions on foreign investment, which further stimulated international investment. For example, in 1961 the former West Germany abolished restrictions imposed on the German steel industry regarding foreign investment, while Japan began to liberalize its outward investment in about 1967. In general, during this period most outward foreign investment was made by the United States and the United Kingdom, who accounted for 50 percent and 16 percent respectively of total world FDI.[4]

1 For a definition of FDI in the 1960s, see International Monetary Fund, *IMF Balance of Payments Yearbook*, IMF, Washington, D.C., 1964, Vol. 16, p. 10.

2 For a definition of foreign direct investment, see the World Bank Data Portal; available at: http://data.worldbank.org/indicator/BX.KLT.DINV.CD.WD. See also Organisation for Economic Co-operation and Development, *OECD Benchmark Definition of Foreign Direct Investment*, 4th ed., OECD 2008, especially ch 3, "Main Concepts and Definitions of Foreign Direct Investment," pp. 39–57; available at: http://dx.doi.org/10.1787/9789264045743-5-en.

3 See Andreas F. Lowenfield, *International Private Investment*, Matthew Bender, New York, 1982, p. 1.

4 See Stefan Robock and Kenneth Simmonds, *International Business and Multinational Enterprises*, Richard D. Irwin, Inc., Homewood, Illinois, 1983, p. 2.

The third phase started in the early 1970s and lasted until the mid-1990s. During this phase, Japan and Western Europe achieved remarkable economic development that was even able to counterbalance that of the United States. As a result, US influence in the world economy was comparatively weakened, as was reflected by the decrease in its share of global investment and the increase of Japan's and the Western European countries' FDI inflows to the United States. This was closely related to the United States' abandonment of the obligation to exchange US dollars for gold while adopting a floating exchange rate system, which subsequently led to a significant depreciation of the international value of the US dollar. That depreciation enabled foreign investors to acquire US enterprises at a lower cost and made it more economical to manufacture products within the United States than to export to it. Investment outflows from the United States and the United Kingdom decreased to 40 percent and 12 percent of the world total respectively, while foreign investment inflows to these two countries nearly doubled. During the same period, foreign investment outflows from Japan and the former West Germany increased by fivefold and fourfold, respectively.[5]

Generally speaking, before the late 1970s international investment was mainly made between developed countries, as three-fourths of total world investment was made within the developed world, while one-fourth was made from developed to developing countries.[6] So far as developed countries were concerned, Canada had long been an ideal host country for foreign investment. Although its gross domestic product ("GDP") only accounted for 2 percent of the world total, it attracted 14 percent of the total foreign investment. At the same time, with its decreasing outflow of investment, the United States accepted more and more FDI. The United Kingdom and other Western European countries also became important FDI host countries. In comparison, Japan ranked as the developed country that hosted the least amount of FDI, mainly because its domestic policies did not encourage FDI and any foreign investor proposing to enter the Japanese market had to do so in the form of a joint venture or technology transfer.

Another feature of FDI before the late 1970s was its close connection with geography and history. Investment between geographically neighboring countries, such as the United States and Canada or the Western European countries, was quite active. Investors from countries such as the United Kingdom and France tended to invest in those countries having historical connections with their home countries, e.g. previous British colonies or the Commonwealth countries and the former French colonies. Investment from developed countries to developing countries mainly concentrated on oil-exporting countries and tax havens, which together absorbed about one-fourth of the world total FDI. The so-called tax havens are those countries which attract FDI by means of low tax rates, including Brazil, Mexico, Argentina, Peru, Trinidad and Tobago, India, Malaysia,

---

5 Ibid., p. 28.
6 Id.

Singapore, Hong Kong, and the Philippines, etc., which accounted for around 60 percent of the FDI to the developing world.

Another feature of international investment from the early 1970s to the mid-1990s was that investment was broadly made among developed, developing and socialist countries alike. This, on the one hand, reflected the fact that the economic interdependence of the international community was becoming more developed while, on the other hand, developing countries had become more mature in terms of protecting their state sovereignty while accepting foreign investment. Meanwhile, the development of worldwide economic interdependence made socialist countries, including China, aware that international cooperation was necessary to develop their domestic economies. After the 1980s, the total investment outflows from market economies reached US$500 billion per year. Although Eastern European countries did not release statistics on the amount of their foreign investments, they had established more than 700 manufacturing and trading companies in other countries by 1976. Therefore, their total amount of foreign investment would have been considerable.[7] In this period, host countries, both developed and developing, also invested in other countries. For example, in 1980 the Kuwait Investment Authority acquired 10 percent of the shares of the Volkswagen Corporation's subsidiary in Brazil, as well as 14 percent and 25 percent respectively of the shares of the German enterprises Benz Corporation and Korf-Stahl Steel Company.[8] Other developing countries and territories, including Brazil, Hong Kong, India, Mexico, the Philippines, and South Korea, also invested overseas.

The fourth phase is that which has run from the mid-1990s to the present. The international community in this phase is characterized by widespread economic integration. Of course, economic integration is attributable to many elements, including the technology revolution marked by information technologies that have impacted many traditional concepts and customs. The establishment of the World Trade Organization ("WTO") and regional organizations, as well as the conclusion of such treaties as the Energy Charter Treaty, has undoubtedly legalized, institutionalized, and internationalized the changes in international economic transactions and exchanges brought about by technology developments. State borders are no longer a significant barrier to investment, and the traditional notion of state sovereignty is undergoing notable restriction.

This period has seen a profound expansion of FDI worldwide. From 1996 to 2000, global FDI inflows increased rapidly and reached the historical peak of US$1413 billion in 2000. FDI inflows in 2000 were 20 times higher than they were in 1980. The average annual growth rate of FDI inflows between 1980 and 2000 was some 16 percent higher than that of world GDP (in current US dollar values).[9] After three years of shrinkage, FDI began to recover in 2004. That

---

7   See United Nations, *Transnational Corporations in World Development*, UN, New York, 1978, p. 53.

8   See *The Wall Street Journal* (June 6, 1980).

9   Laza Kekic and Karl P. Sauvant (eds.), *World Investment Prospects to 2010: Boom or Backlash?*, The Economist Intelligence Unit Ltd., London, 2006, p. 22.

year saw a 22 percent increase over 2003, amounting to US$801.7 billion. In 2005, the global FDI inflows increased to US$954.8 billion, a 19 percent increase over that of 2004.[10] According to the United Nations Conference on Trade and Development ("UNCTAD"), the total value of global FDI inflows increased to US$1510 billion in 2011 but then fell to US$1350 billion in 2012; UNCTAD also forecast that the overall sum invested in FDI projects would be no higher than US$1450 billion in 2013, whilst in 2014 and 2015 this figure would grow to US$1600 billion and US$1800 billion, respectively.[11]

Developed countries continue to be both the major origins and destinations of global FDI. It is worth noting, however, that the investment inflow to developing countries has improved substantially. In 2006, more than 90 percent of FDI went to developed countries and more than 90 percent of cross-border merger and acquisitions in developed countries were concluded by firms from other developed countries.[12] In 2012, investment inflows to developing countries for the first time exceeded those to developed countries, accounting for 52 percent of all FDI, while developed countries received only 42 percent.[13] Except for 1990–1991, 1998, and 2002–2003, the FDI outflow from developing and transitional economies has increased steadily. The capital outflow from these countries and territories (excluding offshore financial centers) increased from US$4 billion in 1985 to a peak of US$462 billion in 2010, which accounted for 32 percent of the world total.[14] In 1990, only six developing and transition economies reported outward FDI stocks of more than US$5 billion; but by 2011, that threshold had been exceeded by 49 developing and transition economies of which 24 reported outward FDI stocks of more than US$10 billion.[15] South-South FDI has increased rapidly in the past 15 years. The FDI among developing and transitional economies increased from US$2 billion in 1985 to US$60 billion in 2004, which mainly took the form of intra-regional investment.[16] In 2011, UNCTAD noted that outward FDI from transition economies into extractive industries in developing countries was continuing to expand and that 65 percent by value of FDI projects of the BRICs countries (Brazil, Russia, India, and China) were invested in developing and transition economies.[17] According to the statistics released by the

10 Ibid., Table 1, p. 19.
11 For further information, see UNCTAD, *World Investment Report 2013, Global Value Chains: Investment and Trade for Development*, United Nations, New York and Geneva, 2013, p. ix; available at: http://www.unctad.org/en/PublicationsLibrary/wir2013_en.pdf.
12 UNCTAD, *World Investment Report 2006*, United Nations, New York and Geneva, 2006, p. 87; available at: http://www.unctad.org/en/docs/wir2006_en.pdf.
13 *World Investment Report 2013, supra*, note 11, p. ix.
14 United Nations Conference on Trade and Development, *World Investment Report 2012: Towards a New Generation of Investment Policies*, United Nations, New York and Geneva, 2012, p. xiv and Annex Table I.1; available at: http://www.unctad-docs.org/files/UNCTAD-WIR2012-Full-en.pdf. The year 2011 saw a slight decline in FDI outflows from developing countries and transitional economies, to US$457 billion, which was still 27% of the world total; id.
15 Ibid., Annex Table I.2.
16 *World Investment Report 2006, supra*, note 12, p. 21.
17 *World Investment Report 2012, supra*, note 14, p. 5.

Chinese Ministry of Commerce, China's outflow of capital was very close to the total amount of the inflow of capital in 2013.[18]

Cross-border mergers and acquisitions were the main source of the sharp increase of FDI in 1999–2001 and 2004–2005. The value of transnational mergers and acquisitions rose by 88 percent in 2004, to US$716 billion, and the number of deals rose by 20 percent, to 6134.[19] The value of transnational mergers and acquisitions within the developed world accounted for three-fourths of the world total for the period from 2002 to 2005.[20] However, in 2005, companies from Western Europe, especially France, took the place of US companies, becoming the top investors.[21] Although the value of mergers and acquisitions worldwide shrank in 2003, 2009 and again in 2012, it has continued increasing in the emerging markets since 2002.[22] In 2010, there were 5405 cross-border mergers and acquisitions, the total value of which amounted to US$338 billion. Of these, developed countries' TNCs accounted for 3644 at a value of US$216 billion.[23]

In any event, the developments in FDI outlined above may be attributed to many elements, among which the establishment of the WTO and the advancement of information technology are the key ones. In addition, the continuous opening-up of more national markets, the increasing importance of the knowledge economy in domestic production, and the progressive liberalization of foreign investment regulations, as well as the gradual development of the international legal regime on foreign investment, are also important reasons for the substantial increases and changes in this field.

II. Impacts of national laws on investment

With the ever extending reach of globalization, which has made foreign investment an important component of the domestic economy of every country, it is now difficult to distinguish whether a country is an investment home country or host country. Meanwhile, national laws also have influences, more or less significant, on international investment. In general, national laws, policies, and regulations on foreign investment can be classified as either restrictive or encouraging measures, through which a host country can directly require foreign investors to change the means of investment or can alter important economic elements for them so as to induce foreign investment according to its own design. Generally

---

18   For details, see: http://news.sohu.com/20140116/n393633748.shtml.
19   *World Investment Report 2006, supra*, note 12, p. 1.
20   Kekic and Sauvant (eds.), *supra*, note 9, Table 4, p. 23.
21   Ibid., p. 22.
22   Compared with previous patterns, contemporary FDI inflows to emerging market economies are more often made by means of mergers and acquisitions instead of by greenfield investment; ibid., p. 23.
23   See *World Investment Report 2011: Non-Equity Modes of International Production and Development*, United Nations, New York and Geneva, 2011, Annex Tables I.3 and I.4; available at: http://www.unctad-docs.org/ UNCTAD-WIR2011-Full-en.pdf.

speaking, when deciding whether to make new investment or expand its business scope, an enterprise, no matter whether domestic or foreign, would balance the advantages and disadvantages and compare the prospective profits to be reaped by its changing strategy. Therefore, if the host country takes the potential profit and risk of the enterprises into account when adopting corresponding measures, it would, at least in theory, influence the decision-making of both domestic enterprises and foreign investors. In general, the following factors can reduce cost and enhance productive efficiency:

1. Reducing the cost of capital, labor, technology, energy, etc.
2. Reducing other costs by adjusting tariffs and import quotas, reducing trade barriers, and restricting investment by other companies and/or
3. Increasing the actual after-tax income by providing subsidies, tax reductions, or tax exemptions to the company.

As for investment risk, the host country can affect the market situation and lower the risks of investment by ensuring the supply of raw materials, stabilizing market prices, providing risk guarantees, or restricting other companies from investing in the same industry. The extent to which, or in which aspect, a host country might adopt restrictive or encouraging measures depends on its actual situation, as well as on other political and economic considerations.

In this globalized era, although every country encourages FDI, none adopts a totally *laissez-faire* policy in this regard. They all preserve the power to supervise and even to terminate foreign investment when necessary. The most common supervisory measures include reviewing foreign investment projects or proposals to ensure the true intent of foreign investors and the consistency of the proposed investments with the general aims and strategy of domestic economic development. Most developing countries have such provisions in their laws. Some developed countries, such as Australia and Canada, also stipulate the procedures and authorities to review foreign investment projects or proposals. For instance, the Canadian Foreign Investment Review Act has very concrete reviewing standards, and comprehensive regimes regarding foreign investment reviewing have also been established by some countries in Latin America.

In order to prevent their domestic economies from being controlled by foreign enterprises, many countries restrict the mergers and acquisitions of domestic enterprises (especially those of considerable scale) with or by foreign investors. The United States, Japan, Canada, Australia, and some developing countries, including the People's Republic of China, have established regimes to review such proposed mergers and acquisitions.

There are also restrictions on the economic activities open to foreign investment. Perhaps owing to the special economic interests of a host country, the significance of a certain economic sector to its economy or for other reasons, most countries impose restrictions on those economic activities in which foreign investment is acceptable, generally including the construction and production of facilities and material for national defense, transportation, communications, public facilities, banking, insurance and public media such as newspapers, radio stations, television broadcast facilities, etc.[24]

Although investment has become an important factor of every country's economic development, for one reason or another some countries still have requirements regarding the percentages of shares that must be owned by domestic enterprises, at least in certain industries. For instance, when China joined the WTO, it maintained its restrictions on foreign investors in the basic telecommunications sector by stating that "[f]oreign service suppliers will be permitted to establish joint venture value-added telecommunication enterprises. … Foreign investment joint ventures shall be no more than 30 per cent."[25] Thereafter, the foreign share in such joint ventures was scheduled to increase but was not to go beyond 49 percent of the total ownership.[26] The Provisions on Administration of Foreign-Invested Telecommunications Enterprises also stipulate:

> The proportion of foreign investment in a foreign-invested telecommunications enterprise providing basic telecommunications services (excluding radio paging) shall not exceed 49% in the end. The proportion of foreign investment in a foreign-invested telecommunications enterprise providing value-added telecommunications services (including radio paging in basic telecommunications services) shall not exceed 50% in the end.[27]

These kinds of requirements are adopted to ensure that control of sensitive industries will be maintained in the hands of local enterprises. Similar measures relating to other industries may also have the effect of enhancing the capabilities of domestic enterprises, establishing an economy dominated by local enterprises and acquiring comparatively advanced industrial technologies and management skills by means of co-management and co-ownership.

Of course, there are also some disadvantages in requiring domestic participation in foreign-invested enterprises. Given that foreign enterprises with a leading position in the international market might not be willing to cooperate with domestic companies owing to financial or technology concerns, the restrictions on foreign shareholding could have a negative effect. Regarding the ownership of a foreign-invested enterprise, the Chinese Equity Joint Venture Law stipulates that a foreign party should own no less than 25 percent of the total shares. Although

---

24 It has been comparatively recently that individual countries have relaxed restrictions on foreign-invested banks and insurance companies. Since the 1980s, developed countries, led by the United States, have strongly advocated that restrictions on foreign investment in the service industries, including banking and insurance, should be relaxed. This request was finally realized by the establishment of the World Trade Organization and the General Agreement on Trade in Services.

25 See World Trade Organization, Protocol on the Accession of the People's Republic of China, Annex 9, Schedule CLII—People's Republic of China: Part II—Services, Basic Telecommunication Services, adopted on November 10, 2001.

26 Ibid.

27 Article 6 of the Provisions on Administration of Foreign-Invested Telecommunications Enterprises, adopted on December 11, 2001, as amended in 2008 by the State Council of China.

this may encourage investment by foreign enterprises of medium or large size in China, it might also have a negative impact on small businesses or individual investors, or even frustrate their investment in China. Apart from legal and policy restrictions, the regulations of foreign investment revenues, remittance controls and limitations on the payment of service fees by host governments could also influence foreign investment.

The exchange rate regime of a host country directly affects the structure of foreign investment and the industries involved. If the domestic currency is over-valued, foreign investors purchasing imported products with it would actually be subsidized by the host government. On the other hand, there would be an invisible additional tax for the exports denominated in that currency. Under these circumstances, foreign investors would most likely try to increase imports as much as possible for the sake of the subsidies offered by the host government but reduce exports and remit their incomes as profits directly out of the host country.

It is clear then that host country exchange rates established to "overvalue" the domestic currency will directly result in increased imports and decreased exports. In addition, since most foreign investors well understand this economic fact and have made a set of comprehensive strategies and measures in that regard, the host country will have to spend a large amount of human and financial resources to make up for this defect. Foreign investors, especially transnational corporations, can, of course, transfer their assets and capital easily.

In order to attract foreign investment, many countries, particularly develop-ing countries, provide favorable treatment to foreign investors by means of their national laws and administrative measures. In fact, the most important element in the encouragement of foreign investment is the political and economic situation of the host country, namely the so-called investment environment. This includes such "natural" elements as population, market preferences, and culture, as well as such "non-natural" elements as the tax regime, the labor market, conditions for foreign entrance and restrictions on the activities of foreign investors. Of course, when considering whether a certain element or measure has an encouraging or discouraging effect on foreign investors, one must analyze it from a comprehensive and global perspective. Whether the investment environment in the host county is favorable requires its comparison with that of other countries. Even in this globalized era, most foreign investors are TNCs with independent information-analysis and decision-making systems that allow them to adjust their investment strategies according to changing situations anywhere in the world.

Experience shows that different policies and measures, because of their specific effects on foreign investment in different economic sectors and industries, must be carefully considered and put into practice. For example, in order to attract foreign investment, some host countries provide foreign investors with preferential loans, the direct effect of which is to encourage foreign enterprises to borrow from the host government as much as possible. Backed by preferential governmental loans, foreign enterprises may be willing to invest in fields of high risk. Although the return on investment in the actual business operations may be less than in other circumstances, the overall profits earned may not be reduced as a result of the preferential loans. Domestic enterprises are thus put in an inferior position and cannot compete with the foreign-invested enterprises subsidized by preferential loans. In such a scenario, the host country's economy will inevitably rely heavily on foreign-invested enterprises and overall economic development is likely to suffer as a result.

Another common measure taken by host countries to encourage foreign investment is tax reduction or exemption. Although this may increase the foreign enterprises' income, the actual benefit they obtain may depend on the tax regime of their home country. Under some circumstances, the tax privileges provided by the host country may play a role in transferring the investors' capital to their home country. Donations and subsidies offered by the host country may also lead to similar results if they are not dealt with properly. In consideration of the tax regime of the investor's home country, many host countries, especially developing countries, therefore place more emphasis on the local reinvestments of foreign-invested enterprises when offering tax reductions or exemptions.

Although all the encouraging or restrictive measures adopted by host governments are enacted to serve general purposes, under certain circumstances some measures may conflict with each other. For example, a preferential tax rate or tax exemption may be used to promote foreign investment inflows. Meanwhile, in order to facilitate the operation of foreign-invested projects, a host country may require domestic participation in the projects. This is helpful for the foreign-invested enterprises in understanding the legal and political regime, as well as the culture of the host country. The two measures do not run parallel with each other, however. Owing to the domestic participation requirement, when considering and calculating prospective profits, a foreign-invested enterprise has to take the potential difficulties and expenses involved with the cooperation into account. Generally, a foreign-invested enterprise may transfer its real income to overseas branches by means of transfer pricing in order to evade the foreign exchange controls or tax policies of the host country. However, where there is domestic participation, the domestic partner may oppose the transfer of real income that may involve a financial loss for it. In this sense, the preferential tax may conflict with the domestic participation requirement. There is always a disparity between the presumed preferential treatment provided by the host government and the real concerns of the foreign investors.

According to a World Bank study, tax reductions or exemptions were the primary measures taken by host countries to encourage foreign investment, followed by national treatment. However, for foreign investors, their major concerns include whether a long-term investment plan can be made and implemented, whether their capital and earnings can be freely remitted outside the host country and whether national treatment is provided. Strictly speaking, it is impossible that there should be no conflict between host countries' promotional policies and measures and foreign investors' needs. However, for the purpose of attracting foreign investment, a host country must make its best efforts to minimize such conflicts.

International investment is subject to the laws and policies of not only the host countries but also those of the foreign investors' home countries, including foreign exchange regulations, laws on equity and securities investment, regulations on the extension of loans, the tax regime, antitrust laws, etc. In addition, guarantees against political risks provided to enterprises engaging in foreign investment, investment insurance and the explanation and publication of agreements or arrangements concluded with foreign governments, as well as other related regulations on commercial transactions, are also important for enterprises in their foreign investment decision-making.

Foreign exchange controls are now mainly adopted by developing countries. Except for the United States, most developed countries had also imposed strict restrictions on foreign exchange flow after World War II. At that time, the United States also maintained domestic financial policy restrictions regarding foreign investment by US enterprises. For example, the Foreign Direct Investment Office of the US Department of Commerce had imposed strict restrictions on the extension of loans for foreign investments made by US enterprises in developing countries on preferential terms. Those companies engaging in foreign investment had to make any reinvestments by using their overseas profits. This policy also led US companies to resort to the European financial market for loans in European currencies. The purpose of this policy was to resolve the United States' balance of payments problem that existed at that time.

Owing to a similar serious balance of payments problem, the United Kingdom had also imposed strict restrictions on the FDI of domestic enterprises and loans made for such purposes during the post-war era. Except for export credit loans, loans for foreign investment could not get approval from the UK Government. Later, with the improvement of the balance of payments situation, the restrictive measures were gradually abolished. However, apart from direct restrictions imposed by the government, enterprises engaging in foreign investment were also exposed to exchange rate risks. The depreciation and appreciation of local currencies by host country governments would also indirectly influence foreign investments. The appreciation of the US dollar after World War II prompted US enterprises' foreign investment. Similarly, the appreciation of the Japanese yen in the 1980s also encouraged Japanese enterprises to invest abroad to lower their production costs and maintain their shares in overseas markets.

Governmental encouragement and restriction of foreign investment is also reflected in the supervision of other institutions by central banks. All central banks, including those of the United States, Japan, China, and the European countries, conduct effective supervision of commercial banks and other financial institutions, even though some measures or policies may be adopted and implemented unofficially. Generally speaking, most measures are enacted to encourage foreign investment by domestic enterprises, but some may also be restrictive. For example, according to US regulations, a member bank of the Federal Reserve Bank or any other commercial bank shall neither make equity or security investments in any domestic or foreign corporation, nor lend to an individual borrower, an amount in excess of 10 percent of its capital.[28] The Banking Ordinance of

---

28 See United States Code, Title 12 Section 84(A)(1) [12 U.S.C. § 84(A)(1)].

Hong Kong stipulates that a bank shall not lend more than 25 percent of its capital to any company or individual. It is obvious that these domestic banking laws and regulations have a major impact on the foreign investment activities of local enterprises.

As noted above, the tax regime of an investor's home country is of great significance to foreign investment. It can offset any tax preferences provided by the host countries and thus restrain foreign investment. Of course, a home country may change its tax regime to promote foreign investment. If the tax paid to the host country by a local enterprise engaging in foreign investment is recognized by its home country—that is, the tax paid to the host country can be deducted from the taxes payable in the home country or payment of income tax can be deferred—the enterprise would certainly be willing to invest overseas. This arrangement not only enables foreign investors not to pay home country income taxes immediately but also lowers their risks.

Antitrust laws and other similar laws of investors' home countries also have significant impacts on international investment. At present, many national laws apply not only to domestic conduct but also to conduct in other countries. For example, US antitrust law applies to all domestic activities as well as those that are carried out overseas but have an impact on the US market.[29] Because domestic antitrust laws also govern the lawfulness of their actions overseas, US enterprises often hesitate to undertake foreign investment owing to the vagueness of the criteria used to determine whether or not they have violated those laws. For example, consider two US companies who have invested in a foreign country to set up a new establishment together. According to the US antitrust law, if the production and distribution of the newly established company is involved in competition in the US market, the investment may be illegal. It is easier for an activity to be regarded as monopolistic where a company engaging in foreign investment has a dominant power over domestic raw materials and markets. Cooperative arrangements or general agent agreements between enterprises may also relate to the antitrust law of the investor's home country or that of the product exporting country.

As their social, economic and legal systems are different, some countries restrict domestic enterprises from exporting specific products or technologies to certain countries in international investment and trade, especially for the high-tech trade. Some of these restrictions are the result of strategic security considerations, while others are the result of the implementation of international treaty obligations. This is generally the case for nuclear material and technology export restrictions.

---

29 For instance, Section 6 of the Sherman Antitrust Act of 1890 stipulates that it shall not apply to foreign trade and commerce, unless—
   (1) such conduct has a direct, substantial, and reasonably foreseeable effect—
      (a) on trade or commerce which is not trade or commerce with foreign nations, or on import trade or import commerce with foreign nations; or
      (b) on export trade or export commerce with foreign nations, of a person engaged in such trade or commerce in the United States; and
   (2) such effect gives rise to a claim under the provisions of sections 1 to 7 of this title, other than this section.

Some export restrictions adopted by developed countries apply not only to domestic companies but also to their subsidiaries in third countries. No matter what may be the reason for technology and equipment export restrictions, such policies can become barriers to international investment.

Sometimes, enterprises invest abroad to manufacture products that will be sold on the domestic market of their home country. They will take into account the home country's customs system, its tariff rates and other import-related costs, as well as customs clearance procedures, etc. Some home countries encourage domestic enterprises to import raw materials or semi-finished products in order to alleviate shortages in domestic supplies. In order to protect domestic industries from competition with cheap foreign products, a home country usually does not encourage companies investing abroad to import their finished products for sale on the domestic market. To achieve this purpose, apart from tariff quotas and other measures directly related to import restriction, it may also adopt policies and measures not directly related to imports. The requirement that government agencies should mainly purchase domestically produced products is an example. The conclusion of the WTO Agreement on Government Procurement, which regulates procurement by its signatories' governments and their agencies, has an indirect influence on the investment environment of related countries and territories.

Of course, a home country can also encourage enterprises investing abroad to import their products or raw materials by means of preferential measures. For example, some developed countries grant the GSP (Generalised System of Preferences) to imports from developing countries, reducing or eliminating import tariffs on certain products. Such preferential treatment is also applicable to the finished or semi-finished products that result from the foreign investments of enterprises in the importing country. A home country can also encourage or inhibit foreign investment through export credit guarantees. In order to reduce the foreign investments made by domestic enterprises that are related to competition in the domestic market, the home country may refuse to provide government preferential loans or risk insurance for such investments.

Most domestic laws on stock exchanges require listed companies (foreign-invested companies are mostly listed companies) to disclose their balance sheets and other critical business information to the government and the public. In this regard, the US laws are most comprehensive and specific.[30] The negotiable instruments laws in some countries also require companies investing abroad to disclose contracts or other arrangements concluded with foreign partners or enterprises to the government and the public. Such a requirement is likely to violate a confidentiality agreement between an enterprise and its foreign partner or the host government. In addition, when obtaining loans, such as syndicated bank lending, the enterprise investing abroad may have to provide the creditor with its balance sheet and disclose its financial situation. It may not pose any difficulty for

---

30 In this regard, the most important US laws include the Securities Act of 1933 and the Securities Exchange Act of 1934, as well as their subsequent amendments.

an investor to provide commercial information to the creditor under conditions of confidentiality. However, some companies in the host country are unable to provide more detailed information because of the laws of their home country or for other reasons.

In order to promote foreign investment by their domestic enterprises, some home countries have entered into bilateral agreements with host countries, providing political risk guarantees and other guarantees to their domestic investors. The US Export-Import Bank, the US Overseas Private Investment Corporation and the UK Export Credit Guarantee Department are among the typical government agencies providing such guarantees. The direct effect of government guarantees against political risks is to reduce or eliminate such risks for overseas investment companies. In case of greater political risks, the government guarantee enables enterprises investing overseas to obtain more preferential loans that are usually unavailable to them by other means.

It is important for government institutions to provide political risk insurance because investors generally do not know exactly how things stand owing to the distances between the relevant investment projects and the home country, as well as any possible cultural differences. Political risk insurance can enhance their confidence and therefore expand foreign investment. In addition, such financial incentives as low-interest loans or loan guarantees provided by the home country also play a significant role in promoting foreign investment.

Apart from economic laws and regulations, the criminal laws of home countries also have an important influence on foreign investment. For example, in 1977, the United States passed the Foreign Corrupt Practices Act, stipulating that any person who directly or indirectly bribes foreign government officials may commit an illegal act. Although such acts are illegal in many countries, the related laws of the home country may make them punishable there as well. The Foreign Corrupt Practices Act also forbids US companies from excluding any property from their account books or falsifying accounts in order to cover up expenses related to corrupt activities. Such a provision is significant to the facilitation of foreign investment. In practice, host countries merely punish those who are bribed rather than those who bribe them. Related laws of the home country can crack down on bribery more effectively. If all home countries enacted laws similar to those of the United States or took such international action as concluding an international convention to fight against economic crimes, there would be a better environment for international investment and a more level playing field. In this regard, the Convention on Combating Bribery of Foreign Public Officials in International Business Transactions, concluded by OECD members, entered into force on February 15, 1999. At present, 39 countries have officially ratified it. The Convention aims to strengthen cooperation among the contracting parties and to crack down on bribery in international business activities by requiring the adoption of appropriate and effective domestic laws.

Home countries' laws on environmental protection, security and other issues may also affect foreign investment. They may exclude the possibility of importing products manufactured by overseas companies. The raw materials or semi-finished products may fail to meet the standards required by the importing government and therefore cannot be imported. In extending loans, some financial institutions and banks of home countries require that the projects concerned do not adversely affect the ecological balance of the host countries. Export-import banks in some countries also review and supervise investment projects to ensure that the natural environment will not be polluted. Although the influence of such laws and regulations on international investment is not very obvious, it cannot be overlooked in the decision-making of companies investing abroad.

In the first decade of the twenty-first century, economic globalization has further strengthened the interdependence of the international community. The development of high technology, especially information technology, has changed the essence of this interdependence. That is, technological elements have increased significantly in both transnational trade and investment. In this case, how to protect the intellectual property rights of foreign investors has become a critical issue. It can be said that in the information age the makeup of the international investment environment is also changing, as more emphasis has been attached to the legal protection of intellectual property rights in host countries.

III. International legal regimes

International investment involves transnational flows of funds, technologies, equipment, labor, and other factors. It is therefore inevitably subject to the laws of both home countries and host countries. In this highly globalized era, attracting foreign investment has become an important policy of all countries. In order to create a better environment for foreign investment and to compete with other countries for limited foreign capital and technologies, individual countries have tried nearly all means, among which entering into bilateral investment protection treaties is considered to be a most effective one. According to UNCTAD, by June 2013, 2860 bilateral investment treaties ("BITs") had been entered into and 340 other agreements had provisions on investment.[31] In 2010 alone, a total of 54 new BITs were concluded. At the end of 2010, the international investment agreements ("IIAs") universe contained 6092 agreements, including 2807 BITs, 2976 double taxation treaties, and 309 "other IIAs." Twenty of the 54 BITs signed in 2010 were between developing countries and/or transition economies, a trend possibly related to developing countries' growing role as outward investors.[32] These figures show that international investment has been comprehensively expanded and that individual countries have taken the acquisition of foreign investment to be an important means to develop their domestic economies. The conclusion of BITs demonstrates a country's desire to encourage foreign investment. With the increasing number of such treaties, their contents have also changed significantly

---

31 UNCTAD, *International Investment Policymaking in Transition: Challenges and Opportunities of Treaty Renewal*, IIA Issues Note, No. 4, June 2013, p. 1.
32 *World Investment Report 2011*, *supra*, note 23, p. 100. Beginning with the *World Investment Report 2012*, UNCTAD has no longer included double taxation treaties among its universe of IIAs.

over the last few decades. For instance, only toward the end of the 20th century had China agreed to the provision of investor–state arbitration in its BITs.

International investment involves a wide range of business activities, from capital input, export and import of equipment and technology, customs duties and other taxes, and intellectual property protection, to enterprise registration and operation, corporate mergers and acquisitions, product quality standards, labor treatment, environmental protection and dispute settlement, etc. These commercial activities are subject to the regime of international investment law.

Insofar as the international legal regime is concerned, however, different from the situation of international trade and international finance, there is no international organization or one single multilateral institution comprehensively coordinating or regulating transnational investment treaties. International norms regarding international investment are scattered among a number of individual treaties of major international organizations, such as the Agreement on Trade-Related Investment Measures of the WTO, the resolutions or guidelines of other international organizations, BITs, etc. These multilateral and bilateral documents constitute the main content of international investment law.

Since the end of the Cold War, especially after the 1990s, international investment law has been greatly enriched. With the development of globalization, in order to attract more foreign investment, some countries had to make concessions on their sovereignty. For example, in 1991, the signatories to the Andean Pact, who had been quite wary of FDI, withdrew Resolution No. 24, which had strictly restricted foreign investment. The World Bank also passed the Guidelines on the Treatment of Foreign Direct Investment (hereinafter "the Guidelines") in 1992.[33] Although the Guidelines were drafted by experts and are not legally binding, they do have significant influence on the international community. The Guidelines are characteristic of a changing attitude of international organizations, whose focus has shifted from the responsibilities of foreign investors and multinational companies to regulating the treatment given by host countries to foreign investors, including the standards of compensation for nationalizations or expropriations. In addition, the Guidelines aim at the progressive development of international investment norms rather than merely summing up the general investment practice of the international community.[34]

The Guidelines recognize a state's right to nationalize properties within its territory, including those of foreigners. However, they also advocate that nationalization or expropriation, as well as measures with similar effects, should be consistent with relevant legal procedures and carried out for the public interest, in good faith, and without any discrimination based on nationality, as well as

---

33 For the full text of the Guidelines on the Treatment of Foreign Direct Investment, see I. F. I. Shihata, *Legal Treatment of Foreign Investment: The World Bank Guidelines*, Martinus Nijhoff, Dordrecht and Boston, 1993.

34 After the United Nations suspended negotiations on the Code of Conduct of Transnational Corporations in 1992, the status and role of the Guidelines on the Treatment of Foreign Direct Investment became more significant. For more about the background and significance of the Guidelines, see ibid.

that the original property owners should be given "full, effective and prompt" compensation.[35] This has actually attached four preconditions to nationalization. In case a country fails to fully meet any of them, the original owner of the property nationalized can claim that the nationalization was in contravention of international law. However, some preconditions, such as the public interest, are difficult to define objectively.

With regard to the standards of compensation for nationalization, the Guidelines have fully endorsed the three principles insisted on by the developed countries but opposed by the developing ones, that is, that compensation be "full, effective and prompt." Moreover, they even specifically provide for the methods and standards to calculate and assess the value of nationalized properties.

The Energy Charter Treaty, signed in 1994, also has a far-reaching impact on international investment. The negotiation of the Treaty started with the collapse of the former Soviet Union. The developed countries of Western Europe wanted to enter into arrangements with the newly independent Eastern European and Central Asian countries on energy exploitation and trade.[36] The negotiations were initially conducted between the EU and Eastern European countries. Owing to its fear that the EU would dominate the exploitation of vast energy resources in Eastern European countries and control the global energy markets, the United States actively joined in the negotiations, followed by Canada, Australia, and Japan.[37]

The Energy Charter Treaty includes important provisions on energy-related international investment and trade. For example, the signatories committed to improve the transparency of their national laws and to undertake obligations to give foreign investors non-discriminatory treatment and most-favored-nation ("MFN") treatment in the negotiation of any energy investment. After entering into the host country, foreign investment should enjoy MFN treatment, national treatment and fair and equitable treatment. Meanwhile, full compensation should be given to foreign investors whose investments are expropriated.[38] In fact, the most noteworthy provision of the Energy Charter Treaty is its mandatory dispute settlement mechanism. According to Article 26, any individual investor can submit its dispute with a host country to international arbitration without the specific consent of the host country. In other words, no signatories to the Energy Charter Treaty were allowed to make reservations to the mandatory provision on

35 See Part VI of the Guidelines on the Treatment of Foreign Direct Investment.
36 This was actually a continuation of the Havana Charter regime, originally proposed by the United States and the European developed countries after World War II, which it took as its core. It took the collapse of the former Soviet Union and the independence of its Member countries to bring this to fruition.
37 For the history and impact of the Energy Charter Treaty, see T. W. Wälde, "Introductory Note to The European Energy Charter Conference, Final Act, Energy Charter Treaty, Decision and Energy Protocol on Energy Efficiency and Related Environmental Aspects," *I.L.M.*, Vol. 33, 1995, pp. 360–67.
38 The "full, effective and prompt" compensation represents the compensation standards of nationalization advocated by the developed countries.

international arbitration. This is unprecedented in the practice of international treaties and economic transactions.[39]

The WTO also has considerable impact on international investment. The Agreement on Trade-Related Investment Measures (the "TRIMs Agreement") is the most relevant one, the purpose of which is "to promote the expansion and progressive liberalization of world trade and to facilitate investment across international frontiers so as to increase the economic growth of all trading partners, particularly developing country Members, while ensuring free competition." In implementing the TRIMs Agreement, "particular trade, development and financial needs of developing country Members, particularly those of the least-developed country Members" shall be taken into account.[40] Accordingly, the TRIMs Agreement aims to coordinate investment laws and policies of WTO members so as to ensure that the implementation of investment measures will not be trade-distorting and restrictive. For example, no investment measure can be inconsistent with the requirements of national treatment or the quantitative restrictions of the General Agreement on Tariffs and Trade ("GATT").[41] The TRIMS Agreement also sets out an illustrative list, indicating what kinds of measures are prohibited by the WTO.

Another WTO Agreement that has direct impacts on international investment is the General Agreement on Trade in Services (the "GATS"), which covers nearly all aspects of service products except for the production phase. In addition, sometimes the supply of services can hardly be distinguished from investment. The establishment of banks, insurance companies, financial institutions and transportation agencies, etc. is not only within the scope of trade in services but also has the nature of investment. In consideration of the WTO's requirements on national treatment and transparency, together with its compulsory dispute settlement mechanism, it is undeniable that the GATS has a substantial impact on FDI.[42]

Another international organization that directly relates to FDI is the World Intellectual Property Organization ("WIPO"). One of the characteristics of contemporary international investment is its high technology element, which calls for more effective protection. Agreements of the WIPO and related WTO provisions regarding intellectual property rights have constituted a safety net at the international level. These international norms not only play a role at the international level but also have a direct impact on the legislation and implementation of national laws.

---

39 As of early 2014, 53 parties had signed the Energy Charter Treaty, most of which are European countries. Another 24 countries, including China and the United States, and 10 international organizations such as the World Bank, the WTO and the Association of Southeast Asian Nations had the status of observers, as does the Palestinian National Authority. See "Members and Observers" on the Energy Charter Treaty website at: http://www.encharter.org/index.php?id=61.

40 Preamble to the TRIMs Agreement.

41 Article 2, TRIMs Agreement.

42 WTO rules regarding product quality, sanitary standards, quarantine standards, environmental protection, and intellectual property rights, etc. are also closely related to FDI.

In addition to multilateral treaties and norms, bilateral investment promotion and protection treaties and agreements on avoiding double taxation and tax evasion concluded by many countries are also important components of the international norms regulating FDI. It is under the provisions of the more than 2,800 existing BITs that most investor–state disputes are settled.

IV. Features of contemporary international investment law

International investment law has been most probably the fastest developing legal sector over the last two decades, and some of its features have evolved to significantly distinguish contemporary international investment law from that which existed in the past. Such features are mainly reflected in the process of resolving disputes, especially in the awards of the arbitral tribunals established by the International Centre for Settlement of Investment Disputes ("ICSID"). The ICSID, which was established under the ICSID Convention of 1965, has played an irreplaceable role in investor–state dispute settlement and has become the most important institution for the settlement of investment disputes. Many free trade agreements ("FTAs"), such as the Energy Charter Treaty and the North American Free Trade Agreement ("NAFTA"), as well as BITs, include provisions enabling investors to submit their disputes with host countries to the ICSID. This is even the case for those countries that did not join the ICSID Convention, as the disputing parties can resort to the Additional Facilities of the ICSID. With the comparative decline in state sovereignty, more and more countries have accepted the ICSID Rules of Procedure for Arbitration Proceedings. As of November 1, 2013, there were 158 Member states to the ICSID Convention,[43] and by early February 2014 there had been a total of 461 cases registered under the ICSID Convention, of which 278 had been completed, with an additional 183 cases pending decision.[44] The ICSID also administered 67 investor–state disputes under the United Nations Commission on International Trade Law ("UNCITRAL") rules between mid-2004 and the end of 2013. There are also other arbitral institutions involved in resolving investment disputes, including the International Chamber of Commerce, the Stockholm Arbitration Court and the Permanent Court of Arbitration. Some of these institutions have their own arbitration rules and others, like the Permanent Court of Arbitration, adopt the Arbitration Rules of the United Nations Commission on International Trade Law.

A. Cross-application of treaty and national law

A unique feature of current investment law is that almost all matters are subject to both treaties and the local laws of host states, sometimes even those of home

---

43 See the ICSID website; available at: http://icsid.worldbank.org/ICSID/FrontServle t?requestTy pe=ICSIDDocRH&actionVal=ContractingStates&ReqFrom=Main.

44 See the "Lists of ICSID Cases" on the ICSID website at: https://icsid.worldbank.org/ICSID/ FrontServlet?requestType=CasesRH&actionVal=ListCases.

states. Therefore, for the purpose of establishing the rights of foreign investors and breaches by host states of their obligations, arbitral tribunals are unavoidably called upon to interpret both international agreements and national laws when deciding investor–state disputes. In this regard, the Vienna Convention on the Law of Treaties ("VCLT"), which is generally accepted as reflecting the customary rules for treaty interpretation, plays an important role.[45] Article 31(3) of the VCLT provides that in interpreting a treaty, "[t]here shall be taken into account … together with the context: any relevant rules of international law applicable in the relations between the parties." The rules of international law in this context include customary international law as well as adopted international treaties. According to this rule, many of the contents of international investment law, such as fair and equitable treatment, depend on their usage in general international law. Moreover, multilateral and bilateral investment treaties usually set up quality requirements for investors; some even provide that the qualified investment must be made in accordance with the domestic laws of host countries. Whether the investor is a national (a juridical person or a natural person) of a contracting party and whether the investment concerned is consistent with the domestic law of the host country shall be determined in accordance with the laws of both the investor's home country and the host country. Therefore, the entirety of international investment law, international law and the relevant domestic law comprise indispensable constituents of the integrated system of investment law.

Fraport v. Philippines[46] is a case in point. It involved the Germany–Philippines BIT, according to which the term "investment" was defined to include any kind of asset "recognized by the respective laws and regulations of either Contracting State" and "in accordance with its Constitution, laws and regulations."[47] By means of secret shareholder agreements, the Claimant, Fraport, had intentionally evaded the Philippines Anti-Dummy Law, which imposed restrictions on foreign shareholders and management in the public utility industry. In the tribunal's view, there could be both de facto investment and de jure investment, but only the latter was entitled to BIT protection. Owing to the secret shareholder agreements that were intended to circumvent the Anti-Dummy Law of the host country, Fraport could not claim to have made an investment "in accordance with law" nor claim that high officials of the respondent had subsequently waived the legal requirements and validated Fraport's investment because the respondent's officials could not have known of the violation. Because there was no "investment in accordance with law," the investment could not enjoy the protection provided under the BIT.[48] The tribunal attached much importance to the principle of good faith

45 The Draft Articles on Responsibility of States for International Wrongful Acts, adopted by the 56th Session of the UN General Assembly in 2001, has always been invoked to determine whether an act could be attributable to the host government.
46 See *Fraport A.G. Frankfurt Airport Services Worldwide v. Philippines*, ICSID Case No. ARB/03/25, Award (August 16, 2007).
47 See Germany–Philippine BIT, Article 1(1); available at: http://www.unctad.org/sections/dite/iia/docs/bits/germany_philippines.pdf.
48 See *Fraport v. Philippines, supra*, note 46, para. 401.

and applied Article 26 of the VCLT, which provides that "[e]very treaty in force is binding upon the parties to it and must be performed by them in good faith." In other words, based on the principle of good faith, the contracting parties to a BIT are only obliged to protect lawful investment and not any investment made by fraud.[49] Similarly, the tribunal in *Inceysa Vallisoletana S.L. v. El Salvador*[50] also held that the consent to ICSID jurisdiction under the El Salvador–Spain BIT should not be effectively extended to an investment made by fraudulent means and which was inconsistent with the host country's domestic laws.

In fact, many provisions of multilateral and bilateral investment treaties are similar or identical and are usually drafted on the basis of several leading investment treaties with some minor revisions. They thus have an inherent consistency in terms of legislative object, legislative technique, general principles, etc. In interpreting treaty clauses, tribunals always refer to other relevant treaties or model treaties. In the *Enron v. Argentina* case, the tribunal held:

> [T]he interpretation of a bilateral treaty between two parties in connection with the text of another treaty between different parties will normally be the same, unless the parties express a different intention in accordance with international law. A similar logic is found in Article 31 of the Vienna Convention in so far as subsequent agreement or practice between the parties to the same treaty is taken into account regarding the interpretation of the treaty. There is no evidence in this case that the intention of the parties to the Argentina-United States Bilateral Treaty might be different from that expressed in other investment treaties invoked.[51]

In *Siemens v. Argentina*, with regard to the respondent's argument that "the dispute settlement clause departed from the standard bilateral investment treaty of Germany and was a clause specially negotiated and hence which should be differentiated from the rest," the tribunal held:

> The end result of the negotiations is an agreed text and the legal significance of each clause is not affected by how arduous was the negotiating path to arrive there. The Tribunal feels bound, in its interpretation of the Treaty, by the expressed intention of the parties to promote investments and create conditions favorable to them.[52]

Therefore, other treaties between the contracting states or their own model treaties can constitute valid evidence in interpreting an investment treaty. Given the

---

49 Of course, the principle of good faith is also a general principle of international law. Article 26 of the VCLT, which specifies this principle, reflects customary international law.

50 See *Inceysa Vallisoletana S.L. v. Republic of El Salvador*, ICSID Case No. ARB/03/26, Award [on Jurisdiction] (August 2, 2006).

51 See *Enron Corporation and Ponderosa Assets L.P. v. Argentina*, ICSID Case No. ARB/01/3, Decision on Jurisdiction (January 14, 2004), para. 47.

52 See *Siemens A.G. v. Argentine Republic*, ICSID Case No. ARB/02/8, Decision on Jurisdiction (August 3, 2004), para. 106.

absence of explicit provisions in the basic treaty, some clauses of other relevant treaties or model treaties can be used to prove the object and the meaning of certain wording of the basic treaty, as well as the trend in the treaty practice of the contracting states.

B. Precedential effect of previous decisions

A phenomenon of international investment is that arbitral tribunals charged with resolution of investor–state disputes actively interpret BITs, FTAs and the domestic laws of both host and home countries, which has resulted in a huge jurisprudence on international investment law. In theory, decisions of arbitral tribunals only bind the parties to the particular case in dispute. In practice, however, previous awards, court judgments such as those of the European Court of Human Rights, and the reports of the panels and Appellate Body of the WTO are often referred to by disputing parties and in the awards of tribunals.

The common law doctrine of *stare decisis* is not applicable to international investment arbitration, as a previous award is not binding for subsequent disputes. This principle is generally recognized by every arbitral tribunal. In practice, however, almost all of them have unexceptionally quoted the reasoning of previous awards or even adhered to the legal interpretations of previous tribunals. The tribunal in *AES Corp. v. Argentina* stated, with regard to the value and status of previous cases:

> Each decision or award delivered by an ICSID Tribunal is only binding on the parties to the dispute settled by this decision or award. There is so far no rule of precedent in general international law; nor is there any within the specific ICSID system for the settlement of disputes between one State party to the Convention and the National of another State Party.[53]

Meanwhile, it also observed:

> Each tribunal remains sovereign and may retain, as it is confirmed by ICSID practice, a different solution for resolving the same problem; but decisions on jurisdiction dealing with the same or very similar issues may at least indicate some lines of reasoning of real interest; this Tribunal may consider them in order to compare its own position with those already adopted by its predecessors and, if it shares the views already expressed by one or more of these tribunals on a specific point of law, it is free to adopt the same solution.[54]

In the *Saipem v. Bangladesh* case, the tribunal considered that "following the precedents" was a duty "to harmonious development of investment law." It noted:

---

53 See *AES Corporation v. Argentine Republic*, ICSID Case No. ARB/02/17, Decision on Jurisdiction (April 26, 2005), para. 23; available at: http://ita.law.uvic.ca/documents/AES-Argentina-Jurisdiction_000.pdf.

54 Ibid., para. 30.

The Tribunal considers that it is not bound by previous decisions. At the same time, it is of the opinion that it must pay due consideration to earlier decisions of international tribunals. It believes that, subject to compelling contrary grounds, it has a duty to adopt solutions established in a series of consistent cases. It also believes that, subject to the specifics of a given treaty and of the circumstances of the actual case, it has a duty to seek to contribute to the harmonious development of investment law and thereby to meet the legitimate expectations of the community of States and investors towards certainty of the rule of law.[55]

The tribunal in *SGS v. Philippines*, however, indicated that according to Article 53(1) of the ICSID Convention awards rendered under it were only binding on the parties. It further stated that:

> … although different tribunals constituted under the ICSID system should in general seek to act consistently with each other, in the end it must be for each tribunal to exercise its competence in accordance with the applicable law, which will by definition be different for each BIT and each Respondent State. There is no hierarchy of international tribunals, and even if there were, there is no good reason for allowing the first tribunal in time to resolve issues for all later tribunals.[56]

The *Impregilo ad hoc* annulment Committee even considered: "A tribunal is entitled to and often quotes from other decisions in deriving or in support of its own reasoning and quoting from rulings of other arbitral tribunals certainly constitutes a valid form of reasoning."[57]

In fact, such an explanation is nothing rare in the judgments made by common law courts. When departing from the doctrine of *stare decisis*, a court will almost always try to justify itself by alleging the differences in the facts or applicable laws between the case with which it is dealing and the precedents. The substantial inclination towards common law practice appears to have become another feature of international investment law.

C. Emphasis on preambles

Article 31(1) of the VCLT provides that "[a] treaty shall be interpreted in good faith in accordance with the ordinary meaning to be given to the terms of the treaty in their context and in the light of its object and purpose." This has become

---

55 See *Saipem S.p.A. v. People's Republic of Bangladesh*, ICSID Case No. ARB/05/07, Decision on Jurisdiction and Recommendation on Provisional Measures (March 21, 2007), para. 67 (footnotes omitted).

56 *SGS Société Générale de Surveillance S.A. v. Republic of the Philippines*, ICSID Case No. ARB/02/6, Decision of the Tribunal on Objections to Jurisdiction (January 29, 2004), para. 97.

57 *Impregilo S.p.A. v. Argentine Republic*, ICSID Case No. ARB/07/17, Decision on Annulment (January 24, 2014), para. 156.

the "Golden Rule" for international arbitral tribunals in treaty interpretation. However, on many occasions, tribunals have placed too much emphasis on the objectives of a treaty without taking the intent of the contracting parties into full account. As a result, these tribunals have often failed to give due consideration to the substantive treaty provisions but have focused on the preambles of the relevant BITs, which has resulted in unnecessary obligations being imposed on host countries.

In the *Noble Ventures v. Romania* case, the tribunal acknowledged that its interpretation was only justified in terms of the treaty's "object and purpose."[58] Similarly, on the basis of the relevant treaty's object and purpose, the tribunal in *Tokios Tokelés* reached the conclusion that the "foreign investors," who were in fact Ukrainian nationals, were entitled to BIT protection, as this would encourage investment inflows to Ukraine.[59] The *Tza Yap Shum v. Peru*[60] Tribunal stated that it "shall" interpret the terms of the BIT "in good faith in accordance with the meaning to be given to the terms of the treaty in their context and in the light of its object and purpose."[61] Yet it failed to give due consideration to the clear and plain language of Article 8(3) of the BIT and stated:

> It may be assumed, in accordance with the wording of the Preamble of the BIT, that the purpose of including the entitlement to submit certain disputes to ICSID arbitration is that of conferring certain benefits to promote investments. Had the Contracting Parties really had the intention of excluding such important issues as those listed in Article 4 from the arbitral proceeding, the Tribunal would determine so, although with certain skepticism with regard to whether such mechanism could possibly help attracting foreign investment.[62]

What the tribunal did was to replace the contracting parties' agreement with its own assumptions on what is needed to attract foreign investment. This kind of interpretation is not helpful for promoting international investment law and will weaken the confidence and trust of BIT contracting parties in international investment settlement mechanisms. In fact, where the parties have deliberately restricted ICSID jurisdiction to ascertaining the amount of compensation for expropriation, a tribunal is not permitted to enlarge its scope of jurisdiction by assumption or by guessing at the intent of the contracting parties or, even worse, by alleging that "a determination of other important matters related to the alleged expropriation" is needed. The question is what the contracting parties have agreed to authorize the

58 See *Noble Ventures, Inc. v. Romania*, ICSID Case No. ARB/01/11, Award (October 12, 2005), para. 52.
59 See *Tokios Tokelés v. Ukraine*, ICSID Case No. ARB/02/18, Decision on Jurisdiction (April 29, 2004).
60 *Tza Yap Shum v. Republic of Peru*, ICSID Case No. ARB/07/6, Procedural Order (July 21, 2009).
61 Ibid., para. 153.
62 Id.

tribunal to decide and not what, in the tribunal's view, is relevant or important for it to decide.[63]

It is true that foreign investors consider international arbitration to be an important dispute settlement mechanism and even a more favorable mechanism than litigation in the courts of the host state. Yet arbitral tribunals may not ignore the clearly stipulated provisions of a BIT, as was done in the *Tza Yap Shum* case, and restructure, in accordance with their own desires, a dispute settlement mechanism. BITs and FTAs should be interpreted according to the VCLT, in particular Articles 31 and 32 thereof, which reflect the customary rules of treaty interpretation. Unless arbitral tribunals and other dispute settlement bodies follow the rules and principles correctly and strictly, many undesirable decisions and awards are likely to be the result. This is very important for a country such as China, which has accepted investor–state arbitration as a means to settle its disputes with foreign investors only recently.

Of course, the text establishing a BIT's object and purpose is important. Nevertheless, it will diminish the due effect and function of substantive provisions to overly emphasize the object and purpose of a BIT. The importance of the text relating to the BIT's object and purpose is that when a provision on substantive issues is unclear, this text can throw light on the understanding of the unclear provision.

Moreover, contracting parties should be free to impose whatever they consider to be proper limitations on the rights enjoyed by foreign investors while still providing protection to them and their investments for the sake of promoting foreign investments. Any tribunal that fails to respect such freedom of the contracting parties could actually distort their intentions, especially as those are expressed in a treaty's object and purpose. The tribunal in the *Plama v. Bulgaria* case seemed to observe and comment on this tendency in international arbitral practice by indicating that "the placing of undue emphasis on the 'object and purpose' of a treaty will encourage teleological methods of interpretation [which], in some of its more extreme forms, will even deny the relevance of the intentions of the parties."[64]

In practice, not only the object and purpose of a BIT is significant to the interpretation of the rights and obligations of the disputing parties, but similar provisions in multilateral treaties are also important. For example, the tribunal in *Malaysian Historical Salvors v. Malaysia*[65] stated that to determine whether the contract to salvage the cargo of a British vessel that sank in 1817 was a

---

63 The proliferation of annulment applications, as to be discussed in Chapter 2 of this book, cannot be said to have nothing to do with such arbitration decisions. Regarding the grounds of annulment under the ICSID mechanism, see Article 52(1)(b) of the ICSID Convention.

64 See *Plama Consortium Ltd. v. Republic of Bulgaria*, ICSID Case No. ARB/03/24, Decision on Jurisdiction (February 8, 2005), para. 193. Apart from Article 31, the tribunal also referred to the supplementary interpretational rule provided in Article 32 of the VCLT. See also *Noble Ventures, supra*, note 58, para. 50.

65 *Malaysian Historical Salvors Sdn. Bhd. v. Malaysia*, ICSID Case No. ARB/05/10, Award (May 17, 2007); available at: http://icsid.worldbank.org/ICSID/FrontServlet?requestType=CasesRH&actionVal=showDoc&docId=DC654_En&caseId=C247.

qualified investment a series of precedents needed to be analyzed by the tribunal. It found that two approaches were adopted by international arbitral tribunals following the *Salini* case,[66] that is, the "typical characteristics approach" and the "jurisdictional approach." Following the jurisdictional approach created by itself, the *Malaysian Historical Salvors* Tribunal analyzed the terms of the contract one by one and came to the conclusion that:

> Unlike the Construction Contract in Salini which, when completed, constituted an infrastructure that would benefit the Moroccan economy and serve the Moroccan public interest, the Tribunal finds that the [present] Contract did not benefit the Malaysian public interest in a material way or serve to benefit the Malaysian economy in the sense developed by ICSID jurisprudence, namely that the contributions were significant.[67]

No treaty has provided that "benefit to local economic development" is the prerequisite for a transaction to be qualified as investment. The *Malaysian Historical Salvors* Tribunal based its approach mainly on the provision about a treaty's object and purpose contained in the preamble to the ICSID Convention: "Considering the need for international cooperation for economic development ...." The contract concerned did not significantly contribute to the local economy and was thus not considered by the tribunal to be an investment within the meaning of Article 25 of the ICSID Convention. Therefore, the tribunal held that it did not have jurisdiction over the dispute. The problem here is that the tribunal failed to address the issue of whether or not the contract was an investment covered by the Malaysia–United Kingdom BIT but only drew its conclusion on the basis of the preamble to the ICSID Convention. As a result, the claimant initiated an ICSID annulment proceeding on the basis that "the Tribunal has manifestly exceeded its powers," and the award was annulled two years after the composition of the *ad hoc* Committee.[68]

The problem encountered by the *ad hoc* Committee was that the Malaysia–United Kingdom BIT defined the term "investment" in a broad manner, according to which the contract would surely qualify as an investment. It then had to address the issue of whether the tribunal established by the disputing parties had the power to, or should, refuse to exercise jurisdiction over the case because the transaction concerned was inconsistent with the Preamble to the ICSID Convention. The Committee considered that the fact that the term "investment" did not mean "sale" comprises "the outer limits" on ICSID jurisdiction, while its inner content should be defined by the disputing parties to a case submitted to ICSID arbitration.[69] The Committee also observed that the strict application

---

66 *Salini Costruttori S.p.A. and Italstrade S.p.A. v. Kingdom of Morocco*, ICSID Case No. ARB/00/4.

67 *Malaysian Historical Salvors, supra*, note 65, para. 131.

68 *Malaysian Historical Salvors Sdn. Bhd. (Applicant) and the Government of Malaysia (Respondent)*, ICSID Case No. ARB/05/10, Decision on the Application for Annulment (April 16, 2009).

69 Ibid., para. 72.

of the four elements raised in the *Salini* case, that is, that ICSID would not have jurisdiction unless all of them were satisfied, would exclude some investment disputes from ICSID jurisdiction. This would not be a desirable result where the related BIT or the disputing parties had consented to resolve their dispute through the ICSID. Therefore, the Committee considered that the ICSID should advance with the times: "If very substantial numbers of BITs across the world express the definition of 'investment' more broadly than the Salini Test, and if this constitutes any type of international consensus, it is difficult to see why the ICSID Convention ought to be read more narrowly."[70]

The annulment decision was made by the majority of the *ad hoc* Committee. Judge Shahabuddeen, one of the Committee members, issued a Dissenting Opinion, holding that the term "investment" under the ICSID Convention must have its outer limits, that is, that it must contribute to local economic development on the basis of the first sentence of the Preamble to the ICSID Convention.[71] He was of the view that the wording "[c]onsidering the need for international cooperation for economic development" evidenced that contributing to local economic development was the prerequisite for a qualified investment and that if it did not do so a transaction could not be an investment covered by the ICSID Convention. Judge Shahabuddeen even justified his conclusion on the basis of the fact that the ICSID was established under the auspices of the International Bank for Reconstruction and Development.

It is obvious from the cases mentioned above that, notwithstanding the significance of a treaty's preamble and purpose in the interpretation of its substantive clauses, over-emphasizing their role would probably lead to undesirable results. For instance, regardless of the wording of a treaty's object and purpose as contained in its preamble, should it not be possible for the contracting parties to establish provisions different from those contained in the preamble in the substantive part of a treaty? Sometimes, the contracting parties may choose to establish limitations in the concrete and substantive clauses, as the wording of the provisions reflecting the treaty's objectives and the preamble could be too broad. Moreover, all treaties are concluded after months or years of negotiation. Any political event or economic problem that comes up during the negotiation may lead the contracting parties to introduce different provisions into a treaty. In fact, once the contracting parties have agreed on certain provisions, such as the preamble or the objectives, in order to avoid the recurrence of any difficulties which may have come up in those previous negotiations, they will probably tend to establish necessary provisions in other clauses, that is, the substantive or concrete clauses. This may result in apparent inconsistencies within a treaty or contract, especially between the preamble and the substantive part. Unfortunately, a lack of intergovernmental negotiating experience on the part of arbitrators, who are always experts in international investment law, combined with the incapability of

---

70 Ibid., para. 79.
71 See *Malaysian Historical Salvors Sdn. Bhd. (Applicant) and the Government of Malaysia (Respondent)*, ICSID Case No. ARB/05/10, the Dissenting Opinion of Judge Shahabuddeen (February 19, 2009).

the disputing parties to provide the preparatory work of the BIT, has led tribunals to attach too much importance to the principles of international law without giving enough consideration to the true meaning of the substantive treaty clauses.

D. Formation of case law

Whether or not previous arbitral awards have the de facto effect of precedents, it is quite clear that all disputing parties and arbitral tribunals frequently refer to previous awards, regardless where and by whom they were made. It has also become a normal phenomenon that investment tribunals quote the judgments of national and international courts,[72] which is similar to the practice of the WTO, where panels refer to the reports of other panels and the Appellate Body, while the Appellate Body quotes its own previous reports. There have been cases where international investment arbitral tribunals have referred to and quoted the reports of WTO Expert Panels and the Appellate Body. This has actually resulted in the emergence of a body of international investment case law, with the cross-references and quotation of previous awards and reports among different tribunals, arbitral institutions, and dispute settlement bodies in various fields. The emergence and development of international investment case law are historical necessities.

The emergence of international investment case law has had a significant effect on the development of international investment law. First of all, comparatively consistent rules of interpretation have been gradually formed. New rules were derived from the fundamental principles codified in the VCLT. Second, some general legal principles, such as *bona fides*, *pacta sunt servanda*, and *nova constitutio futuris formam imponere debet non praeteritis*, have been widely recognized in the international arena and applied by more and more international arbitral tribunals. Third, international laws have been further localized. The concrete provisions of international investment treaties regarding qualified investments and investors, fair and equitable treatment and full protection and security, as well as those on indirect and creeping expropriation and standards on compensation for expropriation, have been generally absorbed by domestic laws.

The formulation of international investment case law has been helped by the development of science and technology. Since the 1950s, the development and wide prevalence of communication and information technologies, especially the rapid development of the Internet, have substantially enhanced the efficiency of information transmission. The time needed for material analysis, investigation, evidence collection and hearings has been shortened. The published final judgments and arbitral awards can be widely disseminated within the international community for the very first time.

The advanced communication and information technologies enable lawyers

---

72 For example, the tribunal in *Técnicas Medioambientales Tecmed S.A. v. United Mexican States*, ICSID Case No. ARB(AF)/00/2, quoted (at para. 22) a judgment made by the European Court of Human Rights when discussing whether or not expropriation should be based on the public interest.

and arbitrators to easily access previous awards and find useful contents to quote to support their views in the arbitrations. One of the best strategies for the lawyers representing the disputing parties is to quote the decisions made by other tribunals to justify their claims. As a matter of fact, all the disputing parties have unexceptionally quoted precedents, seeking to convince the tribunals handling their cases. Tribunals are also inclined to cite previous awards to avoid being criticized for not giving adequate reasoning in their awards. Therefore, the precedents are increasingly more widely spread and quoted, and this is now playing a more important role in the international investment regime.

Based on the choice of the disputing parties, traditional arbitrations were conducted secretly without publicizing the awards. However, in the field of international investment, especially for investor–state dispute settlement, there has to be considerable transparency. On the one hand, this is because nowadays the acts of state governments are subject to a high level of scrutiny, which requires enhanced transparency. Accordingly, a government's involvement in an arbitration, the arbitral results, and the legitimacy of its acts are all related to the outcome of upcoming elections. On the other hand, some awards are submitted to domestic courts by the disputing parties for review or implementation. The fundamental requirement here is to publicize all the documents, including those arbitral awards that may be in dispute.[73] It is against this background that the ICSID has explicitly committed to publicize all its arbitral awards, which in turn prompts regional organizations and *ad hoc* tribunals to publicize their awards as well, such as in the case of the awards made under the NAFTA. All these awards can be widely and timely discussed in some open forum, such as on the Internet, and the commentators influence each other. At the same time, such publicity places huge pressure on the arbitrators, because everyone wants his/her decision to be widely supported, or at least not to be challenged. The safest way to achieve this is to follow the precedents and practices of other tribunals, for by doing so, even when it goes wrong, the tribunal concerned will not be alone.

Within an extremely small circle, the ideas of scholars and experts in this field interact. They firmly believe that economic development depends on international cooperation, including international investment, and that a favorable investment environment is essential to attract foreign investments. Such a perception is manifested by arbitrators connecting the concrete obligations and the broad provisions on a treaty's purpose when interpreting a BIT on the basis of VCLT Article 31. Naturally, they will come to their conclusions regarding what a

---

73 According to ICSID Arbitration Rules, for a dispute between a contracting state and a national of another contracting state, the disputing party who is not satisfied with the arbitral award may apply to establish an *ad hoc* committee to make the final decision. If one of the disputing parties is not an ICSID contracting state or a national of a contracting state, the dispute shall be resolved according to the ICSID Additional Facility Rules and the award made is not subject to ICSID annulment proceedings. However, the disputing parties can resort to domestic courts for remedies. For example, in *Metalclad Corporation v. United Mexican States*, ICSID Case No. ARB(AB)/97/1, Mexico, who was the losing party, brought suit in the Superior Court of British Columbia, seeking an order of annulment.

host country should do to provide foreign investors with a stable and predictable investment environment. This interpretive approach itself is fine, but the problem is that sometimes extensive interpretation without striking a balance between the rights and obligations of foreign investors and those of the host country may finally encourage, if it has not already done so, the abuse or improper exercise of their rights by foreign investors.

In an investor–state dispute, the foreign investor, as the one who contracted with a sovereign state and invested capital in the host country, always tries to give the public an impression that it is the weak party, no matter how strong it may actually be. It is human nature to sympathize with the weak, and this is no less true of arbitrators. Driven by such compassion, a tribunal may be inclined to follow the investor's logic and come to the conclusion that the host country has breached its treaty obligations.

Those legal experts and scholars who were educated in developed countries with advanced economies and highly efficient governments often lack awareness and understanding of the cultures of many host countries. It is common that these countries do not act in a manner which is natural and simple in the eyes of these arbitrators. However, the complexity of the problems encountered by a host government may go far beyond the knowledge of any arbitrator. The culture of a host country may also be very different from that with which the arbitrators are familiar. Therefore, an act or omission of the host country in question may not be appreciated or understood by the arbitrators. All these things could indirectly influence the decision-making of tribunals. In some cases in which developing countries have prevailed, the local lawyers representing the host governments usually have enjoyed high reputations in the international community.

Notwithstanding the foregoing obvious defects of international investment arbitral awards, their influence is ever increasing with the growth in the number of cases. How to respond to the formation of international investment case law has posed an inevitable challenge to the international community.

It goes without saying that the emerging features of international investment law are not limited to the foregoing. There have been new developments in other areas. The scope of application of the MFN clause to be discussed later is just one such example.

To sum up, international investment is subject to the influences of many factors and has experienced different developing stages. Before the 1990s, it was mainly concentrated in natural resources exploitation and the manufacturing industries and was carried out mainly among developed countries. With the development of science and technology, especially information technologies, economic globalization has become the main trend of the contemporary world. Against this background, profound progress has been made in international investment in terms of its breadth, depth and patterns. Although the developed countries still remain the most important host countries, developing countries have also made significant achievements, not only in attracting foreign investment (in terms of both quantity and quality) but also in making their own investments abroad. Notwithstanding the lack of an international organization to coordinate transnational investment, a number of multilateral treaties, FTAs and BITs have constituted a comprehensive network of rules which not only encourage but also regulate international investment. In addition, the jurisprudence established with the contribution of decisions and awards of arbitral tribunals, both institutional and *ad hoc*, is perhaps the most important factor in enforcing the treaty rights and obligations of the parties, including foreign investors. The combination of the above has given international investment law a binding force that it did not have before. This development has also made the study of international investment law more interesting and significant than ever before.

2 The control system pertinent to direct foreign investment

Investment is always accompanied by risks, both commercial and non-commercial. The transnational nature of international investment further increases the risks to which investors are exposed. Differences in culture and business environment; changes in the political, military, or economic situation of host countries; or even the occurrence of natural disasters may result in special risks for foreign investors. In order to strengthen investors' confidence, the international community has established various control mechanisms. Some of these were set up unilaterally by home countries to encourage their domestic entities' overseas investments; some were established through bilateral treaties between home and host countries; and yet others were established by multilateral agreements. No matter whether the mechanism is unilateral, bilateral, or multilateral, it is non-commercial risks that these control mechanisms aim at dealing with.

Insofar as the functions of these control mechanisms are concerned, some of them provide insurance to cover political and non-commercial risks; some offer measures for promotion and protection of direct foreign investment; and still others exist to resolve investor–state disputes. This chapter will first examine the domestic investment insurance systems set up unilaterally by some developed countries and the multilateral insurance mechanism—the Multilateral Investment Guarantee Agency. It will then discuss the bilateral investment protection mechanisms with emphasis on the bilateral investment agreements and free trade agreements entered into by China. The last section will be devoted to the system for resolving investor–state disputes. As the following chapters will deal with various issues of international investment, which are related one way or another to the arbitration mechanisms, the focus of this chapter will be on the ICSID annulment procedures only.

I. The insurance system for foreign investment

The insurance system for direct foreign investment has developed hand-in-hand with the signing of bilateral investment treaties ("BITs"). The most important foreign investment insurance system was formulated by the developed countries on a unilateral initiative. In the late 1980s, the World Bank made efforts to conclude a multilateral mechanism for encouraging the flow of capital from the developed to developing countries. The end result was the establishment of the Multilateral Investment Guarantee Agency ("MIGA").

A. The national insurance system

In order to facilitate overseas private investment, many developed countries have tried to protect their own investors by establishing domestic investment guarantee systems. The sovereign immunities acts adopted by individual countries are all parts of the overseas private investment protection system. Moreover, the Western developed countries have also set up agencies responsible for overseas investment promotion to provide their nationals and companies who invest abroad with various facilities and assistance, as well as different forms of insurance. The US Overseas Private Investment Corporation ("OPIC") is a typical example in this regard.

OPIC was established in 1969 as a result of the 1961 Foreign Assistance Act.[1] Its main purpose was to provide insurance against political risks for US nationals or corporations investing in developing countries.[2] The investment insurance offered by OPIC can be traced back to the Marshall Plan after World War II. In order to encourage private enterprises to invest in European countries and in the recovery of those economies damaged during the War, the US Government assured private investors that the investment returns they earned in European countries could be directly exchanged into US dollars.[3] This guarantee of currency exchange was based on the US Economic Cooperation Act of 1948.[4] This law was amended several times, expanding its coverage so that the guarantee provided by the US Government was extended from currency exchange to cover risks relating to expropriation, war, insurrection, and revolution. Except for the currency exchange guarantee, these guarantees were only applicable to investments made by US nationals in developing countries. According to the traditional understanding of Western developed countries, investments in developing countries were subject to higher political risks, especially in the sense that the interests of investors might be directly impacted by nationalization, expropriation, war, or revolution.

In 1961, the United States adopted the Foreign Assistance Act and established the Agency for International Development ("USAID"), which is responsible for supervising and implementing US foreign assistance and private investment. In 1969, the US Congress amended the Foreign Assistance Act, officially establishing

---

1 Foreign Assistance Act of 1961 (Public Law 87-195), 22 USC 2191(1976); available at: http://www.opic.gov/sites/default/files/statute1.pdf.

2 OPIC provides loan guarantees and loans for investments made by US nationals and enterprises in developing countries and transitional economies.

3 Such a currency exchange guarantee was necessary and attractive because the currencies of European countries were not freely convertible at that time. It was not until the end of the 1950s that the developed Western European countries began to adopt freely convertible currency systems.

4 62 Stat. 137.

OPIC as an independent agency. OPIC was authorized to extend loans to private enterprises, individuals and investment agencies. The insurance premiums for the guarantees it provided were its main funding source. As an independent governmental agency, its authorizations and activities are defined by law for specified time periods which can be extended by authorization from the US Congress. Since its establishment, the US Congress has continually extended its term, expanded the insurance coverage and increased the number of eligible host countries.[5]

The fundamental guiding principle for OPIC's insurance services for private enterprises is that the provision of insurance shall be consistent with the risk management principle of the insurance business. For the sake of reducing risk, it also provides separate insurance and reinsurance in cooperation with other insurance companies. Differently from general insurance companies, OPIC gives priority to weak and small enterprises, especially for those private investments made in friendly least developed countries and territories, on the condition that the investments are consistent with the needs of the host countries' and territories' economic development and support the enhancement of local social and economic living standards.

When issuing guarantees, OPIC takes into account the degree to which the related country or territory allows the presence of domestic and foreign private enterprises, as well as the conditions, capacity, and willingness of that country's government to permit private enterprises to be fully developed. In addition, it encourages competition and assists the US Government in resolving problems with the balance of payments. Under these general principles, OPIC focuses on investments in least developed countries and territories with per capita incomes of less than US$984 (in 1986 US$) and restricts its activities in relation to investments in countries and territories with per capita incomes equal to or higher than US$4269 (in 1986 US$).[6]

Those who may obtain OPIC insurance include US nationals, corporations, partnerships, or other commercial entities registered in the United States and legal persons registered overseas if 95 percent of their shares are held by US nationals or enterprises. If a qualified natural or juridical person cooperates with an unqualified investor to invest in a project, the qualified investor may only apply for OPIC insurance for its own part of the overall investment. In most cases, the foreign countries or territories where OPIC provides investment insurance have concluded agreements with it under which the host countries promise investment protection and grant subrogation to OPIC.

In practice, OPIC only provides guarantees to new investment projects, although this may include the expansion, modernization, technical improvement, and development of existing investment projects. Investors must register with

---

5 See, for example, Overseas Private Investment Corporation Reauthorization Act of 2011 (H.R. 2762); available at: http://www.gpo.gov/fdsys/pkg/BILLS-112hr2762ih/pdf/BILLS-112hr 2762ih.pdf.

6 See Foreign Assistance Act of 1961, as amended, *supra*, note 1, Section 231.

OPIC before actually making their investment so that OPIC can negotiate with them regarding any problems that might arise with the insurance and obtain the investor's commitment. Investors must provide specific information on the insured project when applying for insurance, including the project's effects on the US economy and employment,[7] its influence on the economic development of the host country, the use of local capital and raw materials, the time needed for construction, its impact on the local environment, and its compliance with human rights, including workers' rights.[8]

A special feature of OPIC is that it encourages both traditional and comparatively novel investment methods, including investment by the provision of funds, materials or services, by the conclusion of agreements, joint ventures, or transfers of franchises, or even product sharing to reduce risk. Moreover, related investment projects must have the participation of host governments or local enterprises because OPIC considers that this kind of arrangement is safer than direct equity investment, being less likely to be expropriated by the host country.

OPIC requires that the investors bear at least 10 percent of the risk, which means that only up to 90 percent of the investment can be insured. The insurance provided by OPIC covers direct capital investment and contractual rights or rights under pledge agreements enjoyed by investors. The returns on the investment insured are also insurable. Therefore, for equity investments, OPIC typically issues insurance commitments equal to 270 percent of the initial investment: 90 percent representing the original investment and 180 percent to cover future earnings.[9] The longest term for the insurance provided by OPIC is 20 years. In general, OPIC offers insurance policies to cover three types of risks: currency inconvertibility; nationalization or expropriation; and political violence (including terrorism). In addition, it also offers several insurance products with coverage tailored to meet special investment insurance needs, as well as discounted rates and a streamlined approval process for small businesses.

Risk of currency inconvertibility refers to the risk that because of discriminatory policies of the host country US investors may have to change local currencies into US dollars at a comparatively less favorable or lower exchange rate, or even suffer losses because the host government refuses to change the local currency into convertible foreign currencies. As one of the main insurance types provided by OPIC, this covers both the principal and returns on the investment.

OPIC insurance is mainly concerned with political risks, including risks of nationalization and expropriation. According to the provisions of the Overseas Private Investment Corporation Act, expropriation refers to cancellation of the contract concerned, refusing to recognize its effect, or damaging the contractual

---

7   Investment projects that will result in losses of US jobs or that would move an active business from a depressed region of the United States to an overseas location cannot be insured by OPIC.

8   See "OPIC Policies" on the OPIC website; available at: http://www.opic.gov/doing-business-us/OPIC-policies. See also "Finance Eligibility Checklist;" available on the OPIC website at: http://www.opic.gov/doing-business-us/applicant-screener/finance-eligibility-checklist.

9   See "Extent of Coverage" on the OPIC website at: http://www.opic.gov/what-we-offer/political-risk-insurance/extent-of-coverage.

rights enjoyed by investors, provided that the related actions of the host country have a serious negative impact on the ongoing operation of the insured investment project and are not the result of the fault or illegal acts of the investors. In general, the insurance contracts signed between OPIC and investors always list those actions of the host country that may be considered to constitute expropriation.

An investor's entitlement to compensation under the insurance contract mainly depends on whether he has actually been deprived of rights to use and manage the investment project concerned. Once OPIC confirms its contractual obligation to pay compensation for the losses suffered by an investor, the amount of the compensation will be calculated on the basis of the initial investment and the investment returns before the expropriation. After making the payment, OPIC will take the investor's place and undertake all his/her rights through subrogation. The investor is obligated to cooperate with OPIC in claiming compensation from the host country. If any compensation paid by the host country is more than that paid by OPIC to the investor, the investor is entitled to the surplus.

The insurance contracts signed by OPIC generally provide that the insured investor should inform OPIC when he/she is aware that his/her investment is exposed to the risk of expropriation. For up to one year after the expropriation, the investor is obligated to take reasonable action to prevent or resist the activities of the host government. Where there is expropriation, the private investor should initially consult and negotiate with the host government. Although such negotiation is conducted between the host government and the investor, the latter is actually under the direction of OPIC, including in regard to such matters as the acceptable conditions of compensation, etc.

Investment losses resulting from political violence are not common. In this category, OPIC insures against risks of declared or undeclared war; hostile actions by national or international forces; revolution, insurrection, and civil strife; and terrorism and sabotage. It has established certain general rules for making a determination if one of these has occurred. Among the factors determining whether war or insurrection has occurred, for example, the organized nature of the actors is most important, requiring that the activities were systemically conducted by an organization with a certain political purpose. According to traditional understanding, the insurance provided by OPIC against losses caused by war refers to the direct armed conflict or confrontation between a host country and another country, no matter whether or not either had formally declared war. Although the US courts have tried to distinguish the definitions of revolution and insurrection in some cases, OPIC considers both to be challenges encountered by a host government from organized internal opposition forces. Therefore, in order to be compensated under this type of insurance, investors have to prove that the opposition forces in the host country were organized and proposed to overthrow the current regime and establish a new one. In addition, investors must prove that the losses they suffered were caused by members or direct actions of the organized force.

In July 2003, OPIC began to offer "stand-alone terrorism insurance to support the international war against terrorism and further protect American businesses abroad. Previously, terrorism coverage was only available under OPIC's broader political violence coverage."[10] It offered protection against violent acts undertaken by individuals or groups that do not constitute national or international armed forces with the primary intent of achieving a political objective. Coverage included protection against the use of chemical, biological, radiological, or other weapons of mass destruction. OPIC offered to provide terrorism insurance for up to 10 years, and it was available for both investments and returns on investment.[11]

It is clear that OPIC has proven helpful in the conduct of foreign investment by US nationals and enterprises and in the encouragement of the cross-border flow of US capital. It has been welcomed by private investors as well as host countries. Of course, OPIC also encounters some problems that are common in the insurance business. For example, although the insurance contract signed with the investor has detailed and clear provisions, when losses do occur disputes over the related legal issues or facts may arise and one party may submit the dispute to international arbitration.[12]

B. The multilateral insurance system

MIGA was established in accordance with the Convention Establishing the Multilateral Investment Guarantee Agency (the "MIGA Convention"), adopted at the 1985 Annual Meeting of the World Bank and opened for signature in October 1985. The Convention entered into force in 1988 and, by the end of 2013, 180 countries had become MIGA members, among which 25 were developed countries and 155 were developing countries.[13]

The purpose of MIGA is to encourage international investment between its member countries, especially productive investment in developing countries, "supplementing the activities of the International Bank for Reconstruction and Development, the International Finance Corporation and other international development finance institutions."[14] In order to achieve the above objective, the Agency shall:

> (a) issue guarantees, including coinsurance and reinsurance, against non-commercial risks in respect of investments in a member country which flow from other member countries;

---

10 "OPIC Offers Stand-Alone Terrorism Insurance to Protect U.S. Businesses Overseas," OPIC Products, May 2005, p. 1; available at: http://www.opic.gov/sites/default/files/docs/hl05insurance-terrorism.pdf.

11 Apparently, this program has been discontinued and similar insurance is once again only available under the broader political violence coverage as no reference to it appears any longer on the OPIC website.

12 For important investment claims cases involving OPIC and related arbitration, see Chen An et al., *Five Well-known International Investment Disputes*, Lujiang Press, Xiamen, 1986 (in Chinese).

13 See the MIGA website at: http://www.miga.org/whoweare/index.cfm?stid=1789.

14 See MIGA Convention, Article 2; available at: http://treaties.un.org/doc/Publication/UNTS/Volume%201508/volume-1508-I-26012-English.pdf.

(b) carry out appropriate complementary activities to promote the flow of investments to and among developing member countries;

(c) exercise such other incidental powers as shall be necessary or desirable in the furtherance of its objective.[15]

In summary, MIGA's work includes investment guarantees for non-commercial investment risks and investment-related consultation. It is obliged to pay compensation to holders of guarantees in accordance with guarantee contracts and is entitled to subrogation from investors to enable it to claim compensation against host countries.

Article 14 of the MIGA Convention provides that MIGA may only guarantee investments to be made in the territory of a developing member country. It is further provided in Article 12(a) that investments for MIGA guarantees include equity interest, including non-equity investment such as medium- or long-term loans made or guaranteed by holders of equity in the enterprise concerned. In accordance with Article 12(b), with the special majority approval of the board of directors the scope of eligible investments can be extended to any other medium- or long-term form of investment.

In general, equity investment refers to the acquisition of shares in a corporation with juridical personality or those of other economic entities. If the investor has the right to acquire profits from the corporation concerned or to take part in the distribution of related interests in the liquidation process, this shall be considered to constitute an equity interest. Even if the related company has not been registered as an independent juridical person but the investor has certain ownership rights to some of its operating assets, the investment concerned shall be regarded as an equity investment. In addition, medium- or long-term loans made by equity holders to a corporation, as well as loan guarantees made under specific circumstances, shall also be deemed to comprise direct investment. The specific circumstances here mean the repayment of loans that mainly or totally depend on the profits of the project concerned or on sales of products, or where the lender has the right to transfer the creditor's right to preference shares or ordinary shares of the corporation concerned.[16]

Nonequity direct investment may include cases where an investor acquires stocks of an enterprise without investing cash or materials in it or where returns on the investment depend on the success of the enterprise or project concerned; that is, if the project fails, the investor would not get his/her investment back. In accordance with Article 1.05 of the MIGA Operational Regulations, nonequity direct investments include:

1. production-sharing contracts
2. profit-sharing contracts

---

15   Ibid.
16   For more details on what shall be considered to be equity direct investment projects, see Article 1.02–1.04 of the MIGA Operational Regulations; available at: http://www.miga.org/docu ments/Operations-Regulations.pdf.

3. management contracts
4. trademarks, know-how, franchising and technical assistance contracts
5. patent licensing agreements
6. turn-key contracts
7. operation leasing agreements for a period of at least three years
8. subordinated debentures
9. other forms of non-equity direct investment where returns depend on performance and
10. guarantees and other securities provided for loans.

Only new investments, the implementation of which begins subsequent to the registration of the application for the guarantee by MIGA, may enjoy its guarantees. Such investments may include investments made to modernize, expand, or develop an existing investment and investments made to assist economic adjustment in the host country, such as taking over its state-owned shares.

It is provided in Article 13 of the MIGA Convention that any natural or juridical person may be eligible to receive MIGA guarantees if: (1) such natural person is a national of a member other than the host country; (2) such juridical person is incorporated in and has its principal place of business in a member other than the host country; and (3) such juridical person operates on a commercial basis.

Needless to say, MIGA was established primarily to provide guarantees to juridical person investors, especially large corporate investors. It is thus of great importance to establish which corporations or enterprises are eligible to receive MIGA guarantees. At present, different domestic laws have different provisions on the same type of economic entity. For example, partnerships have a juridical personality under German and Swiss laws, while pursuant to the relevant provisions in other domestic laws this is not the case. In order to deal with this problem, MIGA's Operational Regulations provide that partnerships without juridical personality should be deemed to be unincorporated associations and branches and, as such, are not eligible for guarantees.[17] The owners of these economic entities, however, may apply for investment guarantees on their own. Partnerships or other economic organizations with juridical personality may apply directly to MIGA for guarantees. Consistently with the traditional principle of overseas investment guarantees provided by Western countries, an investor may only apply for MIGA guarantees for part of the investment instead of the whole project concerned.

Apart from juridical personality, it is also of great importance to determine the nationality of a natural person and the nationality or principal place of business of a juridical person. Because MIGA commits itself to promote transnational investment, natural or juridical persons applying for its guarantees should normally not have the nationality of the host country. However, the applicant must have the nationality of, or have its principal place of business in, a member country other than the host country. This provision of the MIGA Convention avoids the controversial and knotty problem of determining the nationality of transnational

17 See Article 1.14 of the Operational Regulations.

corporations and expands the coverage of the guarantees provided by MIGA. In accordance with the MIGA Convention, upon the joint application of the investor and the host country, as well as the approval of the board of directors by special majority, a natural person who is a national of the host country or a juridical person which is incorporated in the host country may also be eligible to receive MIGA guarantees, provided that the capital invested is transferred from outside the host country.[18]

The ownership rights of a juridical person investor are also an important issue for international investment guarantees and insurance. In the traditional practice of Western countries, an overseas investment insurance company usually does not provide guarantees and insurance to investors that are not private enterprises or not mainly owned by private persons. However, Articles 1.17 and 1.18 of the Operational Regulations have set up more flexible rules in this regard, according to which the ownership right of an investor shall be determined by referring to the beneficial rather than the record ownership. If the shares are held by a stock-broker or bank, the customer of that stockbroker or bank shall be deemed to be the owner. In accordance with the Operational Regulations, the registered owner of a corporation shall be deemed to be its actual beneficiary and owner, while for a corporation owned by more than one person, its owners should be deemed to be the natural or juridical persons that do not have the nationality of the host country.

In addition, a juridical person investor may be owned by a private person or by a MIGA member country.[19] This enables an investment intermediary or joint venture established in a third country, which is common in present investment practice, to receive MIGA guarantees. When proposing to invest abroad, in order to disperse or reduce risks, many investors will first establish a corporation in a third country other than the host country, part or most of the shares of which are owned by a local government or governmental organization. Because of such governmental participation, domestic investment insurance agencies of Western countries usually will not provide guarantees or insurance for investments made by these kinds of organizations. However, the above provisions in the MIGA Convention will encourage investors to make investments through various means.

1 Membership and voting rights in MIGA

The prerequisite for membership of MIGA is membership of the World Bank. Members of the Agency are categorized into developed countries and developing countries, with the former category including Australia, Austria, Belgium, Canada, the Czech Republic, Denmark, Finland, France, Germany, Greece, Iceland, Ireland, Italy, Japan, Luxembourg, the Netherlands, New Zealand, Norway, Portugal, Slovenia, Spain, Sweden, Switzerland, the United Kingdom

18 MIGA Convention, Article 13(c).
19 See Articles 1.14 and 1.18 of the Operational Regulations.

and the United States, and the latter category including 155 countries from Asia, Africa, Eastern Europe, the Middle East, and Latin America.[20]

MIGA's authorized capital stock is one billion Special Drawing Rights (SDR 1,000,000,000), which is divided into 100,000 shares having a par value of SDR 10,000 each. Each member must subscribe to no less than 50 shares.[21] The number of shares of capital stock subscribed by each member is set forth in Schedule A to the MIGA Convention. In case the admission of a new member would require additional shares, the Council of Governors is authorized to increase MIGA's total shares by special majority.

For the subscription of shares, each member is obliged to pay for 10 percent of its shares in cash and an additional 10 percent in the form of non-negotiable, non-interest-bearing promissory notes or similar obligations to be encashed. The remaining 80 percent shall be subject to call by MIGA when such funds are required to meet its obligations. Payment for subscriptions should be made in freely usable currency, except that payments by developing countries may be made in their own currencies up to an amount equal to 25 percent of the paid-in cash portion of their subscriptions.

MIGA has adopted the weighted voting system of the World Bank. Each member country has 177 basic votes plus one subscription vote for each share of stock it holds. It is provided in the MIGA Convention that the aggregate sum of votes belonging to the two categories of membership, that is, developed countries and developing countries, should be approximately equal.[22] In case any member fails to fulfill its obligations under the Convention, the MIGA board of directors may suspend its membership, which does not exempt it from fulfilling its obligations.

2 Characteristics of MIGA

One of MIGA's main characteristics, and also one of its missions, is to promote investment in developing countries, including investment flows from developed to developing countries and investments made between developing countries. This objective can best be achieved by a multilateral investment guarantee mechanism co-established by developing and developed countries. Most developed countries have currently established state agencies to provide guarantees for domestic enterprises against risks of their overseas investments. However, except for a few countries such as India, similar state agencies have not been set up in the developing countries to provide risk guarantees for domestic investors, which actually results in investors from developing countries holding an inferior position in competition

20 For the specific categorization of developing and developed countries, see Schedule A to the MIGA Convention.

21 In accordance with Article 5 of the MIGA Convention: "All payment obligations of members with respect to capital stock shall be settled on the basis of the average value of the SDR in terms of United States dollars for the period January 1, 1981 to June 30, 1985, such value being 1.082 United States dollars per SDR."

22 See Article 39 of the MIGA Convention.

with those from developed countries. One of the objectives of the Agency is to level the playing field for investors from developing and developed countries to improve investment cooperation in developing countries. In order to realize this objective, the MIGA Convention expressly provides that in determining those projects to be guaranteed, the board of directors should take due consideration of the shares of the respective member and the need to apply more liberal limitations in respect of investments originating in developing countries.[23] Throughout its operations, the Agency should attach special attention to the significance of facilitating investment between developing member countries.

Investment risk may be guaranteed by MIGA only with the host country's prior approval. In accordance with its needs and domestic situation, the host country may extend or reduce the coverage of the investments to be guaranteed or restrict the scope of risks to be covered.

At present, the objective of most overseas investment risk guarantee agencies is to stimulate domestic economic development, such as to increase exports, and promoting the economic development of host countries is only their second consideration. However, MIGA expressly takes promotion of the economic development of host countries as its primary goal and as an important criterion for the issuance of guarantees. It is expressly provided in Article 12 of the MIGA Convention that the Agency should determine the economic soundness of the investment, its contribution to the development of the host country, the consistency of the investment with the declared development objectives and priorities of the host country, and the compliance of the investment with the host country's laws and regulations. Whether or not the related investment can enjoy fair and equitable treatment and legal protection in the host country is also an important factor for the issuance of a guarantee. In fact, the above two criteria are complementary to each other. The former means that MIGA should take the contribution of a related project to the economic development of the host country as one of the criteria for the issuance of a guarantee, whilst the latter tries to reduce the risk of the guaranteed project to its minimum. In general, investment projects consistent with the development objectives and legal provisions of the host country will be exposed to fewer non-commercial risks.

The economic soundness of a project mainly depends on whether the technology employed by the investor complies with the requirements and feasibility of the project, as well upon the availability of sufficient funding and whether or not the project can produce enough profits to pay both expenses and dividends for shareholders. The contribution of a project to the economic development of the host country mainly depends on whether it will assist the host country to increase its export capacity and domestic production. Generally speaking, the following factors may all constitute criteria affecting these two aspects of a project: employment rates; transfer of technology; supply of raw materials; export capacity; diversity of economic development; social welfare; financial revenues; foreign exchange income; etc. When considering the contribution of an investment project to the

---

23 See Articles 2 and 23 of the MIGA Convention.

economic development of the host country, alternatives should be considered to assess whether the same objective can be achieved by other means or measure, and then the two measures or two projects should be compared to determine which one is more economically reasonable.

(1) RISK GUARANTEES

The types of guarantees provided by MIGA include: currency inconvertibility and transfer restrictions; expropriation and similar measures; breach of contract; war and civil disturbance; non-honoring of a sovereign financial obligation; and non-honoring of a financial obligation by a state-owned enterprise.[24] Although these sorts of investment risks are almost all covered by the overseas investment insurance agencies of individual countries, there is still disagreement regarding the definitions of currency risk and risks of breaches of contract by host countries, as well as whether or not those non-economic risks suffered by investors that may be attributable to their own actions or failure to act are eligible for the guarantees. MIGA has made clear provisions for the above issues.

For example, the investor's inability freely to convert his investment returns, liquidated assets of a related bankrupt enterprise, and other incomes to freely usable currency or to transfer related incomes out of the host country in accordance with its laws should be deemed currency transfer risks. Both the actions of the host country, such as expressly restricting currency conversion and transfer by law, regulation, or administrative order, as well as passively restricting the currency conversion and transfer by such means as long-term delay of the responsible governmental institution in assisting investors in the currency conversion and transfer, may contribute to currency transfer risks.[25]

In addition, MIGA also provides guarantees against the potential exchange rate discrimination suffered by investors in converting the currency of the host country into other currencies. This kind of guarantee mainly deals with the various exchange rate systems adopted by the host country to restrict or prevent investors from transferring the investment returns abroad, that is, using discriminatory or unfavorable exchange rates for the currency transfer. However, if the host country has various exchange rate systems and specific provisions regarding the transfer of every single currency, unless those provisions had been violated, the investors would not be entitled to compensation from MIGA.

For the investment risks of expropriation and similar measures, MIGA guarantees have the following characteristics: they cover official expropriation or similar measures conducted or adopted by the host country, as well as indirect or creeping expropriation. Indirect or creeping expropriation means that, although the

---

24 See Article 11 of the MIGA Convention; and MIGA, *Annual Report*, 2013, p. 60, Box 1; available at: http://www.miga.org/resources/index.cfm?aid=3554.

25 It is provided in Article 1.24 of the MIGA Operational Regulations that a passive restriction is a failure by the host country's exchange authority to act on conversion and/or transfer within 90 days from the date on which the investor applies for such conversion and/or transfer.

measures adopted by the host country do not constitute a direct expropriation of the investor's assets, given their potential aggregate impact on the investor a series of actions taken by the host country would have the same effect as expropriation and, thus, each single action should be deemed to constitute expropriation. In general, indirect expropriation includes increases in income taxes, increases in tariffs, minimum salary standards, employee training, and other compulsory regulations. However, before confirming the occurrence of indirect expropriation, the investor has to prove that the actions taken by the host country have led to serious losses of the related enterprise or have made its ongoing profitable operation impossible.[26]

These provisions for MIGA coverage mark significant progress in international investment guarantees. They ensure the interests of foreign investors, on the one hand, and specifically provide for those circumstances under which investment risks and losses cannot be guaranteed and compensated, on the other hand. Meanwhile, it is also stipulated that those measures of general application which the host governments normally take for the purpose of regulating economic activity in their territories should not be deemed to be expropriation or similar measures.[27]

The MIGA guarantee against risk of the breach of contract by the host country is an innovation in the international investment insurance business. Providing guarantees and compensation for potential losses resulting from the breach by the host government of a contract strengthens investors' confidence. A host country may breach a contract as either a sovereign or an ordinary business partner. The related contracts include natural resources exploration contracts, agreements regarding taxes, patent rights, basic infrastructure, and contracts concerning the supply of raw materials entered into by the host government or governmental agencies with foreign investors. To some extent, the guarantee against the breach of contract by the host country covers the procedural aspects, including whether the investor can submit any dispute to a court or tribunal with jurisdiction independent from the administrative departments of the host country, whether the judgment or award can be reached in a reasonable period of time and whether the judgment or award in favor of the investor can be implemented within a reasonable period of time.[28]

As to the guarantee against risks of war and civil disturbance, Article 1.50 of the Operational Regulations stipulates that the occurrence of such risk does not require that the host country be a party to the event or that the event has to take place within the territory of the host country. This provision is a breakthrough in the present international insurance system, which will facilitate international investment. If a military conflict takes place in a country neighbouring the host

---

26 See Articles 1.29–1.41 of the MIGA Operational Regulations.
27 See Article 11(a)(ii) of the MIGA Convention.
28 According to Article 1.44(iii) of the Operational Regulations, if an award in favor of the investor is not enforced within 90 days after the day when it was made, the legitimate interests of the related investor should be deemed to have been impaired.

country, whose location is so close to the investment project that the conflict affects the project's ordinary operation or causes direct damage to it, the requirements for the guarantee against war and civil disturbance risk will be satisfied and the investor will be entitled to compensation from MIGA. Moreover, for an investment project that seriously relies on international shipping or land transportation (for example, investment in an inland country), if the military conflict or civil disturbance seriously disturbs the transportation or transportation hub and the operation of the related investment project encounters difficulties or even cannot continue as a result, the investor could request MIGA to compensate him/her for any losses thus suffered.

MIGA also offers guarantees against the risks that a government or a state-owned enterprise may fail to honor an unconditional financial payment obligation or guarantee. Unlike its coverage for breach of contract, these types of coverage do not require a final arbitral award or court decision as a precondition to payment of a claim. The essential condition of such coverage is, however, that the underlying project must meet all of MIGA's normal eligibility requirements. The coverage for failure by a state-owned enterprise to meet its obligations was only added in fiscal year 2013.[29]

Another characteristic of MIGA guarantees is that if the non-commercial risks or losses are attributable to the investor, MIGA will not be obliged to pay compensation.[30] This reflects the efforts made by developing countries in the UN and other international organizations for years to establish the stability of international investment and, especially, efforts to force transnational corporation investors to adhere strictly to the laws of the host countries.

The assessment of investment risk depends on the specific condition of the project concerned, rather than on the economic and political situation in the host country.[31] Accordingly, even a project in a host country whose economy develops slowly or whose investment environment is comparatively poor can be eligible for the guarantees. This is obviously beneficial for enabling developing countries with heavy debt burdens or those undergoing economic adjustment to absorb foreign investment.

(2) INVESTMENT CONSULTATION

MIGA not only provides guarantees to investment projects established in developing countries but also acts as an intermediary and promoter of international investment, assuming some responsibility for the communication of accurate information between investment host countries and home countries, as well as among investors. Owing to MIGA's special status, especially its close connection with the World Bank, it knows well the conditions of home countries as well as situations in host countries, including their investment policies, administrative agencies,

29 MIGA, *Annual Report*, 2013, *supra*, note 24, p. 60, Box 1, and p. 2.
30 See Article 11(c) of the MIGA Convention.
31 See Article 3.05 of the Operational Regulations.

and investment environments, and also is aware of the needs and requirements of individual governments and private investors. Therefore, MIGA has inherited advantages in improving the investment environment of host countries and assisting foreign investors and their home countries effectively to coordinate with host countries. Therefore, Article 23 of the MIGA Convention stipulates that:

> [T]he Agency shall carry out research, undertake activities to promote investment flows and disseminate information on investment opportunities in developing member countries, with a view to improving the environment for foreign investment flows to such countries. The Agency may, upon the request of a member, provide technical advice and assistance to improve the investment conditions in the territories of that member.

By conducting investment investigation and research, MIGA is able to provide information regarding overseas investment opportunities for investors, assess the investment environment of member countries or even the feasibility of related projects, and decide whether to provide risk guarantees based on actual research results. It can hardly make the right decisions on investment guarantee issuance if it does not have enough reliable investment information. Practice shows that both MIGA's capacity and effectiveness is considerable. The research data it collects may constitute a base both for individual member countries to make their investment policies and laws and for private investors to make effective foreign investments. The policy consultation offered by MIGA may be achieved by encouraging member countries to conclude investment protection agreements, discussing investment policies and the legal environment with member countries, and conducting wide conversation and consultation within the Council regarding international investment. This may assist an investment host country to understand defects in its domestic investment environment and policy or legal measures that may need improvement. Technical assistance plays an important role after the above-mentioned policy decisions have been made. MIGA may offer member countries detailed and concrete plans and measures to implement new and better investment laws through such technical assistance.

(3) RELATIONSHIP WITH INTERNATIONAL ORGANIZATIONS INCLUDING THE WORLD BANK

MIGA possesses full juridical personality and independent assets, but it maintains close connections and coordinates with the World Bank, the International Financial Corporation ("IFC") and the ICSID. MIGA may also use the facilities and staffs of these institutions.[32] Meanwhile, on the premise of confidentiality, MIGA exchanges information with the World Bank, the IFC and the ICSID so as to promote international investment. These provisions exist to coordinate the investment policies of these institutions and avoid repeated work so as to make efficient use of limited resources. For example, the development plans and

---

32 See, especially, Section III and Article 7.08 of the Operational Regulations.

policies which the World Bank and the IFC endeavour to implement shall obtain MIGA's support, which means that the policies of these individual institutions to encourage international capital flows and international investment should be consistent with each other.

The relationship between MIGA and the ICSID is reflected not only in their complementary roles but also in the procedures of dispute settlement. In accordance with the provisions of the MIGA Convention, MIGA is entitled to acquire subrogation from private investors. In case a dispute arises between MIGA and the host country regarding subrogation, the two parties should first try to settle it by negotiation and consultation. If agreement cannot be reached in this way, they may submit the dispute for mediation or arbitration, where ICSID mediation or arbitration rules shall be applied.[33]

In principle, MIGA encourages the resolution of investment disputes through flexible, non-judicial, non-litigious means. If any member country refuses to accept the ICSID mediation or arbitration rules, it may enter into another dispute settlement arrangement with MIGA, but that arrangement must be adopted by a special majority of the Council[34] and must be made before MIGA decides to provide guarantees to investment projects in that country.

The fact that the MIGA Convention was ratified by many countries and entered into force soon after its adoption evidences that the establishment of MIGA was consistent with the needs of the international community and reflects the desire of individual countries to improve both their domestic and the overall international investment environment. Practice has shown that its establishment has been of great help in promoting the all-around development of international investment, especially in the sense of promoting international capital flows from developed countries to developing countries.

MIGA's influences on the national investment, development and overall economic environments of its member countries are mainly represented in the following aspects. First, by signing and ratifying the MIGA Convention, individual countries express their attitude on non-commercial risks to foreign investors, that is, their good faith to cooperate with foreign investors, which is definitely helpful for the improvement of their investment environment. Second, MIGA research enables governments and the enterprises of member countries to obtain materials and information on international investment, including the policies and measures adopted and to be adopted by other countries, so that they may not only understand the investment environment in other countries but also improve their own. Third, through participation in MIGA, individual countries can obtain timely technical assistance and conduct continuous consultations regarding how to attract foreign investment.

---

33 For dispute settlement, see Chapter IV and Annex II of the MIGA Convention.
34 See Article 57 and Annex II of the MIGA Convention.

(4) NEWEST DEVELOPMENTS

In fiscal year 2011, MIGA's Council of Governors approved substantial changes to the MIGA Convention, the first amendment of the Convention since 1988. The most important change was to allow MIGA to insure project debt even it does not insure a portion of the equity investment. Previously, MIGA had to refuse guarantees to lenders who were concerned about project risk when the equity investor was not eligible for or interested in purchasing coverage. In particular, this allows MIGA to guarantee loans to public sector recipients, whose equity is not traded. The amendments also extend MIGA's political risk insurance to new foreign investors who acquire existing investments. Previously, it was not authorized to provide such coverage, despite the potential developmental benefits of having a new private sector operator. [35]

MIGA reported that there was evidence of solid demand for the extended coverage and that there were a number of prospective deals under review that were eligible for MIGA coverage because it could now provide coverage for lenders even when not covering a related equity investment. MIGA had long considered this to have been the most serious constraint it faced when trying to expand its business. It further noted that its expanded capacity arrived at an opportune moment because "[i]n the aftermath of the financial crisis, the private [political risk insurance] industry has become more conservative and the need for multilateral providers has grown commensurately," especially for certain investments of major importance to development, such as infrastructure projects.[36]

Since it began effective operations in 1990, MIGA has supported 727 projects and has issued 1143 guarantees in a total amount of US$30 billion.[37] In fiscal year 2013, MIGA said that it had provided a record US$2.8 billion in new guarantees, continuing a 6-year period of growth. It has identified the following four strategic priorities to guide its work:

- investments in the world's poorest countries
- South-South investments
- investments into conflict-affected countries[38] and
- complex projects, i.e. those that involve project finance, structured finance or other multi-sourced deals, as well as those dealing with challenging environmental and social considerations, including projects in the infrastructure sectors and those in extractive industries.[39]

It is for all these reasons that the work of MIGA has won wide support from most developed and developing countries. Of course, problems with its decision-making

35 MIGA, *FY12-14 Strategy: Achieving Value-Driven Volume*, 2011, pp. 17–18; available at: http://www. miga.org/documents/MIGA_FY12-14_Strategy.pdf.
36 Ibid., pp. 38–39.
37 MIGA, *Annual Report*, 2013, *supra*, note 24, p. 2.
38 In June 2013, MIGA launched a Conflict-affected and Fragile Economies Facility to increase support to this priority area; see ibid., p. 14.
39 Id.

procedures and their transparency, as well as the overly strong influence of the developed countries remain to be solved. With the further enhancement of the developing countries' strength within the international community, as well as the interdependence among individual countries, MIGA's activities are likely further to facilitate the development of international investment.

II. The bilateral protection system

Apart from the insurance provided unilaterally by an investor's home or host country, BITs signed between different countries constitute perhaps the most important part of the international investment protection system. Because individual countries attach a great deal of importance to improvement of the investment environment and the enhancement of investors' confidence by such means, by June 2013, more than 3200 agreements had been entered into, of which 2860 are BITs and the rest other types of investment-related agreements, such as free trade agreements and economic partnership agreements.[40] Since there are now 178 countries that have signed BITs, and their domestic situations and environments differ a great deal, the principles and standards provided in individual BITs also differ from each other.

As the biggest and most active investment home country, the United States has played a leading role in protecting overseas investors. It has a long history of concluding treaties of friendship, commerce and navigation with other countries,[41] which not only provided systemic guarantees for related contracting states in terms of their relationships in navigation and trade but also stipulated standards of protection for the investment interests of nationals or corporations from one state in the other state. Initially, the purpose of concluding such treaties was to facilitate the trade and ocean shipping connections between the contracting states. With the continuous increase of US overseas investment, especially after World War II, this kind of treaty began to take the protection of US overseas investment as its main purpose.

Owing to the inherited limits of treaties of friendship, commerce, and navigation, the US Trade Representative ("USTR") publicized the adoption of a model BIT on January 11, 1982. Based on the Model BIT, the US Government signed its first two BITs later that year with Egypt and Panama. Based on the negotiations with these two countries, the United States further revised the 1982 Model BIT. On January 21, 1983, it publicized a new and revised version of the Model BIT between the US Government and another country on investment

---

40 UNCTAD, *International Investment Policymaking in Transition: Challenges and Opportunities of Treaty Renewal*, IIA Issues Note, No. 4, June 2013, p. 1.

41 For systemic analysis of the treaties of friendship, commerce and navigation signed between the United States and other countries, see Herman Walker, Jr., "Modern Treaties of Friendship, Commerce and Navigation," 42 *Minn. L. Rev.* 805, 1958; idem., "Treaties for the Encouragement and Protection of Foreign Investment: Present United States Practice," 5 *Am.J.Comp.L.* 229, 1956; Robert R. Wilson, "Access-to-Court Provisions in U.S. Commercial Treaties," 47 *Am. J. Int'l L.* 20, 1953.

encouragement and protection. After several revisions, the most recent publicized Model BIT is the 2012 version.[42]

As one of the most important home and host countries for foreign direct investment ("FDI"),[43] China's practice is in line with the trend in this aspect. China started its long march toward modernization in 1978 by encouraging the inflow of foreign capital and technology and reforming its domestic economy.[44] Within the short span of 35 years, it has become the most active and largest developing host country for FDI[45]—a result of its economic reforms and its opening up to the outside world. By June 2013, China had entered into more than 128 BITs[46] and several free trade agreements ("FTAs"). In April 2008, China not only entered into an FTA with New Zealand, its first FTA concluded with a developed country,[47] and a trilateral investment agreement with South Korea and Japan,[48]

---

42 See US Department of State, "Model Bilateral Investment Treaty," Fact Sheet (April 20, 2012); available at: http://www.state.gov/r/pa/prs/ps/2012/04/188199.htm. The text of the 2012 US Model BIT is available at: http://www.ustr.gov/sites/default/files/BIT%20text%20for%20 ACIEP%20Meeting.pdf.

43 According to UNCTAD Statistics, mainland China received the second-largest inflows of FDI in 2012; the United States received the most, although if the total received by both mainland China and Hong Kong were combined, the United States would fall to second place; see UNCTAD, *World Investment Report 2013: Global Value Chains: Investment and Trade for Development*, United Nations, New York and Geneva, 2013, p. 3, Figure I.2. Mainland China was also the third-largest source of FDI in 2012, although the combined investment outflows of mainland China and Hong Kong are second only to those of the United States; see ibid., p. 6, Figure I.6. According to the statistics released by the Ministry of Commerce of China on January 16, 2014, in 2013, China's direct outbound investment to other countries reached US$90.17 billion, whilst it had attracted US$117.586 billion of foreign investment in the same period of time. It was projected that by the end of 2014, China's outbound investment would surpass inbound investment. For details, see: http://news.sohu.com/20140116/n393633748.shtml.

44 After the death of Chairman Mao Zedong in 1976, Deng Xiaoping came to power. The Chinese Communist Party held a meeting at its 3rd Plenary Session of the 11th Central Committee at which it declared an end to the notorious Cultural Revolution and abandoned large-scale political change. It also announced that the country would embark on domestic economic reforms and open itself to the outside world. For a more detailed discussion, see Guiguo Wang, *Wang's Business Law of China* (4th ed.), Butterworths, 2003, pp. 5–11.

45 According to UNCTAD, global FDI inflows rose by 11% in 2013, to an estimated US$1.46 trillion; the inflows to China in 2013 were estimated to be US$127 billion, which again ranked China the second-largest recipient of FDI in the world, closing the gap with the United States to some US$32 billion. See UNCTAD, *Global Investment Trends Monitor*, No. 15 (January 28, 2014), pp. 1–6; available at: http://unctad.org/en/PublicationsLibrary/webdiaeia2014d1_en. pdf.

46 For details, see UNCTAD, "Bilateral Investment Treaties signed by China," June 1, 2013; available via the UNCTAD website at: http://unctad.org/en/Pages/DIAE/International%20 Investment%20Agreements%20(IIA)/Country-specific-Lists-of-BITs.aspx?Do=1,50.

47 China and New Zealand started by carrying out a feasibility study for concluding an FTA. The two countries signed the FTA on April 7, 2008. See Free Trade Agreement between the Government of New Zealand and the Government of the People's Republic of China; available at: http:// chinafta.govt.nz/1-The-agreement/2-Text-of-the-agreement/0-downloads/NZ-ChinaFTA-Agreement-text.pdf [hereinafter "2008 China–New Zealand FTA"].

48 China, South Korea and Japan signed an Agreement among the Government of the People's Republic of China, the Republic of Korea and the Government of Japan for the Promotion,

but also started negotiations on a BIT with the United States, its most important trading partner.[49]

A very important issue in China's effort to attract foreign investment has been its treatment of foreign investors, in particular with respect to the issues of whether foreign investment might be expropriated and, if so, whether compensation would be paid and what the standard for such compensation would be, including the method of assessing foreign investment assets.[50] These questions arose because the Chinese Government had nationalized foreign and Chinese private enterprises after its establishment in 1949.[51] Also, since the People's Republic of China had assumed the seat of China at the United Nations, it had always followed the policies of developing countries with respect to South-South and North-South issues.[52]

Facilitation and Protection of Investment on May 12, 2012. The provisional translation of the Agreement is available at: http://www.meti.go.jp/english/press/2012/pdf/0513_01a.pdf.

49 At the closing of the 5th U.S.–China Strategic and Economic Dialogue in early July 2013, it was announced that the two countries would start negotiating a BIT to regulate their bilateral investment. This is the first time that China has agreed to negotiate a BIT that includes all stages of investment and sectors. For more details, see Betsy Bourassa, "U.S. and China Breakthrough Announcement on the Bilateral Investment Treaty Negotiations" (July 15, 2013); available at: http://www.treasury.gov/connect/blog/Pages/U.S.-and-China-Breakthrough-Announcement-. aspx. Once the United States–China BIT is concluded, it will have a significant effect on China's investment laws and system, as investors and investments from other countries could demand the same treatment received by US investors through operation of the MFN clause in other BITS with China. For discussion of this issue, see Chapter 7 of this book—"The relative standards of treatment."

50 These are still paramount issues for foreign investors, although the form and scale of expropriation have changed over time. Open nationalization or expropriation is no longer the principal issue, but regulatory taking has become a concern of the contemporary world. This is evidenced in the ICSID arbitrations relating to Argentina, Mexico, etc.

51 After the establishment of the People's Republic in 1949, China expropriated all private enterprises, a process essentially completed by 1957, when the country started the Anti-Rightists Movement. For discussion of China's political and economic situation, in particular regarding expropriations, see George N. Ecklund, "Protracted Expropriation of Private Business in Communist China," 36 *Pac. Aff.* 238–49, 1963.

52 At the 6th Special Session of the UN General Assembly in 1974, Deng Xiaoping, then Vice Premier of the People's Republic of China, expounded upon the theory of three worlds and stressed the need for establishing a new international economic order. For discussion of the preparation and formulation of the "three worlds" theory, see Zhang Guoxin, "On Deng Xiaoping and the Theory of the Three Worlds;" available at: http://gxgc.ahlib.com/datalib/qikan/2005/2005_06/qikan.2005-03-10.8820460920. Soon after assuming its seat at the UN, the People's Republic of China joined the Group of 77, afterwards known as "the G77 plus China." China shared the views of developing countries expressed in the 1974 Charter of Economic Rights and Duties of States, the 1990 Declaration on International Economic Co-operation, in particular the Revitalization of Economic Growth and Development of the Developing Countries, etc. and contributed to their adoption. The G-77 and China started their formal relationship in their preparations for the UN Conference on Environment and Development held in Rio in June 1992, at which they jointly put forward a position paper. Thereafter, this cooperation model has been referred to as "The G-77 and China." Recent examples of cooperation between the G-77 and China include: (1) the insertion of the principle of Common but Differentiated Responsibility into the United Nations Framework Convention on Climate Change ("UNFCC"), the Rio Declaration and the Agenda in the 21st century, (2) the third Rio UN Sustainable Conference in 2012, and (3)

At first, the Chinese Government tried to ease the concern of foreign investors over expropriation through the enactment of domestic laws.[53] For instance, Article 2 of the Chinese Foreign Joint Venture Law provides: "The State shall not nationalize or requisition any joint ventures. Under special circumstances, in the interest of the public, the State may requisition a joint venture in accordance with legal procedures and appropriate compensation shall be made."[54] It should be pointed out, however, that when China started its policy on domestic reforms and opening to the outside world 35 years ago, concerns relating to expropriation of foreign investment were quite different from those arising in the 21st century.[55] Even taking that into account, the Chinese legal provisions could not ease the concern of foreign investors, as at that time the rest of the world and China were entirely unknown to each other. For instance, expropriation for public purposes had already been commonly accepted by Western countries when the Chinese Foreign Joint Venture Law was adopted. Yet, Chinese scholars were still debating whether nationalization was an exercise of sovereignty and, if so, what should be the standard of compensation.[56] Regarding the standard for compensation, China

China's participation in the annual Ministerial Meeting of the G-77. For details, see http://www. dailypost.vu/content/g-77-and-china-symbol-solidarity-among-developing-countries.

53 Some scholars argued that the concern about macro-political risks such as expropriation misunderstood the *zeitgeist* of post-Mao China and that, as part of its commitment to reform, China had paid less attention to its theoretical right to seize foreign assets and the ensuing legal implications than to its ability to attract foreign investment. See David L. Weller, "The Bureaucratic Heavy Hand in China: Legal Means for Foreign Investors to Challenge Agency Action," 98 *Colum. L. Rev.* 1238, 1998.

54 At the same time, Article 5 of the Wholly Foreign-Owned Enterprises Law states that the state shall not nationalize or requisition any foreign-owned enterprises. Under special circumstances, however, the same Article provides that where the public interest so requires, foreign-owned enterprises may be requisitioned through legal procedures and appropriate compensation shall be made. Article 5 of the Regulations of the People's Republic of China on Sino-foreign Cooperation in the Exploitation of Continental Petroleum Resources prescribes that the state shall not expropriate the investments and income of foreign enterprises that participate in the cooperative exploitation of continental petroleum resources but that under special circumstances, the state may, according to the needs of the public interest, expropriate a portion or all of the petroleum due to foreign enterprises in connection with their cooperative contracts.

55 Currently, the international community is paying increasing attention to creeping expropriation or indirect expropriation. As a result, changes in exchange rates, repatriation policies, adoption and amendment of laws relating to taxes, prices, labor, import and export, foreign control of certain types of companies, etc. may all lead to disputes involving creeping expropriation. A renegotiated contract may also result in suspicion of indirect expropriation if the terms thereof become less favorable to the foreign investors in question. For discussions of these issues as they relate to China, see Pat K. Chew, "Political Risks and U.S. Investment in China: Chimera of Protection and Predictability?" 34 *Va. J. Int'l L.* 615, 1994; Timothy A. Steinert, "If the BIT Fits: The Proposed Bilateral Investment Treaty between the United States and the People's Republic of China," 2 *J. Chinese L.* 451, 1988. Even Chinese scholars have admitted that an indirect expropriation is not impossible in China; see Zeng Huaqun, *WTO and the Development of Foreign Investment Law of China*, Xiamen University Press, 2006, p. 290.

56 See Wang Xuan, "Permanent Sovereignty of States toward Natural Resources," *Chinese Yearbook of International Law*, Chinese Society for International Law, 1982, pp. 99–114; Mei Ruao, "Legal Protection of International Investment," *Chinese Yearbook of International Law*, Chinese Society

took the developing countries' view, that is, "appropriate compensation," which begged the question rather than resolved it.[57]

In addition to the issues relating to expropriation, there were other hurdles in Chinese law to be overcome for foreign investments, including Chinese law being the governing law in foreign investment contracts,[58] although investment disputes among contracting parties may be resolved either within or outside China.[59] No right relating to investor–state arbitration was to be found in Chinese law.[60]

Naturally, what the Chinese Government did was welcomed by foreign investors who at the same time expected China to adopt more measures geared toward protecting their interests.[61] For instance, the Joint Venture Law only mentioned compensation for nationalization but did not specify what were the related rights and interests of joint ventures. Also, it was not stated in detail what forms of investment other than joint ventures would be considered as FDI and would therefore be entitled to the same treatment in case of nationalization.[62]

Unless these questions were answered, the skeletal Chinese laws mentioned

for International Law, 1982, pp. 115–44; Ni Zhengyu, "On the Theory and Practice of State Immunity," *Chinese Yearbook of International Law*, Chinese Society for International Law, 1983, pp. 3–30; and Chen Tiqiang, "State Sovereign Immunity and International Law," *Chinese Yearbook of International Law*, Chinese Society for International Law, 1983, pp. 31–53.

57 It is interesting to note that in his Separate Opinion in *CME Czech Republic B. V. v. Czech Republic*, an UNCITRAL award issued in 2003, Professor Ian Brownlie suggested relying on 1974 UN General Assembly Resolutions regarding "appropriate" compensation as the standard for assessing the Czech Republic's liability. See *CME Czech Republic B.V. v. Czech Republic*, Separate Opinion on the Issues at the Quantum Phase of: CME v. Czech Republic by Ian Brownlie, C.B.E., Q.C., (March 13, 2003); available at: http://italaw.com/sites/default/files/case-documents/ita0181.pdf.

58 Article 2 of the Chinese Foreign Joint Venture Law stipulates that joint venture agreements, contracts, and articles of association are subject to relevant Chinese laws.

59 Article 15 of the Chinese Foreign Joint Venture Law provides that parties to Chinese-foreign joint ventures may, by agreement, have their disputes resolved by a Chinese arbitration body or another arbitration body, which is interpreted to mean a foreign arbitration body, and where there is no agreement on arbitration, a disputing party may bring the case to a Chinese court. In practice, most Chinese foreign joint venture contracts contain provisions for settling disputes by arbitration tribunals within China, in particular by the China International Economic and Trade Arbitration Commission.

60 Having recognized the limits of traditional remedies available to foreign investors against host countries, such as local court proceedings and diplomatic protection, the World Bank started to create a special mechanism for resolving investor–state disputes in 1961. In 1965, the executive directors of the World Bank adopted the text of the Convention on the Settlement of Investment Disputes between States and Nationals of Other States, which entered into force in 1966 after the deposit of 20 ratifications. For more on the Convention, see P. F. Sutherland, "The World Bank Convention on the Settlement of Investment Disputes," 28 *Int'l & Comp. L.Q.* 367–400, 1979.

61 See Stanley Lubman, "Looking for Law in China," 20 *Colum. J. Asian L.* 1, 2006; Jerome Alan Cohen and Stuart J. Valentine, "Foreign Direct Investment in the People's Republic of China: Progress, Problems and Proposals," 1 *J. Chinese L.* 161, 1987.

62 There are differences under the Chinese Constitution with regard to protection against expropriation of foreign-owned properties as opposed to the expropriation of domestically owned private properties. See Yasheng Huang, "One Country, Two Systems: Foreign-Invested Enterprises and Domestic Firms in China," 14 *China Econ. Rev.* 404, 2003.

above would be of little use to foreign investors.[63] The solution of the problem rested on the formation of international mechanisms for the protection of FDI in China.

The first step that China took in creating international mechanisms to deal with FDI was the conclusion of BITs.[64] The first group of BITs that China entered into included those with Germany (1983),[65] France (1984),[66] and Norway (1984).[67]

All these BITs had the common feature of being brief in nature. For instance, the China–Norway BIT has only nine articles, which outline the desire of both parties to promote bilateral investment and a few concepts such as investment and investors. It emphasizes the right of subrogation in case of expropriation and repatriation of investment. Most-favored-nation ("MFN") treatment is provided for but not national treatment.

Further improvements were made after China had gained some experience with foreign investment treaties and had become more familiar with international practice. An example is the China–United Kingdom BIT entered into in 1986,[68] in which the Hull formula for compensation for expropriation was accepted. The

---

63 Chinese practice in the 1980s and 1990s was that when a law was adopted by the National People's Congress, implementation provisions would be enacted by the State Council; further detailed rules could also be promulgated by the ministries in charge under the State Council. Even so, Chinese laws adopted in those years were quite brief compared with those in the United States and other developed countries. For a detailed account of China's law-making practices, see Wang, *supra*, note 44.

64 At that time, lawyers and scholars from the United States and elsewhere often advised the Chinese Government on foreign investment issues, although such advice was given unofficially. The Chinese Government also sent its officials as visiting scholars to foreign countries to study. At least three heads of the Law and Treaties Department of the Ministry of Foreign Trade and Economic Cooperation, predecessor of the Ministry of Commerce of China, studied in the United States. Such exchanges greatly helped China to understand the needs of foreign investors. Therefore, to make use of BITs as means for promoting foreign investment was not unthinkable for the Chinese Government.

65 Agreement between the People's Republic of China and the Federal Republic of Germany on the Encouragement and Reciprocal Protection of Investments (1983).

66 Agreement between the Government of the People's Republic of China and the Government of the French Republic on the Reciprocal Encouragement and Protection of Investments (1984); available at: http://www.unctad.org/sections/dite/iia/docs/bits/france_china_fr.pdf.

67 Agreement between the Government of the People's Republic of China and the Government of the Kingdom of Norway on the Mutual Protection of Investments (1984); available at: http://www.unctad.org/sections/dite/ iia/docs/bits/china_norway.pdf.

68 Agreement between the Government of the United Kingdom and Northern Ireland and the Government of the People's Republic of China concerning the Promotion and Reciprocal Protection of Investments; available at: http://www.unctad.org/sections/dite/iia/docs/bits/ uk_china.pdf. China and the United Kingdom signed a Joint Declaration on the Question of Hong Kong in 1984, according to which the United Kingdom agreed to return Hong Kong to China by 1997 and China agreed to maintain the capitalist system of Hong Kong thereafter for 50 years. That was considered by China as a friendly move. Therefore, it was understandable that China was prepared to make more concessions in its BIT with the United Kingdom than it did in BITs with other states.

overall contents of that BIT were also determined in more detail than had been the case with previous investment treaties.

With the help of the above laws and BITs, China achieved good results in attracting foreign investment in the 1980s.[69] In 1992, the Chinese leader Deng Xiaoping took a tour of the southern part of China to advocate for further reform.[70] Thereafter, the Chinese Government formally announced that it would gradually adopt a market economy with Chinese characteristics, which triggered another wave of inflow of foreign investment.[71]

These newly revised BITs represent China's current position on international investment law. They constitute a new generation of BITs with China's participation. Significant changes that have been built into these BITs relate, inter alia, to the definition of investment and investors, the treatment of foreign investment, expropriation, compensation, and dispute settlement—in particular, investor–state arbitration.

The FTAs to which China is a party are also important to foreign investment. China did not participate in FTAs until quite recently. The first FTA negotiated by China was with the Association of South East Asian Nations ("ASEAN") in November 2001.[72] One year later, a framework agreement was entered into, laying out the FTA plan in stages.[73] The parties agreed to implement an early harvest agreement relating to trade in goods, together with a dispute settlement mechanism to be established by July 2005, whilst negotiations on trade in services were aimed to be completed in January 2007 for implementation in July 2007.[74] The objective of the early harvest agreement was to establish a full FTA by 2010

---

69 In the 1980s, China signed 19 BITs, which made it an attractive destination for foreign investment.

70 After the Tiananmen movement of June 4, 1989, foreign countries imposed economic sanctions on China. Within the country and among the leadership, there were doubts as to whether further opening of the country would be in its best interests. Deng Xiaoping, whilst without an official position at that time, followed the steps of the late Chairman Mao Zedong, toured the more liberal-minded southern part of China, and used his personal influence to call upon the leadership for further reform.

71 Article 15 of the Constitution of the People's Republic of China reads: "The State practices a planned economy on the basis of socialist public ownership. It ensures the proportionate and coordinated growth of the national economy through overall balancing by economic planning and the supplementary role of regulation by the market." The 1993 Amendment to the Constitution changed the words "planned economy" into "socialist market economy."

72 At the invitation of the Malaysian Government, the Chinese Foreign Minister Qian Qichen attended the 24th ASEAN Ministerial Meeting in 1991, which started the bilateral dialogue. China then participated in the 25th ASEAN Ministerial Meeting at the invitation of the ASEAN Standing Committee. In 1996, China became a full member of the dialogue at the 29th ASEAN Ministerial Meeting. The formation of an FTA between China and ASEAN was suggested by the Chinese Premier Zhu Rongji at the China–ASEAN Summit on November 6, 2001.

73 The Framework Agreement on Comprehensive Economic Cooperation between the People's Republic of China and the Association of South East Asian Nations was signed on November 4, 2002 in Phnom Penh and entered into force on July 1, 2003. The Framework Agreement contains 16 articles to set out the principles of cooperation between the parties and to outline a timetable for implementation.

74 The early harvest program was stipulated in Article 6 of the Framework Agreement.

for the six original ASEAN members and in 2015 for the remaining four members.[75] Investment is part of the overall China–ASEAN FTA.

The most comprehensive FTA that China has entered into is that with New Zealand, which was preceded by the China–Pakistan FTA.[76] In general, China's FTA with Pakistan is much less comprehensive than that with New Zealand insofar as bilateral investments are concerned. Both FTAs aim at establishing a mechanism for promoting cross-border direct investment.[77] One of the objectives of the China–New Zealand FTA is to "substantially increase investment opportunities."[78] At the same time, the China–Pakistan FTA requires the parties to "encourage investors of the other Party to make investments in its territory."[79] However, the China–Pakistan FTA requires that investments be made "in accordance with [each Party's] laws and regulations" in order to qualify for protection, whilst the China–New Zealand FTA does not include the same requirement.

In addition to Chapter 11, which deals exclusively with investment issues, the China–New Zealand FTA places emphasis on "creating new opportunities for … investment."[80] This is intended to echo the objectives of the FTA, requiring specific actions on the part of the parties. Such actions include a policy dialogue and exchanges of information, providing assistance and facilities to business persons, etc.[81] The implementation of this obligation requires positive and concrete actions by the parties, which include cooperation and information exchange between government institutions, business groups and industrial associations, and the holding of investment marts.[82]

Another distinct feature of the China–New Zealand FTA is its emphasis on the special interests of small and medium-sized enterprises. This is a reflection of the economic and business reality of the bilateral relationship: because of the size

---

75 As its objective, the Framework Agreement wishes to strengthen and enhance economic, trade and investment collaboration by progressively relaxing trade and other barriers. To achieve this purpose, Articles 2 and 3 provide a timetable for a gradual integration of ASEAN members into their FTA with China.

76 The Free Trade Agreement between the Government of the People's Republic of China and the Government of the Islamic Republic of Pakistan was entered into on November 24, 2006; text available at: fta.mofcom.gov.cn/pakistan/xieyi/fta_xieyi_en.pdf.

77 For the purpose of promoting bilateral investment, the China–New Zealand FTA requires the establishment of a Committee on Investment, whilst the China–Pakistan FTA has no such arrangement. This difference in arrangements shows that China and New Zealand give bilateral investments a more important role. See China–New Zealand FTA, *supra*, note 47, Article 150.

78 Ibid., Article 2. Other objectives that are investment related include "promote conditions for fair competition in the free trade area," to "provide for the protection and enforcement of intellectual property rights," and to "eliminate barriers to trade in … services."

79 China–Pakistan FTA, *supra*, note 76, Article 47.

80 China–New Zealand FTA, *supra*, note 47, Article 173(b).

81 Ibid., Article 175.2. No similar provisions are found in the China–Pakistan FTA. This is a reflection of China's caution in committing to the establishment of a comprehensive mechanism which it may not be able to handle.

82 Ibid., Article 176.2(a) and (c).

of the New Zealand market, it is more attractive to the small and medium-sized Chinese entities; also, the majority of Chinese business entities are relatively small. Therefore, to promote investment by such enterprises is in the interests of both China and New Zealand.[83]

While negotiating with some countries to conclude new BITs, China has been actively engaged in amending its existing BITs since 2002.[84] In comparison with the BITs signed by China in the 1980s and 1990s, the new generation of BITs reflects new developments in many aspects.

Like the investment agreements entered into by other countries, the contemporary BITs and FTAs signed by China all contain provisions relating to investor–state arbitration. For that purpose, China became a state party to the Convention on the Settlement of Investment Disputes between States and Nationals of Other States (the "ICSID Convention") on February 6, 1993.[85] This was, however, considered a small step in ensuring the protection of foreign investors, as China had made a reservation that it "would only consider submitting to the jurisdiction of ICSID disputes over compensation resulting from expropriation or nationalization."[86] Thereafter, China accelerated the process of concluding new BITs and amending the existing ones. The most recently renegotiated BITs include the China–Germany BIT (December 2003),[87] the China–Finland BIT (November 2004),[88]

83 Most of the provisions of Chapter 14 on Cooperation are related to small and medium-sized enterprises. These provisions require the contracting parties to take government measures for the promotion of cooperation between small and medium-sized enterprises of both countries.

84 Since 2002, China has concluded 36 new or renegotiated BITs with the following countries: Côte d'Ivoire (2002), Bosnia and Herzegovina (2002), Trinidad and Tobago (2002), Djibouti (2003), Germany (2003), Guyana (2003), Benin (2004), Finland (2004), Latvia (2004), Sweden (2004), Tunisia (2004), Uganda (2004), Belgium and Luxembourg (2005), Czech Republic (2005), Equatorial Guinea (2005), Guinea (2005), North Korea (2005), Madagascar (2005), Portugal (2005), Spain (2005), Vanuatu (2006), India (2006), Russian Federation (2006), Costa Rica (2007), Cuba (2007), France (2007), Romania (2007), Seychelles (2007), Slovakia (2007), South Korea (2007), Colombia (2008), Mali (2009), Malta (2009), Switzerland (2009), Chad (2010), and Libya (2010).

85 China signed the ICSID Convention on February 9, 1990 and deposited its instrument of ratification on January 7, 1993; it became a member state on February 6, 1993. As for China's reservation, see ICSID official document No. ICSID 8-D.

86 The reservation made by China was considered by some as a reluctance to accede to international arbitration; see, for example, Mark A. Cymrot, "Investment Disputes with China," *Dispute Res. J.*, Aug.–Oct. 2006; available at: http://findarticles.com/p/ articles/mi_qa3923/is_200608/ ai_n16779631.

87 The Agreement between the People's Republic of China and the Federal Republic of Germany on the Encouragement and Reciprocal Protection of Investments was signed on December 1, 2003 and entered into force on November 11, 2005; text available at: http://www.unctad.org/ sections/dite/iia/docs/bits/china_germany.pdf.

88 The Agreement between the Government of the Republic of Finland and the Government of the People's Republic of China on the Encouragement and Reciprocal Protection of Investments was signed on November 15, 2004 and entered into force on November 15, 2006; text available at: http://www.unctad.org/sections/dite/iia/docs/bits/china_finland.pdf.

the China–Spain BIT (November 2005)[89] and the China–Portugal BIT (December 2005).[90]

Dispute settlement mechanisms in China's earlier BITs usually excluded the jurisdiction of the ICSID. Even for those BITs where ICSID jurisdiction was permitted, disputes that could be subject to international arbitration were limited to those involving the scope of expropriation and compensation,[91] a practice that has changed dramatically in recent years. In 1998, China entered into a BIT with Barbados whereby disputes between a foreign investor and the host state are permitted first to be settled through friendly negotiation and, if no solution can be reached within a reasonable period of time, upon the investor's discretion, they then may be submitted to the ICSID for arbitration.[92] Similar provisions can be found in most recent BITs to which China is a party. These BITs do not exclude the jurisdiction of the ICSID in relation to such important issues as the denial of benefits to foreign investors with capital from the host country or investments that are controlled or owned by domestic entities of the host country, prudent financial supervisory measures adopted by the host country, significant safety exceptions, etc.[93] Such changes in Chinese BIT practice have a great deal to do with the

89 The Agreement between the People's Republic of China and the Spanish Kingdom on the Encouragement and Reciprocal Protection of Investments was signed on November 14, 2005 and entered into force on July 1, 2008; text available at: http://www.unctad.org/sections/dite/iia/docs/bits/spain_china_sp.pdf (in Spanish).

90 The Agreement between the People's Republic of China and the Republic of Portugal on the Encouragement and Reciprocal Protection of Investments was signed on December 9, 2005 and entered into force on July 26, 2008; text available at: http://www.unctad.org/sections/dite/iia/docs/bits/china_portugal_por.pdf (in Portuguese).

91 For example, Article 9(3) of the 1994 China–Iceland BIT states: "If a dispute involving the amount of compensation for expropriation cannot be settled within six months after resort to negotiations as specified in paragraph 1 of this Article, it may be submitted at the request of either party to the International Centre for Settlement of Investment Disputes (ICSID) or to an *ad hoc* arbitral tribunal. Any dispute concerning other matters between an investor of either Contracting Party and the other Contracting Party may be submitted by mutual agreement to an *ad hoc* arbitral tribunal. The provisions of this paragraph shall not apply if the investor concerned has resorted to the procedure specified in paragraph 2 of this Article." Article XII(2) of the 1988 China–Australia BIT provides: "If the dispute has not been settled within three months from the date either party gave notice in writing to the other concerning the dispute, either party may take the following action: (a) in accordance with the law of the Contracting Party which has admitted the investment, initiate proceedings before its competent judicial or administrative bodies; and (b) where the parties agree or where the dispute relates to the amount of compensation payable under Article VIII, submit the dispute to an Arbitral Tribunal constituted in accordance with Annex A of this Agreement."

92 Agreement between the Government of the People's Republic of China and the Government of Barbados on the Encouragement and Reciprocal Protection of Investments, Article 8. This Agreement was signed on July 20, 1998 and entered into force on October 1, 1999; text available at: http://www.asianlii.org/cn/legis/cen/laws/ abtgotprocatgobctearpoi1447/.

93 For example, Article 9 of the 2003 China–Germany BIT provides that: "(1) Any dispute concerning investments between a Contracting Party and an investor of the other Contracting Party should as far as possible be settled amicably between the parties in dispute. (2) If the dispute cannot be settled within six months of the date when it has been raised by one of the parties in dispute, it shall, at the request of the investor of the other Contracting State, be submitted for arbitration. (3) The dispute shall be submitted for arbitration under the Convention of 18 March 1965 on the

fact that in recent years more and more Chinese entities have begun to invest overseas.[94] China is no longer only the largest developing host country of foreign investments but also an important capital exporting state. For the purpose of protecting its own natural and legal persons investing overseas, it is necessary for China to accept investor–state arbitration as a norm of international investment law.

The China–Pakistan FTA and the China–New Zealand FTA also provide for investor–state arbitration. Both FTAs make amicable settlement through negotiation a prerequisite for the submission of a dispute to international arbitration, the period of which is six months.[95] Thereafter, the investor concerned may decide to submit its dispute through other means. Under the China–Pakistan FTA, the alternate means include submitting the dispute to a competent domestic court of the host country and arbitration at the ICSID; once a local court is chosen, submitting the same dispute to the ICSID for arbitration is excluded.[96] The China–New Zealand FTA also authorizes investors to submit disputes to the ICSID for arbitration. At the same time, investors may make use of ICSID conciliation or UNCITRAL arbitration procedures.[97] Before availing themselves of international arbitration, a three-month advance notice condition must be satisfied. The purpose of this provision is to afford the host country an opportunity to require the investor concerned to go through administrative review procedures, which must already exist in the laws and regulations of the host country.[98] The administrative review process may not in any event exceed three months.

Host countries always welcome investors to submit their disputes to local courts, whilst investors in most cases prefer international arbitration. Under the China–New Zealand FTA, an investor, having submitted its dispute to a local court of the host country, may later decide to resort to international arbitration provided that it has withdrawn its case from the domestic court before a final judgment is reached.[99] This arrangement is in contrast with that under the China–Pakistan FTA.

The China–New Zealand FTA also has detailed rules on arbitration procedures, which have the effect of modifying the domestic laws of the parties and the

Settlement of Investment Disputes between States and Nationals of other States (ICSID), unless the parties in dispute agree on an *ad hoc* arbitral tribunal to be established under the Arbitration Rules of the United Nations Commission on International Trade Law (UNCITRAL) or other arbitration rule."

94 By 2012, China's FDI outflow had increased to US$84 billion in 2006, and its outward FDI stock had reached US$509 billion. Part of this overseas expansion involves considerable investment in other developing and transition economies. See UNCTAD, *supra*, note 43, at pp. 6 and 218.

95 See Articles 152 and 153 of the China–New Zealand FTA, *supra*, note 47, and Article 55(1) and (2) of the China–Pakistan FTA, *supra*, note 76.

96 Article 55(2) of the China–Pakistan FTA, ibid.

97 Article 153(2) of the China–New Zealand FTA, *supra*, note 47.

98 Id.

99 Ibid., Article 153(3).

ICSID Rules of Arbitration.[100] One such modification is that the period for submission of disputes is limited to three years from "the time at which the disputing investor became aware, or should reasonably have become aware, of a breach of obligation" by the host country, which has caused loss or damage to the investor or its investments.[101]

Challenges to the jurisdiction of an arbitral tribunal and objections to arbitration on the basis that the claim is without merit have become common tactics in international arbitration. According to the ICSID Convention, a precondition for ICSID's jurisdiction is that the dispute in question is legal in nature: "The jurisdiction of the Centre shall extend to any legal dispute arising directly out of an investment, between a Contracting State … and a national of another Contracting State."[102] In practice, what may constitute a legal dispute has been given a wide interpretation. In *Saipem*,[103] Bangladesh argued that the existence of a legal dispute within the meaning of the above provision presupposed the "existence of a cause of action" and that, since its dispute with the claimant concerned an arbitral award issued by the International Chamber of Commerce, it did not constitute a legal dispute.[104] The tribunal, however, held that a dispute over an arbitral award satisfied the requirement as "it involves a disagreement about legal rights or obligations."[105] The underlying principle was that:

> … the rights embodied in the ICC Award were not created by the Award, but arise out of the Contract. The ICC Award crystallized the parties' rights and obligations under the original contract. It can thus be left open whether the Award itself qualifies as an investment, since the contract rights which are crystallized by the Award constitute an investment within Article 1(1)(c) of the BIT.[106]

100 Article 153(4) of the China–New Zealand FTA clearly states that the provisions of the FTA on dispute settlement prevail over both ICSID and UNCITRAL arbitration and conciliation procedures.
101 Ibid., Article 154(1).
102 ICSID Convention, Article 25(1).
103 *Saipem S.p.A. v. People's Republic of Bangladesh*, ICSID Case No. ARB/05/07, Decision on Jurisdiction and Recommendation on Provisional Measures (March 21, 2007); available at: italaw.com/sites/default/files/case-documents/ita0733.pdf.
104 The BIT between Bangladesh and Italy defines "investment" in its Article 1(1) as "any kind of property invested," including "credit for sums of money or any right for pledges or services having an economic value connected with investments."
105 *Saipem*, *supra*, note 103, para. 94. Obviously, the *Saipem* Tribunal was influenced by the Report of the Executive Directors of the World Bank on the Convention, which stated that where there exists a dispute involving the determination of the existence of legal rights of a party or the scope thereof, there is a legal dispute. See *Report of the Executive Directors on the Convention on the Settlement of Investment Disputes Between States and Nationals of Other States*, World Bank (March 18, 1965), para. 26; available at: http://www.worldbank.org/icsid/staticfiles/basicdoc/partB-section05.htm#03.
106 *Saipem*, ibid., para. 127. In the view of the tribunal, "the notion of investment pursuant to Article 25 of the ICSID must be understood as covering all the elements of the operation, that is not only the ICC Arbitration, but also *inter alia* the Contract, the construction itself and the Retention Money;" ibid., para. 114.

What is the response of China to this issue? The China–New Zealand FTA requires that a state party that wishes to raise objections to jurisdiction must file its submission no later than 30 days after the constitution of the tribunal.[107] The tribunal must decide on the issue of these objections first and must give the parties a reasonable opportunity to present their views and observations.[108] With regard to the interpretation of the FTA, the state party to a dispute may request the tribunal to seek a joint interpretation by the parties thereto. The joint interpretation, which must be reached within 60 days, has binding force on the tribunal. Where a joint interpretation is not reached, the tribunal should decide the issue on its own account.[109] This looks like a balanced arrangement: on the one hand, it requires the state party to disputes to take actions without delay and, on the other hand, the FTA contracting parties may give joint interpretations. It is always the Chinese position that those who have participated in the law-making should know best the meaning of the provisions thereof.

With government accountability in respect of arbitration growing, the China–New Zealand FTA permits a state party to an investment dispute to make public all documents relating to arbitration, except those specifically designated as confidential information when submitted to the arbitral tribunal.[110]

The tribunal's award is final and may be in the form of (a) monetary damages plus interest or (b) restitution of property, in which case the state party may choose to pay monetary damages in lieu of restitution.[111] Although costs and fees may be included in an award, no punitive damages may be awarded.[112] Also, a "disputing party may not seek enforcement of a final award until all applicable review procedures have been completed."[113]

III. The ICSID dispute settlement system

Investment dispute resolution is different from commercial dispute resolution; the former involves a foreign investor and a host state, whilst the latter usually involves private entities as disputing parties. It is, of course, possible that an investment dispute—an investor–state dispute—may be resolved through the domestic courts of the host state. Understandably, no foreign investor would prefer, if it has a choice, to submit its dispute with the host state to the local courts. As an alternative, most—if not all—of the modern BITs provide for investor–state arbitration to be conducted by a third body, which may, as in commercial arbitration, follow its own arbitration rules or adopt the UNCITRAL arbitration rules. Currently, BITs and the investment chapter of FTAs usually stipulate that investor–state disputes shall

---

107 China–New Zealand FTA, *supra*, note 47, Article 154(2).
108 Ibid., Article 154(3). When making a decision, the tribunal must consider whether either the claim or the objection was frivolous or manifestly without merit.
109 Ibid., Article 155.
110 Ibid., Article 157.
111 Ibid., Article 158(1).
112 Ibid., Article 158(3).
113 Ibid., Article 158(5).

be submitted to the International Centre for Settlement of Investment Disputes ("the ICSID" or "the Centre"), the Permanent Court of Arbitration ("the PCA") or another arbitration institution or an *ad hoc* tribunal. Among these institutions, the ICSID is the most popular for the handling of investor–state disputes.

With regard to the rules governing arbitration proceedings, where an arbitration institution—like the ICSID—has its own regulations, the dispute, once submitted to it, would be subject to the rules and procedures of the institution. At the same time, where an *ad hoc* tribunal or the PCA is to conduct the arbitration, the UNCITRAL rules would be followed. As in commercial arbitration, party autonomy is the key in all investor–state arbitration. Unless there is consent by all the disputing parties with regard to the arbitration body and the arbitration rules, no jurisdiction may be exercised by any tribunal. Insofar as arbitration rules are concerned, although they appear to be diversified among various institutions, they have much more in common than they have differences, and the latter usually only relate to the detailed procedures. In such circumstances, this part will only discuss the ICSID mechanisms, for two reasons. In the first place, the ICSID arbitration rules are similar to—or at least not very different from—those of other institutions. Second, there is an annulment procedure in the ICSID mechanisms that does not exist elsewhere.

A. ICSID arbitration mechanisms

The ICSID was established by the Convention on the Settlement of Investment Disputes between States and Nationals of Other States,[114] which has an Administrative Council as its governing body.[115] The establishment of the ICSID was based on recognition of the "need for international cooperation for economic development, and the role of private international investment therein" and that "the possibility that from time to time disputes may arise in connection with such investment between Contracting States and nationals of other Contracting States."[116]

Regarding dispute settlement, the Centre maintains a panel of conciliators and a panel of arbitrators with members designated by the contracting states to the Convention. Where a dispute is submitted to the ICSID, an arbitral tribunal will be constituted, either with a sole arbitrator or any uneven number of

---

114 The Convention, formulated under the auspices of the International Bank for Reconstruction and Development (the World Bank), came into force on October 14, 1966. By the end of 2013, there were 158 countries which were contracting parties to the Convention. For details, see "List of Contracting States and Other Signatories of the Convention (as of November 1, 2013);" available at: https://icsid.worldbank.org/ICSID/FrontServle t?reques tType=ICSIDDocRH& actionVal=ShowDocument&language=English.

115 Regarding the functions and powers of the Administrative Council, see Article 6 of the ICSID Convention.

116 The Preamble of the ICSID Convention. The Convention is complemented by Regulations and Rules adopted by the Administrative Council.

arbitrators.[117] Where the disputing parties cannot agree on the number or the method of appointment of arbitrators, a tribunal shall consist of three arbitrators—each disputing party appointing one arbitrator and the presiding arbitrator to be appointed by agreement of the parties.[118] If either party fails to appoint an arbitrator or the parties fail to reach an agreement on appointing the third arbitrator within 90 days after the registration of the request for arbitration, the chairman of the ICSID shall appoint the arbitrators from among the members of the panel to fill any vacancies.[119] The disputing parties, however, may appoint anyone to serve as arbitrators. As a general rule, no majority of arbitrators may have the nationality of either disputing party. In practice, this never happens, because after each disputing party makes its own appointment, the third arbitrator is almost always a national of a third country.

Arbitral tribunals are judges of their own competence and as such may determine their jurisdiction themselves.[120] Tribunals are required to conduct arbitration proceedings in accordance with the rules of law agreed by the parties and, in the absence of such agreement, with the "law of the Contracting State party to the dispute ... and such rules of international law as may be applicable."[121] In any event, a tribunal may not find "*non liquet* on the ground of silence or obscurity of the law."[122]

As with commercial arbitration, investor–state arbitration at the ICSID is carried out by consent of the disputing parties. In general, BITs and FTAs are the source of consent by the state party to a dispute, whilst the investor's consent may be confirmed by its request for arbitration.[123] A recent and controversial issue in respect of consent is interpretation of the most-favored-nation clause to be discussed later in this book.

Although ICSID tribunals are judges of their own competence, their jurisdiction is qualified by Article 25 of the Convention, according to which the jurisdiction of tribunals is confined to legal disputes "arising directly out of an investment, between a Contracting Party ... and a national of another Contracting State." In practice, the respondent host states often invoke this provision to challenge the jurisdiction of tribunals. Such challenges range from determination of qualified investments and investors to whether a dispute in question "arises directly" from a qualified investment.[124] To complicate the issue of jurisdiction even further, a contracting state may exclude certain classes of disputes from application of the ICSID Convention.[125]

---

117 Article 37(2)(a) of the ICSID Convention.
118 Ibid., Article 37(2)(b).
119 Ibid., Article 38.
120 Ibid., Article 41.
121 Ibid., Article 42(1).
122 Ibid., Article 42(2).
123 For discussion of this issue, see Chapter 5 on "Consent as a condition of jurisdiction" in this book.
124 These issues will be examined in detail in the chapters to follow.
125 Article 25(4) of the ICSID Convention.

Another unique and important feature of the ICSID system is its annulment mechanism.

B. Annulment procedure under the ICSID mechanism

Investor–state arbitration under the ICSID on the one hand reflects the finality of arbitration by requiring the contracting parties to recognize and enforce arbitral awards,[126] while on the other hand it provides a remedy for curing the mistakes of investment arbitration tribunals—an annulment procedure. Article 52(1) of the ICSID Convention provides:

> (1) Either party may request annulment of the award by an application in writing addressed to the Secretary-General on one or more of the following grounds:
> (a) that the Tribunal was not properly constituted;
> (b) that the Tribunal has manifestly exceeded its powers;
> (c) that there was corruption on the part of a member of the Tribunal;
> (d) that there has been a serious departure from a fundamental rule of procedure; or
> (e) that the award has failed to state the reasons on which it is based.

The annulment procedure represents a compromise of the ICSID arbitration system with commercial arbitration mechanisms;[127] in commercial arbitration, many countries have laws authorizing their domestic courts to set aside arbitral awards.[128] Being of that nature, the ICSID annulment mechanism is designed to be used only in extraordinary circumstances.

1 General issues re annulment

The most important issue relating to the ICSID annulment procedure is how to distinguish annulment from appeal. To start with, the annulment procedure under the ICSID is not an appeal procedure. As such, a successful application for annulment only results in invalidation of the original award. In other words, an *ad hoc* annulment committee may annul an award partially or in its entirety but it may not amend or substitute the award with its own decisions. In practice it is very difficult to ensure that:

---

126 See Articles 53–54 of the ICSID Convention.
127 Hans van Houtte, "Article 52 of the Washington Convention: A Brief Introduction," in Emmanuel Gaillard and Yas Banifatemi (eds.), *Annulment of ICSID Awards*, Juris Publishing, Inc., 2004, at p. 14. See also ICSID, *Documents Concerning the Origin and the Formulation of the Convention*, Vol. II, 1969, pp. 849–50.
128 This practice is, however, not without restrictions, as the 1958 New York Convention on the Recognition and Enforcement of Foreign Arbitral Awards does not permit its contracting parties to set aside arbitral awards made in other contracting parties' territories.

On the one hand, they should not fall into the temptation to uphold the award because of solidarity with their fellow ICSID arbitrators. On the other hand, they should also be careful not to create an impression that they are better minds than the arbitrators whose award they have to review.[129]

It has been the practice from the first annulment decision that all *ad hoc* committees, almost without exception, stress the importance of distinguishing annulment from appeal and acknowledge their own limited functions. For instance, the *Klöckner ad hoc* Committee expressly said:

> It is clear that "error in judicando" could not in itself be accepted as a ground for annulment without indirectly reintroducing an appeal against the arbitral award, and the ad hoc Committee under Article 52 of the Convention does not, any more than the Permanent Court of Arbitration in the *Orinoco* case, have the "duty … to say if the case has been well or ill judged, but whether the award must be annulled."[130]

In reality, however, *ad hoc* annulment committees have often acted beyond the limits set by the ICSID Convention. Ironically, the *Klöckner ad hoc* Committee is among those which have been severely criticized for having exceeded their authority under the ICSID Convention by re-examining the merits of the cases.[131] In this regard, an often quoted paragraph of the *Klöckner ad hoc* Committee's decision reads:

> To summarize, while the Award contains *some* reasoning on the conditions for applying the exception based on non-performance, the question may be asked whether these reasons are sufficient or "sufficiently relevant." It is not necessary to answer this, since on the question of the *effects* of the exception based on non-performance, the Award does not state the legal grounds nor does it state the rules of civil law (reinforced by references to scholarly opinion and case law comparable to those which the Award cited on the general principle) which could justify its conclusion. In reality, everything occurs as if the Arbitral Tribunal had considered the *exceptio non dimpleti contractus* as a ground for *extinguishing* obligations under French law. On the basis of the Award's own citations, [its] conclusion does not necessarily follow, nor does it conform to the understanding the [Annulment] Committee may have of this area of law.[132]

---

129 Van Houtte, *supra*, note 127, at p. 14.
130 *Klöckner Industrie-Anlagen GmbH v. Republic of Cameroon* ("*Klöckner I*"), ICSID Case No. ARB/81/2, Decision on Annulment (May 3, 1985), para. 61 (emphasis in original).
131 See Jason Clapham, "Finality of Investor-State Arbitral Awards: Has the Tide Turned and Is There a Need for Reform?" 26 *J. Int'L Arb*. 437, 2009, at pp. 454–56; and W. Michael Reisman, "The Breakdown of the Control Mechanism in ICSID Arbitration," 1989 *Duke L. J.* 739, at pp. 755–81.
132 *Klöckner I*, *supra*, note 130, para. 171 (emphasis in original).

It is evident that the *Klöckner ad hoc* Committee was in effect assessing the substantive reasons given by the original tribunal or the merits of the original award. The impression was given that the award was annulled because the *ad hoc* Committee disagreed with the reasons given by the tribunal for its award. The criticisms that it functioned as an appeal body rather than as an annulment committee were basically true.[133] At the same time, it may also be true that as the first ICSID annulment committee the *Klöckner ad hoc* Committee was breaking new ground and its mistakes are understandable, if not forgivable.

Indeed, another annulment decision which is also considered as part of the first group of ICSID annulment decisions—that in *Amco v. Indonesia*[134]—has also been criticized.[135] Like the *Klöckner I ad hoc* Committee, the *Amco I ad hoc* Committee was viewed as having intruded into the affairs of the original arbitration tribunal by reviewing the merits of the case.

In the second generation of ICSID annulment decisions, including those in *MINE*,[136] *Klöckner II* and *Amco II*,[137] the *ad hoc* annulment committees have been considered to have acted with less intrusion into the original tribunals' awards. The representative decisions of the third generation include those in *Wena Hotels*[138] and *Vivendi*,[139] in which the *ad hoc* annulment committees are also considered to have properly performed their functions.[140] This conclusion, however, may be correct only insofar as the final decisions of the *ad hoc* annulment committees are concerned. In other words, those *ad hoc* annulment committees did not annul the original awards. If an examination is made of the way in which the *ad hoc* annulment committees performed their duties, it is obvious that several of the

---

133 See for instance, George R. Deaume, "The Finality of Arbitration Involving States: Recent Developments," 5 *Arb. Int'l* 21, 1989, p. 32; Mark B. Feldman, "The Annulment Proceedings and the Finality of ICSID Arbitral Awards," 2 *ICSID Rev Foreign Inv. L. J*. 85, 1987; Jan Paulsson, "ICSID's Achievements and Prospects," 6 *ICSID Rev Foreign Inv. L. J*. 380, 1991, pp. 388 *et seq.*; and Reisman, *supra*, note 131.

134 *Amco Asia Corp. v. Republic of Indonesia*, ICSID Case No. ARB/81/1, Decision on Annulment (May 16, 1986), 1 *ICSID Rep*. 509, 1993.

135 Christoph Schreuer, "Three Generations of ICSID Annulment Proceedings," in Gaillard and Banifatemi (eds.), *supra*, note 127, at pp. 17–19; text also available at: https://www.google. com.hk/?gws_rd=cr&ei=_Xg9Uq2yLoq9iAeg_oFQ#q=Christoph+Schreuer%2C+Three+ Generations+of+ICSID+Annulment+Proceedings%2C+in+ANNULMENT+OF+ICSID+ AWARDS+17.

136 *Maritime International Nominees Establishment (MINE) v. Republic of Guinea*, ICSID Case No. ARB/84/4, Decision on Annulment (December 22, 1989), para. 5.05.

137 The *Klöckner II* and *Amco II* decisions were not published.

138 *Wena Hotels Limited v. Arab Republic of Egypt*, ICSID Case No. ARB/98/4, Decision on Annulment (February 5, 2002), para. 57.

139 *Compañia de Aguas del Aconquija S.A. and Vivendi Universal S.A. (formerly Compagnie Générale des Eaux) v. Argentine Republic*, ICSID Case No. ARB/97/3, Decision on Annulment (July 3, 2002) ("*Vivendi I*, Annulment Decision"), para. 65.

140 For discussion of the three generations of ICSID *ad hoc* annulment Committee decisions, see Walid Ben Hamida, "Two Nebulous ICSID Features: The Notion of Investment and the Scope of Annulment Control: Ad Hoc Committee's Decision in Patrick Mitchell v. Democratic Republic of Congo," 24 *J. Int'l Arb*. 287, 2007, at p. 301; Van Houtte, *supra*, note 127, at pp. 11–16; and Schreuer, *supra*, note 135.

committees intruded one way or another into the substantive issues of the cases. For instance, regarding Article 52(1)(e) of the ICSID Convention—failure to state reasons—the *Wena Hotels ad hoc* Committee commented:

> If the award does not meet the minimal requirement as to the reasons given by the Tribunal, it does not necessarily need to be resubmitted to a new Tribunal. If the *ad hoc* Committee so concludes, on the basis of the knowledge it has received upon the dispute, the reasons supporting the Tribunal's conclusions can be explained by the *ad hoc* Committee itself.[141]

Although this passage could be said to be no more than *obiter dictum*, it shows the extent to which the *Wena Hotels ad hoc* Committee was prepared to go. Where an *ad hoc* annulment committee can "explain" the reasons of a tribunal, it is no longer conducting an annulment but an appeal.

The *Wena Hotels ad hoc* Committee's attitude, in fact, is not unique, and that is one reason why some commentators consider that the trend is that *ad hoc* committees are overstepping their limits. Schreuer noted that: "[i]n part this is due to the inflationary nature of requests for annulment. In large measure this is due to an extensive interpretation of the grounds for annulment and a tendency of some ad hoc committees to take an expansive view of their functions."[142] The expansive role assumed by some ICSID *ad hoc* annulment committees is also partly the result of the fact that at present the losing parties very often institute annulment proceedings to, at least, postpone the enforcement of the award and, with a bit of luck, to overturn it.[143] As more and more legal counsel are familiar with ICSID arbitration, increasingly creative techniques are employed, one of which is the attempt to expand the grounds for annulment. As a result, even in a passive way, *ad hoc* annulment committees are bound to expand their functions. Another technique is to raise as many grounds for annulment as possible,[144] although in general three grounds—manifest excess of powers, serious departure from a fundamental

---

141 *Wena Hotels*, Annulment Decision, *supra*, note 138, para. 83.
142 Christoph Schreuer, "From ICSID Annulment to Appeal: Half Way Down the Slippery Slope," *The Law and Practice of International Courts and Tribunals 10*, Martinus Nijhoff, 2011, pp. 211–25, at p. 213. According to Schreuer: "In 2010 ICSID ad hoc Committees have rendered eight decisions on annulment. Four of these decisions led to the annulment of the respective awards. In four cases the awards survived." Id.
143 According to one ICSID report, up to June 2013 there had been 47 annulment applications registered, of which 14 were discontinued, 13 were either fully or partially supported, and 20 were rejected. See ICSID, *The ICSID Caseload – Statistics (Issue 2013-2)*, p. 17.
144 On this issue, Schreuer commented: "In *Rumeli* and *Helnan* the Requests for annulment are each based on four aspects of the Awards. In *Sempra* the ad hoc Committee noted that Argentina had raised 'a number of issues' each of which, on Argentina's case, constituted one or more grounds for the Award's annulment in its entirety. The Request in *Enron* listed more aspects of the Award that in Argentina's view deserved annulment than one can reasonably count—a veritable area bombardment. ... In *Sempra* the Request listed four grounds, adding improper constitution of the Tribunal. The Request in *Vivendi II* initially invoked all five grounds ..." See Schreuer, *supra*, note 142, at p. 214 (footnotes omitted).

rule of procedure, and failure to state reasons—are the most common grounds alleged by the requesting parties.

With regard to the way *ad hoc* committees conduct annulment proceedings, there is no uniform practice. Some committees follow the organization of the grounds under Article 52(1) of the ICSID Convention, whilst others do not adopt such an approach. For instance, in the *Fraport* annulment proceedings,[145] the applicant—Fraport—raised three grounds for annulment, namely: manifest excess of powers; serious departure from a fundamental rule of procedure; and failure to state reasons.[146] The *ad hoc* Committee went through all the grounds raised by the applicant. In fact, even after it had found that the tribunal had committed a serious departure from a fundamental rule of procedure which would annul the award in its entirety,[147] it continued to analyze whether or not it had to state reasons. In *Impregilo*,[148] the applicant—Argentina—organized its claims on five grounds that the tribunal had: (1) manifestly exceeded its powers; (2) manifestly exceeded the material limits of its competence; (3) abrogated the normative content of the standard on fair and equitable treatment; (4) failed to state the reasons on which the award was based and exceeded its powers in deciding on the defenses based on the extraordinary situation faced by Argentina by failing to clarify its meaning; and (5) compensation. On each ground, Argentina argued on excess of powers, serious departure from a fundamental rule of procedure, failure to state reasons, etc. Despite such organization by the applicant, the *ad hoc* annulment Committee decided to organize its own analysis in accordance with the order of Article 52(1) of the ICSID Convention.[149]

The *Sempra ad hoc* Committee adopted a very different approach. In its view:

> Once an ad hoc committee has concluded that there is … one instance … which warrants annulment of the Award in its entirety, this will be the end of the ad hoc committee's examination … it is unnecessary to consider whether there are other grounds—whether in respect of the same matter or other matters—that may also lead to annulment.[150]

The reason given by the *Sempra ad hoc* Committee for this ruling is that once an award is annulled in its entirety, it would lose the effect of *res judicata* and therefore any further examination becomes unnecessary. This approach is in line with the principle of judicial/arbitral economy and should be supported. After all, any further review done by an *ad hoc* annulment Committee will have a direct effect on the time and money spent by the parties.

In addition to these approaches, there are annulment decisions that are not

145 *Fraport v. Philippines*, ICSID Case No. ARB/03/25, Decision on Annulment (December 23, 2010).
146 Ibid., para. 32.
147 Ibid., para. 247.
148 *Impregilo S.p.A. v. Argentine Republic*, ICSID Case No. ARB/07/17, Decision on Annulment (January 24, 2014).
149 Ibid., para. 114.
150 *Sempra v. Argentina*, ICSID Case No. ARB/02/16, Decision on Annulment (June 2010), para. 78.

organized in accordance with the order of Article 52(1) of the ICSID Convention. A recent example is *Malicorp v. Egypt*,[151] in which the *ad hoc* Committee examined the allegation of serious departure from a fundamental rule of procedure first and then failure to state reasons and manifest excess of powers. The most complicated structure of organization is perhaps the annulment decision in *Vivendi II*.[152] As the case was brought to an *ad hoc* annulment Committee for a second time, the Committee went out of its way in examining various aspects of the decisions of the first tribunal, the first *ad hoc* Committee and the second tribunal. Consequently, this made its own decision very difficult to follow. Another annulment decision with a similar pattern is that in *Enron v. Argentina*.[153] Although there is no requirement that *ad hoc* annulment committees must adopt a certain structure in their analysis, it is important for them to give clear reasons for each ground of annulment alleged by applicants.

In any event, among all the issues discussed above, the most important one is still the distinction between annulment and appeal. As the *ad hoc* Committee in *Amco II* said: "[i]t is incumbent upon *Ad Hoc* Committees to resist the temptation to rectify incorrect decisions or to annul unjust awards."[154] In reality, however, it is increasingly the case that *ad hoc* annulment committees fail to resist the temptation to function as appeal bodies. The most recent annulment decision to appear before completion of this book—that in *Impregilo*—is most probably an exception, wherein the *ad hoc* annulment Committee time and time again stated that it was not in a position to annul the original award because it was not an appeal body.[155]

2 Tribunal not properly constituted

The ground that the tribunal is not properly constituted is not often invoked to annul an award. In *Vivendi II*, Argentina challenged the impartiality of Professor Gabrielle Kaufmann-Kohler—one of the arbitrators—because she simultaneously served as a member of the board of directors of UBS, Vivendi's single largest shareholder.[156] The *ad hoc* Committee viewed the matter as a "most serious shortcoming" but also considered that "Professor Kaufmann-Kohler's exercise of

151 *Malicorp Limited v. Arab Republic of Egypt*, ICSID Case No. ARB/08/18, Decision on the Application for Annulment (July 3, 2013).
152 *Vivendi (II) v. Argentina*, ICSID Case No. ARB/97/3, Decision on Annulment (August 10, 2010).
153 *Enron v. Argentina*, ICSID Case No. ARB/01/3, Decision on Annulment (July 30, 2010).
154 *Amco v. Indonesia*, Resubmitted Case: Decision on Annulment (December 3, 1992), para. 1.18, quoted from Schreuer, *supra*, note 142, at p. 213.
155 With regard to whether or not the tribunal should have applied the MFN clause to dispute settlement procedures, the *ad hoc* annulment Committee first stated that where there were treaty provisions regulating the matter and the tribunal failed to apply such provisions, there would be grounds for it to annul the award. As that was not the case, the *ad hoc* annulment Committee ruled that it had "no authority to determine whether or not the Tribunal should apply Article 3.1 of the BIT in order to establish its jurisdiction to review the merits of the dispute." See *Impregilo, supra*, note 148, paras. 136–37 and 141.
156 *Vivendi II*, Annulment Decision, *supra*, note 152, paras. 20–21.

independent judgment … was in the circumstances not impaired."[157] Apparently, the *Vivendi II ad hoc* Committee's decision was based on its judgment that there would be no "demonstrable difference in outcome" and, consequently, it "would be unjust to deny the Claimants the benefit of the Award."[158]

There are at least two questionable issues in this decision. In the first place, the impression given by the *Vivendi II ad hoc* annulment Committee is that the outcome of the award played a part in its decision on the proper constitution of the tribunal, which should not be a consideration. By saying that there would be no "demonstrable difference in outcome," the *Vivendi II ad hoc* annulment Committee apparently admitted that, had the award been different, the constitution of the tribunal might have been considered improper. This is a demonstration of the consideration by the *Vivendi II ad hoc* annulment Committee of the substantive issues of the case. Once an *ad hoc* annulment committee touches upon the outcome of the award, it has crossed the limits of annulment and stepped over into the boundary of appeal. Second, the actual function of the arbitrator should not be a concern either, as again it involves the substance of the arbitral proceedings. In fact, the *Vivendi II ad hoc* Committee also took into account the length of the case when making its decision,[159] which is also irrelevant and very unfortunate, to say the least.

In *Azurix*,[160] Argentina requested the annulment of the arbitral award on the ground that the tribunal was not properly constituted because its president, Andres Rigo Sureda, was "immersed in various conflicts of interest which cast reasonable doubts on his impartiality."[161] The alleged conflicts included, as contended by Argentina, that Rigo Sureda had been employed as a consultant by the law firm that represented Azurix in another investor–state dispute, in which Azurix also appointed an arbitrator who had then served as legal counsel in the case between Azurix and Argentina. Argentina alleged that Rigo Sureda had failed to disclose his possible conflicts and that by virtue of those conflicts, there was a serious departure from a fundamental rule of procedure.[162] It should be pointed out that, during the arbitration proceedings, Argentina requested the tribunal to disqualify Rigo Sureda in accordance with Article 57 of the ICSID Convention but that proposal was rejected by the tribunal.

The *Azurix ad hoc* Committee interpreted Article 52(1)(a)—tribunal not properly constituted—as a ground for annulment relating to procedures and said that, in its view, the quality of the arbitrators and proposals for disqualifying arbitrators should follow the procedures established under ICSID provisions other than Article 52(1)(a). Accordingly, where a proposal to disqualify an arbitrator is "rejected in accordance with the procedure established in Article 58 of the

157 Ibid., para. 238.
158 Ibid., para. 240.
159 Ibid., para. 241.
160 *Azurix Corp. v. Argentine Republic*, ICSID Case No. ARB/01/12, Decision on the Application for Annulment (September 1, 2009).
161 Ibid., para. 249.
162 Ibid., paras. 252–53.

ICSID Convention and ICSID Arbitration Rule 9," in the *ad hoc* Committee's view, "it cannot be said that the tribunal was 'not properly constituted' by reason of non-compliance with the first sentence of Article 57."[163] This distinction of the functions between Article 52 and other provisions relating to disqualification of arbitrators is very important, for otherwise Article 52 would serve to provide new opportunities for challenging members of tribunals. In fact, the *Azurix ad hoc* Committee also ruled that even in cases where new evidence became available or known to a party subsequent to the rendering of an arbitral award, the party should seek revision of the award pursuant to Article 51. The role of an *ad hoc* annulment committee in such cases is to review whether or not decisions have been made in accordance with the procedures for revision of arbitral awards and whether or not such decisions have been made by the authorized bodies.[164] It therefore rejected the applicant's request to annul the award on the ground that there were conflicts of interest on the part of one arbitrator.

Obviously, the *Azurix ad hoc* Committee adopted quite a measured and correct approach. It confined its functions to reviewing whether or not the established procedures had been followed rather than whether such procedures had been correctly followed. This measured approach keeps the annulment procedure within its established limits. At the same time, it should be noted that, had the *Vivendi II ad hoc* Committee taken the same approach, it would not have annulled the award. The key difference between the two cases is that the *Azurix ad hoc* Committee correctly refused to review the decision by the tribunal insofar as the procedures had been followed, whilst the *Vivendi II ad hoc* Committee actually engaged in substantive review. Notwithstanding the end result, the *Vivendi II ad hoc* Committee's conduct was more like an appeal proceeding than an annulment, which should be avoided by all *ad hoc* annulment committees.

3 Manifest excess of powers

Manifest excess of powers is often invoked as a ground for annulment. An important issue is the definition of the word "manifest."[165] Annulment committees have interpreted the term "manifest" as "obvious" or "readily recognizable." For instance, the *Wena Hotels ad hoc* Committee considered that the term "manifest" "must be self-evident rather than the product of elaborate interpretations one way or the other. When the latter happens the excess of power is no longer manifest."[166] In a similar tone, the *CDC ad hoc* Committee stated that "even if a Tribunal exceeds its powers, the excess must be plain on its face for annulment

---

163 Ibid., para. 280.
164 Ibid., para. 281.
165 The word "manifest" was not present in the Preliminary Draft of the ICSID Convention and was first added in the First Draft. Its inclusion is said to be a result of the insistence of Germany, which feared that without the qualifier, arbitral awards might run the risks of being frustrated. See Christoph H. Schreuer et al., *The ICSID Convention: A Commentary*, 2nd ed., Cambridge University Press, 2001, p. 938.
166 *Wena Hotels*, Annulment Decision, *supra*, note 138, para. 25.

to be an available remedy."[167] At the same time, in the *CDC ad hoc* Committee's view, "[a]ny excess apparent in a Tribunal's conduct, if susceptible of argument 'one way or the other,' is not manifest."[168] This is, of course, by no means the end of the issue.

Even with regard to the term "manifest," there are different interpretations. In *Lucchetti*, for instance, the *ad hoc* Committee considered that "the word 'manifest' should be given considerable weight also when matters of jurisdiction are concerned."[169] At the same time, it noted that an *ad hoc* annulment committee is "not charged with the task of determining whether one interpretation is 'better' than another, or indeed which among severable interpretations might be considered the 'best' one" and that it was only concerned "with the process by which the Tribunal moved from its premise to its conclusion."[170] It then decided that "[t]he interpretation of Article 2 adopted by the Tribunal is clearly a tenable one," although "there are other tenable interpretations."[171] Clearly, the *Lucchetti ad hoc* Committee strictly adhered to the principle of annulment. By doing so, regardless of the outcome of the annulment proceedings, so long as the tribunal has exercised its jurisdiction within the limit of its powers, for example by conducting a "tenable" interpretation of the relevant treaty, an ICSID *ad hoc* annulment committee should not intrude into the decisions made by the tribunal. This approach is different from that taken by the *Vivendi I ad hoc* Committee.

In *Vivendi I*, in considering what might constitute a manifest excess of powers, the *ad hoc* Committee emphasized the outcome of the tribunal's decision, rather than the process itself. In its view, where "the failure to exercise a jurisdiction is clearly capable of making a difference to the result,"[172] a manifest excess of powers has occurred. Yet, in order to ascertain whether a difference might be made by an error in establishing jurisdiction, an *ad hoc* annulment committee must go into the substance of the disputed facts, in which it ends up functioning as an appeal body, which should be avoided. In the end, the *Vivendi I ad hoc* Committee decided:

---

167 *CDC Group plc v. Republic of Seychelles*, ICSID Case No. ARB/02/14, Decision on the Application for Annulment (June 29, 2005), IIC 48 (2005), at para. 41. The *Lucchetti ad hoc* Committee observed that, "[m]oreover, a request for annulment is not an appeal, which means that there should not be a full review of the tribunal's award;" and that "the word 'manifest' should be given considerable weight also when matters of jurisdiction are concerned." See *Empresas Lucchetti, S.A. and Lucchetti Peru, S.A. v. Republic of Peru*, ICSID Case No. ARB/03/4 (also known as: *Industria Nacional de Alimentos, A.S. and Indalsa Perú S.A. v. Republic of Peru*), Decision on Annulment (September 5, 2007), at para. 101.

168 *CDC Group*, Annulment Decision, ibid., para. 41.

169 *Lucchetti*, Decision on Annulment, *supra*, note 167, para. 101.

170 Ibid., para. 112.

171 Id.

172 *Vivendi I*, Annulment Decision, *supra*, note 139, at para. 86. Looking to the "clear and serious implications" of the decision and "the surrounding circumstances," the *ad hoc* Committee felt obliged to characterize the refusal of jurisdiction as a "manifest" error. The *CMS ad hoc* Committee appears to have taken the same approach when considering Argentina's argument that the tribunal in that case had exceeded its jurisdiction; see *CMS v. Argentina*, ICSID Case No. ARB/01/08, Decision on Annulment (September 25, 2007).

[T]he Committee concludes that the Tribunal exceeded its powers in the sense of Article 52(1)(b), in that the Tribunal, having jurisdiction over the Tucumán claims, failed to decide those claims. Given the clear and serious implications of that decision for Claimants in terms of Article 8(2) of the BIT, and the surrounding circumstances, the Committee can only conclude that that excess of powers was manifest.[173]

The *Soufraki ad hoc* Committee took yet another approach. It first stated that "the term 'manifest' is a strong and emphatic term referring to obviousness."[174] It then concluded that "a manifest excess of powers implies that the excess of power should at once be textually obvious and substantively serious."[175] Unfortunately, the *Soufraki ad hoc* Committee did not further explain how the test that it proposed would work. For instance, what is the requirement to annul an award that is textually obvious? Is that different from the findings of the *Repsol ad hoc* Committee that "exceeding one's powers is *'manifest'* when it is *'obvious by itself'* simply by reading the Award, that is, even prior to a detailed examination of its contents?"[176]

At the same time, in looking into whether an excess of powers is "substantively serious," should an *ad hoc* annulment committee conduct a substantive examination of the facts involved? In a way, the *Soufraki ad hoc* Committee further complicated the already diversified views on what may meet the requirement of "manifest," rather than resolving any. Nevertheless, the *Malicorp ad hoc* Committee concurred with the *Soufraki* annulment decision, holding that it understood "'manifest' to mean both obvious and serious" and that it did "not believe that these two terms are inconsistent to the extent that what has serious and substantial implications is also clear and obvious."[177] The *Malicorp ad hoc* Committee, however, did not conduct a substantive review of the tribunal's decision in the case.

In addition to definition of the term "manifest," what may constitute an excess of power is equally important. In this regard, ICSID *ad hoc* annulment committees are in agreement. It is now quite well settled that both exercise of powers such as that of a jurisdiction that a tribunal does not have and/or a refusal or failure to assume the jurisdiction that a tribunal should have exercised are considered to be excess of powers. This was explicitly put by the *Malicorp ad hoc* Committee, approving the *Vivendi I ad hoc* Committee's decision that:

> The most significant excess of powers ... occurs when the Tribunal exceeds the limits of its jurisdiction. This may be the case where a tribunal "exercises a jurisdiction which it does not have under the relevant agreement or treaty

---

173 *Vivendi I*, Annulment Decision, ibid., para. 115.
174 *Hussein Nuaman Soufraki v. United Arab Emirates*, ICSID Case No. ARB/02/7, Decision on the Application for Annulment (June 5, 2007), para. 39.
175 Ibid., para. 40.
176 *Repsol YPF Ecuador S.A. v. Empresa Estatal Petróleos del Ecuador (Petroecuador)*, ICSID Case No. ARB/01/10, Decision on Annulment (January 8, 2007), para. 36 (emphases in original).
177 *Malicorp*, Decision on Annulment, *supra*, note 151, para. 56.

and the ICSID Convention, read together, but also if it fails to exercise a jurisdiction which it possesses under those instruments."[178]

This is so, said the *Malicorp ad hoc* Committee, because "[i]t is not within the tribunal's powers to refuse to decide a dispute or part of a dispute that meets all jurisdictional requirements of Art. 25."[179] In practice, for an excess of the jurisdictional limits to occur, this may be a result of a tribunal's failure to apply the proper law or "acting *ex aequo et bono* without agreement of the parties."[180] A failure to exercise jurisdiction may also involve application of proper law and, as a result, a tribunal may find itself lacking jurisdiction over the dispute. In both scenarios, there is a question of how to define the proper law—a legal system such as a treaty or a national law, or merely a provision of a treaty or a national law. Specifically, the question is whether an award may be annulled on the ground that the tribunal applied the law incorrectly.

Commentators argue that to permit annulment committees to overturn incorrect applications of the law is contrary to the spirit of the finality of arbitral awards and that such an idea was specifically rejected by the drafters of the ICSID Convention.[181] In other words, an annulment committee must respect the award where the tribunal has applied the right law, even though the application itself may be incorrect. Some annulment committees agree with this principle in theory and, at the same time, propose a condition that such incorrect application or misapplication must not be "of such a nature or degree as to constitute objectively (regardless of the Tribunal's actual or presumed intentions) its effective non-application."[182] In this regard, the *Soufraki ad hoc* Committee stated:

> [O]ne must also consider that a tribunal goes beyond the scope of its power if it does not respect the law applicable to the substance of the arbitration under the ICSID Convention. It is widely recognized in ICSID jurisprudence that failure to apply the applicable law constitutes an excess of power. The relevant provisions of the applicable law are constitutive elements of the Parties' agreement to arbitrate and constitute part of the definition of the tribunal's mandate.[183]

The *Soufraki ad hoc* Committee also noted that "ICSID ad hoc committees have commonly been quite clear … that a distinction must be made between the

---

178 Ibid., para. 47, citing *Vivendi I*, Annulment Decision, *supra*, note 139, at para. 86.
179 Ibid., para. 47, citing Schreuer et al., *supra*, note 165, at p. 947.
180 ICSID, "Background Paper on Annulment for the Administrative Council of ICSID," (August 10, 2012), para. 94; available at: http://icsid.worldbank.org/ICSID/FrontServlet?requestType= ICSIDNewsLettersRH&actionVal=ShowDocument&DocId=DCEVENTS11. See also, in general, Gaëtan Verhoosel, "Annulment and Enforcement Review of Treaty Awards: To ICSID or Not to ICSID," 23 *ICSID Review* 119, 2008, pp.119–54.
181 See Antonio Parra, *The History of ICSID*, Oxford University Press USA, 2012, p. 87.
182 *Amco Asia*, Resubmitted Case: Decision on Annulment, *supra*, note 154, para. 7.19.
183 *Soufraki*, Annulment Decision, *supra*, note 174, para. 45.

failure to apply the proper law, which can result in annulment, and an error in the application of the law, which is not a ground for annulment."[184] Practice unfortunately does not support such a positive conclusion as that stated by the *Soufraki ad hoc* Committee. As at least one commentator has said: "the distinction between non-application of the proper law and its erroneous application is melting away."[185]

In *Duke Energy*, for instance, the *ad hoc* Committee clearly considered the proper application of the law to refer to the application of the right system of law and not merely a particular provision of law, holding:

> [T]he obligation upon a tribunal under Article 42(1) of the ICSID Convention to apply, *inter alia, "the law of the Contracting State"* is a reference to the whole of that law, such as the Tribunal may determine to be relevant and applicable to the issue before it, and not to any particular portion of it.[186]

By contrast, the *ad hoc* Committee in *Malaysian Historical Salvors* ("*MHS*")[187] took a rather different approach. In that case, the sole arbitrator decided that the claimant's activities did not meet the requirements of "investment" under the *Salini* test.[188] As the tribunal had adopted the double-barreled approach to determining its jurisdiction, on the basis of its finding that there was no "investment" within the meaning of the *Salini* test, it declined jurisdiction without considering the definition of "investment" under the BIT. The *ad hoc* Committee first identified the issue in the case as that of determination of "the meaning of the treaty term 'investment' as that term is used in Article 25(1) of the ICSID Convention—but also in Article 1 of the [BIT] … because that instrument is the medium through which the Contracting States involved have given their consent to the exercise of jurisdiction of ICSID."[189] It then went on to say that it was not generally accepted that a BIT's provisions on investor–state arbitration "could be rendered nugatory by a restrictive definition of a deliberately undefined term of the ICSID Convention."[190]

In the end, the majority of the *MHS ad hoc* Committee annulled the award in its entirety. The majority's grounds for doing so included: (a) the tribunal "failed to take account of and apply" the term "investment" as defined in the BIT and limited its interpretation to the criteria of investment under the ICSID Convention; (b) the tribunal, through its analysis of the criteria, "elevated them to jurisdictional conditions;" and (c) the tribunal failed to take account of the *travaux* of the ICSID

---

184 Ibid., para. 85.
185 Schreuer, *supra*, note 142, at p. 217.
186 *Duke Energy International Peru Investments No. 1 Ltd. v. Republic of Peru*, Decision on Annulment (March 1, 2011), para. 212 (emphasis in original).
187 *Malaysian Historical Salvors Sdn. Bhd. v. Government of Malaysia*, ICSID Case No. ARB/05/10, Decision on Annulment (April 16, 2009).
188 The "*Salini* test" for the existence of an "investment" is discussed in Chapter 4 on "Determination of Investments" in this book. It is derived from the decision on jurisdiction in *Salini Costruttori S.p.A. and Italstrade S.p.A. v. Kingdom of Morocco*, ICSID Case No. ARB/00/4, Decision on Jurisdiction (July 23, 2001).
189 *MHS*, Decision on Annulment, *supra*, note 187, para. 58.
190 Ibid., para. 62.

Convention.[191] Obviously, the *MHS ad hoc* Committee regarded the proper law to be applied as the "proper rule"—an expansive approach. It even blurred the distinction between a misapplication of law and application of the wrong law. The *ad hoc* Committee's analysis of the *travaux* relating to the ICSID Convention is an example. Under the Vienna Convention on the Law of Treaties ("VCLT"), tribunals are not required to take account of the *travaux* in every instance of treaty interpretation. By doing so, the *MHS ad hoc* Committee functioned as an appeal body rather than as an annulment committee.

This unfortunate approach of the *MHS ad hoc* Committee was, however, shared by the *Sempra ad hoc* Committee. In *Sempra*, the key question at the tribunal stage was the relationship between Article XI of the United States–Argentina BIT relating to measures necessary to deal with emergencies and Article 25 of the International Law Commission ("ILC") Articles on State Responsibility on the "state of necessity." The tribunal ruled that the ILC Articles reflected the customary international law and, as such, Article XI of the BIT was inseparable from and had to be applied in the light of the customary international law. Accordingly, as the tribunal held that the requirements for a "state of necessity" under the ILC Articles were not met, there was no need to examine whether the requirements were met under Article XI of the BIT.[192]

The *Sempra ad hoc* Committee found that "whether a state of necessity justifies exoneration from state responsibility will become an issue only where liability is not already precluded under Article XI of the BIT. As a general rule, a treaty will take precedence over customary international law."[193] As the tribunal had considered Article 25 of the ILC Articles rather than Article XI of the BIT to be the "primary law," in the *Sempra ad hoc* Committee's view it had made a "fundamental error in identifying and applying the applicable law."[194] The *ad hoc* Committee thus held that the tribunal's failure to conduct its review on the basis of the applicable legal norm constituted an excess of powers and the award was annulled.[195]

Unlike in the *MHS* case, in which the tribunal was found to have failed to identify and apply a rule—the definition of "investment" under the relevant BIT—the *Sempra* Tribunal did correctly identify and apply the law and rules, namely, Article XI of the BIT and Article 25 of the ILC Articles. Yet, in the opinion of the *Sempra ad hoc* Committee, the tribunal failed to apply the rules correctly by reversing what the *ad hoc* Committee saw as the correct relationship between Article XI of the BIT and Article 25 of the ILC Articles. Clearly, in this case, the *Sempra ad*

191 Ibid., para. 80.
192 *Sempra v. Argentina*, ICSID Case No. ARB/02/16, Award (September 28, 2007), paras. 376 and 388.
193 Ibid., Decision on Annulment, *supra*, note 150, para. 176.
194 Ibid., para. 208. The *Sempra ad hoc* Committee stated: "The Tribunal ha[d] held, in effect, that the substantive criteria of Article XI simply cannot find application where rules of customary international law – as enunciated in the ILC Articles – do not lead to exoneration in case of wrongfulness, and that Article 25 'trumps' Article XI in providing the mandatory legal norm to be applied." Id.
195 Ibid., paras. 208 and 209.

hoc Committee failed to distinguish misapplication of law from application of the wrong law, which is again not permissible under the ICSID mechanism.[196]

The fact is that even before the award in *Sempra* was issued, the annulment decision of the *CMS ad hoc* Committee[197] had been published. So there can be no doubt that the *Sempra ad hoc* Committee was aware or ought to have known that there had been other views. In *CMS*, the tribunal took a similar position on the relationship between a treaty provision—again Article XI of the relevant BIT—and international law—again Article 25 of the ILC Articles. The *CMS ad hoc* Committee found that "Article XI and Article 25 are substantively different" and that "[o]n that point, the Tribunal made a manifest error of law."[198] Yet, the *CMS ad hoc* Committee said that although the tribunal had applied Article XI of the BIT defectively, it had applied it and, hence, there was no manifest excess of powers.[199] After extensive analysis of the errors made by the tribunal, the *CMS ad hoc* Committee concluded:

> [This Committee] has only a limited jurisdiction under Article 52 of the ICSID Convention. In the circumstances, the Committee cannot simply substitute its own view of the law and its own appreciation of the facts for those of the Tribunal. Notwithstanding the identified errors and lacunas in the Award, it is the case in the end that the Tribunal applied Article XI of the Treaty. Although applying it cryptically and defectively, it applied it. There is accordingly no manifest excess of powers.[200]

The significance of the *CMS* annulment decision is its delineation of the distinction between annulment and appeal. Even though the *ad hoc* Committee severely criticized the decision of the tribunal, it did not annul the award because the tribunal had identified and applied the right law. Unfortunately, a number of ICSID *ad hoc* annulment committees have chosen not to adopt this practice and instead have chosen not to distinguish between erroneous application and failure to apply the proper law.

The *Enron* case is an example. In examining the tribunal's decision on fair and equitable treatment, the *ad hoc* Committee stated that it was:

> … satisfied that the Tribunal, in finding that there was a breach of the fair and equitable treatment clause in Article II(2)(a) of the BIT, purported to interpret that provision in accordance with general international law treaty interpretation principles and to apply it to the facts of the case as found. In

---

196 In fact, the *Sempra ad hoc* Committee even openly stated that: "[a]s a general proposition, [it] would not wish totally to rule out the possibility that a manifest error of law may, in an exceptional situation, be of such egregious nature as to amount to a manifest excess of powers;" ibid., para. 164.

197 *CMS v. Argentina*, Decision on Annulment, *supra*, note 172. This decision was delivered on September 25, 2007, just three days before the *Sempra* award.

198 *CMS v. Argentina*, Decision on Annulment, ibid., para. 130.

199 Ibid., paras. 128–36.

200 Ibid., para. 136.

so doing, the Tribunal applied the applicable law, whether or not it did so correctly.[201]

With regard to the tribunal's treatment of the umbrella clause, the *Enron ad hoc* Committee used the identical words to confirm its satisfaction.[202] The gist of the issue in the *Enron* case was whether the measures taken by Argentina during the economic crisis were the "only way" to cope with the situation, as Argentina had pleaded necessity as its defense.

The *ad hoc* Committee in *Enron*, although it was satisfied with the tribunal's identification and application of relevant law to the facts of the case, found the tribunal to have failed to apply customary international law because it had "applied an expert opinion on an economic issue," which in the view of the *ad hoc* Committee amounted "to a failure to apply the applicable law."[203] Specifically, the *Enron ad hoc* Committee stated:

> [T]he Award clearly suggests that the Tribunal accepted the expert evidence … to the effect that Argentina's own "misguided" policies contributed to the magnitude of the economic crisis, and that from this the Tribunal directly concluded that the measures adopted by Argentina "contributed to the situation of necessity."[204]

By doing so, in the view of the *ad hoc* Committee, the tribunal "did not in fact apply Article 25(2)(b) of the ILC Articles,"[205] because an economist's view that a state policy had contributed to the economic crisis should not by itself be considered a legal conclusion. The *ad hoc* Committee elaborated how the tribunal should have conducted its reasoning.[206] Clearly, what the *Enron ad hoc* Committee was not satisfied with was the tribunal's interpretation, in particular its reliance on an economist's expert evidence. Such matters unquestionably belong, however, to the category of errors in law which, if proven, cannot serve as a basis upon which an ICSID *ad hoc* annulment committee may annul an award; nor may it annul an award by equating anything to non-application of the proper law.[207] It is therefore unquestionable that the *Enron ad hoc* Committee misinterpreted the provisions of Article 52(1)(b) of the ICSID Convention.

---

201 *Enron*, Annulment Decision, *supra*, note 153, para. 314.
202 Ibid., para. 344.
203 Ibid., para. 377.
204 Ibid., para. 392.
205 Ibid., para. 393.
206 Id.
207 In the *Enron* case, the *ad hoc* Committee said that: "the parties in their arguments before the Tribunal do not appear to have expressly identified and argued the issue of the legal definition of the expression 'contributed to the situation of necessity' in Article 25(2)(b) of the ILC Articles. However, the Committee again considers that the Tribunal is nonetheless required to apply the applicable law." Ibid., para. 392.

3 Serious departure from a fundamental rule of procedure

As a ground for annulment, a serious departure from a fundamental rule of procedure, by definition, is concerned with the procedures that tribunals are required to follow. For instance, the right to be heard exists in most jurisdictions and is recognized as a procedural right of the disputing parties in arbitration. When this ground is invoked, the issues that must be determined are whether the rule allegedly breached by a tribunal is fundamental; and then the question is whether the breach, having been proven, is serious. Regarding what may constitute a fundamental rule of procedure, the *Fraport ad hoc* Committee held that this term was "intended to denote procedural rules which may properly be said to constitute 'general principles of law', insofar as such rules concern international arbitral procedure."[208]

On the other hand, the *MINE ad hoc* Committee commented on what may constitute a serious departure by saying:

> In order to constitute a ground for annulment the departure from a "fundamental rule of procedure" must be serious. The Committee considers that this establishes both quantitative and qualitative criteria: the departure must be substantial and be such as to deprive a party of the benefit or protection which the rule was intended to provide.[209]

The *Wena Hotels ad hoc* Committee interpreted the term "fundamental" as "a set of minimal standards of procedure to be respected as a matter of international law."[210] Relying on this definition, the *ad hoc* Committee further concluded: "In order to be a 'serious' departure from a fundamental rule of procedure, the violation of such a rule must have caused the Tribunal to reach a result substantially different from what it would have awarded had such a rule been observed."[211]

The *Wena Hotels* standard was adopted by the *ad hoc* Committee in *Continental Casualty*, which also cited the *MINE ad hoc* Committee's decision that for a departure to be serious it must cause a substantially different result or must "deprive a party of the benefit or protection which the rule was intended to provide."[212] One common feature of *ad hoc* committees' consideration of this issue is that they all place emphasis on the result by attempting to ascertain the seriousness of the departure. As a result, even where there are departures, so long as the result of such departures is not substantial, they may not be regarded as "serious."

The consequential effect of the *ad hoc* committee decisions discussed above is that not every procedural rule of the ICSID Convention is fundamental and

---

208 *Fraport*, Annulment Decision, *supra*, note 145, paras. 186–87.
209 *MINE*, Decision on Annulment, *supra*, note 136, para. 5.05.
210 *Wena Hotels*, Annulment Decision, *supra*, note 138, para. 57.
211 Ibid., para. 58.
212 *Continental Casualty Company v. Argentine Republic*, ICSID Case No. ARB/03/9, Decision on the Application for Partial Annulment (by both Parties) (September 16, 2011) para. 96, citing *MINE*, Decision on Annulment, *supra*, note 136, para. 5.05.

not every departure or breach thereof may be serious.[213] For instance, the *Azurix ad hoc* Committee decided that: "it [was] not a serious departure from a fundamental rule of procedure for a tribunal to decline to consider an issue that it consider[ed] to be irrelevant, merely because one of the parties consider[ed] it to be important."[214] The *Continental Casualty ad hoc* Committee also observed that: "no fundamental rule of procedure requires a tribunal to give express consideration to *every* argument or issue advanced by a party in support of its position in relation to a particular question."[215]

Arbitration practice shows that the right to be heard has been unanimously regarded as a fundamental rule of procedure. In the *Wena Hotels* annulment proceedings, the applicant—Egypt—alleged that it had not been offered an opportunity to address the issue of compound interest.[216] The *ad hoc* Committee observed that the record showed that Wena Hotels had requested on various occasions an award of interest at an appropriate rate, and the applicant was invited to reply to Wena Hotels' claims and arguments. Based on the record, the *ad hoc* Committee concluded that both parties "must have been aware of the possibility" that compound interest might be awarded as "appropriate" interest.[217]

The *Vivendi I ad hoc* Committee, facing a complaint that the applicants had had no opportunity to present their arguments on a decisive point, stated that the applicants had "had ample opportunity to consider and present written and oral submissions on the issues and that the oral hearing itself was meticulously conducted to enable each party to present its point of view. The Tribunal's analysis of issues was clearly based on the materials presented by the parties and was in no sense *ultra petita*."[218] The *ad hoc* Committee thus found that the tribunal had committed no departure from any fundamental rule of procedure.

The *Fraport* annulment case also involved the determination of a serious departure from a fundamental rule of procedure. An issue in dispute was whether the tribunal's failure to provide the claimants an opportunity to comment on the documents that had been submitted by the respondent to the prosecutor of the Philippines—who later decided that the domestic law the tribunal had applied for its award was no longer valid—constituted a serious departure from a fundamental rule of procedure. The *Fraport ad hoc* Committee decided that the tribunal, having estopped the parties from making further submissions, continued its deliberation and "proceeded to make extensive use in its Award of the documents which had been produced in the prosecutor's investigation."[219] Also, the tribunal had drawn

---

213 See, for example, *Azurix*, Annulment Decision, *supra*, note 160, para. 50; *Enron*, Annulment Decision, *supra*, note 153, para. 70; *MINE*, Annulment Decision, ibid., para. 5.06; and *MTD Equity Sdn. Bhd. and MTD Chile S.A. v. Republic of Chile*, ICSID Case No. ARB/01/7, Annulment Decision (May 21, 2007), para. 49.

214 *Azurix*, Annulment Decision, ibid., para. 244.

215 *Continental Casualty*, Annulment Decision, *supra*, note 212, para. 97 (emphasis in original).

216 *Wena Hotels*, Annulment Decision, *supra*, note 138, para. 66.

217 Ibid., para. 69.

218 *Vivendi I*, Annulment Decision, *supra*, note 139, para. 85.

219 *Fraport*, Annulment Decision, *supra*, note 145, para. 224.

an inference that the prosecutor's awareness of the secret shareholder agreements which were not submitted to him might have made a difference to its decision that the claimants had not committed a criminal offense.[220] In these circumstances, the tribunal's refusal to accept additional submissions from the parties was considered by the *Fraport ad hoc* Committee to be "incompatible with the fundamental obligation on the Tribunal to permit both parties to present their case."[221] Thus, presentation of its case by a party is, in the *Fraport ad hoc* Committee's view, a fundamental rule of procedure. The question that followed was whether or not the tribunal's departure from this rule was serious.

The *Fraport ad hoc* Committee held that the failure on the part of the tribunal to accept fresh submissions in light of new materials was serious in nature.[222] It is also apparent that the size of the new materials (1900 pages) and the fact that the prosecutor's decision involved interpretation of the domestic law all played a part in the *ad hoc* Committee's decision.[223]

Regarding a serious departure from a fundamental rule of procedure, *Malicorp* was one of the most recent annulment cases before completion of this book. Malicorp Limited, a British company, made an investment in Egypt with the help of a Build-Operate-Transfer ("BOT") contract with the Egyptian Civil Aviation Authority for the construction, management, operation, and transfer of the Ras Sudr International Airport. The dispute arose from the termination of the BOT contract. The *Malicorp* Tribunal decided in favor of the respondent. Malicorp then requested annulment of the award on the grounds, inter alia, that there had been a serious departure from a fundamental rule of procedure.[224] Malicorp contended specifically that the tribunal had allowed the respondent to submit a hard copy of its PowerPoint slides but did not accept the applicant's *dossier de plaidoirie*, thereby committing a violation of the *principe du contradictoire*.[225]

The *ad hoc* Committee in *Malicorp*, whilst acknowledging the utmost importance of adhering to proper procedures, stated that for an award to be annulled on this ground, the departure must be serious.[226] In its view, whether the departure is serious depends on whether or not it constitutes a violation of the "fundamental rules necessary to ensure a full and fair hearing."[227]

The *Malicorp ad hoc* Committee considered the *principe du contradictoire* to be a rule of procedure that ensures equality of the parties in an adversarial proceeding, which was "closely related to the right to be heard."[228] In other words, the *ad hoc* Committee decided that the *principe du contradictoire* was a fundamental rule of

220 Ibid., paras. 225–30.
221 Ibid., para. 230.
222 Ibid., para. 235.
223 Ibid., paras. 236–46.
224 *Malicorp*, Annulment Decision, *supra*, note 151, para. 22.
225 Ibid., para. 23.
226 Ibid., para. 28.
227 Ibid., para. 30.
228 Ibid., para. 36.

procedure. The remaining question was whether the tribunal did violate the rule. In this regard, the Committee opined:

> Printed copies of slides or visual aids used at the hearing are routinely submitted to tribunals for ease of reference, provided they contain only information that is already in the record. There is no reason to believe that such printed copies would unduly influence the Tribunal or have any persuasive impact beyond the effect of the initial presentation.[229]

On the other hand, the claimant's dossier was voluminous. The *Malicorp ad hoc* Committee considered that "it was well within the Tribunal's discretion to admit … [the] PowerPoint slides … while refusing to admit … [the Claimant's] *dossier de plaidoirie*."[230] The *ad hoc* Committee therefore did not find that the tribunal had committed a serious departure from a fundamental rule of procedure.

In addition to the right to be heard, there have been instances in which complaints were raised relating to the way that tribunals had dealt with the issues. In *Klöckner I*, for instance, the claimant challenged the tribunal for not having had a serious deliberation among the arbitrators.[231] The reason given was that there was total divergence between the award and the dissenting opinion. The *ad hoc* Committee did not support the claimant, commenting that the minority arbitrator and the majority of the tribunal had prepared their drafts "within the same time limit" and therefore they could not have benefited from each other's draft.[232] The claimant in *Klöckner I* also alleged that there was a lack of impartiality on the part of the majority of the tribunal, which repeatedly used harsh words about the claimant. On this point, the *ad hoc* Committee held that the "wording and repetition simply show the high idea the Tribunal had of the duties of cooperation and mutual disclosure of parties to such a legal relationship and reflect a high moral conception."[233] It goes without saying that the challenge made by Klöckner—the claimant—was serious. However, unless such complaints can be established with evidence, it is impossible for an *ad hoc* annulment committee to support them.

Similarly, in *Enron*, the claimant contended that the tribunal's admission of a late submission of expert evidence was a violation of the disputing parties' agreement—party autonomy—on the conduct of the arbitration in the First Session. As party autonomy or consent is the prerequisite for arbitration, the alleged breach of the agreement was raised to the level of a serious departure from a fundamental rule of procedure. The *ad hoc* Committee found that the principle of party autonomy was indeed a fundamental rule of procedure.[234] Yet it did not agree that every departure from the principle of party autonomy was serious.[235] In the end,

---

229 Ibid., para. 96.
230 Ibid., para. 99.
231 *Klöckner I*, Annulment Decision, *supra*, note 130, paras. 84–86.
232 Ibid., para. 86.
233 Ibid., para. 98.
234 *Enron*, Annulment Decision, *supra*, note 153, para. 195.
235 Ibid., para. 197.

the *ad hoc* Committee found that the tribunal's acceptance of the expert evidence did not violate the agreement because it was admitted in the extraordinary circumstances prescribed by the agreement.[236] It could be imagined that, had the *ad hoc* Committee not considered that the admission of evidence was done in extraordinary circumstances, the departure could have been considered "serious," taking into account the nature of the principle of party autonomy.

These examples illustrate how easily an award can be challenged on grounds of a serious departure from a fundamental rule of procedure. This is so because it is difficult to determine precisely what rule may be regarded as "fundamental" and which departure may be considered as "serious" in practice. Understandably, the losing party is likely to challenge a trivial matter that may arguably be overlooked or improperly handled by the tribunal as a matter of departure from a fundamental rule. At the same time, as Schreuer said: "almost any procedural rule can somehow be traced back to one or another broader principle that may be described as fundamental."[237] In such circumstances, even an apparently unimportant rule at the initial stage may be expanded into a rule of fundamental importance. This has become a real challenge to all tribunals.

4 Failure to state reasons

Failure to state reasons, as a ground for annulment, may involve a complete lack of reasons. Article 48(3) of the ICSID Convention requires investment tribunals to deal with every question raised by the parties and to state the reasons upon which an award is based. Other than this requirement, no detailed standard relating to reasons has been laid down and thus it is left up to each tribunal to decide how extensively it must present its reasoning in an award. In the contemporary world, it is expected that a statement of reasons or a reasoned decision is a basic requirement in judicial and arbitration proceedings.[238] The history of the ICSID Convention shows that the founding fathers voted not to permit a disputing party to waive the requirement of reasons in an arbitral award.[239] In practice, ICSID *ad hoc* annulment committees have ruled that a waiver of the statement of reasons would not bar a party from seeking annulment of the award in question.[240]

The requirement of reasons in an award, notwithstanding Article 52(e) of the ICSID Convention, does not qualify the ground "failure to state reasons" as it does with regard to other grounds. This triggers several questions. In the first

---

236 Ibid., para. 196.
237 Schreuer, *supra*, note 142, at p. 221.
238 For discussions of the issue, see Schreuer et al., *supra*, note 165, p. 996.
239 By a vote of 28 to 3, a proposal to permit disputing parties to waive the requirement of a reasoned award was rejected. See ICSID, *History of the ICSID Convention: Documents Concerning the Origin and the Formulation of the Convention on the Settlement of Investment Disputes between States and Nationals of Other States*, Washington D.C., Vol. II, p. 816.
240 For instance, the *ad hoc* Committee in *MINE* said: "A waiver of the requirement in an arbitration agreement would therefore not bar a party from seeking an annulment for failure of an award to state reasons." See *MINE*, Annulment Decision, *supra*, note 136, para. 5.10.

place, what is the scope of the failure to state reasons? Does it include, for instance, insufficient reasons and contradictory reasons in an award? Second, as Article 48(3) of the ICSID Convention stipulates that tribunals must deal with every question raised by the parties, does the failure to deal with every question fall into the category of excess of power or failure to state reasons or any other grounds for annulment? The most important question, in any case, is how investment tribunals interpret these provisions.

In practice, tribunals have interpreted the requirement to state reasons as a minimum standard. In other words, so long as there are reasons given in an award, it will satisfy the requirement. This was addressed by the *ad hoc* Committee in *MINE* as follows:

> In the Committee's view, the requirement to state reasons is satisfied as long as the award enables one to follow how the tribunal proceeded from Point A. to Point B. and eventually to its conclusion, even if it made an error of fact or of law. This minimum requirement is in particular not satisfied by either contradictory or frivolous reasons.[241]

The principle pronounced in the *MINE* decision was explicitly adopted by the *Wena Hotels ad hoc* Committee, which added that: "[t]he ground for annulment of Article 52(1)(e) does not allow any review of the challenged Award which would lead the ad hoc Committee to reconsider whether the reasons underlying the Tribunal's decisions were appropriate or not, convincing or not."[242] In the *Wena Hotels ad hoc* Committee's view, failure to state reasons, as a ground for annulment, is "based on the Tribunal's duty to identify, and to let the Parties know, the factual and legal premises leading the Tribunal to its decision."[243] Accordingly, once reasons leading to the decisions are given, the tribunal in question should be considered to have fulfilled its duties and, regardless of the decisions so made, they cannot be challenged. Some ICSID *ad hoc* annulment committees, however, have treated the ground of failure to state reasons as a guarantee for avoiding the arbitrariness of arbitral awards.[244]

As mentioned earlier, the ICSID Convention does not set out the ground of failure to state reasons with any qualifiers, unlike in the case of other grounds. This omission has led to the question of whether or not insufficient reasons would constitute a ground for annulment. Early ICSID *ad hoc* annulment committee decisions do not seem to have hesitated to discuss the inadequacy of reasons offered by tribunals in their arbitral awards. For instance, in *Klöckner I*, the *ad hoc* Committee found that the tribunal did not have a discussion "of the conditions of the seller's warranty under Article 1641 *et seq.* of the Civil Code, or of the provisions of Article

---

241 Ibid., para. 5.09.
242 *Wena Hotels*, Annulment Decision, *supra*, note 138, para. 79.
243 Id.
244 On this point, the *Fraport ad hoc* Committee said: "The obligation to give a reasoned award is a guarantee that the Tribunal has not decided in an arbitrary manner." See *Fraport*, Annulment Decision, *supra*, note 145, para. 250.

9 of the Turnkey Contract on the equipment warranty, and in particular of the warranty period set forth in Article 9(2)."[245] In its view, these items were conditions of the equilibrium of reciprocal contractual undertakings. One of the reasons that the *Klöckner I ad hoc* Committee has been criticized so severely is that it functioned as an appeal body. Where an *ad hoc* annulment committee observes the limits of its power, the insufficiency of reasons in an original award would not be a question at all.

In practice, however, it is easy for an *ad hoc* annulment committee to go beyond the limits of its powers. Even in a decision that has received approval from the commentators—the *Wena Hotels* annulment decision—the *ad hoc* Committee, although it did not annul the award, went so far as to review the adequacy of the reasons given by the tribunal. It stated, for instance: "The explanation thus given for not determining the respective obligations of Wena and ERC under the leases is sufficient to understand the premises on which the Tribunal's decision is based in this respect."[246] With regard to the determination of the rate of interest, the *Wena Hotels ad hoc* Committee also acted as if it were reconstructing the reasons for the award. Such practice is not only not in compliance with the function of an *ad hoc* annulment committee assigned by the ICSID Convention but also risks aligning the annulment mechanism with that of appeal.

It is commonly accepted that contradictory reasons may cancel each other out. As such, where an award is given based on contradictory reasons, it should be regarded as not having given reasons, and this would be a ground for annulment. This was first confirmed by the *ad hoc* Committee in *Klöckner I*, which said: "As for 'contradiction of reasons', it is in principle appropriate to bring this notion under the category 'failure to state reasons' for the very simple reason that two *genuinely* contradictory reasons cancel each other out."[247] At the same time, the *Klöckner I ad hoc* Committee did not consider that ambiguities in language would make the relevant reasons contradictory of each other.[248] Indeed, in practice, tribunals have a duty to consider the arguments of both parties and various possibilities before making conclusions. As this is the case, unless there is clear contradiction, an *ad hoc* annulment committee should be careful in holding that the reasons given in an award are contradictory. This was clearly stated by the *Vivendi I ad hoc* Committee when it said that: "tribunals must often struggle to balance conflicting considerations, and an ad hoc committee should be careful not to discern contradiction when what is actually expressed in a tribunal's reasons could more truly be said to be but a reflection of such conflicting considerations."[249] In other words, unless the contradiction is genuine, *ad hoc* annulment committees should not rule the reasons to be contradictory of each other. In this regard, the *CDC ad*

245 *Klöckner I*, Annulment Decision, *supra*, note 130, para. 162.
246 *Wena Hotels*, Annulment Decision, *supra*, note 138, para. 86.
247 *Klöckner I*, Annulment Decision, *supra*, note 130, para. 116 (emphasis in original).
248 Ibid., para. 123.
249 *Vivendi I*, Annulment Decision, supra, note 139, para. 65.

hoc Committee suggested interpreting arbitral awards in the same way in which laws are interpreted.[250]

The *Malicorp ad hoc* Committee also urged that caution be taken in holding the reasons for an award to be contradictory. It stated that "an award must be upheld unless the logic is so contradictory as to be 'as useful as no reasons at all'."[251] The *Malicorp ad hoc* Committee also emphasized, relating to contradictory reasons as a failure to state reason, that applicants have "a high burden" to prove how different parts of the analysis of an award would cancel each other out.[252] As the *Malicorp* annulment decision is the most recent in this regard, it shows, at least to a certain extent, that ICSID *ad hoc* annulment committees are careful in annulling arbitral awards on the ground of contradictory reasons. This is understandable because, as in the case of insufficient reasons, in order to establish that different parts of the analysis of a tribunal are contradictory to each other an *ad hoc* annulment committee must reconstruct the reasons of the tribunal. In doing so, there is a danger of blurring the distinction between annulment and appeal mechanisms. After all, a lack of reasons is not the same as a lack of sufficient reasons or a lack of non-contradictory reasons.

In conclusion, the development of direct foreign investment has benefited greatly from the unilateral insurance mechanisms created by the developed countries. The establishment of MIGA has improved the environment for international investment through its issuance of guarantees.[253] The most important phenomenon of international investment law over the last six decades and more has been the conclusion of BITs that provide for direct investor–state arbitration of disputes. With such an arrangement, foreign investors have been actively bringing their disputes with the host states to international arbitration—ICSID being the institution most often relied upon.

Finality is still an important feature in investor–state arbitration. At the same time, ensuring the correctness of arbitral awards is equally important, for without a mechanism of remedy to rectify the errors of arbitral tribunals, the arbitration system cannot be sustained. The annulment procedure is thus a compromise between the finality of investment arbitration and an appeal mechanism for rectifying the errors of arbitral tribunals. As is often the case in any system, there are inherent risks within the ICSID annulment mechanism, one of which is an *ad hoc* annulment committee assuming the functions of an appeal body. In this connection, earlier ICSID annulment decisions showed an assertiveness on the part of the *ad hoc* annulment committees, whilst in more recent cases committees have

---

250 The *CDC ad hoc* Committee said that: "[i]n construing awards, as in construing statutes and legal instruments generally, one necessarily should construe the language in issue, whenever possible, in a way that results in consistency;" see *CDC*, Annulment Decision, *supra*, note 167, para. 81.

251 *Malicorp*, Annulment Decision, *supra*, note 151, para. 45.

252 Ibid., para. 42.

253 In the fiscal year of 2013, MIGA issued US$2.8 billion in investment guarantees for projects in the developing member countries, US$1.5 billion of which was for new businesses. See MIGA, *Annual Report*, 2013, *supra*, note 24.

apparently recognized the importance of distinguishing annulment from appeal. The *Impregilo ad hoc* annulment Committee is an example.

That said, it is not difficult to discern that ICSID *ad hoc* annulment committees have often functioned as if they were appeal bodies. This happened, for instance, in *Vivendi II*, in which the central question was whether or not the failure of an arbitrator to disclose her directorship in a peripherally related financial institution constituted an annullable ground. The *ad hoc* Committee, although it did not find the arbitrator's relationship to be sufficient grounds for annulment,[254] went out of its way to elaborate on arbitrators' ethics.[255] Similarly, in *Fraport*, the *ad hoc* Committee was critical of the way the tribunal interpreted the relevant BIT in conjunction with the national law of the Philippines and indicated that the tribunal's method of treaty interpretation was not in accordance with the VCLT.[256] One may wonder if it is appropriate for an *ad hoc* annulment committee to offer such teachings as if it is superior to the tribunal, or at least to give that appearance.[257]

Inconsistency of *ad hoc* annulment committee decisions is another inherent risk of the ICSID mechanism. As all the *ad hoc* annulment committees are comprised of members who are chosen from among individuals with varied backgrounds— cultural, legal, and otherwise—and appreciation of laws and law enforcement, the consistency of their decisions cannot be ensured or even expected. Because annulment decisions are routinely publicized and cited by disputing parties, as well as by tribunals and other *ad hoc* annulment committees, such decisions are discreetly gaining precedential effect.[258]

The international community is becoming increasingly concerned about the above-mentioned problems. Suggestions have been made to improve the mechanism, including institution of an appeal body, making the Appellate Body of the World Trade Organization the appeal body for investment disputes, introducing a security collateral requirement for discouraging likely abuse of the ICSID annulment mechanism, etc.[259] No immediate solution, however, is available. It is hoped that with more and more people, especially those involved in decision-making, becoming aware of the issues, the world will be ready to agree on improving the system.

254 *Vivendi II*, Annulment Decision, *supra*, note 152, para. 239.
255 Ibid., paras. 218–32.
256 *Fraport*, *supra*, note 145, paras. 98, 99, and 107.
257 This has been criticized by scholars and practitioners alike. See, for example, Schreuer, *supra*, note 142, at p. 224.
258 For instance, the *Impregilo ad hoc* annulment Committee considered that a tribunal—likewise an *ad hoc* annulment committee—was entitled to quote previous decisions by other tribunals in their own reasoning. See *Impregilo*, *supra*, note 148, para. 156.
259 For further discussion on the subject, see Chapter 11 of this book.

3 Determination of foreign investors

Foreign investors are the key players in international investment and international investment law. All preferential treatments, grants and protections offered by bilateral investment treaties ("BITs") in respect of foreign investment eventually benefit their owners—the foreign investors. All investment-related dispute resolution mechanisms unavoidably involve foreign investors as participants. Therefore, to determine which and what kinds of investors are qualified as foreign investors who are protected under the BITs and multilateral investment protection schemes is of utmost importance.

Contemporary BITs and the investment chapters of free trade agreements ("FTAs") usually identify what kinds of natural persons and juridical persons are covered in principle, but often do so without specifying detailed requirements. In these circumstances, it may be difficult to determine whether or not a natural person is a qualified investor, especially if he/she possesses dual or multiple nationalities. It may be even more complicated to determine the nationality of a juridical person. Most investments today are made by juridical persons in the form of companies or other entities. In the past, owing to a lack of advanced communications technology and transportation technology, incorporating a company in a foreign country was not an easy process, nor was transferring funds across borders. With the deepening of globalization and the progress made in science and technology, especially in telecommunications and information technology and Internet innovation, it is now a very simple process to set up an entity abroad and have capital moved across borders, even though some countries still maintain restrictions on capital movement.

The business environment that has emerged against the background of globalization has thus presented new issues for the determination of foreign investors. For instance, where a national of a state establishes an overseas company and then uses the foreign company as a vehicle to make an investment in his home country, is this investment a "foreign investment" and the foreign entity a "foreign investor"? Very often, host states require foreign investments to be made in a certain form, such as local-foreign joint ventures or locally established subsidiaries. These joint ventures and subsidiaries are—as they are established according to the host state's laws—juridical persons of the host state. Should such "local entities" be treated as foreign investors? Also, where a person—natural or juridical—only owns a minority shareholding in an entity that has made investments in a foreign country, and when the majority shareholders and the entity itself fail to take actions to protect their investment, is the minority shareholder entitled to resort to the international mechanisms of investment protection that are available to foreign investors?

All these questions relate to the issue of the jurisdiction or competence of arbitral tribunals, because unless a person is considered to be a qualified foreign investor, the tribunal in charge may ultimately not have jurisdiction over the dispute and no protection may be afforded. Therefore, in the interests of both claimants and respondents—for the purpose of either establishing or denying jurisdiction—tribunals may be requested to pierce the corporate veil of investors. The jurisdiction of tribunals may also be affected by provisions on exhaustion of local remedies and denial of benefits, among others.

This chapter will first discuss the general issues relating to qualified investors. It will then consider such specific issues as indirect investors and minority shareholders, the necessity of piercing the corporate veil, and denial of benefits by analyzing the arbitral awards made by tribunals under the canons of international law. The last part is devoted to the Chinese practice in this area. Because China has not been actively involved as a respondent in international investment arbitration, despite it being the largest direct foreign investment recipient among the developing countries and a rapidly growing capital exporter, the discussion will be restricted to China's treaty practice.

I. Qualified investors as a jurisdictional issue

Investors are subjects of international investment protection. For purposes of determining qualified investors, reference must be made not only to bilateral but sometimes also to multilateral conventions.[1] In 1982, in *Sumitomo*, a case involving the interpretation of the United States–Japan Treaty on Friendship, Commerce and Navigation, the US Supreme Court ruled that the subsidiary established by its Japanese parent company incorporated and operated in the United States under US laws was a US company instead of a Japanese company and thus could not enjoy the benefit of the Treaty.[2] This approach, however, is no longer the general practice under BITs. Even the US Model BIT clearly defines subsidiaries controlled by juridical persons of one contracting party and constituted and operated in another contracting party as qualified "investors" with the same rights as their parent companies.[3] Had this provision been applicable in the *Sumitomo* case,

---

1 For instance, where a BIT authorizes claimants to bring their disputes with the host state to ICSID for arbitration, as ICSID tribunals' jurisdiction is confined to legal issues directly arising from an investment under Article 25 of the ICSID Convention, tribunals need to consider whether the scope of "investment" under Article 25 is the same as that under the BIT.

2 *Sumitomo Shoji America, Inc. v. Avagliano*, 457 U.S. 176 (1982); available at: http://www.leagle.com/xmlResult.aspx?xmldoc=1982633457US176_1622.xml&docbase=CSLWAR1-1950-1985.

3 2004 US Model BIT, Article 1; available at: http://www.state.gov/documents/organization/117601.pdf.

the Japanese subsidiary would not have been deemed to be a US company and thus would have been entitled to the benefit of the Treaty.

Regarding both natural and juridical persons, determination of nationality is a prerequisite for the jurisdiction of arbitration tribunals in investment disputes. Traditionally, international law has permitted sovereign states to exercise diplomatic protection on condition that there is a genuine link between the individual concerned and his/her nationality.[4] Contemporary BITs, however, do not contain provisions dealing with the genuine link test of nationality. The jurisprudence of investment law is also opposed to the application of the test.[5] This was illustrated in the case of *Micula v. Romania*,[6] in which the nationality of the claimant was doubted by the respondent. Regarding the application of the *Nottebohm* requirement of a genuine link for determining the nationality of the claimant, the tribunal held: "There is little support for the proposition that the genuine link test has any role to play in the context of ICSID proceedings. The ICSID Convention requires only that a claimant demonstrate that it is a national of a 'Contracting State.'"[7] This has seemingly become the standard approach taken by investment tribunals, as was observed by Schreuer when he said that:

> … even in BIT cases involving dual nationality tribunals will not apply a doctrine of effective or dominant nationality. Therefore, it appears that at least as far as arbitration under BITs is concerned, *Nottebohm* has been laid to rest and a doctrine of genuine link will not overcome treaty provisions defining nationality in term of the nationality legislation of the countries concerned.[8]

In practice, tribunals seldom openly denounce the principle of a genuine link when determining nationality. Insofar as natural persons are concerned, tribunals are more willing to rely on the provisions of the relevant treaty—bilateral and multilateral—in ascertaining nationalities.[9] The *Champion Trading Company* case[10] is a good example.

---

4 See, for example, the *Nottebohm case* (*Liechtenstein v. Guatemala*), ICJ, Judgment (November 18, 1953) and Judgment (April 6, 1955), *ICJ Reports*, 1955; available at: http://www.icj-cij.org/docket/files/18/2674.pdf; and *Barcelona Traction, Light and Power Company, Limited* (*Belgium v. Spain*), ICJ, Judgment (July 24, 1964) and Judgment (February 5, 1970), *ICJ Reports*, 1970, pp. 3–357.

5 See, for example, *Waguih Elie George Siag and Clorinda Vecchi v. Arab Republic of Egypt*, ICSID Case No. ARB/05/15, Decision on Jurisdiction (April 11, 2007); and *Hussein Nuaman Soufraki v. United Arab Emirates*, ICSID Case No. ARB/02/7, Award (July 7, 2004).

6 *Ioan Micula, Viorel Micula, S.C. European Food S.A., S. Starmill S.R.L. and S.C. Multipack S.R.L. v. Romania*, ICSID Case No. ARB/05/20, Decision on Jurisdiction and Admissibility (September 24, 2008).

7 Ibid., para. 100.

8 Christoph Schreuer, "Nationality of Investors: Legitimate Restrictions vs. Business Interests," *ICSID Review Foreign Investment Law Journal*, Vol. 24, Issue 2, 2009, pp. 521–27, at 522.

9 For discussions on the nationality of natural persons as investors, see Organisation for Economic Co-operation and Development, *International Investment Law: Understanding Concepts and Tracking Innovations* 10, 2008.

10 *Champion Trading Company, Ameritrade International, Inc., James T. Wahba, John B. Wahba, Timothy T.*

The respondent in the *Champion Trading Company* case maintained that the three individual claimants, who had by birth acquired both US and Egyptian nationalities, could not invoke the Convention because they were Egyptian nationals.[11] On their part, the non-corporate claimants argued that under international rules nationality requires a real and effective link between the national and the state in question and that since they had had no real and effective link with Egypt they should not be treated as Egyptian nationals.[12] The tribunal cited the landmark decision of the International Court of Justice of April 6, 1955 in the *Nottebohm* case that:

> According to the practice of States, to arbitral and judicial decisions and to the opinions of writers, nationality is a legal bond having as its basis a social fact of attachment, a genuine connection of existence, interests and sentiments, together with the existence of reciprocal rights and duties. It may be said to constitute the juridical expression of the fact that the individual upon whom it is conferred, either directly by the law or as the result of an act of the authorities, is in fact more closely connected with the population of the State conferring nationality than with that of any other State. Conferred by a State, it only entitles that State to exercise protection vis-à-vis another State, if it constitutes a translation into juridical terms of the individual's connection with the State which has made him its national.[13]

Yet the tribunal chose to rely on the Iran–United States Claims Tribunal's decision[14] that this principle also "contained an important reservation that the real and effective nationality was indeed relevant 'unless an exception is clearly stated'." It then concluded that it was faced with such a clear exception.[15] The exception referred to is the provision of Article 25(2)(a) of the ICSID Convention, which excludes dual nationals from invoking protection under the Convention against the host state. In holding that it had no jurisdiction over the individual claimants, the tribunal did not exclude the possibility of tribunals exercising jurisdiction in similar situations when circumstances so justified. Whether the *Champion Trading Company* Tribunal was in favor of doing away with the principle of an effective link was not clarified. In the circumstances of the case, however, it was reasonable for it to consider the issue of nationality by taking into account the outer limits of the ICSID Convention.

Soufraki v. United Arab Emirates[16] is another case that involved the issue of nation-

Wahba v. Arab Republic of Egypt ("*Champion Trading*"), ICSID Case No. ARB/02/9, Decision on Jurisdiction (October 21, 2003).
11 Ibid., para. 3.2.
12 Ibid., para. 3.3.
13 *Nottebohm case* 1955, *supra*, note 4, p. 23.
14 Decided in Iran–United States Claims Tribunal Case No. A/18 of April 6, 1984 (5 Iran-U.S.C.T.R.-251).
15 *Champion Trading*, *supra*, note 10, para. 3.4.1.
16 *Soufraki v. United Arab Emirates*, ICSID Case No. ARB/02/7, Award (July 7, 2004). After the award was delivered, the claimant initiated proceedings to annul it. The *ad hoc* Committee decided to

ality. The claimant in that case—Mr Soufraki—entered into a concession contract with the Dubai Department of Ports and Customs for developing, maintaining and operating the Port of Al Hamriya and its surrounding area for a term of 30 years. In May 2002, the claimant, based on the BIT between Italy and the United Arab Emirates, filed a request for arbitration with ICSID. The respondent challenged the jurisdiction of the tribunal on grounds that the claimant possessed no valid nationality of Italy and was therefore not a national of another ICSID contracting party. The claimant produced two Italian passports and five certificates issued by the Italian authorities confirming his Italian nationality. Upon examination, however, it was revealed that in accordance with Italian law the claimant had lost, automatically and spontaneously, his Italian nationality when he acquired Canadian nationality in 1991. As that was the case, the tribunal concluded that the Italian authorities' certificates were issued without the knowledge that Mr Soufraki had ceased to be an Italian national and that those documents therefore could not be relied upon.[17] It was also evident that the claimant could have reinstated his Italian nationality but that he had made no attempt to do so. The tribunal in the end ruled that it had no jurisdiction to hear the case.[18]

It is also noteworthy that the *Soufraki* Tribunal opined, almost as a postscript, that "had Mr. Soufraki contracted with the United Arab Emirates through a corporate vehicle incorporated in Italy, rather than contracting in his personal capacity, no problem of jurisdiction would now arise. But the Tribunal can only take the facts as they are and as it has found them to be."[19]

The difference between the *Champion Trading Company* case and the *Soufraki* case is that, in the former, the natural person claimants indeed had Egyptian nationality and, in the latter, the claimant's Italian nationality had been lost and he had not taken any measures to restore it. In both cases, the tribunals relied on the formal laws of the respondents in determining the nationality of the investors. Where a person holds the nationality of the host state, e.g. being a person with dual nationality, Article 25(2)(a) of the ICSID Convention will be held to apply. These and other arbitral decisions clearly show that the determination of nationality is still a matter of domestic law. The effect of the ICSID Convention is to exclude the possibility of nationals instituting arbitration against their own state.

In relation to determination of the nationality of juridical persons, however, the situation is not as clear as that of natural person investors. In the first place, the nationality of a juridical person may be determined by its place of incorporation or by the place of its corporate seat, depending on domestic laws and the provisions of the relevant BITs.[20] Insofar as multilateral treaties are concerned, under

dismiss Soufraki's annulment request on June 5, 2007; see *Hussein Nuaman Soufraki v. United Arab Emirates*, ICSID Case No. ARB/02/7, Decision of the *ad hoc* Committee on the Application for Annulment of Mr Soufraki (June 5, 2007), para. 139.

17   Award, ibid., paras. 66–68.
18   Ibid., para. 86(a).
19   Ibid., para. 83.
20   In practice, both the place of incorporation and the place of the corporate seat are mentioned in BITs. There are advantages and disadvantages for applying either test. For discussions on the

Article 25 of the ICSID Convention, tribunals' jurisdiction is confined to disputes "between a Contracting State … and a national of another Contracting State" in which the parties "consent in writing to submit" their disputes to the ICSID for arbitration.[21] The national of another contracting state can be either a natural person or a juridical party. The ICSID will not register a dispute if the natural person party had the nationality of the state party when the dispute is submitted.[22] However, there are slightly different rules for a juridical person party. Generally speaking, a juridical person party has the "nationality" of the state where it is organized or registered.[23] In practice, as mentioned earlier, most international investment disputes are between host states and foreign investors who are doing business in some legal form within the host state's territory. In such cases, the ICSID takes a considerably practical approach. Where a juridical person with the nationality of the state party to the disputes is under the control of foreign capital and is therefore recognized by both parties as deserving of treatment as a national of the other contracting state, the ICSID will accept jurisdiction over the case.[24]

This provision was tested in the very first case submitted to ICSID arbitration, *Holiday Inns v. Morocco*.[25] The claimants were Holiday Inns S.A., registered in Switzerland, and the Occidental Petroleum Corporation, a US company. The case was registered by the ICSID on December 22, 1971. The parties reached a settlement agreement later on and, pursuant to a joint request by the parties, the tribunal rendered a procedural order noting the discontinuation of the case on October 17, 1978. Nevertheless, the opinions expressed by the tribunal are still of significance in tracing the history of investor–state investment arbitration in general and ICSID arbitration in particular.

The facts of this case were as follows. In 1966, in order to promote its tourism industry, especially the hotel industry, the Government of Morocco asked the

---

matter, see UNCTAD, "Scope and Definition," *UNCTAD Series on Issues in International Investment Agreements II*, 2011, pp. 80–84.

21 Article 25(1) of the ICSID Convention.

22 See Article 25(2) of the ICSID Convention.

23 Georges R. Delaume, "ICSID Arbitration and the Courts," *American Journal of International Law*, Vol. 77, 1983, pp. 795–96, at 794.

24 See Article 25(2)(b) of the ICSID Convention, which provides that: "… any juridical person which had the nationality of a Contracting State other than the State party to the dispute on the date on which the parties consented to submit such dispute to conciliation or arbitration and any juridical person which had the nationality of the Contracting State party to the dispute on that date and which, because of foreign control, the parties have agreed should be treated as a national of another Contracting State for the purposes of this Convention."

25 *Holiday Inns S.A. and Others v. Morocco*, ICSID Case No. ARB/72/1. Six years after the case was registered with the ICSID, the parties to the dispute reached an amicable settlement and, by joint request, the case was withdrawn. As a result, there is no record in the files of ICSID, although the tribunal issued eight decisions on, inter alia, jurisdiction and consent, before the case was withdrawn. The most comprehensive narrative and analysis of the case, according to this author's knowledge, can be found in an article by Pierre Lalive, "The First 'World Bank' Arbitration (*Holiday Inns v. Morocco*)— Some Legal Problems," 51 *BYBIL* 123, 1980; available at: http://bybil. oxfordjournals.org. The factual statements of the case herein are either quoted or summarized from Lalive's article.

Occidental Petroleum Corporation to introduce a first-rate US business in that field whose experience, organization and know-how could be used to improve the service quality of the hotel industry in Morocco. Occidental thus invited representatives of the US corporation Holiday Inn of America to visit Morocco. Both Holiday Inn and the Government of Morocco considered that the hotel industry of Morocco was promising and thus concluded a Basic Agreement on December 6, 1966 to establish four Holiday Inn hotels in Morocco.

A joint venture responsible for the construction and management of the four Holiday Inn hotels was established by the Government of Morocco, the Occidental Petroleum Corporation and Holiday Inn of America. The Government of Morocco provided tens of millions of US dollars in mortgage loans to the Occidental Petroleum Corporation and Holiday Inn of America for the construction and made a commitment that the joint venture would enjoy preferential treatment in such areas as duties exemptions, bonuses and foreign exchange transfer facilities. The Occidental Petroleum Corporation and Holiday Inn of America promised to construct hotels of five-star category and operate them. They also promised that the cost of construction would not exceed the amount fixed by the joint venture and, if that did not prove possible, they would be responsible for any excess costs.[26]

For the sake of tax avoidance and other considerations, like many other foreign investors do, the Occidental Petroleum Corporation established a wholly owned subsidiary, the Occidental Hotels of Morocco, as the cooperator in the joint venture. Also, Holiday Inns S.A., Glarus, Switzerland was established by Holiday Inn of America to participate in the joint venture project. The Moroccan Government was aware of and did not raise any objection to these arrangements. As a matter of fact, the Basic Agreement allowed the parties to transfer their contractual obligations and rights to their subsidiaries or affiliated companies. On the day of the conclusion of the Basic Agreement, the Occidental Petroleum Corporation and Holiday Inn of America also signed letters of guarantee in which they respectively promised "to assume all responsibilities of guarantors to warrant all commitments and liabilities and the true and complete fulfillment of all obligations which the signatories to the Basic Agreement had entered or would enter into."[27] It should be pointed out that the Occidental Petroleum Corporation and Holiday Inn of America were the signatory parties to the Basic Agreement. The Occidental Hotels of Morocco and Holiday Inns S.A. had not been established at that time. According to Article 14 of the Basic Agreement, disputes arising from the contract should be submitted to the ICSID.

Soon after the entering into force of the Basic Agreement, differences with respect to culture, politics, and other matters began to arise between the host government and the foreign investors. The most important differences concerned two matters. First, in order to obtain the governmental loans to construct the hotels, Holiday Inn of America had to establish another four companies, but it was required to transfer 49 percent of the shares of each company to the Moroccan

26 Lalive, ibid., at 125–27.
27 Ibid., at 128.

Government directly or indirectly when it applied for the land on which to build the hotels. Second, according to the agreement signed by the parties, the constructor might withdraw the money, that is, the governmental loans, from the special account administered by a specialized governmental agency. However, the governmental agency always delayed such payments and eventually directly refused to make any payments. Behind these apparent discrepancies lies the fact that the project had been approved by the former Minister of Tourism, whereas the new Minister of Tourism considered that the Moroccan Government was at a disadvantage in the agreement and was not in favor of the project. He thus unilaterally reinterpreted it. Finally, the Occidental Petroleum Corporation and Holiday Inn S.A. submitted the dispute to ICSID for arbitration on December 22, 1971. One of the issues to be resolved by the tribunal was its jurisdiction.

The jurisdiction of the tribunal became an issue because among the six claimants, five were registered in Morocco. Legally speaking, these companies were not nationals from "another Contracting State" and, thus, the respondent— the Moroccan Government—contended that the tribunal did not have jurisdiction over the dispute. In summary, Morocco's argument was based on Article 25(2)(b) of the ICSID Convention that the claimants were not nationals of another contracting party and there was no agreement to treat them as foreign nationals. Article 25(2) provides:

> (b) any juridical person which had the nationality of a Contracting State other than the State party to the dispute on the date on which the parties consented to submit such dispute to conciliation or arbitration and any juridical person which had the nationality of the Contracting State party to the dispute on that date and which, because of foreign control, the parties have agreed should be treated as a national of another Contracting State for the purposes of this Convention.

The above provision, commented Lalive, "constitutes in itself a relatively bold departure from the traditional principles of international law, according to which a State cannot be sued internationally by its own nationals."[28] As the matter was of much importance to investment host states, "the question had to be decided 'whether such an agreement must be expressed or whether it may be implied'."[29] In this regard, Lalive observed that:

> … had the drafters of the Convention wished to request *express* agreement, they would have said so in the text, in the interest of legal certainty. The absence of any precision or qualification might thus lead one to assume that, according to general principles of the law of contract, consent or agreement may be either express or tacit, unless otherwise required. On the other hand … a State's consent to international adjudication of disputes with its own

---

28 Ibid., at 140.
29 Ibid., at 139 (footnote omitted).

nationals is an act of such impact and importance as to deserve unequivocal expression.[30]

In the end, in a ruling that expressed the same sentiment as Lalive, the tribunal ruled that the domestic nationals, that is, the Holiday Inns companies created in Morocco, could not be parties to the proceedings of the ICSID arbitration. At the same time, however, the tribunal noted that:

> … the situation of the H.I.S.A. [Holiday Inns in Morocco] companies may have to be taken into account in judging the performance of the obligations which the Agreement of December 5, 1966 and the additional related agreements have created for the Government of Morocco and for the companies which are Parties to the present arbitration.[31]

The underpinning of the decision was that to treat a juridical person of the host state as a "foreign investor" was an exceptional provision in the Washington Convention, which required the express consent of the parties unless all the related circumstances had precluded such necessity, which was obviously not applicable in this case.

The findings of the *Holiday Inns* Tribunal, however, can only serve as an historical event of investment arbitration and cannot throw any light on contemporary investment law, even though the case was decided less than 30 years ago. In this short span of time, international investment law has undergone drastic changes. Contemporary BITs generally treat locally incorporated entities as foreign investors owing to them being under foreign control.[32] As a result, it is very unlikely that companies such as Holiday Inns would fail to be treated as foreign investors under modern BITs. In practice, however, there are issues of another kind. *ČSOB v. Slovak Republic* ("*ČSOB*")[33] is an example.

In the *ČSOB* case, the claimant—Československa Obchodni Banka, A.S. ("ČSOB")—was a commercial bank organized under the laws of the Czech Republic, the creation of which was a result of the dissolution of the former Czechoslovakia. For the purposes of privatizing ČSOB, which would also be in charge of foreign exchange matters for both the Czech and Slovak Republics, the Ministry of Finance of the Slovak Republic, the Ministry of Finance of the

---

30 Id. (emphasis in original).
31 Ibid., at 142.
32 For discussions on this issue, see Giorgio Sacerdoti, "The Concept of Foreign Investment and the Definition of the Investor in Recent BITs," *Recueil des Cours, Collected Courses*, Tome/Vol. 269, 1997, The Hague Academy of International Law, ch 2. In discussing the definition of investors, Professor Sacerdoti examined a number of treaty provisions and especially such clauses.
33 *Československa Obchodni Banka, A.S. (ČSOB) v. Slovak Republic*, ICSID Case No. ARB/97/4, Decision on Jurisdiction (May 24, 1999). After the issuance of this decision, the tribunal issued a second decision on jurisdiction on December 1, 2000 and the award on December 29, 2004. The award on merit was not published by ICSID; it is available, however, on the website of international treaty arbitration (ita), at: http://www.italaw.com/cases/238.

Czech Republic, and ČSOB had reached an "Agreement on the Basic Principles of a Financial Consolidation of Československa Obchodni Banka, A.S." ("Consolidation Agreement") on 19 December 1993. Under the Consolidation Agreement, a collection company was to be established in each republic, which was to accept assignments of non-performing loan portfolio receivables with an obligation to pay ČSOB the face value of such receivables. As a means of refinancing, ČSOB provided loans to both collection companies for the nominal amount of the receivables. In order to ensure that ČSOB would recover all the non-performing receivables, the Slovak Republic guaranteed the payment to ČSOB of whatever amount the Slovak collection company established under its laws could not collect on the receivables assigned to it.

The dispute arose from the performance of the Consolidation Agreement—the claimant alleged that the respondent had breached its obligations under the Agreement by failing to pay the guaranteed amount. The respondent raised objections on the tribunal's jurisdiction. One of these objections was that ČSOB was an agent of the Czech Republic and therefore not a "national of another contracting state", according to the terms of Article 25 of the ICSID Convention. ČSOB was, in fact jointly owned by the Czech Republic (65 percent) and the Slovak Republic (24 percent). The tribunal first referred to Broches, one of the framers of the Convention, who said that: "for purposes of the Convention a mixed economy company or government-owned corporation should not be disqualified as a 'national of another Contracting State' unless it is acting as an agent for the government or is discharging an essentially governmental function."[34] In the view of the tribunal, on its own, the fact of state ownership would not affect the status of ČSOB as a juridical person—a national—of the Czech Republic because "such ownership or control alone will not disqualify a company under the here relevant test from filing a claim with the Centre as 'a national of another Contracting State'."[35] The issue of control may not affect the qualification of an entity as a national of another contracting state where the shareholders involved are not nationals of the host state. Otherwise, as will be discussed elsewhere (see Chapter 4), control may become a jurisdictional issue for a tribunal. In *ČSOB*, however, one of the minority shareholders was the host state itself, which makes the case distinguishable from others.

The respondent contended that the claimant had been "discharging essentially governmental functions throughout its existence" and thus was an agent of the government.[36] The tribunal accepted that, for much of its existence, the claimant "acted on behalf of the State in facilitating or executing the international banking transactions and foreign commercial operations the State wished to support."[37] Yet, at the same time, it pointed out that the "focus must be on the *nature* of these

---

34 *ČSOB v. Slovak Republic*, Decision of Jurisdiction, ibid., para. 17, citing A. Broches, *The Convention on the Settlement of Investment Disputes between States and Nationals of Other States*, 135 Hague Recueil des Cours 331, 1972. at 354–55.

35 *ČSOB v. Slovak Republic*, Decision on Jurisdiction, ibid., para. 18.

36 Ibid., para. 19.

37 Ibid., para. 20.

activities and not their *purpose*."[38] Based on this analysis, even if a given activity or transaction was performed to carry out a policy of the state, so long as the transaction was commercial in nature, the claimant should not be disqualified as a national of another state under Article 25 of the ICSID Convention. It was the view of the tribunal that the claimant might take advantage of the government policies and preferences in performing its commercial functions. Because the Consolidation Agreement was considered to be a commercial transaction, the tribunal concluded that the respondent's challenge to its jurisdiction had failed.[39] The significance of this decision is that there are still a good number of foreign investors which have the dual function of implementing state policies and conducting business as business. The emphasis on the *nature* of specific transactions, the approach taken by the *ČSOB* Tribunal, is in line with contemporary international law relating to state immunity.[40]

Vacuum Salt v. Ghana[41] illustrates the issue of determining nationality from another angle. The claimant was incorporated in Ghana with the majority of its shares held by nationals of the host state. The tribunal in that case held that Article 25(2)(b) set an objective limit to ICSID jurisdiction on the basis of "foreign control."[42] Accordingly, anything beyond the limit set by the above provision could not confer jurisdiction.[43] This is so despite an agreement between parties to treat a claimant as a foreign national. In the view of the tribunal, the 20 percent shareholding by Greek nationals did not amount to foreign control.[44]

The *Vacuum Salt* decision may be compared with that in *Aguas del Tunari SA v. Bolivia*,[45] in which the tribunal analyzed in detail what might constitute control both directly and indirectly. In that case, the question of actual control by Dutch nationals of a Bolivian company—the claimant—was at issue, and Bolivia challenged the jurisdiction of the tribunal on this ground. Bolivia alleged that the Dutch holding companies were only shell companies whose ultimate owner was a US company. The tribunal, however, considered that the Dutch companies were in actual control of the Bolivian claimant and that it was unnecessary to pierce the corporate veil any further.[46] The *Aguas del Tunari* Tribunal did not elaborate on what basis a corporate veil may or may not be pierced. Like some other ICSID tribunals, it did so no more or no less than was necessary to establish its jurisdiction. In so doing, it once again demonstrated the importance of assessing the issue of piercing the corporate veil.

---

38 Id. (emphases added).
39 Ibid., para. 27.
40 For discussions on this issue, see Chapter 10 of this book.
41 *Vacuum Salt Products Ltd. v. Republic of Ghana*, ICSID Case No. ARB/92/1, Award (February 16, 1994); 9 *ICSID Review Foreign Investment Law Journal* 72, 1994.
42 Ibid., para. 36.
43 Id.
44 Ibid., para. 53.
45 *Aguas del Tunari, S.A. v. Republic of Bolivia*, ICSID Case No. ARB/02/3, Decision on Jurisdiction (October 21, 2005).
46 Ibid., paras. 206–32.

II. Piercing the corporate veil of foreign investors

Natural persons are the ultimate foreign investors and may enter into host countries by various means. They can invest in the host countries by themselves as natural persons, through the corporations they have established in their home countries, or even through subsidiaries set up in the third countries. With regard to the capital and technology invested, in certain fields the host countries may require investments to take the form of a joint venture or other corporate bodies— that is, foreign investments being made in the form of juridical persons of the host country. The diversity of the forms in which foreign investments are made illustrates the importance of determining the nationality of foreign investors. As discussed earlier, the ICSID only handles disputes between a contracting state and a national of another contracting state. The ICSID Convention, however, does not stipulate explicitly the criteria for ascertaining the nationality of investors. Faced with specific cases, tribunals must resolve the differences between the parties by employing different techniques.

To a large extent, foreign investors may, on the basis of treaty protections[47] and domestic preferential treatments, including tax reductions and exemptions, choose to establish an entity in a convenient jurisdiction. In fact, even investors who are nationals of a host state may set up a subsidiary in a foreign country and use it as an investment vehicle to invest in their home country. For one reason or another, the question as to whether or not the corporate veil of foreign investors should be pierced is often raised before tribunals. Yet the decisions made by tribunals on the issue are often unsatisfactory. *Tokios Tokelės v. Ukraine*[48] is one of the earliest cases involving the issue.

The facts of the case are as follows. Tokios Tokelės was a company registered under the laws of Lithuania. It established a wholly owned subsidiary—Taki Spravy—under the laws of Ukraine in 1994 to engage in "the business of advertising, publishing, and printing, and related activities in Ukraine and outside its borders."[49] The initial investment consisted of office furniture, printing equipment, and the construction of and repairs to office facilities. It also reinvested the profits in Taki Spravy. The claimant alleged that owing to its publication of a book that favorably portrayed a leading Ukrainian opposition politician—Yulia Tymoshenko—its investment had been subjected by the Ukrainian Government to "a series of unreasonable and unjustified actions," including: (1) numerous and invasive investigations under the guise of enforcing national tax laws; (2) unsubstantiated actions in domestic courts; (3) placing the assets of Taki Spravy under administrative arrest; (4) unreasonable seizure of financial and other documents;

---

47 For instance, the BITs entered into by the Netherlands are considered to provide wide protections and, as a result, foreign investors may be attracted by such favorable provisions and decide to set up entities in that country; see Roos van Os and Roeline Knottnerus, *Dutch Bilateral Investment Treaties: A Gateway to "Treaty Shopping" for Investment Protection by Multinational Companies*, SOMO, Amsterdam, October 2011.

48 *Tokios Tokelės v. Ukraine*, ICSID Case No. ARB/02/18, Decision on Jurisdiction (April 29, 2004).

49 Ibid., para. 2.

and (5) false accusations of Taki Spravy engaging in illegal activities.[50] By these actions, the claimant contended, the Ukrainian Government had breached its obligations under the Ukraine–Lithuania BIT.

The respondent challenged the jurisdiction of the ICSID tribunal on the ground that, inter alia, the claimant was not a juridical person of the other contracting party—Lithuania—within the meaning of the ICSID Convention. It was undisputed that 99 percent of the claimant's shares were owned by Ukrainian nationals who also controlled two-thirds of its management.[51] Because the respondent's arguments amounted to a request that the tribunal pierce the claimant's corporate veil, that is, reveal the genuine investors in the case, the tribunal began its analysis by quoting Broches, one of the founders of the ICSID Convention, to the effect that the purpose of Article 25(2)(b) is not to define corporate nationality but to

> … indicate the outer limits within which disputes may be submitted to conciliation or arbitration under the auspices of the Centre with the consent of the parties thereto. Therefore the parties should be given the widest possible latitude to agree on the meaning of 'nationality' and any stipulation of nationality made in connection with a conciliation or arbitration clause which is based on a reasonable criterion.[52]

The tribunal also referred to Schreuer's opinion that the contracting parties to the ICSID Convention should enjoy broad discretion in defining corporate nationality:

> … "[d]efinitions of corporate nationality in national legislation or in treaties providing for ICSID's jurisdiction will be controlling for the determination of whether the nationality requirements of Article 25(2)(b) have been met" and that "[a]ny reasonable determination of the nationality of juridical persons contained in national legislation or in a treaty should be accepted by an ICSID commission or tribunal."[53]

With regard to Lithuanian juridical person "investors," Article 1(2) of the Ukraine–Lithuania BIT provides that they include "any entity established in the territory of the Republic of Lithuania in conformity with its laws and regulations," reflecting terminology which is common in many BITs. In addition, the BIT further stipulates in Article 1(2)(c) that a juridical person in respect of either contracting party may be "any entity or organization established under the law of any third State which is, directly or indirectly, controlled by nationals of that Contracting Party or by entities having their seat in the territory of that Contracting Party; it being understood that control requires a substantial part in the ownership." On the basis

---

50 Ibid., para. 3.
51 Ibid., para. 21.
52 Ibid., para. 25, citing Aron Broches, "The Convention on the Settlement of Investment Disputes between States and Nationals of Other States," 136 *Recueil des Cours* 331, 1972-II, at 361.
53 Ibid., para. 26, citing Christoph H. Schreuer, *The ICSID Convention: A Commentary*, 2001, at 286.

of these provisions, Tokios Tokelės would fall into the category of Lithuanian juridical persons. The question was whether its corporate veil should be pierced.

The tribunal considered that the control test should not be applied to determine "investors" in this case because the object and purpose of the BIT was to "intensify economic cooperation to the mutual benefit of both States" and "create and maintain favourable conditions for investment of investors of one State in the territory of the other State."[54] This reasoning, however, begs the real question. If, for the purpose of encouraging investment, the source of capital should not be looked into, why does it matter who controls an investor, as any investment may contribute to the object and purpose of the BIT? Apparently to overcome this uncertainty, if not its unpersuasiveness, the *Tokios Tokelės* Tribunal drew inferences from the previous arbitral decision in *SGS v. Philippines*, in which the tribunal also adopted a broad interpretation relating to investment protection.[55]

The *Tokios Tokelės* Tribunal also sought support from the *Amco Asia* case, in which the tribunal stated that the concept of nationality in the ICSID Convention was "based on the law under which the juridical person has been incorporated, the place of incorporation and the place of the social seat."[56] The *Amco Asia* Tribunal considered that the only exception to this rule is in determining the nationality of a juridical person of the host state when that juridical person is under "foreign control," but that there is no exception to the rule in respect of determining the nationality of the foreign controller.[57]

To support its conclusion, the *Tokios Tokelės* Tribunal also invoked the ICJ's decision in *Barcelona Traction*:[58]

> In that case, the International Court of Justice ("ICJ") stated, "the process of lifting the veil, being an exceptional one admitted by municipal law in respect of an institution of its own making, is equally admissible to play a similar role in international law." In particular, the Court noted, "[t]he wealth of practice already accumulated on the subject in municipal law indicates that the veil is lifted, for instance, to *prevent the misuse of the privileges of legal personality*, as in certain cases of *fraud* or *malfeasance*, to *protect third persons* such as a creditor or purchaser, or to *prevent the evasion of legal requirements or of obligations*."[59]

54 See ibid., paras. 31–32.
55 *SGS Société Générale de Surveillance S.A. v. Republic of the Philippines*, ICSID Case No. ARB/02/6, Decision on Jurisdiction (January 29, 2004). In paragraph 116 of the decision, the tribunal stated that as the preamble of the BIT was "to create and maintain favourable conditions," to resolve any uncertainties, interpretation should favor investments.
56 *Amco Asia Corp. and Others v. Republic of Indonesia*, ICSID Case No. ARB/81/1, Decision on Jurisdiction (September 25, 1983), 1 *ICSID Reports* 389, at 396.
57 Id.
58 *Barcelona Traction, Light and Power Co., Ltd. (Belgium v. Spain)*, I.C.J. 3 (February 5, 1970). For discussions on the impact of the *Barcelona Traction* case on international investment law, see F. A. Mann, "The Protection of Shareholders' Interests in the Light of the Barcelona Traction Case," *Am. J. Int'l L.*, Vol. 67, 1973, pp. 259–74.
59 *Tokios Tokelės*, Decision on Jurisdiction, *supra*, note 48, at para. 54, citing *Barcelona Traction*, ibid., para. 58 (emphases added by the *Tokios Tokelės* Tribunal).

It seems that the *Tokios Tokelės* Tribunal attached much importance to the fact that Tokios Tokelės had been in operation for six years before the Ukraine–Lithuania BIT entered into force and that "there [was] no evidence in the record that the Claimant used its formal legal nationality for any improper purpose."[60] Since the shareholders of Tokios Tokelės did not establish a foreign corporation for the purpose of instituting arbitration proceedings at ICSID against their own government, it would be unfair to deny jurisdiction in the circumstances.

The *Tokios Tokelės* Tribunal's decision not to pierce the claimant's veil was criticized by the dissenting president of the tribunal, Professor Prosper Weil, because the "assumption [flies] in the face of the object and purpose of the ICSID Convention and system as explicitly defined both in the Preamble of the Convention and in the *Report of the Executive Directors*."[61] In Weil's view, the tribunal's interpretation was not consistent with Article 31 of the Vienna Convention on the Law of Treaties ("VCLT") that "[a] treaty shall be interpreted … in accordance with the ordinary meaning to be given to its terms in their context and *in the light of its object and purpose*," which the International Court of Justice has repeatedly indicated as expressing the status of contemporary customary international law on the matter of treaty interpretation.[62] The dissenting opinion fiercely stated:

> It is indisputable, and indeed undisputed, that the object and purpose of the ICSID Convention and, by the same token, of the procedures therein provided for are not the settlement of investment disputes between a State and its own nationals. It is only the international investment that the Convention governs, that is to say, an investment implying a transborder flux of capital. This appears from the Convention itself, in particular from its Preamble which refers to "the role of private international investment" and, of course, from its Article 25. This appears also from the passages in the *Report of the Executive Directors* quoted above.[63]

Unsurprisingly, Weil also drew support from Schreuer, who wrote:

> The basic idea of the Convention, as expressed in its title, is to provide for dispute settlement between States and foreign investors … Disputes between a State and its own nationals are settled by that State's domestic courts …

---

60 *Tokios Tokelės*, Decision on Jurisdiction, ibid., para. 56.
61 *Tokios Tokelės*, Decision on Jurisdiction, Prosper Weil, Dissenting Opinion, para. 6. The "Report of the Executive Directors on the Convention" stated that the object of the ICSID Convention was "designed to facilitate the settlement of disputes between States and foreign investors" for the purpose of "stimulating a larger flow of private international capital into those countries which wish to attract it." See "Report of the Executive Directors on the Convention of the Settlement of Investment Disputes between States and Nationals of Other States" [hereinafter, "Report of the Executive Directors"], Doc. ICSID/2, 1 *ICSID Reports* 23, 1993, para. 9.
62 Ibid., para. 19.
63 Id.

The Convention is designed to facilitate the settlement of investment disputes between States and nationals of other States. It is not meant for disputes between States and their own nationals. The latter type of dispute is to be settled by domestic procedures, notably before domestic courts.[64]

To be fair to the *Tokios Tokelės* Tribunal, there are no definite criteria to determine whether it is necessary, or under what exceptional circumstances, to pierce the corporate veil. It is true that the purpose of the ICSID Convention is to resolve disputes between a contracting state and a foreign national. The question is at what stage and according to what criteria a corporate veil should be lifted. Actually, it could be argued with equal force that for a tribunal to take steps to pierce the corporate veil of foreign investors is not in compliance with Article 31 of the VCLT, as it looks beyond the plain meaning of the treaty provisions, unless the BIT in question stipulates otherwise.

In any event, the *Tokios Tokelės* decision has triggered many discussions and critiques. For instance, one commentator stated:

> To allow disputes between national investors, although disguised under the form of foreign [sic] and their own States to be settled before ICSID arbitral tribunals not only jeopardizes the ICSID system and opens the door to judicial chaos, but also damages the reputation and development of international law of foreign investment.[65]

With regard to jurisprudence in this aspect, there are other cases that either support or oppose the views of the *Tokios Tokelės* Tribunal. In a number of other cases, tribunals have emphasized the importance of relying on the terms of the treaties in question. For instance, in *Rompetrol v. Romania*,[66] a Romanian national and a US national owned, respectively, 80 percent and 20 percent of a holding company incorporated in Switzerland, which in turn was the 100 percent shareholder of a company organized under the laws of the Netherlands—the Rompetrol Group N.V. The Dutch company owned 51 percent of the shares of a Romanian company—Rompetrol S.A. The respondent claimed that despite the fact that the claimant's formal nationality met the requirements of the BIT,[67] the tribunal should apply the test of actual control. In other words, the respondent maintained that the actual control of the claimant was in the hands of a Romanian national. Therefore, it argued, the tribunal should not exercise jurisdiction over the dispute. The tribunal held that, according to the BIT, a test of nationality by way of

64 Id., citing Schreuer, *supra*, note 53, p. 158, para. 165, and p. 290, para. 496.

65 See Omar E. Garcia-Bolivar, "Protected Investments and Protected Investors: The Outer Limits of ICSID's Reach," *Trade, Law and Development*, Vol. II, No. 1, 2010, pp. 145–68, at 167.

66 *Rompetrol Group N.V. v. Romania*, ICSID Case No. ARB/06/3, Decision on Jurisdiction (April 18, 2008).

67 The Netherlands–Romania BIT contained a broad definition of investors, in accordance with which Article 1(b)(ii) provides that the term investors: "shall comprise with regard to either Contracting Party: … ii. Legal persons constituted under the law of that Contracting Party."

incorporation for legal persons should be applied. In such circumstances, it was not necessary for the tribunal to pierce the corporate veil and reveal the actual control or the effective link between nationality and the company.[68]

Saluka v. Czech Republic[69] is another case in which the tribunal, by referring to the provisions of the BIT, refused to pierce the corporate veil of the claimant, which was incorporated in the Netherlands but was owned by Japanese investors. The respondent challenged the jurisdiction of the tribunal on the grounds that Saluka was a mere shell company. The tribunal held that incorporation in the Netherlands was sufficient for determining nationality of the claimant.[70] The tribunal, however, was sympathetic that there was no real connection between the respondent and the claimant, which was "in reality a mere shell company controlled by another company which [was] not constituted under the laws of" the respondent.[71] Despite the fact that there may be "abuses of the arbitral procedure" and "treaty-shopping," which "can share many of the disadvantages of the widely criticized practice of 'forum shopping',"[72] the tribunal decided that the "predominant factor" that must guide its "exercise of its functions is the terms in which the parties to the Treaty now in question have agreed to establish the Tribunal's jurisdiction."[73] As the contracting parties to the Treaty had chosen "to limit entitled 'investors' to those satisfying the definition set out in Article 1," they then

> … cannot in effect impose upon the parties a definition of 'investor' other than that which they themselves agreed. That agreed definition required only that the claimant-investor should be constituted under the laws of (in the present case) the Netherlands, and it is not open to the Tribunal to add other requirements which the parties could themselves have added but which they omitted to add.[74]

ADC v. Hungary also upheld the criterion of incorporation as the determinative factor for nationality of juridical persons.[75] In this case, the claimants were companies incorporated in Cyprus, albeit controlled by Canadian entities. Hungary, appealing to the "genuine-link" test of customary international law for establishing nationality,[76] requested that the tribunal pierce the claimants' corporate veil. The tribunal, however, held that the terms of the BIT must

---

68 *Rompetrol v. Romania, supra,* note 66, paras. 3 and 78.
69 *Saluka Investments BV v. Czech Republic,* UNCITRAL, Partial Award (March 17, 2006).
70 Ibid., paras. 229 and 241.
71 Ibid., para. 240.
72 Id.
73 Ibid., para. 241.
74 Ibid. The tribunal in *Petrobart* took a similar approach. See also *Petrobart Limited v. Kyrgyz Republic,* Arbitration No. 126/2003, Arbitration Institute of the Stockholm Chamber of Commerce, Award of March 29, 2005; available at: http://italaw.com/cases/documents/826.
75 *ADC Affiliate Ltd. and ADC & ADMC Mgmt. Ltd. v. Hungary,* ICSID Case No. ARB/03/16, Award (October 2, 2006), paras. 334–41, 350, 357–59.
76 Ibid., para. 336.

apply and found no requirement for a genuine link therein.[77] Thus, it found "no scope for consideration of customary law principles of nationality, as reflected in *Barcelona Traction*, which in any event are no different. In either case inquiry stops upon establishment of the State of incorporation, and considerations of whence comes the company's capital and whose nationals, if not Cypriot, control it are irrelevant."[78]

Similarly, in *Rumeli v. Kazakhstan*, the tribunal was also faced with the challenge that the claimant was merely a shell company. The tribunal held that: "the BIT does not provide a basis for looking beyond a company on the alleged basis that it would be a shell company and does not exclude such companies from its scope of application from the moment it [sic] is incorporated in another contracting State."[79]

The tribunal in the *TSA Spectrum* case[80] took a different approach. In brief, the facts of the case are as follows. Thales Spectrum de Argentina S.A.—TSA—was a company incorporated in Argentina, which was a wholly owned subsidiary of TSI Spectrum International N.V. ("TSI").[81] TSI and the National Commission of Telecommunications of the Argentine Republic ("CNC") entered into a Concession Contract on June 11, 1997, according to which TSA was to provide radio spectrum administration, monitoring, and control services to CNC, which, in turn, was obliged to create a unified database.

On January 26, 2004, CNC declared the Concession Contract terminated for reasons, inter alia, that TSA had breached the contract in regard to the provision of an integrated information system and had unduly enriched itself.[82] Therefore, on March 25, 2004, TSA wrote to CNC to request amicable negotiations with a view to reverse CNC's previous decision. CNC rejected TSA's request on May 14, 2004.[83] Seven months later, TSA wrote to the President of Argentina, stating that "since more than 30 days had passed without an express reply from the Secretary of Communications, TSA's request should be considered rejected according to Argentine law. Ten days later, TSA filed a request for arbitration with ICSID on December 20, 2004.[84]

One of the disputes between TSA as claimant and the Argentine Government as respondent was whether the claimant qualified as a juridical person of the Netherlands under Article 25(2)(b) of the ICSID Convention. TSA contended that it was a wholly owned subsidiary of TSI, which was incorporated under the law of the Netherlands and was domiciled there. Therefore, it was entitled to be

---

77 Ibid., paras. 357 and 359.
78 Ibid., para. 357.
79 *Rumeli Telekom A.S. and Telsim Mobil Telekomikasyon Hizmetleri A.S. v. Republic of Kazakhstan*, ICSID Case No. ARB/05/16, Award (July 29, 2008), para. 326.
80 *TSA Spectrum de Argentina S.A. v. Argentine Republic*, ICSID Case No. ARB/05/5 (December 19, 2008).
81 Ibid., para. 1.
82 Ibid., para. 9.
83 Ibid., para. 11.
84 Ibid., para. 23.

treated as a foreign investor in accordance with the Netherlands–Argentina BIT and Article 25(2)(b) of the ICSID Convention. In other words, pursuant to the agreement of the parties to the BIT and because its total capital was held by TSI, a national—juridical person—of the Netherlands, it should be treated as a foreign investor.[85] The respondent, on its part, however, challenged the contention of the claimant by pointing out that TSI was "controlled by an Argentinian national, Mr. Jorge Justo Neuss, who held, directly or indirectly, a majority of its shares, starting with 51%, increasing over time to near totality."[86] The question facing the tribunal was whether, in these circumstances, TSI's corporate veil should be pierced.

The tribunal first opined that whether it, as an ICSID tribunal, had jurisdiction over the case could not be decided by the BIT in question. In its view, the jurisdictional matter could only depend on whether the conditions of Article 25(2)(b) of the ICSID Convention were satisfied.[87] It then decided that, in order to apply the second part of Article 25(2)(b), it was necessary to pierce the corporate veil of TSI and that the relevant time for doing so was the date on which the parties consented to submit the dispute to arbitration. As TSA sent its letter to the President of Argentina on December 10, 2004, informing him of its intent to initiate arbitration, this was the date on which the consent to arbitration of both parties was reached.[88] Based on the evidence available, the tribunal concluded that: "whatever interpretation [was] given to the BIT between Argentina and the Netherlands, including the Protocol to the BIT, TSA [could] not be treated, for the purposes of Article 25(2)(b) of the ICSID Convention, as a national of the Netherlands because of absence of 'foreign control'."[89]

The only conclusion that could be drawn from the information and evidence available to the tribunal was that the ultimate owner of TSA on and around the date of consent was the Argentinean citizen Mr Jorge Justo Neuss. It therefore followed that, whatever interpretation was to be given to the BIT between Argentina and the Netherlands, including the Protocol to the BIT, TSA could not be treated, for the purposes of Article 25(2)(b) of the ICSID Convention, as a national of the Netherlands because of its lack of "foreign control" and that the Arbitral Tribunal therefore lacked jurisdiction to examine TSA's claims.

It should be pointed out that, in reaching its decision, the *TSA* Tribunal referred to the views expressed by the *Vacuum Salt Products Ltd v. Ghana* Tribunal that:

> … the parties' agreement to treat Claimant as a foreign national "because of foreign control" does not *ipso jure* confer jurisdiction. The reference in Article 25(2)(b) to "foreign control" necessarily sets an objective Convention limit beyond which ICSID jurisdiction cannot exist and parties therefore lack

---

85 Ibid., para. 158.
86 Ibid., para. 159.
87 Ibid., para. 156.
88 Ibid., para. 160.
89 Ibid., para. 162.

power to invoke same no matter how devoutly they may have desired to do so.[90]

Certainly, the *TSA* Tribunal was aware of the "strict constructionist interpretation in spite of the control of the foreign companies by nationals of the host States" adopted in both *Tokios Tokelès v. Ukraine* and *Rompetrol Group N.V. v. Romania*.[91] In particular, it commented that such an interpretative approach had not been generally accepted and had been criticized even "by the dissenting President of the *Tokios Tokelès* Tribunal."[92] The *TSA* Tribunal considered that the text of the second clause of Article 25(2)(b) permitted the piercing of the corporate veil in cases of foreign control. Its reasoning was that, in order to apply the second clause of Article 25(2)(b), "the existence and materiality of this foreign control have to be objectively proven in order … to establish ICSID jurisdiction."[93] The scrutiny of foreign control should not stop at merely piercing the first layer of the corporate veil. In order to achieve the "objective identification of foreign control up to its real source," the tribunal held that "the same criterion" should be adopted in piercing the second layer of the corporate veil.[94]

In the *TSA* case, the claimant, by invoking the decision in the *Tokios Tokelès* case, requested the tribunal to overlook the nationality of TSI's shareholders. The tribunal, however, indicated that while the problem of piercing the corporate veil had been discussed by the *Tokios Tokelès* Tribunal, it did not allow this to be done because it was of the view that the justifications considered for doing so in the *Barcelona Traction* case were not relevant in the *Tokios Tokelès* case. The *TSA* Tribunal, however, noted that:

> [The *Tokios Tokelès*] case differs from the present one, since there was no ostensible attempt to conceal the true controller of the company, taking advantage of the rights that a Dutch controlling shareholder could have in an Argentine company. Alternatively, the comments made by Professor Weil in his dissent should be applied. According to these comments, only a genuinely foreign investment should be protected by the ICSID mechanism.[95]

The *TSA* Tribunal further considered that Article 25(2)(b) of the ICSID Convention was an important exception to the underlying principle of the Convention, that is, that it should only be applicable to disputes between parties of diverse nationalities and not to those between a state and its own national investors.[96] The key to this exception or the prerequisite to its application was "foreign control," which justified the extension of the ambit of the ICSID Convention. In support of

90 *Vacuum Salt v. Ghana, supra*, note 41, para. 36.
91 *TSA v. Argentina, supra*, note 80, para. 146.
92 Id.
93 Ibid., para. 147.
94 Id.
95 Ibid., para. 118.
96 Ibid., para. 139.

this argument, the tribunal cited the statement of the *Vacuum Salt* Tribunal that: "[t]he reference in Article 25(2)(b) to 'foreign control' necessarily sets an objective Convention limit beyond which ICSID jurisdiction cannot exist."[97]

The approach of the *TSA* Tribunal emphasized the purposes and objectives of Article 25(2)(b) of the ICSID Convention. By doing so, it had to sacrifice the plain meaning of the BIT provisions. In its analysis, the *TSA* Tribunal divided Article 25(2)(b) into two parts. In its view, the first part "uses the formal legal criterion, that of nationality, whilst the second uses a material or objective criterion, that of 'foreign control' in order to pierce the corporate veil and reach for the reality behind the cover of nationality."[98] It held that once the contracting parties to the ICSID Convention agreed to use the second part, they became bound by the limitation imposed by the clause and could not extend the ICSID jurisdictional limits. This view is in agreement with that of Broches, who considered that the purpose of the control test is to expand the jurisdiction of the Centre:

> There was a compelling reason for this last provision. It is quite usual for host States to require that foreign investors carry on their business within their territories through a company organized under the laws of the host country. If we admit, as the Convention does implicitly, that this makes the company technically a national of the host country, it becomes readily apparent that there is need for an exception to the general principle that that the Centre will not have jurisdiction over disputes between a Contracting State and its own nationals. If no exception were made for foreign-owned but locally incorporated companies, a large and important sector of foreign investment would be outside the scope of the Convention.[99]

In fact, for purposes of avoiding or preventing potential abuse of the ICSID mechanisms, to interpret Article 25(2)(b) in accordance with its objectives is no more problematic than is the approach of a strict constructive interpretation. The question is one of consistency. In practice, tribunals have displayed a wide discretion in employing any means of interpretation without giving persuasive reasons for doing so. For instance, in *SOABI v. Senegal*,[100] the claimant was a company incorporated in Senegal but controlled by a Panamanian company owned by Belgian nationals. The respondent objected to the jurisdiction of the tribunal on grounds that Panama was not a contracting party to the ICSID Convention and therefore maintained that the claimant could not resort to ICSID Arbitration to resolve their dispute. The tribunal observed that the purpose of Article 25(2) (b) of the ICSID Convention was to facilitate foreign investment through entities incorporated in the host state. Based on its findings, the tribunal held that Belgian

---

97 Id., citing *Vacuum Salt v. Ghana, supra*, note 41, at para. 36.

98 Ibid., para. 140.

99 See Broches, *supra*, note 52, para. 25, at 358–59.

100 *Société Ouest-Africaine des Bétons Industriels (SOABI) v. Republic of Senegal*, ICSID Case No. ARB/82/1, Decision on Jurisdiction, 2 *ICSID Reports* 182–83 (August 1, 1984).

nationals, instead of a Panamanian company, were in effective control of the claimant and it therefore had jurisdiction over the case.

The *Champion Trading* case also involved determination of the nationality of the investors, both as natural persons and juridical persons. Regarding its decision on the juridical person investors' nationality, the tribunal emphasized the importance of faithful interpretation of treaties by giving ordinary meaning to relevant provisions in accordance with Article 31 of the VCLT. Accordingly, the tribunal considered that as neither the Egypt–United States BIT nor the ICSID Convention contained "any exclusion of dual nationals as shareholders of companies of the other Contracting State," it ruled that it had jurisdiction over the corporate claimants.[101] Unfortunately, the tribunal did not conduct any analysis in respect of corporate nationality. It is apparent, however, that it took for granted that the incorporation of the two companies in the United States gave them the nationality of that country and there was no need to explore further whether the shareholding in those companies by individuals with dual nationalities would have any impact on their corporate nationality. The tribunal therefore implicitly adopted the place of incorporation as the determinative factor in deciding corporate nationality—an approach that the *Tokios Tokelės* Tribunal and others also took.

In *Yukos Universal v. Russian Federation*,[102] the tribunal was requested to pierce the corporate veil of the claimant—Yukos Universal—which was incorporated under the laws of the Isle of Man in the United Kingdom and was a large shareholder of Yukos Oil Incorporated ("Yukos Oil")—a Russian company. Yukos Oil was one of the largest oil concerns of Russia and was jointly owned by both Russian and foreign owners. In 2003, Russia started investigations into the operation of Yukos Oil, which led to arrests, legal charges, and the imprisonment of a number of key officials of the company on grounds of embezzlement, tax evasion, money laundering, forgery, and fraud.[103] Apparently fearing the situation in Russia, the majority of the remaining Yukos Oil officials fled the country. In 2006, Yukos Oil went bankrupt. As a large shareholder, Yukos Universal instituted arbitration proceedings with the Permanent Court of Arbitration in The Hague, alleging that Russia had breached its obligations under the Energy Charter Treaty ("ECT").

The respondent challenged the tribunal's jurisdiction by maintaining that the ownership structure of Yukos Universal should disqualify it from benefiting from the ECT. Specifically, whilst the claimant's shareholding of over 50 million shares (amounting to 2.25 percent of the total shares) of Yukos Oil was not challenged, the respondent argued that Yukos Universal was wholly owned by GML, a company incorporated in Gibraltar, and in turn GML was owned by a number of trusts whose beneficiaries included Russian nationals and former senior executives of Yukos Oil (amounting to 59.5 percent of the shares of GML).[104] In the

---

101 *Champion Trading, supra*, note 10, para. 3.4.2.
102 *Yukos Universal Limited (Isle of Man) v. Russian Federation*, PCA Case No. AA 227, Interim Award on Jurisdiction and Admissibility (November 30, 2009).
103 Ibid., para. 49.
104 Ibid., paras. 463 and 483.

respondent's view, trustees of the trusts were nominal owners only, the economic interest of the ownership of GML having always remained with the "Russian oligarchs."[105]

The tribunal first pointed out that the claimant was incorporated in the Isle of Man; the United Kingdom had extended the application of the ECT to the Isle of Man when accepting that Treaty's obligations; the claimant was duly incorporated and in existence at the time it filed its claims pursuant to ECT Article 26.[106] The tribunal then stated that: "[o]n its face, Article 1(7)(a)(ii) of the ECT contains no requirement other than that the claimant company be duly organized in accordance with the law applicable in a Contracting Party."[107] As that was the case, "in order to qualify as a protected Investor under Article 1(7) of the ECT, a company is merely required to be organized under the laws of a Contracting Party."[108] The *Yukos Universal* Tribunal, like that in *Saluka*,[109] by basing its decision on international rules for interpreting treaties, held that it was "bound to interpret the terms of the ECT, including Article 1(7), not as they might have been written but as they were actually written."[110] It further stated that there were:

> … no general principles of international law that would require investigating how a company or another organization operates when the applicable treaty simply requires it to be organized in accordance with the laws of a Contracting Party. The principles of international law, which have an unquestionable importance in treaty interpretation, do not allow an arbitral tribunal to write new, additional requirements—which the drafters did not include—into a treaty, no matter how auspicious or appropriate they may appear.[111]

The approach taken and the international principles relied upon by the *Yukos Universal* Tribunal were not questionable. Tribunals should deal with the disputes before them by reading the plain meaning of the relevant Treaty provisions. In this regard, the tribunal's decision was in line with applicable international law. For instance, in its advisory opinion in the *Acquisition of Polish Nationality* case, the Permanent Court of International Justice ("PCIJ") stated: "To impose an additional condition for the acquisition of Polish nationality, a condition not provided for in the Treaty … would be equivalent not to interpreting the Treaty, but to reconstructing it."[112]

The jurisprudence in relation to the determination of the nationality of investors indicates that the majority of tribunals has been prepared to rely on the provisions of the BIT and was not in favor of piercing the corporate veil. It is also noteworthy

---

105 Ibid., para. 483.
106 Ibid., para. 404.
107 Ibid., para. 411.
108 Id.
109 See *Saluka Investments v. Czech Republic*, *supra*, note 69.
110 *Yukos Universal v. Russian Federation*, *supra*, note 102, para. 413.
111 Ibid., para. 415.
112 See *Acquisition of Polish Nationality*, Advisory Opinion (1923), PCIJ Ser. B, No. 7, p. 20.

that in such cases jurisdiction could be confirmed without anything further. At the same time, whenever jurisdiction was at issue, piercing the corporate veil would be conducted to the extent that jurisdiction could be established. Whether or not this phenomenon is coincidental is unknown. As most BITs provide that investors of the other contracting party are those entities established in accordance with the laws of that party, there is nothing wrong in using the place of incorporation as a determinative factor in ascertaining the nationality of corporate entities. Such an approach is also in line with Article 31 of the VCLT. Even though this may result in treaty shopping and abuse of the arbitration process in some cases, this should not be the basis for tribunals to depart from the well recognized rules of treaty interpretation. It should also be noted that Sinclair has raised the theoretical question of:

> … whether the network of bilateral investment treaties, coupled with the ICSID Convention, have [sic] entirely departed from the traditional rules of diplomatic protection and replaced these with a legal framework in which their own rules of jurisdiction *ratione personae* comprehensively and exclusively govern to the exclusion of rules of general international law.[113]

He further notes that in the context of direct arbitration in place of diplomatic protection:

> The bond of nationality appears to have diminished in significance to a mere formality.
>
> …
>
> Yet, in entering into investment treaties states generally act upon a desire to create favourable conditions for greater investment flows between the Contracting States in the mutual hope that this will increase their prosperity and the prosperity of their nationals. These goals might suggest that as between an investor and the state under whose treaty of protection it seeks to gain protection there is the need for a bond of more substance than mere nationality on paper.[114]

At the same time, others consider that "States know well the options available to them to delimit nationality. Furthermore, the consequences of these different choices have been thoroughly discussed and debated for some time."[115] Therefore, in their view, to rely on the treaty provisions for determining the nationality of investors is no problem. In any event, it is unacceptable if tribunals are only prepared to pierce the corporate veil when there is prima facie no sup-

---

113 Anthony C. Sinclair, "Nationality of Individual Investors in ICSID Arbitration," *International Arbitration Law Review*, 2004, 7(6), pp. 191–95, at 194.

114 Id.

115 See, for example, Paul M. Blyschak, "Yukos Universal v. Russia: Shell Companies and Treaty Shopping in International Energy Disputes," *Rich. J. Global L. & Bus.*, Vol. 10, 2010–2011, pp. 179–210, at 199.

port or inadequate support for their jurisdiction and, once jurisdiction can be established based on the control of investors, then cease piercing the corporate veil any further.

III. *Jus standi*: indirect investors and minority shareholders

Determination of foreign investors also involves the *jus standi* of minority shareholders and indirect investments, where a foreign investor makes an investment in a host country by establishing or participating in an existing company but without holding the majority shares of the entity. In most cases, BIT provisions on foreign investment, and hence investors, are broad enough to cover such investors. Yet, in practice, the respondent states often question indirect investments as qualified investments and minority investors as qualified investors.[116] In such cases, the respondent states always argue that the investors have no *jus standi*.

The matter is further complicated by the provisions of Article 25 of the ICSID Convention, which define the jurisdiction of the tribunals established thereunder. In practice, a number of cases concern the interpretation of the above provisions, in particular whether the first sentence of Article 25(2)(b) includes indirect investors and, if the answer is "yes," whether minority shareholders are qualified as shareholders. With regard to "foreign control" in the second sentence of Article 25(2)(b), the question is what constitutes such "foreign control." Another question is where an entity established under the laws of the host state is controlled by more than one person (foreign investors), whether the status of "foreign control" is affected.

Arguably, *CMS v. Argentina*[117] was the first ICSID case involving the *jus standi* of minority shareholders that was brought before an international investment tribunal. The claimant—CMS Gas Transmission Company ("CMS")—was an entity incorporated in the United States which, during the privatization of Argentina's state-owned companies beginning in 1989, purchased from the Argentine Government 25 percent of the shares of Transportadora de Gas del Norte ("TGN"), an Argentine company. In 1992, TGN obtained a license for the transportation of gas. Later, CMS purchased an additional 4.42 percent that had been assigned to an employee share program, thus bringing its ownership of TGN to 29.42 percent.[118] In response to the economic and financial crisis in Argentina in the late 1990s, the Argentine Government took various measures affecting gas companies in late 1999. It was against these measures that the claimant brought the arbitration at ICSID, claiming that its business had suffered a material adverse impact and the respondent had breached guarantees to protect its investment in

---

116 For discussions on state practice relating to the standing of shareholders in arbitration and the evolution of international law rules in this regard, see Patrick Dumberry, "The Legal Standing of Shareholders Before Arbitral Tribunals: Has Any Rule of Customary International Law Crystallised?," *Michigan State Journal of International Law*, Issue 18, Vol. 3, 2010, pp. 353–74.

117 *CMS Gas Transmission Company v. Republic of Argentina*, ICSID Case No. ARB/01/8, Decision of the Tribunal on Objections to Jurisdiction (July 17, 2003).

118 Ibid., paras. 18–19.

TGN. The respondent objected to the jurisdiction of the tribunal on grounds of a lack of *jus standi* on the part of the claimant.

The respondent contended specifically that TGN was the licensee and the claimant was only a minority shareholder of TGN. It further argued that only TGN could claim for any damage suffered as a result of the Argentine measures but that TGN was an Argentine company which was not a foreign investor under the Argentina–United States BIT. Therefore, in the respondent's view, what the claimant claimed for was indirect damages[119] and it should not be permitted to arbitrate the case before an ICSID tribunal since that "would imply that the shareholders have standing different from that of the company."[120]

The claimant's argument was that it was "not claiming for any rights pertaining to TGN but for the rights associated with its investment" in TGN.[121] In its view, because of its participation in TGN, it was an investor under the BIT and therefore had rights to the protection of its investment in accordance with the Treaty. As such, it had right of action—*jus standi*.[122]

As *CMS* was an early case on the issue of minority shareholder as foreign investor, the tribunal was understandably very careful in expressing its opinion. It first analyzed the issue from the point of view of international law and concluded that the judgment of the International Court of Justice in the *Barcelona Traction* case[123] was not directly relevant. At the same time, the tribunal considered the judgment in the *Elettronica Sicula* case[124] as evidence that the ICJ accepted "the protection of shareholders of a corporation by the State of their nationality in spite of the fact that the affected corporation had a corporate personality under the defendant State's legislation."[125] Then the tribunal concluded that in contemporary international law, diplomatic protection is preserved as a residual mechanism for protecting an individual's rights and that the prevailing arrangements were represented by the ICSID Convention in relation to the protection of foreign investors. The decisions of the Iran–United States Claims Tribunal and the rules and decisions of the United Nations Compensation Commission were relied on as further examples to support the above position. Finally, the *CMS* Tribunal agreed with the respondent that the decisions in all the above cases were the results of *lex specialis*—specific treaty arrangements. Nevertheless, the tribunal pointed out that "*lex specialis* in this respect is so prevalent that it can now be considered the

---

119 Ibid., para. 36.
120 Ibid., para. 37.
121 Ibid., para. 39.
122 Ibid., para. 43.
123 *Barcelona Traction, supra*, note 58. In that case, the Belgian shareholders of a Canadian company suffered losses as a result of government measures of Spain. The issue before the ICJ was whether, under customary international law, Belgium could exercise diplomatic protection over its nationals/shareholders. Although the ICJ denied Belgium's *jus standi*, it did not pronounce on whether shareholders had independent rights from their company under international law; ibid., para. 90.
124 *Case Concerning the Elettronica Sicula S.p.A. (ELSI) (United States of America v. Italy)*, Judgment of July 20, 1989, *ICJ Reports*, 1989, 15.
125 *CMS v. Argentina, supra*, note 117, para. 44.

general rule, certainly in respect of foreign investments and increasingly in respect of other matters."[126]

Because international law could only shed light on the general approach to protecting shareholders as investors, the *CMS* Tribunal turned to the ICSID Convention. Even though Article 25 thereof fails to define either "investor" or "investment," the tribunal pointed out that:

> There is indeed no requirement that an investment, in order to qualify, must necessarily be made by shareholders controlling a company or owning the majority of its shares. It is well known incidentally that, depending on how shares are distributed, controlling shareholders can in fact own less than the majority of the shares. The reference that Article 25(2)(b) makes to foreign control in terms of treating a company of the nationality of the Contracting State party as a national of another Contracting State is precisely meant to facilitate agreements between the parties, so as not to have the corporate personality interfering with the protection of the real interests associated with the investment.[127]

The tribunal then concluded that there was no bar for it to exercise jurisdiction under the terms of the ICSID Convention. Yet, as for the specific meaning of "investment" and "investor," the tribunal then examined the relevant provisions of the Argentina–United States BIT, Article I(1) of which provides that an investment includes "a company or shares of stock or other interests in a company or interests in the assets thereof." As the definition of the term "investment" was very broad, anybody, whether a natural or juridical person, who has made an investment in shares would qualify as an "investor" under the BIT. In addition, there had been other tribunal decisions supporting the broad definition of investments and investors, so the *CMS* Tribunal had no difficulty in concluding that the dispute before it arose directly from an investment made by the claimant and that there was no bar to its exercise of jurisdiction under the BIT. In the tribunal's view, the claimant had *jus standi* because, according to the specific provisions of the BIT, whether "the protected investor is in addition a party to a concession agreement or a license agreement with the host State is immaterial for the purpose of finding jurisdiction."[128] The *CMS* Tribunal further commented that the origin of the shares made no difference as to whether or not they constituted an investment and that what the BIT was concerned with was the protection of the rights of foreign investors.[129]

As the first decision in a case involving minority shareholders as foreign investors, the *CMS* Tribunal's decision is very important. In contemporary investment practice, many foreign investors may not choose or be able to be majority

---

126 Ibid., para. 48.
127 Ibid., para. 51.
128 Ibid., para. 65; see also ibid., para. 68.
129 Ibid., para. 69.

shareholders. Unless minority shareholders' interests are protected, there would be a major loophole in the international investment protection mechanism. For instance, where a foreign minority shareholder makes an investment in a company incorporated in accordance with the laws of the host state and the latter has violated its obligations under the BIT but the local company, for one reason or another, refuses or fails to take action against the host state, unless the minority shareholder is recognized as a qualified foreign investor, it may not be able to resort to protection under any procedures except through the local courts, which most foreign investors do not regard as being able to provide adequate protection. *GAMI v. Mexico*[130] is a case involving precisely such a situation.

In the *GAMI* case, GAMI Investments Inc.—the claimant—was a US investment corporation wholly owned by another US company named Great American Management and Investments, Inc. GAMI owned 14.18 percent of the shares of Grupo Azucarero Mexico SA de CV ("GAM"), which was a Mexican holding company whose remaining shareholders were Mexican nationals.[131]

GAM, by acquiring sugar mills from the Government of Mexico in the late 1980s and early 1990s in the context of a privatization program, owned five sugar mills by 1997.[132] In 2001, it was Mexico's fourth largest sugar producer. Beginning in 1999, the sugar industry experienced a crisis, as a result of which GAM filed for a *suspensión de pagos* (suspension of payments) on May 9, 2000. This judicial procedure was intended to allow the restructuring of GAM's debt and its avoidance of bankruptcy.[133] Subsequently, the Mexican Government issued a decree on September 3, 2001 formally to expropriate 22 sugar mills, including the five owned by GAM.[134]

GAM then challenged the constitutionality of the Expropriation Law and the Expropriation Decree, in relation to three of its five mills, by means of *amparo* proceedings before the relevant Mexican administrative courts. On February 9, 2004, the Tribunal Colegiado en Materia Administrativa del Primer Circuito rendered a *Sentencia de Amparo en Revision* (the "*Sentencia*") in favor of GAM, holding the Expropriation Decree to be unlawful and therefore ineffective with regard to the three mills.[135]

The claimant's complaints were not that its shareholding was adversely affected by the Mexican Government's measures. Rather, the claimant's claims, being derivative in nature, related to the reduction in value of its shareholding which resulted from the Mexican Government's measures. As there was no contract between the claimant and the respondent, these claims were based on the fact that the claimant was an investor under Article 1105 of the North American Free Trade Agreement ("NAFTA").

---

130 *GAMI Investments, Inc. v. Government of the United Mexican States*, NAFTA Chapter 11 Arbitration under the UNCITRAL Rules, Final Award (November 15, 2004).
131 Ibid., para. 1.
132 Ibid., para. 12.
133 Ibid., para. 16.
134 Ibid., para. 17.
135 Ibid., paras. 18–20.

Regarding jurisdiction, there were two issues, namely: (1) whether the claimant was a qualified investor, even though it only held a 14.18 percent equity interest in GAM; and (2) whether, as a minority shareholder, the claimant could make a separate claim where the majority of shareholders had decided not to take any actions in respect of the government measures.

With regard to the first issue, the heart of the question was "whether governmental acts or omissions that adversely affect GAM may be pleaded as breaches of NAFTA because they had the result of reducing the value of GAMI's stake in GAM."[136] The claimant contended that NAFTA Article 1110 did not require majority shareholding in order to qualify as an investor.[137] It also made reference to other tribunals' findings on the issue, including *AIG v. Iran*[138] and *Liamco v. Libya*.[139]

The *GAMI* Tribunal first reviewed international practice on the issue, including the ICJ decision in *ELSI*,[140] in which it was held that US shareholders of an Italian corporate entity were entitled to international jurisdiction when seeking to hold Italy liable for an alleged violation of a treaty,[141] and the decision of the annulment Committee in *Vivendi*.[142] The tribunal then stated that if the claimant were a 100 percent shareholder of GAM, it would be allowed to seek relief for alleged treaty breaches under NAFTA without being required to seek relief before the Mexican courts.[143] Therefore, the fact that it was only a minority shareholder should not affect its right to seek relief from international arbitral tribunals. In the tribunal's view, it was not decisive whether or not the host state had taken any measures directly affecting the claimant's shareholding. The issue was "whether a breach of NAFTA leads with sufficient directness to loss or damage in respect of a given investment."[144]

As to the fact that GAM's majority shareholders had decided not to resort to the Mexican courts for remedies, the tribunal stated:

> The owners of the other 85.82% shares might for reasons of their own have chosen not to cause GAM to seek relief before the Mexican courts. (They might simply have been defeatists. Or they might have made their separate

---

136 Ibid., para. 27.
137 Ibid., para. 28.
138 4 Iran–US Claims Tribunal Reports 96 (1983), in which the claimant held a 35% interest and was awarded damages.
139 20 *I.L.M.* 1 (1977), in which the claimant's 25.5% interest in three oil concessions were compensated for nationalization.
140 *ELSI, supra*, note 124.
141 See *GAMI v. Mexico, supra*, note 130, para. 30.
142 See ibid., para. 32. From that decision, the *GAMI* Tribunal quoted the following text: "*it cannot be argued that CGE did not have an 'investment' in CAA from the date of the conclusion of the Concession Contract, or that it was not an 'investment' in respect of its own shareholding, whether or not it had overall control of CAA. Whatever the extent of its investment may have been, it was entitled to invoke the BIT in respect of conduct alleged to constitute a breach …*" (emphasis in original).
143 *GAMI v. Mexico, supra*, note 130, para. 37.
144 Ibid., para. 33.

peace with the Government and abandoned any complaint in return for offsetting benefits.) That would not disentitle GAMI.[145]

The tribunal's reasoning was based on the fact that international treaties very often require states to accord foreign investors more preferential treatment than that available to their own citizens. At the same time, citizens may enjoy many other rights that are not available to foreign investors.[146] In the circumstances of the present case, whatever the Mexican shareholders of GAM did or did not do was entirely immaterial insofar as the claimant was concerned. Indeed, the *GAMI* Tribunal stated:

> They [GAM's Mexican shareholders] may have complaints about inciden-tal losses caused by the wrongful expropriation notwithstanding its reversal. They may be dissatisfied with the compensation to be offered on account of the two mills whose expropriation was unchallenged. They may be sanguine or apprehensive about Mexican judicial acceptance of such complaints. But this is the relief that is available to them. They are Mexican nationals and do not have standing under Chapter 11 of NAFTA. GAMI however is entitled to seek international relief from a NAFTA Tribunal on account of a wrongful expropriation.[147]

It is generally accepted that the jurisdiction of an international arbitration tribunal should not be affected by the fact that the same question has been addressed in a national court. The two bodies exercise their jurisdiction in accordance with different authorities and apply different sets of rules. This is strikingly clear in the comments made by the *GAMI* Tribunal in relation to the different treatments that foreign investors and citizens of the host states may be accorded. Where the same principle and analogy are applied, one would find the dissenting opinion in the *Tokios Tokelės* case to be convincing. It would be illogical, and in fact wrong, that whilst foreign investors' rights under treaties are considered as fundamentally different from those of nationals of the host states, the nationals may be treated as foreign investors simply because they have set up an entity in a foreign country through which funds are transferred out and then back to the same country. It follows then that there may be a need to pierce the corporate veil in cases where a national of the host state is alleged to hold shares in a foreign investor that has made investments in the host state.

In *Sempra v. Argentina*,[148] the claimant asserted that the respondent had adopted measures that had changed the general regulatory framework established for foreign investors in a way which had severely affected its investment in two

---

145 Ibid., para. 37.

146 On this point, the *GAMI* Tribunal quoted the decision in the *Hopkins* case (US-Mexican Claims Commission, IV *UNRIAA* 41, at 47 (1926)); ibid., para. 38.

147 Id.

148 *Sempra Energy International v. Argentine Republic*, ICSID Case No. ARB/02/16, Decision on Objection to Jurisdiction (May 11, 2005).

natural gas distribution companies. The claimant in that case had participated in Argentina's vast privatization program of its natural gas industry and owned 43.09 percent of the share capital of Sodigas Sur S.A. ("Sodigas Sur") and Sodigas Pampeana S.A. ("Sodigas Pampeana"). The balance of the share capital of the two companies was owned by Camuzzi—another foreign company. The two Argentine companies—Sodigas Sur and Sodigas Pampeana—in turn, held 90 percent and 86.09 percent, respectively, of the shares in Camuzzi Gas del Sur S.A. ("CGS") and Camuzzi Gas Pampeana S.A. ("CGP"), licensees for natural gas distribution.[149]

The respondent raised the question as to why "Sempra had not claimed as an Argentine company—presumably Sodigas—if in fact it considered that it had control of that company."[150] The underpinning of the respondent's argument was that where foreign investors are permitted to claim as shareholders, the second sentence of ICSID Article 25(2) would be made redundant and therefore a contradiction would exist between the two sentences of that Article.[151] The tribunal, however, considered that there was "no such contradiction" because "where various investor companies resort to arbitration, some can do so as shareholders and others as companies of the nationality of the state that is a party to the dispute, on the basis of the various corporate arrangements and control structures."[152] The tribunal therefore concluded that, under the second sentence of Article 25(2)(b), an investor was entitled to bring an ICSID arbitration. It did not even consider it necessary to address the matter of how foreign control was exercised.[153] As to the question of whether more than one foreign investor may have their participation combined in order to establish control, the tribunal's view was that where foreign investors make initial and subsequent investments which result in a joint operation, "it is then presumable that their participation has been viewed as a whole, even though they are of different nationalities and are protected by different

---

149 Ibid., para. 19.
150 Ibid., para. 43.
151 ICSID Article 25(2) reads as follows: "'National of another Contracting State' means: (a) any natural person who had the nationality of a Contracting State other than the State party to the dispute on the date on which the parties consented to submit such dispute to conciliation or arbitration as well as on the date on which the request was registered pursuant to paragraph (3) of Article 28 or paragraph (3) of Article 36, but does not include any person who on either date also had the nationality of the Contracting State party to the dispute; and (b) any juridical person which had the nationality of a Contracting State other than the State party to the dispute on the date on which the parties consented to submit such dispute to conciliation or arbitration and any juridical person which had the nationality of the Contracting State party to the dispute on that date and which, because of foreign control, the parties have agreed should be treated as a national of another Contracting State for the purposes of this Convention."
152 *Sempra v. Argentina, supra*, note 148, para. 44. The tribunal also cited the *Lucchetti* case (*Empresas Lucchetti, S.A. and Lucchetti Peru, S.A. v. Republic of Peru*, ICSID Case No. ARB/03/4 (also known as *Industria Nacional de Alimentos, A.S. and Indalsa Perú, S.A. v. Republic of Peru*), Award (February 7, 2005), in which Empresas Lucchetti, S.A. petitioned as a foreign investor and Lucchetti Peru petitioned as a Peruvian company; see id.
153 Ibid., para. 46.

treaties."[154] In such cases, all the foreign investors must have the right, one way or another, to institute arbitration under the pertinent treaties. Such control, of course, cannot be jointly exercised with local or national investors.

The second issue in the *Sempra* case was whether the alleged loss suffered by the claimant was indirect and hence should not be protected. This issue arose because the claimant had no direct contractual relationship with the respondent and the guarantees and promises had all been made by the respondent to the licensees. The tribunal did not find this situation problematic because the claimant's investment was made in the Argentine companies through which funds were channeled to the licensees. Thus, even though the investment was indeed indirect, the effect of protection under the BIT should not be adversely affected. The tribunal stated: "In this connection, if one were to conclude anything different, one would be depriving the Treaty of any effect since it was signed with the precise intention of guaranteeing the investments that would be made in the privatization process, by means of the specific modality with which they were made."[155]

It should be noted that the tribunal in *GAMI*, in considering the loss allegedly suffered by the claimant in that case, stated: "The fact that a host state does not explicitly interfere with share ownership is not decisive. The issue is rather whether a breach of NAFTA leads with sufficient directness to loss or damage in respect of a given investment. Whether GAM can establish such a prejudice is a matter to be examined on the merits. Uncertainty in this regard is not an obstacle to jurisdiction."[156] This was a precedent that the *Sempra* Tribunal could rely upon, because in both cases what the claimants requested was compensation for losses suffered by their indirect investments. In such circumstances, unless it could be established that the alleged loss suffered was attributable to the measures of the host state, no compensation could be awarded. In fact, this test is applicable even in assessing losses suffered by direct investments.

The third issue facing the *Sempra* Tribunal was the claimant's *jus standi*. The respondent challenged the tribunal's jurisdiction on the ground that the claimant, as a minority shareholder "did not control the licensees" and therefore had suffered no direct losses and that, even if there had been any losses suffered, they could only be indirect and derivative losses.[157] In essence, the respondent's argument was based on the fact that the claimant was only a shareholder with which it had no direct contractual relations. The tribunal first decided that the BIT's

154 Ibid., para. 54.
155 For details of the tribunal's discussion, see ibid., para. 69.
156 Ibid., para. 75, quoting *GAMI v. Mexico, supra,* note 130 para. 33. This position also has the support of the *Enron* case, in which the tribunal considered that the matter was related to consent to arbitration and held: "If consent has been given in respect of an investor and an investment, it can be reasonably concluded that the claims brought by such investor are admissible under the treaty. If the consent cannot be considered as extending to another investor or investment, these other claims should then be considered inadmissible as being only remotely connected with the affected company and the scope of the legal system protecting that investment." See *Enron Corporation and Ponderosa Assets, L.P. v. Argentine Republic,* ICSID Case No. ARB/01/3, Decision on Jurisdiction (January 14, 2004), para. 52.
157 *Sempra v. Argentina, supra,* note 148, para. 90.

definition of investment was so broad that its protection would extend to the claimant. In support of this conclusion, it cited the decision of the *Enron* Tribunal that: "The Tribunal must accordingly conclude that under the provisions of the Bilateral Investment Treaty, broad as they are, claims made by investors that are not in the majority or in the control of the affected corporation when claiming for violations of their rights under such treaty are admissible."[158] Consequently, the *Sempra* Tribunal adopted the same approach—to hold that the claimant was under the protection of the Argentina–United States BIT.

As to the question of whether a breach of contract may constitute a breach of a BIT, the *Sempra* Tribunal considered that certain breaches would be purely contractual in nature and others merely violations of treaties. What is more common, in the tribunal's view, are cases which "originate in a violation of a contractual obligation that at the same time amounts to a violation of the guarantees of the treaty."[159] The tribunal therefore dismissed the respondent's objections[160] and held that it had jurisdiction over the case.

It should be pointed out that the *ad hoc* annulment Committee annulled the *Sempra* Tribunal's award but, at the same time, upheld that tribunal's decision relating to jurisdiction. In this regard, the *ad hoc* Committee stated that: "[s]hareholders may claim under the BIT—as distinct from what was the case in the *Barcelona Traction* case—simply because this BIT extends such rights to 'investors' as defined therein, a right which does not exist under customary international law."[161]

The *ad hoc* Committee considered that the dispute involved two distinctive issues. It its view, the first issue was whether the claimant was entitled to claim under the BIT and the ICSID Convention for damages to its investment in the companies that were partly and indirectly owned by it, and the second issue was whether acts or omissions on the part of the respondent had caused any damage to the two local companies and thence to the claimant. It said that: "[t]he first issue is one of jurisdiction, while the second issue relates to the merits of the dispute."[162] Therefore, although the *ad hoc* Committee annulled the *Sempra* award, it upheld the findings of the tribunal with regard to minority shareholders' rights under the BITs and the ICSID Convention. This further illustrates the extent to which support may be given to minority shareholders' *jus standi* in investment arbitration practice.

The position of international arbitration on the protection of minority shareholders and indirect investors is further demonstrated in the decision in *Impregilo*.[163]

158 *Enron v. Argentina*, *supra*, note 156, para. 49.
159 *Sempra v. Argentina*, *supra*, note 148, para. 95 (footnote omitted).
160 The respondent in the *Sempra* case also challenged the jurisdiction of the tribunal on other grounds, including that a renegotiation of the licenses was in process, that there was a lack of evidence on the status of the investors and that the dispute has been submitted to national courts.
161 *Sempra Energy International v. Argentine Republic*, ICSID Case No. ARB/02/16, Decision on the Argentine Republic's Request for Annulment of the Award (June 29, 2010), para. 103.
162 Ibid., para. 104.
163 *Impregilo S.p.A. v. Argentine Republic*, ICSID Case No. ARB/07/17, Award (June 21, 2011).

In that case, the claimant—Impregilo—was one of the parties in a consortium that was granted a concession for water and sewage services in Argentina. The consortium, in turn, incorporated a company—AGBA—in the host state, which entered into a concession contract with Argentina.[164] The arbitration was instituted under Article 1(1)(b) of the Argentina–Italy BIT. One of the questions facing the tribunal was whether Impregilo, being a shareholder in the direct investor, was qualified as a foreign investor.[165] The tribunal treated the matter in a summary fashion, because in its view there was "a substantial case-law showing that claims such as those presented by Impregilo enjoy protection under the applicable BITs."[166] It had no hesitation in deciding that it had jurisdiction over the case on the ground that Impregilo was an investor protected by the Argentina–Italy BIT.

Quite often, respondent states argue that where a shareholder seeks relief independently in accordance with the applicable BIT and the company of which it is a shareholder may also claim through local proceedings, there is a possibility of double compensation. When that happens, it would be unfair to the respondent state and may constitute unjust enrichment to the investor. It should be noted, however, that the *Impregilo* Tribunal considered the danger of double compensation in the case to be theoretical. It stated: "It seems obvious that if compensation were granted to AGBA at domestic level, this would affect the claims that Impregilo could make under the BIT, and conversely, any compensation granted to Impregilo at international level would affect the claims that could be presented by AGBA before Argentine courts."[167] Yet it did not elaborate how an international tribunal, including itself, could coordinate with local courts or other bodies of the host state so that double compensation could be avoided.

In fact, in assessing the damages that were allegedly suffered by Impregilo, the tribunal opined that: "it cannot be established with certainty in what situation AGBA – and thus Impregilo – would have been, had the Argentine Republic's breach of the fair and equitable treatment standard not occurred."[168] Nevertheless, it found that Argentina had contributed to some extent to the negative development of the concession, even though it was not convinced that the business of AGBA would succeed in any event.[169] In these circumstances, it was quite certain that had AGBA resorted to local remedies it would not have been granted any damages. Hence, there would not be any danger of double compensation, as there would be no compensation anyway. Perhaps that was the reason that the tribunal considered the issue to be purely theoretical. It would have made better contributions to the development of investment law had the tribunal further elaborated this point.

Although different investment arbitration tribunals may take differing positions regarding assessment of damages and, hence, determination of compensation, a

164 Ibid., para. 137.
165 Ibid., para. 138.
166 Ibid., para. 140.
167 Ibid., para. 139.
168 Ibid., para. 371.
169 Ibid., paras. 374–78.

consensus has been established that foreign investors who are minority shareholders of companies organized pursuant to the laws of the host states are qualified investors under the ICSID Convention and most, if not all, BITs. Views to this effect are found in the decisions of many arbitral tribunals and ICSID *ad hoc* committees. For instance, the *ad hoc* Committee in *CMS* stated: "The Committee observes that, as regards shareholder equity, the BIT contains nothing which indicates that the investor in capital stock has to have a majority of the stock or control over the administration of the company. Investments made by minority shareholders are covered by the actual language of the definition, as also recognized by ICSID arbitral tribunals in comparable cases."[170] Indeed, no BIT requires that a foreign investor must own a majority interest in a company of the host state in order to be treated as a foreign investor.[171] This was also confirmed in the *El Paso* case, in which it was decided that the rights of shareholders were derived from their shareholding and any claim to those rights was not affected by the quantity or volume of the shares so held.[172] Where a host state requires that foreign investors must use certain vehicles in making an investment,[173] the protection of shareholders' interests, including those of minority shareholders, is not only equitable but also of the utmost importance because, in such circumstances, the local entity in which a foreign investor has invested may refuse to take action against its own government even if it may be treated as a qualified investor owing to foreign control in accordance with Article 25(2)(b) of ICSID Convention. The practice of investment arbitration illustrates that the provision of protection to shareholders, including minority shareholders, has acquired general recognition.[174] This is so

170 *CMS Gas Transmission Company v. Argentine Republic*, ICSID Case No. ARB/01/8, Decision of the *ad hoc* Committee on the Application for Annulment (September 25, 2007), para. 73.
171 In this regard, national laws may require a minimum shareholding by foreign investors in local entities. For instance, the Chinese Foreign Equity Joint Venture Law provides that the minimum investment that a foreign investor must make in such a venture is 25% of the total registered capital. See Guiguo Wang, *Wang's Business Law of China*, 4th ed., LexisNexis, 2003, ch 8.
172 The *El Paso* Tribunal made a distinction between the action that the company's home country may take and that which the home country of the shareholders may take. It stated: "It has generally been assumed that, as long as the company's home State was in a position to claim on the international level, by way of diplomatic protection, the shareholders' national States could not claim for any infringement of the rights of the company, or could do so only if the shareholders' rights had become immediate rights against the host State as a result of the disappearance of the company itself." See *El Paso Energy International Company v. Argentine Republic*, ICSID Case No. ARB/03/15, Award (October 31, 2011), para. 207.
173 For instance, under Chinese law, foreign investments may only be made in the form of Chinese foreign joint ventures, Chinese foreign contractual ventures and wholly foreign-owned enterprises, and all such entities must be established as Chinese juridical persons. For details, see Wang, *supra*, note 171.
174 The following cases, with the exception of *Goetz* case, in which the claimant held the majority shares of the local company, all held in favor of protecting minority shareholders: *Lanco International, Inc. v. Argentine Republic*, ICSID Case No. ARB/97/6, Preliminary Decision on Jurisdiction (December 8, 1998), para. 10; *Antoine Goetz and Others v. Republic of Burundi*, ICSID Case No. ARB/95/3, Award (February 10, 1999), para. 89; *Emilio Agustin Maffezini v. Kingdom of Spain*, ICSID Case No. ARB/97/7, Decision on Jurisdiction (January 25, 2000), paras. 65–70; *Alex Genin and Others v. Republic of Estonia*, ICSID Case No. ARB/99/2, Award (June 25, 2001),

despite the fact that some tribunals consider the availability of shareholder protection to be *lex specialis*, as was stated by the *CMS ad hoc* Committee.[175]

In theory, it is unquestionable that all shareholders should be treated equally and no-one should be treated differently merely because the person holds a small number of shares or is an indirect shareholder. In practice, however, the matter may not be that simple. In *Enron*, the tribunal considered the claimant's indirect ownership of 35.263 percent of the shares of an Argentinean company to be qualified for protection under the BIT. At the same time, it commented that; "[t]he Tribunal notes that while investors can claim in their own rights under the provisions of the treaty, there is indeed a need to establish a cut-off point beyond which claims would not be permissible as they would only have a remote connection to the affected company."[176] The *Enron* Tribunal's concern was not unfounded, as may be seen by taking into account subsequent developments in this regard.

The *Abaclat* case[177] is illustrative in this respect. The dispute in that case arose from Argentina's announcement of the deferral of over US$100 billion of external bond debt owed to both non-Argentine and Argentine creditors on December 21, 2001 and the restructuring of its sovereign debt. Subsequently, eight major Italian banks—underwriters of the Argentine bonds—established Task Force Argentina ("TFA") under Italian law. With the funding of its member banks, TFA was to "represent the interests of the Italian bondholders in pursuing a negotiated settlement with Argentina."[178] Those bondholders who wished to be represented by TFA were required to sign a mandate with TFA. On January 14, 2005, Argentina launched the Exchange Offer 2005, pursuant to which bondholders could exchange certain bonds, on which Argentina had suspended payment in 2001, for new debt that Argentina would issue. The new bonds would offer either the same principal but a lower interest rate than the non-performing debt, a reduced principal but a higher interest rate, or a principal and interest rate falling between the two other bond options. The claimants in *Abaclat* were Italian bondholders who did not accept the Argentine debt exchange offer.

Having not been successful in its negotiations with Argentina, TFA decided to initiate arbitration proceedings at ICSID in accordance with the Italy–Argentina BIT. To secure the approval of the bondholders, TFA requested them to sign a

para. 324; *Azurix Corp. v. Argentine Republic*, ICSID Case No. ARB/01/12, Decision on Jurisdiction (December 8, 2003); *LG&E Energy Corp., LG&E Capital Corp. and LG&E International, Inc. v. Argentine Republic*, ICSID Case No. ARB/02/1, Decision on Objections to Jurisdiction (April 30, 2004), para. 89; *Enron Corporation and Ponderosa Assets L.P. v. Argentine Republic*, ICSID Case No. ARB/01/3, Decision on Jurisdiction (Ancillary Claim) (August 2, 2004), paras. 28–32; *Siemens A.G. v. Argentine Republic*, ICSID Case No. ARB/02/8, Decision on Jurisdiction, (August 3, 2004), paras. 136–44; and *Pan American LLC and BP America Production Company v. Argentine Republic*, Joined ICSID Case Nos. ARB/03/13, ARB/04/8, Decision on Preliminary Objections (July 27, 2006), paras. 209–22.

175 *CMS v. Argentina*, *supra*, note 117, para. 69.

176 *Enron v. Argentina*, *supra*, note 156, para. 52.

177 *Abaclat and Others v. Argentine Republic*, ICSID Case No. ARB/07/5, Decision on Jurisdiction and Admissibility (August 4, 2011).

178 Ibid., para. 66.

new mandate which advised them, among other things, that if they participated in the mandate they could not at the same time conduct other legal proceedings—meaning that they could not sue the member banks of TFA at the same time. In April 2010, well after the ICSID arbitration proceedings had commenced in 2006, Argentina launched another debt exchange offer in an effort to "restructure and cancel defaulted debt obligations of Argentina represented by Pre-2005 Eligible Securities, to release Argentina from any related claims, including any administrative, litigation or arbitral claims and to terminate legal proceedings against Argentina in respect of the tendered Eligible Securities in consideration for the issuance of New Securities and, in certain cases, a cash payment."[179] A large number of bondholders accepted this debt exchange offer, thereby reducing the number of claimants in *Abaclat* from 180,000 to 60,000.

Neither the ICSID Convention nor the Italy–Argentina BIT contains specific provisions relating to "mass claims." The tribunal first considered the objective requirements for a "qualified" investor of another contracting state under Article 25(2)(b) of the ICSID Convention. It then concluded that a qualified investor may be determined by the contracting parties.[180] In this regard, the Italy–Argentina BIT, like many others, provides only in general terms the definition of an investor as "any individual or corporation of one Contracting Party that has made, makes or undertakes to make investments in the territory of the other Contracting Party." In this case, however, that definition was supplemented by an Additional Protocol, which specified:

> (a) Individuals of each Contracting Party who, when making an investment, maintained their domicile for more than two years in the Contracting Party in the territory of which the investment was made, cannot benefit of this Agreement.
> (b) The domicile of an investor will be determined in compliance with laws, regulations and provisions of the Contracting Party in the territory of which the investment was made.

Hence, in order for the claimants to benefit from the protection of the BIT, they must first of all have Italian nationality. Insofar as a juridical person is concerned, it must be "an entity incorporated in compliance with the legislation of Italy, having its office in the territory of Italy and being recognized thereby."[181] The tribunal pointed out:

> The ICSID Convention does not define the concept of juridical person, and does in particular not expressly require a non-natural investor to have specific legal personality. Thus, although this question is controversial, the Tribunal finds that the ICSID Convention does not provide for a clear "yes or no"

179 Ibid., para. 92.
180 Ibid., para. 281.
181 Ibid., para. 413.

answer and that the specific requirements regarding the legal personality of a non-natural investor therefore eventually depends on the scope *rationae personae* of the relevant BIT and the legal capacity required for a non-natural investor to acquire an investment protected by the BIT under the law applicable to such investor and to sue or be sued in its own name with regard to such investment.[182]

Regarding the test of legal capacity to be qualified under the BIT and the ICSID Convention, the tribunal considered "the statutory right to litigate in their own names, and that their constituents all have the requisite nationality" as the basic requirements.[183]

In the *Abaclat* case, the claimants made collective or mass claims, and neither the Italy–Argentina BIT nor the ICSID Convention addresses this issue. Facing Argentina's challenge of its jurisdiction on this ground, the tribunal considered that the mass claims derived from the nature of the investment made and that "it would be contrary to the purpose of the BIT and to the spirit of ICSID to interpret this silence as a 'qualified silence' categorically prohibiting collective proceedings."[184] It further stated that: "[a]ssuming that the Tribunal has jurisdiction over the claims of several individual Claimants, it is difficult to conceive why and how the Tribunal could loose [sic] such jurisdiction where the number of Claimants outgrows a certain threshold."[185] Yet, at the same time, it agreed that certain adaptations of the rules relating to procedures and proceedings were needed.

What then are the adaptations required in order to conduct a mass claims arbitration? In the *Abaclat* Tribunal's view, it

> … would need to implement mechanisms allowing a simplified verification of evidentiary material, while this simplification can concern either the depth of examination of a document (e.g. accepting a scanned copy of an ID document instead of an original), or the number of evidentiary documents to be examined, and if so their selection process (i.e. random selection of samples instead of a serial examination of each document).[186]

In the end, the question is still how "fairness" to all the parties, both procedurally and substantively, can be ensured. For instance, whilst a random selection of samples may be a practical solution of the case, what measures should be taken so that the accuracy of information is ensured? The issues that the *Abaclat* case raised are unique, but nonetheless ones that the international community must face. They include that of whether a holder of a single share in a private company may start

182 Ibid., para. 417 (footnotes omitted).
183 Id.
184 Ibid., para. 519.
185 Ibid., para. 490.
186 Ibid., para. 531.

international investment arbitration proceedings. The question is whether ICSID and the mechanisms under many BITs in practice entertain such arbitration requests. In such circumstances, the contracting parties' intent relating to the purposes of these mechanisms is no longer relevant. Another issue is that if a group of holders of a single share, as in the *Abaclat* case, is permitted to make a mass claim at ICSID, how can the accuracy of such information as the verification of each claimant be ensured. This issue has important implications: although each individual claimant, as in the *Abaclat* case, may undertake not to make similar claims in national courts, unless each claimant's particulars can be confirmed, it may be difficult to prevent double claims—one through arbitration and the other through national courts.[187] In addition, does it matter if an investor is remotely indirect? In other words, where an entity is the direct investor and there are several layers of companies between the investor and the shareholder, would the investor be qualified to resort to arbitration?

Needless to say, *jus standi* is an important issue in international investment law. With advanced information and communication technology developing and the investment tools diversifying and innovating every day, ordinary individuals are provided with investment opportunities. Many such investors are less sophisticated and hence require more protection, including investor–state arbitration. The question is whether the existing mechanisms are capable of handling disputes like that in the *Abaclat* case. The other question is the procedures for such cases. Currently, no BITs or FTAs or multilateral instruments contain specific provisions. Faced with the issues at hand, however, tribunals have to invent the procedure, which is, to say the least, unsatisfactory. In the long-term interest of international investment, the international community must take measures to deal with these and other issues relating to *jus standi*.

IV. Denial of benefits

"Denial of benefits" is an important provision in some treaty arrangements; it is also closely related to the concept of piercing the corporate veil. In order to prevent free-riders taking advantage of treaty protections, some treaties stipulate explicitly that no protection may be accorded to certain groups of individuals and entities.[188] In this regard, the ECT and the United States–Dominican Republic–Central America Free Trade Agreement ("DR–CAFTA") are examples. They contain provisions permitting their contracting parties not to extend the rights and

---

187　With regard to the rights of portfolio investors to BIT arbitration, concerns have been expressed that unless systemic reforms are implemented, "crucial parts of the system could disintegrate;" see Joseph D'Agostino, "Rescuing International Investment Arbitration: Introducing Derivative Actions, Class Actions, and Compulsory Joinder," *Virginia Law Review*, Vol. 98, 2012, pp. 177–229.

188　For a discussion of the operation of the denial of benefits clause, see Rachel Thorn and Jennifer Doucleff, "Disregarding the Corporate Veil and Denial of Benefits Clauses: Testing Treaty Language and the Concept of 'Investor'," in Michael Waibel et al. (eds.), *The Backlash against Investment Arbitration*, Wolters Kluwer, 2010, Pt I, ch 1.

advantages of those treaties to certain entities. Article 17 of the ECT, for example, stipulates that:

> Each Contracting Party reserves the right to deny the advantages of this Part to:
> (1) a legal entity if citizens or nationals of a third state own or control such entity and if that entity has no substantial business activities in the Area of the Contracting Party in which it is organized.

Article 10.12.2 of the US–DR–CAFTA also permits its contracting parties to "deny the benefits of [Chapter 10 of the DR–CAFTA] to an investor of another Party that is an enterprise of such other Party and to investments of that investor if the enterprise has no substantial business activities in the territory of any Party, other than the denying Party and persons of a non-Party, or of the denying Party, own or control the enterprise."

A common feature of the above provisions is the requirement of "substantial business activities." With regard to the "control" requirement, the ECT's provisions permit a contracting party to deny the Treaty's benefits to nationals of the host state, whilst the US–DR–CAFTA's provisions refer to persons of the "denying Party." In theory, these treaty provisions do not have any effect on non-contracting parties. Nevertheless, as case law and the cross-referencing of arbitral awards deriving from different treaties and tribunals are a distinctive feature of contemporary international investment law, the practices relating to the ECT and US–DR–CAFTA provisions may provide guidance, or at least examples, for determining what constitutes "substantial business activities" and qualified investors in other investment arbitration contexts.

Pac Rim Cayman v. El Salvador[189] was the first US–DR–CAFTA case involving interpretation of provisions on denial of benefits. The claimant in the case was Pac Rim Cayman LLC, a legal person organized under the laws of Nevada, USA but wholly owned by Pacific Rim Mining Corporation, a legal person organized under the laws of Canada. The claimant advanced several claims against the respondent both on its own behalf and on behalf of its subsidiary companies, who were legal persons organized under the laws of the respondent and who were the owners of certain rights in mining areas located in the northern part of El Salvador. The respondent contended that the claimant had no "substantial business activities" in the USA and was owned and controlled by persons of Canada—a non-DR–CAFTA party.[190] It therefore objected to the tribunal's jurisdiction on the grounds, inter alia, of its right to deny benefits to the claimant pursuant to US–DR–CAFTA Article 10.12.2.

The *Pac Rim Cayman* Tribunal stated that in accordance with the object and purpose of US–DR–CAFTA, two conditions must be satisfied in order to invoke the

---

189 *Pac Rim Cayman LLC v. Republic of El Salvador*, ICSID Case No. ARB/09/12, Decision on the Respondent's Jurisdictional Objections (June 1, 2012).
190 Ibid., para. 4.7.

denial of benefit provisions. They are that the claimant has no substantial business activities in the country of its registration and that the claimant is owned or controlled by persons of a non-DR–CAFTA party.[191] The tribunal also took into consideration whether there was a time by which the respondent should have elected to deny benefits and, if so, whether that deadline was met by the respondent in the case.

It was undisputed that the group of companies of which the claimant was a part carried on business activities in the United States. The question was whether the group's business activities would satisfy the requirement of substantial business activities. The tribunal emphasized that "CAFTA Article 10.12.2 relates not to the collective activities of a group of companies, but to activities attributable to the 'enterprise' itself"—the claimant.[192] For this, the tribunal, apparently being convinced by the evidence that the claimant itself had no employees, no office space, no bank account, no board of directors, no tangible property, made nothing, performed no exploration activities, and paid no taxes in the United States,[193] held that the claimant "did not and does not have substantial activities in the USA."[194] This holding is reasonable since, within a group of companies, each member has a separate and independent juridical personality. Yet, if the parent company of the claimant had been incorporated in the United States and had instituted the arbitration, instead of the claimant itself, the outcome would have been different. In such a case, the parent company would be an indirect investor and would be entitled to claim its own rights.

In investment practice, it is often the case that an investor may be a holding company. Should the decision of the *Pac Rim Cayman* Tribunal gain general application, there would be a potential danger that a holding company might be disqualified as an investor on the grounds of not carrying out substantial business activities. The *Pac Rim Cayman* Tribunal, however, did endeavour to address this issue by distinguishing between a general holding company—one that owns all or substantially all of the shares of its subsidiaries—from the situation of the claimant in the present case. In its view, a holding company's commercial purpose was "to own shares in its group of companies, with attendant benefits as to control, taxation and risk-management for the holding company's group of companies."[195] It then went on to say that a holding company usually had "a board of directors, board minutes, a continuous physical presence and a bank account."[196] As the claimant had failed to prove that it had any of these features, the traditional concept of a "holding company" could not help its case.

Another issue in the *Pac Rim Cayman* case was that the claimant was wholly owned and controlled by its parent company—Pacific Rim, a company organized under the laws of Canada, which was not a party to the US–DR–CAFTA. The

191 Ibid., para. 4.61.
192 Ibid., para. 4.66.
193 Ibid., para. 4.68.
194 Ibid., para. 4.78.
195 Ibid., para. 4.72.
196 Id.

claimant contended, however, that a majority of the shares of the Canadian company was held by "both natural and legal persons, [who] reside or at least have postal addresses in the USA."[197] The tribunal considered that as the "requirements for US citizenship or permanent allegiance to the USA cannot be met by adducing mere US postal addresses,"[198] this could not be relied upon as evidence to prove the nationality of shareholders in the Canadian parent company. In the end, the tribunal held that the respondent had satisfied the second condition for denying benefits, that is, that the claimant was "owned or controlled by persons of a non-CAFTA Party."

The timeliness of El Salvador's decision to exercise its right of denial of benefits was also considered by the tribunal. Since no deadline for the exercise of that right is stipulated in the US–DR–CAFTA, the tribunal had no difficulty in finding that the respondent had done so on time. It noted, however, that under different arbitration rules the conclusion might be different. In other words, where the applicable arbitration rules have specific time limitations on the exercise of the right to deny benefits as a challenge to the jurisdiction of an arbitral tribunal over investment disputes, such denial of benefits must be made before the stipulated deadline. In the present case, the tribunal held that because in accordance with ICSID Arbitration Rule 41, any objection to jurisdiction including objecting to jurisdiction by invoking denial of benefits provisions "shall be made as early as possible" and "no later than the expiration of the time limit fixed for the filing of the counter-memorial," the respondent was found to have raised the issue in time.[199] This decision is significant because most BITs and other treaties do not stipulate a precise deadline for the respondent state to raise objections to jurisdiction.

Plama v. Bulgaria[200] was another case concerning denial of benefits, but in this case the issue arose from provisions of the ECT. There were two issues, that is, the scope of application of ECT Article 17 (a jurisdictional issue) and the time of application. The claimant argued that the respondent's reliance on Article 17(1) to deny it the advantages under Part III of the ECT was a disguised objection to jurisdiction and in essence a defense on the merits.[201] Were the claimant's reasoning followed, the consequence would be that the respondent's consent to arbitration should not be affected by the denial of benefits. In its response, the respondent contended that "Article 17 is not a reservation. Rather Article 17 contains substantive provisions of the treaty which qualify, limit or narrow the scope of the Contracting Parties' Part III obligations."[202] In addition, the respondent contended that it was not necessary for it to give advance notice of its exercise of

---

197 Ibid., para. 4.80.
198 Ibid., para. 4.81.
199 Ibid., para. 4.92.
200 *Plama Consortium Limited v. Republic of Bulgaria*, ICSID Case No. ARB/03/24 [ECT], Decision on Jurisdiction (February 8, 2005).
201 Ibid., para. 41.
202 Ibid., para. 64; the condition, as admitted by the respondent, was satisfaction of all the requirements of the ECT.

the right under Article 17 as it was self-implementing.[203] Therefore, an investor should not have any reasonable expectation that the host state would be bound by obligations under Part III of the ECT once the conditions for denial of benefits are met. The claimant, however, argued that it was entitled to ECT Part III benefits until and unless they were validly denied.[204]

The tribunal considered that under ECT Article 17, a contracting state could only deny the advantages under Part III on condition that the entity in question was owned or controlled by persons from a third country which was not a party to the ECT and that it had no substantial business activities in the country in which it is organized—the so called two-limb analysis.[205] As Article 26 on dispute resolutions belongs to Part V of the ECT, the denial does not extend to the issue of jurisdiction.[206] In the tribunal's view, Article 17—which is entitled "Non-Application of Part III in Certain Circumstances"—refers to "the substantive advantages conferred upon an investor by Part III of the ECT,"[207] whilst Article 26 provides "a procedural remedy for a covered investor's claims; and it is not physically or juridically part of the ECT's substantive advantages enjoyed by that investor under Part III."[208] The tribunal therefore considered the language to be unambiguous. The purpose of ECT Article 26 is, as a remedy, to resolve "wide-ranging, complex and highly controversial disputes" such as "citizenship, nationality, ownership, control and the scope and location of business activities."[209]

With regard to the implementation of ECT Article 17, after having considered the views of both parties, the tribunal pointed out that "the existence of a 'right' is distinct from the exercise of that right."[210] It considered that the language of the Article was not only unambiguous but also "consistent with the different state practices of the ECT's Contracting States under different bilateral investment treaties: certain of them applying a generous approach to legal entities incorporated in a state with no significant business presence there (such as the Netherlands) and certain others applying a more restrictive approach (such as the USA)."[211] As a multilateral treaty, the ECT Article 17 was to accommodate such different state practices by means of its permissive terms.

As state practices differ, in the tribunal's view, before advantages are denied, an investor must be informed of a state's decision to do so. For this conclusion, the tribunal sought support from NAFTA Article 1113(2), which also provides for a denial of benefits and requires a form of prior notification and consultation. It stated that, although the wording of the two documents was "materially different," NAFTA Article 1113(2) would support the tribunal's interpretation

203   Ibid., para. 84.
204   Ibid., para. 91.
205   Ibid., para. 143.
206   Ibid., para. 147.
207   Id.
208   Ibid., para. 148.
209   Ibid., para. 149.
210   Ibid., para. 155.
211   Id.

as "not unreasonable as a practical matter."[212] This interpretation is again very much pro-investor. If the NAFTA and ECT provisions are different, they should certainly be interpreted differently according to Article 31 of the VCLT. The tribunal held that, in order to implement the provision on denial of benefits, the contracting party concerned must make a prior announcement of its intention to do so.[213] However, if such notice can be made in a general announcement in order to satisfy the requirements, as the *Plama* Tribunal asserted, foreign investors may not be informed in practice. Most importantly, what the tribunal has done is to add a procedural requirement—prior notice—to ECT Article 17.

The *Plama* Tribunal also discussed whether any denial of benefits under ECT Article 17 should be considered to have a retrospective or prospective effect. It ruled that both Sections 1 and 2 of that Article suggested a prospective effect. For this, in addition to the text of the Article,[214] it placed emphasis on the Treaty's object and purpose as stipulated in Article 2 to be "the establishment of '… *a legal framework in order to promote long-term co-operation in the energy field … in accordance with the objectives and principles of the Charter*'."[215] In its view, for the purpose of establishing a long-term cooperation, putative foreign investors should be informed in advance whether or not they are entitled to certain advantages.

The *Plama* Tribunal was also faced with the question of determining whether the claimant had "substantial business activities" in the country of its registration. The claimant admitted that it had no substantial business activities in the place of its incorporation—Cyprus. Yet it argued that its parent company had substantial business activities there. Like the *Pac Rim Cayman* Tribunal, the *Plama* Tribunal ruled that: "this shortfall [lack of substantial business activities] cannot be made good with business activities undertaken by an associated but different legal entity, Plama Holding Limited ('PHL'), even where PHL owns or controls the Claimant."[216] In the end, the tribunal decided that it had jurisdiction in the case, whilst leaving the matter as to whether or not the respondent had the right to deny the claimant advantages under Part III to be decided at the merits stage.[217]

It should be noted that the *Plama* Tribunal's conclusion on jurisdiction was different from that of the *Pac Rim Cayman* Tribunal.[218] This was so largely because of

212 Ibid., para. 157.
213 The tribunal elaborated that: "[t]he exercise would necessarily be associated with publicity or other notice so as to become reasonably available to investors and their advisers. To this end, a general declaration in a Contracting State's official gazette could suffice; or a statutory provision in a Contracting State's investment or other laws; or even an exchange of letters with a particular investor or class of investors." Id.
214 Ibid., para. 159.
215 Ibid., para. 161 (emphasis in original).
216 Ibid., para. 169.
217 In respect of the burden of proof, the tribunal said that "the burden of proof on the merits is significantly different from the burden applied to a jurisdictional issue;" ibid., para. 167.
218 Sinclair considered that the *Plama* decision had practical consequences that "Article 17 can offer a good defence for Host States to claims brought by mailbox companies, but a State must exercise its right prior to the time when an investment is made;" see A. C. Sinclair, "Investment

the difference in a single word: "Part" in Article 17(1) of the ECT and "Chapter" in Article 10.12 of the DR–CAFTA. The two treaties have an analogous structure. The differences are as follows: in the ECT, provisions on dispute resolution and denial of benefits appear in different "Parts" of the Charter, whilst the provisions on denial of benefits refer to "Part III;" in the DR-CAFTA, the provisions on dispute resolution and denial of benefits appear in the same Chapter 10, though in different "Sections" of the "Chapter" and the provisions on denial of benefits refer to Chapter 10. One may consider that it is unfortunate that such a "small" difference in text has made such a big difference in effect. Yet treaty provisions must be interpreted faithfully. Of course, one may assume that, had Article 17(1) of the ECT read "Treaty" instead of "Part," the *Plama* Tribunal might have ruled similarly to the *Pac Rim Cayman* Tribunal on this matter; or had Article 10.12 read "Section" instead of "Chapter," the *Pac Rim Cayman* Tribunal might have ruled as the *Plama* Tribunal did.

AMTO v. Ukraine was another case involving interpretation of ECT Article 17. In that case, in addition to challenging the control and ownership of the claimant, the respondent contended that because Article 26 of the Treaty only deals with breaches of obligations, its application should be excluded from interpretation of Article 17, which provides for the rights of contracting parties. In its view, the tribunal had no jurisdiction because of a lack of *ratione materiae*.[219] In reaching its conclusion that the respondent could not in the circumstances exercise its right under Article 17 to deny the claimant the advantages of Part III of the ECT,[220] the tribunal reasoned that the respondent's argument that Article 17 was not subject to arbitration because it only dealt with "rights," not "obligations," had "a terminological basis."[221] It went on, however, to observe:

> A dispute regarding an obligation includes a dispute relating to the existence of an obligation, Indeed, this is the essence of the *competence/competence* principle in international arbitration. The State might assert "rights," "powers," "privileges" or "immunities" to deny, annul or evade an obligation, but the legal description of the objection does not detach it from the Claimant's assertion of the existence and breach of an obligation.[222]

Protection for 'Mailbox Companies' under the 1994 Energy Charter Treaty," *Transnational Dispute Management*, Vol. 2, Issue 5, November 2005, pp. 1–6, at 6. For discussion of the denial of benefits clause of the ECT, also see Loukas A. Mistelis and Crina Mihaela Baltag, "Denial of Benefits and Article 17 of the Energy Charter Treaty," *Penn. State Law Review*, Spring 2009, Vol. 113, p. 1301; and Elvira R. Gadelshina, "Burden of Proof Under the 'Denial-of-Benefits' Clause of the Energy Charter Treaty: *Actori Incumbit Onus Probandi?*" *Journal of International Arbitration*, Vol. 29, No. 3, 2012, pp. 269–84.

219 *LLC AMTO v. Ukraine*, Arbitration Institute of the Stockholm Chamber of Commerce, Arbitration No. 080/2005, Final Award (March 26, 2008), §26(h). The respondent also criticized the decision of the *Plama* Tribunal on prospective application of Article 17 of the ECT.

220 Ibid., §70.

221 Ibid., §60.

222 Id.

In other words, whilst ECT Article 17 addresses the rights of contracting parties, the exercise of such rights must be in compliance with their obligations. In fact, in every system governed by the rule of law, an exercise of right must be subject to certain conditions. ECT Article 17 therefore cannot be beyond the reach of arbitration under ECT Article 26.

In its analysis, the *AMTO* Tribunal adopted the two-limb approach introduced by the *Plama* Tribunal.[223] With regard to the question as to whether or not the claimant had satisfied the substantial business activities requirement, the claimant proved that it had paid residents' income tax, internal VAT and entrepreneurial activity risk state fees and had made obligatory social insurance payments in Latvia and that it had employed two full-time employees. Based on these facts, the tribunal considered the claimant had substantial business activities there.[224] Its reasoning on this issue was that the word "substantial" under the ECT meant "of substance, and not merely of form. It does not mean 'large', and the materiality not the magnitude of the business activity is the decisive question."[225] Considering that neither the ECT nor the Final Act of the European Energy Charter Conference defines the word "substantial," the *AMTO* Tribunal's ruling is helpful in formulating consistent interpretations of Article 17. As other treaties—including the DR–CAFTA and some of the BITs that China has entered into, which will be discussed later—contain similar provisions, arbitral decisions such as *AMTO* may have a spill-over effect on the interpretation of those treaties as well.

The *Petrobart v. Kyrgyz* case[226] also involved the issue of denial of benefits, but there the tribunal did a poor job in its examination of the relevant issues. In that case, the claimant—Petrobart—was a company registered in Gibraltar, but its relationship to Gibraltar was never anything other than its incorporation there.[227] The claimant's incorporation number even indicated that it was organized as a Gibraltar non-resident company, that is, a legal entity incorporated in Gibraltar but owned, managed, and controlled by non-residents. Such an entity is not subject to Gibraltar's local corporate tax, except for profits remitted to Gibraltar, so long as it conducts no business operations in Gibraltar.[228]

The claimant's argument was that it was managed by Pemed Ltd., a company registered in the United Kingdom with its principal office in London and which handled many of Petrobart's strategic and administrative matters.[229] The respondent maintained that the United Kingdom had not ratified the ECT on Gibraltar's behalf and that, therefore, Gibraltar was not a contracting state to the ECT.[230]

---

223 See ibid., §62.
224 Ibid., §§68–69.
225 Ibid., §69.
226 *Petrobart v. Kyrgyz Republic, supra,* note 74.
227 Ibid., §VII.2.C(a), first three paragraphs.
228 Id.
229 Ibid., §VII.3.B, 4th–7th paragraphs.
230 Ibid., §VII.2.C(a), last two paragraphs.

As regards the two individual employees singled out by the Kyrgyz Republic, the claimant maintained that Mr Josif Todorovski was a national of both the United Kingdom and Macedonia and Mr Ratko Zatazelo was a Serbian national who also held permanent residency in France.[231] Moreover, according to the claimant, the respondent misrepresented the scope of Article 17 of the Treaty and read into it more than it can bear.[232]

In its award, the tribunal stated that it attached "weight to the information about Petrobart provided by Petrobart itself which, in the arbitral tribunal's view, contradicts the view that Petrobart is a company owned or controlled by citizens or nationals of a state other than the United Kingdom and that Petrobart has no substantial business in the United Kingdom."[233] Obviously, the tribunal considered the claimant's parent company's business activities in London as if they were those of Petrobart. This decision is contrary to the positions taken by both the *Pac Rim Cayman* and *Plama* Tribunals. Its departure from other arbitral decisions, however, was not well reasoned. Throughout its discussions, the tribunal accepted that Petrobart was a corporation organized in Gibraltar and was consequently at some pains to examine if the ECT applied to Gibraltar. Another problem is that the arbitral tribunal seems to have simply taken Petrobart's word for these facts, without any supporting evidence, while not accepting the testimony of the Kyrgyz Republic and, in fact, rejecting the respondent's seemingly reasonable request that the tribunal ask for documents that might have clarified Petrobart's ownership.[234] It is indeed very unfortunate that the tribunal committed such serious mistakes. One can only hope that such problems will not occur frequently in international investment arbitration.

The *Generation Ukraine*[235] case involved, inter alia, interpretation of Article I(2) of the Ukraine–United States BIT, which provides:

> Each Party reserves the right to deny to any company the advantages of this Treaty if nationals of any third country control such company and, in the case of a company of the other Party, that company has no substantial business activities in the territory of the other Party or is controlled by nationals of a third country with which the denying Party does not maintain normal economic relations.

The claimant, a US company, had made an investment in an office building construction project. The respondent challenged the jurisdiction of the tribunal on the basis of Article I(2) of the BIT. The tribunal first stated that the respondent had the responsibility "to establish the factual basis of the 'third country control', together

231 Ibid., §VII.3.B, 5th paragraph.
232 Id.
233 Ibid., §VIII.3, final paragraph.
234 See ibid., §V, 4th and 5th paragraphs from the end.
235 *Generation Ukraine, Inc. v. Ukraine*, ICSID Case No. ARB/00/9, Arbitral Award (September 16, 2003).

with the other conditions."[236] This was not a surprising requirement because in international arbitration practice it is always the case that the claimant bears the burden of proof. The tribunal then went on to state that "the Respondent is still a long way from displacing the clear manifestation of control by a U.S. national (Mr Laka), who owns 100 percent of the share capital of the Claimant, Generation Ukraine."[237] In the end, the tribunal dismissed the respondent's objection to jurisdiction based on the existence of grounds for a denial of benefits under the BIT. It should be pointed out that the *Generation Ukraine* Tribunal explicitly treated the respondent's jurisdictional objection as an "admissibility objection." This decision is therefore distinguishable from the position taken by the *Pac Rim Cayman* Tribunal, although it is in line with the *Plama* decision.

Indeed, an important issue concerning denial of benefits is whether it is a matter of jurisdiction or admissibility. The difference between the two is that if it is a jurisdictional issue, upon establishing that the respondent is entitled to deny the claimant benefits the tribunal in charge must give up jurisdiction; but if it is an admissibility issue, the tribunal should go ahead with the arbitration proceedings and leave the proof by the respondent of its entitlement to deny benefits to the merits stage. It is very unfortunate that, as in the interpretation of other treaty provisions, the arbitral practice is not consistent in applying the denial of benefit provisions. As not all BITs contain provisions on denial of benefits, the inconsistency of arbitration tribunals in interpreting this clause has not caused as much outcry as have some interpretations of the MFN clause.[238] Yet this should not be a ground for forgiving the inconsistent construction of the clause. Investment arbitration practitioners and scholars of international investment law should encourage and, in fact, ensure that arbitral tribunals will seriously take into account the intent of the parties when interpreting the denial of benefits clause. Arbitral tribunals should feel that they have an obligation to state the reasons for their decisions, notwithstanding that some arbitration rules, unlike those of the ICSID, do not require reasoned decisions. A tribunal's presentation of reasoned decisions, in particular in cases of contradictory decisions made by previous tribunals, should be considered an essential principle of the rule of law. Otherwise, the impact of contradictory interpretations of this or any treaty provision is bound to become more serious.

V. China's practice relating to investors

China's treaty practice on the definition of investors has also been through an evolution. In this regard, the China–Norway BIT, which was among the first of such

---

236 Ibid., para. 15.7.
237 Ibid., para. 15.9. Apparently, the tribunal was not impressed by the disputing parties' performance, as neither of them advanced much helpful analysis but "simply asserted competing semantic points without investigating the ramifications of either approach as a matter of law or policy;" ibid., para. 15.3.
238 For discussions on the inconsistency among international arbitral tribunals in interpreting the MFN clause, see Chapter 7 of this book.

treaties that China entered into, is illustrative. According to the BIT, investors are nationals of the other party. It further defines "Nationals" as natural persons with the nationality of China or Norway and "Companies" as the legal persons of either party.[239] At the time of ratifying the China–Norway BIT, China did not have a company law.[240] The concept of "companies" was unclear. To accommodate both parties, the BIT provides that in the case of China, companies are "economic bodies incorporated and domiciled" in China. In respect of Norway, companies are "judicial persons and sole proprietors domiciled in the territory of Norway, or companies and associations, regardless of whether or not the liabilities of its partners, members or constituents are limited, and regardless of whether their activities are profit-oriented."[241] Protection is accorded by one contracting party to nationals and companies of the other.[242]

The 1986 China–UK BIT[243] was also one of the earlier BITs for China, Article 1 of which provides that "Nationals" means physical persons who have Chinese nationality and physical persons who derive their status as UK nationals under the laws in force and who have the right of abode in the United Kingdom or any territory for whose foreign relations the UK Government is responsible. As for legal persons protected by the treaty, the definitions given in the China–UK BIT and that in the traditional US Friendship, Commerce, and Navigation Treaties are the same, using the incorporated or registered place to determine the nationality of an enterprise. The 2004 US Model BIT provides that an "enterprise of a Party" must not only be constituted or organized under the laws of one of the contracting parties but must also carry out business activities there.[244] It also provides that any contracting party has the right to refuse to protect the investment of an enterprise registered in the other contracting party if it is controlled by nationals of a third country or of the host country.[245] The purpose of this provision is to authorize the contracting parties to deny the protection of the treaty if an enterprise is

239 1984 China–Norway BIT, Articles 3 and 4.
240 Before the promulgation of the Company Law in 1993, different Chinese laws governing enterprises were adopted based on their ownership. Whilst the Chinese Foreign Joint Venture Law was adopted in 1979, the Law of the People's Republic of China on Industrial Enterprises Owned by the Whole People was promulgated in 1988.
241 1984 China–Norway BIT, Article 4(2).
242 In theory, national treatment was mutually applicable to both Chinese and Norwegian investors. As at that time no Chinese entities made investments in Norway, the benefit of this provision was one-sided. Since 1983, Norwegian companies have been investing in China. The main sectors of their investments are post and telecommunications, electronics, machinery, transportation, light industry, agriculture, and environmental protection. Most of the investment projects are located in Eastern coastal cities; see http://www.bergen-chamber.no/publish_files/Wikborg_Rein_China_Summit.pdf.
243 For the Agreement Between the Government of the People's Republic of China and the Government of the United Kingdom of Great Britain and Northern Ireland Concerning the Promotion and Reciprocal Protection of Investments (including the Exchange Notes), see *Chinese Economic News*, Supplementary Issue No. 4 (July 14, 1986); also available at: http://www.unctad.org/sections/dite/iia/docs/bits/uk_china.pdf.
244 See 2004 US Model BIT, Article 1, *supra*, note 3.
245 Ibid., Article 17.

controlled by nationals of a third country or lacks important connections with the other contracting party.

Some of the older generation BITs concluded by China also include a "control" standard, which further expands their coverage. For example, Article 1(4) of the 1985 China–Kuwait BIT stipulates that:

> If natural or juridical persons of a Contracting State have an interest in a juridical person which was established within the territory of a third State, and this juridical person invests in the other Contracting State, it shall be recognized as a juridical person of the former Contracting State. This Paragraph of this Article can be applied only when the said third State has no right or abandons its right to protect the said juridical person.

The definition of investor has been expanded in the new generation of China–foreign BITs. Two approaches have been adopted: one is to define investors of individual countries in specific terms; the other is to stipulate a general definition of investor. Most BITs signed by China in recent years, except for a few BITs such as the 2003 China–Germany BIT and the 2005 China–Portugal BIT, take the second approach. With regard to natural persons as investors, in order to avoid nationality conflicts, the 2003 China–Germany BIT specifically provides that the nationality of a natural person shall be determined by his/her domestic law, and neither Chinese nor German laws recognize dual nationality.

For other investors, the 2003 China–Germany BIT applies to all types of "economic entities" established in China, irrespective of whether or not for profit and whether its liabilities are limited or not, but only if they have their seats in China. In other words, the nationality of Chinese juridical person investors is determined by the dual standard of registered place and seat, while qualified juridical person German investors merely need to have their seats in Germany. However, to use "seat" to determine the nationality of a juridical person is likely to cause disputes, as the word "seat" may refer to the place where the management center is located or where the operating center is located. Where a company is established in China but has its management center in China and its operating center in Germany, should it be treated as a Chinese national or as a German national? It is a Chinese company according to Chinese domestic law.[246] Yet, under the provisions of

---

246 Article 2 of the Company Law of the People's Republic of China reads that "the term 'company' as mentioned in this Law refers to a limited liability company or a joint stock limited company set up within the territory of the People's Republic of China according to the provisions of this Law." Article 10 provides that "a company shall regard its main office as its domicile." According to Article 39 of the General Principles of Civil Law of the People's Republic of China, "a legal person's domicile shall be the place where its main administrative office is located." Article 184 of the Opinions of the Supreme People's Court on Several Issues concerning the Implementation of the General Principles of the Civil Law of the People's Republic of China (For Trial Implementation) provides that "for a foreign legal person, the law of its registration country shall be deemed as its domestic law, and the capacity for civil conduct of a legal person shall be determined according to its domestic law."

the 2003 China–Germany BIT, it may qualify as both a Chinese investor and a German investor. In comparison, the related provision in the 2004 China–Finland BIT[247] is more precise, using the dual standard of place of registration and seat to determine qualified investors of both contracting parties.[248]

According to the China–New Zealand FTA, which contains a chapter on investment, juridical person investors include those "constituted or organized under the law of a Party, and a subsidiary located in the territory of a Party and engaged in substantive business operations there."[249] A plain reading of the above provision would mean that where an entity from one party sets up an enterprise (subsidiary) in the territory of the other party, the subsidiary may not be entitled to the treaty protection unless it engages in substantive business activities. In this respect, the provision is quite in line with the 2004 United States Model BIT and the Ukraine–United States BIT discussed earlier. Where the position is clear for entities that set up subsidiaries in the territory of the other party, there is no similar requirement in relation to natural persons from one party who have constituted or organized entities in the other party. This situation is dealt with in Article 149 (Denial of Benefits), sub-section (b) of which permits a contracting party to deny the benefits to "[i]nvestors of the other Party where the investment is being made by an enterprise that is owned or controlled by persons of the denying Party and the enterprise has no substantive business operations in the territory of the other Party." The word "persons" clearly covers both legal and natural persons.[250] The essence of these provisions is to prevent situations such as that seen in the *Tokios Tokelés* case,[251] where it was held that the control test did not apply to the determination of the nationality of foreign investors.

China's situation concerning investors is in fact more complicated than that which is confined to treaty practices. Chinese laws regard investors from Hong Kong, Macau, and Taiwan as foreign investors who are entitled to preferential treatment, even though under Chinese law these three areas are part of the country. As was discussed in relation to the FTA with New Zealand, the Chinese

247 The China–Finland BIT was signed on November 15, 2004.
248 Under Article 1(2) of the 2004 China–Finland BIT, the term "investor" means, (a) any natural person who is a national of either contracting party in accordance with the laws of that contracting party; (b) any legal entity, including a company, corporation, firm, association, partnership or other organization, incorporated or constituted under the laws and regulations of either contracting party and having its registered office in that contracting party, irrespective of whether or not for profit and whether its liabilities are limited or not.
249 China–New Zealand FTA, Article 135. Natural person investors include those having a permanent residence status in one of the parties. As China does not yet have any law or regulation giving permanent residence status to foreigners, the FTA prescribes that upon China adopting such laws, these provisions will apply. In the China–Pakistan FTA, according to its Article 46(3), "investors" include "(a) natural persons who have the nationality of either Party in accordance with the laws of that Party; (b) legal entities, including companies, associations, partnerships and other organizations, incorporated or constituted under the laws and regulations of either Party and have their seats in that Party."
250 As the "denial of benefit" applies to the matters covered in the entire chapter on investment, all issues including dispute resolution, foreign investors, and investments are likely to be affected.
251 For discussion on *Tokios Tokelés v. Ukraine*, see Section II of this chapter.

Government is concerned about its nationals setting up entities in a foreign country—a party to a BIT or FTA. Yet, there are many companies from the mainland of China that have invested in Hong Kong and Macau. They use such Hong Kong and Macau entities to invest back in the mainland, where they are regarded as foreign investors. There is therefore a clear conflict in the Chinese policy. To encourage mutual investment, mainland China and Taiwan signed an investment pact in 2012, which may also have an impact on who should be treated as foreign investors. It defines "investor" as:

> … a natural person or enterprise of a Party that makes an investment in the other party:
> (1) "natural person of a Party" means a natural person holding the identification document of that Party;
> (2) "enterprise of a Party" means an entity constituted in a Party under the laws and regulations of that Party, including a company, trust, sole proprietorship, partnership, or other organization;
> (3) any entity which is constituted under the laws and regulations of a third party but which is owned or controlled by an Investor as described in subparagraph (1) or (2) of this paragraph is considered an enterprise of a Party.

VI. Conclusions

In the contemporary globalized world, it is common practice for investors to organize their investments in such a way that they can maximize their potential benefits. One way of doing so is to establish a company in a foreign country, in particular in a country that provides better protection both in terms of domestic law and treaties. With the current information and communication technology which has tremendously reduced the cost of and increased the capability for cross-border transfers of funds, treaty shopping is no longer surprising in investment circles. As Schreuer commented:

> It is neither illegal nor improper for an investor of one nationality to establish a new entity in a jurisdiction perceived to provide a beneficial regulatory and legal environment, including the availability of an investment treaty. The establishment of companies so as to obtain benefits from domestic law and treaties is neither unethical nor illegal and is standard practice in international economic relations. Nationality planning has become as much a standard feature of diligent management as tax planning.[252]

There is, of course, nothing wrong in a prudent investor planning so as to maximize the benefits of BITs and other instruments. Yet there are here, as in everything else, limits to doing so. The *Banro v. DR Congo* case[253] offers a cogent example.

252 Schreuer, *supra*, note 8.
253 *Banro American Resources, Inc. and Société Aurifère du Kivu et du Maniema S.A.R.L. v. DR Congo*, ICSID Case No. ARB/98/7, Award (September 1, 2000).

In that case, the claimant was a Canadian company which entered into an investment contract with DR Congo, according to which ICSID arbitration was available in case of disputes. When a dispute occurred, in this and, indeed, in many other cases, it was realized that Canada was not a contracting party to the ICSID Convention and thus the dispute could not be resolved by ICSID. Apparently, in order to cure the defect of jurisdiction, the claimant transferred its investment to its US subsidiary. As the United States was a contracting party to the ICSID Convention, the US subsidiary would be considered a national of another contracting state. Faced with the respondent's challenge of its jurisdiction, the tribunal applied the principle *nemo plus iuris transferre potest quam ipse habet* and held that it had no jurisdiction over the case. This case is comparable to *Phoenix v. Czech Republic,*[254] in which the claimant employed a similar device but where the tribunal denied jurisdiction on the grounds of the absence of a qualified investment. In both cases, what the claimants had done was perceived as an abuse of the arbitration system. To deny them the benefit of international protection is reasonable. In fact, it would be absurd to hold otherwise.

The situation would be different where the host state is aware of an investor's lack of qualification. In accordance with the principle of estoppel, the host state should not be permitted to claim later on that the investor was not qualified. In this regard, *Autopista v. Venezuela*[255] is relevant. The host state in the case was aware that the holding company of the local subsidiary was not from an ICSID contracting party and that a subsequent transfer of the majority shares in the local subsidiary was made to a holding company incorporated in a contracting party. Based on those facts, the tribunal held that where the respondent was aware of the situation and had given its consent to it, it could not challenge the tribunal's jurisdiction.[256]

Needless to say, issues and difficulties in respect of determination of investors are not confined to those discussed above. To say the least, the issue is further complicated by the relatively simplified procedures for establishing juridical persons and the fact of minority shareholders making investments abroad. As was pointed out by Legum: "The reality that foreign capital is highly fungible and the breadth of the definitions of investor and investment thus combine effectively to transform the facially bilateral obligations of the BIT into an obligation that the host state must consider potentially applicable to all investors."[257] In practice, nowadays host states, for the purpose of attracting foreign investments, are likely to assume more obligations than ever before, and tribunals and other bodies in charge of resolving investor–state disputes should also ensure fair treatment of host states.

Treaty provisions cannot, however, keep up with the development of diversifying investment practice. As a result, many unresolved issues are left to arbitration tribunals to deal with. As in other areas of investment law, the performance of

---

254 *Phoenix Action Ltd. v. Czech Republic,* ICSID Case No. ARB/06/5, Award (April 15, 2009).
255 *Autopista Concesionada de Venezuela, C.A. v. Bolivarian Republic of Venezuela,* ICSID Case No. ARB/00/5, Decision on Jurisdiction (September 27, 2001).
256 Ibid., paras. 117–22.
257 Barton Legum, "Defining Investment and Investor: Who is Entitled to Claim?" *Arbitration International,* Vol. 22, No. 4, p. 525.

arbitration tribunals is not satisfactory because, inter alia, there are too many contradictory decisions. Some such decisions apparently resulted from tribunals interpreting relevant provisions either in favor of investors or in order to acquire jurisdiction. For instance, regarding piercing the corporate veil, the trend seems to be that tribunals are prepared to do so to the extent that their jurisdiction can be confirmed. Another technique often used to achieve the same goal is reliance on the purposes and objectives of the provisions without evidentiary support. There is obviously no easy solution to the problem. Yet the investment community is bound to react to the situation. The provisions of the China–New Zealand FTA are clearly more precise and clearer than those found in many BITs. Thus, we will continue to experience and may even expect both inconsistent and contradictory arbitral decisions and, at the same time, better drafted and more definite treaty provisions relating to determination of investors. If those involved in interpreting treaties are prepared to apply faithfully and impartially the provisions of the VCLT, the international community would have more confidence in investment arbitration.

4 Determination of foreign investments

Determination of investment is an important element of international investment law because only qualified investments are protected thereunder. Traditionally, definitions of investments have taken either an asset-based or an enterprise-based approach. Briefly, an asset-based definition emphasizes foreign investors' property interests and rights, whilst an enterprise-based definition focuses on foreign investors' participation in and control of the entities established in the host state.[1] What is common in contemporary bilateral investment treaties ("BITs") and free trade agreements ("FTAs") is the combination of asset-based and enterprise-based definitions in which what may constitute an investment is stipulated in an illustrative list. However, no BIT or FTA contains an exhaustive list of qualified investments. As a result, whether a particular transaction is qualified as a protected investment is subject to interpretation.

This situation is further complicated by the provisions of such multilateral treaties as the ICSID Convention, especially when disputing parties resort to the Convention's arbitration mechanisms. Article 25 of the ICSID Convention provides that the ICSID's jurisdiction "shall extend to any legal dispute arising directly out of an investment" but does not further define what an investment is.[2]

---

1 There are advantages to each definition. For discussion of the definition of asset-based and enterprise-based investment, see UNCTAD, "Scope and Definition," *UNCTAD Series on Issues in International Investment II*, 2011, pp. 21–27. According to UNCTAD, "An enterprise-based approach is useful where the agreement covers pre-entry treatment as well as post-entry treatment, as the act of entry and establishment has to take place through a specific entity rather than through the mere transfer of assets such as goods and/or services. … [T]reaties with an enterprise-based approach often expressly enable a foreign investor to bring claims not only on its own behalf but also on behalf of its enterprise." Ibid., p. 22.

2 As will be discussed later, the negotiating history of the ICSID Convention reflects that the contracting Parties intentionally chose not to define the term "investment." However, there is no consensus among scholars and tribunals as to the reasons for this. Some have held that it is because the contracting Parties failed to reach agreement on this issue, while others maintain that it was deemed unnecessary to define the term. The classic formulation of the former opinion is that expressed in Christoph H. Schreuer, *The ICSID Convention: A Commentary*, Cambridge University Press, Cambridge, UK, 2001, at 121–25, especially at 124. As an example of the latter approach, see Julian Davis Mortenson, "The Meaning of 'Investment': ICSID's *Travaux* and the Domain of International Investment Law," 51 *Harv. Int'l L. J.* 257, 2010.

The ICISID Model Clauses in this regard note that "[t]he fact that the parties consent to submit a dispute to the Centre of course implies that they consider it to arise out of an investment. If the parties wish to strengthen the presumption, they may include an explicit statement to this effect in the consent agreement."[3] Some experts explicitly support this approach.[4] Gaillard, in a similar vein, has expressed the opinion that in cases arising pursuant to investment protection agreements, "except for the claimant's satisfaction of the investment requisite as defined by the treaty on which the claim is based, the concept of investment within the meaning of the ICSID Convention should not give rise to particular difficulty."[5]

However, the ICSID Model Clauses also point out that parties do not have "unlimited" discretion to define a transaction as an "investment." Thus, in practice, some tribunals have considered that for a dispute to be arbitrated at the ICSID, the related transaction must satisfy the requirements of investment under both the applicable BIT and the ICSID Convention. Some have even tried to work out what elements an investment should have in order to be protected. In any event, as determination of a qualified investment is essential for ascertaining the host state's obligations, very often respondents challenge the jurisdiction of tribunals on the ground that the transaction in question is not a qualified investment.

This chapter will examine the treaty practice of states and the arbitration practice of tribunals in respect of determination of investment. The first part will explore legal scholarship and the practice of tribunals (especially ICSID tribunals) in attempting to establish a definition of investment. The second part will examine the special role played by the terminology of the ICSID Convention in determining investment that can be submitted to ICSID arbitration. The third part will discuss the particular provisions of bilateral and multilateral agreements as well as the laws of the host state in qualifying investment for treaty protection, including the impact of investment made in violation of national laws on treaty protection. The fourth part will examine the advantages and disadvantages of arbitral practice treating commercial arbitration awards as investment. The last part discusses Chinese treaty practice relating to and its impact on the definition of qualified investment.

---

3 See ICSID Model Clauses, II.A, "Stipulation that Transaction Constitutes an Investment;" available at: https://icsid.worldbank.org/ICSID/StaticFiles/model-clauses-en/8.htm#a.
4 See, for example, Georges R. Delaume, "ICSID Arbitration and the Courts," *American Journal of International Law*, Vol. 77, 1983, pp. 795–96; and Christoph Schreuer, "Commentary on the ICSID Convention," *ICSID Review Foreign Investment Law Journal*, Vol. 11, 1996, pp. 318–492, at 373, para. 124.
5 Emmanuel Gaillard, "Identify or Define? Reflections on the Evolution of the Concept of Investment in ICISD Practice," ch 22 in Christina Binder et al. (eds.), *International Investment Law for the 21st Century: Essays in Honour of Christoph Schreuer*, Oxford University Press, Oxford UK, 2009, pp. 403–16.

I. Searching for a definition of investment

For any investment to benefit from international protection, it must fall into the definition of investment contained in a relevant treaty—in the contemporary world, a BIT or an FTA. A distinctive feature of modern BITs and FTAs is that they all contain a broad definition of investment, such as "every kind of asset" and "every kind of economic interest." For instance, the 2003 Azerbaijan–Finland BIT in its Article 1 on definition of investment stipulates that: "The term 'Investment' means every kind of asset established or acquired by an investor of one Contracting Party in the territory of the other Contracting Party in accordance with the laws and regulations of the latter Contracting Party …" It then provides an illustrative list of investments, including movable and immovable property, shares, titles or claims to money or rights, etc. The 2003 Botswana–Ghana BIT defines investment as "every kind of asset" and then goes on to give examples of assets that may be considered to be investments.

The trend in contemporary BITs is to expand the scope of "investment." Yet, at the same time, as direct investment continues to be emphasized, portfolio investments are excluded from being qualified for protection under some treaties. An example is the 2000 European Free Trade Association ("EFTA")–Mexico FTA,[6] Article 45 of which provides:

> For the purpose of this Section, investment made in accordance with the laws and regulations of the Parties means direct investment, which is defined as investment for the purpose of establishing lasting economic relations with an undertaking such as, in particular, investments which give the possibility of exercising an effective influence on the management thereof.

The 1998 Framework Agreement on the Association of Southeast Asian Nations ("ASEAN") Investment Area[7] also excluded portfolio investments.[8] This Agreement has been superseded by the ASEAN Comprehensive Investment Agreement (2009),[9] which does not exclude portfolio investments. This represents the trend that the international community is now more relaxed in defining the scope of investments.

---

6 The text of the Free Trade Agreement between the EFTA States and the United Mexican States is available at: http://www.efta.int/~/media/Documents/legal-texts/free-trade-relations/mexico/EFTA-Mexico%20Free%20Trade%20Agreement.pdf.

7 The text of the Agreement is available at: http://www.jus.uio.no/english/services/library/treaties/09/9-02/asean_investment_agreement.xml.

8 Article 2 of the Agreement stipulates: "This Agreement shall cover all direct investments other than:
   a. portfolio investments; and
   b. matters relating to investments covered by other ASEAN Agreements, such as the ASEAN Framework Agreement on Services."

9 The text of the Agreement is available at: http://www.unescap.org/sites/default/files/tisiln-investagreement.pdf.

There are also BITs that require "risk" and other factors for determining investment. For instance, under the 2004 US Model BIT, in order to be qualified as an investment, an asset must have certain characteristics of an investment, "including such characteristics as the commitment of capital or other resources, the expectation of gain or profit, or the assumption of risk." Another example is the 2007 Brunei–Japan Economic Partnership Agreement,[10] which provides that: "Where an asset lacks the characteristics of an investment, that asset is not an investment regardless of the form it may take. The characteristics of an investment include the commitment of capital, the expectation of gain or profit, or the assumption of risk."[11] The 2008 Rwanda–United States BIT[12] also makes the expectation of gain or assumption of risk factors an aspect of determining investment.

In addition to the above issues, whether reinvestment should constitute an investment, whether a change in the form of an investment would disqualify the related transaction as an investment, or whether the investment is made "in the territory" of a contracting party are sometimes addressed in BITs and FTAs.

With globalization ever deepening, the forms of foreign investment are becoming increasingly diversified. Certain transactions which were not possible several years ago owing to restrictions on the movement of capital or the lack of efficient means to do so can now be conducted by private individuals. A case in point is found in the *Abaclat* case,[13] in which Argentina issued government bonds internationally and the bondholders did not transfer such funds to the country directly. The tribunal in that case held that the place of making the investment was not an issue, as it had no difficulty in finding that the investment was made in accordance with the laws of Argentina. This was the case even if banks sold the same bonds in the secondary market in a manner that was not in compliance with the applicable Argentine law.[14] Obviously, the tribunal attached importance to the use of the proceeds by the respondent government. In other words, the funds generated through the issuance of the bonds did reach the territory of Argentina, even though the bondholders themselves may not have been to the country for that purpose. By applying the asset-based approach, the tribunal certainly had no difficulty in finding that the investment had been made in the respondent's territory. This finding is important, because sometimes an investment, by its very nature, cannot be made or activities cannot be conducted in the territory of the host state.

---

10 For the full text of the 2007 Brunei–Japan Economic Partnership Agreement, see: http://www. mofa.go.jp/region/asia-paci/brunei/epa0706/agreement.pdf.
11 Article 56 of the Brunei–Japan EPA provides: "'investments' means every kind of asset owned or controlled, directly or indirectly, by an investor," but Note 10 to that Article stipulates the requirement that to be considered an "investment" under the Agreement, these factors must be present.
12 For the full text of the 2008 Rwanda–United States BIT, see: http://www.ustr.gov/sites/default/files/uploads/agreements/bit/asset_upload_file743_14523.pdf.
13 The essential facts of the case were discussed in Chapter 3 of this book. For the text of the case, see *Abaclat and Others v. Argentine Republic*, ICSID Case No. ARB/07/5, Decision on Jurisdiction and Admissibility (August 4, 2011).
14 Ibid., para. 385.

By applying the principle established by the *Abaclat* Tribunal, such investments should be regarded as having been made in the territory of the host state.[15]

The first case in which the jurisdiction of the ICSID was challenged on the ground of the lack of a qualified investment was *Fedax N.V. v. Venezuela*.[16] The case involved Venezuela's failure to pay six promissory notes that were held by the claimant but which had been issued by the Republic of Venezuela in order to acknowledge its debt for the provision of services under a contract signed in 1988 with Industrias Metalurgicas Van Dam C.A., Venezuela. The claimant acquired the promissory notes by endorsement.

The parties had different views on whether promissory notes were qualified investments under the Netherlands–Venezuela BIT and the ICSID Convention. The respondent contended that the government-issued promissory notes were not investments because the claimant had acquired the notes by way of endorsement from a Venezuelan company.[17] The underpinning of this argument was that there was no direct investment, which was, in the view of the respondent, required by the ICSID Convention.[18] The tribunal first examined the meaning of the term "investment" under Article 25(1) of the ICSID Convention and concluded that owing to difficulties in reaching consensus on the definition of investment, the matter had been left to the consent of the parties.[19] In the circumstances, it decided to adopt a broad approach to the interpretation of Article 25(1), stating:

> [T]he text of Article 25(1) establishes that the "jurisdiction of the Centre shall extend to any legal dispute arising directly out of an investment." It is apparent that the term 'directly' relates in this Article to the "dispute" and not the "investment." It follows that jurisdiction can exist even in respect of investments that are not direct, so long as the dispute arises directly from such transaction. This interpretation is also consistent with the broad reach that the term "investment" must be given in light of the negotiating history of the Convention.[20]

The *Fedax* Tribunal also tried to distinguish the requirements under Article 25(1) of the ICSID Convention from those under the Convention Establishing the Multilateral Investment Guarantee Agency ("MIGA"). It considered the ICSID

---

15 For instance, in both *SGS v. Philippines* and *SGS v. Pakistan*, the tribunals took great pains to search for reasons to determine that the claimants' services constituted investments made in the host states. For details, see *SGS Société Générale de Surveillance S.A. v. Islamic Republic of Pakistan*, ICSID Case No. ARB/01/13, Decision on Objections to Jurisdiction (August 6, 2003), especially paras. 133–40; and *SGS Société Générale de Surveillance S.A. v. Republic of the Philippines*, ICSID Case No. ARB/02/6 Decision on Objections to Jurisdiction (January 29, 2004), especially paras. 99–112.

16 *Fedax N.V. v. Republic of Venezuela*, ICSID Case No. ARB/96/3, Decision of the Tribunal on Objections to Jurisdiction (July 11, 1997), 37 *I.L.M.* 1378 (1998), 5 *ICSID Rep.* 186 (2002).

17 Ibid., para. 25.

18 Ibid., para. 24.

19 Ibid., para. 21.

20 Ibid., para. 24.

and MIGA to be two different systems. Whilst investments under MIGA are confined to direct investment,[21] the tribunal remarked that:

> … ICSID may cover investments which may not be direct if the circumstances so warrant. Even so, MIGA's coverage may eventually extend to "any other medium or long-term form of investment," including loans relating to investments, an alternative which also broadens the scope of the MIGA Convention, and to this extent narrows the differences with the ICSID Convention.[22]

As *Fedax* involved promissory notes, the tribunal also sought support for its position that no jurisdictional obstacle had been raised from comments by scholars on the matter. It specifically cited Georges R. Delaume, who said that although the new types of investment

> … especially those relating to the supply of services are sometimes on the borderline between investment proper and commercial transactions, which would fall outside the scope of ICSID, … loans, or more precisely those of a certain duration as opposed to rapidly concluded commercial financial facilities, were included in the [ICSID] concept of "investment"… [as] evidenced by the first Draft of the Convention.[23]

Having concluded that a broad approach must be taken in interpreting the ICSID Convention, the *Fedax* Tribunal stated that the contracting states did not make any declaration to restrict the coverage of investment in accordance with Article 25(4) of the ICSID Convention, which meant that they had accepted a broad interpretation. However, the tribunal considered that for an investment to be qualified for arbitration at the ICSID it must fall not only into the definition of investment under the ICSID Convention but also that of the applicable BIT—the so-called double-barreled test.[24] It therefore moved on to consider whether the promissory notes were investments under the Netherlands–Venezuela BIT, which

21 See Regulation 1.02 of the Operational Regulations of the Multilateral Investment Guarantee Agency, 1988, as amended, *ICSID Review: Foreign Investment Law Journal*. Vol. 3, 1988, 360, also available at: http://www.miga.org/documents/Operations-Regulations.pdf; Carolyn B. Lamm and Abby Cohen Smutny, "The Implementation of ICSID Arbitration Agreements," *ICSID Review: Foreign Investment Law Journal*, Vol. 11, 1996, p. 64, at 80.

22 *Fedax v. Venezuela, supra*, note 16, para. 27 (footnotes omitted).

23 Ibid., para. 23, citing Georges R. Delaume: "ICSID and the Transnational Financial Community," *ICSID Review: Foreign Investment Law Journal*, Vol. 1, 1986, pp. 237–56, at 239–40. For additional discussion of the issue of promissory notes as investment in the *Fedax* case, see C. Chatterjee, "Investment-related Promissory Notes are Investments under the ICSID Convention: *Fedax NV v. Republic of Venezuela*," *The Journal of World Investment*, Vol. 3, No. 1, 2002, pp. 147–59.

24 The *Fedax* Tribunal, having decided that the promissory notes met the requirements of investment under the ICSID Convention, stated that: "[t]his conclusion, however, has to be examined next in the context of the specific consent of the parties and other provisions which are controlling in the matter;" *Fedax v. Venezuela*, ibid., para. 29.

provided that "the term Investments shall comprise every kind of asset and more particularly though not exclusively …" and made no differentiation between direct investment and indirect investment, contrary to what was suggested by Venezuela. The tribunal concluded that there was "nothing in the nature of the [underlying] transaction, namely the provision of services in return for promissory notes that would prevent it from qualifying as an investment under the Convention and the Agreement."[25]

Yet the issue in *Fedax* was not whether the underlying transaction was qualified as an investment but whether the subsequent endorsement of the notes to foreign holders would satisfy the requirements of a protected investment. Regarding this issue, the *Fedax* Tribunal first adopted the claimant's argument that promissory notes of this kind had "a legal standing of their own, separate and independent from the underlying transactions."[26] It then applied the five criteria of investment originally suggested by Christoph Schreuer—a certain duration, a certain regularity of profit and return, assumption of risk, a substantial commitment, and a significance for the host state's development[27]—and concluded that the endorsement of the promissory notes had met the "basic features of an investment."[28]

As the first case involving a difficult determination of the qualification of an "investment" as a condition for jurisdiction, the *Fedax* decision has several distinctive features. In the first place, it was decided that the term "investment" contained in Article 25(1) of the ICSID Convention must be given a broad interpretation. This approach has subsequently been followed by many tribunals because it is in line with the negotiation history of the Convention, which shows that, after numerous attempts were made to define investment, no consensus was reached. This was confirmed by Broches, who noted that "during the negotiations several definitions of 'investment' were considered and rejected."[29] As a result of such difficulties, the matter was left to the consent of the parties. As a matter of policy, the Report of the Executive Directors stated:

> No attempt was made to define the term "investment" given the essential requirement of consent by the parties, and the mechanism through which Contracting States can make known in advance, if they so desire, the classes of disputes which they would or would not consider submitting to the Centre (Article 25 (4)).[30]

---

25 Ibid., para. 38.
26 Ibid., para. 39.
27 Schreuer, *supra*, note 2, at 372, para. 122.
28 *Fedax v. Venezuela, supra*, note 16, para. 43.
29 A. Broches, "The Convention on the Settlement of Investment Disputes: Some Observations on Jurisdiction," *Columbia Journal of Transnational Law*, Vol. 5, 1966, pp. 261–80, at 268. Broches was general counsel of the World Bank for 20 years until he retired in 1979 and is considered to have been a founder of the ICSID in 1967.
30 "Report of the Executive Directors on the Convention of the Settlement of Investment Disputes between States and Nationals of Other States" [hereinafter, "Report of the Executive Directors"], Doc. ICSID/2, 1 *ICSID Reports*, 1993, p. 23, para. 27.

In other words, it is up to the contracting parties to decide what may constitute an investment and what kinds of disputes may be excluded from ICSID arbitration. In these circumstances, "the requirement that the dispute must have arisen out of an 'investment' may be merged into the requirement of consent to jurisdiction. Presumably, the parties' agreement that a dispute is an 'investment dispute' will be given great weight in any determination of the Centre's jurisdiction, although it would not be controlling."[31] The question that remains is: if the contracting parties have the freedom to define what transactions may constitute an investment, why did the *Fedax* Tribunal have to determine if the underlying transaction—endorsement of promissory notes—constituted an investment under the ICSID Convention?

A second notable feature of the *Fedax* case was its introduction of the double-barreled test for determining the making of an investment. As will be discussed later, this has had a significant impact on subsequent ICSID arbitration practice.

The third distinctive feature of the *Fedax* case was the tribunal's use of the criteria of investment suggested by Schreuer to support its determination that the promissory notes at issue could be considered "investments" pursuant to the Netherlands–Venezuela BIT. This was the first time that an arbitral tribunal had considered that an investment must satisfy certain requirements in order to be protected by the ICSID Convention. Subsequent tribunals, however, have consistently referred to such requirements as the *Salini* test, rather than the *Fedax* test. In any case, this shows that scholars and arbitrators alike consider that there must be some limitations to the definition of investment under the ICSID Convention, notwithstanding that a broad interpretation is desirable.

In *Salini v. Morocco*,[32] the claimant was an Italian company that had been awarded a contract for highway construction in Morocco through competitive bidding. The Moroccan contracting party was the Moroccan State Highways company Société Nationale des Autoroutes du Maroc ("ADM"), which issued the international invitation to tender on behalf of the Moroccan Government. There was a delay in completion of the construction project, and ADM claimed that the delay constituted a breach of the contract, while the claimant maintained that the delay was owing to external causes and not its failure to comply with the contract. In any event, ADM did not pay the claimant in full. Subsequently, Salini filed a Request for Arbitration against Morocco with the ICSID.

One of the issues encountered by the tribunal was the respondent's challenge to its jurisdiction on the ground that the highway construction project was not a qualified investment within the meaning of Article 25(1) of the ICSID Convention. The issue of whether or not the claimant's transaction constituted a qualified investment thus became the prerequisite for establishing ICSID jurisdiction.

The tribunal admitted that the ICSID Convention does not contain a definition of investment and that the contracting parties did not intend to give a definition,

---

31 Broches, *supra*, note 29.
32 *Salini Costruttori S.p.A. and Italstrade S.p.A. v. Kingdom of Morocco (Salini v. Morocco)*, ICSID Case No. ARB/00/4, Decision on Jurisdiction (July 23, 2001).

which was confirmed in the Report of the Executive Directors.[33] It pointed out, however, that the absence of a definition of investment in the ICSID Convention should not be construed to dilute the requirement that a dispute must have arisen "in direct relation to an investment" under the Convention, as agreed by the contracting parties. In the view of the *Salini* Tribunal, the "investment requirement must be respected as an objective condition of the jurisdiction of the Centre."[34]

The *Salini* case was first time in the history of the ICSID Convention that certain criteria—contributions, a certain duration of performance of the contact, and a participation in the risks of the transaction—which have later come to be known as the *Salini* test, were considered as objective elements for the determination of a qualified investment within the meaning of ICSID Article 25(1). The *Salini* Tribunal did not adopt in full the *Fedax* criteria for investment. Instead, it pointed out that there had been "almost no cases where the notion of investment within the meaning of Article 25 of the Convention was raised,"[35] including, obviously, the *Fedax* case.[36]

Notwithstanding the differences in the two decisions—the *Salini* Tribunal considered "the contribution to the economic development of the host state of the investment as an additional condition"[37]—the objective constituent elements of "investment" put forward in *Fedax* and *Salini* are in substance nearly identical. The *Salini* Tribunal, however, also observed that the various elements contained in its test were interdependent. For instance, the risks that an investor may assume depend on the amount committed for a transaction and the duration thereof. Therefore, in the tribunal's view, "these various criteria should be assessed globally even if, for the sake of reasoning," they were analyzed individually in the case.[38] In this and some other respects, the *Salini* Tribunal was careful to make clear in its decision how it had conducted its analysis and to give the reasons for its conclusions, which may have led subsequent tribunals and legal scholars to refer to the criteria as the *Salini* test.[39]

Many subsequent ICSID tribunals have resorted to this *Salini* test in deciding whether the projects concerned were qualified investments. Nonetheless, they have also demonstrated a remarkable disparity in how they have applied the *Salini* criteria—or declined to do so—in determining investment. Gaillard,

---

33 Ibid., para. 51.
34 Ibid., para. 52. In its analysis, the tribunal referred to the writings of unnamed legal scholars, but in particular, Emmanuel Gaillard, "Commentary on the *Fedax* Award," *Journal du Droit International*, 1999, pp. 298 *et seq.*
35 *Salini v. Morocco*, *supra*, note 32, para. 52.
36 Note that in the *Fedax* case, discussed earlier, the tribunal used the Schreuer criteria to determine if the promissory notes at issue could be considered to be investments within the meaning of the relevant BIT, not the ICSID Convention.
37 *Salini v. Morocco*, *supra*, note 32, para. 52.
38 Id.
39 The *Salini* Tribunal also considered that an arbitration request based on a simple sales contract had been refused registration by the Secretary-General of the ICSID. For details of the matter, see I. F. I. Shihata and A. R. Parra, "The Experience of the International Centre for Settlement of Investment Disputes," *ICSID Review: Foreign Investment Law Journal*, Vol. 14, No. 2, 1999, p. 308.

in his thoughtful analysis of ICSID cases up until 2008, identified two major approaches: the "intuitive" approach, according to which "the 'characteristics' allowing the 'identification' of an investment may, in fact, vary from one case to another;" and the "deductive" approach, according to which "there exists a true definition of an investment, and that such a definition is based on constitutive elements or criteria."[40]

In this regard, Gaillard cites the *ČSOB v. Slovak Republic* case as "the first clear example of the application of the intuitive method in ICSID case law."[41] The relevant facts of the case are as follows. Upon the dissolution of the former Czechoslovakia into the two states of the Czech Republic and the Slovak Republic, a commercial bank—Československa Obchodni Banka, A.S. ("ČSOB")—was created with both states as owners. In order to improve the financial position of ČSOB by reducing its non-performing receivables, a collection company was to be established in each Republic. Insofar as the Slovak Republic was concerned, ČSOB assigned its receivables to the collection company in that country. For the purposes of financing, ČSOB provided the Slovakian collection company a loan equaling the nominal amount of the non-performing receivables. Because the total of its operational costs, the principal of the loan and the interest arising therefrom would be far more than the amount it might be able to collect, the Slovak Republic guaranteed the payment by the collection company of the loan advanced by ČSOB. The dispute occurred owing to non-performance of this guarantee by the Slovak Republic.

ČSOB commenced arbitration proceedings at the ICSID, alleging that the Slovak Republic had failed to fulfill the commitment contained in the agreement signed with ČSOB in which it (the Slovak Republic) promised to provide compensation for any losses incurred by the financial management company. The respondent contended that the making of the loan by ČSOB was not an investment on its part. The tribunal considered that an investment was "frequently a rather complex operation, composed of various interrelated transactions, each element of which, standing alone, might not in all cases qualify as an investment."[42] However, to determine whether ČSOB's loan could constitute an investment, the tribunal first examined the definition of investment under the BIT and concluded that: "[a]lthough loans are not expressly mentioned in this list [of

40 Gaillard, *supra*, note 5, p. 407. In a similar vein, Mortenson, *supra*, note 2, at pp. 269–73, refers to the "deferential' approach," which he says "has been highly deferential to host states' ex ante decisions about which categories of economic activity to protect;" and the "restrictive approach," which "scrutinize[s] far more skeptically whether a given economic activity or asset constitutes an 'investment.'" The sole arbitrator in *Malaysian Historical Salvors v. Malaysia*, ICSID Case No. ARB/05/10 (May 17, 2007) [hereinafter "*Malaysian Historical Salvors*, Award"], at paras. 70ff similarly identified what he called the "Typical Characteristics Approach" and the "Jurisdictional Approach."

41 Gaillard, id., referring to *Československa Obchodni Banka, A.S. (ČSOB) v. Slovak Republic*, ICSID Case No. ARB/97/4, Decision on Jurisdiction (May 24, 1999). After the issuance of this decision, the tribunal issued a Second Decision on Jurisdiction on December 1, 2000 and the Award on December 29, 2004. The award on the merits was not published by ICSID; it is available, however, on the website of international treaty arbitration (ita), at: http://www.italaw.com/cases/238.

42 *ČSOB*, Decision on Jurisdiction, ibid., para. 72.

investments under the BIT], terms as broad as 'assets' and 'monetary receivables or claims' clearly encompass loans extended to a Slovak entity by a national of the other Contracting Party."[43]

The tribunal also pointed out that: "the broad meaning which must be given to the notion of investment under the ICSID Convention is opposed to the conclusion that a transaction is not an investment merely because, as a matter of law, it is a loan. This is so, if only because under certain circumstances a loan may contribute substantially to a State's economic development."[44]

There are also other cases in which the tribunals did not find it necessary to establish certain criteria to define what may constitute an investment under Article 25(1) of the ICSID Convention. In *Biwater v. Tanzania*,[45] for instance, the claimant was an operator of water and sewerage services in Tanzania. The BIT categorized investment as "every kind of asset." The respondent accepted that transactions with the claimant fell within the broad definition of investment under the BIT but at the same time argued that the project was a "'loss leader', i.e., an undertaking that was not economically rational standing alone, but that might have led to other profitable opportunities later"[46] and that, as such, it could not be regarded as an investment under Article 25 of the ICSID Convention nor did it satisfy the criteria of "risk" and "substantial commitment."[47]

The tribunal observed that the five criteria of investment were initiated by the *Fedax* Tribunal and restated in the *Salini* case. It considered, however, that there was "no basis for a rote, or overly strict application of the five *Salini* criteria in every case."[48] It further stated that:

> [T]he *Salini Test* itself is problematic if ... the "typical characteristics" of an investment as identified in that decision are elevated into a fixed and inflexible test, and if transactions are to be presumed excluded from the ICSID Convention unless each of the five criteria are satisfied.[49]

In the *Biwater* Tribunal's view, application of the *Salini* test as a "fixed and inflexible" test may do more harm than good to the formulation of international investment law within the context of the ICSID Convention.[50] Doing so would contradict, in certain cases, the intent of contracting parties as that has been expressed in a BIT and even the consensus of the international community on the definition of investment when agreements have been reached to broaden the concept.[51]

---

43 Ibid., para. 77.
44 Ibid., para. 76.
45 *Biwater Gauff (Tanzania) Limited v. United Republic of Tanzania*, ICSID Case No. ARB/05/22, Award (July 24, 2008).
46 Ibid., para. 288.
47 Id.
48 Ibid., para. 312 (emphasis in original).
49 Ibid., para. 314 (emphasis in original).
50 Id.
51 Ibid.

There may be some truth in what the *Biwater* Tribunal said. An important point that was not mentioned by the tribunal is the principle of treaty interpretation. Supposing its interpretation of Article 25 of the ICSID Convention—to leave the definition of investment open-ended—is correct, whether or not there is consensus in the world on the issue should have no bearing on how the Article is interpreted. In any event, the *travaux préparatoires* of the ICSID Convention only indicate that the contracting parties chose not to give "investment" a definition. This does not mean that there should be no criteria for ascertaining whether a transaction constitutes an investment. This having been said, *Biwater* is not the only case that disagrees with *Salini* and others which support the objective criteria approach to the definition of "investment."[52]

The majority of the *ad hoc* Committee in *Malaysian Historical Salvors*[53] was also critical of the use of specific criteria to define investment in the context of the ICSID Convention. Its holding in this regard was based largely on the intent of the drafters of the Convention, especially as demonstrated by the *travaux préparatoires*. It pointed out that:

> It appears to have been assumed by the Convention's drafters that use of the term "investment" excluded a simple sale and like transient commercial transactions from the jurisdiction of the Centre. Judicial or arbitral construction going further in interpretation of the meaning of "investment" by the establishment of criteria or hallmarks may or may not be regarded as plausible, but the intentions of the draftsmen of the ICSID Convention, as the *travaux* show them to have been, lend those criteria (and still less, conditions) scant support.
>
> ...
>
> The preparatory work of the Convention as well as the Report of the Executive Directors thus shows that: (a) deliberately no definition of "investment" as that term is found in Article 25(1) was adopted; (b) a floor limit to the value of an investment was rejected; (c) a requirement of indefinite duration of an investment or of a duration of no less than five years was rejected; (d) the critical criterion adopted was the consent of the parties.[54]

Another ICSID tribunal that refused to apply the *Salini* criteria as definitive in determining investment was that in *Alpha Projektholding v. Ukraine*.[55] In doing so, it relied for support on "a number of tribunals and *ad hoc* committees [that] have treated the *Salini* elements as non-binding, non-exclusive means of

---

52 In *Rompetrol v. Romania*, for example, the tribunal stated: "At a deeper level, though, the Tribunal is not persuaded that there is anything in the rules of treaty interpretation that would justify giving the ICSID Convention overriding effect for the interpretation of the BIT." See *Rompetrol v. Romania*, ICSID Case No. ARB/06/3, Decision on Jurisdiction (April 18, 2008), para. 107.

53 *Malaysian Historical Salvors v. Malaysia*, ICSID Case No. ARB/05/10, Annulment Decision (April 16, 2009) [hereinafter *"Malaysian Historical Salvors* annulment Decision"].

54 Ibid., paras. 69 and 71.

55 *Alpha Projektholding GmbH v. Ukraine*, ICSID Case No. ARB/07/16, Award (November 8, 2010).

identifying (rather than defining) investments that are consistent with the ICSID Convention."[56] It held further that:

> … the elements of the so-called *Salini* test, which some tribunals have applied mandatorily and cumulatively (i.e., if one feature is missing, a claimed investment will be ruled out of ICSID jurisdiction), are not found in Article 25(1) of the ICSID Convention. In applying the criteria in this manner, these tribunals have sought to apply a universal definition of 'investment' under the ICSID Convention, despite the fact that the drafters and signatories of the Convention decided that it should not have one. This Tribunal will not follow that approach and will not impose additional requirements beyond those expressed on the face of Article 25(1) of the ICSID Convention and the UABIT [Ukraine–Austria BIT].[57]

Continuing in this vein, the tribunal in the *Abaclat* case[58] likewise declined to apply the *Salini* criteria. Its reasoning in this regard is particularly worthy of note:

> If Claimants' contributions were to fail the *Salini* test, those contributions – according to the followers of this test – would not qualify as investment under Article 25 ICSID Convention, which would in turn mean that Claimants' contributions would not be given the procedural protection afforded by the ICSID Convention. The Tribunal finds that such a result would be contradictory to the ICSID Convention's aim, which is to encourage private investment while giving the Parties the tools to further define what kind of investment they want to promote. It would further make no sense in view of Argentina's and Italy's express agreement to protect the value generated by these kinds of contributions. In other words – and from the value perspective – there would be an investment, which Argentina and Italy wanted to protect and to submit to ICSID arbitration, but it could not be given any protection because – from the perspective of the contribution – the investment does not meet certain criteria. Considering that these criteria were never included in the ICSID Convention, while being controversial and having been applied by tribunals in varying manners and degrees, the Tribunal does not see any merit in following and copying the *Salini* criteria. The *Salini* criteria may be useful to further describe what characteristics contributions may or should have. They should, however, not serve to create a limit, which [neither] the

---

56 Ibid., para. 313. The footnote refers to the tribunals in *Biwater, supra*, note 45; *MCI Power Group, LC and New Turbine, Inc. v. Republic of Ecuador*, ICSID Case No. ARB/03/6, Award (July 31, 2007); *RSM Production Corp. v. Grenada*, ICSID Case No. ARB/05/14, Award (March 13, 2009); and *ČSOB*, Decision on Jurisdiction, *supra*, note 41; as well as the *ad hoc* Committee in *Malaysian Historical Salvors* annulment Decision, *supra*, note 53.

57 Ibid., para. 311. Footnotes are omitted, although one of them identifies the tribunals that have sought to apply a universal definition of investment under the ICSID Convention as including those in *Joy Mining, infra*, note 63; *Victor Pey Casado, infra*, note 79; and *Patrick Mitchell, infra*, note 72.

58 *Abaclat and Others v. Argentina, supra*, note 13.

Convention itself nor the Contracting Parties to a specific BIT intended to create.[59]

Some ICSID arbitration practice, while accepting that a broad interpretation of the term "investment" is appropriate, has nonetheless shown a tendency to consider that it should not be interpreted too broadly without any restriction. For instance, in *PSEG v. Turkey*,[60] the claimant—PSEG, a US corporation—entered into a build-operate-transfer contract with Turkey and established the project company Konya Ilgin Elektrik. The North American Coal Company ("NACC"), another US corporation, had an option to acquire an ownership interest in the project company. Since the dispute arose from the performance of the contract, PSEG, Konya Ilgin Elektrik and NACC requested ICSID arbitration. NACC claimed that the value of its option had been impaired by actions of the Turkish Government. The tribunal pointed out that neither the ICSID Convention nor the United States–Turkey BIT stipulated whether an option constituted an investment. According to the tribunal, although contemporary investment treaties included a broad definition of investment, "there is a limit to what they can reasonably encompass as an investment."[61] It held that the option enjoyed by NACC should not be deemed to be an investment. It acknowledged, however, that "different circumstances from those which obtain in the present case may lead to a different conclusion."[62]

On the other hand, there is a definite line of ICSID jurisprudence within which tribunals have relied upon certain "criteria" as "objective" measures of whether or not a specific transaction can be deemed an "investment." One such is the *Joy Mining Machinery v. Egypt* case.[63] In that case, one issue in dispute was whether or not certain guarantees that the Egyptian Government failed to pay the claimant constituted investment. The tribunal first of all examined whether or not the guarantees could be considered investment pursuant to the United Kingdom–Egypt BIT. Despite the broad definition of investment contained therein, the tribunal held that interpreting the guarantees in issue as investment "would really go far beyond the concept of investment, even if broadly defined, as this and other treaties normally do."[64] It expanded upon this by saying that: "Even if a claim to return of performance and related guarantees has a financial value it cannot

59 Ibid., para. 364.
60 *PSEG Global Inc. and Konya Ilgin Elektrik Üretim ve Ticaret Limited Sirketi v. Republic of Turkey*, ICSID Case No. ARB/02/5, Decision on Jurisdiction (June 4, 2004); available at: https://icsid.worldbank.org/ICSID/FrontServlet?requestType=CasesRH&actionVal=showDoc&docId=DC631_En&caseId=C212.
61 Ibid., para. 189.
62 Id.
63 *Joy Mining Machinery Limited v. Arab Republic of Egypt*, ICSID Case No. ARB/03/11, Award on Jurisdiction (August 6, 2004); available at: https://icsid.worldbank.org/ICSID/FrontServlet?requestType=CasesRH&actionVal=showDoc&docId=DC647_En&caseId=C229.
64 Ibid., para. 45.

amount to recharacterizing as an investment dispute a dispute which in essence concerns a contingent liability."[65]

One would expect that the tribunal, having determined that there was neither an "investment" nor an "investment dispute" within the meaning of the relevant BIT, would have rested at this point and declined jurisdiction in the case. However, in a remarkable display of "judicial diseconomy," the tribunal went on to examine whether or not the guarantees could be considered "investment" pursuant to ICSID Article 25(1). The tribunal held that investment protected by the ICSID Convention should have the following elements: a certain duration; a regularity of profit and return; an element of risk; a substantial commitment; and should constitute a significant contribution to the host state's development.[66] However, it reached this conclusion not by reference to "the *Salini* test" but on the basis of its analysis of a number of previous ICSID decisions (of which *Salini* was only one) and by reference to Schreuer.[67] In this instance, the tribunal held that the transaction between Joy Mining Machinery and the Egyptian Government was merely a commercial contract which did not satisfy the above requirements and thus was not deemed to be an investment. An international commercial contract, no matter how complicated, could not automatically be transformed into international investment. Were that to be the case, trade and investment, as well as international commercial arbitration and international investment arbitration, would be confused.[68]

Jan de Nul v. Egypt[69] was a case involving a contract between the claimants and the Suez Canal Authority, an Egyptian state entity, for dredging works in the Suez Canal. To determine whether or not this involved an "investment," the tribunal applied the four criteria of the *Salini* test: "(i) a contribution, (ii) a certain duration over which the project is implemented, (iii) a sharing of operational risks, and (iv) a contribution to the host State's development."[70] In this regard, the tribunal noted:

> The only aspect which the Respondent appears to question is whether the duration of the operation is sufficient to qualify as an investment. In response to a specific question by the Tribunal at the hearing on jurisdiction, both parties expressed the opinion that an operation may be characterized as an investment if it lasts at least two years.[71]

---

65 Ibid., para. 47.
66 Ibid., para. 53.
67 Ibid., paras. 51 and 53. The cases considered by the tribunal in this context included, in addition to *Salini*, *Alcoa Minerals of Jamaica v. Jamaica*, ICSID Case No. ARB/74/2, Decision on Jurisdiction and Competence (July 6, 1975); *Amco Asia Corporation et al. v. Indonesia*, ICSID Case No. ARB/81/1, Decision on Jurisdiction (September 25, 1983); *Fedax*, *supra*, note 16; *ČSOB*, Decision on Jurisdiction, *supra*, note 41; *Atlantic Triton Company Limited v. People's Revolutionary Republic of Guinea*, ICSID Case No. ARB/84/1, Award (April 21, 1986); and *SGS v. Philippines* and *SGS v. Pakistan*, both *supra*, note 15.
68 See ibid., paras. 54–62, especially para. 58.
69 *Jan de Nul N.V. and Dredging International N.V. v. Egypt*, Decision on Jurisdiction, ICSID Case No. ARB/04/13 (June 16, 2006).
70 Ibid., para. 91.
71 Ibid., para. 93.

In this case, it is clear that all parties—both claimants and the respondent, as well as the tribunal—felt that the application of the *Salini* criteria was appropriate (and sufficient) to determine the existence of an investment.

Subsequent jurisprudence that adheres to the restrictive or deductive approach to the determination of investment has shown a tendency to limit the essential criteria of a definition of investment to three: contribution, duration, and risk.[72] This is an approach that has been endorsed by Gaillard, who says that it "avoids the risk of reducing the notion of investment to a subjective test and rendering superfluous the requirement of 'investment' under the [ICSID C]onvention."[73] As such, he says, "this approach is the most faithful to both the text and the intention of the drafters of the ICSID [C]onvention."[74]

One of the first tribunals to take this approach was that in *L.E.S.I.–DIPENTA v. Algeria.*[75] The dispute in this case involved a contract for construction of a dam to provide drinking water for the city of Algiers. Numerous problems led to prolonged delays in the course of the construction project and, eight years after it was entered into, the contract was eventually cancelled. Following an additional two years of negotiations to seek compensation for their losses pursuant to the delays and cancellation, the claimants filed for arbitration of the dispute at the ICSID. The respondent objected to the ICSID's jurisdiction on the ground that "the dispute does not fulfill the conditions required by Article 25.1 of the 1965 Washington Convention as needed to bring it within the scope of jurisdiction of ICSID," that is, that it did not arise directly out of an "investment."[76]

In making its determination of investment, the *L.E.S.I.–DIPENTA* Tribunal held that:

> It would seem consistent with the objective of the Convention that a contract, in order to be considered an investment within the meaning of the provision, should fulfill the following three conditions:
> a) the contracting party has made contributions in the host country;
> b) those contributions had a certain duration; and
> c) they involved some risks for the contributor.[77]

On this basis, the tribunal had little difficulty in deciding that "[t]he dispute submitted to the Arbitral Tribunal arises directly out of an investment within the meaning of the Convention."[78]

72 Notable exceptions to this trend can be found, however, in the annulment Decision in *Patrick Mitchell v. Democratic Republic of Congo*, ICSID Case No. ARB/99/7 (November 1, 2006); and the original tribunal's award in *Malaysian Historical Salvors v. Malaysia, supra*, note 40. Both these cases are discussed elsewhere in this chapter.
73 Emmanuel Gaillard, "'Biwater,' Classic Investment Bases: Input, Risk, Duration," *New York Law Journal*, Vol. 240, No. 126 (December 31, 2008).
74 Id.
75 *Consortium Groupement L.E.S.I. DIPENTA v. People's Democratic Republic of Algeria*, ICSID Case No. ARB/03/8, Award (January 10, 2005).
76 Ibid., para. I.48(i).
77 Ibid., para. II.13(iv).
78 Ibid., para. II.15.

Victor Pey Casado v. Chile[79] was a rather complicated case that arose from the closure and confiscation of the assets of a Chilean newspaper by the Pinochet Government in 1973. In addressing the numerous challenges to its jurisdiction over the case, the tribunal undertook to determine if Sr Pey Casado's acquisition of the companies that were owners of the newspaper could be considered an investment in accordance with ICSID Article 25.[80] In carrying out its analysis, the tribunal first noted that "a study of the ICSID jurisprudence shows that there are at least two interpretations of the concept of investment in accordance with the ICSID Convention,"[81] the first of which it said is "content to identify a number of 'characteristics' which permit the conclusion that an investment exists"[82] and the second holds that there is "a true definition of investment which depends upon the satisfaction of specific criteria."[83] Within the latter approach, it noted that some tribunals have relied upon the four *Salini* criteria, while others have held that an investment exists whenever the combination of three elements can be shown: a contribution made in the host state for a certain duration and at a certain degree of risk.[84]

The *Victor Pey Casado* Tribunal clearly placed itself within this latter school of thought. It said:

> This Tribunal, for its part, considers that there is a definition of investment in the sense of the ICSID Convention, and that it is not sufficient to show the presence of some of the habitual 'characteristics' of an investment to satisfy this objective condition of ICSID jurisdiction. Such an interpretation would serve to deprive certain terms of ICSID Article 25 of any meaning, which would be incompatible with the requirement to interpret the terms of the Convention in such a way as to give them effective meaning ... According to this Tribunal, this definition comprises only three elements."[85]

79 *Victor Pey Casado and President Allende Foundation v. Republic of Chile*, ICSID Case No. ARB/98/2, Award (May 8, 2008).

80 Ibid., para. 179.

81 Ibid., para. 231 (free translation secured by the author; in the original: "... *el studio de la jurisprudencia CIADI pone de manifiesto que existen al menos dos interpretaciones del concepto de inversión de acuerdo al Convenio CIADI*" (Spanish); "*L'examen de la jurisprudence CIRDI fait cependant apparaître qu'il existe au moins deux conceptions de la notion d'investissement au sens de la Convention CIRDI*" (French)).

82 Id. (free translation secured by the author; in the original: "*La primera de ellas se limita a identificar un cierto número de 'características' que permitirían concluir la existencia de una inversión*" (Spanish); "*La première se contente d'identifier un certain nombre de 'caractéristiques' qui permettraient de conclure à l'existence d'un investissement*" (French)).

83 Id. (free translation secured by the author; in the original: "...*una verdadera definición de inversión que supone que se satisfagan criterios específicos*" (Spanish); "...*une véritable définition de l'investissement qui suppose la satisfaction de critères spécifiques*" (French)).

84 Id. The Spanish version seems to say that there is always ("*siempre*") an investment where these elements exist in combination.

85 Ibid., para. 232 (free translation secured by the author; in the original: "*Este Tribunal considera, por su parte, que sí existe una definición de inversión de acuerdo al Convenio CIADI y que no basta con señalar la presencia de algunas de las 'características' habituales de una inversion para satisfacer esta condición objetiva de la competencia del Centro. Una interpretación de este tipo significaría privar de sentido alguno a ciertos términos del*

It then clarified that these three elements are "the existence of a contribution, the fact that this contribution will continue for a certain duration, and the fact that it will involve, for whomever has made it, a certain risk."[86]

In the more recent case of *Fakes v. Turkey*,[87] the claimant—Mr Saba Fakes, a dual Dutch and Jordanian national—alleged that he had a contract to acquire shares of a mobile phone company—Telsim—in Turkey. The dispute centered on the receivership and subsequent sale by the Turkish authorities of assets held by Telsim. Regarding the issue as to whether an investment had been made by the claimant, the tribunal stated that the claimant was "never expected (nor did he expect) to make any payments beyond the initial US$3,800"[88] and therefore no investment had been made. In its analysis, the tribunal said that there was no contribution, duration or risk involved in the transaction. Most importantly, the parties to the transaction never had any intention to transfer any rights to the claimant, and there was no actual transfer of rights.[89] In this case, the tribunal confirmed that Article 25 of the ICSID Convention provides for an objective definition of investment. Yet, in the same vein as the cases just discussed, it only considered a contribution, a certain duration, and an element of risk as the essential factors in such an objective test.

Another recent ICSID tribunal dismissed a case (*Global Resource v. Ukraine*) on an expedited basis because the dispute arose out of a sales contract and was therefore "manifestly without legal merit" under the ICSID Convention.[90] In so doing, it noted that "[t]he existing case law has thrown up no uniform approach as to the identification and respective importance of the criteria that may be resorted to by ICSID tribunals having to define an investment for the purposes of Article 25(1)."[91]

In theory, no arbitral decision has precedential effect. In practice, however, as discussed in previous chapters, subsequent tribunals always consider earlier decisions by other tribunals. Through this informal process, arbitral decisions

---

artículo 25 del Convenio CIADI, lo cual no sería compatible con la exigencia de interpretar los términos del Convenio confiriéndoles un efecto útil … Según el Tribunal, dicha definición comprende sólo tres elementos" (Spanish); "*Le présent Tribunal estime pour sa part qu'il existe bien une définition de l'investissement au sens de la Convention CIRDI et qu'il ne suffit pas de relever la présence de certaines des 'caractéristiques' habituelles d'un investissement pour que cette condition objective de la compétence du Centre soit satisfaite. Une telle interprétation reviendrait à priver de toute signification certains des termes de l'article 25 de la Convention CIRDI, ce qui ne serait pas compatible avec l'exigence d'interpréter les termes de la Convention en leur donnant un effet utile … Selon le Tribunal, cette définition ne comprend en revanche que trois éléments*" (French)).

86 Ibid., para. 233 (free translation secured by the author; in the original: "*la existencia de un aporte, el hecho de que dicho aporte implica una cierta duración en el tiempo y el hecho de que dicho aporte comporta ciertos riesgos para quien lo efectúa*" (Spanish); "*l'existence d'un apport, le fait que cet apport porte sur une certaine durée et qu'il comporte, pour celui qui le fait, certains risques*" (French)).

87 *Mr Saba Fakes v. Republic of Turkey*, ICSID Case No. ARB/07/20, Award (July 14, 2010).

88 Ibid., para. 140.

89 Ibid., paras. 136 and 147.

90 See *Global Trading Resource Corp. and Globex International, Inc. v. Ukraine*, ICSID Case No. ARB/09/11, Award (December 1, 2010), paras. 56–58.

91 Ibid., para. 55.

always have impacts on others.[92] It is also evident that the decisions of ICSID tribunals have extended their impact even beyond that system. For instance, in *Romak v. Uzbekistan*,[93] a case decided by the Permanent Court of Arbitration in accordance with the UNCITRAL rules, the BIT in question provides in its Article 1 that investment includes "every kind of assets." The *Romak* Tribunal found that the claimant did not own an investment because its rights were embodied in and arose out of a sales contract. It held that "the term 'investments' under the BIT has an inherent meaning (irrespective of whether the investor resorts to ICSID or UNCITRAL arbitral proceedings) entailing a *contribution* that extends over a *certain period* of time and that involves some *risk*."[94] The tribunal said that it was "further comforted in its analysis by the reasoning adopted by other arbitral tribunals (see, *supra*, paras. 198–204) which consistently incorporates contribution, duration and risk as hallmarks of an 'investment.'"[95]

The *Romak* Tribunal was faced with the question whether a transfer of title to wheat from the claimant to the respondent amounted to an investment. It first observed that an investment contribution could be made in "cash, kind or labor."[96] Nevertheless, it considered that the mere transfer of title over goods in exchange for full payment was not a contribution in any event.[97] Nor was the five month delivery time considered by the tribunal to be a significant duration of the transaction in order to satisfy the definition of an investment. With regard to risks, the tribunal stated that "[a]ll economic activity entails a certain degree of risk,"[98] yet not every risk is investment related, as some of them are pure commercial risks, such as non-performance of contract. In the tribunal's view, the purpose of the transaction plays an important part in determining what constitutes an investment risk. For that purpose, it considered that the "entire economic transaction" should be taken into account.[99] In the case of an investment risk, according to the tribunal, "the investor cannot be sure of a return on his investment, and may not know the amount he will end up spending, even if all relevant counterparties discharge their contractual obligations."[100] It should be noted that in no other cases have the tribunals conducted such a detailed analysis of each of these three elements of

92 For discussions of the role of precedent in ICSID arbitration, see, for example, Jeffery P. Commission, "Precedent in Investment Treaty Arbitration: *A Citation Analysis of a Developing Jurisprudence*," *Journal of International Arbitration* 24(2), 2007, pp. 129–58; August Reinisch, "The Role of Precedent in ICSID Arbitration," *Austrian Arbitration Yearbook*, 2008, pp. 495–510.

93 *Romak S.A. v. Uzbekistan*, PCA Case No. AA280, Award (November 26, 2009).

94 Ibid., para. 207 (emphasis in original).

95 Id. The arbitral tribunals mentioned in the referenced paragraphs are all ICSID tribunals: *Salini, supra*, note 32; *Consortium Groupement L.E.S.I.–DIPENTA v. People's Democratic Republic of Algeria*, ICSID Case No. ARB/03/8, Award (January 10, 2005); and *Victor Pey Casado, supra*, note 79.

96 *Romak v. Uzbekistan*, ibid., para. 214.

97 Ibid., para. 222.

98 Ibid., para. 229.

99 Ibid., para. 211.

100 Ibid., para. 230.

the investment criteria. The *Romak* Tribunal's contribution to the jurisprudence in this regard should be appreciated.[101]

Finally, as a non-ICSID arbitration, the *AMTO v. Ukraine*[102] case is also instructive in relation to how qualified investment may be determined outside that system. The claimant in that case was a limited liability company with its legal address in Latvia. Its main business activity was to act as an investment company. In late 1999, the claimant sought an investment in the nuclear energy industry in Ukraine and decided to buy shares in EYUM-10, the legal successor of a state entity called Erection Division No. 10 of the EYUM Group that had participated in the construction of the Zaporozhskaya AES ("ZAES") nuclear power plant. EYUM-10 became a supplier of services to ZAES. The claimant's total shareholding in EYUM-10 as of March 2003 was 204,165 shares or 67.2 percent of the total share capital.[103]

One of the issues in the case was that the respondent asserted that the arbitral tribunal had no jurisdiction over this dispute because the claimant's shares in EYUM-10 did not constitute a qualified investment under the Energy Charter Treaty ("ECT").[104] In this case, because the arbitration was administered by the Stockholm Chamber of Commerce pursuant to the ECT, the tribunal was able to limit its determination of "investment" to the definition contained in that Treaty.

Article 1(6) of the ECT defines "investment" as:

> ... every kind of asset, owned or controlled directly or indirectly by an Investor and includes:
> (a) tangible and intangible, and movable and immovable, property, and any property rights such as leases, mortgages, liens, and pledges;
> (b) a company or business enterprise, or shares, stock, or other forms of equity participation in a company or business enterprise, and bonds and other debt of a company or business enterprise;
> ...
> (f) any right conferred by law or contract or by virtue of any licences and permits granted pursuant to law to undertake any Economic Activity in the Energy Sector.

101 For further discussion of the *Romak* award and its importance to international investment arbitration in general, see Julien Burda, "A New Step Towards a Single and Common Definition of an Investment? Comments on the Romak versus Uzbekistan Decision," *The Journal of World Investment & Trade*, Vol. 11, No. 6, 2010, pp. 1085–1101.

102 *Limited Liability Company AMTO v. Ukraine* ("*AMTO v. Ukraine*"), SCC Arbitration No. 080/2005, Final Award (March 26, 2008).

103 Ibid., §§15–24.

104 For a brief but thorough discussion of ECT provisions on "investment," see Emmanuel Gaillard, "Investments and Investors Covered by the Energy Charter Treaty," ch 2 in Clarisse Ribeiro (ed.), *Investment Arbitration and the Energy Charter Treaty*, JurisNet, 2006, pp. 54–73, especially pp. 58–66; and for a study of interpretations of these provisions by ICSID tribunals and others, see Anna Turinov, "'Investment' in Energy Charter Treaty Arbitration: Uncertain Jurisdiction," *Journal of International Arbitration*, Vol. 26, No. 1, 2009, pp. 1–23.

A change in the form in which assets are invested does not affect their character as investments and the term 'Investment' includes all investments, whether existing at or made after the later of the date of entry into force of this Treaty for the Contracting Party of the Investor making the investment and that for the Contracting Party in the Area of which the investment is made (hereinafter referred to as the "Effective Date") provided that the Treaty shall only apply to matters affecting such investments after the Effective Date.

"Investment" refers to any investment associated with an Economic Activity in the Energy Sector and to investments or classes of investments designated by a Contracting Party in its Area as "Charter efficiency projects" and so notified to the Secretariat.[105]

The respondent maintained that the claimant's shareholdings were not associated with an economic activity in the energy sector and therefore were not qualified as investment under the ECT.[106] The claimant, on the other hand, contended that EYUM-10 provided and was still providing qualified construction and maintenance services to the nuclear industry in Ukraine. In other words, because EYUM-10's business was associated with the energy sector, the shares held by the claimant were also energy related, which would qualify such shareholding as investment under the ECT.

In its analysis, the *AMTO* Tribunal determined that the shareholding constituted "a kind of asset owned by the claimant within the definition of the first part of Article 1(6) ECT, and in particular constitute[d] 'shares … in a company or business enterprise' …"[107] It pointed out that an "associated activity … must be energy related, without itself needing to satisfy the definition in Article 1(5) of an Economic Activity in the Energy Sector."[108] To apply the above test to the dispute, the tribunal further stated:

> In the present case, ZAES/Energoatom is engaged in an Economic Activity in the Energy Sector as its activity concerns the production of Energy Material and Products, namely electrical energy. EYUM-10 provides technical services—installation, repair and upgrades—directly related to the production of electrical energy. It has provided these services through multiple contracts over a substantial period of time. … The close association of EYUM-10 with ZAES in the provision of services directly related to energy production means that AMTO's shareholding in EYUM-10 is an "investment associated with an Economic Activity in the Energy Sector."[109]

---

105 The full text of the ECT may be found at the website of the Energy Charter at: http://www.encharter.org/fileadmin/user_upload/document.EN.pdf.
106 *AMTO v. Ukraine, supra*, note 102, §26.
107 Ibid., §42.
108 Id.
109 Ibid., §43.

Consequently, the tribunal found the claimant's shareholding in EYUM-10 to be an investment covered under the ECT.

As illustrated in this review of investment jurisprudence, the definition of investment is of utmost importance because it is the crux on which depends the treatment and protection of presumed investment under the domestic laws of host states and BITs, as well as under such multilateral treaties as the ICSID Convention. Jurisprudence on this issue, as in relation to many other matters, is not consistent; nor is the written jurisprudence of international jurists. On the surface, most of the debates have revolved around Article 25 of the ICSID Convention because it gives no definition of the term "investment," whilst in comparison most BITs do further elaborate the term investment to cover "every kind of asset," etc.

At the same time, it has been reported that "the purpose of Section 1 [of the ICSID Convention] is not to define the circumstances in which recourse to the facilities of the Center would in fact occur, but rather to indicate the outer limits within which the Center would have jurisdiction provided the parties' consent had been attained."[110] Where Section 1 of the ICSID Convention is to "indicate the outer limits" of the ICSID's jurisdiction, there must be certain criteria to regulate what is a covered investment under the Convention and what is not. If the definition of investment were left entirely to the consent of the contracting parties, the issue of "outer limits" would become meaningless. One may ask another question: does the term "investment" have any objective meaning? Or is it subject to any interpretation? For instance, when states negotiate a treaty to protect foreign investment, they must have a shared understanding of the term "investment." Even when the term is further defined as "every kind of asset," would that require some other conditions such as risks, duration, or compliance with the domestic law, to name but a few? The problem is that very few tribunals really analyze or pay attention to the objective meaning of the term "investment" itself.

Even among scholars, no firm consensus has emerged. It is instructive in this regard, however, to note that Schreuer, the so-called "father" of the *Salini* criteria said at the very time he first laid them out in 1996 that: "[t]hese features should not necessarily be understood as *jurisdictional requirements* but merely as *typical characteristics* of investments under the Convention."[111] More recently, he has stated that: "The development in practice from a descriptive list of typical features towards a set of mandatory legal requirements is unfortunate. The First Edition of the Commentary cannot serve as authority for this development."[112]

It is indeed unfortunate that investment tribunals are not in agreement as to what constitutes an investment. At the same time, this development is not surprising, since members of investment tribunals have different cultural backgrounds, legal

---

110 ICSID, *History of the ICSID Convention: Documents Concerning the Origin and the Formulation of the Convention on the Settlement of Investment Disputes between States and Nationals of Other States*, ICSID, Washington, D. C., Volume II-1, p. 566.

111 Schreuer, *supra*, note 2, para. 122 (emphases added).

112 Christoph Schreuer, Loretta Maintoppi, August Reinisch, and Anthony Sinclair, *The ICSID Convention: A Commentary* (2nd ed.), Cambridge University Press, Cambridge, UK, 2009, Art. 25, paras. 171–74.

knowledge from dissimilar jurisdictions, and do not necessarily share common practical experiences. Notwithstanding such dissimilarities, the failure, at least by some tribunals, to pay adequate attention to the intent of the contracting parties is an important cause of this unfortunate state of affairs. For instance, it can hardly be pretended that there are no objective criteria for determining investment. In concluding a BIT or an FTA, the contracting parties must have decided what types of transaction should be protected under the bilateral mechanisms. In this regard, the *Salini* test is reasonable.

II. The double-barreled test and contribution to economic development for qualified investment in ICSID arbitration

The failure effectively to resolve the issue of a generally accepted definition or concept of investment has significantly contributed to another debate—whether or not a transaction must fit into the definition of investment contained in both the BIT in question and any definition that can be attributed to the ICSID Convention, the so-called double-barreled test. Those who support the double-barreled test, as will be seen, most often refer to Schreuer, the *Salini* test (either in its original form or as variously truncated or expanded), and the requirement for an objective definition of "investment" under ICSID Article 25(1). Others tend to quote Broches, the former General Counsel of the World Bank, and place an emphasis on the calculated absence of a definition of "investment" in the Convention and the consequent necessity for a broad, even open-ended interpretation of the concept in that context, with an emphasis on the consent of contracting states as expressed in contracts, BITs, FTAs, and other agreements. Yet both Schreuer and Broches confirmed that there were discussions on the definition of investment at the negotiations of the ICSID Convention and that eventually the parties decided not to include a definition of investment in the Convention.

The double-barreled or twofold test for determining qualification of investment occurs only in relation to ICSID arbitration. Article 25 of the ICSID Convention stipulates that a "legal dispute arising directly out of an investment" is the basis for the jurisdiction of an ICSID arbitral tribunal. Those who support the double-barreled test contend that the jurisdiction of an ICSID arbitral tribunal depends on satisfaction of the requirement in respect of investment under both the ICSID Convention and the BIT in question. The failure to meet either one of these tests would mean that the tribunal would not have jurisdiction to hear the case. Ever since it was first invented by the *Fedax* Tribunal, the "double-barreled" test has been applied in ICSID arbitration, although tribunals have demonstrated a significant degree of difference in the rigor and/or qualifications with which they have done so.

ČSOB v. Slovak Republic[113] is an important case relating to the double-barreled test. What is noteworthy here is that in reaching its decision, the *ČSOB* Tribunal made a sweeping statement on the double-barreled test for determining

---

113 *ČSOB v. Slovak Republic*, *supra*, note 41.

investment. It considered the determination of investment under Article 25(1) of the ICSID Convention to be an objective concept. Hence, the agreement of the parties on what constituted an investment was not "conclusive" for determining the tribunal's jurisdiction under that Article. Disputing parties, it said, "may agree on a more precise or restrictive definition" of investment, thereby indicating the limits of their acceptance of ICSID jurisdiction. In other words, the disputing parties' concept of investment may be narrower than the objective concept of investment under Article 25(1) but may not be broader than the latter; that is, they may not submit disputes to ICSID that are not related to investment as that is understood by the Article.

In deciding the issue of jurisdiction, the *ČSOB* Tribunal asserted that "[a] two-fold test must therefore be applied," under which the following two assessments must be made: "whether the dispute arises out of an investment within the meaning of the Convention and, if so, whether the dispute relates to an investment as defined in the parties' consent to ICSID arbitration, in their reference to the BIT."[114] It should be pointed out that, on the one hand, the tribunal agreed that the drafters of the Convention decided to leave the matter—what may constitute an investment—to the contracting parties, but, on the other hand, it preferred the double-barreled test in making its decision on jurisdiction.

The *Phoenix* Tribunal[115] also adopted the double-barreled test for determining qualified investment and applied it in a manner similar to that of the *ČSOB* Tribunal. In its view:

> … BITs, which are bilateral arrangements between two States parties, cannot contradict the definition of the ICSID Convention. In other words, they can confirm the ICSID notion or restrict it, but they cannot expand it in order to have access to ICSID. A definition included in a BIT being based on a test agreed between two States cannot set aside the definition of the ICSID Convention, which is a multilateral agreement. As long as it fits within the ICSID notion, the BIT definition is acceptable, it is not if it falls outside of such definition.[116]

On the basis of the approach to the "double-barreled" test set forth in *ČSOB* and *Phoenix*, one can almost imagine ICSID tribunals drawing up Venn diagrams to determine what the *Phoenix* Tribunal called "the intersection of the two definitions."[117] On the other hand, some of the most recent ICSID tribunals that have tackled this issue have adopted a somewhat more relaxed (if sometimes no less complex) approach. The first to propose this approach was the *Malicorp* Tribunal.[118]

114 Ibid., para. 68.
115 *Phoenix Action, Ltd. v. Czech Republic*, ICSID Case No. ARB/06/5, Award (April 15, 2009).
116 Ibid., para. 96.
117 Ibid., para. 74.
118 *Malicorp Limited v. Arab Republic of Egypt*, ICSID Case No. ARB/08/18, Award (February 7, 2011).

In November 2000, Malicorp, a UK enterprise, entered into a concession contract with the Government of Egypt for the construction, management, operation, and transfer of the Ras Sudr International Airport. Less than a year later, the contract was terminated by the Egyptian Government. In 2004, after failing to reach agreement on compensation for its alleged losses pursuant to the cancellation of the contract, Malicorp filed for arbitration at the Cairo Regional Centre for International Commercial Arbitration ("CRCICA"). In 2006, the CRCICA arbitral tribunal issued an arbitral award dismissing Malicorp's claims for damages for the loss caused by the termination of the contract but ordering the Government of Egypt to reimburse Malicorp for costs, invoices, and the salaries of its employees. For the next four years, Malicorp attempted unsuccessfully to enforce this award against Egyptian assets in France. During that period, it also filed for ICSID arbitration under the terms of the United Kingdom–Egypt BIT.

One of the issues addressed by the *Malicorp* Tribunal, although it must be noted that it was not raised by either party to the arbitration, was whether or not the dispute to be arbitrated arose "directly out of an investment."[119] In that regard, the tribunal noted that "in order for a proceeding based on breach of a treaty to be admissible, the investment to which the dispute relates must pass a double test (also known as the 'double-keyhole approach' or 'double-barreled test')."[120] The definition of "investment" in the United Kingdom–Egypt BIT, the tribunal found, "does not so much stress the contributions made by the party acting, as the rights and assets that such contributions have generated for it."[121] Nevertheless, as ICSID Article 25(1) contains no definition and, despite the fact that several arbitral tribunals have suggested definitions, the *Malicorp* Tribunal was of the opinion that "[s]uch criteria are not at all absolute and must be regarded as attempts to pin down the notion."[122] In its view, the definition of investment contained in the United Kingdom–Egypt BIT and that applicable to the ICSID Convention looked at "investment" from different perspectives and, therefore, they might not necessarily overlap. In these circumstances, the *Malicorp* Tribunal considered that the notion of investment must be understood from the objectives of the BIT and the ICSID Convention, that is, to promote investment by providing it with legal protection. The tribunal said: "The two aspects are thus complementary. There must be '*active*' economic contributions, as is confirmed by the etymology of the word '*invest*,' but such contributions must '*passively*' have generated the economic assets the instruments are designed to protect."[123] In a way, this conclusion is probably the most balanced approach for determining "investment." The approach taken by the *Malicorp* Tribunal is not only applicable to the double-barreled test but also to the determination of investment in general. However, its position that there is no overlapping in the definition of investment under the

---

119 See ibid., para. 106.
120 Ibid., para. 107 (references omitted).
121 Ibid., para. 108.
122 Ibid., para. 109.
123 Ibid, para. 110 (emphases in original).

BIT and the ICSID Convention is not convincing. After all, BITs in general and the ICSID Convention in particular have been created to promote or encourage foreign investment, whilst their functions differ.

The *Abaclat* Tribunal[124] also observed that a number of ICSID arbitral tribunals had applied the "double-barreled" test, that is, that an investment must satisfy the requirements of both the relevant BIT and the ICSID Convention. Making direct reference to the *Malicorp* Award, however, it likewise held that there are "two different aspects [of an investment]: (i) the contribution that constitutes the investment, and (ii) the rights and the value that derive from that contribution"[125] and, moreover, that "[t]hese two aspects are addressed somewhat differently by the BIT and the ICSID Convention as interpreted by a number of arbitral tribunals."[126] In its view, under the double-barreled test, "the definition of investment provided in the BIT focuses on what is to be protected, that is, the fruits and value generated by the investment, whilst the general definitions developed with regard to Article 25 ICSID Convention focus on the contributions, which constitute the investment and create the fruits and value."[127] The two perspectives—that of the ICSID Convention on "contributions" and that of BITs on "fruits and value"—it held to be "complementary."[128] In the end, in order to satisfy the ICSID jurisdiction *rationae materiae*, it is not necessary "that one definition, namely the definition provided by two Contracting Parties in a BIT, has to fit into the other definition, namely the one deriving from the spirit of the ICSID Convention. Rather, it is the investment at stake that has to fit into both of these concepts, knowing that each of them focuses on another aspect of the investment."[129]

The above tribunals attempted to reconcile the terms of both the ICSID Convention and BITs/FTAs in a "complementary" fashion. They also tried to tackle the issue through a complexity of analysis that goes far beyond the simpler method of applying "criteria" to the "investment" under immediate consideration. It is noteworthy, however, that the president of both the *Malicorp* and *Abaclat* Tribunals was the same person. Other tribunals have demonstrated a large degree of disagreement on the criteria of "investment," in particular on the issue as to whether or not a contribution to the economic development of the host state should be a requirement for qualified investment—one of the most controversial criteria for determining investment.

The importance of the criterion "contribution to the economic development of the host State" is that under the double-barreled test, unless it is established that an investment contributes to the development of the host state, some ICSID tribunals have held that it is not qualified for protection and the tribunal in charge does not have jurisdiction to hear the case. Disputes relating to this issue arose from the

124 *Abaclat and Others v. Argentina, supra*, note 13.
125 Ibid., para. 346.
126 Ibid., para. 347.
127 Ibid., para. 350.
128 Ibid., para. 349.
129 Ibid., para. 351.

preamble of the ICSID Convention, which reads, in relevant part: "Considering the need for international cooperation for economic development, and the role of private international investment therein ...."[130] There is no evidence, however, that contribution to economic development constitutes a criterion for protection pursuant to the ICSID Convention.[131] This criterion emerged in Schreuer's early commentary on the Convention: "The fifth feature [that can be said to be typical of investments in ICSID's experience] is the operation's significance for the host State's *development*. This is not necessarily characteristic of investments in general. But the wording of the Preamble and the Executive Directors' Report suggest that development is part of the Convention's object and purpose."[132] As discussed earlier, this criterion was also considered by both the *Fedax* and *Salini* Tribunals, although in a somewhat peremptory manner.[133] It was the tribunal in *ČSOB v. Slovak Republic*,[134] whose decision on jurisdiction was delivered in between these two cases that first made a more extensive analysis of this criterion.

The *ČSOB* Tribunal first noted that the language of the first paragraph of the preamble to the ICSID Convention "permits an inference that an international transaction which contributes to cooperation designed to promote the economic development of a Contracting State may be deemed to be an investment as that term is understood in the Convention."[135] It then went on to examine whether the loan at issue in the case would make economic contributions to the Slovak Republic. In its view, since the transaction including the loan was meant to improve the financial position of ČSOB, which in turn would conduct business in

130 The preambles of many BITs and FTAs use similar language, employing such phrases as "recognizing the need to promote investment based on the principles of sustainable development" (2012 China–Canada BIT); "recognizing that agreement on the treatment to be accorded such investment will stimulate the flow of private capital and the economic development of the Parties" (2004 US Model BIT); "convinced that sustained inflows of new investments and reinvestments will promote and ensure dynamic development of ASEAN economies" (2008 ASEAN Comprehensive Investment Agreement); and the like. Of course, some of these phrases are more susceptible than others to application of the interpretation that they establish an investment's contribution to the host state's economic development as a criterion of protection.

131 Although it should be noted that the Report of the Executive Directors, *supra*, note 30, at para. 9, did make the comment that: "In submitting the attached Convention to governments, the Executive Directors are prompted by the desire to strengthen the partnership between countries in the cause of economic development."

132 Schreuer, *supra*, note 2, pp. 372–73, para. 122 (cross-reference and footnote omitted; the cross-reference is to the same remark of the Report of the Executive Directors cited ibid.).

133 In *Fedax*, *supra*, note 16, "a significance for the host State's development" is identified as one of the five "basic features of an investment" (at para. 43; presumably what is meant here is "basic features of an investment within the meaning of the ICSID Convention"), but the tribunal's analysis consists of only one line: "[M]ost importantly, there is clearly a significant relationship between the transaction and the development of the host State, as specifically required under the Law for issuing the pertinent financial instrument"(id.). In *Salini*, *supra*, note 32, the tribunal merely noted that "[i]n reading the Convention's preamble, one may add the contribution to the economic development of the host State of the investment as an additional condition" (para. 52) and its analysis consists of one short paragraph of three sentences (para. 57).

134 *ČSOB v. Slovak Republic*, Decision on Jurisdiction, *supra*, note 41.

135 Ibid., para. 64.

the Slovak Republic by, inter alia, creating a subsidiary there with ČSOB holding less than 50 percent of the shares, it would contribute to the economic development of the state. Therefore, the transaction had satisfied the requirements of investment under the ICSID Convention.[136] The tribunal also pointed out that: "the broad meaning which must be given to the notion of investment under the ICSID Convention is opposed to the conclusion that a transaction is not an investment merely because, as a matter of law, it is a loan. This is so, if only because under certain circumstances a loan may contribute substantially to a State's economic development."[137]

The *L.E.S.I.–DIPENTA* Tribunal, on the other hand, firmly rejected contribution to economic development as a useful criterion for determining investment. In its view, "it is not necessary that the investment contribute more specifically to the host country's economic development, something that is difficult to ascertain and that is implicitly covered by the other three criteria [contribution, duration and risk]."[138]

The *Patrick Mitchell v. DRC* case[139] involved a considerably detailed analysis of the importance of an investment's contribution to the economic development of the host state, at least on the part of the *ad hoc* Committee that eventually annulled the original award. The claimant, Patrick Mitchell, was a US lawyer who had set up an office in the Democratic Republic of Congo. He claimed that the respondent had expropriated his investment—the law firm—by forcing the closure of the firm and imprisoning two of its lawyers. The respondent objected to the tribunal's jurisdiction on the sole ground that the claimant's activity in the DRC did not qualify as an investment.[140] In particular, it maintained that the claimant's "activity does not constitute a long-term operation nor is it materialized by a significant contribution of resources, and that it is not of such importance for the State's economy that it distinguishes itself from an ordinary commercial transaction."[141] The tribunal, however, noted:

> These elements, while they are frequently present in investment projects, are not a formal requirement for the finding that a particular activity or transaction constitutes an investment. Such a concept, as long as it is not supplemented by the appropriate restrictions, does equally include, under the ICSID Convention, and, as demonstrated, under the BIT, "smaller" investments of shorter duration and with more limited benefit to the host State's economy.[142]

---

136 Ibid., paras. 78–89.
137 Ibid., para. 76.
138 *L.E.S.I.–DIPENTA v. Algeria, supra,* note 95, para. II.13(iv).
139 *Patrick Mitchell v. Democratic Republic of Congo,* ICSID Case No. ARB/99/7, Award (February 4, 2004); Decision on Annulment (November 1, 2006).
140 *Patrick Mitchell,* Award, ibid., para. 32.
141 Ibid., para. 56.
142 Id.

On this basis, the tribunal held that Mitchell's law firm was an investment and ultimately supported the claims made by the claimant. The respondent state then requested to have the award annulled.

Before the *ad hoc* Committee—faced with the challenge of the original arbitral decision on grounds that the tribunal had committed a manifest excess of powers and had failed to state reasons for its conclusions—one of the central issues was whether the setting up and operation of the law firm by the claimant constituted an investment. For a transaction to be a qualified investment, the respondent considered a contribution to the economic development of the state to be an "essential element;" the claimant only regarded it as a supplementary condition to justify the broadening of the concept of investment.

The *ad hoc* Committee first opined that the need for international cooperation for economic development and the role of private international investment referred to in the preamble of the ICSID Convention, as basic principles, imbue the provisions of the Convention, including Article 25.[143] With this in mind, it considered that the contribution of foreign investment to economic development had "always been taken into account, explicitly or implicitly, by ICSID arbitral tribunals in the context of their reasoning … and quite independently from any provisions of agreements between parties or the relevant bilateral treaty."[144] In other words, regardless of the agreements entered into by the contracting parties to BITs, in order to have their disputes with an investor from the other party arbitrated at the ICSID, the underlying transaction must be able to contribute to the economic development of the host state.[145] In this particular case, the *ad hoc* Committee also drew support for its undertaking to treat "contribution to the economic development of the host State" as a criterion of investment from the fact that the DRC–United States BIT stipulates in its preamble that "investment will stimulate the flow of private capital and the economic development of both Parties."[146]

In the end, the *ad hoc* Committee annulled the original award on the grounds of the tribunal's failure to state reasons why Mitchell's law firm could be considered an investment and manifest excess of power in assuming jurisdiction in the case. It appears to have done so largely because the original tribunal had not carried out as extensive an analysis of Mitchell's firm's contribution to the DRC's economic development as the Committee would have liked. It dismissed

---

143 *Patrick Mitchell v. DRC*, Decision on Annulment, *supra*, note 139, para. 28.

144 Ibid., para. 29.

145 In its analysis, the *ad hoc* Committee referred to the decisions in *Salini*, *Fedax*, and *ČSOB*. Regarding *Salini*, the Committee said that it explicitly set economic development as a criterion. It quoted the *Fedax* Tribunal's finding that the promissory notes in that case served a fundamental public interest and that there was "clearly a significant relationship between the transaction and the development of the host State" and the *ČSOB* Tribunal's assertion that "a loan may contribute substantially to a State's economic development." It should also be noted, however, that the *ad hoc* Committee also inaccurately cited Schreuer as considering "the contribution to the economic development of the host State as 'the only possible indication of an objective meaning' of the term 'investment'."See ibid., para. 30, and para. 31, citing Schreuer, *supra*, note 2, at p. 124.

146 Ibid., para. 32.

the tribunal's preference for a broad interpretation of investment and its rejection of "formal requirements" as resulting in an award that was "incomplete and obscure as regards what it considers an investment: it refers to various fragments of the operation, without finally indicating the reasons why it regards it overall as an investment, that is, without providing the slightest explanation as to the relationship between the 'Mitchell & Associates' firm and the DRC."[147]

Yet the *ad hoc* Committee's own reasoning seems to break down at several points. The Committee nowhere defines "economic development" and, in fact, at least once seems to confuse or conflate that concept with a contribution to "the interests of the State."[148] It even seems to confuse evidence of a contribution to the host state's economic development with a given economic transaction's direct relationship with some agency of the host state itself.[149] In all fairness, it should be noted that even though the *ad hoc* Committee considered a contribution to economic development to be an essential characteristic or "unquestionable criterion" of investment, it also said that such contribution does not have to be "sizable or successful."[150]

Probably the most well known and controversial case to address the issue of "contribution to the host state's economic development" as a criterion of qualified investment is *Malaysian Historical Salvors*.[151] In that case, the claimant—Malaysian Historical Salvors Sdn Bhd—was a marine salvage company which entered into a contract with the respondent that called for, inter alia, the claimant's location and salvage of the cargo of the "*Diana*," a British vessel that sank off the coast of Malacca in 1817.[152] The claimant's obligation under the contract included "to utilize its expertise, labour and equipment to carry out the salvage operation, and to invest and expend its own financial and other resources, and assume all risks of the salvage operation, financial and otherwise."[153] Upon the success of the salvage operation, according to the contract, the recovered items would be auctioned and the proceeds would be divided between the claimant and the respondent, based on a formula specified therein.[154]

A dispute arose over distribution of the proceeds of the eventual auction of the recovered items, and the claimant commenced arbitration proceedings in Kuala Lumpur, where its claim was dismissed by the arbitrator. The claimant then challenged the arbitration award in a Malaysian court, which was alleged to have dismissed the petition without hearing the case. The claimant then invoked the ICSID arbitration provisions in the Malaysia–United Kingdom BIT, claiming that it had been denied fundamental and rudimentary due process in the

---

147 Ibid., para. 40.
148 Ibid., para. 39.
149 See ibid., paras. 30 and 31.
150 Ibid., para. 33.
151 *Malaysian Historical Salvors*, Award, *supra*, note 40; and *Malaysian Historical Salvors*, Annulment Decision, *supra*, note 53.
152 *Malaysian Historical Salvors*, Award, ibid., para. 7.
153 Ibid., para. 8.
154 Ibid., paras. 10–11.

Malaysian courts—a violation of the BIT. The question facing the sole arbitrator of the ICSID tribunal was whether the salvage contract constituted an investment.

As a threshold issue, the tribunal considered that the claimant had an obligation to prove that its transaction fell within the definitions of investment contained in Article 25(1) of the ISCID Convention and the BIT.[155] At the same time, it indicated that the word "investment" embodied in Article 25 should be interpreted as "to encourage, facilitate and to promote cross-border economic cooperation and development."[156] After examining a number of ICSID cases in which the tribunals applied the *Salini* test for the determination of investment, the *Malaysian Historical Salvors* Tribunal concluded that the "weight of the authorities" swung in favor of "requiring a significant contribution to be made to the host State's economy" as a condition for determining the existence of an investment.[157]

Because the tribunal considered that the claimant's contract with the respondent was not a "readily recognizable" investment,[158] it placed considerable emphasis on the question of its contribution to the local economy. It considered that the claimant's contract "did not benefit the Malaysian public interest in a material way or serve to benefit the Malaysian economy in the sense developed by ICSID jurisprudence, namely that the contributions were significant."[159] As such, the tribunal concluded that the contract did not make "a sufficient contribution to Malaysia's economic development to qualify as an 'investment' for the purposes of Article 25(1) or Article 1(a) of the BIT."[160] In fact, it went even further, saying that "the Tribunal concludes that there was no substantial contribution [made by the claimant] because the nature of the benefits that the contract offered to Malaysia did not provide substantial benefits in the sense envisaged in previous ICISD jurisprudence."[161] Hence, it dismissed the case for lack of jurisdiction. What is particularly striking is that in its analysis the tribunal did not consider, except in a brief mention, the BIT's provisions on the definition of investment and its impact on the decision. This became the ground for the claimant to challenge the award—that the tribunal had manifestly exceeded its powers by failing to exercise jurisdiction.

The *ad hoc* Committee was divided in its decision on annulment. The majority of the Committee was very critical of the views expressed in the award, in particular with regard to the issue of contribution to the economic development of the host state as a condition of jurisdiction. According to the *ad hoc* Committee, the claimant's contract was an investment under the BIT because it was "one of a kind of asset" and "a claim to money."[162] The *ad hoc* Committee annulled the award because the tribunal failed to take account of and apply the BIT, elevated

155 Ibid., para. 43.
156 Ibid., para. 66.
157 Ibid., para. 123.
158 Ibid., para. 129.
159 Ibid., para. 131.
160 Ibid., para. 143.
161 Id.
162 *Malaysian Historical Salvors*, Annulment Decision, *supra*, note 53, para. 60.

the *Salini* test—in particular the criterion of "a contribution to the economic development of the host State"—to the level of establishing conditions for jurisdiction, and failed to take account of the *travaux préparatoires* of the ICSID Convention relating to the decision to leave "investment" undefined.[163]

In its analysis, the *ad hoc* Committee, after visiting the *travaux*—including the explanation given by Broches[164]—stated that "[g]iven that the ICSID Convention was not drafted with a strict, objective, definition of 'investment', it is doubtful that arbitral tribunals sitting in individual cases should impose one such definition which would be applicable in all cases and for all purposes."[165] It therefore favored a more flexible and pragmatic approach in defining investment.

This position of the majority of the *ad hoc* Committee did not receive the approval of Judge Mohamed Shahabuddeen, the third member of the Committee. The main difference between Judge Shahabuddeen and the majority is whether a contribution to the economic development of the host state should be "a condition of an ICSID 'investment'."[166] In his dissenting opinion, the judge said that: "[i]t is possible to conceive of an entity which is systematically earning its wealth at the expense of the development of the host State. However much that may collide with a prospect of development of the host State, it would not breach a condition – on the argument of the Applicant."[167] Clearly, Judge Shahabuddeen's dissent favors the double-barreled approach, according to which, regardless of the definition of investment under a BIT, the transaction at issue must also fall within the definition of investment in Article 25 of the ICSID Convention in order to avail of its dispute settlement mechanisms.[168] Equally, the dissenting opinion regards a "substantial" or "significant" contribution to the host state's economic development to be a compulsory element of investment and hence a condition of the ICSID's jurisdiction.[169] The question is why tribunals and learned experts on the same Committee differ on such an important issue.[170]

It can actually be detected that the *ad hoc* Committee was sympathetic to the claimant, who, in its view, made a genuine investment but, when being wronged, could not have recourse to any remedies. In this regard, the Committee stated that "unlike some other BITs, no third party dispute settlement options are provided in the alternative to ICSID. It follows that, if jurisdiction is found to be absent under the ICSID Convention, the investor is left without international recourse altogether."[171] It is certainly unfortunate that a foreign investor should have no

163 Ibid., para. 80.
164 See *supra*, note 29.
165 *Malaysian Historical Salvors*, Annulment Decision, *supra*, note 53, para. 79.
166 *Malaysian Historical Salvors v. Malaysia*, ICSID Case No. ARB/05/10, Dissenting Opinion of Judge Shahabuddeen (April 16, 2009), para. 2.
167 Ibid., para. 22.
168 See ibid., paras. 40–47, especially para. 42.
169 See ibid., paras. 33–38 and, especially, para. 65.
170 For one thought-provoking explanation of this phenomenon, see Nitish Monebhurrun, "The Political Use of the Economic Development Criterion in Defining Investments in International Investment Arbitration," *Journal of International Arbitration*, Vol. 29, No. 5, 2012, pp. 567–80.
171 *Malaysian Historical Salvors*, Annulment Decision, *supra*, note 53, para. 62.

access to international remedies. Yet this should not be a reason for the ICSID or other arbitral institutions to step up to provide such remedies unless there are other legal grounds for doing so.

In the *Phoenix* case,[172] the tribunal proposed a simpler economic criterion, that is, that investment must be an operation made in order to develop an economic activity in the host state. In that case, after actions were taken by the Czech Republic against two Czech companies owned by the claimant—a Czech citizen—he fled to Israel, founded a company there and then used that company to purchase the two Czech companies he had previously owned. Before the investment was made, the operations of the two Czech companies had already been terminated for a period of time. The question was whether or not the transaction carried out by the claimant constituted a qualified investment.

The *Phoenix* Tribunal assessed the question of qualified investments— investments under the protection of the ICSID Convention and BITs—first from the object of the ICSID Convention, which is "to encourage and protect international investment made for the purpose of contributing to the economy of the host State."[173] In its analysis, the *Phoenix* Tribunal adopted the position of the tribunal in *Sedelmayer v. Russian Federation* that: "investments are made within the frame of a commercial activity and that investments are, in principle, aiming at creating a further economic value."[174] It stated that as an investment qualified for protection under the BIT and the ICSID Convention, the development of economic activities relating thereto "must have been foreseen or intended, but need not necessarily be successful … otherwise the international protection of foreign investment provided by the BITs would be emptied of its purpose."[175] Yet the claimant had notified the Czech Government of its disputes "even *before the registration of its ownership* of the two Czech companies in the Czech Republic and a mere *two months*" thereafter instituted the ICSID arbitration.[176] Based on these facts, and because virtually "no economic activity in the market place was either performed or even intended" by the claimant, the tribunal concluded that the so-called investment by the claimant was "simply a rearrangement of assets within a family, to gain access to ICSID jurisdiction to which the initial investor was not entitled."[177] It should be noted that the *Phoenix* Tribunal also explicitly stated that the purchase of a bankrupt or inactive company may not necessarily be disqualified as an invest-

---

172 *Phoenix, supra*, note 115, para. 114.

173 Ibid., para. 87, noting that it was observed by the Report of the Executive Directors, *supra*, note 30, at para. 12, that: "… adherence to the Convention by a country would provide additional inducement and stimulate a larger flow of private *international investment* into its territories, which is *the primary purpose* of the Convention" (emphases added by the tribunal).

174 *Sedelmayer v. Russian Federation* (Germany–Union of the Soviet Socialist Republics BIT), *ad hoc* arbitration under the Stockholm Chamber of Commerce arbitration rules, Award (July 7, 1998), para. 224.

175 *Phoenix v. Czech Republic, supra*, note 115, para. 133.

176 Ibid., para. 138 (emphases in original).

177 Ibid., para. 140. The tribunal further commented that "[n]o business plan, no program of re-financing, no economic objectives were ever presented, no real valuation of the economic transactions were ever attempted" by the claimant; id.

ment, providing that there is an intention to make a profit.[178] Its decision was thus based purely on the fact that the transaction carried out by the claimant was not a *bona fide* investment.[179] Therefore, the tribunal held that it had no jurisdiction over the case under the ICSID Convention.[180]

It is unfortunate that arbitration tribunals are so divided in relation to the definition of investment in this regard. The cases examined above show that the main difference between scholars and tribunals is essentially the same as that between the majority view and the dissenting opinion in the *Malaysian Historical Salvors* annulment—whether or not an ICSID investment must make a contribution to the host state's economic development.[181] This goes to the heart of the purpose of foreign investment from the viewpoint of the host state.[182] It can hardly be said that any country would encourage a foreign investment—a general purpose of most BITs—unless there is a local need or it is expected to contribute to the local economy. On the other hand, as some scholars and tribunals have maintained, economic development and any contribution thereto are difficult to define or identify,[183] and the concept seems rarely to be applied to any definition of investment outside ICSID arbitration. The fact that "contribution to the economy of the host State" as an element of investment may be difficult to ascertain cannot, however, be a valid reason to refuse it as a criterion for qualifying protectable investment. In practice, it may not cause as much difficulty as it may seem. Where an investment is made with the approval, implicit or explicit, of the host state, it should be assumed that it can contribute to the local economy. The host state should then be estopped from arguing, later on, that the investment has failed the requirement of contributing to the local economy. The question is the objective and purpose of the ICSID Convention and whether the provisions of its preamble should be given legal force. There is no reason, according to Articles 31 and 32 of the VCLT, not to recognize the legal force of a preamble of a treaty, including that of the ICSID Convention.

---

178 Id.
179 For more discussion on this aspect of the case, see later in this chapter, Section III.A.
180 *Phoenix v. Czech Republic, supra*, note 115, para. VIII.1.
181 In *Victor Pey Casado, supra*, note 79, it was held that although there was a definition of investment under Article 25 of the ICSID Convention, there was no evidence to indicate any characteristic of an investment that could determine the jurisdiction of ICSID tribunals. This would include the contribution to the host state's economic development.
182 UNCTAD considers that the difference in the treatment of a requirement that "investment" under the ICSID Convention must make a contribution to local economic development is the result of two differing approaches to investment law; one regards it as a law of investment protection, pure and simple; and the other treats it as a law of international economic cooperation, in which the interests of both foreign investors and host states should be taken into account. See UNCTAD, "Scope and Definition," *supra*, note 1, p. 65.
183 See, for example, Joseph M. Boddicker, "Whose Dictionary Rules? Recent Challenges to the Term 'Investment' in ICSID Arbitration," 25 *Am. U. Int'l L. Rev.* 1031, 2010, at 1054–55: "Economic development is a nebulous concept, one that is not readily quantifiable and, moreover, is subject to divergent viewpoints" (footnote omitted); and *L.E.S.I.–DIPENTA v. Algeria, supra*, note 95, para. II.13(iv): "…economic development [is] something that is difficult to ascertain."

III. Additional criteria for qualified investments

BITs and FTAs sometimes stipulate other prerequisites for protection of investments, such as that the investment must be made in accordance with laws of the host state. In practice, tribunals have also developed other criteria in determining whether an investment is qualified for protection. These criteria, unlike "contribution to economic development," which has led to tremendous controversies, are not based on the ICSID Convention. Therefore, the outcome of these cases, insofar as determination of qualified investment is concerned, is not dependent on whether the tribunals adopted the double-barreled test, even though in some cases—the *Phoenix* case being one—both "contribution to economic development" and other criteria were considered by the tribunals.

A. Investments made in compliance with law and in good faith ("bona fide")

One of the often raised issues related to "qualified investment" is whether or not such investment is made in accordance with the laws of the host state in cases where the applicable BIT or FTA contains such a requirement. Where a BIT or FTA is silent on the requirement of compliance with local law, is an investment made in violation of local laws or international law principles qualified for protection under the BIT in question under such multilateral mechanisms as the ICSID? For purposes of demonstrating sovereignty, developing countries often insist on stipulating in their BITs that qualifying investments must be made in compliance with the laws of the host state. As will be discussed below, most of China's first-generation BITs contain such requirements. Another example is Article 1(9) of the Investment Agreement for the Common Market for Eastern and Southern Africa (COMESA) Common Investment Area (2007),[184] which provides that "'investment' means assets admitted or admissible in accordance with the relevant laws and regulations of the COMESA Member State in whose territory the investment is made." The effect of such provisions, as the jurisprudence shows, may disqualify the related investment for the protection of BITs and multilateral instruments.[185]

The ASEAN countries took a different approach. In their Comprehensive Investment Agreement (2009), the term "covered investment" is defined, with respect to a Member state, as "an investment in its territory of an investor of any other Member state in existence as of the date of entry into force of this Agreement or established, acquired or expanded thereafter, and has been admitted according to its laws, regulations, and national policies, and where applicable, specifically approved in writing by the competent authority of a Member State." The effect

---

184 For the full text of the COMESA Investment Agreement, see: http://vi.unctad.org/files/wksp/iiawksp08/docs/wednesday/Exercise%20Materials/invagreecomesa.pdf.
185 The *Phoenix* Tribunal, for instance, stated that when considering the validity of an investment, "the laws in force at the moment of the establishment of the investment" must be taken into account. See *Phoenix v. Czech Republic, supra*, note 115, para. 103.

of having a separate provision on the requirement of local law is to emphasize the importance of such requirement. With such provisions, foreign investors are presumed to have been informed of the requirement. The host state respondent in arbitration proceedings would be in a better position to defend its case.

The Convention Establishing the Multilateral Investment Guarantee Agency ("MIGA") also provides that: "[i]n guaranteeing an investment, the Agency shall satisfy itself as to: ... (ii) compliance of the investment with the host country's laws and regulations; (iii) consistency of the investment with the declared development objectives and priorities of the host country."[186] The MIGA is an inter-governmental organization with sovereign states as contracting parties whose purpose is the encouragement of the flow of private capital to the developing countries. Its emphasis on the requirement that foreign investors must observe the local laws of host states in making investments, on the one hand, reflects the position of developing countries and, on the other hand, helps its activities as an investment insurer. Once an investment certificate is issued, it is assumed that the investment can contribute to the development of the host state.

Despite all of the above, it cannot be concluded that a requirement that investment be made in compliance with local law is a common trend of modern BITs. Some BITs and FTAs, such as those entered into by China recently, do not contain such a requirement.

The *Fraport* case[187] involved the Germany–Philippines BIT, according to which the term investment meant any kind of asset "recognized by the respective laws and regulations of either Contracting State" and "in accordance with its Constitution, laws and regulations."[188] The Philippines has a so-called Anti-Dummy Law that restrains the roles of foreign shareholders and management in public enterprises. Fraport, the claimant, intentionally evaded this law by means of secret shareholder agreements. In the tribunal's view, there could be both de facto and de jure investment, but only the latter was entitled to BIT protection. Owing to the secret shareholder agreements that were specifically intended to circumvent the Philippines' Anti-Dummy Law, Fraport could not claim to have made an investment "in accordance with law" nor claim that officials of the respondent subsequently had waived the legal requirements and validated its investment, because the respondent's officials could not have known of the violation. Because there was no "investment in accordance with law," the investment could not enjoy the protection of the BIT.[189] The tribunal attached much importance to the principle of good faith and extended the application of Article 26 of the VCLT, which provides that "every treaty in force is binding upon the parties

---

186 See Article 12(d) of the Convention Establishing the Multilateral Investment Guarantee Agency. The full text of the Convention is available at: http://www.finance.gov.lb/en-US/finance/InvestmentTaxAgreements/Documents/Multilateral%20Investments%20related%20Agreements/MIGA%20convention.PDF.
187 *Fraport AG Frankfurt Airport Services Worldwide v. Republic of the Philippines*, ICSID Case No. ARB/03/25, Award (August 16, 2007).
188 Germany–Philippines BIT, Article 1(1).
189 *Fraport, supra*, note 187, para. 401.

to it and must be performed by them in good faith."[190] In other words, based on the principle of good faith, the contracting parties to a BIT are obliged to protect only lawful investment, not investment made by fraud.[191]

The tribunal held that "[i]n summary, Fraport had been fully advised and was fully aware of the ADL [Anti-Dummy Law] and the incompatibility with the ADL of the structure of its investment which it planned and ultimately put into place with the secret shareholder agreements."[192] Based on the fact that the foreign investor knowingly made an investment not "in accordance" with local law, the *Fraport* Tribunal decided not to have recourse to the interpretative technique that relies upon the objects and purposes of treaties to offer protection to the foreign investor. In its view:

> It is also clear that the parties were anxious to encourage investments, which are the *raison d'être* of the treaty. But while a treaty should be interpreted in the light of its objects and purposes, it would be a violation of all the canons of interpretation to pretend to use its objects and purposes, which are, by their nature, a deduction on the part of the interpreter, to nullify four explicit provisions. Plainly, as indicated by these four provisions, economic transactions undertaken by a national of one of the parties to the BIT had to meet certain legal requirements of the host state in order to qualify as an "investment" and fall under the Treaty.[193]

The tribunal hence ruled that the ICSID had no jurisdiction over the dispute because the Philippines' consent for ICSID arbitration was conditioned on an investment being valid according to the BIT.

In the *Fraport* case, in denying jurisdiction the tribunal stated that it had to ascertain for itself whether for the purpose of its jurisdiction the investment at issue was a protected investment. In its view:

> With respect to a bilateral investment treaty that defines "investment", it is possible that an economic transaction that might qualify *factually and financially*

---

190 The claimant later filed annulment proceedings with the ICSID, and the *ad hoc* Committee decided on December 23, 2010 to annul the tribunal's award on the grounds that the tribunal had relied on "new" material (i.e. material not presented during the course of the arbitral proceedings) in reaching its decision and had committed "a serious departure from the fundamental rule of procedure entitling the parties to be heard." See *Fraport A.G. Frankfurt Airport Services Worldwide v. Republic of the Philippines*, ICSID Case No. ARB/03/25, Decision on the Application for Annulment (December 17, 2010), paras. 180–247.

191 Certainly, the principle of good faith is also a general principle of international law. Article 16 of the VCLT simply specified it and reflected customary international law.

192 *Fraport*, Award, *supra*, note 187, para. 327.

193 Ibid., para. 340. The *Fraport* Tribunal was obviously convinced by the evidence introduced by the foreign investor itself, holding that "[e]ven assuming, however, that the 'preponderance of evidence' test which applies in civil law must yield in the instant case to a 'beyond a reasonable doubt' test because the subject of the 'in accordance' inquiry is a Philippine criminal statute, this is a case in which *res ipsa loquitur*. The relevant facts, all of which are found in Fraport's own documents, are incontrovertible." Ibid., para. 399.

as an investment (i.e., be comprised of capital imported by a foreign entity into the economy of another state which is party to a BIT), falls, nonetheless, outside the jurisdiction of the tribunal established under the pertinent BIT, because *legally* it is not an "investment" within the meaning of the BIT. This will occur when the transaction that might otherwise qualify as an 'investment' fails *ratione temporis*, as occurred in *Empresa Lucchetti S.A. et al v. Republic of Peru*, or fails *ratione personae*, as occurred in *Soufraki v. The United Arab Emirates*. It will also occur when the transaction fails to qualify *ratione materiae*, as occurred in *Inceysa Vallisoletana, S.L. v. Republic of El Salvador*.[194]

The tribunal finally denied jurisdiction with the following statement: "Fraport was consciously, intentionally and covertly structuring its investment in a way which it knew to be a violation of the ADL [Anti-Dummy Law]."[195]

In the more recent case of *Fakes v. Turkey*,[196] discussed in some detail above, in addition to the three definitive elements of investment—contribution, duration and risk—the tribunal regarded the satisfaction of the legality requirement—compliance with the laws of the host state—contained in the BIT as a condition to the consent of the parties.[197] At the same time, the tribunal considered that not every violation of the host state laws "would result in the illegality of the investment."[198] In its view, the domestic law requirement only concerned the admission of investment; once an investment was established, where a foreign investment violates other domestic laws "that are unrelated to the very nature of investment regulation," the host state concerned should take other measures against such violation rather than denying the substantive protection of the foreign investment by declaring that the investment is illegal.[199]

In a similar vein, a number of tribunals have addressed the issue of "good faith" in determining "qualified investment." One of these was the tribunal in *Inceysa v. El Salvador*,[200] which held that in order for an investment to benefit from the BIT, it must be made in good faith, which in the tribunal's view is generally recognized as a general principle of law: "Good faith is a supreme principle, which governs legal relations in all their aspects and content … El Salvador gave its consent to the jurisdiction of the Centre, presupposing good faith behavior on the part of future investors."[201] Because the tribunal found that the claimant had violated the principle of good faith from the time that it made the investment, it considered that the investment was not made in accordance with the laws of the host state

194 Ibid., para. 306 (emphases in original).
195 Ibid., para. 323.
196 *Fakes v. Turkey, supra*, note 87.
197 Ibid., para. 121.
198 Ibid., para. 119.
199 Id.
200 *Inceysa Vallisoletana, S.L. v. Republic of El Salvador*, ICSID Case No. ARB/03/26, Award [on Jurisdiction] (August 2, 2006).
201 Ibid., para. 230.

and hence it had no jurisdiction over the case.[202] It also viewed the violation of the national principle of good faith to constitute a violation of international public policy and held: "It is not possible to recognize the existence of rights arising from illegal acts, because it would violate the respect for the law which … is a principle of international public policy."[203]

A similar position was also adopted in the *Plama* case,[204] where the tribunal was faced with the silence of the relevant treaty on the necessary conformity of a protected investment with the laws of the host country. This did not prevent it from considering that this condition had to be implied:

> Unlike a number of Bilateral Investment Treaties, the ECT [Energy Charter Treaty] does not contain a provision requiring the conformity of the Investment with a particular law. This does not mean, however, that the protections provided for by the ECT cover all kinds of investments, including those contrary to domestic or international law … The Arbitral Tribunal concludes that the substantive protections of the ECT cannot apply to investments that are made contrary to law.[205]

In *Plama*, the tribunal found good faith to be a principle of Bulgarian law and that the deceitful conduct of the claimant in making the investment was not only a violation of the law of the host state but "would also be contrary to the basic notion of international public policy – that a contract obtained through wrongful means (fraudulent misrepresentation) should not be enforced by a tribunal."[206]

In the *Phoenix* case, the tribunal proposed these additional criteria to determine whether or not a transaction constitutes a qualified investment: (1) assets invested in accordance with the laws of the host state; and (2) assets invested *bona fide*.[207] The factual background of this case, discussed previously, led the tribunal to propose these additional criteria. As the purpose of the ICSID Convention is to encourage private international investment or investments from foreign countries, the *Phoenix* Tribunal considered that "a national investment cannot give rise to ICSID arbitration, which is reserved to international investments and that an invalid ICSID clause signed by a national cannot be transformed into a valid ICSID clause by assignment to a foreign investor."[208] At the same time, the *Phoenix* Tribunal held that where a transaction is undertaken "with *the sole purpose* of taking advantage of the rights contained in" an instrument, it would not be qualified for protection under the ICSID and BITs.

It should be noted that the transaction carried out by the claimant was not in

---

202 Ibid., para. 243.
203 Ibid., para. 249.
204 *Plama Consortium Limited v. Republic of Bulgaria*, ICSID Case No. ARB/03/24 (Energy Charter Treaty), Award (August 27, 2008).
205 Ibid., paras. 138–39.
206 Ibid., paras. 143–44.
207 *Phoenix v. Czech Republic, supra*, note 115, para. 114.
208 Ibid., para. 89.

violation of any laws of the Czech Republic. The basis of the tribunal's decision was that what the claimant had done was in violation of the principle of good faith. In this respect, it held that the *Phoenix* case was distinguishable from the *Tokios Tokelės* case.[209]

In its analysis of the application of the principle of good faith, the *Phoenix* Tribunal emphasized that the ICSID Convention and the BIT in question must be read within the requirements of general international law, "such as the principle of non-retroactivity or the principle of *good faith*."[210] It quoted Pauwelyn, who had stated that:

> States in their treaty relations, can contract out of one, more or in theory, all rules of general international law (other than those of *jus cogens*), but they cannot contract out of the system of international law. As soon as States contract with one another, they do so automatically and necessarily within the system of international law.[211]

This approach had the support of the very first case decided by the World Trade Organization ("WTO") Appellate Body, which was also cited by the *Phoenix* Tribunal.[212] Having laid down the basis for its decision, the *Phoenix* Tribunal, most probably for the first time in the history of investor–state arbitration, stated that investment made in violation of the fundamental principles of international law would not confer jurisdiction to the tribunals.[213]

In *Phoenix*, the tribunal also considered that a qualified investment must be made not only in compliance with the laws of the host state but also with the principles of international law. Specifically, the *Phoenix* Tribunal stated that: "States cannot be deemed to offer access to the ICSID dispute settlement mechanism to investments made in violation of their laws."[214]

209 Ibid., paras. 94 and 95. The tribunal noted that the *Tokios Tokelės* Tribunal (see *Tokios Tokelės v. Ukraine*, ICSID Case No. ARB/02/18, Decision on Jurisdiction, 29 April 2004) found no abuse of procedure in the claimant's performance in that case. It further held that: "International investors can of course structure *upstream* their investments [as Tokios Tokelės did,] ... [b]ut on the other side, an international investor cannot modify *downstream* the protection granted to its investment by the host State, once the acts which the investor considers are causing damages to its investment have already been committed [as Phoenix was attempting to do]." Id. (emphases in original). In the present case, it considered that to accept jurisdiction "would go against the basic objectives underlying the ICSID Convention as well as those of bilateral investment treaties;" ibid., para. 144.
210 Ibid., para. 77 (emphasis in original).
211 Id., citing Jost Pauwelyn, "Role of Public International Law in the WTO Law," 95 *AJIL* 535, 2001, at 539.
212 *United States – Standards for Reformulated and Conventional Gasoline*, WT/DS2/AB/R, Appellate Body Report (April 29, 1996), in which (at p.18) the AB stated that "The General Agreement is not to be read in clinical isolation from public international law."
213 *Phoenix v. Czech Republic, supra*, note 115, para. 78. The tribunal stated that "the ICSID Convention's jurisdictional requirements – as well as those of the BIT – cannot be read and interpreted in isolation from public international law, and its general principles;" id.
214 Ibid., para. 101. According to the *Phoenix* Tribunal: "If a State, for example, restricts foreign

Insofar as international law principles are concerned, the *Phoenix* Tribunal considered "good faith" to be a principle that "has long been recognized in public international law, as it is also in all national legal systems."[215] It further elaborated the contents of the principle of good faith by relying on D'Amato, who said that it required parties "to deal honestly and fairly with each other, to represent their motives and purposes truthfully, and to refrain from taking unfair advantage."[216] As an international law principle, would the principle of good faith apply to investor–state disputes? The *Phoenix* Tribunal had no difficulty in determining the applicability of the principle. In its view:

> This principle governs the relations between States, but also the legal rights and duties of those seeking to assert an international claim under a treaty. Nobody shall abuse the rights granted by treaties, and more generally, every rule of law includes an implied clause that it should not be abused.[217]

This holding was in line with the much earlier decision in the *Amco Asia* case, in which the tribunal stated, inter alia, that:

> ... like any other conventions, a convention to arbitrate is not to be construed *restrictively*, nor, as a matter of fact, *broadly or liberally*. It is to be construed in a way which leads to find out and to respect the common will of the parties ... Moreover – and this is again a general principle of law – any convention, including conventions to arbitrate, should be construed in good faith, that is to say by taking into account the consequences of their commitments the parties may be considered as having reasonably and legitimately envisaged.[218]

In fact, the *Phoenix* Tribunal even considered that the silence of a treaty on the principle of good faith should not stop tribunals from adopting it. On this matter, the *Phoenix* Tribunal's position was shared by the *Salini* Tribunal, which considered that it was its duty to "prevent the BIT from protecting investments that should not be protected, particularly because they would be illegal."[219]

An important feature of the above cases is that they all took the dual violation approach, according to which a violation of the national principle of good faith would constitute a violation of international law. In essence, this approach regards

investment in a sector of its economy and a foreign investor disregards such restriction, the investment concerned cannot be protected under the ICSID/BIT system. These are illegal investments according to the national law of the host State and cannot be protected through an ICSID arbitral process." Id.

215 Ibid., para. 107.
216 Id., citing A. D'Amato, "Good Faith," in R. Bernhardt (ed.), *Encyclopedia of Public International Law*, Vol. 7, North-Holland, 1984, Amsterdam, p. 107.
217 Id.
218 *Amco Asia v. Indonesia, supra*, note 67, para. 14 (emphases in original).
219 *Phoenix v. Czech Republic, supra*, note 115, para. 101. In the end, the *Salini* Tribunal actually found that the claimant's investment in that case was lawfully made; see *Salini v. Morocco*, Decision on Jurisdiction, *supra*, note 32, para. 46.

good faith as a general principle of law. The difference between *Phoenix* and other cases involving application of the good faith principle is that in the former there was no deceitful act. Rather, what the claimant had done constituted an abuse of the international system of investment dispute resolution. The *Phoenix* tribunal considered itself to have an obligation "to prevent an abuse of the system … in ensuring that only investments that are made in compliance with the international principle of good faith and do not attempt to misuse the system are protected."[220]

To recognize "good faith" as an essential principle of international law—in particular as a general principle of the laws of nations—is important. As a fundamental principle of investment law, its application is not confined to investors but also to host states. This was confirmed by the tribunal in *Desert Line Projects LLC v. Yemen*.[221] The claimant was a limited liability construction company organized under the laws of the Sultanate of Oman. It constructed a number of asphalt roads in Yemen. In their contracts, there was an arbitration clause according to which the claimant and respondent had submitted their disputes for settlement. After the arbitration tribunal delivered an award, the disputes between the parties over payment continued, which resulted in the claimant signing a settlement agreement with the respondent.

After having received payment pursuant to the settlement agreement, the claimant challenged its validity by arguing that the settlement agreement had been entered into under duress. The respondent contended that the claimant's investment was not "accepted, by the Host Party, as an investment according to its laws and regulations, and for which an investment certificate is issued" as required by Article 1 of the 1998 Oman–Yemen BIT. According to the respondent, no such certificate had ever been issued and no evidence was offered by the claimant to counter that argument.

The tribunal, however, observed that: "the Respondent has not come close to satisfying the Arbitral tribunal that the claimant made an investment which was either inconsistent with Yemeni laws or regulations or failed to achieve acceptance by the Respondent."[222] With regard to the issue that no certificate had been issued in accordance with the BIT, the tribunal had to decide whether the requirement corresponded to "a mere formalism or a material objective."[223] In its view, if the requirement were merely a formality, it would constitute "an artificial trap depriving investors of the very protection the BIT was intended to provide."[224] "It would offend the most elementary notions of good faith, and [be] insulting to the Head of State," the tribunal continued, to imagine that he would first welcome the foreign investment and then would say that no benefit would be offered under the BIT.[225]

---

220 *Phoenix v. Czech Republic*, ibid., para. 113.
221 *Desert Line Projects LLC v. Republic of Yemen*, ICSID Case No. ARB/05/17, Award (February 6, 2008).
222 Ibid., para. 105.
223 Ibid., para. 106.
224 Id.
225 Ibid, para. 119.

184 International Investment Law: A Chinese Perspective

Thus, the respondent was estopped from raising objections to the validity of the investment on the basis of the principle of good faith.

It appears that although it may be expressed in different languages and from different approaches, good faith as a principle of international investment law has been generally recognized.[226] This is important for maintaining the investment protection mechanisms because, otherwise, the host state would be able to abuse the system by unilaterally creating a circumstance that would deprive foreign investors of their protection.[227]

The issue of compliance with domestic laws can be further complicated by the involvement of an intermediary. This occurs when a foreign investor's transaction (investment) is made with a third party, which then engages in an activity not in compliance with the law. *Anderson v. Costa Rica*[228] is a case in point. In that case, 137 individual nationals of Canada made deposits with a currency exchange owned by the Villalobos brothers under a scheme whereby individuals and companies would place funds with the brothers in return for a high interest rate on their deposits, as well as the repayment of the principal amount with stipulated conditions. The business, however, was not authorized by the Costa Rican Government.[229] As a consequence of the arrest and sentencing of the Villalobos brothers and the closure of their business, the claimants commenced ICSID arbitration proceedings under the Additional Facility procedures, alleging that the respondent had breached its domestic law, international law, and the BIT between Costa Rica and Canada and this had caused injuries to their deposits.

The Canada–Costa Rica BIT in its Article I(g) defined "investment" as "any kind of asset owned or controlled either directly, or indirectly through an enterprise or natural person of a third State" and required that it should be in accordance with the laws of the host state. "Money, claims to money, and claims to performance under contract having a financial value" were included as examples

---

226 *Hamester v. Ghana* also recognized good faith as an essential principle underlying the commitment of host States to ICSID arbitration. That tribunal stated: "An investment will not be protected if it has been created in violation of national or international principles of good faith; by way of corruption, fraud, or deceitful conduct; or if its creation itself constitutes a misuse of the system of international investment protection under the ICSID Convention. It will also not be protected if it is made in violation of the host State's law." See *Gustav F.W. Hamester GmbH & Co. KG v. Ghana*, ICSID Case No. ARB/07/24, Award (June 18, 2010), para. 123.

227 See Campbell McLachlan, Laurence Shore, and Matthew Weiniger, *International Investment Arbitration: Substantive Principles*, Oxford University Press, Oxford, UK, 2007, p. 196. Furthermore, the tribunal in the *Ioannis Kardassopoulos* case stated that the host state could not preclude the protection of the BIT "on the ground that its own actions are illegal under its own laws. In other words, a host State cannot avoid jurisdiction under the BIT by invoking its own failure to comply with its domestic laws." *Ioannis Kardassopoulos v. Georgia*, ICSID Case No. ARB/05/18, Decision on Jurisdiction (July 6, 2007), para. 182.

228 *Alasdair Ross Anderson, et al. v. Republic of Costa Rica*, ICSID Case No. ARB(AF)/07/3, Award (May 19, 2010).

229 The Costa Rican Government had been unable to gather sufficient evidence to take any action until it received a request for legal assistance from Canada, which triggered a raid of the Villalobos brothers' business to reveal that they were engaged in the unauthorized activities; ibid., paras. 23–24.

of investment.[230] The claimants argued that their deposits constituted investments under the BIT. At the same time, the respondent challenged the jurisdiction of the tribunal by contending, *inter alia*, that the deposits made by the claimants were not investments.

The tribunal considered that the claimants must establish that their "deposits and resulting legal relationship with the Villalobos brothers" were investments under the BIT.[231] It had no difficulty in recognizing that the deposits made by the claimants were "assets" under the BIT. Yet, it emphasized that the ownership and control of the claimants over the assets must be "in accordance with the laws of Costa Rica."[232] This was so because not all BITs contain such requirements. In the tribunal's view, the very fact that the Canada–Costa Rica BIT had such a requirement was "a clear indication of the importance that they attached to the legality of investments made by investors of the other Party and their intention that their laws with respect to investments be strictly followed. The assurance of legality with respect to investment has important, indeed crucial, consequences for the public welfare and economic well-being of any country."[233]

As the Villalobos brothers had acted in violation of Costa Rican law, the tribunal further observed, their transactions with the claimants were "illegal" and did not result in a relationship that could constitute an investment.[234] The respondent's objection to jurisdiction was therefore supported.

A question remaining is what remedies are available for claimants in such circumstances. It seems that the *Anderson* Tribunal did not show much mercy on the claimants in that case. It commented that prudent investors must always exercise due diligence before making an investment. In its view, an important element of such due diligence is to make any investment in compliance with the law and that such an "obligation is neither overly onerous nor unreasonable."[235] As the claimants had not exercised the expected due diligence when making their investment, they had to be considered to have done so at their own peril. This case is so far the only one that has clearly and specifically stated an investor's obligation in observing the host state laws. Although the tribunal did not elaborate on foreign investors' obligations absent a treaty requirement for complying with domestic law, the strong language it used obviously lends support to the principle of an implied obligation to obey the local law in making investments, as has been decided in other cases.

From the arbitration practice discussed above, it seems that although BITs and FTAs may provide for investments to be made in compliance with the national laws of the host states, such requirement has been interpreted as only relating to the determination of the validity of investment and not the definition of investment. In some cases, essential principles of international law, including the general

---

230 Ibid., para. 46.
231 Ibid., para. 47.
232 Ibid., para. 51.
233 Ibid., para. 53.
234 Ibid., para. 55.
235 Ibid., para. 58.

principle of good faith, have been considered to be applicable hand-in-hand with domestic law.[236] The significance of the fundamental principle of international law is that it not only requires foreign investors to make investments in good faith but also demands observation of the principle by the host states.[237] Thus, where an investment is made and approved by or with the knowledge of a host state, it is not permitted subsequently to challenge the validity of the investment.

B. Investments made "in the territory" of the host state

In addition to being the first case to address the definition of investment, the *Fedax* case[238] was also the first to confront the issue of whether or not the investment had been made "in the territory" of the host state. The tribunal first noted that there was a difference between investments in immovable property and those that were primarily of a financial nature. It held:

> It is a standard feature of many international financial transactions that the funds involved are not physically transferred to the territory of the beneficiary, but put at its disposal elsewhere. … And of course, promissory notes are frequently employed in such arrangements. The important question is whether the funds made available are utilized by the beneficiary of the credit, as in the case of the Republic of Venezuela, so as to finance its various governmental needs. It is not disputed in this case that the Republic of Venezuela, by means of the promissory notes, received an amount of credit that was put to work during a period of time for its financial needs.[239]

Pursuant to the decision of the *Fedax* Tribunal, in determining whether an investment is made in the territory of the host state, as is often stipulated in BITs and FTAs, the nature of the investment should be taken into account. At the

236 In a recent case, the tribunal considered that the reference to the host state's laws contained in the BIT "is a reference to the laws and regulations made by, or under the authority of, the public authorities of the State, and does not extend to purely contractual obligations." Thus, where a foreign investor breaches its contractual obligations, it will not have any effect on the validity of the investment. See *Vannessa Ventures Ltd. v. Bolivarian Republic of Venezuela*, ICSID Case No. ARB(AF)/04/6, Award (January 16, 2013), paras. 134–35.

237 The *RDC v. Guatemala* Tribunal, for instance, also confirmed that the requirement of compliance with domestic law is only concerned with the legality of the investment. In this first arbitration under the United States–Dominican Republic–Central America Free Trade Agreement ("US–DR-CAFTA"), the tribunal stated that its jurisdiction was governed by both the US–DR-CAFTA and Article 25 of the ICSID Convention. See *Railroad Development Corporation (RDC) v. Guatemala*, Second Decision on Objections to Jurisdiction (May 18, 2010), para. 111. With regard to the respondent's argument that the claimant's investment was not a "covered investment" under the US–DR–CAFTA or the ICSID Convention owing to its illegality, which did not create rights, the tribunal stated that even if there were irregularities, the principle of good faith "should prevent the government from raising violations of its own law as a jurisdictional defense" when it knowingly overlooked such defects and endorsed the investment; ibid., para. 146.

238 *Fedax, supra,* note 16.

239 Ibid., para. 41.

same time, what is most important is whether the host state benefits from the investment. As the *Fedax* case involved a promissory note whose beneficiary was the Venezuelan Government, it was relatively easy for the tribunal to draw its conclusion. In other cases, the issue may not be that straightforward.

The *SGS* cases[240] involved more complex issues. In the first of these, *SGS v. Pakistan*, the claimant—Société Générale de Surveillance, S.A. ("SGS"), a Swiss corporation—had entered into an agreement ("the Pre-Shipment Inspection Agreement"), effective January 1, 1995, with Pakistan to provide certain inspection services of goods to be imported into that country "to ensure that goods were classified properly for duty purposes and to enable Pakistan to increase the efficiency of its customs revenues collection and thereby contribute to the national treasury."[241] The Agreement was to have a five-year duration with automatic renewal but was terminated by Pakistan with effect from March 11, 1997.[242] Although SGS did establish two "liaison offices" in Pakistan "to convey information to Pakistan's customs authorities,"[243] it was undisputed that nearly all of SGS's services to Pakistan were provided outside the country.

In its analysis, the *SGS v. Pakistan* Tribunal, giving short shrift to the "double-barreled test," held that the PSI Agreement constituted an investment because it met the Switzerland–Pakistan BIT's definitions of an investment as including a "claim to money" and a "concession under public law" and that the rights exercised by SGS pursuant to the Agreement were "rights given by law" and "by contract."[244] In fact, the tribunal did little to address the issue of "where" the investment was actually made other than to note that even though SGS's actual expenditures in Pakistan were "relatively small, … they involved the injection of funds into the territory of Pakistan for the carrying out of SGS's engagements under the PSI Agreement."[245] In the end, the tribunal held that the PSI Agreement was a qualified investment centered primarily on the fact that it conferred on SGS the power to exercise a part of the public power of the state.[246]

SGS v. Philippines involved a similar set of facts. In this case, SGS concluded in 1991 an agreement ("the CISS Agreement") to perform certain import supervision services to improve the customs clearance and control processes of the Philippines. After several extensions, the arrangement between SGS and the Philippines was finally discontinued in 2000. SGS alleged that CHF 202 million in services remained unpaid at the time the arrangement was discontinued and sought arbitration at the ICSID. Among other objections to the tribunal's

240 *SGS v. Pakistan*, and *SGS v. Philippines*, both *supra*, note 15; and *SGS Société Générale de Surveillance, S.A. v. Republic of Paraguay*, ICSID Case No. ARB/07/29, Decision on Jurisdiction (February 12, 2010).

241 *SGS v. Pakistan*, ibid., para. 11.

242 Ibid., para. 16.

243 Ibid., para 13.

244 Ibid., para. 135.

245 Ibid., para. 136.

246 See ibid., paras. 138–39.

jurisdiction over the case, the Philippines maintained that there was "no investment in the Philippines as required by the BIT."[247] Specifically, it maintained:

> [T]he Tribunal should not be distracted by incidental and minor activities, such as training courses or donation of a certain item of equipment, but instead should have regard to the "integral part of the overall operation." In this case, the delivery of the PSI service, being clearly the "overall operation" of this contract, took place entirely outside the Philippines.[248]

In this instance, and after referring to the *SGS v. Pakistan* Tribunal's approach, the *SGS v. Philippines* Tribunal tackled the question head on. First of all, it noted that "[i]n accordance with normal principles of treaty interpretation, investments made outside the territory of the Respondent State, however beneficial to it, would not be covered by the BIT."[249] However, the tribunal observed that the services provided outside the Philippines by SGS "were not carried out for their own sake but in order to enable it to provide, in the Philippines, an inspection certificate on which BOC could rely to enter goods to the customs territory of the Philippines and to assess and collect the ensuing revenue" and that these operations were organized through SGS's Manila Liaison Office, which was "a substantial office, employing a significant number of people."[250] In consequence, it held that "[a] substantial and non-severable aspect of the overall service was provided in the Philippines"[251] and that "these elements taken together are sufficient to qualify the service as one provided in the Philippines. Since it was a cost to SGS to provide it, this is enough to amount to an investment in the Philippines within the meaning of the BIT."[252]

The *SGS v. Paraguay* case involved nearly identical facts to those in the two previous *SGS* cases, and the tribunal's reasoning for finding that an investment had been made in the territory of the host state was an almost *verbatim* repetition of that presented by the *SGS v. Philippines* Tribunal, on which it noted it had relied heavily.[253]

In *Abaclat*,[254] the respondent argued, among other things, that the investment was not made "in" the territory of Argentina as was required by the

247   *SGS v. Philippines*, *supra*, note 15, para. 17.

248   Ibid., para. 58.

249   Ibid., para. 99 (footnote omitted).

250   Ibid., para. 101.

251   Ibid., para. 102.

252   Ibid., para. 103.

253   See *SGS v. Paraguay*, supra, note 240, at paras. 109–17; see also para. 102. In this regard, the tribunal also referred (at para. 117) to the Decision on Jurisdiction of May 29, 2009 in *Bureau Veritas, Inspection, Valuation, Assessment and Control, BIVAC B.V. v. Republic of Paraguay*, ICSID Case No. ARB/07/9, at para. 104, noting that "in *BIVAC v. Paraguay*, the tribunal likewise had 'little difficulty' in concluding, with respect to a contract virtually identical to the one before the tribunal here, that BIVAC had made an investment in the territory of Paraguay for purposes of the Netherlands-Paraguay BIT's comparable 'in the territory" requirement."

254   *Abaclat and Others v. Argentine Republic*, *supra*, note 13.

BIT.[255] Specifically, in the respondent's view, there was no "sufficiently significant physical and legal connection" between the bonds at issue in the dispute and Argentina because "(i) they did not cause any transfer of money into the territory of Argentina, (ii) they are located outside of Argentina and are beyond the latter's scope of territorial jurisdiction … and (iii) the indirect holding systems of these entitlements implicates a cut-off point beyond which claims are not permissible because they have only a remote connection with the investment."[256] The tribunal held, however, that the place of investment making depends on the nature of the investment in question: "With regard to investments of a purely financial nature, the relevant criteria should be where and/or for the benefit of whom the funds are ultimately used, and not the place where the funds were paid out or transferred."[257]

Determination of qualified investment is an important issue on which depend all the preferential treatments and guarantees promised by contracting parties in contemporary BITs and FTAs (investment chapter). By agreeing to submit investment disputes to international arbitration, from the host states' point of view, they are agreeing to a limitation on their sovereign powers. The question then is whether, in return for this action, the making of investments by foreign investors must be in compliance with laws of the host states. Jurisprudence shows that where a BIT or FTA requires compliance with local laws, it is without question that any making of an investment must be in accordance with the host state's laws, albeit the silence of a BIT or FTA on the matter may lead to different interpretations. Even if there is an explicit requirement for observation of domestic laws, it is only relevant for the "making" of investment insofar as the validity of investment is concerned. Once an investment has been admitted into a host state, the latter should not refuse or decline protection unless the investment was made in violation of its laws and without its knowledge or consent.[258]

Investment arbitration practice also demonstrates that tribunals are quite prepared to apply the fundamental principles of international law, such as good faith. This development is conducive for the formation of international investment law. Whilst countries in the contemporary world are competing for direct foreign investments, this trend will enhance the confidence of both investors and host states.

Another feature of international investment law is that almost without exception contracting parties commit themselves to provide national, fair and equitable

---

255 Article 1(1) of the Argentina–Italy BIT provides: "Investment shall mean … any conferment or asset invested or reinvested by an individual or corporation of one Contracting Party in the territory of the other Contracting Party, in compliance with the laws and regulations of the latter party." Bonds and private or public financial instruments are included in the illustrative list of investments.

256 *Abaclat and Others v. Argentine Republic, supra*, note 13, para. 341.

257 Ibid., para. 374.

258 On this matter, see Anna Joubin-Bret, "Admission and Establishment in the Context of Investment Protection," in August Reinisch (ed.), *Standards of Investment Protection*, Oxford University Press, Oxford, UK, 2008, pp. 9–28, at 27.

and other treatments to investments made "in" the territory of the other contracting party. Whether or not the word "in" had been carefully considered before it became part of the investment protection instrument, practice demonstrates that it has given rise to disputes. Tribunals facing the issue have adopted a practical approach by emphasizing the special nature and features of the investment in question. From the few cases discussed here, it appears that tribunals consider the benefits that the host state has or is to have as an essential factor.[259] With the deepening of globalization, the already existing interdependence among national communities will grow, and that will lead to diversification of forms of investment. The steady progress of science and technology will help enable such development, especially in the area of service-related investment.

IV. Commercial arbitration awards and investments

Investment arbitration and commercial arbitration are two distinctive mechanisms for resolving disputes. Commercial arbitration may deal with any dispute arising from a commercial transaction. It is often the case that in such circumstances the underlying transaction is a commercial contract with either a private party or a state, which may include sale and purchase contracts, joint-venture contracts, turnkey contracts, construction, management, production, concession, revenue-sharing, or other similar contracts. Investment arbitration, on the other hand, is designed for the settlement of disputes between a foreign investor and the government of the country where it has made an investment—the host state— arising from an investment which is protected by a BIT between the investor's home state and the host state. Sometimes a breach of contract may constitute a violation of a BIT in accordance with the so-called umbrella clause.[260] Except in such special cases, commercial contracts are not considered to be investments for the purposes of international dispute resolution.

In practice, BITs may include provisions to specifically exclude commercial transactions from being qualified as investments. For instance, in the 2002 Japan– Singapore EPA, Article 72(a)(v) provides that investments include "claims to money and claims to any performance under contract having a financial value," but then, in a note to that Article, it is stipulated that "for the purposes of this Chapter, … 'claims to money and claims to any performance under contract' …

---

259 For further discussion on the issue of territorial importance in investment making, see Christina Knahr, "Investments 'In The Territory' of the Host State," in Christina Binder et al. (eds.), *International Investment Law for the 21st Century: Essays in Honour of Christoph Schreuer*, Oxford University Press, 2009.

260 In a BIT, an "umbrella clause" is a provision that "create[s] an international law obligation that a host State shall, for example, 'observe any obligation it may have entered into'; 'constantly guarantee the observance of the commitments it has entered into'; 'observe any obligation it has assumed', and other formulations, in respect to investments;" see Katia Yannaca-Small, *Interpretation of the Umbrella Clause in Investment Agreements*, OECD Working Papers on International Investment, No. 2006/3, OECD, Paris, 2006; available at: http://www.oecd.org/investment/ internationalinvestmentagreements/37579220.pdf.

refer to assets which relate to a business activity and do not refer to assets which are of a personal nature, unrelated to any business activity."[261] Canada's 2004 Model BIT provides in Article 1 that "investment does not mean, (X) claims to money that arise solely from (i) commercial contracts for the sale of goods or services by a national or enterprise in the territory of a Party to an enterprise in the territory of the other Party."[262] The advantage of provisions such as this is that they remove any doubt about the definition of investment in this regard. Thus, arbitration tribunals are unlikely to interpret it otherwise.

However, in some recent investment arbitration cases tribunals have been faced with the issue as to whether or not a commercial arbitral award itself constituted an investment. *Saipem v. Bangladesh*[263] is a case in point. In that case, the claimant—a company incorporated in Italy, specializing in oil and gas pipeline construction—entered into a contract with Petrobangla—a Bangladeshi state-owned enterprise—to build a pipeline to carry condensate and gas in northeast Bangladesh in a World Bank-sponsored project. Owing to problems with the local population and other difficulties, the completion date of the project was delayed for one year. Under the contract, Petrobangla had the right to retain an amount equivalent to 5 percent of the total contract price until it issued a final acceptance certificate. As the retained funds were not paid to Saipem in accordance with the above arrangement, it commenced arbitration proceedings at the ICC under the contract.

In the course of the ICC arbitration in Dhaka, Petrobangla first brought an action in a Bangladeshi court to revoke the ICC arbitral tribunal's authority, which request was granted by the Bangladeshi court, then asked another local court to restrain Saipem from proceeding with the ICC arbitration, and finally, after the ICC tribunal continued with the case and rendered an award in favor of the claimant, filed an application before the High Court Division of the Supreme Court of Bangladesh to set it aside. The Supreme Court of Bangladesh denied the application to set aside the award on the ground that there was no award in the eyes of Bangladeshi law and therefore there was nothing to be set aside.[264]

The claimant then submitted a request for arbitration to the ICSID, based on the BIT between Bangladesh and Italy. The first issue facing the tribunal was whether the claimant had made an investment. On this issue, the respondent argued that the criteria established by the *Salini* case and others could not be satisfied. First of all, it argued that the period for the work to be performed was less than one year, that is, that it was a short-term undertaking.[265] The respondent's

261 For the full text of the 2002 Japan–Singapore EPA, see: http://www.mofa.go.jp/region/asia-paci/singapore/jsepa-1.pdf.

262 For the full text of Canada's 2004 Model BIT, see: http://www.dfait-maeci.gc.ca/tna-nac/what_fipa-en.asp#structure.

263 *Saipem S.p.A. v. The People's Republic of Bangladesh*, ICSID Case No. ARB/05/7, Decision on Jurisdiction (March 21, 2007) (hereinafter "*Saipem*, Decision on Jurisdiction"); Award (June 30, 2009) (hereinafter "*Saipem*, Award").

264 *Saipem*, Decision on Jurisdiction, ibid, para. 36.

265 Ibid., para. 101.

second ground of objection was that, because the project was sponsored by the World Bank, the claimant had not needed to put any money into the project and was only required to carry out the work and be paid for its performance under the contract; hence, there was no risk involved.[266]

The respondent also compared this case with *Soabi v. Senegal*,[267] in which the tribunal was of the opinion that the contract concerned, under which the contractor was to be paid as the building project progressed, was not an investment under Article 25 of the ICSID Convention and disputes arising thereunder could therefore not be investment disputes. The *Saipem* Tribunal first noted that there was no provision in Bangladeshi law requiring foreign investors to raise funds by themselves, while the drafting history of the ICSID Convention also suggested that the origin of the funds was irrelevant.[268] It should be noted that, in most other cases, tribunals did not consider the definition of investment under the domestic laws of the host state and would only rely on the relevant BITs and the relevant multilateral treaties such as the ICSID Convention and the ECT. The *Saipem* Tribunal also took this approach, saying that it was "not prepared to consider that the term 'investment' in Article 1(1) of the BIT is defined according to the law of the host State."[269]

The tribunal went on to observe that "Bangladesh's argument appears to refer more … to the fact that the investor did not incur any commercial risk because it received an advance payment."[270] The tribunal disagreed with this argument, holding that the stopping of the works and the necessity to renegotiate the contract, as well as "the contractual mechanism providing for Retention Money," were all examples of inherent risks for the investor.[271]

The tribunal's reasoning is not without question. The origin of the funds would not be a problem if Saipem had itself obtained the loans to finance the project, because it would not then be the host state that would bear the responsibility for paying off such debts. Where the host state provides the necessary funds and makes advance payments for the project, the investor would have less risk, if any, and the nature of that risk is identical to the risk involved in any commercial transaction. In this connection, the tribunal emphasized that for the purpose of determining whether there was an investment under Article 25 of the ICSID Convention, the entire operation should be considered, including the contract, the construction itself, the retention money, the warranty, the related ICC arbitration, and so on.[272] With such considerations, the claimant's transaction was considered to be qualified as an investment.

To take into account the totality of a transaction is reasonable for determining

---

266 Ibid., para. 108.
267 *Société Ouest Africaine des Bétons Industriels (SOABI) v. Senegal*, ICSID Case No. ARB/82/1, Award (February 25, 1988), 2 *ICSID Reports* 190, at para. 219.
268 *Saipem*, Decision on Jurisdiction, *supra*, note 263, para. 106.
269 Ibid., para. 120.
270 Ibid., para. 109.
271 Id.
272 Ibid., para. 110.

the establishment of an investment. What is problematic is the inclusion of the dispute settlement arrangement as a factor of investment. Even though the settlement mechanisms established in a contract form an integral part of the contract, this should not be considered as a factor for ascertaining whether or not an investment has been made. The dispute settlement mechanism certainly involves uncertainty—risks—for the parties. Yet, whether a transaction can constitute an investment has nothing to do with this. In fact, where a transaction meets all the requirements of the relevant BIT and Article 25 of the ICSID Convention, even without a dispute settlement mechanism, it is still a covered investment and should be protected. Even though a decision that results from such dispute settlement procedures may "crystallize" the rights and obligations of the parties concerned, as was held by the *Saipem* Tribunal,[273] such decision itself is not an investment or a part thereof.

The respondent in *Saipem* also argued that:

> ... the fact that the BIT's definition of investment used the word "property" and not "assets" as in other bilateral investment treaties implies a reference to Bangladeshi law. In support of this assertion, Bangladesh submitted that the word "property" was chosen because it was a notion well known in Bangladesh, thus suggesting that the word "property" must be interpreted according to its ordinary meaning in Bangladeshi law. That meaning is allegedly "more specific and narrower than the word 'assets.'"[274]

The tribunal maintained that the interpretation of the ICSID Convention and the BIT should be governed by international law.[275] This approach of interpretation is consistent with the practice of investment arbitration, that is, because such treaties are international instruments they must be interpreted in accordance with international law principles. At the same time, where there is a requirement that investment be made in accordance with domestic laws, the domestic law provisions must be interpreted in accordance with national law principles. The result of this exercise will impact the definition of investment under treaties.

The claimant also argued that the contract was an investment as defined in the BIT and that "the rights accruing from the ICC Award fall squarely within the notion of 'credit for sums of money ... connected with investments' set out in ... the BIT."[276] The respondent maintained that "[t]hese words would normally include bank deposits or book debts on a running account."[277] The tribunal was of the opinion that "[t]his may well be so. However, in their ordinary meaning, the words 'credit for sums of money' also cover rights under an award ordering a

---

273 Ibid., para. 127.
274 Ibid., para. 81 (references omitted).
275 Ibid., para. 78.
276 Ibid., para. 125.
277 Ibid., para. 126.

party to pay an amount of money: the prevailing party undoubtedly has a credit for a sum of money in the amount of the award."[278]

In fact, even if the claimant's undertaking in the building project constituted an investment, it was still necessary to prove that the dispute arose "directly out of" the investment. During the hearings, the respondent objected to the ICSID tribunal's jurisdiction on the ground that, inter alia, the contract was not an "investment" and, even if it was, it had nothing to do with the Bangladeshi Government because the dispute arose from Petrobangla's payment due to the claimant.[279] By referring to the words of the Report of the Executive Directors, the tribunal held that the dispute was legal in nature because it dealt with "'the existence or scope of [Claimants'] legal rights' and with the nature and extent of the relief to be granted to the Claimants as a result of the Respondent's alleged violation of those legal rights."[280] In other words, the rights embodied in the ICC award were not created by the award, but arose out of the contract. The ICC award crystallized the parties' rights and obligations under the original contract.[281]

In addition to the ICSID Convention, the tribunal's jurisdiction was also restricted by the Bangladesh–Italy BIT, Article 9 of which provides that:

(1) Any disputes arising between a Contracting Party and the investors of the other, relating to compensation for expropriation, nationalization, requisition or similar measures including disputes relating to the amount of the relevant payments shall be settled amicably, as far as possible.

(2) In the event that such a dispute cannot be settled amicably within six months of the date of a written application, the investor in question may submit the dispute, at his discretion for settlement to:

 (a) the Contracting Party's Court, at all instances, having territorial jurisdiction;

 (b) an ad hoc Arbitration Tribunal, in accordance with the Arbitration Rules of the "UN Commission on International Trade Law" (UNCITRAL),

 (c) the "International Centre for the Settlement of Investment Disputes", for the application of the arbitration procedures provided by the ICSID Convention of 18th March 1965 on the "Settlement of Investment Disputes between States and Nationals of other States", whenever, or as soon as both Contracting Parties have validly acceded to it.

Literally, the Bangladesh–Italy BIT limits the ICSID's jurisdiction to issues relating only to compensation for expropriation, nationalization, requisition, or similar measures, including the amount of the relevant payments. This is similar to the

278 Ibid. para. 126.
279 Ibid., para. 76.
280 Ibid., para. 95, citing Report of the Executive Directors, *supra*, note 30, at para. 26.
281 Ibid., para. 127.

earlier practices of the former Soviet Union and some Eastern Europe states, as well as China.[282] A number of ICSID tribunals had examined such provisions before, most of which upheld ICSID jurisdiction. Those that denied jurisdiction did so mostly because the investor failed to prove that jurisdiction was appropriate based on prima facie evidence.[283]

In *Saipem*, the tribunal referred to the decision in *Impregilo*, on "whether the facts as alleged by the Claimant, if established, are capable of coming within those provisions of the BIT which have been invoked."[284] In other words, if the dispute alleged by the claimant is within the scope of the BIT, the tribunal should first exercise its jurisdiction. The issue of whether or not the respondent has breached the agreement should then be examined at the merits stage. This approach inevitably involves different standards of "proof" to be applied at the jurisdictional and merits stages. International investment arbitration practice suggests that tribunals tend to apply a lower standard at the jurisdictional stage and a more demanding one in examining the respondent's breach of the agreement.[285] Notwithstanding the reasons behind the application of differed standards, this practice has made it easier for tribunals to assume jurisdiction.

After making its positive decision on jurisdiction, the *Saipem* Tribunal moved on to examine whether or not the respondent had violated its BIT with Italy. The claimant alleged that Bangladesh had violated Article 5 of the BIT, which provides that:

(1) The investments to which this Agreement relates shall not be subject to any measure which might limit permanently or temporarily their joined rights of ownership, possession, control or enjoyment, save where specifically provided by law and by judgments or orders issued by Courts or tribunals having jurisdiction.

282 For discussion on China's practice in this regard, see Guiguo Wang, "China's Practice in International Investment Law: From Participation to Leadership in the World Economy," in Mahnoush H. Arsanjani, Jacob Katz Cogan, Robert D. Sloane, and Siegfried Wiessner (eds.), *Looking to the Future: Essays on International Law in Honor of W. Michael Reisman*, Martinus Nijhoff Publishers, 2011, pp. 845–90.

283 For example, see *Vladimir Berschader and Moïse Berschader v. Russian Federation*, Stockholm Chamber of Commerce (SCC), Award (April 21, 2006); and *RosInvestCo UK Ltd. v. Russian Federation*, SCC Case No. V079/2005, Award on Jurisdiction (October 5, 2007).

284 *Saipem*, Decision on Jurisdiction, *supra*, note 263, para. 84. Regarding the *Impregilo* case, see *Impregilo S.p.A. v. Islamic Republic of Pakistan*, ICSID Case No. ARB/03/3, Decision on Jurisdiction (April 22, 2005). As for the criteria for whether or not the prima facie evidence of jurisdiction is established, see *United Parcel Service of America, Inc. v. Canada*, an arbitration under Chapter 11 of the North American Free Trade Agreement, Award on Jurisdiction (November 22, 2002), paras. 33–37; available at: http://www.naftaclaims.com/Disputes/Canada/UPS/UPSAwardOnJurisdiction.pdf; *Siemens A.G. v. Argentine Republic*, ICSID Case No. ARB/02/8, Decision on Jurisdiction (August 3, 2004), para. 180; *Plama Consortium Limited v. Republic of Bulgaria*, ICSID Case No. ARB/03/24, Decision on Jurisdiction (February 8, 2005), paras. 118–20 and 132; and *Bayindir Insaat Turizm Ticaret Ve Sanayi A.S. v. Islamic Republic of Pakistan*, ICSID Case No. ARB/03/29, Decision on Jurisdiction (November 14, 2005), paras. 185–200.

285 See *Saipem*, Decision on Jurisdiction, ibid., paras. 85–86.

(2) Investments of investors of one of the Contracting Parties shall not be directly or indirectly nationalized, expropriated, requisitioned or subjected to any measures having similar effects in the territory of the other Contracting Party, except for public purposes, or national interest, against immediate full and effective compensation, and on condition that these measures are taken on a non-discriminatory basis and in conformity with all legal provisions and procedures.

The tribunal was of the opinion that "the guarantee against expropriation of Article 5(2) only comes into play if (i) there is an expropriation and (ii) that expropriation is not justified by 'public purposes' or 'national interest,' does not conform to 'all legal provisions and procedures,' is not adequately compensated, or is discriminatory."[286] The respondent did not claim in the hearing that the intervention by the local courts was driven by public purposes or the national interest, and it was common ground that no compensation was paid.[287] Therefore, the tribunal considered that it should first consider whether the respondent had violated Article 5(1) of the BIT.

The tribunal emphasized that the respondent, as a contracting party to the 1958 New York Convention on the Recognition and Enforcement of Foreign Arbitral Awards ("the New York Convention"), was obliged to "recognize" the validity of the arbitration agreement.[288] Based on that obligation, it was the tribunal's opinion that:

> ... it is ... generally acknowledged that the issuance of an anti-arbitration injunction can amount to a violation of the Convention. ... Technically, the courts of Bangladesh did not target the arbitration or the arbitration agreement in itself, but revoked the authority of the arbitrators. ... [This] can amount to a violation of Article II of the New York Convention whenever it *de facto* "prevents or immobilizes the arbitration that seeks to implement that [arbitration] agreement" ...[289]

Accordingly, the *Saipem* Tribunal held that since the parties to the contract chose to arbitrate in Dhaka and to apply Bangladeshi law, the courts of the respondent therefore had supervisory jurisdiction over the arbitration.[290] Those courts' responsibilities are also ascertained by reference to Bangladeshi law. Pursuant to Section V of the Bangladeshi Arbitration Act of 1940, "the authority of an appointed arbitrator is irrevocable except with the leave of the court, unless

---

286 *Saipem*, Award, *supra*, note 263, para. 125.
287 Ibid., para. 126.
288 Ibid., para. 166.
289 Ibid., para. 167, citing *Salini Costruttori S.p.A v. Federal Republic of Ethiopia*, ICC Case No. 10623/ AER/ACS, Award regarding the suspension of the proceedings and jurisdiction of December 7, 2001, 42 *I.L.M.* 609 (2003) and 21 *ASA Bulletin* 82 (2003), paras. 130–31.
290 Ibid., para. 115.

a contrary intention is expressed in the arbitration agreement."[291] Therefore, there seems to have been no violation of Bangladeshi law in the action of the Bangladeshi courts to revoke the authority of the ICC arbitrators. However, in the *Saipem* Tribunal's view, "[i]t is generally acknowledged in international law that a State exercising a right for a purpose that is different from that for which that right was created commits an abuse of rights."[292] It must be noted that *Saipem* was the first case in the history of investment arbitration in which a state was held liable for its courts' abuse of power by revoking the authority of a commercial arbitration body (in this case, the Bangladeshi court, when facing an application to set aside the ICC award, expressed that in its view there was no arbitral award to speak of—i.e. it refused recognition of the award).

The *Saipem* Tribunal's opinion appears to have hinged on the fact that during the ICC hearings Petrobangla raised a number of objections to the proceedings but most of those were rejected.[293] Petrobangla then resorted to the Bangladeshi courts to revoke the authority of the arbitrators on the grounds of "misconduct and breach of the parties' procedural rights."[294] This raised Saipem's concerns that Petrobangla might have colluded with the courts.[295] In the opinion of the tribunal, the Bangladeshi courts had "exercised their supervisory jurisdiction for an end which was different from that for which it was instituted and thus violated the internationally accepted principle of prohibition of abuse of rights."[296] The tribunal also held that the actions of the Bangladeshi courts constituted an instance of "measures having similar effects" within the meaning of Article 5(2) of the BIT and that such indirect expropriation had resulted in substantially depriving the claimant of the benefit of the ICC Award.[297]

The *Saipem* Tribunal was very careful in drawing its conclusions. Understandably, what this ICSID tribunal did was to assume the function of enforcing a commercial arbitral award, which is obviously not the purpose for which the ICSID Convention was designed. Unless it is carefully guarded, the line between commercial arbitration and investment arbitration may be blurred.

A little more than a year after the *Saipem* award, the investment arbitration community was again faced with a request to treat a commercial arbitral award as an investment—in *GEA v. Ukraine*.[298] The claimant, a company incorporated

291 Ibid., para. 139.
292 Ibid., para. 160; in support of this statement, the tribunal cited Alexandre Kiss, "Abuse of Rights," in Rudolf Bernhardt (ed.), *Encyclopedia of Public International Law*, North-Holland, Amsterdam, 1992, Vol. 1, at 5.
293 See ibid., paras. 152–55.
294 Ibid., para. 35.
295 See ibid., para. 41; in the end, the tribunal held that it was "not satisfied that the Bangladeshi courts acted in collusion or conspired with Petrobangla;" ibid., para. 148.
296 Ibid., para. 161.
297 Ibid., para. 129. The tribunal also pointed out that its decision that "the intervention of the Bangladeshi courts ... qualifies as a taking" was also based on the fact that Petrobangla did not have any assets overseas and therefore Saipem could not seek enforcement of the ICC award in other countries in accordance with the New York Convention; ibid., para. 130.
298 *GEA Group Aktiengesellschaft v. Ukraine*, ICSID Case No. ARB/08/16, Award (March 31, 2011).

under the laws of Germany, entered into a conversion contract with a company incorporated in Ukraine that was a former state-owned entity—OJSC Oriana ("Oriana"). According to the conversion contract, the claimant was to provide Oriana each year with 200,000 tons of naphtha fuel for conversion. During the implementation of the conversion contract, some incidents occurred which triggered disputes between the parties in relation to the quality of the raw materials and finished products, as well as a large quantity of "missing" finished products. Subsequently, a settlement agreement and repayment agreement were signed by the parties, both of which contained a dispute settlement mechanism naming the ICC as the institution for arbitration. Not satisfied with the performance of the two agreements with Oriana, the claimant commenced arbitration proceedings at the ICC, which rendered an award largely in favor of the claimant on November 25, 2002.[299] Thereafter, the claimant commenced a prolonged attempt to have the arbitral award enforced in Ukraine. Three years later, when all its petitions had been dismissed by the Ukrainian courts, the claimant instituted an ICSID arbitration alleging that Ukraine had violated its rights under the 1993 Germany–Ukraine BIT.[300]

As in many other investment arbitration cases, an important question facing the tribunal was whether the conversion contract constituted a covered investment, which presumption was challenged by the respondent. The tribunal implicitly adopted the double-barreled analysis. It referred in summary form to the cases that had either supported or opposed the double-barreled approach. It nevertheless considered that investment per se should have "an objective meaning in itself."[301] With the objective meaning in mind, the tribunal first pointed out that in Article 1(1)(e) of the BIT an investment was defined to include "rights to the exercise of an economic activity." It then related the above provision to the last sentence of the Article that "any change to the form in which assets are invested shall not affect their nature as investments" and concluded that the term "investment" should be interpreted in a "broader context of an investment operation."[302] In its view, the conversion contract not only satisfied the requirements of the BIT but also the objective criteria of Article 25 of the ICSID Convention. The question that remained to be answered was the impact that this underlying transaction—a covered investment under both the BIT and the ICSID Convention—had on the ICC award.

On the matter as to whether or not the ICC Award could be construed to be a covered investment, the tribunal considered that the term "investment" itself should have an objective meaning. On that basis, it stated that the "ICC

---

299 Ibid, para. 62.
300 Ibid., para. 7.
301 Ibid., para. 141.
302 Ibid, para. 149. Regarding the conversion contract, the tribunal put it in the broader context as follows: it "was more than just goods against a tolling fee – it established a relationship of 'common interest' whereby KCH (and, ultimately GEA) would, among other things, assist with delivery of logistics and pay for Ukrainian domestic freight, resolve customs issues, and supply the Oriana plant with necessary materials." Id.

Award—*in and of itself*—cannot constitute an investment" because it was a legal instrument for the disposition of rights and obligations arising from the settlement agreement and the repayment agreement, "neither of which was itself an investment."[303] It further stated that even if the ICC award "could be characterised as directly arising out of the Conversion Contract or the Products, … the fact that the Award rules upon rights and obligations arising out of an investment does not equate the Award with the investment itself."[304] In other words, the tribunal treated the ICC award and the underlying investment as two separate matters. This position is in contrast to that taken in both the *Saipem* case, which was decided earlier, and the *White Industries* case, which was decided later.[305] The *GEA* decision, in particular its criticisms of the *Saipem* decision, has indeed raised serious issues for those involved in international investment law to consider.

White Industries[306] was decided by an *ad hoc* arbitral tribunal under the UNCITRAL rules less than two years after the *Saipem* case and less than a year after the *GEA* case. It also involved enforcement of a commercial arbitral award through an investment treaty. The claimant in that case was a company constituted in accordance with the laws of Australia. In the 1970s–1980s, India undertook a major development of its coal resources. For that purpose, it set up a wholly state-owned company—Coal India—which in the name of its subsidiary Central Coalfields Limited entered into a contract with the claimant. Under the contract, the claimant had an obligation to provide services related to the production of coal, including the supply of equipment and technical services. The contract also contained provisions for bonuses and penalties for the claimant, depending on its performance.

A dispute occurred between the claimant and Coal India; the claimant argued that it was entitled to bonuses and Coal India contended that it was entitled to impose penalties. The two parties submitted their disputes to the International Chamber of Commerce for arbitration, and the ICC tribunal awarded the claimant more than A$4 million.[307] Soon thereafter, Coal India applied to an Indian court—the Calcutta High Court—to set aside the award, and that court granted Coal India leave to apply and ordered the matter returnable.[308] Thereafter, with the arbitral award in hand, the claimant applied to the High Court at New Delhi for enforcement of the award. A number of back and forth actions by the claimant and Coal India in different Indian courts followed without substantial result. On July 27, 2010, more than seven years after it had requested enforcement

---

303 Ibid, para. 161 (emphasis in original).

304 Ibid, para. 162.

305 The *GEA* Tribunal considered that the *Saipem* Tribunal had said under one heading that the ICC award was part of the investment, under another heading that it was not an investment, and then under still another heading that it was not necessary to decide whether it was part of the investment. See ibid., para. 163.

306 *White Industries Australia Limited v. Republic of India*, UNCITRAL Case, Final Award (November 30, 2011).

307 See ibid., paras. 3.2.1–3.2.33.

308 Ibid., para. 3.2.35.

of the ICC award, the claimant instituted investment arbitration against the respondent—India—for violation of the Australia–India BIT.[309] Unlike the *Saipem* case, *White Industries* involved non-enforcement of a commercial arbitral award, which was alleged to have constituted a violation of the BIT.

The *White Industries* Tribunal started its analysis by examining whether the claimant was a covered investor and its transaction was a covered investment. The Australia–India BIT defines an investment to mean, inter alia, a "right to money or to any performance having a financial value, contractual or otherwise."[310] The tribunal considered that the double-barreled test "imposes a higher standard than simply resolving whether there is an 'investment' for the purposes of a particular BIT"[311] but that this test was only applicable to cases under ICSID arbitration. The same applied, in its view, to the *Salini* test. Nevertheless, it moved on to analyze how well the claimant's transaction met all the elements of the *Salini* test and concluded that it had "comprehensively satisfied any *ratione materiae* test that may be said to exist under the BIT."[312] With regard to the relationship between the ICC arbitral award and the definition of investment, the *White Industries* Tribunal adopted the position of the *Saipem* Tribunal by concluding that "rights under the Award constitute part of White's original investment (i.e., being a crystallization of its rights under the Contract) and, as such, are subject to such protection as is afforded to investments by the BIT."[313] Then the question that remained was whether the non-enforcement or delayed enforcement of the award would constitute a breach of the BIT. In fact, unless the respondent were to be found to have violated the BIT, there could be no remedy for the claimant.

The tribunal did not find that India had breached the Australia–India BIT by the court actions because there had been no bad faith on the part of the Indian judiciary.[314] In the tribunal's opinion, the delay in the judicial process in India was "not particularly surprising,"[315] even though it was "certainly unsatisfactory."[316] At the same time, in the tribunal's view, the claimant "either knew or ought to have known at the time it entered into the Contract that the domestic court structure in India was overburdened."[317] Therefore, the claimant should not have had any expectation that its award would be enforced in a particular manner or time frame.[318] The matter, however, did not stop there.

The claimant, by relying on the MFN clause in the BIT (Article 4.2), argued that in Article 4(5) of the India–Kuwait BIT, there was a provision that "Each

---

309 Ibid., para. 2.1.1.
310 Ibid., para. 7.3.1, quoting Article 1(iii) of the Australia–India BIT.
311 Ibid., para. 7.4.9.
312 Ibid., para. 7.4.19.
313 Ibid., para. 7.6.10.
314 Ibid., para. 10.4.23. The tribunal stated that the conduct of the Indian courts did not amount to "a particularly serious shortcoming" or "egregious conduct that 'shocks or at least surprises, a sense of judicial proprietary';" id.
315 Ibid., para. 10.4.12.
316 Ibid., para. 10.4.22.
317 Ibid., para. 10.3.14.
318 Ibid., para. 10.3.15.

Contracting State shall in accordance with its applicable laws and regulations, provide *effective means of asserting claims and enforcing rights with respect to investments*" (emphasis added). Based on this provision, the tribunal concluded:

> In these circumstances, and even though we have decided that the nine years of proceedings in the set aside application do not amount to a denial of justice, the Tribunal has no difficulty in concluding the Indian judicial system's inability to deal with White's jurisdictional claim in over nine years, and the Supreme Court's inability to hear White's jurisdictional appeal for over five years amounts to undue delay and constitutes a breach of India's voluntarily assumed obligation of providing White with "effective means" of asserting claims and enforcing rights.[319]

The tribunal then went on to analyze in detail whether there was any ground for the award to be denied recognition and enforcement. With the finding that there was no ground to refuse enforcement of the arbitral award "under the laws of India,"[320] it considered that India had failed to provide "effective means" of asserting claims.[321] Again, it did not explain what the threshold for provision of "effective means" was or the surrounding circumstances to be considered in establishing whether a system failed to provide such "effective means." It should also be noted that in concluding that there was no ground under Indian law to refuse enforcement of the award, the tribunal put itself in the shoes of Indian judges, at least in this respect. One may wonder if the tribunal was qualified to make judgments under Indian law.

The idea that commercial arbitration awards should be treated as investments is new to everybody. BITs, FTAs and multilateral treaties such as the ICSID Convention can offer little help. Tribunals facing the issue, however, must make decisions. Unfortunately, so far no detailed and persuasive analysis has been conducted by tribunals. The *Saipem* Tribunal's "crystallization" theory is interesting. With BITs and FTAs providing very broad definitions of investment, the danger of misuse arises, that is, investment dispute settlement mechanisms being abused for enforcement of commercial arbitral awards. The *GEA* approach to separate commercial arbitral awards from investment—articulating that investment in and of itself must have an objective meaning—is helpful in safeguarding the distinctiveness of the two dispute settlement systems: investment and commerce. Yet, it has also been subject to disagreement.

In *White Industries*, for instance, the tribunal simply regarded the opinion of the *GEA* Tribunal as *obiter dicta* and concluded that it represented "an incorrect departure from the developing jurisprudence on the treatment of arbitral awards."[322] Yet, by the time the *White Industries* Tribunal rendered its decision, there had only

319 Ibid., para. 11.4.19.
320 Ibid., para. 14.2.66.
321 Ibid., para. 14.4.4.
322 Ibid., paras. 7.6.7–7.6.8.

been two well-known cases—*Saipem* and *GEA*. On what basis it then considered the *GEA* decision to be an incorrect departure from "developing jurisprudence" should have been stated. The *White Industries* Tribunal did not even make a serious effort to explain its position.[323] It did admit in a footnote that tribunals in *Mondev*, *Chevron* and *Frontier Petroleum Services* "characterized their findings as providing protection to the subsisting interests" of the claimants in the original investments, rather than categorizing such awards as investment per se.[324] This actually informatively confirms that there is hardly a trend or development to treat commercial awards as investments. That having been said, it is probable that without different considerations, tribunals are likely to assert jurisdiction in cases involving enforcement of commercial arbitral awards. Whether this development will help to promote international investment is a different issue.

V. China's treaty practice on determination of foreign investment

China has been a recipient of large amounts of foreign investment for more than two decades. It is, on the one hand, eager to attract foreign investment and, on the other hand, imposes restrictive measures on foreign investment. Even today, every foreign investment must receive the approval of the Chinese Government

---

323 Although it observed that the *GEA* Tribunal's opinion that the ICC Award in that case did not constitute an investment was *obiter dicta* and continued to consider that "the conclusion expressed by the *GEA* Tribunal represents an incorrect departure from the developing jurisprudence on the treatment of arbitral awards to the effect that awards made by tribunals arising out of disputes concerning 'investments' made by 'investors' under BITs represented a continuation or transformation of the original investment," the *White Industries* Tribunal actually went no further than did the *Saipem* Tribunal, as it "conclude[d] that rights under the Award constitute part of White's original investment (i.e., being a crystallization of its rights under the Contract) and, as such, are subject to such protection as is afforded to investments by the BIT." (*White Industries v. India*, Final Award, *supra*, note 306, para. 7.6.10.) Further, in its footnote 41, the *White Industries* Tribunal noted: "Rather than define awards as 'investments' in and of themselves, tribunals such as *Mondev*, *Chevron* and *Frontier Petroleum Services* have characterized their findings as providing protection to the subsisting interests that [the investor] continued to hold in the original investment." In fact, the sole tribunal that appears to have actually held that a commercial award was, in itself, an investment appears to be *ATA Construction, Industrial and Trading Company v. Hashemite Kingdom of Jordan*, ICSID Case No. ARB/08/2, Award (May 18, 2010), at para. 115, where the tribunal observed that: "measured by the standards in *Saipem*, the Final Award at issue in the present arbitration would be part of an 'entire operation' that qualifies as an investment."

324 *White Industries v. India*, Final Award, ibid., *supra*, note 306, para. 7.6.8. Unfortunately, contrary to the *White Industries* Tribunal's assertion in its footnote 41, the *Frontier Petroleum Services* Tribunal—a UNCITRAL tribunal—nowhere characterized the previous Stockholm awards in that case as anything; it merely noted, *obiter dicta*: "This Tribunal accepts that Claimant's original investment consisted of the payments made to MA and Davidová between April 18, 2001 and August 14, 2001, which were transformed into an entitlement to a first secured charge in the Final Award." It then continued that "by refusing to recognise and enforce the Final Award in its entirety, the Tribunal accepts that Respondent could be said to have affected the management, use, enjoyment, or disposal by Claimant of what remained of its original investment." See *Frontier Petroleum Services Ltd. v. Czech Republic*, UNCITRAL Arbitration, Final Award (November 12, 2010), para. 231.

before it can be made. The reflection of this policy in Chinese BITs is a certain caution in recognizing what may constitute an investment. The trend is that this Chinese policy is becoming more and more relaxed. Take, for example, the 1984 China–Norway BIT, one of the earliest bilateral agreements on investment that China entered into. Regarding the definition of investment, it provides:

> The term "investing" means assets permitted by either contracting party in accordance with its laws and regulations, including, in particular:
> a. Movable and immovable property and other property rights such as mortgages, pledges, liens, usufruct, and other similar rights;
> b. Shares, stock, and debentures of companies or interests in the property of such companies;
> c. Claims to money or to any performance under contract having a monetary value;
> d. Copyrights, industrial property rights (such as patents, trademarks and external designs of industrial products), know-how, and goodwill; and
> e. Concessions conferred by law or under contract permitted by law, including concessions to search for and exploit natural resources.[325]

The definition of "investment" in the China–Norway BIT, although relatively incomplete when compared with those contained in modern BITs, has the effect of filling certain gaps in Chinese law,[326] because in the Chinese legal system international treaty provisions prevail over local laws in cases of conflict.[327] That was

---

325 1984 China–Norway BIT, Article 1.1; available via UNCTAD, Investment Instruments Online, at: http://www.unctadxi.org/templates/DocSearch____779.aspx.

326 None of the Chinese laws contains a detailed definition of foreign "investment." In general, Chinese law regards cash, equipment, technology, and intellectual property rights contributed by foreign investors as investment. Yet it does not define the outer limits of the rights arising from such invested items. For example, Article 5 of the Chinese Foreign Joint Venture Law reads: "Each party to a joint venture may make its investment in cash, in kind or in industrial property rights, etc. The technology and the equipment that serve as the foreign party's investment must be advanced technology and equipment that actually suit our country's needs. If the foreign party causes losses by deception through the intentional use of backward technology and equipment, it shall pay compensation for the losses. The investment of a Chinese partner in a joint venture may include the right to the use of a site provided for the joint venture during the period of its operation. If the right to the use of the site does not constitute a part of the Chinese party's investment, the joint venture shall pay the Chinese Government a fee for its use. The various investments referred to above shall be specified in the joint venture contract and articles of association and the value of each (excluding that of the site) shall be jointly assessed by the parties to the venture."

327 Article 142 of the General Principles of Civil Law of the People's Republic of China provides that where any international treaty concluded or acceded to by China contains provisions differing from those in the laws of the country, the provisions of the international treaty shall apply, unless the provisions are ones with respect to which China has made a reservation. Article 236 of the Chinese Civil Procedure Law provides that where an international treaty ratified or acceded to by the People's Republic of China contains provisions differing from those found in this Law, the provisions of the international treaty shall apply, unless the provisions are ones on which China has announced reservations.

precisely the way BITs were used in the development of the Chinese legal system on the protection of foreign investment.

The 1986 China–United Kingdom BIT gives investment a broader definition than does the 1984 China–Norway BIT. It states that "[i]nvestment means every kind of asset accepted as investment by a contracting party" and that this "includes investments existing at the date of entry into force of this Agreement; and a change in the form in which assets are invested does not affect their character as investments."[328]

In the current generation of Chinese BITs, the definition of "investment" has been further expanded. For instance, the 2003 China–Germany BIT defines investment as "every kind of asset invested directly or indirectly by investors of one Contracting Party in the territory of the other Contracting Party."[329] With the broad definition expanded to include investments made "indirectly," the coverage by the 2003 China–Germany BIT is much wider than that afforded by prior agreements.[330] The 2003 China-Germany BIT also enumerates on a non-exclusive basis assets that should be considered as investment, including:[331]

(a) movable and immovable property and other property rights such as mortgages and pledges;
(b) shares, debentures, stock and any other kind of interest in companies;
(c) claims to money or to any other performance having an economic value associated with an investment;
(d) intellectual property rights, in particular copyrights, patents and industrial designs, trademarks, trade-names, technical processes, trade and business secrets, know-how and good-will;
(e) business concessions conferred by law or under contract permitted by

---

328 1986 China–United Kingdom BIT, Article 1(1)(a).
329 2003 China–Germany BIT, Article 1(1).
330 Article 1(1) of the 1983 China–Germany BIT provides that: "'Investment' means all the assets under the effective laws of the contracting parties, mainly including: (a) ownership rights of movable and immovable property and other property rights such as mortgages and pledges; (b) shares and other kind of interest in companies; (c) claims to money that can be used in creating economic value or to any other performance having an economic value; (d) copyrights, industrial property rights, technical processes, know-how, trademarks and trade names; and (e) concession rights, including concessions to search for, exploit and extract."
331 This is comparable with the recent US Model BIT, under which "'investment' means every asset that an investor owns or controls, directly or indirectly, that has the characteristics of an investment, including such characteristics as the commitment of capital or other resources, the expectation of gain or profit, or the assumption of risk. Forms that an investment may take include: (a) an enterprise; (b) shares, stock, and other forms of equity participation in an enterprise; (c) bonds, debentures, other debt instruments and loans; (d) futures, options, and other derivatives; (e) turnkey, construction, management, production, concession, revenue-sharing, and other similar contracts; (f) intellectual property rights; (g) licenses, authorizations, permits, and similar rights conferred pursuant to domestic law; and (h) other tangible or intangible, movable or immovable property, and related property rights, such as leases, mortgages, liens, and pledges."

law, including concessions to search for, cultivate, extract or exploit natural resources.[332]

Beyond the definition of investment in the 1983 BIT, the current China–Germany BIT includes stocks and shares; business secrets and goodwill; and concessions to search for, cultivate, extract, or exploit natural resources as investments. In addition, the open-ended definition of investment, that is, that it "includes, though not exclusively", may extend the application of the BIT to an as yet unknown extent.[333] In an effort to contain the scope of application within the expectation of the parties, the Protocol to the BIT[334] stipulates that "investments" are those "made for the purpose of establishing lasting economic relations in connection with an enterprise, especially those which [are] allow[ed] to exercise effective influence in its management." The Protocol further defines indirect investments as those "invested by an investor of one Contracting Party through a company which is fully or partially owned by the investor and having its seat in the territory of the other Contracting Party." The Protocol is an integral part of the BIT, and the two agreements were entered into at the same time. The restrictions set forth in the Protocol were a compromise by the parties; a Chinese negotiator told this author that the term "indirect investment" was too indeterminate for China but that Germany insisted on having it included in the BIT.[335] As a result, whilst the BIT explicitly provides for the protection of indirect investment, the Protocol formulates restrictions to narrow down the application of such provisions. This practice also reflects the cultural sensitivity inherent in BIT negotiations.

The 2008 China–New Zealand FTA has an even wider definition of investment than does the 2003 China–Germany BIT. It covers, in addition, "bonds, including government issued bonds, debentures, loans and other forms of debt, and rights derived therefrom" and "any right conferred by law or under contract and any licenses and permits pursuant to law."[336] In comparison, the 2007 China–Pakistan FTA's definition of investment is almost identical with that of

---

332 2003 China–Germany BIT, Article 1(1).
333 In *Fedax v. Venezuela*, for example, as we have seen previously, promissory notes were considered to be qualified investment, and one of the rationales given by the tribunal for reaching this conclusion was that Article 1 of the Netherlands–Venezuela BIT gave an open-ended definition of "investment" by providing that "the term 'investments' shall comprise every kind of asset and more particularly though not exclusively ..." See *Fedax v. Venezuela, supra*, note 16.
334 The Protocol and the BIT between China and Germany were signed on the same day. The preamble of the Protocol states: "On signing the Agreement ..., the plenipotentiaries, being duly authorized, have, in addition, agreed on the following provisions, which shall be regarded as an integral part of the said Agreement."
335 It is also China's practice in international treaty-making that less important provisions and concrete provisions, as well as those that may be amended afterwards, may be stipulated in a separate document, such as a protocol to the main agreement.
336 2008 China–New Zealand FTA, Article 135. The FTA also stipulates that non-interest bearing loans and other forms of debt should be treated as investments, provided that they are registered with the competent authorities of a party.

the 2003 China–Germany BIT.[337] Another notable difference is that, in the 2007 China–Pakistan FTA, it is provided that "any change in the form in which assets are invested does not affect their character as investments provided that such a change is in accordance with the laws and regulations of the Party in whose territory the investment has been made," whilst in both the 2008 China–New Zealand FTA and the 2003 China–German BIT, the words "provided that such a change is in accordance with the laws and regulations of the Party in whose territory the investment has been made" are not included.

The BITs and FTAs that China has entered into list possible assets and activities as investments, a practice common to international investment treaties. As a consequence, what may actually constitute an investment is subject to interpretation in practice, which is also often the source of disputes. Although China has not yet been involved in an investor–state arbitration, related decisions made by arbitral tribunals are of significance in determining how the provisions in China's BITs and FTAs are likely to be interpreted in practice.

China would welcome the application of the *Salini* test, even though the last element thereof has been criticized by some.[338] Whether a given investment contributes to the economic development of a country may be difficult to ascertain. As discussed earlier, Chinese law requires foreign investors to contribute advanced technology which, in the view of China, will contribute to its economic development. Suppose a foreign investor is found to have failed to provide advanced technology and the Chinese Government, local or central, decides to suspend preferential treatment of the foreign investor. The question as to whether the investment concerned is qualified for protection is likely to arise. The tribunal in charge will need to decide whether the Chinese authorities were at fault in approving the foreign investment and, if not, whether the foreign investor acted deceptively. Any major investment will involve a substantial period of preparation, construction and operation before it makes any profit. Where the Chinese Government, after supposedly examining the documents and business plans regarding the foreign investment, approves the project and later on decides that the investment is not qualified to enjoy preferential treatment because the technology invested is not sufficiently advanced, arbitral tribunals are unlikely to be sympathetic.[339] Thus, the

---

337 Article 46 of the 2007 China–Pakistan FTA does not include industrial designs in its definition of investment.

338 For instance, the tribunal in *L.E.S.I and ASTALDI v. Algeria* expressly questioned whether this was a valid separate criterion, saying: "Il ne paraît en revanche pas nécessaire qu'il réponde en plus spécialement à la promotion économique du pays, une condition de toute façon difficile à établir et implicitement couverte par les trois éléments retenus." ("It does not seem, however, necessary that it [a contract] responds more especially to the economic promotion of the country, a condition that in any case is hard to establish and which is implicitly covered by the three other criteria" [author's translation]). See *L.E.S.I. S.p.A. and ASTALDI S.p.A. v. République Algérienne Démocratique et Populaire*, ICSID Case No. ARB/05/3, Decision on Jurisdiction (July 12, 2006), para. 72.

339 For instance, in *Saipem*, the claimant, in supporting its position that the transaction at issue was an investment, argued that it had "invested substantial technical, financial and human resources in the project, which gave a substantial contribution to Bangladesh's economic development, and it

provisions of the relevant BITs are likely to play a crucial role in protecting foreign investors' interests.

The BITs entered into by China prior to the mid-1990s all required that the investment be made "in accordance with the laws and regulations" of the host country. Some of the recently concluded BITs, however, do not include such a requirement. The 2003 China–Germany BIT simply defines investment as "every kind of asset invested directly or indirectly by investors of one Contracting Party in the territory of the other Contracting Party."[340] Article 2, on the Promotion and Protection of Investments, states that: "Each Contracting Party shall encourage investors of the other Contracting Party to make investments in its territory and admit such investments in accordance with its laws and regulations." It then continues to provide for constant protection and security.[341] The 2008 China–New Zealand FTA not only does not require foreign investment to be made by following host country laws but also omits such provisions in the articles stipulating treatment of foreign investments. This is in contrast to the 2007 China–Pakistan FTA, which contains stipulations similar to those contained in China's first-generation BITs,[342] and the 2004 China–Benin BIT.[343] The 2004 China–Benin BIT provides in Article 1 that: "[t]he term 'investment' means every kind of asset invested by investors of one Contracting Party in accordance with the laws and regulations of the other Contracting Party in the territory of the latter." It then gives examples of what may constitute an investment.

There is hardly any official reason to explain why some of China's BITs and FTAs—signed almost at the same time—require investment to be made in accordance with local laws and others do not contain such a requirement. It does appear that the ones which require that investments be made in compliance with domestic laws are those made with developing countries and those without such requirements are those made with developed countries. It could be the case that China is relaxing its policy in this regard. As a result, where its counterpart insists on requiring foreign investment to be made in compliance with the local laws, China would concede to such request, as that was, after all, China's previous practice.

The differences in treaty requirements on the making of investments that are contained in the various agreements entered into by China may lead to problems in practice. It can be argued that because the 2008 China–New Zealand FTA was entered into subsequent to the 2007 China–Pakistan FTA and because the

assumed risks for a significant duration (the performance phase lasted two and a half years);" see *Saipem v. Bangladesh*, Decision on Jurisdiction, *supra*, note 263, para. 100.

340 2003 China–Germany BIT, Article 1(1).
341 Ibid., Article 2(2).
342 Article 46 of the 2007 China–Pakistan FTA provides that the term investment "means every kind of asset invested by investors of one Party in accordance with the laws and regulations of the other Party in the territory of the latter." It should be noted that the 2007 China–Pakistan FTA was concluded before the 2008 China–New Zealand FTA.
343 For the text of the 2004 China–Benin BIT, see: http://unctad.org/sections/dite/iia/docs/bits/China_Benin.pdf.

former does not require investments to be made "in accordance with the laws and regulations of the host country," at the least the Chinese Government was not unaware of the significance of the omission. In practice, of course, this omission may stop China (and also, of course, New Zealand) from claiming an investment to be unqualified for protection on the ground that it was not made in compliance with local laws. As discussed earlier, in *Fraport*,[344] the term "in accordance with the laws and regulations" was interpreted as a condition for the making of an investment and hence a precondition of the consent given by the host country for investor–state arbitration.

The approval processes may work in China's favor as a recipient of foreign capital where the foreign investor fails fully to disclose or deliberately makes false disclosure of the information required by law. In the *Plama*[345] case, for example, where the foreign investors failed to disclose the shareholders of the entity through which the investment was made, the tribunal held that the deliberate concealment of the actual shareholders "amount[ed] to fraud, calculated to induce the Bulgarian authorities to authorize the transfer of shares to an entity that did not have the financial and managerial capacities required" for an oil refinery and that it was contrary to "provisions of Bulgarian law and to international law and that it, therefore, precludes the application of the protections of the ECT."[346]

Based the rulings of the *Fraport* Tribunal, even though Chinese law may require that foreign investments meet certain requirements, including advanced technology, etc., because international treaty provisions prevail over national laws in case of conflict, the provisions of such agreements as the 2008 China–New Zealand FTA may enable foreign investors to avoid strict compliance with Chinese law. The Chinese Government still requires foreign investors to go through an approval process when making an investment, but once approval is given, it will be more difficult for the Chinese Government to argue that a given investment was not made in accordance with Chinese law.

As discussed earlier, in disputes arising under a BIT or other agreement which is silent on the requirement that an investment be made in compliance with local laws, an implied requirement may still be assumed. However, where a foreign investor goes through the examination procedures and no question is raised by the local officials in charge, a presumption may be reached that the transaction has satisfied the requirements of local law. In such cases, the only possible defense available to the host state may be "good faith." Yet, to what extent this defense can be effective is still open to question, as the foreign investor may argue that the host state is estopped from raising such a defence. On balance, the Chinese decision to eliminate the local law requirement in BITs and FTAs may suggest that the Chinese negotiators still assume that there is such an implied requirement. It may nevertheless be difficult to defend such cases in practice.[347]

344 *Fraport v. Philippines, supra*, note 187.
345 *Plama Consortium Limited v. Republic of Bulgaria, supra*, note 204.
346 Ibid., para. 135.
347 This is so because the very act of deleting a previously incorporated condition that is often

Another feature of China's practice in defining foreign investment is that Chinese laws regard reinvestment of earnings from existing foreign investment as also being foreign investment. The purpose of the provision is to encourage foreign investors not to take their earnings back to their home countries. This policy has been extended to BITs. For instance, in the 2004 China–Finland BIT, it is specifically provided in Article 1(1) that "[r]einvested returns shall enjoy the same treatment as the original investment." As foreign investments in China enjoy certain preferential treatments, such as tax exemptions and reductions which are limited to certain periods of time, to treat reinvestment of earnings as foreign investment not only puts such funds under the protection of BITs but also enables the continuing enjoyment of preferential treatments. There are no statistics available to indicate to what extent this Chinese policy has contributed to China's ability to attract foreign investment, but it certainly plays a positive part.

VI. Conclusions

As is the case with other areas of investment law, jurisprudence and the writings of jurists differ in how to define investment. Jurists may always hold different views, which will actually assist the development of international investment law. Different and very often contradictory decisions by tribunals may not help anyone. Insofar as the definition of investment is concerned, the most important question is whether or not the term investment should have any objective meaning. This question actually has nothing to do with the double-barreled test, although it is often phrased as if it does. In the entire jurisprudence of investment law, no one has bothered to check—as the WTO Appellate Body and panels often do—the simple dictionary meaning of "investment" and related terms. In the end, the determination of whether a transaction is a covered investment has been to a large extent subject to the perception of individual panels.[348]

It is also the case that where a different instrument is used, the result would be different—a transaction which is not considered to be an investment according to one instrument may be considered an investment under another. *Petrobart v. Kyrgyz Republic*[349] is an example in this regard. Even though the claimant in that case was badly treated by the Kyrgyz Government, the transaction in question in that case was a sale and purchase contract. The claimant—Petrobart Limited—was a company registered in Gibraltar. On February 23, 1998, Petrobart as supplier

included in the treaties that a country has entered into may not be perceived as demonstrating that it was felt unnecessary or "implied" but rather that it was being actively removed.

348 One scholar has commented that "[t]here is no multilateral grant of authority over objective interpretation granted to individual tribunals sitting in cases of particular investor-State disputes;" D. Krishan, "A Notion of ICSID Investment," in T. J. Grierson Weiler (ed.), *Investment Treaty Arbitration and International Law*, Juris Publishing, Huntington, New York, 2008. By the same token, however, no tribunal is authorized to interpret a treaty provision without considering faithfully its objective meanings.

349 *Petrobart Limited v. Kyrgyz Republic*, SCC Arbitration No. 126/2003, Arbitral Award (March 29, 2005).

and the Kyrgyz Republic joint stock company Kyrgyzgazmunaizat ("KGM") as purchaser concluded a goods supply contract for the supply and transfer of 200,000 metric tons of stable gas condensate over the course of one year on a monthly basis against the payment of US$143.50 (inclusive of VAT) per metric ton of gas condensate. The price was to remain unchanged throughout the life of the contract and was to be paid according to the details of the invoice presented by Petrobart in relation to each separate consignment of goods, within 10 days of the date of the goods' arrival at the station of destination.[350] Petrobart fulfilled part of its obligation under the contract, but KGM paid for only a part of the goods supplied. As a consequence, Petrobart filed a claim with the Bishkek City Court of Arbitration (the "Bishkek City Court"), requesting payment for the remainder of the supplied goods.[351] On December 25, 1998, the Bishkek City Court rendered a ruling in favor of Petrobart in the amount of US$1,499,143 plus an amount of duty calculated in Kyrgyz Soms and, on February 10, 1999, it decided that Petrobart could execute its judgment against the stock and property of KGM.[352]

The claimant contended that its contract should benefit from the investment protection provisions of the ECT. It further claimed that the contract for money and the Bishkek court's judgment represented investments pursuant to Article 1(6) of the ECT. The tribunal first pointed out that the contract between the claimant and the respondent "did not involve any transfer of money or property as capital in a business in the Kyrgyz Republic but was a sales contract. It concerned the sale of goods at an agreed price."[353] The question then was whether the same contract could constitute an investment under the ECT.[354]

The tribunal referred to Article 1(6)(f) of the ECT, according to which "any right conferred by law or contract or by virtue of any licences and permits granted pursuant to law to undertake any Economic Activity in the Energy Sector" may constitute an investment. As to the question of what may constitute an economic activity, under Article 1(5), any economic activity "concerning the exploration, extraction, refining, production, storage, land transport, transmission, distribution, trade, marketing, or sale of Energy Materials and Products" may satisfy the requirement. Based on this definition, the tribunal held that "the gas condensate which Petrobart sold in the Contract [should] be regarded as Energy Materials and Products."[355]

It is true that although the sales contract to which the claimant was a party might arguably fall into the category of an "economic activity" relating to the

---

350 See ibid., p. 4, first 4 paragraphs.
351 Ibid., p. 5, paras. 4 and 5, and p. 6, para. 3.
352 Ibid., p. 6, paras. 6 and 10; see also p. 7, para. 4.
353 Ibid., p. 69, para. 6.
354 This is so because the tribunal believed that: "While in ordinary language investment is often understood as being capital or property used as a financial basis for a company or a business activity with the aim to produce revenue or income, wider definitions are frequently found in treaties on the protection of investments, whether bilateral (BITs) or multilateral (MITs)." Ibid, p. 69, para. 7.
355 Ibid., p. 72, paras. 5–6.

energy sector,[356] it must also be pointed out that the tribunal applied the widest interpretation possible in order to reach its conclusion that it was also an investment under the ECT. The transaction was not an investment in an ordinary sense at all. This has obviously presented the tribunals dealing with the definition of investment with an extremely complicated task. That is perhaps also the reason that the *Petrobart* Tribunal was rather conservative in assessing the damages that the claimant was considered to have suffered.[357]

The limitations—in relation to both bilateral and multilateral treaty provisions—that a tribunal faces in deciding a case notwithstanding, in order to win wider support tribunals still have a great deal of work to do in improving their decision-making. Very often it is felt that more faithfulness to the intentions of the parties is needed in the interpretation of treaty provisions. For instance, no state would encourage investments not made in compliance with its laws nor would it support foreign investments that could not contribute, at least by intent and in theory, to its economy. At the same time, where a transaction per se is not an investment under the relevant BIT and a multilateral instrument such as the ICSID Convention, it should not be converted to or regarded as an investment just because there has been an intervening commercial arbitral award. To cure such defects in relation to the definition of investments, tribunals and scholars should seriously consider whether there is an objective meaning to the term "investment" itself and, if so, what the specifics are.

---

356 The *Petrobart* Tribunal stated that: "It is thus not unusual that claims to money, even if not based on any long-term involvement in a business in another country, are included in treaties within the concept of 'investment'." Ibid, p. 72, para. 3.

357 For a critical discussion of the case see Galina Zukova, "The Award in Petrobart Limited v. Kyrgyz Republic," in Guillermo Aguilar and W. Michael Reisman (eds.), *The Reasons Requirement in International Investment Arbitration*," Martinus Nijhoff Publishers, 2008, ch 11, pp. 323–47.

5   Consent as a condition of jurisdiction

As in commercial arbitrations,[1] an important feature of investor–state arbitration is party autonomy—especially the consent of the parties to arbitration.[2] Yet the way in which consent is given for investment arbitration differs from that for commercial arbitration. For instance, in most cases, consent is not given in an agreement signed by both disputing parties. Instead, the host states often give their consent in local laws, the bilateral investment treaties ("BITs") and free trade agreements ("FTAs") to which they are parties or such multilateral treaties as the Energy Charter Treaty or the North American Free Trade Agreement ("NAFTA"), and each of these is regarded as a standing offer that can be accepted by investors. In such cases, foreign investors are not parties to the international agreements or unilateral declarations. This has been referred to as "international arbitration without privity," which "allows the true complainant to face the true defendant. This has the immense merit of clarity and realism; these virtues, and not eloquent proclamations, are the prerequisites of confidence in the legal process."[3] Some scholars, however, argue that "arbitration is entirely dependent on the consent of the parties evidenced in a written argument [sic] to arbitrate future disputes or in a clause in a contract to arbitrate future disputes arising from the contract. An arbitration agreement could also be made after the dispute

---

1 In commercial arbitration, consent of the disputing parties is essential as it is the prerequisite to an arbitration tribunal's jurisdiction. For discussions on consent or agreement to arbitrate in the context of commercial arbitration, see Philip D. O'Neill, Jr., *International Commercial Arbitration*, West (2012), chs 1–2.

2 For discussions on the history of State consent to ICSID arbitration, see M. D. Nolan and F. G. Sourgens, "The Interplay between State Consent to ICSID Arbitration and Denunciation of the ICSID Convention: The (Possible) Venezuela Case Study," *Transnational Dispute Management*, Vol. 4, Issue 5, September 2007. The authors advocated the theory of offer and acceptance as an analogy to state consent to arbitration.

3 See Jan Paulsson, "Arbitration Without Privity," *ICSID Review—Foreign Investment Law Journal*, Vol. 10, No. 2 (Fall 1995), pp. 232–57, at 256. The underpinning for this proposition, according to Paulsson, is that very often the aggrieved investors cannot hold the party which has breached the contract that they are parties to accountable for the breach. "Even if they can, their local contracting party may often avoid responsibility for the breach by reason of an act of *force majeure* or the like. The injury is caused by a third party, often a governmental authority." Ibid., at 255.

had arisen."[4] The trend is that in investor–state arbitration, privity is no longer an issue. Even those who are critical of the above proposition have to admit that the practice is in favor of arbitration without privity:

> This view has gained acceptance as a result of some arbitrations in which the tribunals found jurisdiction even in the absence of contractual provisions which indicated consent to arbitration of future disputes arising from the contract. Those who are disposed to seeing progress towards the dawn of an age in which private power will be triumphant, see in these developments the beginning of a trend in which foreign investment arbitration could be held even in the absence of privity.[5]

Although in investor–state arbitration privity is not an issue, consent is still essential to prove that the tribunal in question is bestowed the power to arbitrate. Yet the consent to arbitrate may be given by the host state and the foreign investor at different times. It is often the case that the host state will give consent first, which is regarded as an offer. The acceptance of this offer by the investor, and thus its own consent, may be accomplished by its filing of a request for arbitration or by direct notification to the respondent state. As far as the form is concerned, most arbitration rules do not stipulate what may constitute a valid consent. For instance, the ICSID Convention requires consent to arbitration to be in writing. It does not, however, further provide the requirements of writing. Thus, disputing parties have freedom to choose the manner of expressing their consent. Under the ICSID Convention, once consent to arbitration has been given, no party may withdraw such consent unilaterally.[6] Also, unless otherwise stated, any consent to ICSID arbitration shall be deemed to be to an exclusion of any other remedy.[7] At the same time, under local laws and BITs, consent to arbitration may be subject to certain conditions, such as choice of forum (the so-called "fork in the road") or exhaustion of local remedies.[8]

This chapter examines international investment law, in particular arbitration practice, in respect of consent, including the general issues involved, *ratione temporis*, "fork in the road" provisions, exhaustion of local remedies and Chinese treaty practice.

I. Determination of consent

Consent is a precondition of arbitration, regardless of whether it is commercial or investor–state. Consent determines the formation and competence of arbitration

---

4 M. Sornarajah, "Power and Justice in Foreign Investment Arbitration," *Journal of International Arbitration*, 14(3), September 1997, pp. 103–40, at 126.

5 Id.

6 Article 25(1) of the ICSID Convention.

7 For sample consent clauses in BITs and Latin American practice, see F. J. Pascual Vives, "Consent to ICSID Arbitration: Recent Conventional and Arbitral Practice," *Transnational Dispute Management*, Vol. 8, Issue 2, May 2011.

8 Article 26 of the ICSID Convention.

tribunals. It is therefore a foundation of any arbitration system. The Report of the Executive Directors to the ICSID Convention,[9] for instance, describes consent as "the cornerstone of the jurisdiction of the Centre." Delaume summarized the situation as follows:

> The scope of such a consent is within the discretion of the parties. In this connection, it should be noted that ratification of the ICSID Convention is, on the part of a Contracting State, only an expression of its willingness to make use of the ICSID machinery. As such, ratification does not constitute an obligation to use that machinery. That obligation can arise only after the State concerned has specifically agreed to submit to ICSID arbitration a particular dispute or classes of disputes. In other words, the decision of a State to consent to ICSID arbitration is a matter of pure policy and it is within the sole discretion of each Contracting State to determine the type of investment disputes that it considers arbitration in the context of ICSID.[10]

Any determination of the existence of consent involves interpretation of the agreement in question and the relevant arbitration rules. As such, arbitral tribunals are expected to interpret consent clauses in accordance with the true meaning of the treaty provisions.[11] This was observed by the tribunal in *Amco Asia v. Indonesia* when it said that:

> … a convention to arbitrate is not to be construed *restrictively*, nor, as a matter of fact, *broadly* or *liberally*. It is to be construed in a way which leads to find out and to respect the common will of the parties. … Moreover, … any convention, including conventions to arbitrate, should be construed in good faith, that is to say by taking into account the consequences of the commitments the parties may be considered as having reasonably and legitimately envisaged.[12]

As investor–state arbitration involves sovereign states, where the respondent state raises an objection to jurisdiction on the grounds of a lack of consent, tribunals

---

9 *Report of the Executive Directors of the International Bank for Reconstruction and Development on the Convention on the Settlement of Investment Disputes between States and Nationals of Other States* [hereinafter "Report of the Executive Directors"], International Bank for Reconstruction and Development (March 18, 1965).

10 G. R. Delaume, "ICSID Arbitration: Practical Considerations," 1 *Journal of International Arbitration* 101 (1984), at 104–105, quoted from Christoph H. Schreuer et al. (eds.), *The ICSID Convention: A Commentary* (2nd ed.), CUP, 2009, at 190.

11 An early case involving interpretation of provisions on consent is *Alcoa Minerals of Jamaica, Inc. v. Government of Jamaica*, ICSID Case No. ARB/74/2, Decision on Jurisdiction and Competence of Arbitral Tribunal, 1975, unpublished. For discussions on the case, see John T. Schmidt, "Arbitration Under the Auspices of the International Centre for Settlement of Investment Disputes (ICSID): Implications of the Decision on Jurisdiction in Alcoa Minerals of Jamaica, Inc. v. Government of Jamaica," 17 *Harv. Int'l. L. J.* 90, 1976.

12 *Amco Asia et al. v. Indonesia*, Decision on Jurisdiction (September 25, 1983), 23 *I.L.M.* 359 (1984).

must treat the matter of consent with great care. This was noted by the *Mihaly* Tribunal, which said:

> ... the question of jurisdiction of an international instance involving consent of a sovereign State deserves a special attention at the outset of any proceeding against a State Party to an international convention creating the jurisdiction. As a preliminary matter, the question of the existence of jurisdiction based on consent must be examined *proprio motu*, i.e., without objection being raised by the Party. A fortiori, since the Respondent has raised preliminary objections to the jurisdiction, the existence of consent to the jurisdiction must be closely examined.[13]

In such circumstances, as Jan Paulsson once observed, "[a] single incident of an adventurist arbitrator going beyond the proper scope of his jurisdiction in a sensitive case may be sufficient to generate a backlash."[14] Practice shows, however, that there are increasingly fewer arbitral tribunals that would restrain from exercising jurisdiction. The question as to whether this is owing to the growing existence of consent or to a growing desire on the part of tribunals to assert jurisdiction needs to be answered by examining the arbitral decisions.

In practice, for the purpose of attracting foreign investment, states may express in their own national laws their willingness to have their disputes with foreign investors resolved through international arbitration. That is an offer of consent to arbitration. This was tested in *Inceysa v. El Salvador*,[15] in which Article 15 of the El Salvador Investment Law provided that:

> In the case of controversies arising between foreign investors and the State regarding their investment in El Salvador, the investors may submit the controversy to:
> (a) ... ICSID, with the purpose of solving the controversy through conciliation and arbitration ...
> (b) ... the Additional Facility of ICSID; in those cases in which the foreign investor involved in the controversy is a national of a State that is not a contracting party to the ICSID Convention.[16]

The *Inceysa* Tribunal ruled that the above provisions constituted a unilateral offer of consent by El Salvador, although it declined jurisdiction on the ground that the claimant's investment was not qualified to invoke the provisions.[17] The advantage

---

13 *Mihaly International Corporation v. Democratic Socialist Republic of Sri Lanka*, ICSID Case No. ARB/00/2, Award (March 15, 2002), para. 56.

14 Jan Paulsson, "Arbitration Without Privity," in W. Wälde (ed.), *The Energy Charter Treaty: An East-West Gateway for Investment and Trade*, Kluwer, 1996, pp.422–42, at 442.

15 *Inceysa Vallisoletana, S.L. v. Republic of El Salvador*, ICSID Case No. *ARB/03126*, Award [on Jurisdiction] (August 2, 2006).

16 Ibid., para. 331.

17 Ibid., para. 332.

of such a unilateral commitment is that it does not need the assistance of BITs, the negotiation of which often takes time. The disadvantage for foreign investors is that the standard of substantive treatments will have to be determined in accordance with national laws and customary international law. With more and more BITs in force, unilateral consent to arbitration is no longer the main method in expressing consent to arbitration.

In *Holiday Inns v. Morocco*, the respondent denied the existence of consent to arbitrate on a strict interpretation of Article 25(2)(b) of the ICSID Convention. According to Article 25(2)(b), a "national of a Contracting Party" means "any juridical person which *had the nationality* of a Contracting State other than the State party to the dispute *on the date on which the parties consented to submit such dispute to conciliation or arbitration*" (emphases added). Therefore, in the respondent's view, whether or not, on the date the consent to arbitration was given, the juridical person had acquired the nationality of a contracting party other than the host state—Morocco—would be critical in establishing jurisdiction. The reason for this contention was that at the time the Basic Agreement was entered into, Holiday Inns S.S., Glarus—one of the complainants—had not been registered in Switzerland. The situation of the Occidental Petroleum Corporation was the same: it had not yet acquired the status of a juridical person at that time. In fact, when the Basic Agreement was signed, neither Switzerland nor Morocco was a contracting party to the ICSID Convention. Yet the Moroccan Government was fully aware of the fact that it would take some time for the private parties to the Basic Agreement to complete the formal procedures for acquiring a juridical person status in their respective jurisdictions. The question was whether or not, under either international law or the ICSID Convention, a consent to arbitration could be given prior to the state's becoming a contracting party to the Convention.

On the above point, the *Holiday Inns* Tribunal opined that "the Convention allows parties to subordinate the entry into force of an arbitration clause to the subsequent fulfillment of certain conditions, such as the adherence of the States concerned to the Convention, or the incorporation of the company envisaged by the agreement."[18] As to the case at hand, the tribunal further stated that "the only reasonable interpretation of the Basic Agreement is to hold that the Parties when signing the Agreement envisaged that all necessary conditions for jurisdiction of the Centre would be fulfilled and their consent would at that time become fully effective."[19] The tribunal's views and holding are neither surprising nor unreasonable. In international investment, it is often the case that states enter into a BIT long before an investment dispute is brought to arbitration. It is equally no less common that long after a state has entered into a BIT with another state—the time at which it is deemed to have given its consent to arbitration—an entity is established which engages in an investment in the state. It is therefore generally

---

18 Quoted from Pierre Lalive, "The First World Bank Arbitration (Holiday Inns v. Morocco)—Some Legal Problems," 51 *Brit. Y. B. Int'l L.* 123 (1980), at 146.
19 Id.

agreed that for the investor/claimant, the date of giving its consent is the date of its filing of a request for arbitration.[20]

In fact, there was an additional aspect that bothered the *Holiday Inns* Tribunal; that is that the Moroccan Government accepted ICSID jurisdiction in the Basic Agreement and performed the same contract thereafter. It only questioned its consent to ICSID jurisdiction at the arbitration hearing. As the complainants had also relied on this behavior on the part of Morocco, under the principle of estoppel, the state's argument could not stand. Yet, as will be discussed later, estoppel has not been relied upon by complainants in establishing the jurisdiction of tribunals. This is actually not surprising, taking into account that modern BITs all provide for investor–state arbitration, which represents the consent thereto by the host state. Once an investor institutes arbitration proceedings, that act will be construed as an acceptance of the offer contained in the BIT. In such circumstances, the issue of estoppel can hardly arise.[21]

ČSOB v. Slovakia[22] was also concerned with the issue of whether or not consent to arbitration was given but in a unique way. In that case, one of the difficulties in determining consent was that the effectiveness of the BIT between the Czech Republic and Slovakia had not been agreed upon by the parties, whilst Article 8 of the BIT contained an ICSID arbitration clause. There was no question that the claimant had consented to ICSID arbitration by filing its request thereto.

The respondent, however, argued that the BIT had not yet entered into force because Article 12 thereof provided that "each Party shall give notice to the other Party of the completion of the constitutional formalities required for this Agreement to enter into force." Thus, although the Slovak Ministry of Foreign Affairs had published a notice in the Official Gazette on October 22, 1993 announcing the entry into force of the BIT on January 1, 1993, the same Ministry had also published a corrective notice in the same Gazette on 20 November 1997 to announce the invalidity of the BIT. The tribunal considered that the above "language shows that the parties were aware and mutually recognized that the

20 Lalive commented that this interpretation was in compliance with the "balance established by the [ICSID] Convention between the interests of the investment-importing States and those of the investment-exporting States. The former, once they have consented to the jurisdiction of ICSID, are fully protected against diplomatic protection by the latter. From this point of view, it is entirely sufficient that the quality of 'Contracting State' (i.e. the fact of ratification) be checked on the date when the dispute is submitted to arbitration." Ibid., at 144.

21 For discussion on the Venezuelan law relating to consent to arbitrate in investor–state disputes, see G. Lemenez de Kerdeleau, "State Consent to ICSID Arbitration: Article 22 of the Venezuelan Investment Law," *Transnational Dispute Management*, Vol. 4, Issue 3, June 2007. However, in cases where a bilateral or multilateral investment treaty or a domestic foreign investment law has been abrogated or repealed, estoppel may be one of the grounds for establishing consent; see, for example, the comment of the *Rumeli* Tribunal that: "it is also well established in international law that a State may not take away accrued rights of a foreign investor by domestic legislation abrogating the law granting these rights. This is an application of the principles of good faith, estoppel and *venire factum proprium*." *Rumeli Telekom AS and Telsim Mobil Telekomikasyon Hizmetleri AS v. Kazakhstan*, ICSID Case No. ARB/05/16, Award (July 21, 2008), at para. 335.

22 *Československa obchodni banka, A.S. (ČSOB) v. Slovak Republic*, ICSID Case No. ARB/97/4, Decision on Objections to Jurisdiction (May 24, 1999).

signature of the BIT by the two heads of government was not sufficient to bring the treaty into force and that further formalities were required under the respective constitutions."[23]

Another factor to be considered was that the second sentence of Article 12 of the BIT provided that "the treaty shall come into force as of the date of the division of the two Republics."[24] The tribunal agreed with the respondent that this sentence should be read as part of the constitutional requirement for the coming into force of the BIT and that "once the exchange of notices contemplated by the first sentence had taken place, the treaty would be effective as of the date of division, the division being another condition for the coming into force of the BIT."[25] This was so because both states knew that the division would take place on January 1, 1993.

Even though the notice of the Ministry of Foreign Affairs of Slovakia was made ineffective by its corrective notice, there was no exchange of notices by the contracting parties to the BIT. As to whether the said notice could be interpreted as a unilateral declaration, the tribunal held:

> Even if the Notice were to be characterized as a unilateral declaration by the Slovak State, it still needs to be asked whether it was "the intention of the State making the declaration that it should become bound according to its terms,"[26] as required by the international law principles applicable to unilateral declarations. Pursuant to these principles, unilateral assumption of the contractual obligations is "not lightly to be presumed …" and requires "a very consistent course of conduct."[27, 28]

Having found lack of intention on the part of the respondent, the tribunal moved on to consider if consent had been given in the Consolidation Agreement, Article 7 of which provides that "this Agreement shall be governed by the laws of the Czech Republic and the Treaty on the Promotion and Mutual Protection of Investments between the Czech Republic and the Slovak Republic dated November 23, 1992." The question was whether the above provision could be interpreted as consent to ICSID arbitration. The respondent contended that it was a provision on governing law and that because the BIT never came into effect the reference to it

---

23 Ibid., para. 39. This is also in compliance with Article 24(1) of the Vienna Convention on the Law of Treaties ("VCLT"), which provides that "a treaty enters into force in such manner and upon such date as it may provide or as the negotiating States may agree."

24 Ibid., para. 41.

25 Id.

26 Internal footnote no. 9, citing *Nuclear Tests Case (Australia v. France)*, *I.C.J. Reports* 1974, p. 253, at 274, in ibid., para. 46.

27 Internal footnote no. 10, citing *North Sea Continental Shelf Cases*, *I.C.J.* Reports 1969, p. 4, at 25, in ibid., para. 46.

28 Ibid., para. 46. The tribunal in its deliberations also relied on Ian Brownlie, *Principles of Public International Law*, 4th ed., OUP, 1990, pp. 638–39; and B. Cheng, *General Principles of Law as Applied by International Courts and Tribunals*, CUP, 1987, pp. 147 *et seq.*

should be dismissed.[29] The negotiation history showed, however, that at first, the Consolidation Agreement contained no choice of law clause and that only "before it was signed on December 17/19, 1993, the above provision was amended by deleting the words 'after it is ratified' and by replacing it with the date of the signature of the BIT."[30] Also, the Consolidation Agreement contained no separate dispute settlement clause. This, together with a reference to the BIT, which did have a dispute settlement clause, in the view of the tribunal "[could] not be understood to mean that the contested provision was intended to deal exclusively with the governing law question ... if only because by eliminating the phrase relating to the BIT's ratification, the parties made the reference to the BIT and to the consent to arbitration expressed by it effective and unconditional."[31] In other words, had the phrase "after it is ratified" remained in the Consolidation Agreement, it would have been interpreted to mean that the parties' consent was conditioned on the entering into force of the BIT. Since that was not the case, the tribunal stated "by referring to the BIT, the parties intended to incorporate Article 8 of the BIT by reference into the Consolidation Agreement, in order to provide for international arbitration as their chosen dispute-settlement method."[32]

On the whole, this was quite a carefully reasoned decision, in which the tribunal gave the intent of the respondent adequate consideration. As the consent to arbitration was contained in the Consolidation Agreement, there was also an issue as to whether or not the foreign investor had relied on the consent. It would have been unfair to the foreign investor if the decision had been otherwise.

Consent of a state to arbitration may also be established by unilateral declarations of the state.[33] Rule 7 of the International Law Commission's 2006 Guiding Principles on Unilateral Acts of States provides:

> A unilateral declaration entails obligations for the formulating State only if it is stated in clear and specific terms. In the case of doubt as to the scope of the obligations resulting from such a declaration, such obligations must be interpreted in a restrictive manner. In interpreting the content of such obligations, weight shall be given first and foremost to the text of the declaration, together with the context and the circumstances in which it was formulated.[34]

In *Pac Rim Cayman v. El Salvador*,[35] one of the issues was whether provisions in respect of international arbitration under the Investment Law of El Salvador had

29 Ibid., para. 50.
30 Ibid., para. 52.
31 Ibid., para. 54.
32 Ibid., para. 55.
33 For discussion on consent to arbitration in national laws, see Michele Potesta, "The Interpretation of Consent to ICSID Arbitration Contained in Domestic Investment Laws," *Arbitration International*, Vol. 27, Issue 2, pp. 149–69.
34 UN International Law Commission, "Guiding Principles Applicable to Unilateral Declarations of States Capable of Creating Legal Obligations," *Report of the 58th Session*, UN Doc. A/61/10 (2006), p. 369, at 377, para. 7; available at: prawo.uni.wroc.pl/pliki/6987/pobierz.
35 *Pac Rim Cayman LLC v. Republic of El Salvador*, ICSID Case No. ARB/09/12, Decision on the Respondent's Jurisdictional Objections (June 1, 2012).

satisfied the ICSID Article 25 requirement of written consent. Article 15 of the El Salvadorian Investment Law provides:

> In the case of disputes arising between foreign investors and the State, regarding their investment in El Salvador, the investors may submit the dispute to: (a) the International Center for Settlement of Investment Disputes (ICSID), in order to settle the dispute by means of conciliation and arbitration, in accordance with the Convention on Settlement of Investment Disputes Among States and Nationals of other States (ICSID Convention) …[36]

The question was whether Article 15 formulated the respondent's consent to ICSID jurisdiction. Insofar as the nature of national laws on promotion of foreign investments is concerned, the consent to arbitrate contained therein is regarded as a guarantee to foreign investors. As Potesta observed: "[w]hile in their goals and basic structure investment laws are akin to bilateral investment treaties (BITs) or multilateral treaties, these laws raise certain particular problems connected with the fact that they contain assurances given by host states unilaterally to every possible foreign investor."[37] In fact, the issue in the *Pac Rim Cayman* case was not very complicated. In the first place, the Report of the Executive Directors stated that "a host State might in its investment promotion legislation offer to submit disputes … to the jurisdiction of the Centre, and the investor might give his consent by accepting the offer in writing."[38] Second, investment jurisprudence has been quite consistent on this issue. In practice, tribunals and scholars consider unilateral declarations by host states to be standing offers which are subject to acceptance by foreign investors.[39] The *Pac Rim Cayman* Tribunal pointed out that under Article 41(1) of the ICSID Convention, it was "for the Tribunal, as the judge of its competence …, to determine the basis of that competence, whether it be derived from a treaty or a unilateral offer made in legislation and subsequently accepted in writing by the investor."[40]

Another question facing the *Pac Rim Cayman* Tribunal was the applicable rules

---

36 Ibid., para. 5.28.
37 Potesta, *supra*, note 33, at p. 150. He also stated that "in order to amount to a consent agreement, the offer contained in national legislation must be accepted by the investor. This can be done by simply instituting arbitral proceedings." Ibid., p. 153.
38 Report of the Executive Directors, *supra*, note 9, Section 24.
39 See *Mobil Corporation and Others v. Bolivarian Republic of Venezuela*, ICSID Case No. ARB/07/27, Decision on Jurisdiction (June 10, 2010); *Cemex Caracas II Investments B.V. v. Bolivarian Republic of Venezuela*, ICSID Case No. ARB/08/15, Decision on Jurisdiction (December 30, 2010); *Southern Pacific Properties (Middle East) Limited v. Arab Republic of Egypt*, ICSID Case No. ARB/84/3, Second Decision on Jurisdiction (April 14, 1988), 3 *ICSID Reports* 131 (1995); *Inceysa v. El Salvador*, *supra*, note 15; *Zhinvali Development Ltd. v. Republic of Georgia*, ICSID Case No. ARB/00/1, Award (January 24, 2003); and *Tradex Hellas S.A. v. Republic of Albania*, ICSID Case No. ARB/94/2, Decision on Jurisdiction (December 24, 1996).
40 *Pac Rim Cayman*, *supra*, note 35, para. 5.30.

for interpreting Article 15 of the El Salvadorian Investment Law. On this matter, the tribunal relied on the practice of the International Court of Justice in the *Land and Maritime Boundary*[41] and *Fisheries Jurisdiction*[42] cases and decided that unilateral declarations and legislation should be interpreted in accordance with international law.[43] In the view of the tribunal: "declarations must be interpreted as they stand, having regard to the words actually used and taking into consideration 'the intention of the government at the time it made the declaration.' Such intention can be inferred from the text, but also from the context, the circumstances of its preparation and the purposes intended to be served by the declaration."[44]

On that basis, the tribunal then considered what the natural and plain meaning of the provisions of Article 15 of the Investment Law of El Salvador was. It concluded that the wording of Article 15 had the effect of inviting foreign investors to "decide whether to submit their claims to local courts … or to ICSID tribunals."[45] In these circumstances, the intent of El Salvador was "clear and unambiguous," and the tribunal ruled that Article 15 of the Investment Law constituted consent of the respondent to ICSID arbitration. This is so because, in the tribunal's opinion, under the ICSID Convention no specific or uniform wording in expressing consent is required.[46]

The *Pac Rim Cayman* Tribunal's decision was in line with international practice— interpreting unilateral commitments of states in accordance with international law. For instance, in *Cemex v. Venezuela*, the tribunal also stated:

> Unilateral acts by which a State consents to ICSID jurisdiction are standing offers made by a sovereign State to foreign investors under the ICSID Convention. Such offers could be incorporated into domestic legislation or not. But, whatever may be their form, they must be interpreted according to the ICSID Convention and to the principle of international law governing unilateral declarations of States.[47]

Needless to say, to adopt a certain approach in interpreting unilateral declarations and national laws is one thing and whether such interpretation reflects the intent of the states concerned is another.

In *AMTO v. Ukraine*,[48] the respondent challenged the jurisdiction of the tribunal on the grounds of an alleged lack of consent. It maintained that there was "no relevant or appropriate consent on the part of the Claimant to arbitrate" because the

41 *Land and Maritime Boundary between Cameroon and Nigeria*, Preliminary Objections, *ICJ Reports* 1998.
42 *Fisheries Jurisdiction (Spain v. Canada)*, *ICJ Reports* 1998.
43 *Pac Rim Cayman*, *supra*, note 35, para. 5.33.
44 Ibid., para. 5.35 (footnotes omitted).
45 Ibid., para. 5.37.
46 Ibid., para. 5.38.
47 *Cemex v. Venezuela*, *supra*, note 39, para. 79.
48 *Limited Liability Company AMTO v. Ukraine*, SCC Arbitration No. 080/2005, Final Award (March 26, 2008).

222 International Investment Law: A Chinese Perspective

claimant did not submit a separate written consent as required by Article 26(4)(a) of the ECT, which provides: "In the event that an Investor chooses to submit the dispute for resolution …, the Investor shall further provide its consent in writing for the dispute to be submitted." It maintained that "Article 26(4)(a) of the ECT requires a separate written consent on the part of the Investor to be provided to a relevant Contracting Party to the ECT prior to commencement of arbitration, and that submission of a request for arbitration is not sufficient."[49] The respondent further contended that "[a] belated submission of a written consent is invalid … and this defect cannot be cured by ratification of consent itself half a year later and almost a year after the initiation of arbitration."[50]

The tribunal opined that:

> A request for arbitration is by its very nature a consent to arbitrate because a legal proceeding cannot be requested by a party without their own participation in the proceeding. To request legal process is to submit to this process. An unconditional request to initiate arbitration proposed by another is the consent that completes the arbitration agreement and establishes the jurisdiction of the arbitral tribunal.[51]

In the *AMTO* case, as the claimant had made an unambiguous request to submit its disputes with Ukraine for arbitration, such request, said the tribunal, "satisfies the requirement of Article 26(4) that the Investor 'further provide its consent in writing' for this dispute to be submitted to arbitration."[52] This was an expected and inevitable decision. In the first place, the law itself does not stipulate what constitutes consent in writing. Hence, foreign investors could not be alleged to have been informed of the requirements of consent. Second, in practice, participating in arbitration is generally considered to be an expression of consent to arbitration, and nothing more is needed to establish such consent.

The issue of consent considered in the *Generation Ukraine*[53] case is rather uncommon. In that case, the respondent—Ukraine—argued that the claimant's consent to arbitration was defective because it was communicated directly to the ICSID and not to the respondent. Another argument of the respondent was that its acceptance of the ICSID arbitration was "preliminary" in the BIT between Ukraine and the United States.[54] The tribunal stated that "an investor can accept a State's offer" of arbitration by instituting arbitration proceedings without separately informing the host state.[55] It then confirmed that position by quoting Article VI(3)(a) of the ICSID Convention, which provides that "the national or

---

49 Ibid., §26(b).
50 Id.
51 Ibid., §46.
52 Ibid., §47.
53 *Generation Ukraine, Inc. v. Ukraine*, ICSID Case No. ARB/00/9, Arbitral Award (December 16, 2003).
54 Ibid., para. 12.1.
55 Ibid., para. 12.2.

company concerned may choose to consent in writing to the submission of the dispute for settlement by binding arbitration: (i) to the International Centre for the Settlement of Investment Disputes." The host state is informed in such cases by ICSID, which, upon receiving the request for arbitration, has a duty to notify the respondent.

With regard to the respondent's second argument on preliminary consent, Ukraine relied on Article 3(a)(i) of the Ukraine–United States BIT, which conditioned the contracting parties' consent on their acceding to the ICSID Convention by stating "provided that the Party is a party to [the ICSID] Convention." Article VI(4) of the BIT, however, provides:

> Each Party hereby consents to the submission of any investment dispute for settlement by binding arbitration in accordance with the choice specified in the written consent of the national or company … Such consent, together with the written consent of the national or company … shall satisfy the requirement for: (a) written consent of the parties to the dispute for the purposes of [the ICSID Convention].

With the assistance of the above provisions, the *Generation Ukraine* Tribunal correctly concluded that the "the adverb 'hereby' … conveys the finality of the consent to arbitration on the part of the State Parties to the BIT."[56] The proviso in the BIT therefore serves as a condition precedent. The tribunal also stated that this position was "recognised in the very first ICSID arbitration, the *Holiday Inns S.A. v. Morocco* case."[57] As the condition precedent to Ukraine's offer to arbitrate had been satisfied long before the start of the arbitration, the claimant's initiation of the proceedings constituted an acceptance of the respondent's offer.

Tza Yap Shum v. Republic of Peru[58] is perhaps the most notorious case of an arbitral tribunal's distortion of interpretation of consent to arbitration. The claimant investor, who was born in Fujian Province of China but later became a Hong Kong resident, invested in Peru through his company, which was incorporated in the Virgin Islands. He submitted his dispute with regard to tax liens to the ICSID on the basis of the China–Peru BIT.

By far the serious problem in the tribunal's decision was its misinterpretation of the BIT in relation to the scope of consent to arbitration. To start with, Article 8 of the China–Peru BIT reads as follows:

1. Any dispute between an investor of one Contracting Party and the other Contracting Party in connection with an investment in the territory of the other Contracting Party shall, as far as possible, be settled amicably through negotiations between the parties to the dispute.

56 Ibid., para. 12.5.
57 Ibid., para. 12.7.
58 *Tza Yap Shum v. Republic of Peru*, ICSID Case No. ARB/07/6 [hereinafter "the *Tza Yap Shum* case"], Decision on Jurisdiction (June 19, 2009).

2. If the dispute cannot be settled through negotiations within six months, either party to the dispute shall be entitled to submit this dispute to the competent court of the Contracting Party accepting the investment.

3. If a dispute involving the amount of compensation for expropriation cannot be settled within six months after resort to negotiations as specified in Paragraph 1 of this Article, it may be submitted at the request of either party to the international arbitration of the International Centre for Settlement of Investment Disputes (ICSID), established by the Convention on the Settlement of Investment Disputes between States and Nationals of Other Sates, signed in Washington D.C. on March 18, 1965. Any disputes concerning other matters between an investor of either Contracting Party and the other Contracting Party may be submitted to the Centre if the parties to the disputes so agree. The provisions of this Paragraph shall not apply if the investor concerned has resorted to the procedure specified in Paragraph 2 of this Article.

The Peruvian Government rightly argued that according to Article 8(3) of the BIT only disputes "involving the amount of compensation for expropriation" could be submitted to international arbitration and that the tribunal thus had no jurisdiction over the dispute about tax liens. The tribunal, however, without conducting a detailed analysis of the provision according to international law, first of all indicated that Article 8(3) reflected a "certain degree of distrust or ideological unconformity on the part of communist regimes regarding investment of private capital, and maybe also certain concern about the decisions of international tribunals on matters such regimes are not familiar with and over which they had no control."[59]

Such a statement itself was extremely biased and obviously discriminatory, and was clearly a reflection of the tribunal's unwillingness to give full weight to the provisions of the BIT. In any case, it set the tone for the tribunals' subsequent efforts to expand its jurisdiction under the BIT by a combination of tortuous linguistic analysis and a particularly selective consideration of "context." The tribunal's biased attitude toward the ability of the BIT's contracting parties to effectively express their intent—and the limits of their consent—in the BIT (along with its own determination to inform them of what they must have meant) was also evidenced in its somewhat cavalier dismissal of the witness statements of Professor An Chen and two of the original negotiators (Mr Jianghong Fan of China and Ms María del Carmen Vega of Peru), as well as other contemporaneous materials relating to the parties' understanding of the terms they chose.

Concerning the wording in Article 8(3) of the BIT, which permits submission to international arbitration of "dispute[s] involving the amount of compensation for expropriation," the tribunal did concede that "[s]uch wording *seemed* to seek certain limitations."[60] It maintained, however, that "the exact scope of such limitations is a key issue that must be determined."[61] On the one hand, it admitted

59 Ibid., para. 145.
60 Id. (emphasis added).
61 Id.

that one interpretation of Article 8(3) would limit its scope of application to "the determination of the value of the investment." At the same time, it stated that "this phrase may include, in addition to the amount of compensation, a determination of other important matters related to the alleged expropriation. ... For a variety of reasons, the tribunal has decided that ... the broadest interpretation happens to be the most appropriate."[62] In short, even though it recognized that the contracting parties intended this wording to limit those disputes which could be submitted to international arbitration, it finally decided that such limitation must include disputes over "any ... issues normally inherent to an expropriation."[63] As one commentator noted: "...the tribunal was aware of the exact purpose of having such a restrictive phrase ... in the BIT ...[but it] explicitly disregarded the public policy concern by applying an expansive approach without offering a convincing justification."[64]

Chief among the reasons given by the tribunal for its conclusion was its insistence that "a *bona fide* interpretation" of this Article hinged almost exclusively on the word "involving," and it chose to define that word on the basis of the Oxford English Dictionary, which it said defines "involve" to mean "to enfold, envelope, entangle, include." It went even further, stating that "[a] *bona fide* interpretation of these words indicate[s] that the only requirement established in the BIT is that the dispute must 'include' the determination of the amount of a compensation, and not that the dispute must be restricted thereto."[65] In doing so, as noted by Shen: "[i]n spite of its technical reference to the Vienna Convention in the treaty interpretation, the Tribunal indeed relied more on the linguistic interpretation of 'involving' in reaching its expansive jurisdiction."[66]

As a secondary reason for adopting this interpretation, the tribunal appealed to the "context" of Article 8(3). In doing so, however, it appears either completely to have misread or neglected to analyze carefully the immediate context—the other clauses of Article 8. These clauses effectively establish a "fork in the road" provision, which will be discussed later. Suffice it to say here that the *Tza Yap Shum* Tribunal opted to "establish the objective meaning of Article 8 in the overall context of the BIT" and, like many other tribunals, did so by appealing to the preamble of the BIT to establish its overriding objective.[67] That objective, it held "consisted in increasing the flow of private investment between both Contracting Parties" and, to that end, should be read so as "to extend the rights and protections of investors, both in content and form, by the incorporation of protections of international law."[68] The tribunal simply could not accept that the contracting

---

62 Ibid., para. 150.
63 Ibid., para. 188.
64 Wei Shen, "The Good, the Bad or the Ugly? A Critique of the Decision on Jurisdiction and Competence in *Tza Yap Shum v. Republic of Peru*," 10 *Chinese Journal of International Law* 55, 2011, para. 35, p. 74.
65 *Tza Yap Shum*, *supra*, note 58, para. 151.
66 Shen, *supra*, note 64, para. 36, p. 74.
67 *Tza Yap Shum*, *supra*, note 58, para. 187.
68 Id.

parties could have intended in good faith to accomplish the objective of the BIT within the boundaries of limiting the jurisdiction of international arbitral tribunals only to disputes over quantum and such other disputes as both an investor and the host state both agreed to submit to such jurisdiction. Despite clear evidence to the contrary, the tribunal insisted: "Had the Contracting Parties really had the intention of excluding such important issues as those listed in Article 4 from the arbitral proceeding, the tribunal would determine so, although with certain skepticism with regard to whether such mechanism could possibly help attracting foreign investors."[69]

Such an approach to treaty interpretation, that clearly has more to do with establishing jurisdiction than with upholding the will of the contracting parties to a BIT, to say the least, can hardly contribute to the development of international investment law except by setting up a bad example from which other tribunals likewise inclined to adopt an expansionist approach to jurisdiction may draw lessons.

In noting contemporary trends in the jurisprudence of international investment arbitration, it is perhaps noteworthy that another ICSID tribunal, in the *Renta4* case,[70] delivered an analysis of a provision in the 1991 BIT between the USSR and Spain that displays striking similarities to that of the *Tza Yap Shum* Tribunal, although it lacks the gratuitous slur directed at the intentions of "communist regimes" found in the latter. In this case, the issue of Russia's consent to arbitration hinged on interpretation of Article 10(1) of the BIT, which provides that "[a]ny dispute between one Party and an investor of the other Party relating to the amount or method of payment of the compensation due under Article 6 of this Agreement"[71] may be submitted to international arbitration.

As the *Tza Yap Shum* Tribunal did with the word "involving," the *Renta4* Tribunal fundamentally based its interpretation of Article 10(1) of the BIT on a linguistic analysis that gave critical place to the word "due." It stated that: "The plainest proposition to be derived from Article 10(1) is that it allows arbitration with respect to debates about the amount or method of such compensation as may be due under Article 6. The difficulty begins precisely once one asks: Who determines whether compensation is indeed 'due' under Article 6?"[72]

Russia maintained that such determination could only be made by the Russian

---

69 Ibid., para. 153. Article 4 of the BIT provides: "1. Neither Contracting Party shall appropriate, nationalize or take similar measures (hereinafter referred to as "expropriation") against investments of investors of the other Contracting Party in its territory, unless the following conditions are met: (a) for the public interest; (b) under domestic legal procedure; (c) without discrimination; (d) against compensation. 2. The compensation mentioned in Paragraph 1, (d) of this Article shall be equivalent to the value of the expropriated investments at the time when expropriation is proclaimed, be convertible and freely transferrable. This compensation shall be paid without reasonable delay."

70 *Renta4 SVSA et al. v. Russian Federation*, Award on Preliminary Objections, SCC Case No. 24/2007 (March 20, 2009).

71 As quoted ibid., para. 5.

72 Ibid., para. 27.

courts or state-to-state arbitration.[73] The tribunal observed that if such had been the contracting parties' intention, then that could have been stipulated in Article 10 but noted that "there is nothing of the kind."[74] On the other hand, the tribunal held that the existence of an obligation under Article 6 was "the evident predicate to any amount being 'due' and thus the object of the type of debate allowed under Article 10. The existence of the basic predicate of a remedy under Article 10 cannot be deemed outside the purview of a tribunal constituted under that very Article."[75] More forcefully, it held that the text of Article 10 "entrains the power to determine whether there has been a compensable event in the first place"[76] and unanimously asserted that "it has subject matter jurisdiction under Article 10 of the Spanish BIT to decide whether compensation is due by virtue of claims of expropriation raised in this arbitration."[77]

The issue of consent in the *Abaclat* case[78] was unique and complicated. The claimants, the total number of whom at the time of initiation of the arbitration exceeded 180,000, gave their consent to the arbitration through a mandate to an association known as "Task Force Argentina" ("TFA"), which initiated the ICSID arbitration on their behalf with a condition that they would not sue the member banks of TFA at the same time. Facing the challenge made by the respondent, the tribunal referred to general international law and the general principles of law according to which consent must be "genuine and intended, i.e., free from coercion, fraud and/or from any essential mistake."[79] It did not consider that the reasons for giving consent or irrevocability might affect the validity of consent.[80] As each of the claimants had executed written powers of attorney to authorize the arbitration of their claims at ICSID, the tribunal found there was no mistake on their part in giving consent.

Another thorny issue in the *Abaclat* case was whether TFA might have a conflict of interest because, on the one hand, it required the claimants not to sue its member banks as a condition to ICSID arbitration and, on the other hand, it represented the claimants in the ICSID arbitration. The tribunal took note that the mandate "clearly sets forth that during the ICSID arbitration Claimants cannot simultaneously initiate legal claims against the TFA member banks and that the statute of limitation for such claims is not tolled."[81] In fact, the tribunal considered the claimants to be sophisticated investors with sufficient knowledge of investment. In such circumstances, in the view of the tribunal, even if the TFA mandate failed to contain adequate information "or did to some extent misrepresent cer-

---

73   Ibid., para. 58.
74   Ibid., para. 59.
75   Ibid., para. 31.
76   Ibid., para. 39.
77   Ibid., para. 155(i).
78   *Abaclat and Others v. Argentine Republic*, ICSID Case No. ARB/07/5, Decision on Jurisdiction and Admissibility (August 4, 2011).
79   Ibid., para. 436.
80   Ibid., paras. 438–39.
81   Ibid., para. 461.

tain information," the flaw "would have been cured by the subsequent events."[82] It is quite obvious that in most cases, if not all, tribunals zealously assert jurisdiction. *Abaclat* is just one example of such cases.

Millicom v. Senegal[83] also illustrates to what extent a tribunal may go in asserting jurisdiction. In that case, the related treaty provision was Article 10 of the Accord between Luxemburg and Senegal for the protection of foreign investment, which provides:

> The Contracting Party in the territory of which a national of the other Contracting Party makes or intends to make an investment shall assent to any request on the part of such national to submit, for arbitration or conciliation, any dispute that may arise in connection with that investment, to the Centre established by the Washington Convention of 18 March 1965 on the settlement of investment disputes between States and nationals of other States.
>
> …
>
> The jurisdiction of the Centre shall extend to any legal dispute arising directly out of an investment, between a Contracting State (or any constituent subdivision or agency of a Contracting State designated to the Centre by that State) and a national of another Contracting State, which the parties to the dispute consent in writing to submit to the Centre.

The respondent challenged the jurisdiction of ICSID on two grounds, that is: (1) the conclusion of the Accord would not constitute the giving of consent and a specific manifestation of consent was required, and (2) the ICSID only had jurisdiction over natural persons who were nationals of the other contracting party to the Accord. With regard to the first issue, the tribunal correctly stated that in the Accord "it is prescribed that the State not only '*pourra*' ('may') but '*devra*' ('shall') give its consent. Nothing in the wording leads to the conclusion that such decision could be left up to the discretion of the State."[84] The reason given by the tribunal was that the two-step procedure in giving consent was not necessary. Therefore, it held that "[i]t is more reasonable to view this as a unilateral offer and a commitment by Senegal to submit itself to ICSID jurisdiction; the request of Claimant 1 constitutes the '*demande*' ('request') and amounts to acceptance of the offer made by the State; it does not create such consent, it consummates it."[85] The finding of the tribunal on this issue is not surprising at all. However, the tribunal did not rely on the plain meaning of the Accord but instead resorted to "necessary" and "reasonable" analysis, which is not a standard for treaty interpretation under Article 31 of the Vienna Convention on the Law of Treaties ("VCLT"). Whether or not an assertion is reasonable or whether or not a given procedure is necessary

---

82 Ibid., para. 463. The issue of conflict of interest was also left to be dealt with at the merits stage. Ibid., para. 459.
83 *Millicom International Operations B.V. and Sentel GSMSA v. Republic of Senegal*, ICSID Case No. ARB/08/20, Decision on Jurisdiction (July 16, 2010).
84 Ibid., para. 63.
85 Id.

is not relevant in interpreting treaty provisions. More important are the provisions of the relevant treaty. Once the factors of necessity and reasonableness are introduced in interpreting a treaty, this leaves much discretion with the tribunal.

As mentioned earlier, the respondent's second ground to challenge the jurisdiction of the tribunal was a restriction on "nationals," which was based on Article 1 of the Accord that defines nationals as follows: "The term 'nationals' shall comprise with regard to either Contracting Party natural persons having the nationality of that Contracting Party in accordance with its law."

Even without knowing the reasons for their exclusion, it is clear that companies, which are the common vehicle for making investment, are not included in the term "nationals." The claimants considered that the omission of companies in the definition of nationals was "an inadvertency" and should be corrected by the tribunal.[86] The tribunal first stated that "in accordance with Article 31, paragraph 1 of the Vienna Convention, the *terms of the treaty* must be interpreted *in good faith* in accordance with the meaning to be given them *in their context and in light of its object and purpose*."[87] It then said that the text of a treaty "even if apparently 'clear', is not the only factor to be used in interpreting a rule."[88] In its view, the dispute settlement provisions of Article 10 of the Accord "establishes the only means ... to guarantee to investors the effectiveness of the rest of the *Accord*."[89] As such, there was no reason, said the tribunal, to distinguish natural persons from judicial persons in relation to protection. It said that "one cannot see why an investment should be less protected depending on whether it is made by a natural person or a company."[90] It then concluded:

> The term ... "national" ... is used three times: the first two times to designate the person who, having made or intended to make an investment, may take the initiative to bring arbitration proceedings; the third time in the last line in the title of the Washington Convention which is reproduced. It is certain that the third time the term must encompass natural persons and juridical persons since what is mentioned are ... 'nationals' ... within the meaning of the Washington Convention. It is indeed the definition given by this Convention which is relevant, of which Article 25(2) provides a broad definition.
>
> According to the Arbitral Tribunal, the use of the term ... "national" ... in Article 10 must be understood in accordance with the general meaning of the Convention, and not the special meaning of Article 1, which is adapted to the other provisions of the *Accord*.[91]

It must be admitted that the conclusion of the *Millicom* Tribunal is correct, as in international investment practice it is hard to imagine that juridical persons would

86 Ibid., para. 68.
87 Ibid., para. 70 (emphases in original).
88 Id.
89 Ibid., para. 71.
90 Id.
91 Ibid., para. 73.

be excluded from investor–state arbitration, which is an important tool to ensure protection of investments. The correct result does not, however, indicate that the arbitration is a sound one. In its analysis, the *Millicom* Tribunal simply ignored the context of the Accord, which stipulates the treatment of foreign investment. It is true that, as the claimant contended, the omission might be an inadvertency. If the tribunal wished to fill the "gap" or to correct it, it should say so. What the tribunal did, however, was to replace treaty provisions with its own words by using the technique of overly emphasizing the preamble of the Treaty.

Although the same technique has been adopted by other tribunals in the past, there at least existed provisions for them to expansively interpret. In this case, the treaty—Accord—contained no mention of "companies" or "juridical persons;" it was the tribunal which inserted the words so that its jurisdiction was established. The reason given by the tribunal—that if the provisions were interpreted otherwise, companies and juridical persons would not be protected—cannot stand. Such entities could, for instance, resolve their differences through amicable means or resort to the local courts of the host state, even though such means may not be as effective or coercive as ICSID arbitration. What the *Millicom* Tribunal did on this issue paves the way for a very liberal interpretation, to say the least, of any provision that employs the word "national."

The important point here is that only the contracting parties to the Accord could prove whether or not their very intent was to deprive juridical persons of the right to resort to ICSID arbitration, the undesirability of such provisions notwithstanding. At the same time, if tribunals are permitted to exercise discretion to this extent, they will actually be revising and rewriting treaties rather than construing them. That is clearly not permitted under international law.[92] The most recent case that has dealt with the issue of consent is Koza which involves interpretation of Article 8 (1) and (2) of the UK-Turkmenistan BIT relating to dispute resolution, that stipulates a two stage consent—first the disputing parties shall submit their dispute to international arbitration upon satisfying certain conditions and then the disputing parties may agree to refer disputes to either ICSID, ICC or *ad hoc* arbitration. The majority of the Tribunal concluded that under such provisions, Turkmenistan had consented to "international arbitration with UK investors" and had "simply expressed its willingness to consider ICSID arbitration as one of

---

92 For instance, in *Interpretation of Peace Treaties with Bulgaria, Hungary and Romania (Second Phase)*—(Advisory Opinion of the International Court of Justice of 18 July 1950), the International Court of Justice stated: "[T]he first duty of a tribunal which is called upon to interpret and apply the provisions of a treaty, is to endeavour to give effect to them in their natural and ordinary meaning in the context in which they occur. If the relevant words in their natural and ordinary meaning make sense in their context, that is an end of the matter. If, on the other hand, the words in their natural and ordinary meaning are ambiguous or lead to an unreasonable result, then, and then only, must the Court, by resort to other methods of interpretation, seek to ascertain what the parties really did mean when they used these words." See *Case concerning the Arbitral Award of 31 July 1989 (Guinea-Bissau v. Senegal)*, Judgment of November 12, 1991, *ICJ Reports*, 1991, para. 48, p. 69, quoting an earlier pronouncement of the Court in the Advisory Opinion on *Competence of the General Assembly for the Admission of a State to the United Nations, ICJ Reports*, 1950, p. 8.

three options, and only on a case by case basis."[93] Yet, the UK-Turkmenistan BIT contained a MFN clause which specifically covers Article 8. Through operation of the MFN clause, the majority of the Tribunal established its jurisdiction.

II. Effective time of consent

The ascertainment of the existence of consent is of the utmost importance in investor–state arbitration. The time at which such consent becomes effective is equally important. As at least one commentator has observed:

> … the date in which the State expresses its consent in the treaty is not just an offer. It is much more than that and it has special legal effects, including obligations of the host state under the treaty and the prohibition to exercise diplomatic protection by the other Contracting Party. The date of expression of consent for the State is that of the entry into force of the treaty or some other instrument which embodies that consent. When this consent is later matched by the consent of the foreign investor, the required conditions for submitting the dispute to arbitration are met, but the respective expressions of consent do not appear to change their dates.[94]

As that is the case, whether in practice states may be prepared to permit their consent to arbitration to be considered to have been given with retrospective effect often triggers dispute.

For any system governed by the rule of law, a legal prescription should not have retrospective effect. The same principle applies to treaties and international agreements—both bilateral and multilateral. Yet, insofar as BITs are concerned, as the purpose of the instrument is to encourage foreign investment, the protection offered to foreign investment under the terms of a newly negotiated BIT may be made available to investments of investors of the other contracting party even before the relevant BIT enters into force. When it comes to dispute resolution, however, in particular to international arbitration of such disputes, states are reluctant to extend the retroactive application of the BIT to *differences* that occurred before the BIT's effective date.

Maffezini v. Spain[95] is a case in point, in which the Argentina–Spain BIT provides in Article II(2) that: "[t]his agreement shall apply also to capital investments made before its entry into force by investors of one Party in accordance with the laws of the other Party in the territory of the latter. However, this agreement shall not apply to disputes or claims originating before its entry into force." The respondent

---

93 *Garanti Koza LLP v. Turkmenistan*, ICSID Case No. ARB/11/20, Decision on the Objection to Jurisdiction for Lack of Consent, July 3, 2013, para. 38.

94 See *Waguih Elie Georg Siag & Clorinda Vecchi v. Egypt*, ICSID Case No. ARB/05/15, Decision on Jurisdiction (April 15, 2007), Partial Dissent of Francisco Orrego Vicuna, p. 64.

95 *Emilio Agustín Maffezini v. Kingdom of Spain*, ICSID Case No. ARB/97/7, Decision on Jurisdiction (January 25, 2000).

challenged the tribunal's jurisdiction on the grounds that the dispute raised by the claimant took place before the coming into force of the BIT.[96]

The *Maffezini* Tribunal first stated that the International Court of Justice had defined a dispute as "a disagreement on a point of law or fact, a conflict of legal views or interests between parties" and quoted Schreuer that a "dispute must relate to clearly identified issues between the parties and must not be merely academic ... The dispute must go beyond general grievances and must be susceptible of being stated in terms of a concrete claim."[97] The tribunal then observed that:

> ... there tends to be a natural sequence of events that leads to a dispute. It begins with the expression of a disagreement and the statement of a difference of views. In time these events acquire a *precise legal meaning through the formulation of legal claims*, their discussion and eventual rejection or lack of response by the other party. The *conflict of legal views and interests will only be present in the latter stage*, even though the underlying facts predate them. It has also been rightly commented that the existence of the dispute presupposes a minimum of communications between the parties, one party taking up the matter with the other, with the latter opposing the Claimant's position directly or indirectly. This sequence of events has to be taken into account in establishing the critical date for determining when under the BIT a dispute qualifies as one covered by the consent necessary to establish ICSID's jurisdiction.[98]

In this statement, the *Maffezini* Tribunal made a clear distinction between the events that give rise to a dispute and the dispute itself. At the same time, determination of the critical date—the entering into force of the BIT—was important, as it separated "the dispute from prior events that do not entail a conflict of legal views and interests."[99] As a result, any dispute that occurred before the critical date would not qualify for arbitration and hence the tribunal would not have jurisdiction. Because the tribunal considered that "the dispute in its technical and legal sense began to take shape" after the coming into force of the BIT, it ruled that it had jurisdiction.[100] The test for an ordinary dispute to transform into a "technical and legal" dispute that was applied by the tribunal is open to question. For instance, the factors that should be taken into account when examining such a transformation were not explained in the decision. Hence, the matter is left entirely to the discretion of a tribunal.

In *Jan de Nul v. Egypt*,[101] the BIT in question also restricted its application to future disputes. The dispute in the case took place well before the entering into force of the 1992 BIT, which replaced the one of 1977. It was first brought to the local Administrative Court, which rendered a decision that was not in the

---

96 Ibid., para. 90.
97 Ibid., para. 94 (footnotes omitted).
98 Ibid., para. 96 (emphases added; footnotes omitted).
99 Ibid., para. 97.
100 Ibid., para. 98.
101 *Jan de Nul N.V. and Dredging International N.V. v. Arab Republic of Egypt*, ICSID Case No. ARB/04/13, Decision on Jurisdiction (June 16, 2006).

claimant's favor one year after the 1992 BIT became effective. The tribunal correctly said that the dispute before the Egyptian court related to contractual issues and the dispute before it involved alleged investment treaty violations.[102] It then said that "[t]he intervention of a new actor, the Ismaïlia Court, appears here as a decisive factor to determine whether the dispute is a new dispute. As the Claimants' case is directly based on the alleged wrongdoing of the Ismaïlia Court, the Tribunal considers that the original dispute has (re)crystallized into a new dispute when the Ismaïlia Court rendered its decision."[103] In this case, the events that gave rise to the dispute were the same. They were crystallized into a dispute which was before the local court when the BIT was concluded. If the tribunal was right in saying that an old dispute could be recrystallized into a new one just because of local court intervention, then the treaty provision restricting arbitration tribunals from dealing with prior disputes would become meaningless. It is doubtful that such decisions may reflect the intent of the parties to the BIT.

In still another case—*Helnan v. Egypt*[104]—the tribunal went to considerable extremes to try to distinguish "divergences" from "disputes." Article 12 of the Denmark–Egypt BIT provides that:

> The provisions of this Agreement shall apply to all investments made by investors of one contracting party in the territory of the other contracting party prior to or after the entry into force of the Agreement by investors of the other contracting party. It shall, however, not be applicable to divergences or disputes, which have arisen prior to its entry into force.

One of the questions was whether "divergence" and "dispute" as stipulated in the BIT meant different things or were *ejusdem generis*, of a "like nature." The tribunal first observed that: "whenever possible, terms must be interpreted literally and given practical effect, which excludes redundancy. As the parties to the Treaty referred both to '*divergence*' and '*dispute*', it must be assumed that they were not giving the same meaning to these two distinct terms."[105] Then what were the meanings that the treaty parties intended to give to the two terms? The tribunal stated:

> Although, the terms *"divergence"* and *"dispute"* both require the existence of a disagreement between the parties on specific points and their respective knowledge of such disagreement, there is an important distinction to make between them as they do not imply the same degree of animosity. Indeed, in the case of a divergence, the parties hold different views but without necessarily pursuing the difference in an active manner. On the other hand, in case

102 Ibid., para. 117.
103 Ibid., para. 128.
104 *Helnan International Hotels A/S v. Arab Republic of Egypt*, ICSID Case No. ARB 05/19, Decision on Objection to Jurisdiction (October 17, 2006).
105 Ibid., para. 52.

of a dispute, the difference of views forms the subject of an active exchange between the parties under circumstances which indicate that the parties wish to resolve the difference, be it before a third party or otherwise. Consequently, different views of parties in respect of certain facts and situations become a "*divergence*" when they are mutually aware of their disagreement. It crystallises as a "*dispute*" as soon as one of the parties decides to have it solved, whether or not by a third party.[106]

The tribunal did not rely on or refer to any materials relating to the negotiation history of the treaty. One may wonder, then, on what basis the tribunal took the above position.

The dispute between the parties on the issue of jurisdiction was whether the claims would fall within the purview of Article 12 of the BIT and hence whether the tribunal had jurisdiction. The tribunal, on the basis of its theory of crystallization of divergences into disputes, stated that where a dispute crystallized after the coming into force of the BIT, even though it was a continuation of divergences that occurred before the effective date of the BIT, it had jurisdiction over the case.

In the *Helnan* case, the claimant's alleged violations related to the facts and situations that existed prior to the entering into force of the BIT. The tribunal said, however, that those facts and situations "are not and could not be at the origin of the dispute which gave rise to the Claimant's claims"[107] because the parties had modified the terms of their contract after the BIT came into effect. In the tribunal's view, the modification of the contract was an intervening event, which changed the nature of the prior divergences. It stated that: "even if they [divergences] originated from disagreement prior to January 29, 2000 [the date of the BIT coming into force], [they] could not be of the same nature as the divergences which crystallised into the instant dispute which occurred under the Management Contract as modified by the Annex."[108] The tribunal then concluded that it had jurisdiction.

The decision of the *Helnan* Tribunal is not surprising, as almost all ICSID tribunals have been eager to assume jurisdiction over all the cases that have appeared before them. In this case, the BIT excluded both divergences and disputes from the jurisdiction of ICSID if they had arisen before it came into force. Yet the *Helnan* Tribunal invented a theory of the evolution of divergences into disputes by which such divergences changed nature. The BIT uses the word "or" between divergences and disputes. A plain reading of the word "or" in the context indicates that both divergences and disputes are excluded. As that is the case, there is no room for any other interpretation, including some novel theory of the evolution of divergences into disputes or of a change in nature of divergences. In this regard, the interpretation by the *Helnan* Tribunal of the above provision is highly questionable.

106 Id.
107 Ibid., para. 54.
108 Ibid., para. 55.

III. The fork in the road

Consent to arbitration is also affected by the choice of forum provision—the so-called fork in the road—of BITs and FTAs. A typical fork in the road provision is like the one found in the China–Argentina BIT: "Where an investor has submitted a dispute to the aforementioned competent tribunal of the Contracting Party where the investment has been made or to international arbitration, this choice shall be final."[109] The function of the fork in the road provision is to provide a foreign investor with a choice to bring claims before local courts or tribunals of the host state *or* before an international arbitration tribunal. Once a choice is made—local judicial proceedings have started—the international arbitration tribunal should refrain from exercising jurisdiction.[110] *Vivendi*[111] was the first case in which the fork in the road provision was analyzed. Prior to the *Vivendi* award, there was a brief mention of the choice of forum provisions in *Olguin v. Paraguay*, where it was said that "when disputes arise between contracting parties, they should meet to resolve them, and if that is not possible within 6 months, the person making the investment may submit the dispute, *inter alia*, to international arbitration by the International Centre for Settlement of Investment Disputes."[112] The tribunal found, however, that there was no evidence to prove that Olguin had resorted to any judicial bodies to resolve his dispute with Argentina.[113] Therefore, issues relating to the fork in the road provision were not discussed at all in the *Olguin* case.

In *Vivendi*, the claimants were a French company, Compagnie Générale des Eaux, and its Argentine affiliate, Compañía de Aguas del Aconquija, S.A. The dispute arose from a concession contract with the Government of Tucumán, a province of Argentina, for operation of the province's water and sewage system. The complainants alleged that Argentina had violated the Argentina–France BIT

109 Fiona Marshall, "Commentary: *Pantechniki v. Albania* decision offers pragmatic approach to interpreting fork-in-the-road clauses," IISD Investment Treaty News (September 2, 2009); available at: http://www.iisd.org/itn/2009/09/02/commentary-pantechniki-v-albania-decision-offers-pragmatic-approach-to-interpreting-fork-in-the-road-clauses.

110 For discussions on fork in the road provisions, see also Sidley Austin LLP, "ICSID tribunal analyses 'investment' requirement," (September 30, 2009); available at: http://arbitration.practicallaw.com/6-500-3439#; Lee A. Steven and Nicole Thornton, "Two Roads – Two Tribunals: Recent 'Fork-in-the Road' Interpretations," White & Case LLP (December 16, 2009), available at: http://kluwerarbitrationblog.com/blog/2009/12/16/two-roads-%E2%80%93-two-tribunals-recent-%E2%80%9Cfork-in-the-road%E2%80%9D-interpretations; Campbell McLachlan, Laurence Shore, and Matthew Weiniger, *International Investment Arbitration: Substantive Principles*, Oxford International Arbitration Series, OUP, 2007; and Peter Turner, "The Fork in the Road Revisited," in Federico Ortino et al. (eds.), *Investment Treaty Law: Current Issues*, British Institute of International and Comparative Law, London, 2006.

111 *Compañía de Aguas del Aconquija, S.A. & Compagnie Générale des Eaux v. Argentine Republic*, ICSID Case No. ARB/97/3, Award (November 21, 2000) ("Award"); *Compañía de Aguas del Aconquija, S.A. and Vivendi Universal (formerly Compagnie Générale des Eaux v. Argentine Republic)*, ICSID Case No. ARB/97/3, Decision on Annulment (July 3, 2002) ("Annulment Decision").

112 *Olguin v. Republic of Paraguay*, ICSID Case No. ARB/98/5, Decision on Jurisdiction (August 8, 2000), para. 27 (the texts cited are from an English translation available at: http://italaw.com/documents/OlguinParaguay.pdf).

113 Ibid., para. 30.

by having failed to prevent Tucumán from taking certain actions in respect of the concession contract, which had infringed their interests. As a matter of fact, the concession contract contained a provision that all disputes arising therefrom had to be submitted to the contentious administrative courts of Tucumán. On the other hand, the Argentina–France BIT, in its Article 8, provides that where an investor–state dispute cannot be resolved within six months through amicable consultations, the dispute, at the investor's option, may be submitted either to the national jurisdictions of the host state or to arbitration under the ICSID Convention or to an *ad hoc* tribunal pursuant to the Arbitration Rules of the United Nations Commission on International Trade Law.[114] It further states: "Once an investor has submitted the dispute to the courts of the Contracting Party concerned or to international arbitration, the choice of one or the other of these procedures is final."[115]

The tribunal held that the dispute resolution provisions of the concession contract did not "divest" it of jurisdiction to hear the case "because that provision did not and could not constitute a waiver by CGE [the Claimant] of its rights under Article 8 of the BIT" to file an arbitration against Argentina.[116] In the tribunal's view, the claimant's "submission of claims against Tucumán for breaches of the contract … would not … have been the kind of choice by Claimants of legal action in national jurisdictions (that is, courts) against the Argentine Republic that constitutes the 'fork in the road' under Article 8 of the BIT, thereby foreclosing future claims under the ICSID."[117] Unfortunately, the *Vivendi* Tribunal did not explain why the claimant's action in the contentious administrative court would not constitute a choice of a fork in the road. This in fact may be contrary to the requirement that an arbitral tribunal must state the reasons on which it has based its decisions under the ICSID Convention.[118]

The *ad hoc* Committee in the *Vivendi* case, however, took pains to explain how fork in the road provisions should work. It first stated that the term "national jurisdictions" referred to national courts of any kind and that this should not be affected by the fact that the contracting party may be a federal or unitary state.[119] It then concluded that because Article 8 of the Argentina–France BIT referred to disputes "relating to investments," the claimant's allegation did not have to be one of "a breach of the BIT itself" and that "it is sufficient that the dispute relate to an investment made under the BIT."[120]

114 *Vivendi v. Argentina*, Award, *supra*, note 111, page 1.
115 Article 8(2) of the Argentina–France BIT, quoted from *Vivendi v. Argentina*, Annulment Decision, *supra*, note 110, para. 53.
116 *Vivendi v. Argentina*, Annulment Decision, *supra*, note 110, para. 53.
117 Ibid., para. 55.
118 Article 48(3) of the ICSID Convention requires tribunals to state the reasons upon which their awards are based. Conclusions like that of the *Vivendi* Tribunal which are made without discussion of the legal basis are obviously subject to challenge. In fact, the claimant in the *Vivendi* case did argue, in the annulment stage, that the tribunal had failed to state the reasons for its award.
119 *Vivendi v. Argentina*, Annulment Decision, *supra*, note 110, para. 54.
120 Ibid., para. 55.

Before drawing its conclusion, the *ad hoc* Committee analyzed the *Vivendi* Tribunal's decision that "in the view of the Tribunal, the fork in the road set out in Article 8(2) is limited in its application to claims which explicitly 'allege a cause of action under the BIT' or which '[charge] the Argentine Republic with a violation of the Argentine-French BIT'."[121] The *ad hoc* Committee commented on the tribunal's interpretation that "it seems that the Tribunal's conclusion that the fork in the road was never reached in this case is based on an interpretation of Article 8(2) which limits its application exclusively to claims alleging a breach of the BIT, that is, to treaty claims as such."[122] The question was whether or not the *Vivendi* Tribunal's interpretation was too narrow.

In the view of the *ad hoc* Committee, a claim by the claimant for a breach of the concession contract brought before a local court of the respondent "would *prima facie* fall within Article 8(2) and constitute a 'final' choice of forum and jurisdiction."[123] The only condition that the *ad hoc* Committee attached to this conclusion is that the claim was "coextensive" with the dispute under the BIT. In reaching its conclusion, the *ad hoc* Committee emphasized and relied on the merits of the dispute and hence the claim rather than adopting the formalistic approach that has been developed by some later tribunals. It considered that a breach of contractual rights such as those under the concession contract could constitute a breach of treaty obligations at the same time.[124] Yet the *ad hoc* Committee also held:

> A treaty cause of action is not the same as a contractual cause of action; it requires a clear showing of conduct which is in the circumstances contrary to the relevant treaty standard. The availability of local courts ready and able to resolve specific issues independently may be a relevant circumstance in determining whether there has been a breach of international law.[125]

In any event, even the *ad hoc* Committee did not elaborate to what extent and in what circumstances a contractual claim and a treaty claim may be considered to be coextensive. It is a pity that the *ad hoc* Committee failed to take the opportunity to explain the standard it had in mind. At the same time, this shows the difficulty, and in fact the danger, in establishing any such standard.[126]

---

121 Ibid., para. 38.
122 Ibid., para. 42.
123 Id.
124 Ibid., para. 110.
125 Ibid., para. 113.
126 Although submitted fully 15 years after the ICSID began its work, the *Vivendi* case was only the 41st ICSID case. This is not surprising, because the OECD's analysis of 1660 BITs, FTAs and other international agreements with provisions related to investment, published in 2012, shows that a significant number of the early such agreements had either no investor–state dispute resolution mechanism or provided only for access to domestic fora. For more details, see OECD, *Dispute settlement provisions in international investment agreements: A large sample survey*, Organization for Economic Co-operation and Development, Investment Division, Directorate for Financial and Enterprise Affairs, Paris, France, 2012; available at: http://www.oecd.org/investment/internati onalinvestmentagreements/50291678.pdf.

Most arbitral decisions after *Vivendi* surprisingly found that the fork in the road provision of the relevant agreement did not constitute any impediment to their jurisdiction. In this regard, Schreuer, after reviewing a number of awards and decisions,[127] concluded that: "[i]n order to determine whether the choice under such a clause [fork in the road] has been taken, it is necessary to establish not only whether the parties to the two lawsuits are identical but also whether the causes of action in the two proceedings are identical."[128] Schreuer derived his conclusion essentially from *Genin v. Estonia*.[129]

In that case, Mr Genin was the ultimate owner of two companies that were the principal shareholders of the Estonian Innovation Bank ("EIB"), a financial institution with the nationality of Estonia which purchased a branch of Estonian Social Bank Limited. The disputes arose from that purchase and the revocation by the Estonian authorities of EIB's license. EIB, in addition to its lawsuit in a local court against the Social Bank for losses resulting from the share purchase, had also sued Estonia in the Administrative Court of the host state over the revocation of the license. As respondent in the arbitration, Estonia challenged the jurisdiction of the tribunal on the grounds that the EIB's lawsuit constituted a choice of forum which triggered the application of the fork in the road provision and, as a result, the tribunal had no jurisdiction to hear the case.

In its analysis, the tribunal stated that "the lawsuits in Estonia relating to the purchase by EIB of the Koidu branch of Social Bank and to the revocation of EIB's license are not identical to Claimants' cause of action in the 'investment dispute' that they seek to arbitrate in the present proceedings."[130] This is the first limb of the so-called "triple identity test"[131] in respect of the fork in the road provision. In its analysis, the *Genin* Tribunal was obviously overly formalistic in saying that the two judicial and arbitral actions were not "identical." It simply failed to examine the contents of the claims.

As to the second limb of the "triple identity test"—cause of action—the *Genin* Tribunal stated that:

---

127 These decisions include *Olguin*; *Enron Corporation and Ponderosa Assets, L.P. v. Argentine Republic*, ICSID Case No. ARB/01/3, Decision on Jurisdiction (January 14, 2004); *Ronald S. Lauder v. Czech Republic* UNCITRAL, London, Award (September 3, 2001); *Middle East Cement Shipping and Handling Co. S.A. v. Arab Republic of Egypt*, ICSID Case No. ARB/99/6, Award of April 12, 2002; *CMS v. Argentina*, ICSID Case No. ARB/01/8, Decision on Jurisdiction (July 17, 2003); and *Azurix v. Argentina*, ICSID Case No. ARB/01/12, Decision on Jurisdiction (December 8, 2003).

128 Christoph Schreuer, "Traveling the BIT Route: Of Waiting Periods, Umbrella Clauses and Forks in the Road," 5 *J.W.I.T.* 2, April 2004, p. 245, available at: http://www.univie.ac.at/intlaw/pdf/68.pdf.

129 *Alex Genin, Eastern Credit Limited, Inc. and A.S. Baltoil v. Republic of Estonia*, ICSID Case No. ARB/99/2, Award (June 25, 2001).

130 Ibid., para. 331.

131 The "triple identity test" was perhaps most clearly defined in *Victor Pey Casado v. Chile*, ICSID Case No. ARB/98/2, Award (May 8, 2008), para. 483: "The exercise of the irrevocable option supposes the combination of three conditions. The claims filed respectively before national courts and before the arbitral tribunal must at the same time have the same object, the same basis and be submitted by the same parties" (translation provided).

… [this] is perhaps best illustrated by the circumstances of EIB's recourse to the courts in the matter of its license revocation. The effort by EIB to have the Bank of Estonia's decision overturned, and its license restored, was in effect undertaken on behalf of all the Bank's shareholders (including minority shareholders), as well as on behalf of its depositors, borrowers and employees, all of whom were damaged by the cessation of EIB's activities. … The "investment dispute" submitted to ICSID arbitration, on the other hand, relates to the losses allegedly suffered by the Claimants alone, arising from what they claim were breaches of the BIT.[132]

The fact is that what was claimed for in the local court of Estonia obviously included that which was claimed for under the BIT. Where, despite such overlapping, the causes of action are considered not to be identical, it would be very difficult, if not impossible, for the fork in the road provision to be applied.

With regard to the third limb—identical parties—the *Genin* Tribunal considered that "EIB had no choice but to contest the revocation of its license in Estonia, in the interest of all its shareholders, whereas the Claimants submitted to ICSID arbitration an 'investment dispute', as defined by the BIT, seeking compensation for what they claim was a violation of their rights under the BIT."[133] Again, this is a very formalistic approach toward the issue. In international investment, it is common practice that a foreign investor has established or owns an entity in the host state which often joins the foreign investor in investor–state arbitration. In commercial practice and under the law of many jurisdictions, the shareholder—Genin—and his companies are considered to be related persons. The disregard by the *Genin* Tribunal of this well-established commercial practice is, to say the least, a very dangerous precedent.[134]

The *Genin* Tribunal's decision has had a rather devastating effect on the usefulness of the fork in the road provision. For instance, in *CMS*, the respondent contended that because TGN had resorted to the local court, the claimant should be prevented from initiating arbitration proceedings. The tribunal stated that "[d]ecisions of several ICSID tribunals have held that as contractual claims are different from treaty claims, even if there had been or there currently was a recourse to the local courts for breach of contract, this would not have prevented submission of the treaty claims to arbitration."[135] As there had been no submissions by the claimant to local courts in Argentina, the tribunal decided that the

---

132 *Genin v. Estonia, supra*, note 128, para. 332.

133 Ibid., para. 333.

134 Schreuer appears to have approved this kind of practice, saying that "[i]f the claim before the international tribunal alleges a breach of the BIT, the dispute before the domestic courts or administrative tribunals would also have to concern an alleged breach of a right conferred or created by the BIT," and that "[t]he host State that is to be the respondent in the international arbitration must be the defendant in the domestic proceedings;" see Schreuer, *supra*, note 127, p. 248.

135 *CMS v. Argentina, supra*, note 126, para. 80.

fork in the road provision could not be triggered.[136] In *Middle East Cement*, the tribunal went as far as saying that: "[t]he case brought by the Claimant before the Egyptian Courts regarding the alleged nullity of the auction, was not and could not be 'concerning' Egypt's obligations under the BIT, but could only be concerning the validity of the auction under national Egyptian law."[137]

The *Lauder* Tribunal[138] is perhaps one of the tribunals which have most badly misinterpreted the fork in the road provision. That is why it has triggered so much criticism. Ben Hamida, for example, said, in reference particularly to the *Lauder* Tribunal's reasoning: "It is certain that by introducing the criterion of the violated norm [that is, a national rule versus a treaty rule] to define the identity of the dispute, arbitral jurisprudence limits the effect of the [fork in the road] clause."[139] In fact, if the triple identity test is applied, one may wonder about the actual usefulness of the fork in the road clause.

The fact that more problems have been caused than resolved by the so-called triple identity test notwithstanding, it is clear that even some arbitrators have seen this approach as undermining the *effet utile* of fork in the road provisions. In *Chevron II*, the tribunal noted, *obiter dicta*, that:

> It is unlikely that the triple identity test will be satisfied in many cases where a dispute before a tribunal against a State under a BIT and based upon an alleged breach of the BIT is compared with a dispute in a national court. National legal systems do not commonly provide for the State to be sued in respect of a breach of treaty as such, even though actions for breach of a national law giving effect to a treaty might be possible. A strict application of the triple identity test would deprive the fork in the road provision of all or most of its practical effect.[140]

In another vein, it is appropriate to consider here the analysis made by the *Tza Yap Shum* Tribunal of the fork in the road provision contained in Article 8 of the China–Peru BIT.[141] In brief, Article 8(1) of the BIT calls for all disputes, "as far as possible" to be settled amicably through negotiations between the parties. Article 8(2) permits either party to submit the dispute to the competent host state court if, after six months, negotiations fail to settle it. Article 8(3) permits the submission to international arbitration of any "dispute involving the amount of compensation for expropriation" that "cannot be settled within six months after resort to negotiations

136 Id.
137 *Middle East Cement, supra*, note 126, para. 71.
138 *Lauder v. Czech Republic, supra*, note 126.
139 Walid Ben Hamida, "L'Arbitrage Transnational Face à un Désordre Procédural: La Concurrence des Procédures et les Conflits de Juridictions," 3 *TDM* 2, April 2006, para. 110, where the original French reads: "*Il est certain qu'en introduisant le critère de la norme violée pour définir l'identité du litige, la jurisprudence arbitrale limite l'effet de la clause.*"
140 *Chevron Corporation and Texaco Petroleum Company v. Republic of Ecuador (Chevron II)*, UNCITRAL, 3rd Interim Award on Jurisdiction (February 27, 2012), para. 4.76.
141 See *Tza Yap Shum, supra*, note 58, especially paras. 146–61.

as specified in Paragraph 1 of this Article", as well as "[a]ny disputes concerning other matters … if the parties to the disputes so agree." However, it further provides that no dispute may be submitted to the ICSID if the investor has already submitted it to the competent court of the host state in accordance with Article 8(2).

In other words, this Article provides a clear-cut fork in the road provision. After a six-month period of negotiation, should a dispute not be resolved, the investor has a clear choice:

1. it may submit any dispute to the host state's courts or
2. *if* the dispute involves:
   (a) "the amount of compensation for expropriation" or
   (b) "other matters" *and* the host state so agrees,
   it may submit it to ICSID arbitration.

However, if it chooses "option number 1," that choice is final.

Peru presented this in the arbitration as a "three-stage process," namely: "(1) negotiation during a six-month period; (2) investor's choice to submit the dispute to the courts of the State accepting the investment if the dispute cannot be settled; and (3) only after such a court has decided on the matter and if the dispute cannot still be settled with regard to the amount of compensation, investor's entitlement to have access to international arbitration."[142] Peru also mistakenly maintained that "the only disputes that may be submitted to arbitration are those involving the amount of compensation for expropriation owed to an investor, after the occurrence of undue expropriation has been established,"[143] a position that is clearly not upheld by the text.

The nature of the fork in the road in the China–Peru BIT was further confounded by the Expert Opinion of Professor An Chen, who submitted that:

> If a dispute cannot be settled amicably, both the investor and the State accepting the investment may submit the dispute to a competent court of the State accepting the investment. If after such court has concluded that the investment has indeed been expropriated, a dispute between the investor and the State arose involving *the amount of compensation* owed to the investor for the value of the expropriated investment, either party may submit such dispute to ICSID arbitration. However, the Treaty warns that the parties may not turn to international arbitration had they previously failed to submit the dispute involving <u>the amount of compensation for expropriation</u> to domestic courts.[144]

In fact, the text clearly warns the opposite, that is, that the parties may not turn to arbitration if the dispute involving <u>the amount of compensation for expropriation was submitted</u> to the domestic courts.

142 Ibid., para. 158.
143 Id.
144 Ibid., para. 160 (italicized emphasis in original; underlined emphasis added by the tribunal).

In the end, the tribunal failed to perform its own independent analysis of the content and structure of Article 8, the context for determining the meaning of Article 8(3). Instead, it satisfied itself with rejecting both Professor An Chen's analysis and the respondent's argument. The latter interpretation, it held, would lead to the result that "in case either party chose ICSID arbitration to settle a dispute 'involving the amount of compensation for expropriation', such party would be informed that the parties have not consented to submit to such arbitration as the investor would be required to first submit the dispute to the courts of the relevant Contracting Party."[145] On the basis of either the respondent's argument as presented in the decision by the tribunal or the clear text of the Article, it is hard to see how the tribunal reached this conclusion.

To be fair, at one point the tribunal did recognize that "the last sentence [of Article 8(3)] dispels any doubt about whether an investor (of any contracting party), when deciding on a course of action to settle a dispute in accordance with Article 8, finds himself with an irrevocable either-or choice, also known as 'for[k] in the road.'"[146] It did not, however, find this an acceptable situation, observing that "[t]hese provisions, read together, seem to indicate that if and [sic] investor submits a dispute to a competent tribunal of the Contracting State accepting the investment, the investor may not have access to ICSID arbitration at all,"[147] even though that is the very purpose of a fork in the road provision.

The tribunal did hint that it understood very well not only that this was a fork in the road provision but also how that part of Article 8(3) that dealt with "dispute[s] involving the amount of compensation for expropriation" fit into that structure when it noted that "[*p*]*rima facie*, Article 8(3) seems to establish an exception to the procedure established in Article 8(2), namely, the determination of a dispute of expropriation by the courts of the State accepting the investment."[148] It did not, however, pursue this line of reasoning, perhaps because it would have opened the door to a logical contextual interpretation of the term "dispute[s] involving the amount of compensation for expropriation" that it had already decided not to accept.

Much has been made of the ruling by Jan Paulsson, sole arbitrator in the *Pantechniki* case.[149] In that case, C.I. Sarantopoulos, a Greek company, had entered into contracts with the Government of Albania for the construction of roads and bridges in Albania. Risks of losses owing to civil disturbances were allocated to the Albanian Government's General Road Directorate, which was to reimburse C.I. Sarantopoulos for any such losses. In March 1997, the company suffered such losses, for which it claimed compensation of approximately US$4.8 million. A special commission valued the losses at just US$1.8 million. The Ministry of Finance, however, refused to pay any amount, so the company commenced litiga-

---

145 Ibid., para. 159.
146 Id.
147 Ibid., para. 157.
148 Ibid., para. 149.
149 *Pantechniki S.A. Contractors & Engineers (Greece) v. Republic of Albania*, ICSID Case No. ARB/07/21, Award (July 30, 2009).

tion in the Albanian courts to enforce its contractual right to compensation. The Albanian district courts and the Court of Appeal dismissed those claims on the basis that the contractual provisions allocating the risk of losses to the General Road Directorate were contrary to Albanian public policy. Pantechniki (at that time successor in title to C.I. Sarantopoulos) appealed to the Supreme Court of Albania (in July 2007) but almost simultaneously commenced ICSID arbitration (in August 2007), alleging breaches of the Greece–Albania BIT. During the course of the arbitration, Pantechniki withdrew its case before the Albanian Supreme Court before any decision was made.

Article 10(2) of the Greece–Albania BIT contains a fork in the road provision in these terms:

> If such disputes ["any dispute" between the host State and an investor of the other Party "concerning investments or the expropriation or nationalization of an investment" as per Article 10(1)] cannot be settled within six months from the date either party requested amicable settlement the investor or the Contracting Party concerned may submit the dispute to the competent court of the Contracting Party or to an international arbitration tribunal.

Article 10(4) provides for ICSID arbitration after both contracting parties have become parties to the ICSID Convention.

Albania contended that the claimant's submission of the dispute over compensation for its losses from civil disturbances to the Albanian courts was a choice under the fork in the road provision of the BIT which precluded the tribunal's jurisdiction over the dispute. Pantechniki maintained, on the other hand, and in keeping with previous jurisprudence in this regard, that "Article 10(2) [of the BIT] does not apply because: (i) the Claimant's resort to the Albanian Courts was not a choice within the meaning of Article 10(2) of the Treaty; and (ii) the dispute before the Albanian Courts and the dispute before ICSID are not the same dispute."[150]

The tribunal ruled that the claimant's resort to the Albanian courts *was* its choice and then proceeded to examine the "sameness" of the litigation before the Albanian courts and the dispute before the tribunal. In this regard, the tribunal held that: "It is common ground that the relevant test is the one expressed by the America-Venezuela Mixed Commission in the *Woodruff* case (1903): whether or not 'the fundamental basis of a claim' sought to be brought before the international forum is autonomous of claims to be heard elsewhere."[151] The tribunal also

150 Ibid., para. 55.
151 Ibid., para. 61. For clarity, see the final dispositive paragraphs of the *Woodruff* Decision, as found in *Reports of International Arbitral Awards/Recueil des Sentences Arbitrales*, Woodruff Case, 1903–1905, Volume IX, pp. 213–23; available at: http://legal.un.org/riaa/cases/vol_IX/213-223.pdf. "Now, whereas it might be said, as it was said before, that by the terms of the protocol the other party, viz, the Government of Venezuela, had waived her right to have questions arising under the agreement determined by her own courts, and had submitted herself to this Tribunal it is to be considered that even in the case of this claim as a claim against the Venezuelan Government, owned by an American citizen, being a claim that is entitled to be brought before this Commission, the judge, having to deal with a claim fundamentally based on a contract, has to

noted that: "The same facts can give rise to different legal claims. The similarity of prayers for relief does not necessarily bespeak an identity of causes of action. What I believe to be necessary is to determine whether claimed entitlements have the same normative source."[152]

The approach taken by the *Pantechniki* Tribunal is similar with that of the *ad hoc* Committee in the *Vivendi* case. As such, the tribunal did not make a mechanical and formalistic comparison between the proceedings before the local court and that under arbitration. Instead, it emphasized the fundamental basis of the case in the following words:

> Its final submission (in the since abandoned petition to the Supreme Court) was that it was entitled to payment of US$1,821,796 "because the Defendant had recognised and admitted that this amount is due." The logic is inescapable. To the extent that this prayer was accepted it would grant the Claimant exactly what it is seeking before ICSID—and on the same "fundamental basis." The Claimant's grievance thus arises out of the same purported entitlement that it invoked in the contractual debate it began with the General Roads Directorate. The Claimant chose to take this matter to the Albanian courts. It cannot now adopt the same fundamental basis as the foundation of a Treaty claim. Having made the election to seise the national jurisdiction the Claimant is no longer permitted to raise the same contention before ICSID.[153]

The significance of the *Pantechniki* Tribunal's decision is its effect in correcting the formalistic approach adopted by other tribunals. The consequence of focusing on the fundamental basis of a dispute is that where the fundamentals of a case are the

---

consider the rights and duties arising from that contract, and may not construe a contract that the parties themselves did not make, and he would be doing so if he gave a decision in this case and thus absolved from the pledged duty of first recurring for rights to the Venezuelan courts, thus giving a right, which by this same contract was renounced, and absolve claimant from a duty that he took upon himself by his own voluntary action; that he has to consider that claimant knew, at all events ought to have known, when he bought the bonds or received them in payment, or accepted them on whatsoever ground, that all questions about liability for the bonds had to be decided by the common law and ordinary tribunals of Venezuela, and by accepting them agreed to this condition; and Whereas it does not appear that any appeal of that kind was ever made to the Venezuelan courts, it must be concluded that claimant failed as to one of the conditions that would have entitled him to look on his claim as on one on which a decisive judgment might be given by this Commission; and Whereas, therefore, in the consideration of the claim itself it appears out of the evidence itself, laid before the Commission, that claimant renounced—at all events adhered to the renunciation of—the right to have a decision on the claim by any other authority than the Venezuelan judges and pledged himself not to go—at all events, adhered to the promise of not going—to other judges (except naturally in case of denial or unjust delay of justice, which was not only not proven, but not even alleged) and that by the very agreement that is the fundamental basis of the claim, it was withdrawn from the jurisdiction of this Commission.

Wherefore, as the claimant by his own voluntary waiver has disabled himself from invoking the jurisdiction of this Commission, the claim has to be dismissed without prejudice on its merits, when presented to the proper judges."

152 *Pantechniki v. Albania, supra*, note 148, para. 62.
153 Ibid., para. 67.

same or similar, the tribunal should give effect to the fork in the road provision and decline jurisdiction.[154] In any case, the *Pantechniki* Tribunal ultimately decided that: "This conclusion [that the Claimant is not permitted to raise the same contention before ICSID] does not exclude a claim for mistreatment at the hands of the Albanian courts: denial of justice. Such a claim is indeed being presented here. That is a matter of merits."[155] Yet, at the same time, the tribunal stated:

> It is true that arbitrary decisions may constitute unfair and inequitable treatment and that an ICSID tribunal in a general sense has jurisdiction to deal with the merits of such claims. Yet this proposition is immediately defeated if the particular claim of arbitrariness has been voluntarily submitted to another jurisdiction. It transpires on examination that the alleged arbitrariness is said to arise by reason of Albania's refusal to compensate. That is precisely the issue which the Claimant (to its current regret) took to the Albanian courts. I could not rule on it without violating my own jurisdictional constraints.[156]

Thus, the *Pantechniki* award clearly departed from most of the arbitration cases that had been decided previously. The practical approach taken by the tribunal shows that some arbitrators have realized the problems caused by the "triple identity test" and that unless timely corrective work is done, the international community is bound to react strongly. The *Pantechniki* award has also been received positively. For instance, one commentator has said:

> Even if Pantechniki turned on its own particular facts, the decision is sure to be a source of inspiration for States and future tribunals facing claims involving parallel proceedings. The possibility that Pantechniki may be followed means that investors and those who advise them need to be aware, when a dispute first arises, that pursuing certain remedies might have a preclusive effect on potential investment treaty rights. Investors wishing to preserve their treaty rights must exercise caution and carefully study the text of potentially applicable treaties before commencing proceedings before local courts.[157]

---

154 Some commentators say that that arbitrator Paulsson in fact rejected "the distinction between contract claims and treaty claims;" see Gerhard Wegen and Lars Markert, "Investment Arbitration: Food for Thought on Fork-in-the-Road—A Clause Awakens from its Hibernation," Ch V in Christian Klausegger et al. (eds.), *Austrian Yearbook on International Arbitration 2010*, C.H. Beck, Stämpfli & Manz 2010, pp. 269–92, at 276. They go further in speculating that Paulsson "would also have given effect to the fork-in-the-road clause had there been an umbrella clause—provided that the 'fundamental basis' of the parallel proceedings had been the same." Ibid, at 279.

155 *Pantechniki v. Albania, supra*, note 148, para. 68. In fact, it went on to examine claims for failure to provide full protection and security to the claimant's investment and for failure to provide the investor fair and equitable treatment. In respect of the latter, see especially, ibid., paras. 85–88.

156 Ibid., para. 87.

157 Anthony Sinclair, "Fork-in-the-road provisions in investment treaties," Allen & Overy LLP (November 4, 2009); available at: http://www.allenovery.com/AOWEB/Knowledge/Editorial. aspx?contentTypeID=1&contentSubTypeID=7944&itemID=53649&prefLangID=410.

Putting aside the issue of whether or not *Pantechniki* "represents a marked departure from the prevailing jurisprudence,"[158] it is clear that it has had some impact on the pleading in subsequent cases. In the *RSM (II)* case,[159] the relevant BIT between the United States and Grenada contains a fork in the road provision in Article VI(3), which provides in relevant part: "Either party to the dispute may institute proceedings before the Centre provided: (i) the dispute has not been submitted by the national or company for resolution in accordance with any applicable previously agreed dispute settlement procedures …." In terms of the relevant facts and circumstances, *RSM (II)* was nearly identical to the previous *RSM* case in which the claimant had not prevailed.[160] The essential difference between the two cases was that RSM was the sole claimant in the first case whereas it was joined as claimants in *RSM (II)* by the three persons who were its sole shareholders. The respondent maintained that:

> Article VI(3)(i) of the Treaty is intended to prevent the re-litigation of disputes. … [T]hat objective is thwarted if claimants can bring successive cases that, despite raising formally distinct legal causes of action, are *co-extensive*, share the same *fundamental basis*, or derive *from the same origin or source*. That is said to be precisely the situation here – Claimants' Treaty claims being based entirely on the same events that underlay the breach of contract claims submitted to the Prior Tribunal.[161]

Clearly the words "*co-extensive*" and "*fundamental basis*" were references to the *Vivendi* and *Pantechniki* cases, respectively. In this regard, the *Pantechniki* decision at least has shown some precedential significance for interpreting fork in the road provisions.[162]

In *RSM (II)*, the claimants contended that the previous tribunal's decision dealt with contractual issues and what they claimed before the *RSM (II)* Tribunal

---

158 Ibid. The same author stated that "Pantechniki represents a marked departure from the prevailing jurisprudence by adopting a qualitative test that looks at the subject-matter of the claims, as opposed to their legal character."

159 *Rachel S. Grynberg, Stephen M. Grynberg, Miriam Z. Grynberg, and RSM Production Corporation v. Grenada* ("*RSM (II)*"), ICSID Case No. ARB/10/6, Award (December 10, 2010).

160 *RSM Production Corporation v. Grenada*, ICSID Case No. ARB/05/14, Award (March 13, 2009).

161 *RSM (II)*, supra, note 158, para. 4.6.14.

162 For instance, in the still undecided (at the time of writing) case of *Guaracachi v. Bolivia*, the respondent based its pleading, at least in part, on the *Pantechniki* award: "The tribunal in *Pantechniki v. Albania*, instead of applying the formal triple identity test, preferred to compare the remedy sought by the investor before the local courts and the remedy sought before the international arbitral tribunal court to decide whether the fork in the road clause in the treaty should apply." See *Guaracachi America, Inc. and Rurelec PLC v. Plurinational State of Bolivia*, UNCITRAL, Respondent Memorial on Jurisdiction (September 17, 2012) (in Spanish), paras. 315–16 (translation provided). The claimants, on their part, offered a novel reading of the *Pantechniki* decision that the sole arbitrator in that case recognized the triple identity test. For details, see *Guaracachi America, Inc. and Rurelec PLC v. Plurinational State of Bolivia*, UNCITRAL, Claimant Counter-Memorial on Jurisdiction (October 26, 2012), para. 97.

was related to treaty breaches.[163] This was not an entirely disingenuous position to maintain. Given the rigidly formalistic way in which almost all tribunals had approached fork in the road provisions in the past, it was almost certain that the claimants expected to prevail by this pleading. Nevertheless, the tribunal refused even to address the fork in the road issue but dismissed the claims on the ground of *res judicata*.[164] This having been said, it does not mean that the *RSM (II)* Tribunal adopted or was even influenced by the *Pantechniki* Tribunal's findings.

In *Chevron (II)*, the respondent, Ecuador, directly appealed to the *Pantechniki* award to uphold its contention that the claimants had violated the fork in the road provision contained in the United States–Ecuador BIT by bringing their case to ICSID arbitration.[165] It is worthy of note that the tribunal did agree, at least in part, with the shortcomings of applying the "triple identity test" in the context of fork in the road provisions. It said:

> It is unlikely that the triple identity test will be satisfied in many cases where a dispute before a tribunal against a State under a BIT and based upon an alleged breach of the BIT is compared with a dispute in a national court. National legal systems do not commonly provide for the State to be sued in respect of a breach of treaty as such, even though actions for breach of a national law giving effect to a treaty might be possible. *A strict application of the triple identity test would deprive the fork in the road provision of all or most of its practical effect.*[166]

The *Chevron (II)* Tribunal, however, held that it did not have to decide if the case before it and the cases in the domestic courts were the same. The wording of the fork in the road provision in the relevant BIT, it pointed out, "require[d] that, for the fork to be applied, not only must the dispute have been submitted for resolution but also that the dispute was submitted by the 'national or company concerned' for resolution in the national courts."[167] As the claimants had not brought either of the cases before the national courts, nor could the tribunal identify any counterclaim they had submitted in those proceedings that could prevent the arbitration from going forward, it held that the claimant's claims were not precluded by the fork in the road provision in Article VI(3) of the BIT.[168]

---

163 *RSM (II)*, *supra*, note 158, paras. 5.1.2–3.
164 The tribunal stated: "… an essential predicate to the success of each of Claimants' claims is an ability for the Tribunal to re-litigate and decide in Claimants' favour conclusions of fact or law concerning the parties' contractual rights that have already distinctly been put in issue and distinctly determined by the Prior Tribunal. Because the Tribunal has concluded, in the answer to the first question it has considered, that it cannot properly revisit those conclusions, the Tribunal therefore finds that each of Claimants' claims is manifestly without legal merit. Accordingly, the Tribunal is obliged to dismiss each of Claimants' present claims." Ibid., para. 7.2.1.
165 *Chevron Corporationa and Texaco Petroleum Company v. Republic of Ecuador (Chevron II)*, UNCITRAL, Memorial on Jurisdictional Objections of the Republic of Ecuador (July 26, 2010), para. 146 (footnote omitted); see also its full argument in paras. 137–46.
166 *Chevron (II)*, 3rd Interim Award on Jurisdiction, *supra*, note 139, para. 4.76 (emphasis added).
167 Ibid., para. 4.78.
168 Ibid., para. 4.89.

It is interesting to note that both the *RSM(II)* and *Chevron (II)* Tribunals were critical of the triple identity test and both concluded that there was no need to apply the fork in the road provision in their respective case. Whether that was a pure coincidence is not known. It at least shows that the rigid application of the triple identity test has the problem in making the fork in the road clause ineffective, even though other principles may give tribunals more discretion.

In *H&H v. Egypt*,[169] the respondent maintained, inter alia, that the fork in the road provisions of the BIT between the United States and Egypt had been triggered because the claimant had already submitted the same dispute to the local courts in Egypt. In the respondent's view:

> (i) The factual components of the treaty cause of action claim have already been brought before the Cairo Arbitral Tribunal and to the local courts; (ii) The fundamental basis of the claims are the same—the alleged interference by GHE and Claimant's rights under the MOC and the denial of the existence of the purported Option to Buy; and (iii) The treaty claims do not have an autonomous existence outside the contract.[170]

The tribunal, however, instead of taking the opportunity to state its position on the issue, neatly sidestepped the issue in the following way: "The Tribunal is of the view that the allegations related to the fork-in-the-road clause are closely related to the merits of the case. The Tribunal considers that ruling on this matter requires a more thorough analysis of the claims and the merits of the dispute."[171]

In the end, the *H&H* Tribunal decided to join its decision on the fork in the road objection to the merits.[172] In other words, the tribunal converted the question of jurisdiction to one of admissibility. This decision is, however, open to question, as the fork in the road provision relates, without doubt, to jurisdiction and not admissibility. By using its discretion to transform a matter of jurisdiction into one of admissibility, the tribunal ran the risk of excessive exercise of power, which is a ground for annulment under the ICSID Convention. It also confirms the extent to which an arbitral tribunal may make decisions of its own free will.

The above practice shows that the majority of arbitrators still regard the triple identity test as their "Bible" in application of the fork in the road provision. One of the clearest expositions of this appears in *Toto Costruzzioni v. Lebanon*, in which the decision on jurisdiction was delivered less than six weeks after the *Pantechniki* award. It stated that:

> The fork-in-the road clause in Article 7 of the Treaty does not take away jurisdiction from the Tribunal over Treaty claims. In order for a fork-in-the-road clause to preclude claims from being considered by the Tribunal, the Tribunal has to consider whether the same claim is 'on a different road,'

169　*H&H Enterprises Investments, Inc. v. Arab Republic of Egypt*, ICSID Case No. ARB/09/15, Decision on Objections to Jurisdiction (June 5, 2012).
170　Ibid., para. 71.
171　Ibid., para. 79.
172　Ibid., para. 80.

i.e., that a claim with the same object, parties and cause of action, is already brought before a different judicial forum. Contractual claims arising out of the Contract do not have the same cause of action as Treaty claims.[173]

In addition, the *Toto* Tribunal elaborated that where a "State acts in the context of the performance of the contract as a '*puissance publique*,' a violation of the Contract would also constitute a violation of the Treaty."[174] In such circumstances, an international tribunal would have jurisdiction over such a dispute. On the one hand, the *Toto* Tribunal was prepared to examine the substantive aspect—nature of the act—in such circumstances. Yet, at the same time, it still insisted on applying the triple identity test. Before reviewing the damages such an approach may cause to the confidence of host states in the emerging international law governing investment disputes, a question to be asked is what are the objects and purposes of the fork in the road provision?

It is said that the purpose of the fork in the road provision "is to prevent parallel proceedings concerning the same investment dispute from being conducted in different *fora*."[175] It also functions to avoid the payment of multiple damages by host states under different proceedings for the same cause of action.[176] Although some tribunals support these proposed purposes, there may well be difficulties in reaching a consensus in this regard. What is certain is that the fork in the road provision is a treaty obligation which should be interpreted in accordance with Articles 31 and 32 of the VCLT.[177] The first and most important principle is to interpret the provision in good faith—to give effect to the provision rather than to deprive it of the same. As at least one commentator has observed:

> One assumes that when States, the two sovereigns who agreed the treaty, inserted a "fork in the road" provision into a contract, that they meant it to have some effect and it seems to me that to date … there has been a tendency by tribunals to seek—no doubt for very good reasons and we don't know all of them—from the awards or decisions that we see, to deprive those words of a genuine meaning.[178]

In practice, the fork in the road provision has not been given effect to the extent that it should have been. The reason for this lack of enforcement may be manifold.

---

173 *Toto Costruzzioni Generali, S.p.A. v. Republic of Lebanon*, ICSID Case No. ARB/07/12, Decision on Jurisdiction (September 11, 2009), para. 211.
174 Ibid., para. 215.
175 Wegen and Markert, *supra*, note 153, at 272.
176 Ibid., p. 273.
177 Giorgio Sacerdoti pointed out that the fork in the road provisions contained in various treaties "are not in any way identical. Therefore the starting point should be the text of the relevant treaty itself" and that "the interpretation of these clauses based on treaty interpretation is fundamental;" see "The Relationship between Local Courts and Investment Treaty Arbitration," Proceedings of the British Institute of International and Comparative Law Third Investment Treaty Forum Conference, *Transnational Dispute Management*, Vol. 2, Issue 4, August 2005, pp. 17–18.
178 Peter Turner, "The Fork in the Road Revisited," in Federico Ortino et al. (eds.), *Investment Law – Current Issues*, Vol. I, British Institute of International and Comparative Law, 2006, at 177.

In the first place, there is still a prevailing distrust of national courts and the administrative tribunals of host states on the part of investors, and this is shared by many arbitrators and scholars, in particular those in the developed countries.[179] Such a shared distrust can lead to the resistance of both investors and a number of tribunals to give effect to the clause.

The second phenomenon of investment arbitration is that in practice, arbitral tribunals have rarely ruled that they had no jurisdiction, except when that was clearly the case *ratione temporis* or *ratione personae*. In the opinion of many, investment tribunals have a tendency to expand jurisdiction, and some decisions in respect of the MFN clause serve as an example of this.[180] At the same time, the culture and educational background of the arbitrators may also play an important part. For instance, the interpretation of the fork in the road provision has been clearly affected by the principle of *res judicata*[181] and *lis pendens*. As a result, the provision has been subject to very narrow interpretation,[182] even at the risk of running against the will of states parties to such provisions. The formulation of investment law jurisprudence constitutes another factor that affects interpretation of the fork in the road provision. As more and more arbitration decisions are made, and when such decisions lean in one direction or favor one interpretation over another, it becomes more difficult for later tribunals to move away from the "main" trend. This is so despite the fact that, in theory at least, arbitration decisions have no precedential effect.[183]

Taking into consideration all of the above, it is remarkable that the *Pantechniki* Tribunal has opened a new channel for interpreting the fork in the road provision. Against the pressure of investment jurisprudence, the tribunal there said:

179 For instance, Schreuer shows how much he shares this distrust by going so far as to suggest that "if the BIT contains a fork in the road provision, guarantees of effective domestic remedies are traps designed to lure an investor into domestic proceedings with the consequence that the door to international arbitration will be closed forever no matter what the outcome of the domestic proceedings may be;" see Schreuer, *supra*, note 127, at 249.

180 For discussions on the issue, see William Rand, Robert N. Hornick, and Paul Friedland, "ICSID's Emerging Jurisprudence: The Scope of ICSID's Jurisdiction," *N. Y. U. Journal of International Law and Politics*, Vol. 19, 1986–1987, pp. 37–38; John T. Schmidt, "Arbitration Under the Auspices of the International Centre for Settlement of Investment Disputes (ICSID): Implications of the Decision on Jurisdiction in Alcoa Minerals of Jamaica, Inc. v. Government of Jamaica," *Harvard International Law Journal*, Vol. 17, 1976, p. 90.

181 Cremades and Madalena, for example, observed: "… the fork-in-the-road jurisprudence seems to borrow heavily from the criteria developed in the *res judicata* context for determining the identity between one proceeding and another." Bernardo M. Cremades and Ignacio Madalena, "Parallel Proceedings in International Arbitration," 24 *Arb. Int'l* 4, 507–40, at 529. See also *Chevron II*, 3rd Interim Award on Jurisdiction, *supra*, note 139, para. 4.77: "The triple identity test was developed to address questions of res judicata and to identify specific issues that have already been determined by a competent tribunal. It has also been applied to similar questions arising in the broadly comparable context of lis pendens."

182 Pedro J. Martinez-Fraga and Harout Jack Samra, "The Role of Precedent in Defining Res Judicata in Investor–State Arbitration," 32 *Northwestern Journal of International Law & Business* 3, Summer 2012, pp. 419–50.

183 For discussion of the origin of precedent and the common law "triple identity" test, see Martinez-Fraga and Samra, ibid.

"[T]here comes a time when it is no longer sufficient merely to assert that a claim is founded on the Treaty. The tribunal must determine whether the claim truly does have an autonomous existence outside the contract."[184] People may question the scope and precision of the fundamental basis test established in *Pantechniki*,[185] but it will not reduce the contributions made by the sole arbitrator to international investment law by correcting the misinterpretations of the fork in the road provision by other tribunals.[186]

IV. Exhaustion of local remedies

Exhaustion of local remedies refers to treaty provisions that establish a requirement that a foreign investor, before resorting to international arbitration, should try to resolve its disputes with the host state through local procedures, administrative or judicial. Many BITs contain provisions to that effect. The second part of Article 26 of the ICSID Convention on consent of contracting parties to arbitration confirms this practice by providing that: "A Contracting State may require the exhaustion of local administrative or judicial remedies as a condition of its consent to arbitration under this Convention." When deciding the issue as to whether or not local remedies have been exhausted, the time factor and other conditions are often related.

In *TSA Spectrum*, for instance, the BIT between the Netherlands and Argentina in its Article 10 provides:

1) Disputes between one Contracting Party and an investor of the other Contracting Party regarding issues covered by this agreement shall, if possible, be settled amicably.

2) If such disputes cannot be settled according to the provisions of paragraph (1) of this Article within a period of three months from the date on which either party to the dispute requested amicable settlement, either party may submit the dispute to the administrative or judicial organs of the Contracting Party in the territory of which the investment has been made.

3) If within a period of eighteen months from submission of the dispute to the competent organs mentioned in paragraph (2) above, these organs have not given a final decision or if the decision of the aforementioned organs has been given but the parties are still in dispute, then the investor concerned may resort to international arbitration or conciliation. Each Contracting Party hereby consents to the submission of a dispute as referred to in paragraph (1) of this Article to international arbitration.

---

184   *Pantechniki, supra*, note 148, para. 64.
185   Wegen and Markert questioned "whether the sole arbitrator's understanding of the 'fundamental basis' test in the Pantechniki v. Albania award actually corresponds with the considerations contained in the precedents he draws on;" see Wegen and Markert, *supra*, note 153, at 281.
186   Fiona Marshall commented that "The award is especially noteworthy considering that the clause in question does not expressly state that the investor's election to submit a dispute to the courts or arbitration will be final." See Marshall, *supra*, note 108.

According to the above provisions, local remedies may be exhausted by either a "final decision" that has been given by the administrative or judicial organs of the host state or the elapse of an 18-month period. Whether the claimant had exhausted the local remedies before resorting to international investment arbitration was an issue in the *TSA Spectrum* case. The relevant facts concerning the issue of exhaustion of local remedies in that case are as follows. On January 26, 2004, CNC—an Argentine government agency—issued Resolution No. 242/04 and declared the concession contract held by the claimant to be terminated and decided that CNC would itself operate the installations and assets that were the object of the contract.[187] The claimant then sent a letter to CNC requesting the reversal of Resolution No. 242/04—an amicable measure taken by the claimant to resolve the dispute. On May 14, 2004, CNC adopted Resolution No. 1231/04 rejecting the claimant's request.[188] Then, on June 4, 2004, the claimant sent a letter to the Secretary of Communications requesting that Resolution No. 1231/04 be overturned. Finally, on December 10, 2004, the claimant sent a letter to the president of the Argentine Republic stating "that, since more than 30 days had passed without an express reply from the Secretary of Communications, TSA's request should be considered rejected according to Argentine law. TSA therefore notified the Argentine Republic of TSA's consent to the exclusive jurisdiction of ICSID in order that the investment dispute be resolved through binding arbitration."[189]

The claimant contended that the Resolution No. 1231/04 was a final decision under the BIT because, according to Argentine law, after an elapse of 30 days any administrative appeal should be considered as having been rejected. The tribunal first considered that as the term "final decision" appeared in an international treaty, it should be interpreted independently in accordance with international law. Thus, it might be given a different meaning from the same term used in national laws. In the tribunal's view, "a decision should be considered final when there is no legal remedy which would give a party a reasonable chance of having the decision changed."[190] It then stated that when the claimant wrote to the Secretary of Communications requesting it to repeal CNC's Resolution No. 1231/04, it "believed that there was a reasonable chance that Resolution No. 242/04 terminating the Concession Contract would be repealed or amended, or that some other relief might be obtained."[191] Therefore, the tribunal concluded that Resolution No. 1231/04 was not a final decision as that would be considered under the terms of the BIT.[192] Nonetheless, the claimant did not wait for a decision of the Secretary of Communications but resorted to international arbitration

---

187 *TSA Spectrum de Argentina, S.A. v. Argentine Republic*, ICSID Case No. ARB/05/5, Award (December 19, 2008), para. 9.

188 Ibid., para. 11.

189 Ibid., para. 13.

190 Ibid., para. 102.

191 Ibid., para. 103.

192 Id.

at ICSID. The question was then whether it was premature for the claimant to initiate the arbitration.

The *TSA Spectrum* Tribunal considered that: "the purpose of the requirement of a final decision was to limit as far as possible the number of disputes that should be the subject of international settlement." As the purpose of local remedies is to limit "as far as possible" international arbitration of investor–state disputes, it is consequentially logical that the investor and the host state should be given adequate opportunities to have their dispute settled without resorting to such arbitration. Hence, any assumption of a final decision to reject requests made by investors should not be permitted. The *TSA Spectrum* Tribunal indeed held that "when TSA requested ICSID arbitration, there was not yet a 'final decision' within the meaning of Article 10(3) of the BIT. Nor had the eighteen-month period provided for in that Article elapsed."[193] This conclusion was based on the "criterion being whether there is a reasonable chance of having a decision changed within the domestic legal system."[194] Given the tribunal's view that treaty provisions must be interpreted according to international law, whether the application of the above criterion is sound or not must be assessed pursuant to the applicable principles of international law and not those of the national law of Argentina or of any other country.

The tribunal did not elaborate on the basis for the application of the criterion. It is apparent, however, that the decision of the tribunal was influenced by the fact that on May 23, 2005—long after the lapse of the 30-day period under Argentine administrative law as argued by the claimant—the Ministry of Federal Planning, Public Investment and Services rejected the claimant's appeal,[195] which proved that in practice the administrative law rule was not strictly followed. As the tribunal emphasized the purpose of the requirement of the exhaustion of local remedies, whether or not local remedies are exhausted should be assessed in the context and circumstances of a particular case, rather than just on the basis of such legal provisions as the Argentine administrative rules.

Since Resolution No. 1231/04 was decided not to be a final decision under the BIT, the claimant should have not resorted to arbitration. It could, for instance, have brought the case to a court of the host state upon receiving the rejection of the Ministry for Federal Planning, Public Investment and Services. Even if resort to a local court was a possibility, there were only three months remaining of the 18 months required by the BIT. The tribunal considered that it was "most unlikely that a decision by a court giving TSA satisfaction could have been obtained before the expiry of the eighteen months."[196] The *TSA Spectrum* Tribunal took a practical approach in the case. Even if it had decided to dismiss the case, the claimant could have restarted the arbitration immediately. In these circumstances, for purposes

---

193 Ibid., para. 107.
194 Ibid., para. 106.
195 Ibid., para. 14.
196 Ibid., para. 111.

of judicial economy and arbitral efficiency, the tribunal's decision to allow the dispute to go to arbitration was reasonable.

Impregilo is a more recent case that involved interpretation of treaty provisions on local remedies. The claimant—Impregilo S.p.A., a company incorporated in Italy—made an investment in water and sewerage services in the Argentine Province of Buenos Aires by forming a consortium with other international companies. After winning a concession agreement, and in accordance with the bidding rules, Impregilo and its partners incorporated AGBA, which in turn executed the concession contract.[197] The operation of AGBA suffered difficulties in collecting payment, and then the Argentine laws on the country's financial emergency and exchange regime which were adopted in 2002 triggered the arbitration proceedings, as they did in many other cases,.

The Argentina–Italy BIT that the claimant relied on was signed on May 22, 1990 and entered into force on October 14, 1993. The respondent objected to the jurisdiction of ICSID and the competence of the tribunal on the grounds, inter alia, that Impregilo had failed to meet the requirements established in Article 8 of the Argentina–Italy BIT.[198]

The dispute resolution clause contained in Article 8(2) and (3) of the Argentina–Italy BIT, after stipulating that investor–state disputes should be first resolved through friendly negotiations, provides:

> 2. If the dispute cannot be settled amicably, it may be submitted to the competent judicial or administrative courts of the Party in whose territory the investment is made.
> 3. Where, after eighteen months from the date of notice of commencement of proceedings before the courts mentioned in paragraph 2 above, the dispute between an investor and one of the Contracting Parties has not been resolved, it may be referred to international arbitration.

The question for the tribunal was how to interpret the above provisions, especially in their use of the permissive verb "may" in Article 8(2). The respondent contended that the word indicated that:

> … an investor is not required to submit the dispute to a binding resolution system but may continue with the amicable consultations for as long as he wishes or even leave the dispute dormant for an indefinite term. It does not mean, however, that the investor, if he wishes to initiate international arbitration proceedings, is exempted from first submitting the dispute to domestic courts and from then waiting for 18 months before proceeding to international arbitration.[199]

197 *Impregilo S.p.A. v. Argentine Republic*, ICSID Case No. ARB/07/17, Award (June 21, 2011), paras. 13–14.
198 Ibid., para. 49.
199 Ibid., para. 51.

The respondent further argued that: "if amicable negotiations fail, then, pursuant to Article 8(3), an investor may submit the dispute to international arbitration only if it was previously submitted to the jurisdiction of the competent administrative or judicial bodies for at least 18 months."[200]

In the claimant's view, however, as Article 8(2) of the BIT uses the word "may," this means that "the dispute may be submitted to competent judicial or administrative courts of the State of investment."[201] This argument was based on the fact that the BIT did not use the word "shall." Therefore, the claimant argued that "the submission of the dispute to the domestic courts is an option and not a mandatory requirement."[202]

The tribunal considered that Article 8(2) could be subject to two interpretations. The first interpretation would place emphasis on the optional character by relying on the word "may." Hence, a foreign investor may or may not submit its dispute to a domestic court before initiating arbitration proceedings. The second interpretation would give weight to the first part of Article 8(3), according to which a foreign investor "must first bring proceedings before the domestic courts and observe the waiting period of 18 months," before commencing arbitration.[203] In accordance with either interpretation, however, a foreign investor would not be required to bring a dispute to a local court.

The *Impregilo* Tribunal further noted that although international treaty practice varied in such a way that some treaties used the word "may" while others used the word "shall," such "terminological differences between BITs do not necessarily mean that any substantive difference was intended."[204] It further stated that the ambiguity in treaty provisions could be resolved in accordance with Article 31 of the VCLT, that is, in the context of such provisions and, for that purpose, the tribunal considered that Article 8(2) and Article 8(3) should be read together.

Where the first interpretation is followed, a foreign investor does not need to bring any dispute to a local court; he could always resort to international arbitration. At the same time, the tribunal noted that from the viewpoint of the host state, "it must have been desirable to give its courts a first opportunity to resolve dispute with foreign investors."[205] As the first interpretation would deprive the host state of the benefit of resolving disputes through local courts, the tribunal considered the second interpretation to be in compliance with the intent of the contracting parties.

In addition, the tribunal believed that Article 8(3) indicated a general condition for arbitration and that where an exception was permitted, it should have been written into the BIT. Accordingly, the tribunal stated that Article 8(3) "should be considered to set out a general condition that must be complied with

---

200 Ibid., para. 52.
201 Ibid., para. 66.
202 Id.
203 Ibid., para. 82.
204 Ibid., para. 86.
205 Ibid., para. 88.

by the investor who wishes to submit the dispute to international arbitration."[206] This general condition, according to the tribunal's decision, has two limbs. The first limb is that a dispute must be brought to a local court. The second limb is that a period of 18 months must elapse. To support its position, like many other tribunals, the *Impregilo* Tribunal referred to the decisions in the *Maffezini*[207] and *Wintershall* cases,[208] both of which decided that a foreign investor has an obligation to exhaust local remedies before initiating international arbitration proceedings.

The *Abaclat* case[209] also dealt with the exhaustion of local remedy provisions contained in the Argentina–Italy BIT. The tribunal considered that the requirements of negotiation and an 18-month period of litigation before arbitration were "to provide the Host State with an opportunity to address the issue before resorting to international arbitration. Thus, the relevant question is not 'could the dispute have been efficiently settled before the Argentine courts?', but was Argentina deprived of a fair opportunity to address the dispute within the framework of its own domestic legal system because of Claimants' disregard of the 18 months litigation requirement?"[210] With that in mind, the tribunal treated the local remedy provisions as conditions for implementing the respondent's consent to arbitration—not a condition to arbitration—and therefore held that they related to admissibility rather than to jurisdiction.

To justify this determination, the tribunal relied on its own theory of "fairness and efficiency," stating that: "As such, the idea of fairness and efficiency must be taken into account when interpreting and determining how the system is supposed to work and what happens if one part of the system fails or is otherwise disregarded by one party."[211] Yet the tribunal did not elaborate on how to balance the concepts of fairness and efficiency. In its view, the efficiency issue related to the courts of the host state and fairness to the investor's interests. It further said that the issue was "not about whether the 18 months litigation requirement may be considered futile; it is about determining whether Argentina's interest in being able to address the specific claims through its domestic legal system

---

206 Ibid., para. 90.
207 *Emilio Agustin Maffezini v. Spain*, ICSID Case No. ARB/97/7, Decision on Jurisdiction (January 25, 2000). In that case, it was held that "the Contracting Parties to the BIT—Argentina and Spain—wanted to give their respective courts the opportunity, within the specified period of eighteen months, to resolve the dispute before it could be taken to international arbitration;" ibid., para. 35.
208 *Wintershall Aktiengesellschaft v. Argentine Republic*, ICSID Case No. ARB/04/14, Award (December 8, 2008). The tribunal in that case concluded that Wintershall "could not avoid prior compliance with" its obligations to bring the dispute to the Argentine courts "before initiating arbitration proceedings;" ibid, para. 156. In the end, the tribunal decided that it had no competence to entertain Wintershall's claim.
209 *Abaclat v. Argentina, supra*, note 78.
210 Ibid., para. 581.
211 Ibid., para. 579.

would justify depriving Claimants of their interests of being able to submit it to arbitration."[212] In its view, where the local courts, having been provided with the opportunity, cannot resolve the dispute efficiently, the question that should be addressed is whether it would be unfair to deprive the investor of its right to resort to arbitration merely because it disregarded the local remedy requirement.[213]

This, of course, cannot resolve the question as to whether or not a determination of the efficiency of a court system should be decided by third bodies. There are at the moment no commonly accepted rules and standards for judging the efficiency of a judiciary. As the efficiency of any judiciary is affected by various factors, any attempt by third parties to judge the efficiency of a national judiciary begs more questions than it may resolve.

In any case, the approach taken by the *Abaclat* Tribunal is akin to that employed by the *TSA Spectrum* Tribunal. The issue was not whether the foreign investor in question would be deprived of an opportunity to take its dispute to arbitration. Rather, the question was when the foreign investor may institute arbitration proceedings. Any assessment of such a situation should give due consideration to the interests of the host state.

Local remedy requirements are included in BITs not only to encourage the resolution of investor–state disputes through local court proceedings; they are also a recognition of individual state sovereignty, which is furthermore the result of the contracting parties' negotiations. At the same time, where investors who disregard such requirements are barred from initiating arbitration proceedings, they would still be entitled to restart the arbitration once the local remedy requirements are satisfied. When commenting on a similar provision of the North American Free Trade Agreement relating to local remedy requirements, Paulsson stated: "This protects the host State from trigger-happy investors mounting instant challenges to actions of public officials that they feel violate Section A, and gives the State some breathing room to refine or adjust controversial measures."[214]

Some tribunals, as discussed earlier, have considered the issue as a matter of deprivation of the right to arbitrate. This is clearly not in accordance with the intent of the contracting parties to the BITs in question. This once again shows that it is of the utmost importance to recall that the function of international tribunals is to interpret treaty or contract provisions and not to rewrite them so that they can sound better or more logical in their opinion. The purposes and objectives of such provisions may be taken into account in interpreting local remedy requirements only in cases of ambiguity. Where treaty provisions are clear and specific, no guesswork about their purposes and objectives is needed.

212 Ibid., para. 584.
213 The reason for this approach, according to the tribunal, was that it would not do any harm to the host state; ibid., para. 583.
214 Jan Paulsson, *supra*, note 3, at 247. Section A of the NAFTA stipulates the standards of treatment of foreign investments like national and MFN treatment, freedom from performance requirements, right to repatriate without delay and conditions of expropriation.

V. China's treaty practice

As a country which suffered enormously from foreign powers in the past, China is very zealous in preserving its sovereign power, notwithstanding that it is already a significant home country of FDI. As that is the case, the first generation BITs all restricted, to say the best, the jurisdiction of arbitral tribunals to the determination of the amount of compensation. The China–Peru BIT discussed earlier in the context of the *Tza Yap Shum* case, is an example. China's new-generation BITs have accepted the modern international practice in their provisions for investor–state arbitration.[215] For instance, Article 152 of the China–New Zealand FTA in relation to dispute resolution stipulates that "any legal dispute … directly concerning an investment … shall, as far as possible, be settled amicably through consultations and negotiations." For this purpose, "non-binding third-party procedures" may also be employed. Where the disputing parties cannot resolve their dispute through such amicable procedures within six months, the dispute, "unless the parties … agree otherwise … shall, by the choice of the investor, be submitted" to ICSID for arbitration by giving the State party a three-month advance notice.[216] This arrangement for dispute resolution is fully in accord with the contemporary international practice of investment dispute resolution.

What may cause some confusion is the requirement that, upon receiving the arbitration notice, the state party "may" require the investor to "go through any applicable domestic administrative review procedures specified by the laws and regulations" of the host state.[217] Such review procedures may not exceed three months. A plain reading of the language shows that the host state may require foreign investors to go through such procedures provided that those are "specified by the laws and regulations." As Article 153 does not provide any choice to foreign investors when the laws and regulations of the host state require such procedures, foreign investors would have to follow them. This arrangement is further complicated by the provision that where a foreign investor has submitted its dispute to a domestic court of the host state, it may not resort to international arbitration before the case is withdrawn from the domestic court.[218]

Insofar as China is concerned, that the "standard" fork in the road provision, at least as it has been applied—or, more generally, not applied—by arbitral tribunals, is not meeting the need that led to its creation is perhaps best illustrated by the recently agreed China–Canada BIT. This agreement contains no fork in the road provision, but, taken together, its Article 21 and Annex C.21 serve the

---

215 For a more thorough discussion of the evolution of China's BIT practice, see, for example, Guiguo Wang, "Investor–State Dispute Settlement in China," *TDM*, Vol. 8, Issue 5, December 2011. For discussion of the nature of consent in China's BIT practice, see Tong Qi, "How Exactly Does China Consent to Investor–State Arbitration: On the First ICSID Case Against China," 5 *Contemp. Asia Arb. J.* 265, 2012.

216 Article 153(1) of China–New Zealand FTA.

217 Article 153(2) of China–New Zealand FTA.

218 Article 153(3) of China–New Zealand FTA.

same purpose and arguably do so better. In accordance with these provisions, if a Chinese measure is challenged:

> An investor who has initiated proceedings before any court of China with respect to the measure of China alleged to be a breach of an obligation under Part B may only submit a claim to arbitration under Article 20 if the investor has withdrawn the case from the national court before judgment has been made on the dispute.[219]

If a Canadian measure is challenged:

> The investor and, where the claim is for loss or damage to an interest in an enterprise of Canada that is a juridical person that the investor owns or controls directly or indirectly, the enterprise shall waive their right to initiate or continue before any administrative tribunal or court under the law of any Contracting Party, or other dispute settlement procedures, any proceedings with respect to the measure of Canada that is alleged to be a breach referred to in Article 20, except for proceedings for injunctive, declaratory or other extraordinary relief, not involving the payment of damages, before an administrative tribunal or court under the law of Canada.[220]

The current Chinese practice in this regard can only be derived from the provisions of its BITs and FTAs. It has not yet been called upon to articulate its position through arbitration proceedings. In its most recent BITs and FTAs, however, it is clear that China has moved far beyond the "distrust or ideological unconformity on the part of communist regimes regarding investment of private capital" attributed to it by the *Tza Yap Shum* Tribunal.[221] In fact, as an increasingly important source of foreign direct investment and, accordingly, in the interests of its own investors which risk their funds overseas, China has freely adopted the generally accepted international principles and standards that apply to foreign investment, including those related to "consent to arbitration."

In this regard, a comparison of the terms of the 1994 China–Peru BIT and the 2009 China–Peru FTA are particularly pertinent. Disregarding issues of "nationality," which are addressed in Chapter 3 of this book, there is no question but that Mr Tza's claims would have been accepted under the terms of China's most recent "consent to arbitration." But that has been an evolutionary process on the part of a sovereign state in determining its own best position within the international community. It is hardly the responsibility of any independent international arbitral tribunal to determine the position of any sovereign state within that environment or to presume to dictate its own terms of compliance with its peculiar standards.

219 China–Canada BIT, Annex C.21(2).
220 China–Canada BIT, Annex C.21(3).
221 See *Tza Yap Shum, supra,* note 58, para. 145.

It is worthy of note that the China–New Zealand FTA reflects an important innovation in the international practice of investor–state arbitration in its Article 155, entitled "Interpretation of the Agreement," which provides:

1.   The tribunal shall, on request of the state party, request a joint interpretation of the Parties of any provision of this Agreement that is in issue in a dispute. The Parties shall submit in writing any joint decision declaring their interpretation to the tribunal within 60 days of delivery of the request.

2.   A joint decision issued under paragraph 1 by the Parties shall be binding on the tribunal, and any award must be consistent with that joint decision. If the Parties fail to issue such a decision within 60 days, the tribunal shall decide the issue on its own account.

A similar provision appears in China's latest BIT, the 2012 China–Canada BIT, Article 30(1) of which reads, in relevant part: "An interpretation by the Contracting Parties of a provision of this Agreement shall be binding on a Tribunal established under this Part, and any award under this Part shall be consistent with such interpretation."

These provisions are clearly intended to limit the heretofore largely unrestricted discretion of arbitral tribunals to interpret the terms of an investment agreement in accordance with their own concepts of legal theory, as was done, for example in the *Tza Yap Shum*, *Helnan* and *Abaclat* cases, as discussed earlier. Perhaps more importantly, they also ensure that the joint understanding of the contracting parties as to the actual content and intended meaning of the agreement they have negotiated is what will govern any arbitration and, therefore, that the joint will of the contracting parties is represented and respected. In *Tza Yap Shum*, for example, it seems clear that the intentions of both China and Peru at the time they negotiated their BIT were to limit the jurisdiction of international tribunals to disputes only over the determination of the amount of compensation for expropriation, but only the position of Peru was heard in this regard and was ultimately rejected by the tribunal. Had provisions such as this been in place in the China–Peru BIT, the outcome of the case would undoubtedly have been very different.

That such practice is part of a wider international reaction to the free-ranging interpretation of the provisions of investment treaties by international tribunals is evidenced by the fact that both the United Kingdom and the United States have also included in their most recent BITs and/or FTAs provisions making a "joint interpretation" by the contracting parties of any of those agreements' provisions "binding on any tribunal established under" their respective sections on investor–state dispute settlement.[222] It is submitted here, however, that the formulation of the provisions contained in the China–New Zealand FTA are far more effective in serving these purposes than are those found elsewhere.

In conclusion, consent in investor–state arbitration bears some similarities to

222 See, for example, Article 17.2 of the 2006 Great Britain–Mexico BIT or Article 10.22.3 of the 2007 United States–Dominican Republic–Central America FTA.

that in commercial arbitration. At the same time, an essential characteristic of investor–state arbitration is that consent to arbitration may not be expressed in the same document to which the foreign investor is a party. In most cases, it is the host state which consents to arbitration first and has such consent stipulated in its BITs and FTAs or in its own national laws. Consent given through such means is regarded in practice as an offer which may be accepted by investors either in formal written form or through the institution of arbitration proceedings. As all investor–state arbitration involves international obligations of the host state, whether or not there exists valid consent must be construed in accordance with the principles of international law relating to treaty interpretation. Practice in this regard, however, is not satisfactory. As one commentator has observed:

> Two decades of practice that have followed the decision in Asian Agricultural Products show that there is still no uniformity of views among treaty tribunals as to how investment treaties should be interpreted, particularly in the event of ambiguity. A recent study suggests that only 35 out of 98 treaty awards examined contained references to the Vienna Convention, and only a handful of those made active use of the Convention's interpretive guideposts in construing the terms of the applicable BITs. Instead, terms such as "effective," "restrictive," "liberal" or "balanced" interpretation—terms that do not appear anywhere in the text of the Vienna Convention—are more frequently employed by treaty tribunals to read procedural and substantive investment guarantees.[223]

In essence, investment tribunals are perceived to be in favor of protecting investors' interests, or at least more in favor of protecting those interests than the interests of the host states. Whilst there is certainly nothing wrong with protecting the interests of investors, tribunals also have obligations to interpret treaty provisions, in particular dispute settlement clauses, faithfully. As the tribunal in *Inceysa v. El Salvador* acknowledged, the autonomous arbitration clause could not be "interpreted as a manifestation of unrestricted consent by El Salvador to submit to arbitration any type of dispute claimed to be based on the Agreement."[224] It also correctly stated that:

> … the work of the Arbitral Tribunal cannot be arbitrary or anarchic. In this regard, arbitral jurisprudence has developed three fundamental principles that must guide its task: (a) Absence of presumptions in favour or against jurisdiction; (b) Identification of the will of the Contracting States; and (c) Interpretation according to the principle of good faith.[225]

---

223 Yulia Andreeva, "Interpreting Consent to Arbitration as a Unilateral Act of State: A Case Against Conventions," *Arbitration International*, Vol. 27, No. 2, 2011, p. 135.
224 *Inceysa v. El Salvador*, *supra*, note 15, para. 164.
225 Ibid., para. 175.

As arbitrators are paid by the disputing parties, they have an unavoidable conflict of interest whenever jurisdiction is at issue. In these circumstances, the assumption of jurisdiction without just grounds is not only perceived as favoring investors but also as getting business and income for the arbitrators themselves.[226] For these reasons, tribunals should interpret treaty provisions, including those relating to consent, with great care so that the interests of both investors and host states will be well served.[227]

226 For instance, some scholars have observed the tension between host states and foreign investors in respect of proving consent; see, for example, Andreeva, *supra*, note 222.
227 As the *Renta4* Tribunal commented: "Article 31 [of the VCLT] must be considered with caution and discipline lest it become a palimpsest constantly altered by the projections of subjective suppositions. It does not, for example, compel the result that all textual doubts should be resolved in favour of the investor. The long-term promotion of investment is likely to be better ensured by a well-balanced regime rather than by one which goes so far that it provokes a swing of the pendulum in the other direction." See *Renta4 v. Russian Federation*, *supra*, note 70, para. 55.

6 The absolute standards of treatment

Modern bilateral investment treaties ("BITs") and multilateral agreements provide for, among other things, fair and equitable treatment ("FET"), minimum standard of treatment, non-discrimination, and full protection and security, as well as often including an umbrella clause.[1] These standards of treatment—unlike most-favored-nation ("MFN") treatment and national treatment ("NT"), which are dependent on the standards applied by the host state to its own investors or those of third countries—are independent of the standards that a host state applies to domestic investors. In other words, whether or not a violation has been committed needs to be determined in accordance with international law rules and not in accordance with the national laws of the host state. Therefore, there are certain objective requirements of each of these standards of treatment, which means such treatment must comply with certain absolute standards.

The absolute standards of treatment have now become a common feature of modern BITs. Yet these standards overlap with each other. For instance, where a measure results in discrimination against foreign investors, it is by its very nature contrary to FET. In practice, when alleging a breach of FET obligations, foreign claimants usually claim that the host state has violated the obligations relating to full protection and security, non-discrimination, and even the umbrella clause. From the point of view of international investment arbitration tribunals, once a violation of the FET standard is established, there is no need to deal in detail with alleged violations of other absolute standards.

Where a government measure is alleged to have violated one of these treaty obligations, as in other aspects of investment dispute resolution, tribunals are obliged to interpret the provisions on absolute standards of protection in accordance with international law. This chapter will first examine the issues related to the FET standard, including its concept and contents, as well as its relationship with the international minimum standard of treatment, investors' expectations and

---

1 For discussions on the history, state practice, and other issues of FET relating to international investment, as well as its inter-relationship with other absolute standards, especially the minimum standard of treatment, see UNCTAD, *Fair and Equitable Treatment: A Sequel*, UNCTAD Series on Issues in International Investment Agreements II, UN Doc. UNCTAD/DIAE/IA/2011/5, United Nations, New York and Geneva, 2012.

stabilization of the business and legal framework for foreign investment. It will then analyze the practice relating to full protection and security and the umbrella clause. The last part will deal with China's treaty practice regarding these standards.

I. Fair and equitable treatment

A. The concept of FET

Like many other terms of international investment law, the FET standard first emerged as a trade standard. Its first appearance in a multilateral instrument was in the Draft Agreement for the International Trade Organization of 1948.[2] Then, in Article 1 of the Draft Convention on the Protection of Foreign Property proposed by the OECD in 1967, it was stipulated that: "Each Party shall at all times ensure fair and equitable treatment to the property of the nationals of the other Parties."[3]

The Energy Charter Treaty ("ECT") and the North American Free Trade Agreement ("NAFTA"), both to be discussed later, are important multilateral agreements that contain the requirement of FET. The failed Multilateral Agreement on Investment contained a provision on FET in Part IV(1.1), which states: "Each Contracting Party shall accord to investments in its territory of investors of another Contracting Party fair and equitable treatment and full and constant protection and security. In no case shall a Contracting Party accord treatment less favourable than that required by international law."[4] The Energy Charter Treaty, in Article 10(1), provides, in relevant part:

> Each Contracting Party shall, in accordance with the provisions of this Treaty, encourage and create stable, equitable, favourable and transparent conditions for Investors of other Contracting Parties to make Investments in its Area. Such conditions shall include a commitment to accord at all times to Investments of Investors of other Contracting Parties fair and equitable treatment.

Article 1105(1) of the NAFTA, on the other hand, provides: "Each Party shall accord to investments of investors of another Party treatment in accordance with international law, including fair and equitable treatment and full protection and security."[5]

---

2 Article 29(2) of the Havana Charter 1948, in relation to state trading, provides: "With respect to such imports, and with respect to the laws, regulations and requirements … each Member shall accord to the trade of the other Members fair and equitable treatment." See International Trade Organization, The Havana Charter (1948); available at: http://www.wto.org/english/docs_e/legal_e/havana_e.pdf.
3 OECD, *Draft Convention on the Protection of Foreign Property* (1967); available at: http://acts.oecd.org/Instruments/ShowInstrumentView.aspx?InstrumentID=242&Lang=en&Book=False.
4 See Part IV, Investment Protection, of the draft Multilateral Agreement on Investment; available at: http://www1.oecd.org/daf/mai/htm/2.htm.
5 The text of the NAFTA is available at: https://www.nafta-sec-alena.org/Default.aspx.

It is clear that none of the multilateral treaties or drafts of treaties has attempted to further define the term FET, although the NAFTA stipulates "international law" as the threshold. Bilateral investment treaties have done no better in this regard. This situation has made the FET a sort of "catch-all" provision, such that when foreign investors have no specific claims they all allege that the host state has violated its obligations under FET. Another feature of investment dispute settlement that has resulted from the brief statement of the FET obligation in these agreements is that, as in other areas of investment arbitration, tribunals' interpretations differ, even where the provisions on FET in the relevant BITs and the material facts of the cases in dispute are similar or identical. Such differences concern the relationship between FET and the international minimum standard of treatment, the concept and content of FET, the conditions for invoking the FET obligation, etc.

With regard to the concept of FET, the practice of arbitration tribunals can be divided into three categories, namely: equating FET with the international minimum standard of treatment; identifying autonomous requirements for FET; and a position between these two, or deciding the matter on a case-by-case basis.

1. Equating FET with the minimum standard of treatment of aliens under customary international law

On the minimum standard of treatment of aliens under customary international law, tribunals and scholars very often refer to the *Neer v. Mexico*[6] case. In that case, an American was murdered in Mexico when riding on horseback with his wife. However, the murderer was never prosecuted, a fact that was alleged to be due to a lack of effort on the part of Mexico. A US–Mexico Mixed Claims Commission was established to hear the case. It held, in rejecting the US claims, that:

> Without attempting to announce a precise formula, it is in the opinion of the Commission possible to go a little further than the authors quoted, and to hold (first) that the propriety of governmental acts should be put to the test of international standards, and (second) that the treatment of an alien, in order to constitute an international delinquency, should amount to an outrage, to bad faith, to willful neglect of duty, or to an insufficiency of governmental action so far short of international standards that every reasonable and impartial man would readily recognize its insufficiency. Whether the insufficiency proceeds from deficient execution of an intelligent law or from the fact that the laws of the country do not empower the authorities to measure up to international standards is immaterial.[7]

---

6 *L.F.H. Neer and Pauline Neer (U.S.A.) v. United Mexican States*, Award (October 15, 1926), *Report of International Arbitration Awards*, Vol. IV, pp. 60–66; available at: http://legal.un.org/riaa/cases/vol_IV/60-66.pdf.

7 Ibid., para. 4.

This decision has thus most often been regarded by investment tribunals as a pronouncement of customary law on the minimum standard of treatment of aliens and their property over the last two decades. The most important feature of *Neer* is that in order to prove a violation of this minimum standard of treatment, bad faith on the part of the host state may be required.

In practice, tribunals that equate the FET with the minimum standard of treatment under customary international law are regarded as taking a restrictive approach. The clearest example of this is the case of *Genin v. Estonia*.[8] The claimants in this case were Mr Alex Genin, a national of the United States, and two companies owned by him, namely, Eastern Credit Limited, Inc., a US company, and A.S. Baltoil, an Estonian company wholly owned by Eastern Credit. Eastern Credit and Baltoil were principal shareholders of Estonian Innovation Bank ("EIB"), which purchased from the Bank of Estonia—Estonia's central bank—the Koidu branch, a local branch of Estonian Social Bank Limited, an insolvent financial institution, at an auction on August 12, 1994. One month later, EIB informed the Bank of Estonia, in writing, of discrepancies in the Koidu branch's balance sheet that had been furnished to potential purchasers prior to the sale.[9] Thereafter, there were exchanges between EIB and the Bank of Estonia as well as court proceedings relating to both parties' allegations and denials of liabilities. Whilst the court proceedings were going on, the Bank of Estonia revoked EIB's license. Based on the 1994 BIT between the United States and Estonia, the claimants instituted ICSID arbitration proceedings, alleging that the respondent had violated, inter alia, obligations on FET.

In considering the issue as to whether or not the respondent had violated the BIT's FET obligations, the *Genin* Tribunal first stated that under international law the FET standard required the host state to "provide a basic and general standard [of treatment] which is detached from the host State's domestic law."[10] The tribunal further stated that whilst the contents of FET were not clear, it was understood to require an "international minimum standard" that was "separate from domestic law, but that is, indeed, a *minimum* standard. Acts that would violate this minimum standard would include acts showing a willful neglect of duty, an insufficiency of action falling far below international standards, or even subjective bad faith."[11] Thus, the *Genin* Tribunal adopted exactly the standard pronounced by the Mixed Commission in the *Neer* case. In fact, the *Genin* Tribunal went so far as to say that under customary international law, aliens and alien property may be subjected to discriminatory treatment in the absence of a treaty requirement not to do so, such as one of national treatment.[12] In the end, the tribunal found that the withdrawal of EIB's license was not done for the purpose of harming the Bank

8   *Alex Genin, Eastern Credit Limited, Inc. and A.S. Baltoil v. Republic of Estonia*, ICSID Case No. ARB/99/2, Award (June 25, 2001).

9   Ibid., para. 45.

10 Ibid., para. 367. In this respect, the *Genin* Tribunal cited Rudolf Dolzer and Margrete Stevens, *Bilateral Investment Treaties*, Martinus Nijhoff Publishers, 1995, p. 58.

11 *Genin v. Estonia*, ibid., para. 367 (emphasis in original).

12 Ibid., para. 368.

and that it was done without discrimination or arbitrariness.[13] Apparently, the fact that the claimants' investment was in the banking sector, which requires prudent regulation by the host state, especially in the circumstances of Estonia's political and economic transition, was an important factor in this decision.[14]

What should be noted is that in the view of the *Genin* Tribunal, a violation of FET may involve both substantive and procedural aspects, both of which would require bad faith or willfulness. In this regard, the tribunal again echoed the ruling in *Neer* when it said that it did "not regard the license withdrawal as an arbitrary act that violates the tribunal's 'sense of juridical propriety.'"[15] In practice, however, it may be difficult for an investor to prove a procedural irregularity "to amount to bad faith, a willful disregard of due process of law or an extreme insufficiency of action," which were listed as criteria by the tribunal.[16] In other words, tribunals should focus on whether or not a departure from normal procedures is serious rather than the intent of the host state. Another feature of the *Genin* case is that the tribunal did not even consider the international law minimum standard of treatment as an evolving standard. It may be said that the *Genin* case represents perhaps the narrowest view toward FET. In this respect, the *Genin* decision is distinguishable from all other decisions that have equated FET with the minimum standard of treatment of aliens under customary international law.

The *CMS v. Argentina* case[17] is an example. In that case, the claimant—CMS, a US corporation—made an investment in Argentina by holding 30 percent of the shares of a local gas transportation company—TGN. When the investment was made, Argentina made a commitment that TGN could calculate tariffs in US dollars and then convert them to pesos at the prevailing exchange rate, with the tariffs to be adjusted every six months to reflect changes in inflation. When the economic crisis took place in Argentina in the late 1990s, the host state first temporarily suspended and then permanently terminated TGN's right to calculate tariffs in US dollars and to adjust them to reflect inflation, both commitments which had been included in previous Argentine law and in the license granted to TGN. Because the Argentine peso was drastically devalued, the claimant suffered losses and claimed that the Argentine measures were in violation of several of Argentina's obligations under the Argentina–United States BIT, including FET.

With regard to the alleged violation of FET, the *CMS* Tribunal first considered that the FET standard was equivalent to that under customary international law. The tribunal observed that in some cases, a choice between a higher treaty standard and that of equating the FET standard with the international minimum standard might be relevant. It then concluded that in the dispute facing it there was no need to make a choice between a higher treaty standard and the customary

---

13 Ibid., para. 369.
14 Ibid., paras. 370–71.
15 Ibid., para. 371. Here, the tribunal also made reference to the ICJ's definition of "arbitrariness" in the *Elettronica Sicula* or *ELSI* case (*United States v. Italy*), *ICJ Reports* (1989), pp. 15, 73–77.
16 Id.
17 *CMS Gas Transmission Company v. Argentine Republic*, ICSID Case No. ARB/01/8, Award of May 12, 2005.

law standard. Instead, it simply stated: "In fact, the Treaty standard of fair and equitable treatment and its connection with the required stability and predictability of the business environment, founded on solemn legal and contractual commitments, is not different from the international law minimum standard and its evolution under customary law."[18] In other words, in the *CMS* Tribunal's view, the treaty standard of FET and the international minimum standard of treatment were the same, and therefore there was no need to make a choice in applying the FET provisions.

The *CMS* Tribunal's position was similar to that of the Notes of Interpretation of the NAFTA Free Trade Commission ("FTC"), which confirmed the minimum standard of treatment in accordance with international law stipulated in NAFTA Article 1105(1) to prescribe "the customary international law minimum standard of treatment of aliens as the minimum standard of treatment to be afforded to investments of investors of another Party."[19] Accordingly, based on the notes of interpretation, the concept of FET does "not require treatment in addition to or beyond that which is required by the customary international law minimum standard of treatment of aliens."[20] The *CMS* Tribunal took note of the notes of interpretation and the further development of this position reflected in the United States–Chile FTA. Even though it did not explicitly state that it was bound by the notes of interpretation, it apparently followed the standard set by the latter.

In *Merrill & Ring v. Canada*,[21] the tribunal considered that the international minimum standard, since the *Neer* decision, had evolved on two tracks, the first of which focuses on human rights issues whilst the second concerns business, trade and investment.[22] In the tribunal's view, insofar as the first track is concerned, there is no "general rule of customary international law" that applies the *Neer* standard "beyond the strict confines of personal safety, denial of justice and due process."[23] Regarding the second track, the *Merrill & Ring* Tribunal considered that there had been an evolution in the application of the *Neer* standard to business, trade and investment with the outcome that aliens are now entitled to be treated fairly and equitably in relation to their commercial activities, including investment.[24] In these circumstances, even though the contents of the standard developed under the second track may not be defined precisely, as an "open and unrestricted" standard

18 Ibid., para. 284.
19 North American Free Trade Agreement, Notes of Interpretation of Certain Chapter 11 Provisions, NAFTA Free Trade Commission (July 31, 2001); available at: http://www.sice.oas.org/tpd/ nafta/Commission/CH11understanding_e.asp.
20 Id. The Notes of Interpretation further states: "A determination that there has been a breach of another provision of the NAFTA, or of a separate international agreement, does not establish that there has been a breach of Article 1105(1)."
21 *Merrill & Ring Forestry L.P. v. Government of Canada*, NAFTA case under the UNCITRAL Arbitration Rules administered by ICSID, Award (March 31, 2010).
22 Ibid., para. 201.
23 Ibid., para. 204.
24 Ibid., para. 210.

of treatment it protects "against all such acts or behaviour that might infringe a sense of fairness, equity and reasonableness," said the tribunal.[25]

The tribunal's conclusion was that against the "backdrop of the evolution of the minimum standard of treatment," it was "satisfied that fair and equitable treatment has become a part of customary law."[26] So far as equating FET with the minimum standard of treatment under international law, the *Merrill & Ring* Tribunal was of the opinion that equation or "convergence is not really the issue. The situation is rather one in which the customary law standard has led to and resulted in establishing the fair and equitable treatment standard as different stages of the same evolutionary process."[27] The *Chemtura* Tribunal[28] held a view similar to that of the *Merrill & Ring* Tribunal, noting that it would "take account of the evolution of international customary law in ascertaining the content of the international minimum standard."[29] At the same time, it also opined that it must take into account the special circumstances of the case.[30]

In conclusion, it must be noted that even according to the narrow view of the *Neer* standard, there is a baseline level of protection in respect of foreign investment, below which a host state is required not to treat foreign investors and their investment arbitrarily, discriminatorily, or without due process. Some tribunals, however, have ruled that there is an evolution from *Neer* that does not require bad faith on the part of the host state in order to establish a violation of FET. For instance, the *Glamis Gold* Tribunal stated expressly that:

> The Tribunal notes that one aspect of evolution from *Neer* that is generally agreed upon is that bad faith is not required to find a violation of the fair and equitable treatment standard, but its presence is conclusive evidence of such. Thus, an act that is egregious or shocking may also evidence bad faith, but such bad faith is not necessary for the finding of a violation.[31]

It is now well established that there is no need to prove bad faith on the part of the host state to establish a violation of FET according to any approach.[32] As jurisprudence in this respect is not consistent, however, the status of customary international law relating to the matter will remain uncertain.

25 Id.
26 Ibid., para. 211.
27 Ibid., para. 209.
28 *Chemtura Corporation v. Government of Canada*, Ad Hoc NAFTA Arbitration under UNCITRAL Rules, Award (August 2, 2010).
29 Ibid., para. 122.
30 The *Chemtura* Tribunal stated that it "must take into account all the circumstances, including the fact that certain agencies manage highly specialized domains involving scientific and public policy determinations;" Ibid., para. 123.
31 *Glamis Gold v. United States of America*, UNCITRAL Arbitration, Award (June 8, 2009), para. 616.
32 See UNCTAD, *Fair and Equitable Treatment 2011*, *supra*, note 1, at p. 58, where it asserts: "The one point common to all three approaches [to compare FET with the international minimum standard of treatment] is that there is no need for proof of bad faith on the part of the host country authorities, although such proof would be conclusive that a breach had occurred."

2. Broad definition—proactive behaviour and programme of good governance

There are other tribunals that consider FET to not be synonymous with the international minimum standard of treatment. In their view, the presence of a provision assuring FET in an investment instrument requires the host state to be proactive in their treatment of foreign investments. *Tecmed v. Mexico*[33] is the most representative in this regard.

In that case, the claimant—Técnicas Medioambientales Tecmed, S.A.— was a Spanish company that invested, through its two Mexican subsidiaries, Tecmed and Cytrar, in a landfill of hazardous industrial waste in 1996. Following its acquisition of the landfill, the claimant acquired a license that was necessary for the operation of the landfill and which was issued by the Hazardous Materials, Waste and Activities Division of the National Ecology Institute of Mexico, an agency of the Mexican Federal Government within the Ministry of the Environment, Natural Resources and Fisheries ("INE"). Despite the fact that the original license for the landfill had been of an indefinite duration, the new license acquired by the claimant had to be renewed on an annual basis. In 1998, the claimant's request to renew the license was rejected by the INE on the grounds of certain minor breaches in the mode of landfill operation. The claimant therefore instituted arbitration proceedings against Mexico, relying on the BIT between Spain and Mexico, because in the claimant's view the refusal to renew the license was largely due to political circumstances—a change in administration of the local government, which encouraged a movement of citizens against the landfill. In particular, the claimant contended that the INE's refusal to renew its license to operate the landfill constituted, inter alia, a violation of the BIT provision regarding FET.

Under the Spain–Mexico BIT, each party agreed to accord to investments of investors of the other party "fair and equitable treatment according to international law." The tribunal considered that in light of the good faith principle of international law, the provision on FET required the contracting parties to act consistently and transparently and not to take any actions that "affect the basic expectations that were taken into account by the foreign investor to make the investment."[34] In the view of the *Tecmed* Tribunal, a foreign investor expects:

> … the host State to act consistently, i.e. without arbitrarily revoking any preexisting decisions or permits issued by the State that were relied upon by the investor to assume its commitments as well as to plan and launch its commercial and business activities. The investor also expects the State to use the legal instruments that govern the actions of the investor or the investment in conformity with the function usually assigned to such instruments, and not to deprive the investor of its investment without the required compensation. In fact, failure by the host State to comply with such pattern of conduct with respect to the foreign investor or its investments affects the investor's ability

33 *Técnicas Medioambientales Tecmed, S.A. v. United Mexican States* [hereinafter *Tecmed*], ICSID Case No. ARB(AF)/00/2, Award of May 29, 2003.
34 Ibid., para. 154.

to measure the treatment and protection awarded by the host State and to determine whether the actions of the host State conform to the fair and equitable treatment principle.[35]

In other words, according to the *Tecmed* Tribunal, the FET provisions under international law require host states to take proactive actions in order to ensure consistency, transparency and non-arbitrariness in their decision-making. Also, the basis of determination of whether or not a host state has failed to live up to the standard is the investor's expectations when making the investment. In the *Tecmed* case, when the claimant made the investment, the operation permit for the landfill had been granted with an indefinite duration. It was therefore justifiable that the claimant, when acquiring the control of the landfill through auction, would not expect that the license could be revoked two years later. The *Tecmed* Tribunal ruled the respondent to have violated its obligations under FET because, "in spite of the expectations created, and without considering ways enabling [the Claimant] to neutralize or mitigate the negative economic effect of such closing by continuing with its economic and business activities at a different place,"[36] it revoked the claimant's license. In the end, the tribunal concluded that the INE's actions were contradictory, ambiguous, and uncertain and, therefore, prejudicial to the claimant.[37]

The *Tecmed* decision is by far the most assertive in respect of the FET standard. The tests that it offered have often been referred to by other tribunals and commentators. In a way, although one may consider the *Tecmed* decision to be rather radical, its detailing of the tests it applied helps in shaping international investment law in this regard.

Pope & Talbot v. Canada[38] involved interpreting the FET provision under Chapter 11 of the NAFTA. In that case, the claimant was a US company with a Canadian subsidiary that operated three sawmills in Canada for exportation of softwood lumber to the US market. The United States and Canada entered into a five-year Softwood Lumber Agreement ("SLA") in 1996, and the dispute arose from the implementation of the SLA. As the quantity of softwood lumber that sawmills wished to export to the US market far exceeded the limits for free exports established by the SLA, Canada allocated export quotas among the softwood lumber producers. Any exports in excess of the quotas would be subject to an

---

35 Id.

36 Ibid., para. 164.

37 Ibid., para. 172. The tribunal's conclusion was based on the fact that, on the one hand, the claimant was given the assurance that it could operate the landfill until its relocation and that new land, together with a license, would be arranged and, on the other hand, it was denied the issuance of a new license. This not only constituted a breach of the good faith principle under international law but also a contradiction in and of itself.

38 There are several decisions and awards delivered by the tribunal in this case, including *Pope & Talbot Inc. v. Canada*, Interim Award on the Merits of Phase 1 (June 26, 2000) [*Pope & Talbot*, Award on Merits 1] [hereinafter "*Pope & Talbot*, Award on Merits" 2] and *Pope & Talbot Inc. v. Canada*, Award on Damages (May 31, 2002) [hereinafter "*Pope & Talbot*, Award on Damages"].

export fee to be collected by Canada. The claimant alleged that certain aspects of the Canadian regime on softwood lumber exports were in violation of Canada's Chapter 11 obligations under the NAFTA, in particular Article 1105 relating to FET.

The *Pope & Talbot* Tribunal considered that a "possible interpretation of the presence of the fairness elements in Article 1105 is that they are *additive* to the requirements of international law."[39] Having considered the treaty practice among developed nations, the tribunal concluded that "[t]hese treaties evolved over the years into their present form, which is embodied in the [US] Model Bilateral Investment Treaty of 1987. Canada, the UK, Belgium, Luxembourg, France and Switzerland have followed the Model."[40] It further considered the formulation of the FET obligation therein "as expressly adopting the additive character of the fairness elements."[41] In the tribunal's view, the NAFTA is supposed to offer better protections to investors from other contracting parties. Therefore, it doubted that it was the intention of the NAFTA drafters that potential investors "would have no recourse to protection against anything but egregiously unfair conduct."[42] In fact, according to the *Pope & Talbot* Tribunal, even the FTC's Notes of Interpretation do not preclude additive interpretations. In its view, the Notes of Interpretation only concluded that Article 1105 prescribes the customary international law standard to be the minimum standard afforded to foreign investors, and FET should be considered "as part of the minimum standard of treatment that it prescribes."[43]

Was the conclusion of the *Pope & Talbot* Tribunal in contradiction with the Notes Of Interpretation? The tribunal did not think so. In its view: "It is a facet of international law that customary international law evolves through state practice. International agreements constitute practice of states and contribute to the grounds of customary international law."[44] In other words, whilst in 1920 an action or omission might not have been considered an "international delinquency," with the inclusion of the concept of fair and equitable treatment, the same action or omission may today be considered a violation of "'customary' international law."[45]

However, the decision of the *Pope & Talbot* Tribunal is also self-contradictory. On the one hand, it considers the NAFTA Chapter 11 requirement on FET to be additive to the international law requirements. Yet, on the other hand, it states that the requirements of international law have evolved from a lower standard to a higher standard. Where the international standard has been elevated, it then becomes the baseline of customary international law and, according to the notes of interpretation, the Chapter 11 requirement should equate to the international law standard. Any "additive" requirement, as determined by the *Pope & Talbot*

39 *Pope & Talbot*, Award on Merits 2, ibid., *supra*, note 38, para. 110 (emphasis in original).
40 Ibid., para. 111.
41 Id.
42 Ibid., para. 116.
43 *Pope & Talbot*, Award on Damages, *supra*, note 38, para. 53.
44 Ibid., para. 59.
45 Ibid., para. 60.

Tribunal, would be in violation of rather than in compliance with the Notes of Interpretation.

In *Azurix*, the tribunal also observed that the requirement for FET contained in the United States–Argentina BIT "as drafted, permits to interpret fair and equitable treatment and full protection and security as higher standards than required by international law. The purpose of the third sentence is to set a floor, not a ceiling in order to avoid a possible interpretation of these standards below what is required by international law."[46] Nevertheless, the *Azurix* Tribunal added that it

> … does not consider that [this conclusion] is of material significance for its application of the standard of fair and equitable treatment to the facts of the case. … [T]he minimum requirement to satisfy this standard has evolved and the Tribunal considers that its content is substantially similar whether the terms are interpreted in their ordinary meaning, as required by the Vienna Convention, or in accordance with customary international law.[47]

Thus, the *Azurix* Tribunal also appears to have contradicted itself. On the one hand, it said that the FET provision requires a higher standard than that found in customary international law but, on the other hand, it said that the standard was the one required by international law. In this regard, the *Pope & Talbot* Tribunal and the *Azurix* Tribunal took the same view—a self-contradictory approach.

Saluka[48] is another case that adopted the autonomous approach. In the view of the *Saluka* Tribunal, the "customary minimum standard … provides a minimum guarantee to foreign investors, even where the state follows a policy that is in principle opposed to foreign investment;"[49] and, in that context, FET may, in fact, provide no more than "minimal protection."[50] The *Saluka* Tribunal also took into consideration the object of BITs, i.e. promotion of foreign investment. In that context, it said that "investors' protection by the 'fair and equitable treatment' standard is meant to be a guarantee providing a positive incentive for foreign investors. Consequently, in order to violate the standard, it may be sufficient that a State's conduct displays a relatively lower degree of inappropriateness."[51] In the case before it, the *Saluka* Tribunal noted that the formulation of the FET obligation contained in the Netherlands–Czech Republic BIT "omits any express reference to the customary minimum standard" and therefore held that "[t]his clearly points to the autonomous character of a 'fair and equitable treatment' standard such as the one laid down in Article 3.1 of the Treaty."[52]

The *Saluka* Tribunal, however, only emphasized the needs of investors, whilst it ignored the regulatory power of the host state. Such an unbalanced approach

---

46 *Azurix Corp v. Argentine Republic*, ICSID Case No. ARB/01/12, Award (July 14, 2006), para. 361.
47 Id.
48 *Saluka Investments B.V. v. Czech Republic*, UNCITRAL, Partial Award (March 17, 2006).
49 Ibid., para. 292.
50 Id.
51 Ibid., para. 293.
52 Ibid., para. 294.

to protecting investors has been adopted by other tribunals supporting a broad definition of FET. The tribunal in the *MTD* case[53] held such a view.

In that case, the tribunal stated:

> [I]n terms of the [Malaysia–Chile] BIT, fair and equitable treatment should be understood to be treatment in an even-handed and just manner, conducive to fostering the promotion of foreign investment. Its terms are framed as a proactive statement – "to promote," "to create," "to stimulate" – rather than prescriptions for a passive behavior of the State or avoidance of prejudicial conduct to the investors.[54]

In support of this position, the *MTD* Tribunal called upon the opinion of the *Tecmed* Tribunal discussed earlier. The *ad hoc* Committee constituted to consider Chile's request for annulment of the *MTD* award, however, took a critical view of the very broad definition given to FET by the *Tecmed* Tribunal. It noted that "[a]ccording to the Respondent, 'the *TecMed* programme for good governance' is extreme and does not reflect international law. The *TECMED* dictum is also subject to strenuous criticism from the Respondent's experts, Mr. Jan Paulsson and Sir Arthur Watts."[55] It then said:

> The Committee can appreciate some aspects of these criticisms. For example the *TECMED* Tribunal's apparent reliance on the foreign investor's expectations as the source of the host State's obligations (such as the obligation to compensate for expropriation) is questionable. The obligations of the host State towards foreign investors derive from the terms of the applicable investment treaty and not from any set of expectations investors may have or claim to have.[56]

Obviously the *ad hoc* Committee in *MTD* favored a plain-meaning approach in its interpretation of the FET provision rather than reliance on the investor's expectations. In its view, although "legitimate expectations generated as a result of the investor's dealings with the competent authorities of the host State may be relevant to the application of the guarantees contained in an investment treaty,"[57] in the end "the extent to which a State is obliged under the fair and equitable treatment standard to be pro-active is open to debate, but that is more a question of application of the standard than it is of formulation."[58] The *ad hoc* Committee was cautious, however, in approving the *MTD* Tribunal's standard

---

53 *MTD Equity Sdn. Bhd. & MTD Chile S.A. v. Republic of Chile*, ICSID Case No. ARB/01/7, Award of May 25, 2004.
54 Ibid., para. 113.
55 *MTD Equity Sdn. Bhd. & MTD Chile S.A. v. Republic of Chile*, ICSID Case No. ARB/01/7, Decision on Annulment of March 21, 2007, para. 66 (footnote omitted).
56 Ibid., para. 67.
57 Ibid., para. 69.
58 Ibid., para. 71.

for determining FET, stating that its formulation was "defensible" and that "in articulating this standard there is no indication that the Tribunal committed any excess of powers."[59]

In addition to investment tribunals, there are scholars who advocate a broad interpretation of the FET provision and regard it as an independent and autonomous mechanism. Mann, for instance, argues that FET:

> … envisage[s] conduct which goes far beyond the minimum standard and afford[s] protection to a greater extent and according to a much more objective standard than any previously employed form of words. A tribunal would not be concerned with a minimum, maximum or average standard. It will have to decide whether in all the circumstances the conduct in issue is fair and equitable or unfair and inequitable. No standard defined by other words is likely to be material. The terms are to be understood and applied independently and autonomously.[60]

Dolzer and Stevens hold a similar view, that "the fact that parties to BITs have considered it necessary to stipulate this fair and equitable treatment standard as an express obligation rather than relied on a reference to international law and thereby invoked a relatively vague concept such as the minimum standard, is probably evidence of a self-contained standard."[61] They further draw support from the state practice that some treaties refer to international law in addition to FET whilst others do not make such a reference. In their view, such treaty practices "reaffirm that international law standards are consistent with, but complementary to, the provisions of the BIT."[62] These writings by scholars have had an important impact on the decisions of arbitral tribunals, who in order to provide support for their own positions often refer to scholarly writings.

3. The modest approach

In addition to the two approaches discussed earlier, there are other tribunals that take a modest approach. *Mondev v. United States*[63] illustrates this approach. The facts of the *Mondev* case are as follows. The City of Boston, in order to redevelop an area of the city, entered into a tripartite agreement among the Boston Redevelopment Authority, an agency of the City of Boston ("BRA"); Mondev International Ltd., a Canadian company ("Mondev"); and Lafayette Place Associates, a limited partnership registered in Massachusetts and wholly owned by Mondev ("LPA") in 1978. The agreement was established for the development of the area in two

59 Id.
60 F. A. Mann, "British Treaties for the Promotion and Protection of Investments," in *British Year Book of International Law* (1981), Vol. 52, p. 241, at 244.
61 Dolzer and Stevens, *supra*, note 10, at 60.
62 Id.
63 *Mondev International Ltd. v. United States*, ICSID Case No. ARB(AF)/99/2, Award (October 11, 2002).

Phases and provided to LPA, inter alia, a conditional option to purchase the Phase II property. After Phase I of the project was completed, LPA had difficulties in exercising its option, whereby it leased its rights to another Canadian company, which ran into the same difficulties. Among various factors leading to these difficulties were the facts that, beginning in the 1980s, the property market was booming in Boston and the market value for Phase II had skyrocketed, and there was a change in administration in the City, with the new administration viewing the agreement as unfair to Boston. LPA perceived Boston's reluctance to allow the purchase of Phase II as an attempt to avoid its contractual obligations and instituted a lawsuit in the Massachusetts State Court in 1992, alleging, inter alia, that BRA and Boston had failed, in bad faith, to carry out the tripartite agreement. The jury found in favor of LPA and awarded damages totaling US$16 million—US$9.6 million against the City of Boston for breach of contract and US$6.4 million against the BRA for tortious interference. The trial judge affirmed the jury's finding against Boston for US$9.6 million but, based on the Massachusetts Tort Claims Act, exempted BRA from its liability to pay damages.

Both LPA and the City of Boston appealed the trial judge's decision to the Supreme Judicial Court—the highest court in Massachusetts—which decided that neither BRA, on the basis of immunity, nor the City of Boston was liable. The Supreme Judicial Court based its decision on LPA's lack of willingness and ability to perform the contract. After the US Supreme Court denied LPA's petition for *certiorari*, Mondev, LPA's Canadian parent company, initiated arbitration proceedings against the United States for alleged violations of its NAFTA Chapter 11 obligations, including those under Article 1105(1) relating to FET.[64]

During the hearing of the *Mondev* case, the FTC issued its Notes of Interpretation relating to Article 1105, which unavoidably had an impact on the decision in the case, especially in relation to the concept of FET under the NAFTA. The *Mondev* Tribunal adopted an evolutionary view of the international minimum standard of treatment, stating:

> [B]oth the substantive and procedural rights of the individual in international law have undergone considerable development. In the light of these developments it is unconvincing to confine the meaning of "fair and equitable treatment" and "full protection and security" of foreign investments to what those terms—had they been current at the time—might have meant in the 1920s when applied to the physical security of an alien. To the modern eye, what is unfair or inequitable need not equate with the outrageous or the egregious. In particular, a State may treat foreign investment unfairly and inequitably without necessarily acting in bad faith.[65]

---

64 NAFTA Article 1105(1) provides: "Each Party shall accord to investments of investors of another Party treatment in accordance with international law, including fair and equitable treatment and full protection and security."

65 *Mondev v. United States*, *supra*, note 63, para. 116.

The *Mondev* Tribunal based its opinion on the fact that there had been more than 2,000 BITs up to that time that had stipulated the application of FET to foreign investment. In those circumstances, where a tribunal would be faced with a claim by a foreign investor of being unfairly or inequitably treated, the *Mondev* Tribunal was of the opinion that such tribunal "is bound to pass upon that claim on the facts and by application of any governing treaty provisions. A judgment of what is fair and equitable cannot be reached in the abstract; it must depend on the facts of the particular case."[66]

Thus, in the *Mondev* Tribunal's view, the concordant treaty practice of states had evolved customary international law from the 19th century to the time of its hearing of the present case.[67] The *Mondev* decision was undoubtedly much influenced by the FTC's Notes of Interpretation. On the one hand, the tribunal was bound by the Notes, according to which FET under the NAFTA reflects the minimum standard of treatment in customary international law but, on the other hand, it was not convinced that the standard established by the *Neer* case should be adopted, as it stated that a state might act unfairly and inequitably without the necessity of bad faith. The question then arises as to what the modern standard in international customary law actually is. The *Mondev* Tribunal seemed to be of the opinion that the traditional qualifications of outrageousness or egregiousness and bad faith were no longer requirements for the establishment of a violation of FET under customary international law. Yet it did not produce any evidence to prove that that is, indeed, the standard under contemporary international law. Thus, the reasoning of the *Mondev* Tribunal is not convincing.

The tribunal in the *Deutsche Bank* case[68] also adopted the position that FET is not substantially different from that of the minimum standard under customary international law. At the same time, it did not consider that "bad faith" is required in establishing a violation of FET. The *Deutsche Bank* case related to an oil hedging agreement concluded between the bank and Ceylon Petroleum Corporation ("CPC"), a state-owned company of Sri Lanka, on July 8, 2008. A few months later, Sri Lanka's Central Bank initiated an official inquiry into the circumstances surrounding the conclusion of the hedging agreement. Still later, the Supreme Court of Sri Lanka issued an interim order directing CPC to suspend all payments to Deutsche Bank under the hedging agreement. Soon thereafter, the Sri Lankan Central Bank also prohibited the CPC from making any payments to Deutsche Bank pursuant to the hedging agreement. Based on this, Deutsche Bank instituted arbitration proceedings against Sri Lanka for violation, inter alia, of FET under the BIT between Germany and Sri Lanka.

The majority of the tribunal found that Sri Lanka had violated its obligations relating to FET on two grounds: (a) that the Sri Lankan Supreme Court had issued an interim order of suspension of payment "without a proper examination

66 Ibid., para. 118.
67 Ibid., para. 125.
68 *Deutsche Bank AG v. Democratic Socialist republic of Sri Lanka*, ICSID Case No. ARB/09/2, Award (October 31, 2012).

and without giving the banks involved an opportunity to respond;"[69] and (b) that the Sri Lankan Central Bank's investigation and stop-payment order were issued in bad faith. In its analysis, the *Deutsche Bank* Tribunal quoted Schreuer, that:

> [I]t is inherently implausible that a treaty would use an expression such as "fair and equitable treatment" to denote a well-known concept such as the "minimum standard of treatment in customary international law." If the parties to a treaty want to refer to customary international law, it must be presumed that they will refer to it as such rather than using a different expression.[70]

As mentioned earlier, the *Deutsche Bank* Tribunal considered that there was no material difference between the treaty standard of FET and that found in customary international law.[71] The question then is, where the content of the treaty standard of FET and the international minimum standard of treatment are the same or similar, is this by coincidence or because the international minimum standard has evolved, as some arbitral tribunals have stated? It seems that the *Deutsche Bank* Tribunal tried to avoid the issue and, at the same time, to locate itself in a safe position by saying that the treaty standard was autonomous. In this regard, the *Deutsche Bank* Tribunal also considered, referring to the award in *Waste Management II*,[72] that bad faith on the part of the host state is not required in ascertaining a violation of FET. Perhaps, in the tribunal's view, this is the major difference between the treaty standard of FET and the international minimum standard. Yet, by saying that a violation of FET can be established even without a showing of bad faith on the part of the host state, the *Deutsche Bank* Tribunal's decision, like the others discussed in this section, situates itself between the narrow and broad approaches. In the end, a tribunal will have more discretion if it decides to adopt either the narrow or the broad approach.

B. Contents of FET

As discussed earlier, no BIT or FTA has stipulated the contents of FET as it applies to investment. This has left the determination of the contents of FET to arbitral tribunals, as they have no choice but to do so in the course of deciding the cases brought before them. Thus, through arbitration practice, some elements of the contents of FET have been identified. For instance, in the *Lemire* case, the tribunal articulated that FET must be defined on the basis of the wording of the BIT and, at the same time, introduced the following factors for establishing a violation of FET:

69 Ibid., para. 478.
70 Ibid., para. 418, quoting C. Schreuer, "Fair and Equitable Treatment in Arbitral Practice," *Journal of World Investment and Trade* (2005), Vol. 6, p. 357, at 360.
71 Ibid., para. 419, citing as examples *Saluka v. Czech Republic, Azurix Corp. v. Argentine Republic, CMS Gas Transmission Company v. Argentine Republic* and *Occidental v. Ecuador*.
72 *Waste Management, Inc. v. United Mexican States* [hereinafter *Waste Management II*], ICSID Case No. ARB(AF)/00/3, Award (April 30, 2004).

- whether the State has failed to offer a stable and predictable legal framework;
- whether the State made specific representations to the investor;
- whether due process has been denied to the investor;
- whether there is an absence of transparency in the legal procedure or in the actions of the State;
- whether there has been harassment, coercion, abuse of power or other bad faith conduct by the host State;
- whether any of the actions of the State can be labeled as arbitrary, discriminatory or inconsistent.[73]

This comprehensive list points out factors that may constitute parts of FET. As this list presented by the *Lemire* Tribunal is obviously based on previous arbitral practice, it should reflect the contemporary status of the matter. In a particular case, establishment of a violation of FET does not require the host state to have committed all such acts or omissions. Proving the existence of one factor should be sufficient to establish a violation. To some extent, the criteria adopted by the *Lemire* Tribunal have the effect of directing any analysis of the subject.

The tribunal in the *Bosh v. Ukraine* case[74] clearly followed the approach taken by the *Lemire* Tribunal. In *Bosh*, the claimants were Bosh International, Inc. ("Bosh"), a US company, and B&P Ltd Foreign Investments Enterprise ("B&P"), a Ukrainian company in which Bosh held 94.5 percent of the shares. B&P and Taras Shevchenko National University of Kiev entered into a contract for renovation and redevelopment of a property belonging to the university. After commencement of the project, the university conducted an audit and found irregularities which were confirmed by the General Control and Revision Office of Ukraine ("CRO") in its own audit. Because of these irregularities, the university requested B&P to terminate the contract by mutual agreement, failing which the university would bring a lawsuit to terminate the contract. Eventually, the contract was declared terminated by a Ukrainian court.

In hearing the case, the *Bosh* Tribunal adopted the three-step analysis proposed by the *Lemire* Tribunal: (1) whether the action or omission of the host state has violated a certain threshold of propriety, (2) whether the impropriety has caused harm to the foreign investor, and (3) whether there was a causal link between action or omission and harm.[75] The *Bosh* Tribunal also quoted the list of factors that the *Lemire* Tribunal had introduced. Essentially on the basis of the *Lemire* approach, the *Bosh* Tribunal concluded that Ukraine had not breached its FET obligations under the BIT.[76]

What the claimants in the *Bosh* case complained of was not in fact what Ukraine,

---

73 *Joseph Charles Lemire v. Ukraine*, ICSID Case No. ARB/06/18, Decision on Jurisdiction and Liability of January 14, 2010, para. 284.

74 *Bosh International, Inc. and B&P Ltd. Foreign Investment Enterprise v. Ukraine*, ICSID Case No. ARB/08/11, Award (October 25, 2012).

75 Ibid., para. 212, referring to *Lemire v. Ukraine, supra*, note 72, para. 284.

76 *Bosh v. Ukraine, supra*, note 73, paras. 212–14.

including its court, had done, but rather whether it had the power to act as it had done. The main issue in the case was the termination of the contract by the university, which was brought about by the irregularities in its implementation and which was contrary to the local law. It was the university that had initiated the termination of the contract and, as the tribunal correctly decided, the university was not part of the Ukrainian Government and its actions or omissions could not be attributed to Ukraine. The only causal links that could make Ukraine liable were the actions or omissions of CRO and the Ukrainian court. Had either one of them acted inappropriately, Ukraine could have been held liable. As there was no obvious impropriety in the actions of CRO and the Ukrainian court, the *Bosh* Tribunal concluded that Ukraine had not breached its FET obligations. It should be noted, however, that the *Bosh* Tribunal did not conduct a very detailed analysis of the case by giving its own reasons, although it quoted other tribunals extensively. This further confirms that, at least with regard to interpretation of the FET obligations, jurisprudence plays an important part.

The jurisprudence of investment also shows that procedural fairness, non-discrimination, transparency and denial of justice are considered to be the main contents of FET. This does not mean that there is consistency in practice. On the contrary, as the *ad hoc* annulment Committee in *CMS* observed, "the fair and equitable standard has been invoked in a great number of cases brought to ICSID arbitration and … there is some variation in the practice of arbitral tribunals in this respect."[77] Cases discussed hereunder are illustrative rather than conclusive.

1. Procedural fairness

The presence (or absence) of procedural fairness is of utmost importance in determining whether a foreign investor has been treated fairly and equitably. Essentially, procedural fairness requires the host state to provide judicial and administrative procedures under which foreign investors' rights and interests can be adequately heard. This may involve principles of due process and denial of justice, for example.[78] A case that exemplifies this issue is *ADC v. Hungary*.[79]

When addressing the issue of due process in relation to expropriation, the *ADC* Tribunal stated that this principle "demands an actual and substantive legal procedure for a foreign investor to raise its claims against the depriving actions already taken or about to be taken against it."[80] In the tribunal's view, the host state is obliged to maintain such basic legal mechanisms as "reasonable advance notice, a fair hearing and an unbiased and impartial adjudicator to assess the actions in dispute."[81] At the same time, such legal mechanisms "must be of a

---

77 See *CMS Gas Transmission Company v. Argentine Republic*, ICSID Case No. ARB/01/8, Decision of the *ad hoc* Committee on the Application for Annulment of September 25, 2007, para. 299.
78 Denial of justice will be discussed later in this section.
79 *ADC Affiliate Limited and ADC & ADMC Management Limited v. Republic of Hungary*, ICSID Case No. ARB/03/16, Award (October 2, 2006).
80 Ibid., para. 435.
81 Id.

nature to grant an affected investor a reasonable chance within a reasonable time to claim its legitimate rights and have its claims heard."[82] In other words, in the *ADC* Tribunal's view, a host state must first have the legal procedures available and then must make them work in a reasonable way.

Such a due process requirement is required in respect of not only expropriation but also the implementation of FET. With regard to an alleged violation of FET, the *ADC* Tribunal held that this had to be "determined under the specific circumstances of each specific case."[83] As the tribunal found that the respondent had violated the due process requirement by failing to maintain the required legal mechanisms relating to expropriation, it had no hesitation in concluding that the respondent also violated FET. This is not unreasonable because, insofar as the requirement of due process is concerned, no distinction is necessary between implementation of the provisions relating to FET and expropriation.

The *Pope & Talbot* case also involved the issue of procedural fairness. In that case, the tribunal held that Canada's Softwood Lumber Division ("SLD"). in its conduct of verification of certain information regarding the claimant, had violated Article 1105 of the NAFTA. It stated that the relationship between the SLD and the claimant were "more like combat than cooperative regulation," with the end result being that the claimant had been "subjected to threats, denied its reasonable requests for pertinent information, required to incur unnecessary expense and disruption in meeting SLD's requests for information, forced to expend legal fees and probably suffer a loss of reputation in government circles."[84] Thus, the SLD's treatment of the claimant in relation to the verification review process was found to be "nothing less than a denial of the fair treatment required by NAFTA Article 1105,"[85] for which Canada was responsible and liable for damages.

Following a reduction in the fees charged by the Province of British Columbia for timber cut on crown lands (stumpage fees) in 1998, the United States "invoked the dispute resolution provisions of the SLA, making the claim that this reduction had the effect of subsidizing the production and export of lumber from BC and was thus inconsistent with the SLA."[86] Before a decision was issued in the case, Canada and the United States reached an agreement that would increase the fees charged on exports of BC softwood lumber products, and the Government of Canada instituted a "Super Fee" to be charged for large excesses of quotas. Pope & Talbot claimed that, as it was the largest exporter of softwood lumber from British Columbia, "the effect of the Super Fee measures was to act as an export restraint in a manner that was unfair and inequitable."[87]

In the end, the *Pope & Talbot* Tribunal found that whilst all softwood lumber producers in British Columbia had benefited from the reduction of stumpage rates in the province, the "only producers who were to a degree penalized [by the Super

82 Id.
83 Ibid., para. 445.
84 *Pope & Talbot*, Award on Merits 2, *supra*, note 38, para. 181.
85 Id.
86 Ibid., para. 132.
87 Ibid., para. 150.

Fee] were those who had ... exported in excess of quota."[88] The tribunal in the end concluded that the apportionment by Canada of the costs of resolving its dispute with the United States, "given the large number of B.C. producers affected by the settlement as well as the hierarchical treatment of shipment levels under the SLA itself, [did not constitute] a denial of fair and equitable treatment" to the claimant.[89]

RDC v. Guatemala[90] was the first case brought under the Dominican Republic–Central America–United States of America Free Trade Agreement—the DR–CAFTA. The claimant—Railroad Development Corporation—brought arbitration proceedings before ICSID against Guatemala on its own behalf and on behalf of Compañía Desarrolladora Ferroviaria, S.A., a Guatemalan company which did business as Ferrovías Guatemala ("FVG") and was majority-owned and controlled by the claimant. In the business of railway investment and management, the claimant acquired the use of the infrastructure to provide railway services in Guatemala and a 50-year right to rebuild and operate the Guatemalan rail system. Later on, FVG entered into a usufruct contract with Ferrocarriles de Guatemala ("FEGUA"), a state-owned company of Guatemala responsible for providing certain railway transport services and managing the rail equipment and real estate assets. The usufruct contract granted FVG "the use, enjoyment, repair and maintenance of railway equipment owned by FEGUA for the purposes of rendering railway transportation services."[91] However, this contract never went into effect, so FVG and FEGUA entered into a new contract to enable FVG to provide commercial service.

On June 26, 2005, FVG initiated two domestic arbitration proceedings against FEGUA for breach of contract, alleging FEGUA's failure to remove squatters from the rail right of way and its failure to make payments to the Railway Trust Fund. The Attorney General of Guatemala then issued an opinion which stated that the signing of the second contract constituted a violation of rules and procedures required for the legally valid execution of the agreement. Then, on August 25, 2006, the Guatemalan Government issued a resolution declaring that the usufruct contracts were injurious to the interests of the state (the "*lesivo* declaration").

The dispute arose, as alleged by the claimant, from Guatemala's failure (through FEGUA) to remove squatters from the rail right of way and to make the required payments to the Railway Trust Fund, as well from the issuance of the *lesivo* declaration by the respondent. In the claimant's view, Guatemala had violated the minimum standards required by the DR–CAFTA, Article 10.5 of which provides:

> 1. Each Party shall accord to covered investments treatment in accordance with customary international law, including fair and equitable treatment and full protection and security.

---

88 Ibid., para. 153.
89 Ibid., para. 155.
90 *Railroad Development Corporation (RDC) v. Republic of Guatemala*, ICSID Case No. ARB/07/23, Award (June 29, 2012).
91 Ibid., para. 32.

2. For greater certainty, paragraph 1 prescribes the customary international law minimum standard of treatment of aliens as the minimum standard of treatment to be afforded to covered investments. The concepts of "fair and equitable treatment" and "full protection and security" do not require treatment in addition to or beyond that which is required by that standard, and do not create additional substantive rights. The obligation in paragraph 1 to provide:

(a) "fair and equitable treatment" includes the obligation not to deny justice in criminal, civil, or administrative adjudicatory proceedings in accordance with the principle of due process embodied in the principal legal systems of the world; and

(b) "full protection and security" requires each Party to provide the level of police protection required under customary international law.

The claimant also contended that the respondent had breached the minimum standard of treatment, including FET, for its application of the *lesivo* procedure, which, in the view of the claimant, "lacks foundation under substantive Guatemalan law, affords no due process to the investor; [so that] in practice, as was the case here, respondent may use its *lesivo* power in order to avoid or force the renegotiation of valid administrative contracts without compensating the investor."[92]

The *RDC* Tribunal observed that the *lesivo* declaration was used as a measure for the government to not enforce a contractual obligation on the basis of harm to the state.[93] In essence, the issue relating to the *lesivo* declaration was that the government agency FEGUA acted in violation of local procedures and laws. Yet, in the view of the tribunal, the respondent had given no reasons for its failure to approve the original contract.[94] Thus, the *RDC* Tribunal concluded that the respondent had used the *lesivo* remedy "under a cloak of formal correctness allegedly in defense of the rule of law, [but] in fact for exacting concessions unrelated to the finding of *lesivo*."[95] The reasons behind the *RDC* Tribunal's decision included (1) that the respondent was fully aware of the original contract, (2) that FVG had provided services for more than seven years, and (3) that FEGUA had continuously received payments from FVG. In those circumstances, even if there were errors in concluding the contract by FEGUA acting *ultra vires*, the respondent should have corrected those errors.[96] In other words, the respondent should be prohibited from raising the violation of its own law as a defense for not observing its international obligations. Finally, the *RDC* Tribunal concluded that the manner in which the respondent applied the *lesivo* remedy constituted a breach of

---

92 Ibid., para. 48.
93 Ibid., para. 85.
94 Ibid., para. 226.
95 Ibid., para. 234.
96 The *RDC* Tribunal considered that the host state may make mistakes, but, at the same time, it should correct its mistakes which have been relied upon by others in good faith and to their detriment; ibid., para. 116.

the minimum standard of treatment provided for in DR-CAFTA Article 10.5 by being "arbitrary, grossly unfair, and unjust" in nature.[97]

It should be noted that the *RDC* Tribunal's decision was based on the manner in which the *lesivo* remedy was used rather than the *lesivo* remedy itself. The emphasis here on the *de facto* breach of the due process requirement is important, because in most cases the host state may have an apparently modern system of law that includes the principle of due process but that system may not operate in the manner required by contemporary customary international law. Unless such de facto breaches are dealt with adequately, the provisions relating to FET cannot be effectively implemented. In this regard, the *RDC* decision is illustrative of how issues relating to due process should be dealt with.

The *TECO* case[98] also concerns procedural fairness, but in a unique way. In that case, the claimant—TECO Guatemala Holdings LLC—was a US company wholly owned by TECO Energy, Inc., also a US company. The claimant made an investment in the electricity distribution business in Guatemala when the respondent privatized its electric power industry. The dispute arose from an alleged violation by the Guatemalan regulatory authority—National Commission of Electric Energy ("CNEE")—of the Guatemalan law for setting tariffs for distribution of electricity by EEGSA, a company that was in the business of distributing electricity and was partly owned by the claimant.[99] Specifically, the claimant argued that the respondent had violated the FET obligation under the DR-CAFTA on two grounds: (a) modification of the legal and regulatory framework, contrary to its representations; and (b) engaging in unfair and arbitrary actions relating to the tariff review process.[100]

The *TECO* Tribunal noted that investment tribunals should pay deference to a sovereign state's regulatory powers.[101] At the same time, it considered that the deference "cannot amount to condoning behaviors that are manifestly arbitrary, idiosyncratic, or that show a complete lack of candor in the conduction [sic] of the regulatory process."[102] In other words, the deference paid to a state's regulatory power should be conditioned on the action or omission of the state not constituting an abuse of power by, for instance, making arbitrary decisions, disregarding legally required procedures or discriminating against foreign investors.[103] In the *TECO* case, one of the issues was whether CNEE's not taking into account an Expert Commission's advice amounted to a violation of FET. The *TECO* Tribunal ruled that "it would be entirely inconsistent to provide for an expert determination mechanism while at the same time allowing the regulator to disregard the Expert

---

97 Ibid., para. 235.
98 *TECO Guatemala Holdings LLC v. Republic of Guatemala*, ICSID Case No. ARB/10/17, Award (December 19, 2013).
99 Ibid., para. 79.
100 Ibid., para. 265.
101 Ibid., para. 490.
102 Ibid., para. 492.
103 Ibid., para. 587.

Commission's conclusions without any reasons."[104] In its view: "A lack of reasons may be relevant to assess whether a given decision was arbitrary and whether there was lack of due process in administrative proceedings."[105] This was so because the respondent had the duty to give the Expert Commission's conclusions serious consideration. One way to prove that serious consideration has been given is to provide reasons for not taking the advice of the Commission. This was the case even though the findings of the Expert Commission had no binding force.[106]

The uniqueness of the *TECO* decision is that the issue involved in the case was not whether or not the regulatory body had observed the procedures set by the law but rather how use should be made of the advice of a neutral body—an Expert Commission. Even though the Commission was stipulated by the law, there was no explicit requirement under the law that the CNEE was required to take into account the Commission's views in its decision-making process. Under these circumstances, where the regulatory body could make decisions disregarding the advice or conclusions of the Commission, the existence of the latter would be superfluous. At the same time, as the Commission was not an adjudicatory authority, its conclusions or views could not bind the CNEE. The *TECO* Tribunal did not require the CNEE to follow the advice of the Expert Commission but expressly said that CNEE had a duty to state its reasons for not taking into consideration that advice. In this way, the *TECO* decision has enriched the jurisprudence of international investment law by examining procedural fairness from the perspective of indirect legal requirements.

2. Non-discrimination

Non-discrimination is another important component of the FET standard.[107] As the *CMS* Tribunal stated: "Any measure that might involve arbitrariness or discrimination is in itself contrary to fair and equitable treatment."[108] Therefore, it is natural to include non-discrimination as an element of the FET standard. In his comments on the NAFTA, Weiler said:

> There are essentially two types of prohibition against discrimination, contained within four separate provisions of the NAFTA: Articles 1102, 1103, 1105 and 1110. One type of prohibition represents an absolute standard that is informed by international law. The other is a comparative test, designed to ensure fairness in result. Together, the two standards combine to prohibit

---

104 Ibid., para. 584.
105 Ibid., para. 587.
106 Ibid., para. 670.
107 For example, Article 10(1) of the Energy Charter Treaty provides that "investments shall also enjoy the most constant protection and security and no Contracting Party shall in any way impair by unreasonable or discriminatory measures their management, maintenance, use, enjoyment or disposal."
108 *CMS*, Award, *supra*, note 17, para. 290.

any government action that discriminates against foreign investors and their investments in most conceivable manners.[109]

In practice, determination of discrimination must compare similar circumstances and similar cases. For instance, in ascertaining whether a foreign investor has been treated in a discriminatory way, there must be another foreign investor or a local investor who is in the same business and has made an investment in the same or similar business. In such circumstances, where the foreign investor has received worse treatment than the other foreign investor or the local investor, discrimination may be assumed unless the differential treatment is justifiable—for a legitimate state objective. Therefore, in ascertaining whether or not discrimination has occurred, three elements must be considered—like circumstances, different treatment, and justification.

In *Parkerings*,[110] the tribunal concluded that determination of discrimination does not depend upon proof of bad faith on the part of the host state. Yet, for a discrimination to violate international law, it "must be unreasonable or lacking proportionality, for instance, it must be inapposite or excessive to achieve an otherwise legitimate objective of the State."[111] The view of the *Parkerings* Tribunal was shared by the *Siemens* Tribunal, which found that "intent is not decisive or essential for a finding of discrimination, and … the impact of the measure on the investment would be the determining factor to ascertain whether it had resulted in non-discriminatory treatment."[112] In the view of the *LG&E* Tribunal, either intent or discriminatory effects would be sufficient to establish a violation of the non-discrimination requirement. It stated: "In the context of investment treaties, and the obligation thereunder not to discriminate against foreign investors, a measure is considered discriminatory if the intent of the measure is to discriminate or if the measure has a discriminatory effect."[113] In practice, investment tribunals most often place emphasis on the effects of a measure rather than the intent of the authorities in taking it in determining whether the measure is discriminatory.

The "effects test" is a reasonable approach. After all, what is important in determining whether a foreign investment or investor has been treated in a discriminatory manner is the result, which may constitute discrimination even given the good intent of the host state. At the same time, if bad faith is required as a condition, due to lack of information, foreign investors may not be able to prove discrimination even if they have been treated in a discriminatory way. Therefore,

---

109 See Todd Weiler, "Saving Oscar Chin: Non-Discrimination in International Investment Law," in Todd Weiler (ed.), *International Investment Law and Arbitration: Leading Cases from the ICSID, NAFTA, Bilateral Treaties and Customary International Law*, Cameron May, 2005, p. 559.

110 *Parkerings-Compagniet AS v. Lithuania*, ICSID Case No. ARB/05/8, Award (September 11, 2007).

111 Ibid., para. 368.

112 *Siemens A.G. v. Argentine Republic*, ICSID Case No. ARB/02/8, Award (February 6, 2007), para. 321.

113 *LG&E Energy Corp. et al. v. Argentine Republic*, ICSID Case No. ARB/02/1, Decision on Liability (October 3, 2006), para. 146.

either from the operational perspective or that of fairness, the effects test should be adopted.

Another aspect for establishing discrimination is that the investor or investment in question and the comparator-investor/investment must be in like circumstances. The *Parkerings* Tribunal defined "like circumstances" as those where two investors are in the "same economic or business sector" but found that despite similarities in objective and venue, "differences of size" between the claimant and the comparator-investor and the claimant's significant extension of the construction project into a sensitive archaeological and cultural area were "important enough to determine that the two investors were not *in like circumstances*."[114] The tribunal also considered that the archaeological and environmental concerns shown by various local bodies in opposing the claimant's project were valid reasons to justify the respondent's measures.[115]

In the *ADC* case, discussed earlier, the respondent was found to have expropriated the claimants' airport project and replaced the claimants with a British operator. The respondent contended that there were only foreign parties involved in the operation of the airport and therefore there could not have been any discrimination. The *ADC* Tribunal pointed out that in the circumstances of the case comparison must be made between the treatment "received by the Respondent-appointed operator and that received by foreign investors as a whole."[116] In the end, it was held that the respondent committed discrimination against the claimants.[117] Discrimination does not depend on whether or not the parties involved are all foreign investors. The essential factor is whether those in like circumstances are treated in like manner.

In practice, where a foreign investor and another party—either another foreign investor or a domestic investor—are in like circumstances, any differential treatment may not be justifiable. Even obligations under other treaties may not be justifiable grounds for differential treatment. The *Petrobart*[118] case is illustrative in this respect. That case involved a supply and purchase contract for stable gas condensate between the claimant Petrobart, a company registered in Gibraltar, and KGM, a state-owned company of the Kyrgyz Republic. According to a Presidential Decree of the Kyrgyz Republic, the purchase of gas should be funded by the Ministry of Finance, which should be repaid by KGM. When KGM went into bankruptcy proceedings, payments had not been made to Petrobart, and the claimant alleged that the respondent had violated, inter alia, the obligations of Article 10(1) and (7) of the ECT relating to non-discrimination. The ground for the complaint was that the respondent had made payments to satisfy a claim of the Central Asian Bank outside the KGM bankruptcy case. The respondent argued that the payment to the Central Asian Bank was made pursuant to a

114 *Parkerings, supra*, note 109, para. 396 (emphasis in original).
115 Id.
116 *ADC v. Hungary, supra*, note 78, para. 442.
117 Ibid., para. 443.
118 *Petrobart Limited v. Kyrgyz Republic*, Stockholm Chamber of Commerce, Award (March 29, 2005).

bilateral agreement with Uzbekistan. The tribunal ruled that the respondent had "discriminated between the investments of two investors, namely the Central Asian Bank and Petrobart."[119] This holding appears to have been made with good reasons, as the ECT is a multilateral treaty and its status is not lower than that of a bilateral treaty. The two investors—the Central Asian Bank and the claimant—were therefore in similar circumstances. As the claimant was treated worse than the Central Asian Bank, discrimination could easily be established.

Comparison of treatment afforded may also be made where foreign investors and domestic investors are in the same business or economic sector.[120] In the *United Parcel* case,[121] the tribunal found that the claimant, which is a US company in the courier delivery service business, was not in like circumstances with the Canadian governmental postal service because "there are inherent distinctions between postal traffic and courier shipments that require the implementation of different programs for the processing of goods imported as mail and for goods imported by courier."[122]

In *Feldman*, however, the tribunal considered that in certain cases, even when the foreign investor and a national investor are in like circumstances, it may still be justifiable to treat them differently for reasons of "better control over tax revenues, [or to] discourage smuggling, protect intellectual property rights, and prohibit gray market sales, even if some of these may be anti-competitive."[123] As to what may constitute like circumstances, the *Feldman* Tribunal stated that the investors in like circumstances were those engaged in the same business of purchasing cigarettes for export.[124]

In this regard, the UNCTAD Report on National Treatment also offers help. By taking into account the experience of the GATT/WTO, it observed that the determination of like circumstances is not easy in practice.[125] The question whether "like circumstances" exist "needs to be determined in the light of the facts of the case."[126] Citing an OECD report, UNCTAD considered that the most important matters in determining like circumstances include "whether the two enterprises are in the same sector; the impact of policy objectives of the host country in particular fields; and the motivation behind the measure involved."[127]

---

119 Ibid., p. 59.
120 For instance, in *Pope & Talbot*, the tribunal considered that "the treatment accorded a foreign owned investment protected by Article 1102(2) [of the NAFTA] should be compared with that accorded domestic investments in the same business or economic sector." See *Pope & Talbot Inc. v. Canada*, Award on the Merits 2, *supra*, note 38, para. 78.
121 *United Parcel Service of America Inc. v. Government of Canada*, UNCITRAL, Award on the Merits (May 24, 2007).
122 Ibid., para. 98.
123 *Marvin Feldman v. Mexico*, ICSID Case No. ARB(AF)/99/1, Award (December 16, 2002), para. 170.
124 Ibid., para. 172.
125 UNCTAD, *National Treatment*, UN Doc. UNCTAD/ITE/IIT/11 (Vol. IV), 1999, p. 33.
126 Id.
127 Id. Rojas, after examining a number of investment cases, concluded that "there is some support to sustain that two or more investors or investments are in *like circumstances* if they operate in the

The *S.D. Myers* Tribunal considered that the word "sector" has a wide connotation that includes "the concepts of 'economic sector' and 'business sector.'"[128]

It is quite certain that investment arbitration practice tends to agree that discrimination involves differential treatment of foreign investors and nationals or among foreign investors situated in "like circumstances" and that the latter has been decided to mean "being in the same economic or business sectors". Where a given foreign investor is afforded less favorable treatment, discrimination is assumed unless a justification for the difference can be made. This is quite similar to GATT/WTO practice, notwithstanding the fact that like circumstances in investment are more difficult to ascertain and in most cases must be determined by taking into account all relevant factors of the case at issue.

3. Transparency

Transparency is also an important component of FET. BITs and FTAs, however, do not stipulate transparency as being part of the FET requirement. In investment treaty arbitration, tribunals, as with respect to their interpretation of other provisions, have given different interpretations to the standard of transparency. In this regard, the *Tecmed* Tribunal represents those tribunals that have adopted a high standard of requirements. It stated that "[t]he Foreign investor expects the host State to act in a consistent manner, free from ambiguity and totally transparently in its relations with the foreign investor."[129] This holding implies that the host state has positive obligations and that any omission may trigger liabilities. As there is no such assertive requirement in BITs and FTAs, it is arguable whether states have such obligations to act vigorously.

In contrast, the tribunal in *Waste Management II* linked transparency to the international minimum standard of treatment, in particular procedural transparency in the administrative process. It stated that "the minimum standard of treatment of fair and equitable treatment is infringed by conduct attributable to the State and harmful to the claimant if the conduct … involves a complete lack of transparency and candour in an administrative process."[130] Obviously, the formulation "a complete lack of transparency" is very ambiguous and indecisive and its determination therefore must be left to the arbitral tribunals. This standard and that adopted by the *Tecmed* Tribunal stand at the two extremes of the requirement of transparency.

Despite the differences in treaty arbitration practice, it should be pointed out that transparency is a general requirement of any society that is governed by the rule of law and of most multilateral organizations, such as the WTO and the World Bank. Although different tribunals may place an emphasis on certain aspects of

same *sector*" (emphasis in original); see Fernando Gonzalez Rojas, "The Notion of Discrimination in Article 1102 of NAFTA," Jean Monnet Working Paper 05/05, NYU School of Law, 2005.

128   *S.D. Myers Inc. v. Canada*, UNCITRAL, First Partial Award (November 13, 2000), para. 250.

129   *Tecmed, supra*, note 33, para. 154.

130   *Waste Management II, supra*, note 71, para 98.

transparency because of the facts before them, it is commonly understood that transparency relates to the openness of administrative procedures as well as the reasons for substantive decision-making. For instance, it should be known to the public, in particular to foreign investors, what stages of procedures are required to obtain a license, for example, and in what time frame a decision is expected to be made. Another relevant factor is that decisions must be made objectively. For that purpose, where a decision is made, and most importantly where the decision is not in the investor's favor, reasons should be stated in the decision. With these specific requirements, it is irrelevant whether or not transparency requires the host state to be proactive, and it may not be treated as a very flexible standard.[131]

4. Denial of justice

There is no clearly defined concept of denial of justice in international law,[132] although some have observed that its origin can be traced to the medieval rule of private reprisals.[133] Traditionally, authors consider that denial of justice only involves actions and omissions of courts. Contemporary opinions, in particular those relating to international law, believe that "every injury involving the responsibility of the state committed by a court or judge acting officially, or alternatively every such injury committed by any organ of the government in its official capacity in connexion with the administration of justice, constitutes … a denial of justice."[134] The advantage of this approach is that all forms of denial of justice are covered and states cannot escape responsibility merely because the persons or bodies are under different cloaks or titles pursuant to national laws, even though their acts or omissions are imputable to the states. This situation has left much room for the investment treaty arbitration tribunals to further interpret, define and redefine the term "denial of justice," as they have to make decisions facing arguments of the disputing parties.

In contemporary international investment law, denial of justice is considered to be a component of FET by both academics and arbitral tribunals.[135] One of the

---

131 The *Waste Management II* Tribunal stated that "[e]vidently the standard is to some extent a flexible one which must be adapted to the circumstances of each case;" ibid., para. 99.

132 Freeman considered that there were six categories of denial of justice that had evolved within the literature of international law; see Alwyn Freeman, *The International Responsibility of States for Denial of Justice*, Longman, London/New York, 1938, quoted in R. Doak Bishop, James Crawford, and W. Michael Reisman, *Foreign Investment Disputes: Cases, Materials and Commentary*, Kluwer Law International, 2005, p. 976.

133 Jan Paulsson, *Denial of Justice in International Law*, Cambridge University Press, 2009, p. 13.

134 Ibid., at 64.

135 For instance, Dolzer and Schreuer said: "Fair procedure is an elementary requirement of the rule of law and a vital element of FET. It is antithetical to the international delinquency of denial of justice." See Rudolf Dolzer and Christoph Schreuer, *Principles of International Investment Law*, Oxford University Press, 2008, p. 142. The *Jan de Nul* Tribunal also stated that the "fair and equitable treatment standard encompasses the notion of denial of justice;" see *Jan de Nul N.V. and Dredging International N.V. v. Arab Republic of Egypt*, ICSID Case No. ARB/04/13, Award (November 6, 2008), para. 188.

leading cases in investment arbitration in this regard is *Loewen v. United States*,[136] according to which the establishment of a denial of justice should depend on the effect of the actions and omissions of the bodies of the host state administering justice and, hence, proof of bad faith or malicious intent is not necessary. The *Loewen* Tribunal ruled: "Manifest injustice in the sense of a lack of due process leading to an outcome which offends a sense of judicial propriety is enough."[137]

The *Mondev* case, discussed earlier, also involved denial of justice, which, as alleged by the claimant, is an important aspect of the minimum standard of treatment in customary international law, according to which it includes undue delay or denial of access to the competent courts of the host state or manifestly unjust judgments that a foreign investor has suffered. The claimant in *Mondev* articulated three primary grounds to support its claim relating to denial of justice; they included: (1) the Massachusetts Supreme Judicial Court ("SJC") departed significantly from its established jurisprudence by disregarding the contract entered into by the parties; (2) the Court failed to remand the case to the jury; and (3) public authorities engaged in commerce should not be entitled to statutory immunity for intentional torts. The *Mondev* Tribunal, however, was not persuaded by these arguments and consequently dismissed each of the grounds raised by the claimant. It held that the *SJC* decision was not so arbitrary as to rise to the level of denial of justice under customary international law. The tribunal cited, with approval, the decision in *Azinian v. Mexico* that:

> A denial of justice could be pleaded if the relevant courts refuse to entertain a suit, if they subject it to undue delay, or if they administer justice in a seriously inadequate way … There is a fourth type of denial of justice, namely the clear and malicious misapplication of the law. This type of wrong doubtless overlaps with the notion of "pretence of form" to mask a violation of international law.[138]

In the view of the *Mondev* Tribunal, in establishing a denial of justice, the test is not "whether a particular result is surprising, but whether the shock or surprise occasioned to an impartial tribunal leads, on reflection, to justified concerns as to the judicial propriety of the outcome."[139] In making such an assessment, an arbitral tribunal must bear in mind that it is not an appellate court, said the *Mondev* Tribunal. The standard established in the *Mondev* case is this: where, according to "generally accepted standards of the administration of justice," the challenged decision itself is "clearly improper and discreditable,"[140] a denial of justice is proven.

In international investment law, a denial of access to local authorities responsible

---

136 *The Loewen Group, Inc. and Raymond L. Loewen v. United States of America*, ICSID Case No. ARB(AF)/98/3, Award (June 26, 2003).
137 Ibid., para. 132.
138 *Azinian v. United Mexican States* (1999) 39 *ILM* 537, at p. 552.
139 *Mondev, supra*, note 63, para. 127.
140 Id.

for discharging justice is the foremost proof of denial of justice. The *Iberdrola* Tribunal expressed the opinion that denial of access can be established by either "the unjustified refusal of a court to hear a matter within its jurisdiction or any state action taken that has the effect of preventing access to justice," "an undue delay in the administration of justice," or "decisions or actions of State bodies that are evidently arbitrary, unfair, idiosyncratic or delayed."[141] The *Parkerings* Tribunal expressed a somewhat similar view when, in opining on redress for breach of contracts, it stated:

> ... if the contracting party is denied access to domestic courts, and thus denied opportunity to obtain redress of the injury and to complain about ... contractual breaches [in the domestic forum provided in a contract], then an arbitral tribunal is in position, on the basis of the BIT, to decide whether this lack of remedies had consequences on the investment and thus whether a violation of international law occurred. In other words, as a general rule, a tribunal whose jurisdiction is based solely on a BIT will decide over the "treatment" that the alleged breach of contract has received in the domestic context, rather than over the existence of a breach [of contract] as such.[142]

It should be noted that both the *Iberdrola* and *Parkerings* Tribunals considered that an undue delay by the courts in handling their cases may amount to a denial of justice. Justice delayed is justice denied. As the tribunal in *Chevron v. Ecuador (I)* stated: "the delay itself usually evidences the general futility" of the host state's system.[143] Therefore, the likelihood that an international arbitral tribunal will consider an undue delay to be a denial of justice has a positive effect in promoting the rule of law in domestic legal systems.

Suppose, however, that a given judiciary has a reputation of being slow due to inefficiency or congestion of cases and the foreign investor is aware of that situation. It is then possible that an argument can be made that a delay which is viewed as too long in other jurisdictions may not be prolonged in the relevant state. For instance, in *Toto v. Lebanon*, the tribunal observed that "international law has no strict standards to assess whether court delays are a denial of justice."[144]

In fact, not only is it true that international law has no strict standards in this regard, but court delays may involve other factors that cannot be quantified— cultural and otherwise. In this regard, the *White Industries* Tribunal identified the following factors as relevant in determining whether court delays may amount to a denial of justice: "... the complexity of the proceedings, the need for swiftness, the behaviour of the litigants involved, the significance of the interest at stake and the

---

141 *Iberdrola Energia S.A. v. Republic of Guatemala*, ICSID Case No. ARB/09/5, Award (August 17, 2012), para. 432 (free translation by the author from the original Spanish).

142 *Parkerings, supra*, note 109, paras. 316 and 317.

143 *Chevron Corporation and Texaco Petroleum Company v. Ecuador* [hereinafter "*Chevron (I)*], Partial Award on the Merits (March 30, 2010), para. 329.

144 *Toto Costruzzioni Generali S.p.A. v. Lebanon*, ICSID Case No. ARB/07112, Decision on Jurisdiction (September 11, 2009), para. 155.

behaviour of the courts themselves."[145] An important issue in the *White Industries* case was that the claimant was aware or ought to have been aware of the overburdened court structure when it made the investment and therefore it could not be expected to have had any legitimate expectation that enforcement of arbitration awards in the host state would be efficient.[146]

The behavior of litigants is also an important factor, which can delay and prolong court proceedings tremendously.[147] Sometimes, the party anticipating that it will lose the case may try all means to postpone a decision of the court. In such cases, it would be unfair to hold the host state responsible. Some other times, litigation culture itself may cause substantive delays of court proceedings. For instance, common law litigators may spend days in cross-examining witnesses, whereas civil law litigators generally do not need that much time. Therefore, cultural aspects are also important considerations in determining a denial of justice.

Although simple court delay may not amount to a denial of justice, discrimination in violation of local law may constitute a denial of justice according to the *Loewen* Tribunal.[148] Yet, if there are remedies available within the system of the host state, no denial of justice should be determined before such local remedies are exhausted. In other words, before the system of the host state is tested or exhausted, there cannot be a violation of international obligation that may constitute a denial of justice. In the words of the *Loewen* Tribunal: "The principle that a court decision which can be challenged through the judicial process does not amount to a denial of justice at the international level has been linked to the duty imposed upon a State by international law to provide a fair and efficient system of justice."[149] In fact, what the *Loewen* Tribunal articulated was a balanced approach, which, on the one hand, requires the foreign investor to exhaust local remedies and, on the other hand, imposes an obligation on the part of the host state to provide a fair and efficient system in which the foreign investor can exercise his/her right of appeal. As such, where there are conditions attached to making appeals that "render exercise of the right impractical, the exercise of the right is neither available nor effective nor adequate."[150] Also, if a state "burdens the exercise of the right directly or indirectly so as to expose the complainant to severe financial consequences,"[151] the host state should be held liable. Therefore, the issue of whether or not local remedies have been exhausted must be decided by taking into account the specific facts of each case.

145 *White Industries Australia Limited v. Republic of India*, UNCITRAL, Final Award (November 30, 2011), para. 10.4.10.
146 Ibid., paras. 10.3.14–10.3.16.
147 In *White Industries*, for example, the respondent maintained that the long delay of the original case "before the Indian courts is due entirely to White's litigation strategy," although this argument was rejected by the tribunal; see ibid., paras. 10.4.15–10.4.16.
148 On this matter, the *Loewen* Tribunal stated: "A decision which is in breach of municipal law and is discriminatory against the foreign litigant amounts to manifest injustice according to international law." *Loewen, supra*, note 135, para. 135.
149 Ibid., para. 153.
150 Ibid., para. 170.
151 Id.

The *Loewen* Tribunal's position has been shared by other tribunals. In *Jan de Nul*, the tribunal opined that "the respondent State must be put in a position to redress the wrongdoings of its judiciary."[152] In quoting Paulsson with approval, the *Jan de Nul* Tribunal further stated: "In other words, [the State] cannot be held liable unless 'the system as a whole has been tested and the initial delict remained uncorrected"[153] An exception to this rule, said the tribunal, may be when even though there is such a system, it may not provide effective remedies or reasonable prospect of success.[154] The *Iberdrola* Tribunal, in approving the view of the claimant, stated that a "denial of justice is not a mere error in interpretation of local law, but an error that no merely competent judge could have committed and that shows that a minimally adequate system of justice has not been provided."[155]

The general trend in arbitral practice in determining whether a denial of justice has occurred is to require that the matter must have been through the whole system of the host state. This is logical, because where other remedies are available to the claimant, it would be premature for an international arbitral tribunal to hold a state liable for a denial of justice.[156] It is also a recognition of the regulatory power of the host state, which is an important consideration in international investment law.

It is commonly agreed that international investment arbitration tribunals should not function as an appeal body of national court decisions in deciding disputes involving denial of justice, which is both theoretically and practically significant, as well as being politically correct. In *Azinian*, for instance, the tribunal observed:

> The possibility of holding a State internationally liable for judicial decisions does not, however, entitle a claimant to seek international review of the national court decisions as though the international jurisdiction seised has plenary appellate jurisdiction. This is not true generally, and it is not true for NAFTA.[157]

Thus, in ascertaining whether a denial of justice has occurred, the fact to be considered is whether the decision of a court or another body responsible for

---

152 *Jan de Nul*, *supra*, note 134, para. 258.
153 Id.
154 Id.
155 *Iberdrola*, *supra*, note 140, para. 432 (free translation by the author from the original Spanish).
156 Similar views have been expressed by scholars in the field. For instance, Greenwood commented that "the decision of a national court, however badly flawed, will not amount to a denial of justice engaging the international responsibility of the State unless the system of appeals and other challenges which exists in that State either does not correct the deficiencies of the lower court's decision or is such that it does not afford a prospect of correcting those deficiencies which is reasonably available to the alien who has suffered from that decision;" see Christopher Greenwood, "State Responsibility for the Decisions of National Courts," in M. Fitzmaurice and D. Sarooshi (eds.), *Issues of State Responsibility before International Judicial Institutions*, The Clifford Chance Lectures, Vol. 7, Hart Publishing, 2004, pp. 55–73, at 68.
157 *Azinian v. United Mexican States*, *supra*, note 137, para. 99.

discharging justice constitutes a violation of the relevant treaty obligations. In Fitzmaurice's view, insofar as court judgments are concerned, the question is whether "the court [was] guilty of bias, fraud, dishonesty, lack of impartiality, or gross incompetence."[158] In other words, international tribunals should be concerned with the way foreign investors are treated by the courts and other justice enforcement bodies of the host state. Unless gross injustices or misconduct by the courts exist, a violation of treaty obligations may not have been committed and, hence, international investment tribunals should not interfere. At the same time, international tribunals must be culturally sensitive. They should refrain from applying the standards of their own system without due consideration of those of the host state.[159]

Because of the sensitivity in establishing denial of justice, investment treaty arbitration practice shows that tribunals are cautious in confirming its occurrence. On this matter, the *White Industries* Tribunal expressed the view that the standard to be applied must be "stringent" and that, hence, "international tribunals are slow to make a finding that a State is liable for the international delict of denial of justice."[160] The *White Industries* Tribunal also cited the Great Britain–Mexico Claims Commission in its analysis that "[i]t is obvious that such a grave reproach can only be directed against a judicial authority upon evidence of the most convincing nature."[161] This position was shared by the *Chevron (I)* Tribunal, which stated:

> [T]he test for establishing a denial of justice sets ... a high threshold. While the standard is objective and does not require an overt showing of bad faith, it nevertheless requires the demonstration of "a particularly serious shortcoming and egregious conduct that shocks, or at least surprises, a sense of judicial propriety."[162]

Similarly, in *Feldman*, the tribunal held:

> Taking into account, as noted earlier, that the Claimant had unrestricted access, at all material times, to the Mexican courts and administrative procedures, the Claimant's victory in the 1993 Amparo decision, and the availability of revision of the decisions on nullity and assessment filed by the Claimant

---

158 G. G. Fitzmaurice, "The meaning of the term denial of justice," 13 *BYIL* 93, 1932, at pp.113–14.
159 In this regard, the *Waste Management II* case is illustrative. The tribunal in that case stated: "Certain of the decisions appear to have been founded on rather technical grounds, but the notion that the third party beneficiary of a line of credit or guarantee should strictly prove its entitlement is not a parochial or unusual one ... In any event, and however these cases might have been decided in different legal systems, this Tribunal does not discern in the decisions of the federal courts any denial of justice as that concept has been explained by NAFTA tribunals." See *Waste Management II, supra*, note 71, paras. 129 and 130.
160 *White Industries, supra*, note 144, para. 10.4.8.
161 Id., citing *El Oro Mining Railway Company (Great Britain) v. Mexico*, Great Britain–Mexico Claims Commission, Decision No. 55 of June 18, 1931, V RIAA 191, at 198.
162 *Chevron (I), supra*, note 142, para. 244.

in 1998, there appears to have been no denial of due process or justice which could reach in this case the level of a violation of international law.[163]

The distinction between the results of court proceedings and the way that local courts have handled the case is important. It can serve as a standard according to which an alleged denial of justice should be determined. The importance of distinguishing the results of domestic litigation from due process also lies in the fact that investment arbitration tribunals seldom touch on the issue of whether or not treaty standards and customary international law standards are the same.[164] It could be argued that because denial of justice is a component of FET, whatever standard is applied to FET should also be adopted in establishing a denial of justice. Yet, as discussed earlier, any decision relating to denial of justice concerns the host state's regulatory power and is culturally sensitive. It may have significant consequences on the host state's perception of international investment law and the development of the latter and therefore should be made with considerable caution.

5. Stability of the business and legal framework and investors' expectations

Maintenance by the host state of a stable legal and business environment will afford foreign investors with predictability so that they can plan their business. Very often, BITs and FTAs contain, in their preamble, references to such stability. In practice, tribunals have often decided that the stability of the legal and business environment constitutes part of FET. For instance, in *Occidental Exploration and Production Co. v. Ecuador*, the tribunal stated:

> Although fair and equitable treatment is not defined in the Treaty, the Preamble clearly records the agreement of the parties that such treatment "is desirable in order to maintain a stable framework for investment and maximum effective utilization of economic resources." The stability of the legal and business framework is thus an essential element of fair and equitable treatment.[165]

The *CMS* Tribunal held a similar view, stating:

> The Treaty Preamble makes it clear, however, that one principal objective of the protection envisaged is that fair and equitable treatment is desirable "to maintain a stable framework for investments and maximum use of economic

---

163 *Feldman v. Mexico, supra,* note 122, para. 140.
164 In *Iberdrola,* facing the issue of whether or not the treaty standard was wider than that of customary international law, the tribunal said that "the fact that the Treaty includes the obligation of giving the investor a fair and equitable treatment does not mean, per se, as Iberdrola argues, that the standard of denial of justice of the Treaty is broader than that of customary international law;" see *Iberdrola, supra,* note 140, para. 427.
165 *Occidental Exploration and Production Company v. Republic of Ecuador,* UNCITRAL Arbitration, LCIA Case No. UN 3467, Final Award of July 1, 2004, para. 183.

resources." There can be no doubt, therefore, that a stable legal and business environment is an essential element of fair and equitable treatment.[166]

The *LG&E* Tribunal, where the material facts of the case were similar to those in *CMS*, found itself in agreement with the *CMS* Tribunal on this point. It opined:

> In considering the context within which Argentina and the United States included the fair and equitable treatment standard, and its object and purpose, the Tribunal observes in the Preamble of the Treaty that the two countries agreed that "fair and equitable treatment of investment is desirable in order to maintain a stable framework for investment and maximum effective use of economic resources." ... In light of these stated objectives, this Tribunal must conclude that stability of the legal and business framework is an essential element of fair and equitable treatment in this case.[167]

The illogicality and implausibility of the above passage notwithstanding, it is without doubt that a generally stable legal and economic environment would encourage foreign investment, as it reduces the risks of investors. The question is to what extent a host state is obliged to keep its laws and legal system unchanged.

Some tribunals have disagreed with the assertion that a stable legal or business framework is part of FET. For instance, the *El Paso* Tribunal observed:

> ... if the often repeated formula to the effect that "the stability of the legal and business framework is an essential element of fair and equitable treatment" were true, legislation could never be changed: the mere enunciation of that proposition shows its irrelevance. Such a standard of behaviour, if strictly applied, is not realistic, nor is it the BITs' purpose that States guarantee that the economic and legal conditions in which investments take place will remain unaltered ad infinitum.[168]

There is truth in what the *El Paso* Tribunal said. In the first place, it is unthinkable that in order to attract foreign investment, any state would give up its regulatory power to make changes to its legal system. On this point, the *Continental Casualty* Tribunal shared the view of the *El Paso* Tribunal, explicitly stating:

> ... it would be unconscionable for a country to promise not to change its legislation as time and needs change, or even more to tie its hands by such a kind of stipulation in case a crisis of any type or origin arose. Such an implication as to stability in the BIT's Preamble would be contrary to an effective

---

166 *CMS, supra,* note 17, para. 274.
167 *LG&E, supra,* note 112, para. 124.
168 *El Paso Energy International Company v. Argentine Republic,* ICSID Case No. ARB/03/15, Award (October 31, 2011), para. 350.

interpretation of the Treaty; reliance on such an implication by a foreign investor would be misplaced and, indeed, unreasonable.[169]

Another point is that it is common sense that states need to modify their legal systems by adding, deleting and revising laws pursuant to the development of the world and domestic need. Third, taking into account the severity of the obligation, where such a commitment is made, it should be distinctly stipulated rather than merely mentioned in the generally vague preambles to BITs.

Tribunals are aware of the difficulties in strictly emphasizing stability. Those who support this position try to link the stabilization of the legal and business framework with the expectations of foreign investors. In *Eureko v. Poland*,[170] for instance, an *ad hoc* arbitration pursuant to the Netherlands–Poland BIT, during Poland's privatization process the claimant made an investment, through a Share Purchase Agreement ("SPA") in a leading Polish insurance group—PZU—as a minority shareholder. The claimant anticipated becoming the majority share-holder in PZU by way of a public offering, which was reflected in the addenda to the SPA. The public offering, however, never took place. The claimant contended that, *inter alia*, the respondent had violated the provisions of fair and equitable treatment. The *Eureko* Tribunal stated that:

> Eureko's investments, its contractual rights to an IPO, which would have led it to acquire majority control of PZU, have been, in the opinion of the Tribunal, unfairly and inequitably treated by the Council of Ministers and Minister of the State Treasury. Those organs of the RoP, consciously and overtly, breached the basic expectations of Eureko that are at the basis of its investment in PZU and were enshrined in the SPA, and, particularly, the First Addendum.[171]

Apparently the tribunal considered the expectations of the claimant, enshrined in contractual form, to be an important factor, as it was consequential to the respondent's privatization of the insurance sector.[172] The *Eureko* Tribunal apparently came to this conclusion without much detailed analysis of the grounds of the claimant's expectations. It also failed to explain, as other tribunals have done, the prerequisites for establishing an investor's expectations.

In practice, investors' expectations are also subject to certain limitations. In the first place, they must be legitimate and reasonable. In *EDF*, for instance, the tribunal said that it "shares the view expressed by other tribunals that one of the major

---

169 *Continental Casualty Company v. Argentine Republic* [hereinafter "*Continental Casualty*"], ICSID Case No. ARB/03/9, Award of September 5, 2008, para. 258.

170 *Eureko B.V. v. Republic of Poland*, Partial Award (August 19, 2005).

171 Ibid., para. 232.

172 The briefness of the *Eureko* Tribunal's reasoning, in addition to its lack of clarity, was criticized by Fietta; see Stephen Fietta, "Expropriation and the 'Fair and Equitable' Standard: The Developing Role of Investors' 'Expectations' in International Investment Arbitration," *Journal of International Arbitration*, Vol. 23(5), 2006, pp. 375–99, at 390.

components of the FET standard is the parties' legitimate and reasonable expectations with respect to the investment they have made."[173] Then the question becomes one of how to determine whether or not a given investor's expectations are legitimate and reasonable. The *El Paso* Tribunal observed that "the notion of 'legitimate expectations' is an objective concept, that it is the result of a balancing of interests and rights"[174] of both the investor and the host state.

The balancing approach was shared by the *Saluka* Tribunal, which said: "In order to determine whether frustration of the foreign investor's expectations was justified and reasonable, the host state's legitimate right subsequently to regulate domestic matters in the public interest must be taken into consideration as well."[175] In that case, Saluka Investment BV was created by its parent—Nomura Group, a major Japanese company—as an investment vehicle under the laws of the Netherlands. In late 1990s, Nomura entered into an agreement with the Czech Government for the purchase of substantial shares of one of the four largest Czech state-owned banks ("IPB") through privatization of the bank. Nomura then transferred the acquired shares to Saluka. Thereafter, the Czech Government adopted measures to assist three state-owned banks, including Československá Obchodní Banka A.S. ("ČSOB"), but not including IPB because the latter was privately owned.

Soon after the acquisition, the operations of IPB were questioned by the Czech National Bank ("CNB"), which made negative reports on it. By early 2000, IPB was in serious financial difficulties and started to negotiate with the Czech Government and ČSOB to find a solution. As no agreement could be reached to rescue IPB, the Czech Government placed it into forced administration and the Czech Securities Commission suspended the trading of IPB's shares in the market. Subsequently, the CNB approved the sale of IPB to ČSOB. The claimant contended that the respondent had breached its obligations in respect of fair and equitable treatment.

In assessing whether the respondent had breached these obligations, the *Saluka* Tribunal stated: "An investor's decision to make an investment is based on an assessment of the state of the law and the totality of the business environment at the time of the investment as well as on the investor's expectation that the conduct of the host state subsequent to the investment will be fair and equitable."[176] Therefore, in the tribunal's view, FET is closely tied to a foreign investor's legitimate expectations. The *Saluka* Tribunal even considered the investor's legitimate expectations to be the "dominant element" of the FET standard, pursuant to

173 *EDF (Services) Limited v. Romania*, ICSID Case No. ARB/05/13, Award (October 8, 2009), para. 216.
174 *El Paso, supra*, note 167, para. 356. The *El Paso* Tribunal commented that "legitimate expectations cannot be solely the subjective expectations of the investor, but have to correspond to the objective expectations that can be deduced from the circumstances and with due regard to the rights of the State;" ibid., para. 358.
175 *Saluka, supra*, note 48, para. 305.
176 Ibid., para. 301.

which the respondent had "an obligation to treat foreign investors so as to avoid the frustration of investors' legitimate and reasonable expectations."[177]

However, the *Saluka* Tribunal failed to elaborate in what ways a host state may frustrate the investor's legitimate expectations. In fact, it did not analyze the specific contents of FET at all. In its decision, the tribunal simply stated that IPB did not differ "sufficiently drastically from the other Big Four banks with regard to the risks involved in its lending policies"[178] and hence it should have been treated equally with the latter insofar as provision of state aid is concerned. The *Saluka* Tribunal seemed to put much emphasis on what it considered to be the discriminatory effect of the respondent's conduct, stating that "the provision of State aid to specific firms or industries must not be discriminatory or unreasonably harmful for the foreign investor."[179] It did not, however, conduct a detailed analysis of the similarities of IPB and other banks. For instance, IPB was a private bank with foreign investment, whilst the comparator banks were state-owned. Does the host state have the same obligations toward the entities in which it holds shares and private entities, the success of which will not benefit the state directly (as the state is not the owner)? To impose an obligation on the host state in relation to provision of state aid to foreign investors has gone beyond "legitimate expectations," to say the least. Such a conclusion is actually contrary to the *Saluka* Tribunal's announced opinion that the host State's legitimate rights should also be protected, notwithstanding that "consistency, transparency, even-handedness and non-discrimination"[180] are the essential requirements that can legitimately be expected by foreign investors.

Investors' expectations may also be affected by serious negligence on the part of the host government, although this is likely to happen only in very rare cases. In *PSEG v. Turkey*,[181] the claimants were PSEG Global, Inc. ("PSEG"), the North American Coal Corporation—both US companies—and Konya Ilgin Elektrik Üretim ve Ticaret Limited Sirketi, companies that had made investments in the generation of electricity in Turkey when the country privatized its energy sector in the 1980s. The investment was in the form of Build-Operate-Transfer ("BOT") projects. Two years after the investment was made, Turkey's Constitutional Court invalidated a law concerning it because, in its view, the BOT projects constituted a public service that had to be organized under a concession contract. A new law was also enacted, allowing parties to existing concession contracts to convert their instruments to private law contracts and submit disputes to domestic or

---

177 Ibid., para. 302.
178 Ibid., para. 320.
179 Ibid., para. 446.
180 In this respect, the *Saluka* Tribunal stated that "a foreign investor protected by the Treaty may in any case properly expect that the [Government] implements its policies bona fide by conduct that is, as far as it affects the investor's investment, reasonably justifiable by public policies and that such conduct does not violate the requirements of consistency, transparency, even-handedness and non-discrimination;" ibid., para. 307.
181 *PSEG Global Inc. and Konya Ilgin v. Republic of Turkey*, ICSID Case No. ARB/02/05, Award (January 19, 2007).

international arbitration.[182] Subsequently, the investment structure was modified and the claimants and the respondent renegotiated the contracts. The claimants considered that during this process, the respondent showed a change of mind about the project and alleged that its actions and omissions had amounted to a breach of FET.

The *PSEG* Tribunal decided that the respondent had breached its obligations relating to FET by its negligence in handling negotiations with the claimants, saying:

> The fact that key points of disagreement went unanswered and were not disclosed in a timely manner, that silence was kept when there was evidence of such persisting and aggravating disagreement, that important communications were never looked at, and that there was a systematic attitude not to address the need to put an end to negotiations that were leading nowhere, are all manifestations of serious administrative negligence and inconsistency.[183]

Other acts and omissions included demands for renegotiation that went far beyond the purpose required by law and inconsistencies in administration.[184] The *PSEG* decision is rather unique in that the host state's behavior really went far beyond what could have been expected by a reasonable foreign investor. In a normal business environment, no foreign investor would expect that its contract with the host state would be declared invalid by the courts of the host state.

The *PSEG* Tribunal considered that the "aggregate of the situations … raise the question of the need to ensure a stable and predictable business environment for investors to operate in, as required" by the Turkey–United States BIT.[185] In its view, "[s]tability cannot exist in a situation where the law kept changing continuously and endlessly, as did its interpretation and implementation."[186] In this connection, the *PSEG* Tribunal did not consider the respondent's general policy of encouraging foreign investment a promise to guarantee the success of the investment project of the claimant.[187] The underlying premise here is that the change in policy should not be regarded as affecting the stability of the investment environment.

Despite the general trend in upholding stability as a component of FET, using investors' legitimate and reasonable expectations as the standard for assessing if the obligation of stability has been violated is not without disagreements. On this matter, the *CMS ad hoc* annulment Committee opined that "[a]lthough legitimate expectations might arise by reason of a course of dealing between the investor and the host state, these are not, as such, legal obligations, though they may be relevant to the application of the fair and equitable treatment clause contained in

182 Ibid., para. 15.
183 Ibid., para. 246.
184 Ibid., paras. 247–50.
185 Ibid., para. 253.
186 Ibid., para. 254.
187 Ibid., para. 243.

the BIT."[188] It should be noted that the *ad hoc* Committee's view is not only contrary to that of the *CMS* Tribunal but also to the opinion put forth by a number of other tribunals.

The question as to whether or not an investor's expectation is a legal obligation depends on the representations made by the host government and the reliance on such representations by the foreign investor. Where a statement is general in nature, it may not trigger legal obligations, as it is commonly regarded as a policy statement. At the same time, where a communication or statement amounts to a specific commitment, the host government must be held liable for breaching it. In these circumstances, what may constitute a legitimate and reasonable expectation must take into account all relevant factors "in the light of the circumstances of each case."[189]

As the *El Paso* Tribunal noted, all investors want to maximize their benefits, and in order to achieve this purpose, they must rely on a number of factors—economic and legal—but not all of their expectations in this regard can "be considered legitimate and reasonable."[190] In ascertaining whether an expectation is legitimate and reasonable, a host government's promise must be distinguished from other communications, although both may have been relied upon by a foreign investor.

Investors are entitled to expect host states to provide a stable framework for their investment. At the same time, honesty and good faith are essential elements of business activities, including the relations between investors and host states. If an investor makes a false representation or fails to make a full disclosure when it is required by the host state to provide further information or even to make a commitment, then the investor is not entitled to rely on the representations of the host state. In these circumstances, any expectation of the investor cannot be considered to be legitimate or reasonable. In *Thunderbird v. Mexico*,[191] the claimant was in the business of operating gaming facilities and, before making its investment, consulted lawyers in Mexico about setting up its business in the country. However, it was not given any assurance by them of "the certainty necessary to proceed with its proposed operations in Mexico."[192] It nevertheless entered into several contracts for operating gaming facilities. The claimant then wrote to the Director General de Gobierno de la Secretaria de Gobernación ("SEGOB") concerning its proposed gaming operations in Mexico (the "*Solicitud*").[193] The Director General of Government of SEGOB issued a formal response to Thunderbird's *Solicitud* (the "*Oficio*"), in which it stated that "the Federal Law of Games and Sweepstakes of Mexico prohibits gambling and luck related games within the Mexican territory" and that as the claimant's machines were "recreational video game devices

---

188   *CMS* Annulment Committee Decision, *supra*, note 76, para. 89.
189   See *Noble Ventures, Inc. v. Romania* [hereinafter "*Noble Ventures*"], ICSID Case No. ARB/01/11, Award of October 12, 2005, para. 185.
190   *El Paso, supra*, note 167, para. 355.
191   *International Thunderbird Gaming Corporation v. Mexico*, UNCITRAL (NAFTA), Arbitration Award (January 26, 2006).
192   Ibid., para. 43.
193   Ibid., para. 50.

for purposes of enjoyment and entertainment of its users, with the possibility of obtaining a prize, without the intervention of luck or gambling, but rather the user's ability and skillfulness," the host government was "not able to prohibit [their] use."[194] After the investment was made by setting up the gambling facilities, there was a change of government, whereupon the SEGOB started to close down the facilities, which triggered the claimant's allegation of the respondent's breach of the FET obligations under Article 1105 of the NAFTA.

The claimant argued that it had "reasonably relied, to its detriment, upon the assurances provided by SEGOB in the *Oficio*."[195] The *Thunderbird* Tribunal, whilst confirming that the contracting parties of NAFTA had an obligation to honour the legitimate expectations of foreign investors, stated:

> The threshold for legitimate expectations may vary depending on the nature of the violation alleged under the NAFTA and the circumstances of the case. Whatever standard is applied in the present case however – be it the broadest or the narrowest – the Tribunal does not find that the *Oficio* generated a legitimate expectation upon which EDM could reasonably rely in operating its machines in Mexico.[196]

The *Thunderbird* Tribunal observed that the information provided by the claimant in its *Solicitud* was incomplete and inaccurate. Because it was the tribunal's view that the claimant was aware that gambling was illegal under Mexican law before making the investment and still chose to make its investment in gambling, it hence concluded that the *Oficio* could not have "generated a legitimate expectation upon which [the Claimant] could reasonably rely in operating its machines in Mexico."[197] This decision was not surprising, as the *Oficio* was based on misrepresentations by the claimant.

However, the tribunal did not link its discussion, at least not as much as it should have, with Article 1105 of the NAFTA on FET. For instance, in order to establish legitimate expectations, an investor must prove that it relied on the representations of the host state. In most cases, the foreign investors concerned, unlike Thunderbird, do not need to make a disclosure of their intended investment and there can therefore be no question of incomplete or unfaithful disclosure of information on their part. The *Thunderbird* case is quite unusual insofar as the implementation of FET is concerned. It would have made a bigger impact had the *Thunderbird* Tribunal elaborated its decision requiring the foreign investor to act in

---

194 Ibid., para. 55.
195 Ibid., para. 146.
196 Ibid., para. 148.
197 Ibid., paras. 164 and 166. One commentator has stated that any prior knowledge that an investor ought to have should mitigate against a finding of a violation of the FET obligation; see P. Muchilinski, "'Caveat Investor'? The Relevance of the Conduct of the Investor under the Fair and Equitable Treatment Standard," 55 *ICLQ* 527, 2006, at 542.

good faith when invoking the legitimate expectations principle,[198] notwithstand-ing that this is already a well-established principle in international investment law.

As mentioned earlier, in practice it is unrealistic to require any state not to make changes to its system in the face of the frequent changes in the modern world. In this highly globalized world, it is unthinkable that a general stabilization require-ment can be legitimately expected by foreign investors.[199] This was confirmed by the Permanent Court of International Justice ("PCIJ"), whose 80-year-old dictum in the *Oscar Chinn* case still rings true today:

> No enterprise—least of all a commercial or transport enterprise, the success of which is dependent on the fluctuating level of prices and rates—can escape from the changes and hazards resulting from general economic conditions. Some industries may be able to make large profits during a period of general prosperity, or else by taking advantage of a treaty of commerce or of an alteration in customs duties; but they are also exposed to the danger of ruin or extinction if circumstances change.[200]

What the PCIJ was trying to explain is that the business environment changes all the time and that it is unfeasible for any entity to expect an unchanged or unchanging environment. This, of course, does not address the issue of treaty obligations, which must often be deduced from arbitration practice.

Some investment tribunals have taken the approach in regard to the stabiliza-tion clause that not only the interests or expectations of foreign investors but also those of the host state must be taken into account. In other words, the interests and rights of both foreign investors and the host state should be balanced rather than protection being provided merely to the foreign investor. In this connection, the *Parkerings* Tribunal took the view that:

> It is each State's undeniable right and privilege to exercise its sovereign legis-lative power. A State has the right to enact, modify or cancel a law at its own discretion. Save for the existence of an agreement, in the form of a stabiliza-tion clause or otherwise, there is nothing objectionable about the amendment brought to the regulatory framework existing at the time an investor made its investment.[201]

---

198 In this regard, Wälde's Separate Opinion gave a detailed account of the legitimate expectations principle as it relates to FET. In particular, he said: "One can observe over the last years a signifi-cant growth in the role and scope of the legitimate expectation principle, from an earlier function as a subsidiary interpretative principle to reinforce a particular interpretative approach chosen, to its current role as a self-standing subcategory and independent basis for a claim under the 'fair and equitable standard' as under Art. 1105 of the NAFTA." See *Thunderbird v. Mexico*, Separate Opinion of Thomas Wälde, para. 37.

199 See Schreuer, *supra*, note 69, at 374.

200 *Oscar Chinn (United Kingdom v. Belgium)* [hereinafter "*Oscar Chinn*"], Judgment of December 12, 1934, 1934 *P.C.I.J. Rep.*, Series A/B, No. 63, p. 88.

201 *Parkerings*, *supra*, note 109, para. 332.

This view was shared by the *El Paso* Tribunal, which also explicitly criticized the decisions in *CMS* and *LG&E* by stating that in those two cases:

> … the reference to the Preamble said that its object and purpose was to maintain "a stable framework for investment and maximum effective use of economic resources;" however, in determining what these purposes implied for the interpretation of FET, the tribunals in these two cases only retained the first purpose, in order to conclude that a stable legal and business environment is an essential element of fair and equitable treatment, without taking into account the goal that any State has to pursue as well, which is to guarantee to its population maximum effective use of its economic resources.[202]

In any event, it seems that the jurisprudence of investment law in general agrees that unless there are specific commitments made by the host state, the stabilization clause does not have the effect of "freezing of the legal system or the disappearance of the regulatory power of the State."[203] However, how the interests of foreign investors and the host state can be balanced or on what conditions a host state is required not to modify its laws and policies must be decided on a case-by-case basis.

Insofar as protection of the investor's interests is concerned, a distinction must be made between political statements and specific commitments. In order to be a specific commitment, the communication must be specific and have a precise object.[204] Whilst a general communication may not be considered to be a specific commitment, its reiteration, even in different forms, could amount to a specific commitment if the object and purpose of the statement "is to give the investor a guarantee on which it can justifiably rely."[205] By its nature, a specific commitment is not communicated by legislation or policy statements that are generally applicable. A contract and a letter of intent have been considered to be able to convey a specific commitment, as has a person-to-person meeting.[206] Other examples, such as a license, a grant or a promise made by the government, may also lead to specific commitments.[207]

Investors' expectations may also be affected by their awareness of the risks when an investment is made. The *Methanex* decision is most illustrative on this point. The tribunal in that case pointed out:

---

202 *El Paso, supra*, note 167, para. 369.
203 See *Enron Corporation and Ponderosa Assets L.P. v. Argentine Republic*, ICSID Case No. ARB/01/3, Award (May 22, 2007), para. 261. Also, in *El Paso*, the tribunal considered that "FET cannot be designed to ensure the immutability of the legal order, the economic world and the social universe;" *El Paso*, ibid., para. 368.
204 *El Paso*, ibid., para. 377.
205 Id.
206 Ibid., para. 376.
207 In this regard, the *Continental Casualty* Tribunal disregarded all political statements and general legislative statements as not being capable of conveying specific commitments. In its view, even contractual undertakings have to be scrutinized before determining that they amount to specific commitments. See *Continental Casualty, supra*, note 168, para. 261.

Methanex entered a political economy in which it was widely known, if not notorious, that governmental environmental and health protection institutions at the federal and state level, operating under the vigilant eyes of the media, interested corporations, non-governmental organizations and a politically active electorate, continuously monitored the use and impact of chemical compounds and commonly prohibited or restricted the use of some of those compounds for environmental and/or health reasons. Indeed, the very market for MTBE in the United States was the result of precisely this regulatory process. Methanex appreciated that the process of regulation in the United States involved wide participation of industry groups, non-governmental organizations, academics and other individuals, many of these actors deploying lobbyists. Methanex itself deployed lobbyists. Mr. Wright, Methanex's witness, described himself as the government relations officer of the company … Methanex entered the United States market aware of and actively participating in this process. It did not enter the United States market because of special representations made to it.[208]

Thus, as it was well aware of the risks involved but still made an investment in the market, the claimant could not later on claim that its legitimate and reasonable expectation was frustrated. The underpinning logic is that the riskier a market is, the more profits that can be expected. By choosing a riskier market, a foreign investor does so at his own peril. The *Generation Ukraine* Tribunal adopted a similar position, saying that "[t]he Claimant was attracted to the Ukraine because of the possibility of earning a rate of return on its capital in significant excess to the other investment opportunities in more developed economies."[209] In the view of that tribunal, as the claimant was aware of the prospects and potential pitfalls of the Ukrainian market when it made its investment, it had to bear the consequences. In such cases, the investor's expectations, if any, can be neither legitimate nor reasonable.[210]

In conclusion, on the issue of applying the stabilization clause, the essential issues are: (1) whether host states are obliged not to change their laws or modify their legal systems because there is a reference to maintaining a stable framework for foreign investors in the preamble of BITs; (2) determination of investors' legitimate and reasonable expectations; and (3) the relationship between the stabilization clause and investors' legitimate and reasonable expectations. The

---

208　*Methanex v. United States*, UNCITRAL (NAFTA), Final Award (August 3. 2005), para. 9 of Part IV, ch D.

209　*Generation Ukraine Inc. v. Ukraine*, ICSID Case No. ARB/00/9, Award of September 16, 2003, para. 20.37.

210　The *Iran–US Claims* Tribunal took a similar approach in its decision in *Starrett Housing*, saying that "investors in Iran, like investors in all other countries, have to assume a risk that the country might experience strikes, lock-outs, disturbances, changes of the economic and political system and even revolution. That any of these risks materialized does not necessarily mean that property rights affected by such events can be deemed to have been taken." See *Starrett Housing Corporation v. Islamic Republic of Iran*, 4 *Iran–U.S. Cl. Trib. Rep.* 122, 154 (1983), 156.

jurisprudence shows that even though some tribunals have decided in favor of strictly applying the stabilization clause—allowing no changes to the applicable laws—the majority acknowledges the need for host states to exercise their regulatory powers when facing an ever-changing world.[211] Many of these tribunals are, at the same time, of the view that where a host state has made a specific commitment and the investor relied on it, the stabilization clause should come into play. In fact, where a specific commitment is made, such as one that is incorporated into a contract, the foreign investor concerned can seek redress without relying on the obligation of FET.

Jurisprudence on the relationship between the stabilization clause and investors' expectations is most diversified. The most controversial issue is whether an investor's expectations and the interests of the host state should be balanced. In this regard, the *Lemire* Tribunal's decision is noteworthy and distinguishable from others.[212] Its position was that the interests of foreign investors should be "balanced against the legitimate right of Ukraine [the Respondent] to pass legislation and adopt measures for the protection of what as a sovereign it perceives to be its public interest."[213] In the *Lemire* Tribunal's view, the purpose of BITs—"the stimulation of foreign investment and of the accompanying flow of capital"—is not meant to be sought "in the abstract."[214] In other words, in assessing the objectives and purposes of BITs, not only foreign investors' interests and benefits but also those of nationals of both signatory countries—especially those of the host country—should be taken into account.[215]

Although some other tribunals, such as that in *AWG v. Argentina*,[216] have also touched upon the issue of balancing the interests of foreign investors and host states, only the *Lemire* Tribunal has emphasized the interests and benefits of nationals of the host state. International investment is intended to benefit both foreign investors and host countries. Accordingly, the law relating to international investment should protect the rights and interests of both investors and host countries. In resolving disputes, arbitral tribunals are therefore duty bound to look into the

211 Martin considers, however, that the current treaty arrangements regarding the stabilization commitment is not effective; see Antoine P. Martin, "Stability in Contemporary Investment Law: Reconsidering the Role and Shape of Contractual Commitments in Light of Recent Trends," *Manchester Journal of International Economic Law*, Vol. 10, Issue 1, 2013, pp. 38–58.

212 For instance, in *AWG v. Argentina*, the tribunal maintained that its finding of the respondent's breach of the FET obligations was not based solely on the investor's expectations. Yet it said: "It was the existence of such expectations created by host country laws, coupled with the act of investing their capital in reliance on them, and a subsequent, sudden change in those laws that led to a determination that the host country had not treated the investors fair and equitably." See *AWG v. Argentina*, UNCITRAL, Decision on Liability (July 30, 2010), para. 226.

213 *Lemire v. Ukraine, supra*, note 73, para. 273.

214 Ibid., paras. 272 and 273.

215 Ibid., para. 273.

216 The *AWG* Tribunal made a brief mention of the need to "balance the legitimate and reasonable expectations of the Claimants with Argentina's right to regulate the provision of a vital public service;" see *AWG v. Argentina, supra*, note 211, para. 336. However, it went no further in elaborating the significance of the respondent's right to regulate—for what purpose and for whose benefit.

rights of both parties. Only by doing so may BITs be made to serve the purposes for which they are designed.

In any event, in interpreting FET in relation to stabilization of the business and legal environment of the host state, as the *TECO* Tribunal decided, unless there is a stabilization clause, a host state may freely amend its laws and regulations even where that may have an impact on foreign investors. However, where a change to the legal framework is made "in bad faith or with the intent to deprive the investor of the benefits of its investment," the host state must bear international responsibilities.[217] This is a quite balanced view.

At the same time, regarding investors' expectations, both the interests of investors and those of the host state should be taken into account. Whilst almost all tribunals recognize the need for host states to introduce new laws and modify their existing laws in a world of change, actions which may affect the business environment, the question is the consequence of such changes. In other words, when there is a need for the host state to change the environment, is it liable to provide compensation to foreign investors who may be adversely affected by that change? The consequence of those decisions favoring a broad approach is to hold host states liable for a breach of treaty obligations when any needed change in the law has a negative impact on foreign investors. Considering the criticisms that have been made of the broad approach, perhaps the international community should consider an alternative approach, wherein host states would be given the discretion to change their laws but, at the same time, would have the obligation to pay compensation for losses suffered by foreign investors.

II. Full protection and security

The obligation to provide "full protection and security" ("FPS") is found in contemporary BITs and the investment chapters of FTAs. Very often, the FPS standard is stipulated together with that of FET. Treaty terms may differ in referring to the obligation as "full protection and security," "constant protection and security," "protection and security" or "legal protection and security." It is said that the origin of FPS, albeit in varying forms, can be traced back to the 19th and early 20th centuries in the US Friendship, Commerce and Navigation ("FCN") treaties.[218] With the growing influence of the United States after World War II, the US treaty practice was soon adopted by most modern BITs and FTAs and, hence, FPS has become a treaty standard of treatment relating to foreign investments and

---

217 *TECO, supra,* note 97, para. 629.
218 K. Vandevelde, "The Bilateral Investment Treaty Program of the United States," 21 *Cornell Int'l L.J.* 203, 1988, at 204. According to one study, among 22 commercial treaties concluded by the United States before 1920, 14 contained reference to "special protection" and the remaining eight specified "full and perfect protection" of private property; see Robert R. Wilson, "Property-protection Provisions in United States Commercial Treaties," 45 *Am. J. Int'l L.* 84, 1951, at 92–96. See also *Suez, Sociedad General de Aguas de Barcelona S.A., and Vivendi Universal S.A. v. Argentine Republic,* ICSID Case No. ARB/03/19; and *AWG, supra,* note 211, para. 161.

investors. There is no consensus in arbitration practice on its interpretation and application, however.

In general, positions taken by investment treaty arbitration tribunals can be divided into narrow and broad approaches, of which the narrow approach is more in line with the traditional view of international law on the issue. Insofar as the traditional view is concerned, the judgment by the International Court of Justice in *ELSI*[219] is considered an authoritative pronouncement of the position of customary international law. In that case, the United States brought a claim against Italy for violating the FCN treaty between the two countries under which the contracting parties had assumed an obligation to provide investors of the other party "the most constant protection and security." The United States contended that the requisitioning of a US investor's factory by the Mayor of Palermo had constituted a violation of Article V(1) of the FCN. The ICJ ruled that: "[t]he reference in Article V to the provision of 'constant protection and security' cannot be construed as the giving of a warranty that property shall never in any circumstances be occupied or disturbed."[220] In other words, the host state's obligation is confined to providing protection and security from physical interruption. This may involve preventive measures and remedial measures after an interruption of or damage to foreign investments—a standard of due diligence.[221]

Early decisions of investment arbitration tribunals followed the ruling of the ICJ. An example is *AAPL v. Sri Lanka*,[222] in which the Sri Lanka–United Kingdom BIT provided: "Investment of nationals and companies of either Party shall at all times be accorded fair and equitable treatment and shall enjoy protection and security in the territory of the other Party." The *AAPL* Tribunal observed that "similar expressions, or even stronger wordings like the 'most constant protection', were utilized since last century in a number of bilateral treaties concluded to encourage the flow of international economic exchanges and to provide the citizens and national companies established on the territory of the other Contracting Party with adequate treatment for them as well as to their property,"[223] but such a promise was not an "absolute obligation which guarantees that no damages will be suffered, in the sense that any violation thereof creates automatically a 'strict liability' on behalf of the host State."[224] By citing with approval Freeman's statement that "[t]he State into which an alien has entered ... is not an insurer or a guarantor of his security ... [and i]t does not, and could hardly be asked to, accept

219 *Case Concerning Elettronica Sicula S.p.A. (ELSI)*, *(U.S. v. Italy)*, Judgment of July 20, 1989, *I.C.J. Reports* (1989), 15; available at: http://www.icj-cij.org/docket/index.php?p1=3&p2=3&case=76&code=elsi&p3=4.

220 Ibid., para. 108, at 65.

221 According to the often cited words of Freeman: "The 'due diligence' is nothing more nor less than the reasonable measures of prevention which a well-administered government could be expected to exercise under similar circumstances." See A. V. Freeman, *Responsibility of States for the Unlawful Acts of Their Armed Forces*, 88 Recueil des Cours 261, 1956.

222 *Asian Agricultural Products Ltd. (AAPL) v. Republic of Sri Lanka*, ICSID Case No. ARB/87/3, Final Award (June 27, 1990).

223 Ibid., para. 47.

224 Ibid., para. 48.

an absolute responsibility for all injuries to foreigners,"[225] the *AAPL* Tribunal concluded that "the addition of words like 'constant' or 'full' to strengthen the required standards of 'protection and security' could justifiably indicate" a due diligence standard higher than that required by the minimum standard of international law.[226] This standard has been adopted by a number of subsequent tribunals.

In *Enron*, for instance, the tribunal considered that the words "full protection and security" had a limited scope, noting that "there might be cases where a broader interpretation could be justified, but then it becomes difficult to distinguish such situation from one resulting in the breach of fair and equitable treatment, and even from some form of expropriation."[227] In *Saluka*,[228] the Czech Republic–Netherlands BIT promised investors "full security and protection." The respondent, however, took measures to stop trading in the claimant's securities. In determining that the respondent did not violate the FPS obligation, the tribunal stated: "The practice of arbitral tribunals seems to indicate however that the 'full protection and security clause' is not meant to cover just any kind of impairment of an investor's investment but to protect more specifically the physical integrity of an investment against interference by the use of force."[229] The tribunal in *El Paso* likewise regarded the standard of FPS as "no more than the traditional obligation provided for those cases in which the acts challenged may not in themselves be attributed to the Government, but to a third party."[230] Other cases that have adopted a similar rationale include *BG v. Argentina, PSEG v. Turkey, Rumeli v. Kazakhstan* and *Waguih v. Egypt*.[231]

The above cases have the following in common. In the first place, they confine the FPS standard to physical protection and security. Second, they consider that the standard requires vigilance and care, which is composed of both prevention and remediation—that is, the host state has an obligation to ensure that no physical harm is done to foreign investments and investors and, when harm is done, the host state is obliged to take remedial measures. Third, as Brownlie pointed out, none of them has given a definition of due diligence.[232] It is true that it may not be possible for tribunals to formulate a generally acceptable definition of due dili-

---

225 Alwyn V. Freeman, *Responsibility of States for Unlawful Acts of Their Armed Forces*, Sijthoff, Leiden, 1957, p. 14.
226 *AAPL, supra*, note 221, para. 50.
227 *Enron, supra*, note 202, para. 286.
228 *Saluka, supra*, note 48.
229 Ibid., para. 484.
230 *El Paso, supra*, note 167, para. 522.
231 *BG Group Plc. v. Republic of Argentina*, UNCITRAL, Final Award (December 24, 2007), paras. 323–28; *PSEG, supra*, note 180, paras. 258–59; *Rumeli Telekom A.S. and Telsim Mobil Telekomikasyon Hizmetleri A.S. v. Republic of Kazakhstan*, ICSID Case No. ARB/05/16, Award (July 29, 2008), para. 669; and *Waguih Elie George Siag & Clorinda Vecchi v. Arab Republic of Egypt*, ICSID Case No. ARB/05/15, Award (June 1, 2009), para. 447.
232 Brownlie, however, also observed that "obviously no very dogmatic definition would be appropriate, since what is involved is a standard which will vary according to the circumstances;" see I. Brownlie, *Principles of Public International Law*, 4th ed., OUP, 1990, at 454.

gence for all cases, as in each case this should be decided by taking into account all of the circumstances. Yet there should be a generally recognized standard of duty of care that a host state is obliged to follow. Any attempt at unifying the definition of the standard will contribute to its development in international investment law.

In addition to the narrow or traditional approach, there are other tribunals that have adopted a wider scope of FPS in practice. The earliest investment arbitration case relating to FPS, although with some variations, is *AMT v. Zaire*,[233] which involved interpreting Article 11(4) of the Zaire–United States BIT, which provided: "Investment of nationals and companies of either Party shall at all times be accorded fair and equitable treatment and shall enjoy protection and security in the territory of the other party."[234] The *AMT* Tribunal ruled that "the obligation incumbent on [the host state] is an obligation of vigilance, in the sense that [the host state] shall take all measures necessary to ensure the full enjoyment of protection and security of its investment and should not be permitted to invoke its own legislation to detract from any such obligation."[235] It also considered that the host state had an obligation to "show that it has taken all measures of precaution to protect the investment of [the foreign investor] on its territory. … It is thus an objective obligation which must not be inferior to the minimum standard of vigilance and care required by international law."[236] This interpretation has ever since become the standard to be followed by those favoring a broad scope to the definition and contents of FPS, although the minimum standard of vigilance and care established by the *AMT* Tribunal has seldom been mentioned by subsequent tribunals.

In *CME v. Czech Republic*, the tribunal expanded the scope of FPS, stating: "The host State is obligated to ensure that neither by amendment of its laws nor by actions of its administrative bodies is the agreed and approved security and protection of the foreign investor's investment withdrawn or devalued."[237] The precedential effect of the *CME* decision is, however, reduced by the fact, to be discussed in detail later, that the tribunal did not conduct a systematic analysis, as well as in light of the diametrically opposed views of the *Lauder* Tribunal and the dissenting opinion in the *CME* case itself.[238]

The *Azurix* and *Biwater* Tribunals also adopted the broad approach in their interpretation of the FPS standard. The *Azurix* Tribunal placed emphasis on the

---

233 *American Manufacturing and Trading, Inc. v. Republic of Zaire*, ICSID Case No. ARB/93/1, Award (February 21, 1997).

234 Ibid., para. 604.

235 Ibid., para. 605.

236 Id.

237 *CME Czech Republic BV (The Netherlands) v. Czech Republic*, UNCITRAL, Partial Award (September 13, 2001), para. 613.

238 The *Lauder* Tribunal concluded that "none of the facts alleged by the Claimants constitutes a violation by the Respondent of the obligation to provide full protection and security under the Treaty;" see *Ronald S. Lauder v. Czech Republic*, UNCITRAL Arbitration, Final Award (September 2001, para. 309. See also *CME Czech Republic BV (The Netherlands) v. Czech Republic*, UNCITRAL, Dissenting opinion of the Arbitrator JUDr Jaroslav Hándl against the Partial Arbitration Award (September 13, 2001).

word "full" and decided that "when the terms 'protection and security' are qualified by full and no other adjective or explanation, they extend, in their ordinary
meaning, the content of this standard beyond physical security."[239] The tribunal
in *Biwater* viewed the FPS standard as implying "a State's guarantee of stability
in a secure environment, both [sic] physical, commercial and legal."[240] As the
Biwater Tribunal considered it proper to extend the FPS standard to provision of
a secure investment environment, it considered that the standard is not "limited
to a State's failure to prevent actions by third parties, but also extends to actions
by organs and representatives of the State itself."[241] In a way, the *Biwater* decision
is in line with that in *AMT*. "Actions" mentioned in the *Biwater* decision certainly
include legislation and other government measures. In any event, both *Azurix* and
Biwater extended the FPS standard to also include the protection and security of
the investment environment—a subject matter under FET. Thus, the distinction
between FPS and FET standards has become blurred, precisely as was noted by
the *Enron* Tribunal.[242]

In *Siemens*,[243] the applicable BIT stipulates the FPS standard as "legal security
and protection." The tribunal in that case agreed on the approach that "full protection and security is wider than 'physical' protection and security." The reasons
given by the tribunal are:

> It is difficult to understand how the physical security of an intangible asset
> would be achieved. In the instant case, "security" is qualified by "legal." In its
> ordinary meaning "legal security" has been defined as "the quality of the legal
> system which implies certainty in its norms and, consequently, their foresee-
> able application." It is clear that in the context of this meaning the Treaty
> refers to security that it [sic] is not physical. In fact, one may question given
> the qualification of the term "security," whether the Treaty covers physical
> security at all. Arguably it could be considered to be included under "full
> protection," but that is not an issue in these proceedings.[244]

Based on the above understanding, the *Siemens* Tribunal found that Argentina's
"initiation of the renegotiation of the contract for the sole purpose of reducing its
costs, unsupported by any declaration of public interest, affected the legal security
of Siemens' investment"[245] and thus constituted a violation of FPS. The finding
in *Siemens*, like those of other tribunals in recent cases in which the adjective "full"
is used, was based on the ground of the word "legal." Whilst it is true that "legal
security" may have a wider coverage than physical security, it can hardly be true

---

239 *Azurix, supra*, note 46, para. 408.
240 *Biwater Gauff (Tanzania) Ltd. v. United Republic of Tanzania*, ICSID Case No. ARB/05/22, Award
      (July 24, 2008), para. 729.
241 Ibid., para. 730.
242 *Enron, supra*, note 202, para. 286.
243 *Siemens, supra*, note 111.
244 Ibid., para. 303 (footnote omitted).
245 Ibid., para. 308.

that it is not related to physical security. In fact, even if the proposition of the *Siemens* Tribunal that legal security is defined as "the quality of the legal system" is to be accepted, physical security is still covered, as without the guarantee of the legal system no question relating to physical security can be fairly ascertained. In other words, the legal system serves as the basis for the provision and assurance of physical security.

In a way, the award in the *Wena Hotels* case[246] is clear-cut, although it decided that the host state had an obligation to take preventive measures. The *Wena Hotels* Tribunal, in making its decision, did not distinguish FPS from the FET standard, holding that Egypt had violated its obligation to accord Wena's investment "fair and equitable treatment" and "full protection and security." It held that:

> Although it is not clear that Egyptian officials other than officials of EHC directly participated in the April 1, 1991 seizures, there is substantial evidence that Egypt was aware of EHC's intentions to seize the hotels and took no actions to prevent EHC from doing so. Moreover, once the seizures occurred, both the police and the Ministry of Tourism took no immediate action to restore the hotels promptly to Wena's control. Finally, Egypt never imposed substantial sanctions on EHC or its senior officials, suggesting Egypt's approval of EHC's actions.[247]

Thus, according to the *Wena Hotels* decision, under the FPS standard, the host state has an obligation not only to prevent any attacks on foreign investments but also to take remedial measures subsequent to such attacks. In the *Wena Hotels* case, the foreign investor's investment was seized by third parties and the host state was aware of the potential seizure. Yet, it took no action to prevent that from happening. It was equally important that the Egyptian Government took no remedial measures to punish those involved in the seizure. In this case, even according to the traditional and narrow interpretation of FPS, a violation was obvious. It is therefore not surprising that this decision was reached.

In the more recent consolidated cases of *AWG v. Argentina* and *Suez and Vivendi v. Argentina*, three BITs between Argentina and France, Spain, and the United Kingdom were at issue. The Argentina–Spain and Argentina–United Kingdom BITs refer only to "protection" and "protect" without the qualifying word "full" or "fully," whilst the Argentina–France BIT states that investors shall be "fully protected."[248] The claimants understandably relied on the broad interpretation of FPS and contended that in withdrawing certain alleged guarantees made to the concessionaire and its investors, Argentina had withdrawn "the legal protection and security previously granted to an investment"[249] and thus violated

---

246 *Wena Hotels Limited v. Arab Republic of Egypt*, ICSID Case No. ARB/98/4, Award (December 8, 2000).

247 Ibid., para. 84.

248 *AWG, supra*, note 211, para. 168 (in the original French: "*d'une protection et d'une sécurité pleines et entières;*" Article 5.1 of the BIT).

249 Ibid., para. 160.

the FPS provisions, which they maintained included protection against actions that the respondent itself "might take in the exercise of its legal and regulatory authority."[250] The *AMT* Tribunal observed that "under all the applicable BITs, Argentina is obliged to exercise due diligence to protect investors and investments primarily from physical injury."[251] This adherence to the narrow approach was reached after the tribunal considered the specific language of the treaties, the evolution in interpreting the FPS standard by other tribunals and the historical development of the standard under international law. This conclusion could adequately resolve the issue relating to the two BITs between Argentina and the United Kingdom and Spain, as they do not contain the word "full" or "fully," but not entirely that pursuant to the BIT with France, which requires "full and complete" FPS treatment.

The *AWG* Tribunal noted that the Argentina–France BIT provided that FPS was to be provided "in accordance with the principle of just and equitable treatment mentioned in Article 3 of this Accord" and that, accordingly, any interpretation of the FPS standard in this case would depend upon "the interplay and scope of the two standards."[252] Furthermore, it observed that in the Argentina–France BIT, the FET standard and the FPS standard were stipulated in two distinct articles and accordingly concluded that the parties must have intended the two standards to be distinctive from each other.[253] The implication of this interpretation, the tribunal said, is that whilst the FET provisions cover the investment environment, the FPS standard's primary purpose must be to "protect investment from physical harm."[254]

With regard to whether the FET standard and the FPS standard might overlap, the *AWG* Tribunal expressed its opinion that "the concept of full protection and security is included within the concept of fair and equitable treatment, but that the scope of full protection and security is narrower than the fair and equitable treatment."[255] As such, where an action or omission of the host state amounts to a violation of FPS, that would at the same time constitute a breach of FET. Yet a violation of FET may not necessarily constitute a breach of FPS.[256] In this regard, the *AWG* case has made an important contribution to the development of international investment law.

In conclusion, traditionally investment arbitration tribunals have considered the FPS standard to be confined to the physical security of investors and their investments. Recent arbitration decisions can be categorized into narrow and broad groups, with the latter expanding the traditional understanding of FPS, by relying on the word "full" or "legal," to include many of the areas covered

250 Id.
251 Ibid., para. 179.
252 Ibid., para. 170.
253 Ibid., para. 172.
254 Ibid., para. 173.
255 Ibid., para. 171.
256 Id.

by FET.[257] The effect of the jurisprudence has been correctly summarized by an UNCTAD report relating to FPS that said: "[W]hile not an obligation of result, an obligation of good faith efforts to protect the foreign-owned property has been established by these recent cases, without special regard for the resources available to do so."[258] The end result is that more and more tribunals favor expanding the FPS standard to include the stability of the political, legal, and business environment and thus to overlap with the scope of FET. Very few tribunals, however, have tried to resolve this unsatisfactory overlapping—the *AWG* Tribunal serves as an exception. It is, however, very important to recognize the difficulty that the overlapping of the two standards brought about by the broad approach of interpretation of the FPS standard has introduced and to try to work out a solution. The *AWG* decision points in the right direction on this matter.

III. The umbrella clause

Many contemporary BITs and investment chapters of FTAs contain an umbrella clause—a reflection of the principle of *pacta sunt servanda*.[259] According to Sinclair, these umbrella clauses can be traced to proposals of Elihu Lauterpacht in connection with legal advice he gave in 1954 in respect of the Iranian Consortium Agreement.[260] The umbrella clause was introduced into an official document when Article 2 of the OECD Draft Convention on the Protection of Foreign Property of 1967 was adopted, which provided: "Each Party shall at all times ensure the observance of undertakings given by it in relation to property of nationals of any other party."[261] Weil observed that: "[t]he intervention of the umbrella clause transforms contractual obligations into international obligations."[262] In Mann's view, the provision of the umbrella clause is of "particular importance in that it protects the investor against any interference with his contractual rights, whether it results from a mere breach of contract or a legislative or administrative act, and independently of the question whether or no such interference amounts

257 There are also tribunals that have expressed doubt that the word "full" before security or protection would make any difference. For instance, the *Parkerings* Tribunal found: "It is generally accepted that the variation of language between the formulation 'protection' and 'full protection and security' does not make a difference in the level of protection a State is to provide." See *Parkerings, supra*, note 109, para. 354. The *Parkerings* Tribunal cited N. Rubins and S. Kinsella, *International Investment, Political Risk and Dispute Resolution*, OUP, 2005 to justify its position.

258 UNCTAD, *Investor–State Disputes Arising from Investment Treaties: A Review*, Series on International Investment Policies for Development, United Nations, New York and Geneva, 2005, pp. 40–41.

259 It has been estimated that of the more than 2000 BITs in force, approximately 40% contain an umbrella clause; see OECD, "Interpretation of the Umbrella Clause in Investment Agreements," *Working Papers on International Investment*, Number 2006/3, October 2006, at 5.

260 Anthony C. Sinclair, "The Origins of the Umbrella Clause in the International Law of Investment Protection," 20 *Arbitration International*, Issue 4, 2004, pp. 411–34, at 414–18.

261 The Commentary to the Draft Convention stated that "Article 2 represents an application of the general principle of *pacta sunt servanda*: the maintenance of the pledged word," which "also applies to agreements between States and foreign nationals."

262 Prosper Weil, "Problèmes relative aux contrats passes *entre un Etat et un particular*," 128 *Recueil des Cours* (1969-III) 95, at p. 130.

to expropriation."[263] Other commentators also attach importance to the umbrella clause; Dolzer and Stevens, for example, said that it:

> … seek[s] to ensure that each Party to the treaty will respect specific under-takings towards nationals of the other Party. The provision is of particular importance because it protects the investor's contractual rights against any interference which might be caused by either a simple breach of contract or by administrative or legislative acts.[264]

Brower, however, took a different view, that the umbrella clause should only "apply specifically to large-scale investment and concession contracts—in the making of which the state is deliberately 'exercising its sovereignty'—and thus it might be argued that the ordinary commercial contracts are an implied exception to the general rule set forth in Article 2 [of the Draft Convention on the Protection of Foreign Property]."[265]

The above brief review of the history of and literature on the umbrella clause confirms that the majority of commentators consider that the umbrella clause is meant to apply to contracts between a private party and a state or a state agency. The remaining question is how the umbrella clause has been interpreted in practice.

The earliest case in investment arbitration relating to the umbrella clause is *Fedax v. Venezuela*.[266] The most publicized cases on the subject are, however, *SGS v. Pakistan*[267] and *SGS v. Philippines*[268] because both cases dealt with similar

263 F. A. Mann, "British Treaties for the Promotion and Protection of Investments," 52 *British Year Book of International Law* 241, 1981, at 246.

264 Dolzer and Stevens, *supra*, note 10, at 81–82. Other works on this subject include Christoph Schreuer, "Travelling the BIT Route: Of Waiting Periods, Umbrella Clauses and Forks in the Road," 5 *The Journal of World Investment & Trade*, 249–55, 2004; and Stanimir A. Alexandrov, "Breaches of Contract and Breaches of Treaty," 5 *The Journal of World Investment & Trade* 564–72, 2004.

265 C. N. Brower, "The Future of Foreign Investment—Recent Developments in the International Law of Expropriation and Compensation," in V. S. Cameron (ed.), *Private Investors Abroad—Problems and Solutions in International Business in 1975, Southwestern Legal Foundation Symposium Series, Private Investors Abroad*, Matthew Bender, New York, 1976, p. 93.

266 *Fedax N.V. v. Republic of Venezuela*, ICSID Case No. ARB/96/3, Award (March 9, 1998). Article 3 of the The Netherlands–Venezuela BIT in that case provided: "Each Contracting Party shall observe any obligation it may have entered into with regard to the treatment of investments of nationals of the other Contracting Party." The *Fedax* Tribunal found the non-payment by the respondent under contractual obligation to be a violation of the BIT and stated that "the Tribunal is fully satisfied that the purchase by Fedax N.V. of the promissory notes subject matter of the request for arbitration meets the requirement of an investment both under the Convention and the Agreement. It follows that the Republic of Venezuela is under the obligation to honor precisely the terms and conditions governing such investment, laid down mainly in Article 3 of the Agreement, as well as to honor the specific payments established in the promissory notes issued, and the Tribunal so finds." Ibid., para. 29.

267 *SGS Société Générale de Surveillance S.A. v. Islamic Republic of Pakistan*, ICSID Case No. ARB/01/13, Award on Objections to Jurisdiction (August 6, 2003).

268 *SGS Société Générale de Surveillance S.A. v. Republic of the Philippines*, ICSID Case No. ARB/02/6, Decision on Objections to Jurisdiction (January 29, 2004).

facts and almost identical umbrella clauses in the BITs but the decisions in these cases diametrically contradict each other. In the *SGS v. Pakistan* case, the Pakistan–Switzerland BIT in Article 11 provided that: "Either Contracting Party shall constantly guarantee the observance of the commitments it has entered into with respect to the investments of the investors of the other Contracting Party." The central issue was whether the claimant could, on the basis of this umbrella clause, bring its disputes with the host state to ICSID arbitration whilst they were being handled simultaneously by a commercial arbitration body for breaches of the contract between SGS and Pakistan. In other words, the question was whether the umbrella clause had the effect of "elevating a simple breach of contract claim to a treaty claim under international law," as was contended by the claimant.[269]

The tribunal in *SGS v. Pakistan* rejected the claimant's request and declined jurisdiction over the case, giving the following reasons: (a) the "commitments" covered by the umbrella clause were not limited to contractual commitments but could also include "the municipal legislative or administrative or other unilateral measures of a Contracting Party;"[270] (b) if the claimant's request were permitted, the legal consequences would be "so far-reaching in scope, and so automatic and unqualified and sweeping in their operation, so burdensome in their potential impact upon a Contracting Party" that "clear and convincing evidence" that this was the intent of the contracting parties must be shown by the claimant;[271] (c) if the claimant's request were accepted, it would amount to incorporating by reference an unlimited number of state contracts, as well as other municipal law instruments setting out state commitments and the substantive protections of the BIT would become "substantially superfluous;"[272] (d) the umbrella clause was not located among the substantive obligations of the BIT but at the end thereof; and (e) the tribunal should take a prudential approach—*in dubio mitius*.[273] Obviously, the tribunal in *SGS v. Pakistan* took a very conservative view on interpreting the umbrella clause, which is contrary to the majority view expressed by scholars in the field.

What is most debatable is the way that the tribunal in *SGS v. Pakistan* interpreted the umbrella clause. To start with, in accordance with Article 31 of the Vienna Convention on the Law of Treaties ("VCLT"), "[a] treaty shall be interpreted in good faith in accordance with the ordinary meaning to be given to the terms of the treaty in their context and in the light of its object and purpose." An umbrella clause therefore should be interpreted according to this rule. The question then is whether "commitments" in the umbrella clause would cover contracts. In this respect, the tribunal is quite right when it says: "The 'commitments' the observance of which a Contracting Party is to 'constantly guarantee' are not limited to *contractual* commitments. The commitments referred to may be embedded in,

---

269 *SGS v. Pakistan, supra*, note 266, para. 98.
270 Ibid., para. 166.
271 Ibid., para. 167.
272 Ibid., para. 168. The tribunal also stated that it would enable investors to nullify at will any freely negotiated dispute settlement procedures contained in their contract.
273 Ibid., para. 171.

e.g., the municipal legislative or administrative or other unilateral measures of a Contracting Party." However, it then held that such an interpretation would be in opposition to the principle of general international law whereby "a violation of a contract entered into by a State with an investor of another State, is not, by itself, a violation of international law" and that the legal consequences of such a reading would be "so far-reaching …"[274] In fact, there is nothing in the VCLT that suggests that the consequences of interpreting the provisions of a treaty are to be taken into account. Also, there is nothing in the VCLT that encourages use of the interpretive approach of "*in dubio pars mitior est sequenda,* or more tersely, *in dubio mitius,*" which the tribunal asserted to be the "appropriate" one in this case.[275] Treaties may, by nature, change the landscape of international law for their signatories, or else there would be little point in entering into them, a point that the tribunal seems to have overlooked or ignored.

Finally, the tribunal made much of determining "the shared intent of the Contracting Parties to the Swiss–Pakistan Investment Protection Treaty in incorporating Article 11 in the BIT."[276] Pakistan, of course, maintained that the interpretation advanced by the claimant was contrary to its own understanding of the Article. However, what exactly that understanding was, or its own intention in including the provision in the BIT, is never made clear. So, like so many tribunals, the tribunal in *SGS v. Pakistan* took it upon itself, not to ask the other signatory to the BIT, but to determine what the shared intent must have been, or at least, what it could not have been. It is noteworthy that under cover of a letter dated October 1, 2003 and on the letterhead of the State Secretariat for Economic Affairs, Dr Marino Baldi, then Swiss Ambassador for Foreign Economic Relations, submitted to Mr Antonio Parra, then Deputy Secretary-General of the ICSID, what purported to be the official understanding of the Swiss Government of the intent of Article 11 of the Switzerland–Pakistan BIT. The note first expressly raised the question as to why the *SGS v. Pakistan* Tribunal, whilst it "attributed considerable importance to the intent of the Contracting Parties in drafting this Article," did not find it necessary to enquire about the Swiss view of the meaning of this Article, even though it did ask for Pakistan's view. It then expressed "alarm" about "the very narrow interpretation given to the meaning of Article 11," which it said: "not only runs counter to the intention of Switzerland when concluding the Treaty but is quite evidently neither supported by the meaning of similar articles in BITs concluded by other countries nor by academic comments on such provisions."[277] It is therefore not surprising that the *SGS v. Pakistan* decision has triggered a great deal of criticism.[278]

---

274 Ibid., para. 167.
275 Ibid., para. 171.
276 Ibid., paras. 167ff.
277 See "Interpretation of Article 11 of the Bilateral Investment Treaty between Switzerland and Pakistan in the light of the decision of the Tribunal on Objections to Jurisdiction of ICSID in Case No. ARB/01/12 SGS Société Générale de Surveillance SA versus Islamic Republic of Pakistan," *Transnational Dispute Management,* Vol. 1, Issue 3, July 2004.
278 Wälde, for instance, criticized the decision severely. He opined: "Had the tribunal examined pre-

With regard to the umbrella clause, the tribunal in *SGS v. Philippines*, based on grounds radically different from that of the *SGS v. Pakistan* Tribunal, held:

1. "The term 'any obligation' is capable of applying to obligations arising under national law, e.g. those arising from a contract …" and further that "[i]nterpreting the actual text of Article X(2), it would appear to say, and to say clearly, that each Contracting Party shall observe any legal obligation it has assumed, or will in the future assume, with regard to specific investments covered by the BIT;"[279]
2. "… if commitments made by the State towards specific investments do involve binding obligations or commitments under the applicable law, it seems entirely consistent with the object and purpose of the BIT to hold that they are incorporated and brought within the framework of the BIT by Article X(2);"[280] and
3. "Article X(2) [of the BIT] addresses not the *scope* of the commitments entered into with regard to specific investments but the *performance* of these obligations, once they are ascertained."[281]

Finally, the *SGS v. Philippines* Tribunal stated:

> To summarize the Tribunal's conclusions on this point, Article X(2) makes it a breach of the BIT for the host State to fail to observe binding commitments, including contractual commitments, which it has assumed with regard to specific investments. But it does not convert the issue of the extent or content of such obligations into an issue of international law.[282]

Unlike the *SGS v. Pakistan* Tribunal, the *SGS v. Philippines* Tribunal was, for the most part, happy to treat the terms of the relevant BIT as if they meant what they said. It even went to some pains to address the differences between its approach and that of the *SGS v. Pakistan* Tribunal. It expressed the opinion that the latter

---

existing international law on breach of government contracts, including the NIEO controversy between Third-World and Western countries' concepts of contract protection more closely, had it paid more than lip-service to the plain meaning approach mandated by the Vienna Convention, had it related the respect for contractual commitment with the investment promotion purposes of this – like all other – investment treaties and had it paid attention to the now prevailing state practice of including increasingly explicit 'pacta sunt servanda' clauses, it would not have dismissed the explicit text, with no evidence at all of a contrary meaning available from the travaux of this or other comparable treaties, with so much nonchalance." See T. W. Wälde, "The 'Umbrella' (or Sanctity of Contract/Pacta sunt Servanda) Clause in Investment Arbitration: A Comment on Original Intentions and Recent Cases," *Transnational Dispute Management*, Vol. 1, Issue 4, October 2004, pp. 1–87, at 67.

279 *SGS v. Philippines, supra*, note 267, para. 115.
280 Ibid., para. 117.
281 Ibid., para. 126 (footnote omitted, emphases in original).
282 Ibid., para. 128.

tribunal had "failed to give any clear meaning to the 'umbrella clause'"[283] but also was able to show that doing so in the context of the wording contained in the Switzerland–Philippines BIT was eminently possible without the consequences feared by the *SGS v. Pakistan* Tribunal. It noted (omitting the footnote that refers to *SGS v. Pakistan*, Decision on Jurisdiction, para. 166):

> For Article X(2) [of the Switzerland–Philippines BIT] to be applicable, the host State must have assumed a legal obligation, and it must have been assumed vis-à-vis the specific investment—not as a matter of the application of some legal obligation of a general character. This is very far from elevating to the international level all "the municipal legislative or administrative or other unilateral measures of a Contracting Party."[284]

The *SGS v. Philippines* Tribunal also gave little weight to the location of the "umbrella clause" in the BIT, noting that "it is difficult to accept that the same language in other Philippines BITs is legally operative, but that it is legally inoperative in the Swiss–Philippines BIT merely because of its location."[285] Of course, a defender of the approach taken by the *SGS v. Pakistan* Tribunal could argue equally as well that it is precisely *because* this clause has been placed in a less prominent place in this BIT than it occupies in other Philippine BITs that it should be given less importance as a "substantive" provision.

As for the tribunal's reasoning in regard to the interplay between the "umbrella clause" of the Switzerland–Philippines BIT and the operation of the "exclusive jurisdictional provision" of the CISS Agreement, the matter seems somewhat less clear. In the face of Arbitrator Crivellaro's reasoning that: "[i]f our jurisdiction derives from (also) Article X(2) [of the BIT], as unanimously admitted, I see no reason why our Tribunal could not deal with and decide on the merits of the payment claim, including quantum."[286] The majority of the tribunal argued:

> … for present purposes Article X(2) includes commitments or obligations arising under contracts entered into by the host State. The basic obligation on the State in this case is the obligation to pay what is due under the contract, … But this obligation does not mean that the determination of how much money the Philippines is obliged to pay becomes a treaty matter. The extent of the obligation is still governed by the contract, and it can only be determined by reference to the terms of the contract.[287]

---

283 Ibid., para. 125.
284 Ibid., para. 121.
285 Ibid., para. 124.
286 See *SGS Société Générale de Surveillance S.A. v. Republic of the Philippines*, ICSID Case No. ARB/02/6, Decision on Objections to Jurisdiction (January 29, 2004), Declaration (Dissenting Opinion of Antonio Crivellaro), para. 11.
287 *SGS v. Philippines*, Decision on Jurisdiction, *supra*, note 267, para. 127.

This may be considered a fine parsing of the meaning(s) that may be attributed to Article X(2) of the Switzerland–Philippines BIT—or, for that matter, other BITs worded in a similar fashion—but it certainly addresses the concern raised by the *SGS v. Pakistan* Tribunal "that the effect of a broad interpretation would be, inter alia, to override dispute settlement clauses negotiated in particular contracts." In fact, only by doing so, may an investment arbitration tribunal function within the limits defined by treaties and without affecting the dispute settlement procedures of the commercial contract. In such circumstances, after the commercial arbitration tribunal determines the amount that the host state may be obliged to pay the foreign investor and the host state refuses to pay, the foreign investor then has the choice either to institute a treaty arbitration at ICSID or file a lawsuit in a court in the host state or another country for recognition and enforcement of the commercial arbitral award.

Decisions subsequent to the two *SGS* cases mentioned above are by no means consistent. One group of tribunals favors a broad interpretation of the umbrella clause, regarding contractual breaches to constitute treaty breaches through the operation of the umbrella clause. *Eureko*[288] is a case in point. The tribunal in that case stated that "insofar as the Government of Poland has entered into obligations vis-à-vis Eureko with regard to the latter's investments, and insofar as the tribunal has found that the respondent has acted in breach of those obligations, it stands, *prima facie*, in violation of Article 3.5 [the umbrella clause] of the Treaty." The grounds on which the *Eureko* Tribunal based the above conclusion were that the Netherlands–Poland BIT uses in the umbrella clause the words "shall observe" and "any obligation," which, in the view of the tribunal, not only indicate the imperative and categorical nature of the obligations but also a wide coverage of obligations of any kind. In addition, the tribunal considered its interpretation of the umbrella clause to be in line with the object and purpose of the BIT—the encouragement and reciprocal protection of investment.[289] The effect of this interpretation, as expressed by the tribunal, is that breaches of contract may be converted into breaches of the BIT, "since they transgress Poland's Treaty commitment to 'observe any obligations it may have entered into' with regard to Eureko's investments."[290]

The tribunal in *SGS v. Paraguay*[291] adopted a similar approach. It decided that "a failure to meet one's obligations under a contract is clearly a failure to 'observe' one's commitments. There is nothing in Article 11 [the umbrella clause] that states or implies that a government will only fail to observe its commitments if

---

288 *Eureko, supra*, note 169, para. 244.
289 Ibid., para. 248.
290 Ibid., para. 250.
291 *SGS Société Générale de Surveillance S.A. v. Republic of Paraguay*, ICSID Case No. ARB/07/29, Award (February 10, 2012).

it abuses its sovereign authority."[292] In making its decision, the *SGS v. Paraguay* Tribunal referred to *Duke v. Ecuador*[293] and *Burlington v. Ecuador*.[294]

In *Duke v. Ecuador*, the tribunal observed that: "[w]hether an umbrella clause in a BIT necessarily elevates any breach of contract by a State to the level of a breach of treaty is a controversial question."[295] With regard to another, but related, issue—if abuse of power by the host state is needed in order to call the umbrella clause into play—the *Duke* Tribunal considered that although language to that effect appeared in some cases, "a majority of decisions do not formulate such distinction."[296]

Similarly, the *Burlington* Tribunal decided that "umbrella clauses may apply even if no exercise of sovereign power is involved."[297] Thus, the *SGS v. Paraguay* Tribunal held that in the case before it, it was irrelevant whether or not the host state's action was in the nature of a sovereign state act when it came to ascertaining any breach of the umbrella clause.

The broad approach to interpretation of the umbrella clause aims to offer foreign investors the maximum protection by elevating contractual obligations to treaty obligations.[298] It therefore serves as a guarantee to foreign investors that any disputes arising from their agreements with the host state may be settled through international arbitration if they cannot be resolved otherwise. This in itself may serve as an encouragement, if not exactly coercion, to the host state, which must think twice before breaching any obligation that it has assumed.

On the other hand, there are inherent difficulties with this broad approach. In the first place, the umbrella clause may have the effect of replacing contracts entered into between an investor and the host state, at least insofar as dispute settlement procedures are concerned. Then the question arises as to why contracting parties would still stipulate dispute settlement procedures in their contracts. Another question is to what extent may the umbrella clause operate? In other words, does it cover disputes arising only from investments or does it cover any disputes arising from "any obligations"? Finally, where every contractual breach is, through operation of the umbrella clause, transformed into a treaty breach, there might be a flood of cases—as some commentators have expressed their concern—that investment tribunals may not be able to handle.[299] Unless these

---

292 Ibid., para. 91.
293 *Duke Energy Electroquil Partners & Electroquil S.A. v. Republic of Ecuador*, ICSID Case No. ARB/04/19, Award (August 18, 2008).
294 *Burlington Resources Inc. and Others v. Republic of Ecuador and Empresa Estatal Petróleos del Ecuador (PetroEcuador)*, ICSID Case No. ARB/08/5, Decision on Jurisdiction (June 2, 2010).
295 *Duke v. Ecuador, supra*, note 292, para. 319.
296 Ibid, para. 320.
297 *Burlington v. Ecuador, supra*, note 293, para. 190.
298 Another case that adopted the broad approach is *Noble Ventures v. Romania*, in which the tribunal concluded that the only way to give effect to the umbrella clause is to internationalize or transform a contract breach to a treaty breach; see *Noble Ventures, supra*, note 188, para. 54.
299 See Heikki Marjosola, "Public/Private Conflict in Investment Treaty Arbitration—A Study on Umbrella Clauses," *Helsinki Law Review*, 2009, pp. 103–34, at 127.

questions are answered satisfactorily, the broad approach may be considered undesirable.[300]

In practice, the majority of investment arbitration decisions have adopted a relatively narrow approach, although they have relied upon different grounds. In *Joy Mining*,[301] for instance, the tribunal refused to apply the umbrella clause for the transaction at issue on the ground that the transaction was not an investment protected under the applicable BIT. The dispute in this case arose out of a "Contract for the Provision of Longwall Mining Systems and Supporting Equipment for the Abu Tartur Phosphate Mining Project", executed on April 26, 1998 between Joy Mining Machinery Limited and the General Organization for Industrial and Mining Projects of the Arab Republic of Egypt ("IMC"). Following various disagreements between the parties, the contract was amended by an agreement of November 8, 2000 ("Amendment Agreement").[302] The company was paid the full purchase price of the equipment in accordance with the contract, but bank guarantees established by the claimant were not released by IMC.[303]

Joy Mining maintained that the contract and its participation in the Longwall Mining Project constituted an investment under the terms of the ICSID Convention, that pursuant to the terms of the contract and the Amendment Agreement it was entitled to the release of the guarantees, and that IMC's refusal to release them was a breach of the contract, a breach attributable to Egypt.[304] Further, Joy Mining argued that "[b]ecause of the 'umbrella clause' included in Article 2(2) of the Treaty, any breach of Egypt's underlying obligations under the Contract also amount[ed] to breaches of the Treaty."[305]

The tribunal first examined whether the bank guarantees under the contract could constitute an investment under the Egypt–United Kingdom BIT. It concluded that the bank guarantees were "simply a contingent liability"[306] and that to consider a contingent liability a protected investment "would really go far

---

300 The broad approach has also been criticized by investment tribunals. The *Pan American Energy* Tribunal, for instance, in relation to the *SGS v. Philippines* case, commented that "the interpretation given in SGS v. Philippines does not only deprive one single provision of far-reaching consequences, but renders the whole Treaty completely useless: indeed, if this interpretation were to be followed—the violation of any legal obligation of a State, and not only any contractual obligation with respect to investment, is a violation of the BIT, whatever the source of the obligation and whatever the seriousness of the breach—it would be sufficient to have a so-called 'umbrella clause' and a dispute settlement mechanism, and no other articles setting standards of protection of foreign investments in any BIT. If any violation of any legal obligation of a State is *ipso facto* a violation of the treaty, then that violation needs not amount to a violation of the high standards of the treaty of 'fair and equitable treatment' or 'full protection and security'." See *Pan American Energy and BP Argentina Exploration Company v. Argentina*, ICSID Case No. ARB/04/8, Decision on Preliminary Objections (July 27, 2006), para. 105.
301 *Joy Mining Machinery Limited v. Arab Republic of Egypt*, ICSID Case No. ARB/03/11, Award on Jurisdiction (August 6, 2004).
302 Ibid., para. 15.
303 Ibid., para. 19.
304 Ibid., paras. 22–39.
305 Ibid., para. 68.
306 Ibid., para. 44.

beyond the concept of investment, even if broadly defined, as this and other treaties normally do."[307] The importance of this conclusion is that in the view of the tribunal, a sales contract—regardless of its complexity—must be distinguished from investment contracts, as the former is a central feature of international trade, which involves different developments in respect of governing law and conceptual issues.[308]

Insofar as the umbrella clause is concerned, the *Joy Mining* Tribunal observed that: "an umbrella clause inserted in the Treaty, and not very prominently, could not have the effect of transforming all contract disputes into investment disputes under the Treaty, unless of course there would be a clear violation of the Treaty rights and obligations or a violation of contract rights of such a magnitude as to trigger the Treaty protection."[309] It then went to say that "[t]he connection between the Contract and the Treaty is the missing link that prevents any such effect."[310] What was the missing link? Article 2(2) of the Egypt–United Kingdom BIT reads, in relevant part: "Each Contracting Party shall observe any obligation it may have entered into with regard to investments of nationals or companies of the other Contracting Party." As the *Joy Mining* Tribunal concluded that the bank guarantees were not a protected investment, the contract's requirement that IMC release them could not be an "obligation … with regard to investments." It was unfortunate that the *Joy Mining* Tribunal did not make this point on the missing link more clearly. Equally, the tribunal did not explain in what circumstances a contract breach may reach such "magnitude" as to trigger treaty protection. In fact, the plain meaning of the umbrella clause does not seem to imply anything like "seriousness" of a contract breach to elevate it to a treaty breach.

In addition to the existence of a qualified investment, in invoking the umbrella clause a claimant must of course first establish that the acts or omissions being complained of are attributable to the host state. In *Bosh v. Ukraine*, an important issue was whether the respondent had breached its obligations regarding the umbrella clause. Article II(3)(c) of the Ukraine–United States BIT provides: "Each Party shall observe any obligation it may have entered into with regard to investments." The *Bosh* Tribunal considered that the "obligation is incumbent on 'each Party' to the BIT to 'observe any obligation it may have entered into with regard to investments.'"[311] As to whether the contract entered into between the claimant and the Taras Shevchenko National University of Kiev could constitute an obligation of Ukraine, however, it was the view of the *Bosh* Tribunal that the university was not a government agency and hence contracts entered into by the university could not be attributable to the respondent. To support its position, the tribunal referred to the decision in *SGS v. Philippines* that although "to fail to observe binding commitments, including contractual commitments, which it had

---

307 Ibid., para. 45.
308 Ibid., para. 58.
309 Ibid., para. 81.
310 Id.
311 *Bosh v. Ukraine*, *supra*, note 73, para. 243.

assumed with regard to specific investments" would constitute a breach of the umbrella clause, this very umbrella clause "did not have the effect of converting the extent or content of such obligations into an issue of international law."[312] In the end, the *Bosh* Tribunal decided that the claimants had the obligation to have their rights and obligations under the 2003 contract determined in accordance with the procedures stipulated in the contract.[313]

In a way, the *Bosh* Tribunal's decision is in line with the ruling in the *BIVAC* case that the obligations mentioned in the umbrella clause were "not limited to international obligations, or non-contractual obligations" and that they were "undoubtedly capable of being read to include a contractual arrangement entered into by BIVAC and the Ministry of Finance of Paraguay, whereby the alleged breaches of the Ministry are attributable to the State."[314] Yet, in the view of the *BIVAC* Tribunal, where the obligations under a contract may be, through operation of the umbrella clause, transferred into treaty obligations, the transfer must be the totality of the contractual obligations. That means, according to the tribunal, that the transfer "would include not only the obligation to make payment of invoices in accordance with the requirements of the Contract, but also the obligation (implicit if nothing else) to ensure that the Tribunals of the City of Asunción were available to resolve any 'conflict, controversy or claim which arises from or is produced in relation to' the Contract."[315]

Some other tribunals have considered that before invoking the umbrella clause a claimant must first follow through with the procedures for dispute settlement stipulated in the relevant contract. In *Swisslion v. Macedonia*,[316] for instance, the tribunal, after having observed that the nature of the commitments made by the claimant were themselves "susceptible of different and conflicting interpretations,"[317] concluded:

> At the end of the day, there were issues pertaining to the investor's compliance with the contract on which reasonable persons could disagree. The Ministry did not unilaterally terminate the contract, but rather put the issue before the courts. The Tribunal is therefore unable to find that in resolving to seek the termination of the contract and in submitting the matter to the jurisdiction of the courts, as provided for in the contract, the Ministry breached any obligation to constantly guarantee the observance of its commitments.[318]

312 *SGS v. Philippines, supra*, note 267, para. 128, quoted in *Bosh, supra*, note 73, para. 247.
313 *Bosh*, ibid., para. 251.
314 *Bureau Veritas, Inspection, Valuation, Assessment and Control BIVAC B.V. v. Paraguay*, ICSID Case No. ARB/07/9, Decision on Jurisdiction of May 19, 2009, para. 141.
315 Ibid., para. 142.
316 *Swisslion DOO Skopje v. The Former Yugoslav Republic of Macedonia*, ICSID Case No. ARB/09/16, Award (July 6, 2012).
317 Ibid., para. 323.
318 Ibid., para. 324.

Thus, as in the *Bosh* case, the *Swisslion* Tribunal impliedly adopted the position of the *SGS v. Philippines* Tribunal that under the umbrella clause the parties must go through the dispute settlement procedures established in the relevant contract before resorting to BIT claims.

It should be noted that the difference between *Bosh* and the *BIVAC* and *SGS v. Philippines* cases is that the former did not involve a contract of which the host state was a party. The *Bosh* Tribunal correctly held that the actions and omissions of the university were not attributable to the respondent. Therefore, compared with *BIVAC* and *SGS v. Philippines*, the *Bosh* Tribunal in essence declined jurisdiction based on lack of privity, although it dealt with the issue through attribution of the actions of the university.

There are a number of other cases where tribunals have rejected the application of the umbrella clause in accordance with the principle of privity. For instance, in *Azurix*,[319] the claimant's subsidiary—ABA—entered into an agreement with the Argentine Province of Buenos Aires, whilst Azurix itself was not a party to the agreement. The *Azurix* Tribunal stated the following with regard to the claimant's request to invoke the umbrella clause:

> While Azurix may submit a claim under the BIT for breaches by Argentina, there is no undertaking to be honored by Argentina to Azurix other than the obligations under the BIT. Even if for argument's sake, it would be possible under Article II(2)(c) to hold Argentina responsible for the alleged breaches of the Concession Agreement by the Province, it was ABA and not Azurix which was the party to this Agreement.[320]

In other words, in the view of the tribunal, Azurix could not rely on the umbrella clause of the BIT against the respondent because it was not a party to the Concession Agreement. Thus, the *Azurix* Tribunal regarded privity as a precondition for invoking the umbrella clause. This position was shared by the tribunal in the *Siemens* case, which was decided some time later.[321] Dealing with similar provisions of an umbrella clause, the *Siemens* Tribunal faced the same situation as that in *Azurix*, that is the parties to the underlying contract were Argentina and SITS—the latter being Siemens' subsidiary. The tribunal explicitly stated that "[t]he Claimant is not a party to the Contract and SITS is not a party to these proceedings."[322] Therefore, Siemens could not invoke the umbrella clause to claim against the respondent. In fact, the *Siemens* Tribunal went as far as saying that unless there was an abuse of power by the host state—"interference with the operation of the contract"—a breach of contract should not be considered a breach of an investment treaty.[323]

In yet another case—the *CMS* annulment proceedings—Argentina challenged

319 *Azurix, supra*, note 46.
320 Ibid., para. 384.
321 *Siemens, supra*, note 111. In *Azurix* and *Siemens*, the umbrella clauses of the respective BITs read similarly. Moreover, both tribunals were chaired by Andrés Rigo Sureda.
322 *Siemens*, ibid., at para. 204.
323 Ibid., 248.

the tribunal's decision on grounds of manifest excess of powers by permitting CMS to invoke the umbrella clause despite the fact that CMS was not a party to the applicable instruments.[324] The *ad hoc* Committee criticized the broad interpretation the *CMS* Tribunal gave to the umbrella clause and annulled the award for failure to state reasons—including its failure to state the reasons for adopting its broad interpretation of the umbrella clause. Thereafter, the *ad hoc* Committee made the following observations in the context of its analysis in respect of the umbrella clause:

> The effect of the umbrella clause is not to transform the obligation which is relied on into something else; the content of the obligation is unaffected, as is its proper law. If this is so, it would appear that the parties to the obligation (*i.e.*, the persons bound by it and entitled to rely on it) are likewise not changed by reason of the umbrella clause.[325]

Obviously, the *CMS ad hoc* Committee endorsed the *Azurix* and *Siemens* Tribunals' decisions by expressly stating the conditions for invoking the umbrella clause. The contribution made by the *CMS ad hoc* Committee is that for the first time in history it made it clear that "any obligation" stipulated in an umbrella clause must have a specific obligor and obligee—parties to the obligation. Such parties may not be changed by reason of the umbrella clause. According to this principle—the principle of privity—only those who are parties to the underlying contract/agreement may benefit from the umbrella clause of an applicable BIT.

The *CMS ad hoc* Committee's position received the full approval of the *Burlington* Tribunal, a recent case in which the claimant's subsidiary entered into a contract with the host state. The *Burlington* Tribunal, having examined previous investment arbitration decisions, concluded that the claimant "may not rely on the Treaty's umbrella clause to enforce against Ecuador its subsidiary's contract rights."[326] In fact, there was a difference between the *CMS* case and the *Burlington* case in that whilst the claimant in the *CMS* case was a minority shareholder, Burlington wholly owned its Ecuadorian subsidiary. The *Burlington* Tribunal, however, did not think that the difference in shareholding could make a difference in applying the umbrella clause.[327]

In a nutshell, the narrow approach does not exclude the application of the umbrella clause to contractual obligations. In fact, some tribunals have even considered that the purpose of the umbrella clause is to elevate contract claims to treaty claims. At the same time, they have maintained that whether the transaction in question is a qualified investment should be ascertained; that the parties

---

324 The *ad hoc* Committee annulled the tribunal's award for failure to state reasons but not for manifest excess of powers. See *CMS Gas Transmission Company v. Argentine Republic*, Annulment Proceeding, Decision of the *ad hoc* Committee on the Application for Annulment of the Argentine Republic of September 25, 2007, para. 46.

325 Ibid., para. 95.

326 *Burlington, supra*, note 293, para. 220.

327 Ibid., para. 229.

should observe all of their obligations under the contract, including any dispute settlement procedures established therein; and that there is privity of the parties to the contract, which serves as the link between a private contract and the umbrella clause. In general, the narrow approach emphasizes a concrete and detailed analysis of the case in question and is more cautious than the broad approach.

The above having been said, the issues surrounding implementation of the umbrella clause are far from being resolved because, as the *Continental Casualty* Tribunal observed, the interpretation of umbrella clauses "remains controversial and … there is a lack of consistency."[328] Even among the decisions which took either the so-called broad approach or the narrow approach, there can hardly be said to be any consistency. What is worse is that, as noted by the *Burlington* Tribunal, "the views expressed in these cases are supported by few reasons, if any."[329]

Among all tribunal decisions on this issue, however, those that have taken the broad approach require further reconsideration because, as the *Hamester* Tribunal noted: "the consequence of an automatic and wholesale elevation of any and all contract claims into treaty claims risks undermining the distinction between national legal orders and international law" and "this is not a result that is in line with the general purpose of the ICSID/BIT mechanism for the international protection of foreign investments."[330] The essence of the problem is that none of the tribunals so far has seemed to be keen on drawing a line between contractual commitments qualified to be under the protection of the umbrella clause and those which are not so qualified, despite appeals made by various people.[331] The reluctance of investment tribunals to make such a distinction has been criticized as a failure on their part to fulfill their duties.[332] It is submitted that tribunals and scholars should further clarify the function of the umbrella clause. Whilst the usefulness of the umbrella clause is not in doubt, what the treaty contracting parties intend to do with it is important. Some commentators argue that the umbrella clause can help stabilize the relationship between a host state and foreign investors.[333]

---

328 *Continental Casualty*, *supra*, note 168, para. 296.
329 *Burlington*, *supra*, note 293, para. 233.
330 *Gustav F W Hamester GmbH & Co KG v. Republic of Ghana* [hereinafter "*Hamester*"], ICSID Case No. ARB/07/24, Award (June 18, 2010), para. 349. In this case, contracts were entered into between the investor and a state entity. The tribunal found those contracts did not fall within the scope of an umbrella clause. See id.
331 Gaillard, for instance, commented: "In light of the increasing number of investment treaty arbitrations involving underlying contractual breaches, it might make sense to better define the borders between the dispute settlement mechanisms of the investment treaty and the underlying contract." See Emmanuel Gaillard, "Investment Treaty Arbitration and Jurisdiction Over Contract Claims—the SGS Cases Considered," in Todd Weiler (ed.), *International Investment Law and Arbitration: Leading Cases from the ICSID, NAFTA, Bilateral Treaties and Customary International Law*, Cameron May, pp. 325–46, at 345.
332 See Bjorn Kunoy, "Singing in the Rain: Developments in the Interpretation of Umbrella Clauses," *The Journal of World Investment & Trade*, Vol. 7, 2006, pp. 275–300, at 299.
333 See Stephan W. Schill, "Enabling Private Ordering: Function, Scope and Effect of Umbrella Clauses in International Investment Treaties," 18 *Minn. J. Int'l L.* 1, 2009, at 12, in which he argued: "The primary function of the umbrella clause … [is that it] allows investors to initiate

Another issue that requires clarification is whether attribution, which is related to privity, is a factor in determining the liability of the host state.[334] In other words, in holding a host state responsible, is it necessary to establish a link that the breach is attributable to the state?

IV. China's practice on absolute standards of treatment

Most of China's recently concluded BITs contain the relative treatment standards—either national treatment or MFN treatment with better treatment applicable—as well as the fair and equitable treatment standard.[335] These standards were incorporated into the 2003 China–Germany BIT, applicable to "investments and activities associated with such investments." It should be noted, however, that it is far from clear what may constitute an activity associated with or relating to an investment. The explanation given in the Protocol to the China–Germany BIT offers little assistance in this regard. It sets out: "[T]he following shall more particularly, though not exclusively, be deemed 'activity' within the meaning of Article 3(2): the management, maintenance, use, enjoyment and disposal of an investment."[336] Whatever purpose it may try to serve, the term "though not exclusively" should be interpreted to include any activity that may be reasonably justified as related to an investment.

Concerning the treatment standards, the 2005 China–Portugal BIT, in which reference is made to international law, is typical. Article 10(1) of this Agreement states, in relevant part:

treaty-based arbitration for the breach of promises made by the host State vis-à-vis the investor. By offering enforcement mechanisms on the level of international law, umbrella clauses stabilize the relationship between the host State and foreign investors *ex post* against opportunistic host State behavior."

334　For an analysis of this issue, see Michael Feit, "Attribution and the Umbrella Clause – Is there a Way out of the Deadlock?" 21 *Minn. J. Int'l L.* 21, 2012, pp. 21–41.

335　For example, Article 3 of the 2005 China–Portugal BIT provides: "(1) Investments of investors of each Contracting Party shall at all times be accorded fair and equitable treatment in the territory of the other Contracting Party. (2) Each Contracting Party shall accord to investments and activities associated with such investments by the investors of the other Contracting Party treatment not less favorable than that accorded to the investments and associated activities of its own investors. (3) Neither Contracting Party shall subject investments and activities associated with such investments by the investors of the other Contracting Party to treatment less favorable than that accorded to the investments and associated activities of the investors of any third State." Article 3 of the 2005 China–Czech Republic BIT reads: "(1) Each Contracting Party shall in its territory accord to investments and returns of investors of the other Contracting Party treatment which is fair and equitable and not less favorable than that which it accords to investments and returns of its own investors or to investments and returns of investors of any third State, whichever is more favorable. (2) Each Contracting Party shall in its territory accord to investors of the other Contracting Party, as regards management, maintenance, use, enjoyment or disposal of their investment, treatment which is fair and equitable and not less favorable than that which it accords to its own investors or to investors of any third State, whichever is more favorable."

336　Protocol to the Agreement between the People's Republic of China and the Federal Republic of Germany on the Encouragement and Reciprocal Protection of Investments, Article 3; available at: http://www.unctadxi.org/templates/DocSearch.aspx?id=779.

… if the provisions of law of either Contracting Party or obligations under international law existing at present or established hereafter between the Contracting Parties in addition to the present Agreement contain regulations entitling investments by investors of the other Contracting Party to a treatment more favourable than is provided for by the present Agreement, such regulations shall, to the extent that they are more favourable, prevail over the present Agreement.[337]

Such provisions may raise more questions than they resolve, as what may constitute an international standard is, to say the least, very uncertain. The situations that might be regulated by the above provision could include, for example, China joining the Energy Charter Treaty and thereby being required to give pre-investment national treatment to foreign investors who are nationals of a contracting state of the ECT.[338] In that circumstance, China would be obliged to grant pre-investment national treatment to investments of investors from Portugal. Yet, at the moment, Portugal is already a Member of the ECT[339] and is thus, through the operation of Article 10(1) of the China–Portugal BIT quoted above, obliged to afford pre-investment national treatment to investments of investors from China, although China has no such obligations because MFN treatment is relative in nature.

Fair and equitable treatment has also become a standard clause in China's recent BITs. The 2003 China–Germany BIT, the 2004 China–Finland BIT, the 2005 China–Spain BIT and the 2005 China–Portugal BIT have all adopted largely the following language: "Investments of investors of each Contracting Party shall at all times be accorded fair and equitable treatment in the territory of the other Contracting Party."[340] The 2006 China–Russia BIT followed these precedents, even though it adopted a slightly different wording.[341]

The 2008 China–New Zealand FTA puts FET and FPS in the same paragraph and requires the parties to accord such treatment "in accordance with commonly accepted rules of international law."[342] It further elaborates that FET includes "the

---

337   2005 China–Portugal BIT, Article 10(1); available at: http://www.chinahotelsreservation.com/china_law/Agreement_between_china_ law_the_Government526.html. Other BITs featuring the same provisions include the 2004 China–Tunisia BIT, the 2002 China–Bosnia BIT and the 2001 China–Netherlands BIT (2001).

338   Article (2) of the ECT provides: "Each Contracting Party shall endeavour to accord to Investors of other Contracting Parties, as regards the Making of Investments in its Area, the Treatment described in paragraph (3)," which stipulates Treatment to include national and MFN treatment.

339   For the list of ECT Members and Observers, see: http://www.encharter.org/index.php?id=61.

340   2003 China–Germany BIT, Article 3(1); 2004 China–Finland BIT, Article 3(1); 2005 China–Spain BIT, Article 39(1); and 2005 China–Portugal BIT, Article 3(1).

341   Article III(1) of the 2006 China–Russia BIT provides that "each Contracting Party shall ensure in its territory fair and equitable treatment of the investments made by investors of the other Contracting Party and activities in connection with such investments."

342   2008 China–New Zealand FTA, Art. 143(1). This arrangement of wording is very different from other FTAs and BITs that China has entered into. Whether or not this will become the practice of China is worth observing.

obligation to ensure that, having regard to general principles of law, investors are not denied justice or treated unfairly or inequitably in any legal or administrative proceeding affecting the investments of the investor," whilst FPS "requires each Party to take such measures as may be reasonably necessary in the exercise of its authority to ensure the protection and security of the investment."[343] Under the China–New Zealand FTA, FET and FPS require the host government not to take any measures that may result in unreasonable or discriminatory treatment against the "management, maintenance, use, enjoyment and disposal of the investments." This is by far the most extensively elaborated provision on the subject that China has committed itself to. However, the China–New Zealand FTA also stipulates that the violation of other articles "does not establish that there has been a violation" of the article on FET and FPS.[344] This is so because the FET requirement is bound to have a significant impact on the laws and legal systems of the host country. What is fair and equitable, in the absence of any treaty obligations, would entirely be decided by administrative and judicial bodies. With the provisions of the China–New Zealand FTA, China must ensure that its decision-making complies with internationally recognized practice, in particular due process.

With regard to the umbrella clause, a good number of BITs that China has entered into contain provisions similar to those found in other modern BITs. An example is Article 2(2) of the China–United Kingdom BIT, which provides: "Each Contracting Party shall observe any obligation it may have entered into with regard to investments of nationals or companies of the other Contracting Party." The Trilateral Investment Agreement among China, South Korea and Japan stipulates in its Article 5(2): "Each Contracting Party shall observe any written commitments in the form of an agreement or contract it may have entered into with regard to investments of investors of another Contracting Party." Thus, it can be said that almost in every aspect, Chinese BITs are in line with the contemporary BITs that have been entered into by other countries.

As China is yet to be a respondent in any investment arbitration, the interpretation of the above provisions remains to be seen.[345] Yet, based on the interpretation of other BITs by international investment tribunals, it is quite certain that what China has committed to in its recent BITs is in line with the contemporary practice of other main players in international investment.

In conclusion, the absolute standards of treatment, including FET, FPS and the umbrella clause, have now been widely incorporated into BITs and the investment chapters of FTAs. The adoption of these absolute standards of treatment

343 Ibid., Article 143(2) and (3).
344 As mentioned earlier, the China–New Zealand FTA puts FET and FPS in a single Article—Article 143. In BITs that China has signed recently and in the 2006 China–Pakistan FTA, FET is provided for in one article, while protection and security are guaranteed in another. Also, instead of "full," these agreements use the adjective "constant" before the words "protection and security."
345 Although China was named as respondent in one ICSID case, the proceedings were suspended and eventually discontinued without the constitution of a tribunal; see *Ekran Berhad v. People's Republic of China*, ICSID Case No. ARB/11/15.

has notably enhanced the protection of foreign investors and hence has helped promote international investment. Yet there are areas that need to be improved so that the potential of the absolute standards of treatment can be realized. For instance, in relation to FET, FPS or the umbrella clause, there is hardly any consistent view on the contents and scope of such standards.[346] This inconsistency is largely a result of the decisions of investment tribunals; whenever different views are expressed by tribunals, they are likely to lead to discussions among scholars and other commentators, which may in turn affect the decision-making of subsequent tribunals. In practice, however, it is almost impossible to unify results or to expect tribunals to come up with consistent decisions. The current problem is that even where the issues in dispute are the same and the relevant provisions in the BITs concerned are very similar, different tribunals have reached diametrically opposite conclusions. Even worse is that the tribunals concerned may not give adequate reasons for their decisions.

It may, of course, be argued that as the history of investor–state arbitration is short, such inconsistency is unavoidable. Whilst this may be true, unless the situation is improved, the confidence in arbitration of both investors and host states may be affected. In this regard, many consider that the uncertainty in respect of FET led the United States to abandon its insistence on its previous position that FET requires treatment in addition to or beyond that which is required by the international minimum standard of treatment.[347] A possible solution, in addition to the comments and suggestions at the end of each section of this chapter, is for tribunals carefully to state the reasons for their decisions so that others are informed of why a decision has been made in a certain way.

In this regard, tribunals should be clear themselves about the reasons they articulate. At the least, they should try not to make self-contradictory statements. This, for instance, happened in *LG&E* when the tribunal stated:

> The Tribunal observes in the Preamble of the Treaty that the two countries agreed that "fair and equitable treatment of investment is desirable in order to maintain a stable framework for investment and maximum effective use of economic resources." … In light of these stated objectives, this Tribunal must conclude that stability of the legal and business framework is an essential element of fair and equitable treatment in this case.[348]

346 See Christoph Schreuer, "Fair and Equitable Treatment in Arbitral Practice," *The Journal of World Investment & Trade*, Vol. 6, No. 3, June 2005, p. 357. See also UNCTAD, *Bilateral Investment Treaties*, ST/CTC/65 (1988), p. 42; idem, *Fair and Equitable Treatment: A Sequel*, *supra*, note 1; OECD, *Fair and Equitable Treatment Standard in International Investment Law*, 2004; available at: http://www.oecd.org/dataoecd/22/53/33776498.pdf; Mahnaz Malik, *The Full Protection and Security Standard Comes of Age: Yet Another Challenge for States in Investment Treaty Arbitration?*, International Institute for Sustainable Development, Winnipeg, Manitoba, Canada, 2011; and Katia Yannaca-Small, *Interpretation of the Umbrella Clause in Investment Agreements*, OECD Working Papers on International Investment, Number 2006/3, OECD, Paris, 2006.

347 See 2004 US Model BIT, Article 5, as supplemented by Annex A. The identical Article and Annex appear in the most recently concluded US BITs.

348 *LG&E*, *supra*, note 112, para. 124.

This passage has been frequently cited or repeated by other tribunals. Yet it is internally illogical, because where FET is "desirable in order to maintain a stable framework for investment," it is not logically tenable for the "stable framework for investment" or "stability of the legal and business framework" to be an essential part of FET. In other words, if the "stability of the legal and business framework" is the object or purpose that may be achieved with the contribution of FET, it cannot at the same time be part of FET. Unfortunately, mistakes of this kind are not unusual. Hopefully, as tribunals gain more experience, the situation will improve.

7 The relative standards of treatment

An important feature of international investment law is promoting cross-border capital flow by means of host states' offers of protection to foreign investors and investments. Bilateral investment treaties ("BITs") and the investment chapters of free trade agreements ("FTAs"), as well as multilateral treaties involving foreign investments contain, almost without exception, most-favored-nation ("MFN") treatment and national treatment ("NT").[1] Both of these are actually relative standards of treatment because by nature they provide foreign investors and their investments with treatment equivalent to that provided to either parties from a third country or nationals of the host state. In other words, even though country X and country Y may both provide foreign investors MFN treatment and NT, the actual standard of such treatment may differ in the two countries. By offering a standard of treatment that differs from that offered by other countries, a host state is not in violation of international obligations. As such, the relative standards of treatment differ from the absolute standards of treatment, which are judged against international standards under international law, including BITs.

This chapter will first examine the history of MFN treatment and the principles for interpreting the relevant treaty provisions. This will be followed by an examination of the practice of investment dispute arbitral tribunals in regard to this standard. The chapter will then discuss the issues relating to NT. As jurisprudence—based on the cases decided by arbitral tribunals—plays an increasingly important role in formulating international investment law, despite its inconsistency, substantial parts of this chapter will be devoted to scrutinizing the often contradictory awards. Some alternatives will be proposed following the discussion of MFN treatment and NT. Thereafter, the Chinese treaty practice regarding these standards will be examined.

---

1 It has been observed that the "general obligations undertaken by the governments [in BITs] often require them to provide ... (4) national treatment (i.e., treatment as favourable as that provided to citizens of the host country), and (5) most favoured nation treatment (i.e., treatment as favourable as that given to citizens of other countries);" see R. Doak Bishop, James Crawford, and W. Michael Reisman, *Foreign Investment Disputes: Cases, Materials and Commentary*, Kluwer Law International, 2005, p. 1007.

I. The history of the MFN clause and the applicable interpretation principles

A. *The history of MFN treatment*

Most-favored-nation treatment is one of the oldest principles of international law and has always been the product of political and economic compromise. Although the MFN clause is found in almost all international treaties, its significance was first recognized and realized in the field of international trade. More specifically, MFN treatment usually is applicable to the following trade-related acts of states: tariffs on imports, exports, and goods in transit, as well as all kinds of duties and taxes; the customs rules, procedures, and charges relating to the import, transit, storage, and transportation of goods; the issue of import licenses; the duties, charges, and procedures for port entry and exit, as well as the anchoring of ships; and the conditions relating to immigration, trademarks, and railway transport.[2]

As an international law principle, the MFN clause can be traced back to the beginning of the 13th century. At that time, it had already been incorporated into international treaties. A prominent example was the treaty signed between Frederick II and the city of Marseille on November 8, 1226. It stated that citizens of Marseille could enjoy the privileges granted by Frederick II to the citizens of Pisa and Genoa.[3] The MFN clause became widely used in world trade in the 16th century. At that time, England and the Netherlands became competitors of Spain and Portugal in international commercial trade. Moreover, France and the Scandinavian Peninsula gradually became growing powers that competed against the Hanseatic League and the declining Italian Republic. Thus, Spain, Portugal, England, the Netherlands, and France became rivals.[4] They were resentful of each other and refused to cooperate. In order to obtain a competitive edge, all these countries strove to be treated no less favorably than a third country in economic exchanges. This explains why MFN status has always had both a political and an economic flavor.

At the dawn of the 17th century, international economic exchanges became more intensified, and the treaties relating to trade and commerce increased in number. On January 29, 1642, Article 4 of the Treaty signed between the Kingdom of England and Portugal stipulated that English nationals would enjoy the same exemptions and privileges that Portugal granted to nationals of other

---

2 This is so because in modern times to carry out international economic exchanges in the form of trade in goods, trade in services and investment, the items mentioned are essential. As most, if not all, treaties relating to trade and investment contain an MFN clause, the MFN principle applies to such a wide range of activities.

3 Stanley Kuhl Hornbeck, "The Most Favoured Nation Clause in Commercial Treaties," *Bulletin of the University of Wisconsin*, No. 343, *Economics and Political Science Series*, Vol. 6, No. 2 (1910), pp. 336ff. It is said that this treaty was the first written international document relating to MFN treatment.

4 Eugene F. Rice, *The Foundations of Early Modern Europe, 1460–1559*, 2nd ed., Norton, New York, 1994.

nations.[5] This was a rather innovative creation at that time because the MFN clause in the 17th century usually listed the rights enjoyed by specific countries. In addition, at the end of the 17th century, international treaties relating to trade usually distinguished between religious and non-religious countries. For example, Article 3 of the commercial treaty between the Kingdom of England and Portugal stated that the MFN status accorded should not be lower than that given to other Christian countries.[6]

Early MFN clauses contained conditions and were based on the principle of reciprocity, requiring the contracting parties to accord treatment no less favorable than that given to a third country, irrespective of whether the treatment was given prior to or after the signing of the treaty. Unconditional MFN and preferential treatment given without being based on the principle of reciprocity emerged in the late 18th century.[7] During the first half of the 19th century, conditional MFN treatment was prevalent in Europe. Nevertheless, during the second half of the 19th century, changes in the world economic situation resulted in dramatic changes in the European countries, which began to favor unconditional MFN treatment. Needless to say, there is no free lunch anywhere. The motivation for giving unconditional MFN treatment was to maintain the dominant position in world trade of the countries which granted it rather than a sign of friendship or assistance to the economic development of other countries.

At that time, the policy of unconditional MFN treatment stood in sharp contrast with the isolationist policy of the United States. In the 18th and 19th centuries, the United States regarded conditional MFN as its basic policy of foreign trade.[8] After the American War of Independence, although the United States became a legal entity in political affairs, it did not attain equal status with Europe in world economic affairs. France, Spain and Great Britain attempted to drive the United States out of their spheres of influence so that it could not conduct free trade with their colonies. On the other hand, these European countries wanted to enter the US market. The United States therefore adopted a closed-door policy with high tariffs. It refused to give any benefit to the European countries unless they agreed to open their markets on similar terms.[9] In 1778, the United States and France signed a Treaty of Amity and Commerce providing for mutual MFN treatment.[10] It is fair to say that the conditional MFN

---

5 Hugh O. Davis, *America's Trade Equality Policy*, American Council on Public Affairs, Washington, D.C., 1942, p. 2.

6 Id.

7 For discussions of the MFN clause prior to modern times, including the practice of the United Sates, the United Kingdom and other European countries, see Hornbeck, *supra*, note 3.

8 In this regard, Hornbeck stated: "In contrast with the guarantee of immediate, unconditional extension of favours to the co-contractor contained in the majority of modern European treaties, this clause expressly says that the second party shall enjoy the favour only in case it is freely extended to a third party, and that in case it is given for a compensation the second may not be excluded from it but may have the right to demand it." Ibid., pp. 350–51.

9 See Davis, *supra*, note 5, p. 3.

10 The MFN clause signed by the United States generally provided that the contracting parties agreed to give the benefits and privileges accorded to or that would be accorded to the countries or

policy adopted by the United States increased its bargaining power and paved the way for widening trade relations with the European countries on an equal footing. The vast US market and the bargaining power of the United States formed the basis for this development.

In any event, the divergence between the United States and Europe on MFN treatment changed after World War I. At the end of the War, the United States progressed from being an importer of European industrial products and capital and an exporter of raw materials to Europe to a country which exported industrial goods and capital to Europe. In the 20th century, the foreign trade policies of the United States underwent tremendous changes. In international trade, the United States began to support the notion of unconditional MFN treatment. It actively advocated that all countries should be treated on an equal basis in respect of import restrictions, especially in terms of tariffs and other duties.[11]

The decision of the United States Customs Court in *John T. Bill Co. v. United States* was a reflection of US policy at that time.[12] On October 14, 1925, John T. Bill Co. sued the United States, alleging that the tariffs it imposed on bicycle parts imported from Germany were contrary to the Treaty between the United States and Germany. Article 7 of that Treaty stated that the contracting parties should unconditionally accord each other treatment no less favorable than that given to third countries. Both parties also agreed to give each other treatment no less favorable than that given to third countries in relation to tariffs of exported goods and other trade.

John T. Bill Co. claimed that the Treaty between the United States and Germany provided for unconditional MFN treatment; thus, bicycle parts imported from Germany should not be subject to tariffs higher than those applied to like products imported from other countries. At that time, the United States levied a duty at the rate of 30 percent *ad valorem* on bicycle parts imported from other countries, whilst the rate of duty was 50 percent on bicycle parts imported from Germany. Judge Garrett ruled that the United States could give preferential treatment to other countries, provided that it would be treated in similar terms,[13] although unconditional MFN treatment was more consistent with the interests and fundamental policies of the United States, because conditional MFN treatment would be unable to ensure that the United States products and merchants would be treated on an equal footing in foreign markets. He also pointed out, however, that the MFN clause in the Treaty between the United States and Germany was reciprocal in nature and, because it provided for reciprocal unconditional MFN

nationals of other countries, provided that the above privileges were given without consideration or based on the principle of mutuality. See ibid., p. 9.

11 The Customs Act adopted by the US Congress in 1922 authorized the President to enter into unconditional MFN treatment provisions. The US Trade Act of 1934 reiterated the above authorization.

12 *John .T Bill Co. Inc., Victor Distributing Co v. United States*, 104 F 2d 67 (1939).

13 Id.

treatment, the Customs Court held that the unfair treatment given to the products imported from Germany violated its treaty obligations.[14]

The MFN principle plays an important role in international trade; when countries negotiate the terms and conditions of MFN treatment, they all hope to restrict the applicability of the MFN provisions so as to prevent a third party from benefiting. Countries also restrict the application of MFN treatment by specifically excluding certain products.

Following World War II, apart from restrictions in the form of tariffs, many countries also introduced non-tariff barriers in international trade, such as anti-dumping regulations, countervailing duty provisions, import license requirements, or export restrictions. These non-tariff restrictions were the biggest obstacles in international trade at that time. Traditionally, the MFN clause was only applicable to import tariffs and did not affect non-tariff barriers. The Tokyo Round of multilateral trade negotiations extended the applicability of the MFN principle to other agreements.[15] However, as the agreements concluded at the Tokyo Round were only applicable to the signatories, their practical effect was limited. Since the coming into force of the World Trade Organization ("WTO"), the MFN principle has applied to all the WTO Agreements covering trade in goods, trade in services, intellectual property, and non-tariff barriers. This is a significant development of the MFN principle.[16]

Another use of the MFN principle in the contemporary world is in service of bilateral political purposes.[17] The MFN principle has now become a normal trade relationship between countries which have diplomatic relations and therefore has become the minimum standard of treatment. With the mutual interdependence of the countries in the international community intensifying, MFN treatment has never been withdrawn in recent decades. As more and more countries enter the WTO, with MFN treatment as a fundamental principle thereof, any nation that might try to unilaterally give or withdraw MFN status would encounter significant obstacles.[18] In relation to international investment, the MFN clause can be found literally in every BIT and FTA, as well as the treaties and agreements on intel-

---

14 Id.
15 For a discussion of the Tokyo Round, see Chapter 1, "From GATT to WTO." As discussed earlier, at the Tokyo Round, a number of separate agreements were reached and the MFN principle became applicable to each of them.
16 See Article 1 of the GATT, Article 4 of the TRIPS Agreement and Article 2 of the GATS. As the Agreement on Agriculture, the Agreement on the Application of Sanitary and Phytosanitary Measures, the Agreement on Technical Barriers to Trade, etc. are annexes to the GATT, the MFN principle is equally applicable to them.
17 For a number of years before China joined the WTO, the United States would review China's human rights situation before giving the latter MFN status on a yearly basis. The situation was improved by the Clinton Administration when it delinked human rights from the determination of MFN status in the late 1990s.
18 Actually, as MFN is the cornerstone of the WTO and is unconditionally applicable to all of the WTO Agreements, any attempt to impose a condition on the application of MFN treatment might constitute an abolition or reduction of the benefits to which a Member is entitled and, therefore, be a violation of the WTO Agreement.

lectual property. Thus, it is certain that MFN treatment has become an essential principle in all economic exchanges—a principle of international economic law.

B. Principles of interpretation

The MFN clause is embodied in international treaties and agreements. As one of the oldest principles of international law, its interpretation—and, in particular, its potential and possibly divergent interpretation—has caused concern within the international community. As early as September 1924, the Assembly of the League of Nations passed a Resolution for the "Progressive Codification of International Law" and set up a Sub-Committee to consider the possibility of "an international agreement concerning the principal means of determining and interpreting the effects of the Most-Favoured-Nation clause in Treaties." [19] The Sub-Committee reported:

> The majority of members of the Committee responded to the original question put to the Sub-Committee with a negative answer: "it would not seem either necessary or desirable even if it were practicable to endeavour to frame a code provision to govern the case."[20]

As the work of the Sub-Committee was inconclusive, the matter was not picked up again until after World War II. Soon after the establishment of the United Nations, its Secretary General, in a memorandum entitled "Survey of International Law in Relation to the Work of Codification of the International Law Commission," stated:

> The divergent interpretations of the most-favoured-nation clause continue to cause difficulties, and it may be necessary to reconsider the view expressed by the League of Nations Committee of Experts that the subject, which it discussed in detail on the basis of a thorough report, can be best dealt with by way of bilateral agreements.[21]

The effort of the UN finally resulted in the publication by its International Law Commission of the Draft Articles on Most-Favored-Nation clauses, which define MFN treatment as follows:

---

19 See Endre Ustor, Special Rapporteur of the ILC, *Yearbook of the International Law Commission*, 1969, Vol. II, p. 170, Document A/CN.4/213 (April 18, 1969); "Second Report on the Most-Favoured-Nation Clause", *Yearbook of the International Law Commission*, 1970, Vol. II, p. 204 (March 9 and May 18, 1970), Document A.CN.4/228 and Add. 1.

20 See "Second Report on the Most-Favoured-Nation Clause", ibid., para. 90.

21 United Nations, Memorandum submitted by the Secretary-General, *Survey of International Law in Relation to the Work of Codification of the International Law Commission*, extract from the Book of the ILC, 1949. Document A/CN.4/1/Rev.1, para. 91, United Nations Publications, 1948, Vol. 1, pp. 52–53.

> Most-favoured-nation treatment is treatment accorded by the granting State
> to the beneficiary State, or to persons or things in a determined relationship
> with that State, not less favourable than treatment extended by the granting
> State to a third State or to persons or things in the same relationship with that
> third State.[22]

Therefore, the right of the beneficiary state to MFN treatment arises only from
a valid agreement between the granting state and the beneficiary state, and the
rights acquired are confined to those falling within the subject matter of the
agreement. The beneficiary state can be a third state itself or persons or things in
the same relationship with that third state.[23] The beneficiary state acquires MFN
rights whenever more favorable treatment is offered by the granting state to the
persons or things of a third state, but only insofar as its persons or things, as well
as the relationship of the persons or things of the third state with that state, are
of the same category.[24] It is evident from the Draft Articles that MFN treatment
was not then considered a natural right of a state. The grant and enjoyment of
MFN treatment was to be achieved through negotiations between the countries
concerned. Also, MFN treatment is only applicable where the persons and things
are in the same or similar circumstances. In other words, MFN treatment is not
applicable to situations where the relevant persons or matters are not of the same
type or of the same nature.

As an integral part of most international treaties and agreements, the MFN
clause should be interpreted in accordance with the rules laid down in Articles
31 and 32 of the Vienna Convention on the Law of Treaties ("VCLT"), that
is, a treaty "shall be interpreted in good faith in accordance with the ordinary
meaning to be given to the terms of the treaty in their context and in the light of
its object and purpose." In this regard, the International Court of Justice ("ICJ")
has considered Articles 31 and 32 of the VCLT to represent customary international law in several of its pronouncements.[25] For instance, in *Interpretation of Peace
Treaties with Bulgaria, Hungary and Romania (Second Phase)* – (Advisory Opinion of
the International Court of Justice of July 18, 1950), the ICJ stated that "[i]t is the
duty of the Court to interpret the Treaties, not to revise them."[26] In the view of
the Court, if the text of a convention is sufficiently clear in itself, there is no need

---

22 Article 5 of UN Report of the International Law Commission, *Draft Articles on Most-Favoured-Nation
Clauses*, July 1978. "Granting State" means a state which has undertaken to accord MFN treatment while "beneficiary State" means a state to which a granting state has undertaken to accord
such status.

23 Ibid., Articles 8 and 9.

24 Ibid., Article 10.

25 The ICJ "has also emphasised that interpretation is not a matter of revising treaties or of reading
into them what they do not expressly or by necessary implication contain, or of applying a rule of
interpretation so as to produce a result contrary to the letter or spirit of the treaty's text;" see Sir
Robert Jennings and Sir Arthur Watts (eds.), *Oppenheim's International Law*, Vol. I (parts 2 to 4), 9th
ed., Oxford University Press, Oxford, UK, pp. 1271–72.

26 *ICJ Reports*, 1950, p. 229.

to resort to the preparatory works of the treaty in question. On this matter, the Court stated:

> [T]he first duty of a tribunal which is called upon to interpret and apply the provisions of a treaty, is to endeavour to give effect to them in their natural and ordinary meaning in the context in which they occur. If the relevant words in their natural and ordinary meaning make sense in their context, that is an end of the matter. If, on the other hand, the words in their natural and ordinary meaning are ambiguous or lead to an unreasonable result, then, and then only, must the Court, by resort to other methods of interpretation, seek to ascertain what the parties really did mean when they used these words.[27]

Again, in *Qatar v. Bahrain*,[28] the ICJ specifically recalled what it had said in the *Case Concerning Territorial Dispute Libyan Arab Jamahiriya/Chad*:

> [I]n accordance with customary international law, reflected in Article 31 of the 1969 Vienna Convention on the Law of Treaties, a treaty must be interpreted in good faith in accordance with the ordinary meaning to be given to its terms in their context and in the light of its object and purpose. Interpretation must be based above all upon the text of the treaty. As a supplementary measure recourse may be had to means of interpretation such as the preparatory work of the treaty and the circumstances of its conclusion.[29]

The approach of the ICJ to the interpretation of treaties has been followed by arbitral tribunals in trade and investment. For instance, in *Wintershall*,[30] the tribunal stated:

> The carefully-worded formulation in Article 31 [of the VCLT] is based on the view that the text must be presumed to be the authentic expression of the intention of the parties. The starting point of all treaty-interpretation is the elucidation of the meaning of the text, not an independent investigation into the intention of the parties from other sources (such as by reference to the *travaux préparatoires*, or any predilections based on presumed intention).[31]

As will be discussed later, in practice, even though tribunals follow the same principles of treaty interpretation, the results still differ. In addition to the customary

27 *Case concerning the Arbitral Award of 31 July 1989 (Guinea-Bissau v. Senegal)*, Judgment of November 12, 1991, *ICJ Reports*, 1991, para. 48, p. 69, quoting an earlier pronouncement of the Court in the Advisory Opinion on *Competence of the General Assembly for the Admission of a State to the United Nations*, *ICJ Reports*, 1950, p. 8.
28 *Case concerning Maritime Delimitation and Territorial Questions between Qatar and Bahrain*, *ICJ Reports*, 1995.
29 Ibid., p. 18, para. 33.
30 *Wintershall Aktiengesellschaft v. Argentine Republic*, ICSID Case No. ARB/04/14, Award of December 8, 2008; available at: http://icsid.worldbank.org/ICSID/FrontServlet?requestType=CasesRH&actionVal=showDoc&docId=DC1492_En&caseId=C39.
31 Ibid., para 78.

international law principles on treaty interpretation illustrated in Articles 31 and 32 of the VCLT, an MFN clause must be interpreted in accordance with the more specific principle of *ejusdem generis*. In accordance with this principle, as stated by one US court, where "general words follow enumerations of particular classes or persons or things, the general words shall be construed as applicable only to persons or things of the same general nature or kind as those enumerated."[32]

Insofar as interpreting the MFN clause per se is concerned, the ICJ was seized with the issue in the following cases: the *Anglo-Iranian Oil Company* case *(Jurisdiction)*,[33] the *Case Concerning Rights of Nationals of the United States of America in Morocco*,[34] and the *Ambatielos Case (Merits)*.[35] In the *Anglo Iranian Oil Company* case, the ICJ stated that "a third party treaty, independent of and isolated from the basic treaty, cannot produce any legal effect" between the contracting parties to the basic treaty.[36] In the *Case Concerning Rights of Nationals of the United States of America in Morocco*, the ICJ said that the MFN clause represented the principle of equality of treatment in the field of foreign trade.

In *Ambatielos*, one of the issues involved was whether Greek nationals were, as the Greek Government contended, entitled to treatment according to "justice, right and equity" by virtue of the MFN clause contained in a treaty between Greece and the United Kingdom. The majority decision of the ICJ did not pronounce upon the issue directly.[37] The joint dissenting opinion of four ICJ judges, on the other hand, stated: "At this stage we meet Article X of the Treaty of 1886 which has been invoked by the Hellenic Government. This Article contains a most-favoured-nation clause which, in its opinion, embodies certain references to the requirements of the proper administration of justice."[38] In the view of the

---

32 *Walling v. Peavy-Wilson Lumber Co.*, D.C., 49 F.Supp. 846, at 859.

33 *Anglo-Iranian Oil Company Case (United Kingdom v. Iran)*, Judgment of 22 July 1952, *ICJ Reports*, 1952, p. 93. ("*Anglo-Iranian*").

34 *Case Concerning Rights of Nationals of the United States of America in Morocco (France v. United States of America)*, Judgment of 27 August 1952, *ICJ Reports*, 1952, p. 176.

35 *Ambatielos Case (Greece v. United Kingdom)*, Merits: Obligation to Arbitrate, Judgment of May 19, 1953, *ICJ Reports*, 1953 ("*Ambatielos I*").

36 *Anglo-Iranian Oil Co.*, *supra*, note 33, p. 109.

37 See Ustor, *supra*, note 19, "Second Report", p. 209. It contains the following: "61. In the course of the proceedings before the International Court of Justice (in the *Ambatielos Case*) the parties referred to a most-favoured-nation clause embodied in the treaty of commerce of 1886 and a national treatment clause of the same treaty granting 'free access to the Courts of Justice'. They differed widely on the scope and effect of the most-favoured-nation clause and on the meaning of the term 'free access to the Courts of Justice'.

62. The Court itself (i.e. the majority) did not decide on the substance of the dispute. Thus no discussion of the substantive issues, which would throw light on the problems connected with the operation of a most-favoured-nation clause, is to be found in the judgment of the Court. They are dealt with in great detail in the written and oral submissions of the parties and in the joint dissenting opinion of four members of the Court, Judge McNair, then President of the Court, and Judges Basdevant, Klaestad and Read."

38 *Ambatielos I*, dissenting opinion by Sir Arnold McNair, President, and Judges Basdevant, Klaestad, and Read, *ICJ Reports*, 1953, p. 34.

four ICJ judges, under Article X, only commerce and navigation were covered by the MFN clause because "it makes no provision concerning the administration of justice."[39] Even though Article XV, paragraph 3, concerned free access to the Courts, because "that Article contains no reference to most-favoured-nation treatment,"[40] the ICJ judges concluded that the MFN clause did not apply; they found that it could not be extended to the administration of justice, which was not expressly stipulated. To apply the MFN clause to the administration of justice, in the view of the judges, would constitute an "extensive interpretation" of the MFN clause in question.[41]

The joint dissenting opinion in *Ambatielos I* also said:

> [I]t is necessary not to lose sight of the fact that in this case the Court has to decide, on the basis of the meaning to be attributed to the free access clause, what is the extent of the obligation to arbitrate arising from the Declaration of 1926. With two interpretations of Article XV, paragraph 3, before us, we cannot subscribe to the one which would extend it to the production of evidence and thereby enlarge the obligation to submit to arbitration. It is particularly difficult to accept an interpretative extension of an obligation of a State to have recourse to arbitration. The Permanent Court in the *Phosphates in Morocco* case stated that a jurisdiction clause must on no account be interpreted in such a way as to exceed the intention of the States that subscribed to it.[42]

As the majority of the ICJ refrained from exercising jurisdiction, a Commission of Arbitration was established to deal with the dispute between Greece and the United Kingdom. In its award— *Ambatielos II*[43]—the Commission of Arbitration said that in the Treaty of 1886 the application of the MFN clause was defined to include "all matters relating to commerce and navigation." It went on to say:

> It would seem that this expression has not, in itself, a strictly defined meaning.
>
> …
>
> Therefore, it cannot be said that the administration of justice, in so far as it is concerned with the protection of these rights, must necessarily be excluded from the field of application of the most-favoured-nation clause,

39 Id.
40 Id.
41 Id.
42 Ibid., p. 33, where reference is made to the *Phosphates in Morocco Case (Italy v. France)*. In that case, the PCIJ observed that it was advisable in case of doubt to give a restrictive interpretation of a clause in a treaty because such a clause "must on no account be interpreted in such a way as to exceed the intention of the States that subscribed to it;" PCIJ Ser. A/B No. 74, 1938, p. 14.
43 *Ambatielos Case (Greece v. United Kingdom)*, Award of March 6, 1956, United Nations, Reports of International Arbitral Awards, Vol. XII, 1963, p. 87. ("*Ambatielos II*").

when the latter includes "all matters relating to commerce and navigation". The question can only be determined in accordance with the intention of the Contracting Parties as deduced from a reasonable interpretation of the Treaty.[44]

Clearly, the Commission of Arbitration did not intend to pronounce "a view on the general question as to whether the most-favoured-nation clause can never have the effect of assuring to its beneficiaries treatment in accordance with the general rules of international law."[45] The MFN clause in that case was expressly confined to "any privilege, favour or immunity which either Contracting Party has actually granted or may hereafter grant to the subjects or citizens of any other State" and, as such, it "would obviously not be the case if the sole object of those provisions were to guarantee to them treatment in accordance with the general rules of international law."[46] Yet, despite the wish of the Commission, its opinion has been relied upon in resolving trade and investment disputes. This has a great deal to do with common law methods that tribunals (including the Appellate Body of the WTO) have employed in their proceedings and the techniques adopted by lawyers in such cases. This development of dispute resolution relating to trade and investment has led to an ever-growing jurisprudence—case law—to which the advancement of science and technology, in particular computer and Internet technology, has made essential contributions.

II. MFN jurisprudence relating to investment

Insofar as cross-border investment is concerned, MFN treatment is, without exception, stipulated in all the BITs and the investment chapters of FTAs. There had been very few cases involving the implementation of the clause until the *Maffezini* case, before which it had been understood that the MFN clause was only concerned with substantive treatment. Ever since, however, there have been debates among scholars in respect of the role that the clause may play. Investment tribunals also divided in their positions toward the scope of application of the MFN clause. Among these differing views, the most thorny question is whether or not the MFN clause should apply to dispute resolution procedures. As this is the single most important and hotly debated issue in regard to MFN treatment in investment law, this section will first examine the cases supporting the extended approach and then analyze those decisions that have rejected such extended application, along with their respective reasoning.

---

44 Ibid., p. 107. This view of the Commission of Arbitration has been heavily relied upon by tribunals that have favored extension of the MFN clause to dispute settlement procedures, as will be discussed later.

45 Ibid., p. 106.

46 Id.

A. Cases supporting extension of the MFN clause to dispute resolution procedures

For decades, the MFN clause was considered to be applicable only to substantive treatment and not to procedural matters, such as the mechanisms relating to dispute settlement. The *Maffezini* case,[47] which involved an Argentine investor's dispute with the Government of Spain, was a turning point. In that case, the Argentine investor brought its dispute with the Spanish Government to arbitration with the ICSID. Article X of the BIT between Argentina and Spain reads:

1. Disputes which arise within the terms of this Agreement concerning an investment between an investor of one Contracting Party and the other Contracting Party shall, if possible, be settled amicably by the parties to the dispute.
2. If the dispute cannot thus be settled within six months following the date on which the dispute has been raised by either party, it shall be submitted to the competent tribunal of the Contracting Party in whose territory the investment was made.
3. The dispute may be submitted to international arbitration in any of the following circumstances:
   (a) at the request of one of the parties to the dispute, if no decision has been rendered on the merits of the claim after the expiration of a period of eighteen months from the date on which the proceedings referred to in paragraph 2 of this Article have been initiated, or if such decision has been rendered, but the dispute between the parties continues;
   (b) if both parties to the dispute agree thereto.
4. In the cases foreseen in paragraph 3, the disputes between the parties shall be submitted, unless the parties otherwise agree, either to international arbitration under the March 18, 1965 Convention on the Settlement of Investment Disputes Between States and Nationals of Other States or to an ad hoc arbitral tribunal established under the Arbitration Rules of the United Nations Commission on International Trade Law (UNCITRAL).

   If after a period of three months following the submission of the dispute to arbitration by either party, there is no agreement to one of the above alternative procedures, the dispute shall be submitted to arbitration under the March 18, 1965 Convention on the Settlement of Investment Disputes Between States and Nationals of Other States, provided that both Contracting Parties have become parties to the said Convention. Otherwise, the dispute shall be submitted to the above mentioned ad hoc tribunal.

---

47 *Emilio Agustín Maffezini v. Kingdom of Spain*, ICSID Case No. ARB/97/7, Award (November 13, 2000).

Before bringing the dispute for arbitration, however, Maffezini had not resorted to the local courts. Spain therefore challenged the jurisdiction of the ICSID Tribunal. The claimant argued that under the BIT foreign investors were permitted to avail of international arbitration in the end and that the requirement of local remedies should not therefore be a bar to international arbitration. In particular, it argued that in the 18-month period, the local court might not make a decision and, even if a decision were made, the foreign investor might not agree with it. In a word, in the view of the claimant, the local court requirement is merely a procedure that may or may not be followed. Regarding this matter, the tribunal held:

> [I]t must now be asked whether a party to a dispute, which has not referred the case to a domestic court, as required by Article X(2), must be deemed to have waived or forfeited the right to submit the matter to international arbitration. Here it is to be noted that paragraph 2 provides that the dispute "shall be submitted" (*será sometida*) to the competent tribunals of the State Party where the investment was made, and that paragraph 3(a) then declares that the dispute "may be submitted" (*podrá ser sometida*) to an international arbitral tribunal at the request of a party to the dispute in the following circumstances: if the domestic court has not rendered a decision on the merits of the case within a period of eighteen months or if, notwithstanding the existence of such a decision, the dispute continues.[48]

In the view of the tribunal, the purpose of the requirement was to give the local courts an opportunity, within a specified period of time, to resolve the dispute between a foreign investor and the host government.[49] Despite the argument of the claimant that the above could not have been the intended meaning of the provision because after the 18-month period the foreign investor would still have the right to bring its dispute to international arbitration, the tribunal further stated that had the claimant relied solely on that argument, it would have concluded that it lacked jurisdiction owing to failure on the part of the claimant first to submit its dispute to Spanish courts as required by Article X(2) of the BIT.[50] In the view of the tribunal:

> [W]hile it is true that the parties would be free to seek international arbitration after the expiration of the eighteen-month period, regardless of the outcome of the domestic court proceeding, they are likely to do so only if they were dissatisfied with the domestic court decision. Moreover, they would certainly not do so if they were convinced that the international tribunal would reach the same decision. … Claimant's interpretation of Article X(2) would deprive this provision of any meaning, a result that would not be compatible with generally accepted principles of treaty interpretation, particularly those of the Vienna Convention on the Law of Treaties.[51]

48 Ibid., para. 34.
49 Ibid., para. 35.
50 Ibid., para. 36.
51 Id.

The claimant, however, also relied on Article IV of the Argentina–Spain BIT to evade the application of Article X of the BIT. Article IV reads: "In all matters subject to this Agreement, this treatment shall not be less favorable than that extended by each Party to the investments made in its territory by investors of a third country." The claimant contended that Article 10(2) of the Chile–Spain BIT imposed no condition of local remedies before international arbitration and that, by operation of the MFN clause, it should not be required to resort to the local court procedures of Spain before submitting its dispute to arbitration. The question was whether the scope of Article IV was wide enough to permit such an interpretation.

The tribunal first stated that, although the words "all matters subject to this Agreement" did not

> … refer expressly to dispute settlement as covered by the most favored nation clause, … today dispute settlement arrangements are inextricably related to the protection of foreign investors, as they are also related to the protection of rights of traders under treaties of commerce. … [S]uch arrangements, even if not strictly a part of the material aspect of the trade and investment policy pursued by treaties of commerce and navigation, were essential for the adequate protection of the rights they sought to guarantee.[52]

It went on to say that "[i]nternational arbitration and other dispute settlement arrangements have replaced these older and frequently abusive practices of the past."[53] Therefore, the tribunal concluded that:

> … if a third party treaty contains provisions for the settlement of disputes that are more favorable to the protection of the investor's rights and interests than those in the basic treaty, such provisions may be extended to the beneficiary of the most favored nation clause as they are fully compatible with the *ejusdem generis* principle.[54]

The *Maffezini* Tribunal considered that the MFN provision of the base treaty was broad enough to cover procedural issues such as dispute settlement. One of the reasons given for this was that among all the BITs that the tribunal examined and to which Spain was a party, only the Argentina–Spain BIT's MFN clause stipulates "all matters subject to this Agreement."[55] Consequently, the tribunal concluded that the contracting parties intended the MFN clause to extend to dispute resolution. It was, of course, to say the least, a very bold move to give the clause such broad meaning.

Apparently, the *Maffezini* Tribunal was also concerned about the consequences

52 Ibid., para. 54.
53 Ibid., para. 55.
54 Ibid., para. 56.
55 Ibid., para. 60.

of its decision. It therefore tried to impose some limitations on the application of the MFN clause by stating:

> As a matter of principle, the beneficiary of the clause should not be able to override public policy considerations that the contracting parties might have envisaged as fundamental conditions for their acceptance of the agreement in question, particularly if the beneficiary is a private investor, as will often be the case. The scope of the clause might thus be narrower than it appears at first sight.[56]

Subsequent to the *Maffezini* case, there have been other cases which supported that tribunal's decision, albeit with different reasons. For instance, in *Impregilo*,[57] Article 8(3) of the BIT between Argentina and Italy contains a jurisdictional requirement that has to be fulfilled before an ICSID tribunal can assert jurisdiction. The tribunal found the "time-bound prior-recourse-to-local-courts-clause" to be mandatory.[58] On the other hand, Article 3(1) of the BIT provides that:

> Each Contracting Party shall, within its own territory, accord to investments made by investors of the other Contracting Party, to the income and activities related to such investments and to all other matters regulated by this Agreement, a treatment that is no less favorable than that accorded to its own investors or investors from third-party countries.[59]

The tribunal concluded that the term "treatment" was broad enough to embrace "procedural matters such as dispute settlement."[60] In its analysis, the tribunal also relied on the wording "all other matters regulated by this Agreement," which it considered to be wide enough to cover dispute settlement matters.

In *Hochtief v. Argentina*,[61] the tribunal also allowed the investor, through operation of the MFN clause in the Argentina–Germany BIT (as the base treaty), to bypass the 18-month local court requirement before bringing its claims to international arbitration. In its analysis, the tribunal noted the implicit limitations of a MFN clause as stated by the International Law Commission in its Commentary on its Draft Articles on Most-Favored-Nation Clauses. It then went on to state that "the MFN clause cannot create a right to go to arbitration where none otherwise exists under the BIT. The argument can be put more generally: the MFN clause stipulates how investors must be treated when they are exercising the rights given

---

56 Ibid., para. 62. The tribunal envisaged a number of situations where the operation of the MFN clause should be limited; for details, see ibid., para. 63.

57 *Impregilo S.p.A. v. Argentine Republic*, ICSID Case No. ARB/07/17, Award (June 21, 2011); available at: http://italaw.com/documents/Imgregilov.ArgentinaAward.pdf.

58 Ibid., para. 94.

59 Ibid., para. 96.

60 Ibid., para. 99.

61 *Hochtief AG v. Argentine Republic*, ICSID Case No. ARB/07/31, Decision on Jurisdiction (October 24, 2011).

to them under the BIT but does not purport to give them any further rights in addition to those given to them under the BIT."[62] To answer the question as to whether or not bypassing the requirement of an 18-month litigation in local courts would constitute "a distinct or new right" or "rather a matter of the manner in which those who already have a right to arbitrate are treated,"[63] the *Hochtief* Tribunal concluded:

> … it cannot be assumed that Argentina and German (sic) intended that the MFN clause should create wholly new rights where none otherwise existed under the Argentina-Germany BIT. The MFN clause stipulates a standard of treatment and defines it according to the treatment of third parties. The reference is to a standard of treatment accorded to third parties, not to the extent of the legal rights of third parties. Non-statutory concessions to third party investors could, in principle, form the basis of a complaint that the MFN obligation has not been secured.[64]

Is the 18-month local litigation period a right or a provision relating to treatment? The *Hochtief* Tribunal admitted that "there is no established criterion to distinguish for this purpose between a 'right' and 'treatment in relation to the exercise of a right'."[65] Yet it considered that "there are several indications that the 18-month pre-arbitration litigation requirement should be regarded as a matter of the treatment of investors in exercising their rights in relation to dispute settlement and not as the subject of a distinct right."[66] In the tribunal's view, under the Argentina–Germany BIT, as the claimant would ultimately have the right unilaterally to submit its claims to international arbitration after it had been through the 18-month litigation period, whilst investors under the Argentina–Chile BIT may unilaterally bring a dispute to international arbitration immediately, investors under both BITs have the same right. Therefore, the tribunal supported the claimant's position.

In *Impregilo*, the BIT with a third party that was at issue was the Argentina–United States BIT, which does not require local court litigation. The question facing the tribunal was whether international arbitration was more favorable when compared with local court procedures. It addressed the issue by examining "whether a *choice* between domestic proceedings and international arbitration, as in the Argentina–US BIT, is more favorable to the investor than compulsory domestic proceedings before access is opened to arbitration." [67] The answer was then quite obvious, as no one would argue that a treaty which allows a choice is not more favorable than one which does not.

The tribunal also examined and attached importance to the provision "all

---

62 Ibid., para. 79.
63 Ibid., para. 80.
64 Ibid., para. 81.
65 Ibid., para. 82.
66 Ibid., para. 83.
67 *Impregilo, supra*, note 57, para. 101 (emphasis in original).

other matters regulated by this Agreement." As to the question of whether or not the principle of *ejusdem generis* would exclude the application of the MFN clause from dispute settlement, the tribunal stated that "all other matters" should not be interpreted as "all similar matters" or "all other matters of the same kind."[68] It concluded that in all previous arbitral decisions, when dealing with treaty provisions such as this one, international investment dispute tribunals had extended the application of the MFN clause to dispute settlement.[69] As in *Maffezini*, the *Impregilo* Tribunal in the end ruled that "all other matters" should override the term "the income and activities related to such investments," which might have limited the application of the MFN clause. It also stressed the importance of maintaining consistency in interpreting treaty provisions, saying that "the Arbitral tribunal finds it unfortunate if the assessment of these issues would in each case be dependent on the personal opinions of individual arbitrators. The best way to avoid such a result is to make the determination on the basis of case law whenever a clear case law can be discerned."[70]

It is idealistic to maintain that international investment case law is clear or that arbitral tribunals follow the case law. The reality is that the jurisprudence of investment law is by no means consistent. Even arbitrators on the same tribunal often have different views. In *Impregilo*, for example, the minority arbitrator in her dissenting opinion severely criticized decisions rendered by previous investment tribunals on the application of the MFN clause. In her view, "unless specifically stated to the contrary, the qualifying conditions put by the State in order to accept to be sued directly on the international level by foreign investors cannot be displaced by an MFN clause, and a conditional right to ICSID cannot magically be transformed into an unconditional right by the grace of the MFN clause."[71]

Another issue of interest in *Impregilo* was Argentina's contention that the words "within its own territory" should limit the scope of the MFN clause. The tribunal stated that: "the question as to what legal protection Argentina shall give to foreign investors is in no way an issue over which Argentina has no power to decide, nor is it tied to any particular territory."[72] Thus, in the tribunal's view, the application of the MFN clause was not limited by the provision of "within its own territory," which is common phrasing in BITs and FTAs.

The most difficult issue that had to be dealt with in *Impregilo* was the fact that, subsequent to the signing of the Argentina–United States BIT, some of the BITs concluded by Argentina with other countries continued to contain a jurisdictional requirement similar to that of the Argentina–Italy BIT. The implication of this practice, as argued by Argentina, was that Argentina did not intend to have such provisions replaced or revised through the operation of the MFN clause.

---

68 Id.
69 Ibid., paras. 103 and 108.
70 Ibid., para. 108.
71 *Impregilo S.p.A. v. Argentine Republic*, Concurring and Dissenting Opinion, Brigitte Stern, para. 99.
72 *Impregilo*, Award, *supra*, note 57, para. 100.

Unfortunately, the *Impregilo* Tribunal did not elaborate on the issue. Rather, it stated that "the argument becomes less persuasive in the present case, because the Italy–Argentina BIT (signed on 22 May 1990) preceded the Argentina–US BIT (signed on November 14, 1991)."[73] It is common knowledge that when negotiating with another country on an unequal footing, a weaker country may be "bullied" into agreeing to special provisions or arrangements. In such circumstances, a broad interpretation of the MFN clause will not reflect the intent of the weaker country in relation to its granting of MFN treatment to other countries.

Tribunals in several other cases simply considered the local remedy requirements as procedural in nature and, as such, lacking in any impact on their jurisdiction. In *Ethyl v. Canada*, for instance, the tribunal questioned whether the "NAFTA Parties intended" that the six-month waiting requirement "must be fulfilled prior to or simultaneously with delivery of a Notice of Arbitration in order for a Tribunal's jurisdiction to attach."[74] In fact, in the *Ethyl* Tribunal's view, the six-month waiting period rule was "analogized to the international law requirement of exhaustion of remedies, which [was] disregarded when it [was] demonstrated that in fact no remedy was available and any attempt at exhaustion would have been futile."[75] In other words, the *Ethyl* Tribunal considered that where the end result would be the same, the rule establishing the waiting period could be overlooked. The question then is why would the contracting parties have agreed to such rule and, in any case, should an arbitral tribunal have the authority to disregard the arrangement and, if so, on what basis.

In *Bayindir Insaat v. Islamic Republic of Pakistan*, Pakistan admitted that "the notice requirement cannot constitute a prerequisite for jurisdiction."[76] The tribunal in *SGS v. Pakistan* also concluded that the consultation requirement was procedural rather than jurisdictional in nature. As such, compliance "with such a requirement is, accordingly, not seen as amounting to a condition precedent for the vesting of jurisdiction."[77]

The *Suez*[78] Tribunal, on the other hand, found "no basis for distinguishing dispute settlement matters from any other matters covered by a bilateral investment treaty."[79] From its point of view, the dispute settlement mechanisms are important issues under the BIT and form an integral part thereof. As such, dispute settlement procedures may not be excluded from the application of the MFN

73 Ibid., para. 102.
74 *Ethyl Corp. v. Canada*, UNCITRAL Award (June 24, 1998), 38 *I.L.M.* 708 (1999), para. 74.
75 Ibid., para. 84.
76 *Bayindir v. Pakistan*, ICSID Case No. ARB/03/29, Decision on Jurisdiction (November 14, 2005), para. 99; available at: http://italaw.com/documents/Bayindr-jurisdiction.pdf.
77 *SGS Société Générale de Surveillance S.A. v. Islamic Republic of Pakistan*, ICSID Case No. ARB/01/13, Decision on Objections to Jurisdiction (August 6, 2003), para. 184; available at: http://italaw.com/documents/SGSvPakistan-decision_000.pdf.
78 *Suez, Sociedad General de Aguas de Barcelona S.A. and Vivendi Universal S.A. v. Argentine Republic*, ICSID Case No. ARB/03/19, Decision on Jurisdiction (August 3, 2006); available at: http://www.italaw.com/documents/SuezVivendiAWGjurisdiction.pdf.
79 Ibid., para. 59.

clause. Similarly, in *Hocktief*,[80] the tribunal considered the phrase "the management, utilization, use and enjoyment of an investment" to be broad enough to include recourse to dispute settlement.[81] In the view of the *Hocktief* Tribunal, the operation of the MFN clause enables the claimant "only to reach the same position as it could reach, by its own unilateral choice and actions, under the Argentina–Germany BIT, but to do so more quickly and more cheaply, without first pursuing litigation in the courts of Argentina for 18 months."[82] Nevertheless, the tribunal went on to state:

> The MFN provision does not permit the selective picking of components from each set of conditions, … The Claimant in this case cannot rely upon the lack of an 18-month litigation period in the Argentina-Chile BIT and ignore the fact that Article 10(2) of the Argentina-Chile BIT imposes a 'fork in the road' provision: it must rely upon the whole scheme as set out in either Article 10 of the Argentina-Chile BIT or Article 10 of the Argentina-Germany BIT.[83]

The essential issue is that the contracting parties to a basic treaty have agreed on a certain procedure for the resolution of disputes. Where such procedures may or may not be followed, tribunals have a duty to explain on what basis such agreed provisions/procedures may be replaced through operation of the MFN clause.

The above cases more or less followed the approach of *Maffezini*. There are also cases in which the tribunals came to the same conclusion by a different approach. In *Siemens*,[84] the German claimant had failed to submit its dispute to the Argentine courts, which was a precondition for international arbitration under the Argentina–Germany BIT. The claimant contended, as in the *Maffezini* case, that there was no similar requirement in the Argentina–Chile BIT and that, by operation of the MFN clause, it should be permitted to submit its dispute to arbitration without going through the local court procedures, as was required by the Argentina–Germany BIT. There were, however, no provisions referring to "all matters" in the Argentina–Germany BIT. This distinction of *Siemens* from *Maffezini* notwithstanding, the tribunal considered the special dispute resolution mechanisms of the Argentina–Germany BIT to constitute part of the treatment to which foreign investors were entitled and, therefore, to be covered by the MFN clause. The tribunal found that "the administration of justice," when viewed in connection with the protection of the rights of investors, must not be excluded

---

80 *Hochtief A.G. v. Argentine Republic*, ICSID Case No. ARB/07/31, Decision on Jurisdiction (October 24, 2011); available at: http://italaw.com/documents/Hochtief_v_Argentina_Jurisdiction_24Oct2011_En.pdf.

81 Ibid., para. 68.

82 Ibid., para. 85.

83 Ibid., para. 98.

84 *Siemens AG v. Argentina*, Decision on Jurisdiction, ICSID Case No. ARB/02/8 (August 3, 2004); available at: http://www.italaw.com/documents/SiemensJurisdiction-English-3August2004.pdf.

from the application of the MFN clause.[85] It considered this to be particularly so when the MFN clause in question covers "all matters relating to commerce and navigation.[86] In the view of the *Siemens* Tribunal, to enable investors to have access to dispute resolution mechanisms is "part of the treatment of foreign investors and investments," as well as an advantage.[87] In response to Argentina's argument that its BIT with Germany was specially negotiated and should not be replaced by virtue of the MFN clause, the tribunal stated that: "the purpose of the MFN clause is to eliminate the effect of specially negotiated provisions unless they have been excepted. It complements the undertaking of each State Party to the Treaty not to apply measures discriminatory to investments under Article 2 [of the BIT]."[88]

What is striking in the *Siemens* decision is that the express intention of the contracting parties to the basic BIT was overridden by the tribunal's broad interpretation of the BIT's object and purpose. Such an interpretation is consistent with neither Articles 31 and 32 of the VCLT nor the principle of *ejusdem generis*. It is also inconsistent with the decision in *Maffezini*. Perhaps the most striking feature of the *Siemens* decision is that when the tribunal was faced with Argentina's argument that where the claimant was entitled to different treatment under its treaty with a third party it should also be subject to the entire set of dispute settlement procedures, including the so-called "fork-in-the-road," it ruled that the MFN clause "relates only to more favourable treatment," the fact that "the disadvantages may have been a trade-off for the claimed advantages"[89] notwithstanding. Having gone this far, the persuasiveness of the Tribunal was reduced to its minimum.

In *RosInvestCo*,[90] the tribunal first defined expropriation as interference with the use and enjoyment by the investor of the investment concerned and then stated that "the submission to arbitration forms a highly relevant part of the corresponding protection for the investor by granting him … procedural options of obvious and great significance compared to the sole option of challenging such interference before the domestic courts of the host state."[91] Based on this reasoning, as in the *Siemens* case, the *RosInvestCo* Tribunal found the MFN clause to be applicable to dispute resolution procedures.

B. Cases opposing extension of the MFN clause to dispute resolution procedures

Since the decision in *Maffezini*, there has been considerable debate as to whether or not the MFN clause should be applied to procedural matters, such as dispute

85 Ibid., para. 101.
86 Id.
87 Ibid., para. 102.
88 Ibid., para. 106.
89 Ibid., para. 120.
90 *RosInvestCo UK Ltd. v. Russian Federation*, SCC Case No. ARBV079/2005, Award on Jurisdiction, October 2007; available at: http://www.italaw.com/documents/RosInvestjurisdiction_decision_2007_10_000.pdf.
91 Ibid., §130.

resolution. Such disagreement on the matter is also reflected in, and even intensified by, the jurisprudence of investment. In *Salini*,[92] the issues involved included an alleged failure to pay amounts owed to the Italian claimant, who had been involved in a dam project in Jordan. The claimant brought the dispute to ICSID arbitration pursuant to the Jordan–Italy BIT. The Jordanian Government argued, inter alia, that the dispute was commercial in nature and that, in accordance with Article 9(2) of its BIT with Italy, such disputes should be settled with the procedures stipulated in the commercial contract. The claimant argued that by virtue of the MFN clause of the Jordan–Italy BIT, because the Jordan–United States and Jordan–United Kingdom BITs did not contain any provisions restricting investors from bringing treaty claims based on contracts, it should be permitted to bring its dispute to arbitration.

The tribunal first examined the decision in *Ambatielos II*, which was heavily relied upon by the *Maffezini* Tribunal. It noted that the Commission of Arbitration in *Ambatielos II* actually confirmed the principle of *ejusdem generis* for interpreting the MFN clause—the clause could only attract matters belonging to the same category of subjects as that to which the clause itself relates—and concluded that, in that case, because the MFN clause spoke of "all matters relating to commerce and navigation," the Commission of Arbitration extended its application to the "administration of justice." In the *Salini* Tribunal's view, the "administration of justice" related to substantive treatment and could therefore be incorporated from other treaties. It further considered that doing so was different from importing dispute resolution procedures from other treaties, which was the issue before it.[93]

The tribunal then went on to examine the differences between *Salini* and *Maffezini*. It stated that because the MFN clause of the BIT between Italy and Jordan did not stipulate "all rights or all matters covered by the agreement" and the claimant had failed to submit convincing evidence to support the application of the MFN clause to dispute resolution procedures, the intention of the BIT's contracting parties "was to exclude from ICSID jurisdiction contractual disputes between an investor and an entity of a State Party in order that such disputes might be settled in accordance with the procedures set forth in the investment agreements."[94] In other words, in the tribunal's view, where a treaty does not stipulate "all matters" or "all rights," the principle of *ejusdem generis* should apply. The MFN clause should thus be limited in its operation to those matters and things that belong to the same category. The tribunal also pointed out, as evidence supporting its conclusion, that some MFN clauses, such as those contained in the United Kingdom's BITs, expressly stipulate that they apply to dispute settlement procedures. In the end, the *Salini* Tribunal held that the MFN clause of

92 *Salini Costruttori S.p.A. and Italstrade S.p.A. v. The Hashemite Kingdom of Jordan*, ICSID Case No. ARB/02/13, Decision on Jurisdiction (November 9, 2004) ("*Salini*"); available at: http://www. italaw.com/documents/salini-decision_000.pdf.
93 Ibid., para. 112.
94 Ibid., para. 118.

the Jordan–Italy BIT "does not apply insofar as dispute settlement clauses are concerned."[95]

In *Plama*,[96] the second paragraph of Article 3 of the Bulgaria–Cyprus BIT expressly stipulates that the MFN clause does not apply to the privileges extended by the contracting parties to members of economic communities and unions, a customs union, or an FTA of which one party is a member. The tribunal considered that the word "privileges" "may be viewed as indicating that MFN treatment should be understood as relating to substantive protection."[97] Therefore, procedural issues such as dispute resolution procedures should not be covered. The tribunal did not even attach any significance to the international trend of favoring arbitration in investment dispute settlement. In its view, what was important was that a prerequisite to arbitration had been established by mutual consent of the parties and that "such an agreement should be clear and unambiguous."[98] It also emphasized the principle of good-faith interpretation of treaties and strongly opposed replacing "a procedure specifically negotiated by parties with an entirely different mechanism."[99]

The *Plama* Tribunal also commented on the decision in *Maffezini*, whose application of the MFN clause appeared to be primarily for the purpose of harmonizing the dispute settlement mechanisms in the field of investment. In its view, what the *Maffezini* Tribunal did was counterproductive to the harmonization of international investment law, of which dispute settlement procedures form a part. It was also "puzzled" by the public policy limitations suggested by *Maffezini* and stated that:

> … the principle with multiple exceptions as stated by the tribunal in the *Maffezini* case should instead be a different principle with one, single exception: an MFN provision in a basic treaty does not incorporate by reference dispute settlement provisions in whole or in part set forth in another treaty, unless the MFN provision in the basic treaty leaves no doubt that the Contracting Parties intended to incorporate them.[100]

Thus, the *Plama* decision serves as another major piece of case law opposing the decision of the *Maffezini* Tribunal.

In both *Salini* and *Plama*, what the tribunals did was to limit the application of the MFN clause to substantive treatments. Yet those tribunals did so by different means. Even though they both disagreed with the *Maffezini* decision, the *Salini* Tribunal did not directly criticize it, whilst the *Plama* Tribunal expressed clear disapproval of the decision. In so doing, the *Plama* Tribunal set out clear principles

---

95 Ibid., para. 119.
96 *Plama Consortium Limited v. Republic of Bulgaria*, ICSID Case No. ARB/03/24, Decision on Jurisdiction (February 8, 2005); available at: http://www.italaw.com/documents/plamavbulgaria.pdf.
97 Ibid., para. 191.
98 Ibid., para. 198.
99 Ibid., para. 209.
100 Ibid., para. 223.

relating to interpretation of MFN clauses. In consequence, as the following discussions show, its reasoning has often been referred to.

In *Telenor Mobile*,[101] the tribunal expressly stated that "[i]n the absence of language or context to suggest the contrary," the MFN clause referred to "the investor's *substantive rights* in respect of the investments."[102] The tribunal in *Société Générale v. Dominican Republic*[103] took a similar position. It stated:

> Each Treaty defines what it considers a protected investment and who is entitled to that protection, and definitions can change from treaty to treaty. In this situation, resort to the specific text of the MFN Clause is unnecessary because it applies only to the treatment accorded to such defined investment, but not to the definition of "investment" itself.[104]

The tribunal in *Tecmed v. Mexico* was faced with a different issue. It eventually refused to introduce, through the operation of the MFN clause relied on by the claimant, a provision of the Mexico–Austria BIT, according to which investments made before the entry into force of the BIT were also to be protected. The tribunal stated that "matters relating to the application over time of the Agreement, which involve more the time dimension of application of its substantive provisions rather than matters of procedure or jurisdiction, due to their significance and importance, go to the core of matters that must be deemed to be specifically negotiated by the Contracting Parties."[105]

It therefore considered such matters to be important to the contracting parties in concluding an agreement to offer substantive protection to foreign investors. As such, the tribunal held that neither the regime for protecting foreign investment nor its operation may be "impaired" by the MFN clause.[106] Implicitly, the *Tecmed* Tribunal considered that the application of the MFN clause should be in strict compliance with the principle of *ejusdem generis*.

The tribunal in *Hicee v. Slovak Republic*[107] took a view similar to that of the *Plama* Tribunal. It rejected the investor's attempt by operation of the MFN clause to expand the notion of investment in the BIT. The *Hicee* Tribunal stated that "the clear purpose of [the MFN clause] is to broaden the scope of the substantive protection granted to the eligible investments of eligible investors; it cannot

101 *Telenor Mobile Communications A.S. v. Republic of Hungary*, ICSID Case No. ARB/04/15, Award (September 13, 2006); available at: http://www.italaw.com/documents/Telenorv. HungaryAward_002.pdf.

102 Ibid., para. 92 (emphasis in original).

103 *Société Générale v. Dominican Republic*, UNCITRAL, LCIA Case No. UN 7927, Preliminary Objections to Jurisdiction (September 19, 2008); available at: http://www.italaw.com/documents/SGJurisdiction.pdf.

104 Ibid., paras. 40–41.

105 *Técnicas Medioambientales Tecmed, SA v. United Mexican States* ("*Tecmed*"), ICSID Case No. ARB(AF)/00/2, Award (May 29, 2003), para. 69; available at: http://www.italaw.com/documents/Tecnicas_001.pdf.

106 Id.

107 *Hicee BV v. Slovak Republic*, UNCITRAL, Partial Award (May 23, 2011).

legitimately be used to broaden the definition of the investors or the investments themselves."[108] Therefore, at least by implication, in the view of the *Hicee* Tribunal, the application of the MFN clause should not be extended to such procedural matters as jurisdiction.

Some other tribunals have considered the local remedy requirement, be it comprised of a waiting period or otherwise, to be a matter of jurisdiction and have opposed the application of the MFN clause to dispute resolution. In *Enron*,[109] the tribunal declared that the six-month negotiation period was very much jurisdictional in nature and "[a] failure to comply with that requirement would result in a determination of lack of jurisdiction."[110] The *Burlington*[111] Tribunal agreed with some other tribunals, including *Maffezini*, in holding that local remedies were meant to afford the host government an opportunity to resolve any disputes amicably. It then went on to say that to allow the investor to forego the local remedy procedures would deprive the host government of that opportunity. Based on that conclusion, it ruled that the failure to satisfy the local remedy requirement was adequate to defeat the tribunal's jurisdiction.[112] The *Telefónica*[113] Tribunal, however, regarded the local remedy requirement "as a temporary bar to the initiation of arbitration" or a matter of inadmissibility, which "would result in the Tribunal's temporary lack of jurisdiction."[114]

The *Wintershall*[115] Tribunal regarded BIT provisions relating to dispute settlement as comprising a standing offer of the host state, in which "the eighteen-month requirement of a proceeding before local courts … [was] an essential preliminary step to the institution of ICSID Arbitration."[116] Therefore, in order to access ICSID arbitration, the investor must accept the entire terms of the standing offer and first satisfy the local remedy requirement. Like the *Enron* and *Burlington* tribunals, the tribunal in *Wintershall* also found the recourse to local court proceedings to be a matter which was jurisdictional in nature.[117] The failure on the part of the investor to satisfy the requirement therefore meant a lack of jurisdiction on the part of the tribunal.

108 Ibid., para. 149.
109 *Enron Corporation and Ponderosa Assets, L.P. v. Argentine Republic*, ICSID Case No. ARB/01/3, Decision on Jurisdiction (January 14, 2004); available at: http://www.italaw.com/documents/Enron-Jurisdiction.pdf.
110 Ibid., para. 88.
111 *Burlington Resources Inc. v. Republic of Ecuador*, ICSID Case No. ARB/08/5, Decision on Jurisdiction (June 2, 2010); available at: http://www.italaw.com/documents/BurlingtonResourcesInc_v_Ecuador_Jurisdiction_Eng.pdf.
112 Ibid., para. 315.
113 *Telefónica S.A. v. Argentine Republic*, ICSID Case No. ARB/03/20, Decision of the Tribunal on Objections to Jurisdiction (May 25, 2006); available at: http://www.italaw.com/documents/DecisiononJurisdictionTelefonica.pdf.
114 Ibid., para. 93.
115 *Wintershall, supra*, note 30.
116 Ibid., para. 160.
117 Ibid., para. 172.

In a more recent case, *Daimler v. Argentina*,[118] the tribunal clearly said that: "[a]ll BIT-based dispute resolution provisions ... are by their very nature jurisdictional. The mere fact of their inclusion in a bilateral treaty indicates that they are reflections of the sovereign agreement of two States – not the mere administrative creation of arbitrators."[119] In the tribunal's view, such an arrangement is a condition upon which a sovereign state has given consent to investor–state arbitration, which may lead to compensation owed to the investor from the state.[120] From this point of view, it considered a BIT dispute settlement mechanism that includes an arrangement for resorting to local remedies to be a condition precedent for jurisdiction of arbitration tribunals.

Its reasoning was that where a particular dispute settlement mechanism is contained in a specific BIT that has been negotiated by the contracting sovereign states, one should not assume or interpret such provisions in a way that they would be modified. Thus, the question of whether or not the MFN clause should be applied to both procedural and substantive matters is not important. It stated:

> [A] claimant wishing to raise an MFN claim ... lacks standing to do so until it has fulfilled the domestic courts proviso. *To put it more concretely, since the Claimant has not yet satisfied the necessary condition precedent to Argentina's consent to international arbitration, its MFN arguments are not yet properly before the Tribunal.* The Tribunal is therefore presently without jurisdiction to rule on any MFN-based claims *unless* the MFN clauses themselves supply the Tribunal with the necessary jurisdiction.[121]

It should be pointed out that, although the *Daimler* Tribunal reached the same conclusion as the *Plama* Tribunal did, it did not agree with the reasoning of the latter, in particular the latter's reference to the *Maffezini* case. In that regard, the *Plama* Tribunal stated:

> The decision in *Maffezini* is perhaps understandable. The case concerned a curious requirement that during the first 18 months the dispute be tried in the local courts. The present Tribunal sympathizes with a tribunal that attempts to neutralize such a provision that is nonsensical from a practical point of view. However, such exceptional circumstances should not be treated as a statement of general principle guiding future tribunals in other cases where exceptional circumstances are not present.[122]

The *Daimler* Tribunal, however, questioned the *Plama* Tribunal's approach. In its view, where the ground of "nonsensical" provisions is adopted, "the 18-month

---

118 *Daimler Financial Services AG v. Argentine Republic*, ICSID Case No. ARB/05/1, Award (August 22, 2012).
119 Ibid., para. 193.
120 Ibid., para. 199.
121 Ibid., para. 200 (emphases in original).
122 *Plama, supra*, note 96, para. 224.

domestic courts requirement" would be subject to waiver by arbitral tribunals. Yet the *Plama* Tribunal failed to explain "in what sense the requirement was 'curious,' 'nonsensical,' or 'exceptional,'" commented the *Daimler* Tribunal.[123] Moreover, the *Daimler* Tribunal expressed the opinion that:

> … the requirement for waiving treaty-based jurisdictional pre-requisites in international law is not nonsensicality but futility. Sovereign States are free to agree to any treaty provisions they so choose—whether concerning substantive commitments or dispute resolution provisions or otherwise—provided these provisions are not futile and are not otherwise contrary to peremptory norms of international law.[124]

Among the decisions that have been made in investment arbitrations, the *Daimler* Tribunal's position relating to the MFN clause is perhaps the most explicit and straightforward. Notwithstanding whether or not its view has been affected by the criticisms of *Maffezini* and other cases giving the MFN clause a broad application, it is indisputable that the international community has shown more and more concern about the consequential impact of extending the MFN clause to dispute settlement arrangements. In this regard, the *Daimler* Tribunal's view is a positive response to the concerns of the international community and can healthily contribute to the development of international investment law.

In summary, the practice in those cases where tribunals have supported the extension of application of the MFN clause to dispute resolution has been inclined to treat the recourse to local court proceedings or a waiting period as a procedural matter. Although these tribunals have relied on such treaty provisions as "all matters subject to this Agreement," "the administration of justice," etc., the basis of this approach is that the MFN clause is designed to ensure equal and non-discriminatory treatment of all investors. This competitive approach will naturally result in making the MFN clause a super-treaty provision,[125] which will inevitably lead to treaty-shopping by investors. However, since this approach takes protection of foreign investors as the primary function of BITs and FTAs, neither treaty-shopping nor the transformation of the MFN clause into a super-treaty provision is of any great concern to its supporters.

The other approach, as taken by the tribunals in *Salini, Plama, Wintershall, Daimler,* etc., considers that all treaty provisions are specially negotiated and should therefore be given precise meaning. In practice, the tribunals that have taken this approach have tended to emphasize the *ejusdem generis* principle and limit the operation of the MFN clause to substantive treatments. In their view, the requirement of local remedies is a prerequisite for jurisdiction. They attach

---

123 *Daimler, supra,* note 118, para. 196.
124 Ibid., para. 198.
125 For further discussion of this issue, see "Most-Favoured-Nation Clause—Report of the Working Group," International Law Commission, Fifty-ninth session, Geneva, A/CN.4/L.719 (July 20, 2007), p. 11.

significance to the consideration that where a BIT or other treaty grants an investor the right to choose a mechanism in dispute resolution, it must assume all the pertinent rights and obligations thereof, rather than be given an opportunity to pick and choose. Another common feature of the reasoning of those tribunals that have refused to apply the MFN clause to dispute resolution is a reliance on good faith interpretation or giving treaty provisions their plain meaning in accordance with Article 31 of the VCLT.

III. National treatment in investment

National treatment ("NT"), like MFN treatment, is also one of the oldest standards of treatment that originated in international treaties on trade. It is reported that the first treaties providing NT to foreign and local traders can be traced back to the Hanseatic League in the 12th and 13th centuries.[126] This section will examine how this standard of treatment on cross-border trade has evolved in the context of investment and how investment tribunals have applied the standard.

A. Status of NT in investment treaties

National treatment is now part of almost all contemporary BITs. Its importance in international investment law, however, did not become clear until the late 1990s through the results of investment dispute arbitrations. Although the reasons for a steadily increasing number of investor–state arbitrations involving NT provisions cannot be confirmed with absolute evidence, they could be manifold. In the first place, with globalization increasingly deepening and spreading, enterprises from the countries that are traditional investment host states are now making investments in the developed countries, which do not provide more favorable treatment to foreign investors. In fact, foreign investors in these latter countries may encounter less favorable treatment, or at the least treatment that they may perceive as such.[127] Second, traditional investment recipients, with their own economies growing, have gradually reduced the favorable treatment they have previously offered to foreign investments and begun to treat foreign investors and domestic investors equally.[128] In these circumstances, a host state's revision of existing measures and adoption of new measures may be challenged as violations of NT provisions.

---

126   VerLoren van Themaat, *The Changing Structure of International Economic Law*, Martinus Nijhoff, 1981, pp. 16ff.

127   For instance, a number of Chinese companies have run into difficulties in their investments in the United States and Canada. For details relating to Huawei, see: http://techcrunch.com/2013/12/03/huawei-usproblems/; and for those relating to Sinopec, see: http://business.financialpost.com/2013/12/07/life-after-cnoocs-nexen-deal-is-chinas-honeymoon-with-canadas-oil-patch-over/?__lsa=f896-9576.

128   In this regard, DiMascio and Pauwelyn commented: "Developing-country hosts of foreign investment gradually increased their domestic standards, often exceeding the original benchmark set by earlier international minimum standards. As the treatment of domestic investors thereby rose above the 'mere' international minimum, the discipline of national treatment gained importance and attracted investors' renewed attention." See Nicholas DiMascio and Joost Pauwelyn,

In the past, NT was considered to be applicable to foreign investors only after their investments were made or after their entry into the market. For example, the 2012 Trilateral Investment Agreement between China, South Korea, and Japan, in its Article 3, provides: "Each Contracting Party shall in its territory accord to investors of another Contracting Party and to their investments treatment no less favorable than that it accords in like circumstances to its own investors and their investments with respect to investment activities."[129] Some recent BITs, however, contain NT provisions that apply to pre-entry activities.[130]

Another feature of contemporary NT is that very often the BIT in question provides such treatment separately to investments and investors. The Germany–Namibia BIT[131] is an example, Article 3 of which stipulates:

(1) Neither Contracting Party shall subject investments in its territory owned or controlled by nationals or companies of the other Contracting Party to treatment less favourable than it accords to investments of its own nationals or companies or to investments of nationals or companies of any third State.

(2) Neither Contracting Party shall subject nationals or companies of the other Contracting Party, as regards their activity in connection with investments in its territory, to treatment less favourable than it accords to its own nationals or companies or to nationals or companies of any third State.

The above phraseology of NT is not uncommon. It is also often the case that NT and MFN treatment are stipulated in the same provision. Still other BIT provisions require that whichever—NT or MFN treatment—is more favorable should apply. The Energy Charter Treaty ("ECT") contains such a provision in its Article 10(7), albeit extending NT or MFN treatment to the operations of foreign investments/investors only after they enter the host country:

Each Contracting Party shall accord to Investments in its Area of Investors of other Contracting Parties, and their related activities including management, maintenance, use, enjoyment or disposal, treatment no less favourable than

"Nondiscrimination in Trade and Investment Treaties: Worlds Apart or Two Sides of the Same Coin?", *American Journal of International Law*, Vol. 102, 2008, pp. 48–89, at 67.

129 See Agreement among the Government of the People's Republic of China, the Government of the Republic of Korea and the Government of Japan for the Promotion, Facilitation and Protection of Investment entered into on May 13, 2012; text available at: http://www.mofa.go.jp/announce/announce/2012/5/pdfs/0513_01_01.pdf.

130 According to an UNCTAD report, such BITs are typically the ones "entered into by Canada and the United States (apart from the Friendship Commerce and Navigation ("FCN") treaties of the United States), [which] have extended national treatment to the pre-entry stage so as to ensure market access for foreign investors on terms equal to those enjoyed by national investors." See UNCTAD, *Report on National Treatment 1999* (hereinafter "UNCTAD Report"), UN Doc. UNCTAD/ITE/IIT/11, Vol. IV, p. 4.

131 The text of the Germany–Namibia BIT is available at: http://arbitrationlaw.com/files/free_pdfs/germany-namibia_bit.pdf.

that which it accords to Investments of its own Investors or of the Investors of any other Contracting Party or any third state and their related activities including management, maintenance, use, enjoyment or disposal, whichever is the most favourable.

Regarding the making of investments, however, ECT contracting parties are required to "endeavour to accord" national treatment. In other words, the matter is left to the discretion of the contracting parties. Also it should be noted that the ECT does not include the wording "in like circumstances" as do the NAFTA and many BITs.

According to Article 1102(1) of the NAFTA, contracting parties are required to "accord to investors of another Party treatment no less favorable than that it accords, in like circumstances, to its own investors with respect to the establishment, acquisition, expansion, management, conduct, operation, and sale or other disposition of investments." Article 1102(2) deals with investments from other contracting parties by providing: "Each Party shall accord to investments of investors of another Party treatment no less favorable than that it accords, in like circumstances, to investments of its own investors with respect to the establishment, acquisition, expansion, management, conduct, operation, and sale or other disposition of investments."

At the same time, NAFTA Article 1102(3) stipulates that the treatment provided to foreign investments and investors by states or provinces of its members should be "no less favorable than the most favourable treatment accorded, in like circumstances, by that state or province to investors, and to investments of investors, of the Party of which it forms a part." This provision is to confirm that local governments of the contracting parties also have the obligation to accord NT to investments and investors from other contracting parties. The reference to "the most favourable treatment accorded," however, is not immediately clear, as in the provisions relating to the national obligation only the phrase "no less favourable" is used. As will be discussed later, this provision does not leave the sub-authorities of NAFTA contracting parties with a lower level of obligations than the parties themselves. Under the law of treaties, once an obligation is assumed by the central government—federal or unitary—it binds the entire country. The significance of the NAFTA provision on NT relating to local governments is that "where a subnational authority has a constitutional power to make investment policy,"[132] a clearly stated obligation will oblige the local governments to grant the most favorable treatment that they accord to their nationals from other provinces and states to foreign investors.[133] In case a non-NAFTA state enters into a

---

132 UNCTAD Report, *supra*, note 130, p. 25.

133 In this regard, the UNCTAD Report stated: "Such power may be used to grant preferential treatment to local, as opposed to out-of-sub-division investors, as, for example, where a host sub-national authority is seeking to encourage the growth of local small and medium-sized firms. A question that arises is whether a subnational authority has to extend such preferential treatment to foreign inward investors on the basis of the national treatment standard, regardless of how it treats national investors from outside the sub-division." Id.

BIT with one of the NAFTA members and the BIT's provision on NT is not as clear as that of NAFTA, investors from the non-NAFTA state may, through the operation of the MFN clause, claim the same treatment as nationals from other NAFTA members receive, unless the BIT itself contains provisions to exclude such invocations.

The purpose of NT is to ensure non-discrimination against foreign investments and investors. From the above brief review of treaty practice, it is certain that as an extension of treatment standards on trade, NT in the case of investments is only applicable "in like circumstances," as opposed to "like products" in the case of trade. The most important question is how to establish "like circumstances" and "less favourable" treatment. This having been said, some BITs do not contain the words "like circumstances" or similar references. A related issue is whether "intent" on the part of the host state to discriminate against foreign investors is required or whether discriminatory "effect" is sufficient. The third question is whether precedents arising from trade tribunals, such as the tribunals and Appellate Body of the WTO, can serve as a reference for settling investment disputes. All these questions must be answered in practice.

B. Competition as a necessary condition for like circumstances

Before examining the jurisprudence of investment relating to NT, it should be noted that foreign investors operate in a wide range of economic sectors. As such, it must be asked what factors should be taken into account in determining "like circumstances," as no BITs or multilateral treaties further define the term and, in fact, some even forego the term. Some commentators consider that because NT is intended to protect foreign investors and because BITs do not provide what "particular risks" of foreign investors must be protected, "[i]n order to ensure coherence and effective operation, the different treaty standards should be matched to particular risks faced by foreign investors."[134] As will be seen in the following discussion, the decisions of investment tribunals in regard to this issue are, as may be expected, far from consistent.

S.D. Myers was the earliest case involving interpretation of NT provisions under the NAFTA, in which the claimant was a US company engaged in the business of exporting polychlorinated biphenyl ("PCB") waste from Canada to the US for destruction by high temperature incineration at its facility in the US State of Ohio. When S.D. Myers "entered" the Canadian market by establishing Myers Canada in 1993, "there was only one credible Canadian competitor: Chem-Security."[135] Also at that time, the US–Canada border was closed "to the import and export of PCBs and PCB waste for disposal" by action of the US

---

134 Jürgen Kurtz, "The Use and Abuse of WTO Law in Investor–State Arbitration: Competition and its Discontents", *Transnational Dispute Management*, Vol. 8, Issue 3, September 2011, pp. 749–71, at 764.

135 *S.D. Myers v. Canada*, First Partial Award (November 13, 2000), para. 112.

Government taken in 1980.[136] On the Canadian side, "the PCB Waste Export Regulations 1990 ... effectively banned the export of PCB waste from Canada to all countries other than the USA[, although under] these regulations exports to the USA were permitted with the prior approval of the US EPA."[137] In effect, then, in 1993, S.D. Myers entered a "market" that did not actually exist and was unlikely to eventuate unless its lobbying efforts with US and Canadian officials were successful. They were successful enough that on October 26, 1995, the US EPA issued a special exemption (called an "enforcement discretion"), valid from November 15, 1995 to December 31, 1997, that would allow S.D. Myers to import PCBs and PCB waste from Canada into the US for disposal if it met certain detailed conditions contained in the "enforcement discretion." Shortly thereafter, similar "enforcement discretions" were also granted to "about nine other US companies," although the import ban itself remained in effect and any imports to the USA were technically contrary to US law. Literally within days, the Canadian Minister of the Environment signed an interim order that had the effect of banning the export of PCBs from Canada.

Following its review of the documentary evidence and testimony, the tribunal was "satisfied that the Interim Order and the Final Order favoured Canadian nationals over non-nationals" and, further, "that the practical effect of the Orders was that SDMI and its investment were prevented from carrying out the business they planned to undertake, which was a clear disadvantage in comparison to its Canadian competitors."[138] Moreover, it held that "the documentary record as a whole clearly indicates that the Interim Order and the Final Order were intended primarily to protect the Canadian PCB disposal industry from U.S. competition."[139]

The tribunal's analysis of the concept "in like circumstances" played a key role in its eventual decision in regard to the respondent's NT obligations under the NAFTA. It first observed: "In considering the meaning of 'like circumstances' under Article 1102 of the NAFTA, it is similarly necessary to keep in mind the overall legal context in which the phrase appears."[140] And, indeed, the tribunal did examine this principle in some detail.[141] In the end, however, unlike the *Pope & Talbot* Tribunal, which was carrying out its work almost simultaneously (see discussion of that case below), the *S.D. Myers* Tribunal gives no evidence in its award of having actually applied the principle in any meaningful way in the context of the specific case before it.

Instead, the tribunal rather perfunctorily determined "likeness" on the basis of a "business perspective."[142] In its view, determination of "likeness" requires an inquiry into the competitive relationship between domestic and foreign investors.

---

136 Ibid., para. 101.
137 Ibid., para. 100.
138 Ibid., para. 193.
139 Ibid., para. 194.
140 Ibid., para. 245.
141 Ibid., paras. 246–50.
142 Ibid., para. 251.

It stated that in order to establish whether less favorable treatment is accorded to a foreign investor, the foreign investor and the comparable domestic investor must be in the same sector, which "has a wide connotation that includes the concepts of 'economic sector' and 'business sector.'"[143] The *S.D. Myers* Tribunal then concluded that, from a business perspective, "SDMI and Myers Canada were in 'like circumstances' with Canadian operators" because they "all were engaged in providing PCB waste remediation service."[144] The rationale the tribunal gave is that SDMI was in a position to attract potential customers from the Canadian operators.[145] The *S.D. Myers* Tribunal's decision was in essence based on its establishment of the competitiveness of the claimant and domestic comparators. Clearly, this decision bears some features of trade tribunals' decisions on "like products."

Whilst making competitiveness the benchmark for ascertaining "like circumstances" is understandable, the *S.D. Myers* Tribunal's decision seems to have been rather rushed—without reasonable analysis. For instance, it could be said that a foreign investment that undertook to destroy PCBs at a facility in Canada is "in like circumstances" with a domestic investment that does the same, but is a foreign investment that carries out the activity abroad really "in like circumstances," even though they may be in competition one way or the other? In other words, is a foreign automobile manufacturer whose sole activity in country X is to buy parts for export to its home country Y for the purpose of manufacturing automobiles there "in like circumstances" with a domestic automobile manufacturer that buys parts in country X and uses them to manufacture automobiles there? For purposes of comparison within country Y, the foreign company is nothing more than a purchaser and exporter of automobile parts, and is certainly not an automobile manufacturer. Likewise, in the present case, it seems that for the purposes of comparison within Canada, S.D. Myers was nothing more than a purchaser of PCBs or an agent for arranging their eventual destruction; it was not, in Canada, a "provider of PCB waste remediation services." Therefore, whilst the *S.D. Myers* Tribunal made a good start by applying "competitiveness" as its benchmark for determining "like circumstances," it misapplied the principle in the end.

The tribunal in *Pope & Talbot* also strongly endorsed competitiveness as a necessary condition of likeness in an NT inquiry. The claimant in that case was a US company[146] whose investment was a Canadian wood products company that manufactured and sold softwood lumber. It harvested timber in the Canadian province of British Columbia and operated three softwood lumber mills in the southern interior of that province.[147] On May 29, 1996, Canada and the United States entered into a bilateral agreement, the Softwood Lumber Agreement ("SLA"), that was retroactive to April 1, 1996, intended to last until March 31, 2001, and established a limit on the free export into the United States of softwood

---

143 Ibid., para. 250.
144 Ibid., para. 251.
145 Ibid., para. 251.
146 *Pope & Talbot v. Government of Canada*, Interim Award on Merits—Phase One (June 26, 2000); Interim Award on Merits—Phase Two (April 10, 2001); Interim Award-Phase 1, para. 2.
147 Ibid., para. 4.

lumber first manufactured in the provinces of, inter alia, British Columbia.[148] The arbitration arose from the claimant's contention that the manner in which Canada had chosen to implement the SLA constituted a breach of certain provisions of NAFTA Chapter 11, among which was Article 1102 regarding NT.[149]

The tribunal considered that the plural form used in the phrase "investments of investors" in Article 1102(2) "permits individual investors and investments to maintain claims of denial of national treatment based upon a comparison of the treatment they receive with the treatment received by host country investors and investments," that is, that "the language of Article 1102(2) [does not require] claimants to show whether and how many other foreign owned investments may fall within the 'like circumstances' as themselves."[150] In other words, a foreign investor/claimant only needs to prove that it alone has received treatment less favorable than a domestic investor without having an obligation to establish that the whole system or a scheme of the host state is in violation of NT obligations. The tribunal also dismissed the differences between the wording of NAFTA Article 1102(3) and that of Article 1102(2) by saying that: "the Tribunal believes that the language of Article 1102(3) was intended simply to make clear that the obligation of a state or province was to provide investments of foreign investors with the best treatment it accords any investment of its country, not just the best treatment it accords to investments of its investors."[151] This conclusion is in line with the principle of international law in respect of treaty interpretations.

In this particular case, the *Pope & Talbot* Tribunal, based on the history of "the approximately twenty-year ongoing softwood lumber trade dispute between Canada and the United States,"[152] found that the joint United States–Canada "decision to implement the SLA through a regime effecting controls only against exports to the United States from covered provinces was reasonably related to the rational policy of removing the threat of CVD [countervailing duty] actions."[153] Consequently, it further held that "the producers in the non-covered provinces were not in like circumstances with those in the covered provinces."[154] As for softwood producers/exporters in the three other covered provinces (Pope & Talbot operated only in British Columbia ("B.C.")), the tribunal held: "It was the underlying economics of the softwood lumber industry in Canada that placed the Investment and other producers in B.C. in unlike circumstances to those in the other covered provinces."[155] Logically, then, as a result of these analyses and conclusions, the only investors or investments "in like circumstances" to those of the claimant were other softwood producers/exporters in British Columbia and, in that regard, the tribunal held that the claimant "received treatment no

---

148 Ibid., para. 6.
149 Ibid., paras. 7 and 41–44.
150 *Pope & Talbot*, Interim Award-Phase 2, *supra*, note 146, para. 38.
151 Ibid., para. 41.
152 Ibid., para. 86.
153 Ibid., para. 87.
154 Ibid., para. 88.
155 Ibid., para. 93.

less favorable than that accorded Canadian-owned producers throughout B.C.," and "determine[d] that Canada ha[d] not been in breach of its obligation to the Investor under Article 1102 of NAFTA."[156]

This case is perhaps most notable for its careful examination and determination of "like circumstances." It seems to have carefully, rationally, and with good reason gone beyond the standards of determination most often applied in trade disputes (same business or economic sector) to consider the "overall legal context" within which NT is to be applied in a specific case, as well as the "underlying economics" of a widespread industry that could cast different enterprises engaged in the same industry into "differing circumstances."[157] By so doing, the *Pope & Talbot* Tribunal distinguished itself from the *S.D. Myers* Tribunal, which gave "like circumstances" a wider connotation by including activities which are in the same business sector but are nonetheless different. Together with its reasoned and careful analysis on the scope of "like circumstances," the investor-to-investor comparison approach adopted by the *Pope & Talbot* Tribunal is not only logical but also in line with the "plain meaning" rule of treaty interpretation.

C. Liberal interpretation of like circumstances

There have been cases where tribunals clearly went beyond the limits of expected interpretation of "like circumstances." *Occidental v. Ecuador*,[158] for instance, not only represents a departure from competitiveness as a necessary condition in an NT enquiry but also very widely interpreted the provision. In that case, the claimant ("OEPC"), a US company, alleged that the respondent had breached its obligation under the United States–Ecuador BIT to provide OEPC "treatment not less favorable than that accorded to Ecuadorian exporters."[159]

The claimant maintained "that the meaning of 'in like situations' does not refer to those industries or companies involved in the same sector of activity, such as oil producers, but to companies that are engaged in exports even if encompassing different sectors."[160] The respondent, on the other hand, argued "that 'in like situations' can only mean that all companies in the same sector are to be treated alike and this happens in respect of all oil producers."[161] The tribunal, in the end, ruled in favor of the claimant's interpretation. It held that the term "'in like situations' cannot be interpreted in the narrow sense advanced by Ecuador as the purpose of national treatment is to protect investors as compared to local producers, and this cannot be done by addressing *exclusively the sector* in which that particular activity

---

156 See, in their entirety, ibid., paras. 96–104 and 194.
157 In the end, the Tribunal did not see any particular effects of any conceivable inter-relationship between Articles 1102 and 1105 in the present case; see ibid., paras. 117–18 and footnote 99.
158 *Occidental Petroleum Corporation and Occidental Exploration and Production Company v. Republic of Ecuador*, LCIA Case No. UN3467 (UNCITRAL), Award of July 1, 2004.
159 Ibid., para. 36.
160 Ibid., para. 168.
161 Ibid., para. 171.

is undertaken."[162] What matters and is extremely bothersome is that the tribunal decided that the comparison should go beyond the sector in which a foreign investor is engaged. The tribunal failed, however, to explain why, for the purpose of implementing the NT provisions, comparison between a protected foreign investor and a local producer "cannot be done by addressing exclusively the sector in which that particular activity is undertaken."[163] Of course, the purpose of national treatment, that is, protecting investors as compared to local producers, *can* be done by addressing exclusively the sector in which that particular activity is undertaken. That, in fact, is precisely how the overwhelming majority of investment tribunals have approached the application of the principle of "in like situations/circumstances" in the context of NT.

The *Occidental* Tribunal concluded that "the fact is that OEPC has received treatment less favorable than that accorded to national companies."[164] In fact, the claimant cited only an unspecified "number of companies involved in the export of other goods, particularly flowers, mining and seafood products" in this respect.[165] It is indeed a broad stretch to say that because OEPC (and all petroleum exporters, including domestic ones) did not receive VAT refunds but national exporters of roses did receive them, that "OEPC has received treatment less favorable than that accorded to national companies." It seems that the tribunal based its decision entirely on the fact that Ecuadorian law granted the right to VAT tax credits and refunds to all exporters.

In addition, the *Occidental* Tribunal further stretched its interpretation of NT provisions and confused the issue when it said that "the purpose of national treatment in this dispute … is to avoid exporters being placed at a disadvantage in foreign markets because of the indirect taxes paid in the country of origin."[166] This is surely a novel interpretation of the "purpose" of NT. That may well have been the "purpose" of the Ecuadorian tax law, but it is certainly a stretch to identify that as also a purpose of NT. Had the law specifically limited VAT tax credits or refunds to exporting manufacturers and not to "producers" or specifically excluded mining, petroleum, or gas extraction or any natural resources exploitation, NT would never have been an issue. It was precisely because the law was meant to apply to "all exporters" that OEPC even conceivably had a claim here. Even though this can be inferred from the award as a whole, the tribunal failed to make that clear in the most pertinent discussions. Most probably this analysis explains why the *Occidental* decision has attracted so much criticism.[167]

---

162 Ibid., para. 177 (emphasis added).
163 Ibid., para. 173.
164 Ibid., para. 177.
165 Ibid., para. 168.
166 Ibid., para. 175.
167 In this regard, Bjorklund for instance, commented: "The *Occidental* tribunal's conclusion was unusual. While the like circumstances determination is indeed flexible and must depend on the circumstances of any particular case, the lack of any competitive relationship between the comparators would ordinarily be a difficult hurdle to overcome with respect to the like-circumstances determination." See Andrea K. Bjorklund, "National Treatment", p. 40; text available at: http://

The *Siemens*[168] decision was also unusual. In that case, the claimant essentially alleged that the respondent had violated Article 2(3) of the Argentina–Germany BIT prohibiting "arbitrary or discriminatory" measures rather than NT provisions. The tribunal appears to have accepted that the claimant's claim of "abritrary" measures was made in the context of Article 2(3) and, based on the "ordinary meaning" of the word "arbitrary," upheld that claim. However, on the other hand, the tribunal considered the claim of "discriminatory" measures solely in the context of NT. Perhaps this is what was intended by the claimant.[169] However, it does seem that in the context of the case, insofar as it is revealed in the award, that any NT claim was ancillary to a more general claim of discriminatory measures that would have more appropriately been considered under Article 2(3) of the BIT and on the basis of the same interpretative principles that the tribunal applied to the claim of "arbitrary" measures. The tribunal failed to do so and, on the other hand, seems to have considered that "discrimination" could arise only in the context of NT.

In that regard, the *Siemens* Tribunal neatly side-stepped the issue. It first expressed the opinion that "intent is not decisive or essential for a finding of discrimination, and that the impact of the measure on the investment would be the determining factor to ascertain whether it had resulted in non-discriminatory treatment."[170] It then went on to say: "The Tribunal considers that, while there are aspects in the actions of Argentina that seem discriminatory, the allegations of the Claimant have not been fully substantiated."[171] Finally, in a sudden urge towards judicial/arbitral economy, it held: "Given the holdings of the Tribunal under other protections of the Treaty, the Tribunal finds it unnecessary to determine whether Argentina breached the non-discriminatory treatment obligation."[172] This is at best unsatisfactory, as it adds nothing to the jurisprudence of either NT or discrimination in general in the investment context but perhaps reveals how difficult some tribunals find it to deal with these issues or their distinctions effectively.

D. The principle of judicial/arbitral economy

Investment arbitration is a very time consuming and expensive exercise, whilst one of the reasons to have disputes resolved through arbitration is its perceived

www.scribd.com/doc/64822832/Bjorklund-A-K-%E2%80%98National-Treatment%E2%80%99.

168 *Siemens, supra*, note 84.

169 This conclusion is based on the Tribunal's comment that: "As regards discriminatory treatment, according to Siemens, the criterion is whether the foreign investor has been treated less favorably than domestic investors or investors of other nationalities; *de facto* discrimination is sufficient even without violation of the host State's domestic law. Siemens argues that the measures taken towards Siemens' investment were not of a general nature; the Contract is the only significant contract terminated which involved a foreign investor and the only foreign investment terminated unilaterally under the 2000 Emergency Law." See ibid., para. 316.

170 Ibid., para. 321.

171 Id.

172 Id.

promptness and cost savings. Tribunals facing disputes are at the same time expected to render reasoned decisions. Thus, striking a balance among these different expectations and reality is a challenge for all tribunals. One way of resolving the issue is perhaps the adoption of the principle of judicial/arbitral economy. Insofar as interpretation of NT provisions is concerned, where a decision on "like circumstances" is made, the proceedings may be stopped unless the finding is positive.

On the other hand, where a tribunal takes up the issue of treatment first and finds different treatment to exist, no violation of NT may eventually be established because the underlying prerequisite for provision or application of NT is "like circumstances." This latter approach was adopted by the *Pope & Talbot* Tribunal. In that case, the tribunal first considered "the legal context of Article 1102" and endorsed competition as a condition for determining "like circumstances," stating that "[i]n evaluating the implications of the legal context ... as a first step, the treatment accorded a foreign owned investment protected by Article 1102(2) should be compared with that accorded domestic investments in the same business or economic sector."[173] Instead of first conducting an analysis of whether the claimant and a domestic investor were in "like circumstances," the *Pope & Talbot* Tribunal decided on a three step examination: (1) whether there is a difference in treatment, (2) justification by the host state of its policies, and (3) determination of whether the claimant and a domestic comparator were in like circumstances.[174]

The *ADF* Tribunal[175] adopted a similar approach and considered the US Buy America Act not to be in violation of its NT obligations. In its analysis, the tribunal compared the claimant's investment with those of US investors as investments in "like circumstances" and found that steel "fabricated in the United States is *not* treated differently, depending on the nationality of the investor owning such steel. Indeed, the Canadian investor's steel and a U.S. investor's steel, if fabricated in Canada, are treated in the same manner and both are excluded from use in the Springfield Interchange Project."[176] Therefore, no violation of NT existed.

This approach shows that the *Pope & Talbot* and *ADF* Tribunals were outcome-based to some extent. In other words, in their view, if there was no difference in treatment, no other analysis need be conducted. Whilst there is nothing wrong with this, in practice, there can hardly be an instance in which a claimant will bring a case before an arbitration tribunal without feeling that he/she has been treated less favorably or that there is a difference in treatment. Therefore, in cases involving allegedly less favorable treatment, the focus is almost always on whether or not the comparators are in like circumstances. From the point of view of judicial economy, tribunals should decide "like circumstances" first.

For example, in *GAMI v. Mexico*, the claimant challenged the expropriation by Mexico of a sugar mill in which it had invested on grounds of violation of NT

173 *Pope & Talbot*, Interim Award-Phase 2, *supra*, note 146, para. 78.
174 Ibid., para. 79.
175 *ADF Group Inc v. United States*, ICSID Case No. ARB(AF)/00/1, Award (January 9, 2003).
176 Ibid., para. 156 (emphasis in original).

under the NAFTA. The tribunal concluded it was not persuaded "that GAMI's circumstances were demonstrably so 'like' those of non-expropriated mill owners that it was wrong to treat GAMI differently."[177] In the view of the *GAMI* Tribunal: "It is not conceivable that a Mexican corporation becomes entitled to the anti-discrimination protections of international law by virtue of the sole fact that a foreigner buys a share of it."[178] Thereafter, there was no need to discuss whether or not the treatment received by the claimant was different or even the rationale of the host state's measure.

The *Methanex* Tribunal[179] was not convinced by the claimant's claim that a California State ban on methyl tertiary butyl ether ("MTBE") had constituted a violation of NT. In that case, the only effective competitor of MTBE was ethanol, as other oxygenates were not yet commercially viable. The *Methanex* Tribunal rejected the claimant's argument that it was in like circumstances with producers of ethanol, which had received more favorable treatment, rather than with producers of methanol or producers of MTBE because, in its view, it "would be as perverse to ignore identical comparators if they were available and to use comparators that were less 'like', as it would be perverse to refuse to find and to apply less 'like' comparators when no identical comparators existed."[180] The *UPS* Tribunal, by majority, decided that importation of goods by post and importation of goods by courier were not in like circumstances and held that the different characteristics meant that the difference in treatment was not a violation of NT.[181]

The tribunal in the *Champion* case[182] also clearly showed its endorsement for judicial/arbitral economy. In that case, the claimants, two US companies (the claims of three individuals who were originally also claimants in the case were held to be outside ICSID jurisdiction because those persons held dual US/Egyptian citizenship), were shareholders in a cotton trading and processing company ("NCC") incorporated in Egypt. They alleged that Egypt had violated the United States–Egypt BIT by taking a series of measures in the cotton industry that affected their investment. The tribunal rightly held that: "there is a significant difference between a company which opts to buy cotton from the Collection Centres at fixed prices and a company which opts to trade on the free market, whether or not the company is privately-owned or State-owned or whether the company is national or foreign."[183] This difference, it said, meant that: "NCC cannot be compared with other cotton trading companies regarding the Settlements."[184] Further, it held: "Since the Arbitral Tribunal came to the conclusion that the

177 *GAMI Investments Inc. v. Mexico*, UNCITRAL, Final Award (November 15, 2004), para. 114.

178 Ibid., para. 116.

179 *Methanex v. United States of America*, UNCITRAL, Award (August 3, 2005).

180 Ibid., Part IV, Ch. B., para. 17.

181 *United Parcel Service of America, Inc v. Canada*, UNCITRAL, Award (May 24, 2007), para. 99.

182 *Champion Trading Company and Ameritrade International, Inc. v. Arab Republic of Egypt*, ICSID Case No. ARB/02/9, Award (October 27, 2006).

183 Ibid., para. 154.

184 Ibid., para. 155.

companies were not in a like situation, it does not need to analyze the other requirements which prohibit discrimination on the grounds of nationality."[185]

E. Determination of less favorable treatment

An important question in respect of NT is whether or not a foreign investor has received "less favourable" treatment. In practice, however, as most tribunals start their analysis with "like circumstances," whenever the claimant and domestic comparator are found not to be alike there is no need to proceed to examine whether the treatment involved is less favorable. This, of course, does not mean that determination of what treatment may be considered less favorable is considered to be less important.

In practice, there are always debates as to whether a distinction should be made between de jure and de facto "less favourable treatment." In connection with this is the question of whether discriminatory intent is required for a finding of a violation of NT. Most investment tribunals have considered de facto differential treatment to be as significant as de jure differential treatment.[186] The *S.D. Myers* Tribunal, for instance, considered intent "important" but not "decisive on its own."[187] In its view, what is more important is the actual effect on foreign investors of the measure in question. The reason for this conclusion apparently was: "The word 'treatment' suggests that practical impact is required to produce a breach of Article 1102, not merely a motive or intent."[188] The view of the *S.D. Myers* Tribunal was shared by the *Occidental* Tribunal, which held that intent was not essential and that what mattered was the result of the policy in question.[189] In fact, it is understandable why tribunals should place emphasis on the actual effect without distinguishing de jure from de facto discrimination. After all, what an investor is concerned about is not the formality but the treatment's effects on its investment.

Other tribunals were either ambivalent or opposed to making intent a condition for establishing an NT violation. The *Siemens* Tribunal, after reviewing investment arbitration practices, concluded that "intent is not decisive or essential for a finding of discrimination, and that the impact of the measure on the investment would be the determining factor to ascertain whether it had resulted in non-discriminatory treatment".[190] Similarly, the *Thunderbird* Tribunal also emphasized that there was no need for the claimant to demonstrate that any less favourable treatment accorded to it was "motivated because of nationality."[191]

---

185 Ibid., para. 156.
186 For instance, the *Feldman* Tribunal maintained that de facto different treatment was contrary to the NT obligation under Article 1102 of the NAFTA; see *Marvin Roy Feldman Karpa v. United Mexican States*, ICSID Case No. ARB(AF)/99/1, Award (December 16, 2002), para. 184.
187 *S.D. Myers, supra*, note 135, para. 254.
188 Id.
189 *Occidental, supra*, note 158, para. 177.
190 *Siemens, supra*, note 84, para. 320.
191 *International Thunderbird Gaming Corp. v. Mexico*, UNCITRAL, Award (January 26, 2006), paras.

The *Methanex* Tribunal serves as an exception in this regard, having stated:

> In order to sustain its claim under Article 1102(3), Methanex must demonstrate, cumulatively, that California intended to favour domestic investors by discriminating against foreign investors and that Methanex and the domestic investor supposedly being favored by California are in like circumstances.[192]

Yet, in the end, the *Methanex* Tribunal still made its decision on the basis of the effects of the disputed measure.

Regarding the standards for determining "treatment no less favorable," in *Pope & Talbot*, Canada maintained that "no denial of national treatment may be found in a *de facto* case, unless the measures in question disproportionately disadvantage foreign investors."[193] In that case, Canada also argued that in *S.D. Myers* the finding of a de facto breach of NT "'clearly' was based on the disproportionate effect of the export ban,"[194] but the tribunal disagreed, asserting that "[o]nce the *Myers* tribunal found that the claimant and its Canadian competitors were in 'like circumstances,' the finding of a denial of national treatment was a foregone conclusion."[195] In fact, it is hard to determine which interpretation is correct here because the *S.D. Myers* Tribunal, having identified this factor to be taken into account, never seriously addressed it.[196]

The respondent in the *Pope & Talbot* case maintained that different standards should be applied to de jure and de facto "treatment" in determining if such treatment was "no less favourable" and that, in the case of de facto discrimination, the standard was "disproportionate effect." The tribunal, however, pointed out that under that proposed standard:

> A violation of Article 1102 could then only be found if the differing treatment between the class of [foreign] investments and their [domestic] competitors in like circumstances is "disproportionately" in favour of the domestic investments, whatever that might mean.

> Simply to state this approach is to show how unwieldy it would be and how it would hamstring foreign owned investments seeking to vindicate their Article 1102 rights. Only in the simplest and most obvious cases of denial of national treatment could the complainant hope to make a case for recovery.[197]

175–76. Nonetheless, the tribunal required the claimant to show "the reason why there was a less favourable treatment;" ibid., para. 177.
192 *Methanex, supra*, note 179, Part IV, Ch B, para. 12.
193 *Pope & Talbot*, Interim Award-Phase 2, *supra*, note 146, para. 55.
194 Ibid., para. 65.
195 Ibid., para. 66.
196 See *S.D. Myers, supra*, note 135, paras. 252–56.
197 *Pope & Talbot*, Interim Award-Phase 2, *supra*, note 146, paras. 71–72.

Although it is understandable why the *Pope & Talbot* Tribunal rejected Canada's argument, the respondent did raise an important issue. This can be considered from the viewpoint of host states' exercise of their regulatory powers, through which differential treatment of foreign investors and domestic investors may be a result because of the purpose of the measure. Where such measures are not aimed at foreign investors but nonetheless have adverse effects on them, the question is then to what remedies the foreign investors should be entitled. In this regard, McDougal, Lasswell, and Chen suggested that: "whether a particular differentiation of aliens and nationals has a reasonable basis in the 'common interest of the larger community' must … depend not only upon the value primarily at stake in the differentiation but also upon many particular, and varying features of the context in which the differentiation is made."[198] Most probably, even if this may not affect the obligation on the part of the host state to pay compensation for the damages suffered by foreign investors, lack of "bad faith" on the part of the host state should be recognized. More importantly, the recognition of host states' regulatory powers will help strengthen the international system governing international investment.

Feldman[199] is a very unusual case, in addition to its being the first international investment arbitration in which violation of NT was clearly and directly asserted by the claimant and seriously considered by the tribunal. The case concerned the refusal of Mexican tax authorities to rebate excise taxes applied to tobacco products exported from Mexico by Corporación de Exportaciones Mexicanas, S.A. de C.V. ("CEMSA"), a Mexican company which the claimant owned and controlled, and the tax authorities' refusal to recognize CEMSA's right to a rebate of excise taxes for prospective exports.[200]

The claimant contended that Mexico had discriminated against CEMSA in the 1998–2000 period by permitting at least three other firms, owned by Mexican nationals ("and possibly some others"), that were resellers of cigarettes in "like circumstances" with CEMSA to obtain rebates for taxes on exported cigarettes during periods when such rebates were denied to the claimant, notwithstanding the fact that like the claimant they did not fulfill the requirements of the Mexican tax law to obtain such rebates.[201] The tribunal correctly concluded that the resellers, whether domestic or foreign, were "in like circumstances" with CEMSA, whether or not they had received tax rebates in violation of the law or, at the very least, by making submissions for rebates that were not "in good faith."

With regard to the issue of "treatment less favorable," the majority of the *Feldman* Tribunal held that "it is not self-evident … that any departure from national treatment must be *explicitly* shown to be a result of the investor's nationality."[202] Therefore, in its view, "it is sufficient to show less favorable treatment for

---

198 M.S. McDougal et al., *Human Rights and World Public Order: The Basic Policies of an International Law of Human Dignity*, Yale University Press, New Haven, Connecticut, 1980, pp. 761–65.

199 *Feldman, supra,* note 186.

200 Ibid., para. 1.

201 Ibid., paras. 23 and 155.

202 Ibid., para. 181 (emphasis in original).

the foreign investor than for domestic investors in like circumstances."[203] Yet, without much analysis, the tribunal decided that "the Claimant in our view has established a presumption and a *prima facie* case that the Claimant has been treated in a different and less favorable manner than several Mexican owned cigarette resellers, and the Respondent has failed to introduce any credible evidence into the record to rebut that presumption."[204]

What the tribunal appears to be saying here is: "If a domestic investor can obtain a benefit to which it is not entitled by acting with a lack of good faith, then a foreign investor should also obtain the same benefit if it acts with a similar lack of good faith." That is a very unfortunate interpretation of the concept of "less favourable treatment." What the tribunal did was to treat the benefits allegedly received by domestic resellers through violating the law—illegal benefits—as legal benefits/treatment and compared such treatment with that received by foreign investors. This is logically incorrect. In every society, someone may benefit more one way or the other than others by breaking the law. Yet such illegal benefits are not the same as those accorded by law, which is required by international obligations. The *Feldman* Tribunal's conclusion was, to say the best, a serious misinterpretation of the concept.[205]

In fact, it is hard to tell on what basis the tribunal made this determination because even it conceded that "[t]he extent of the evidence of discrimination on the record is admittedly limited," consisting in fact of only three documents: "[a] statement of Mr. Diaz Guzman, [a] 'mystery' memorandum from SHCP's files, and [a] tax registration statement for Mercados Regionales, owned by the Poblano Group."[206] This decision of the *Feldman* Tribunal is in sharp contrast with that of the *GAMI* Tribunal, which considered that mere differential treatment alone could not result in a successful national treatment claim. It further stated in relation to the expropriation of a sugar mill with American investment that "[i]t is not conceivable that a Mexican corporation becomes entitled to the antidiscrimination protections of international law by virtue of the sole fact that a foreigner buys a share of it."[207]

The dissenting Arbitrator Covarrubias in the *Feldman* case strongly disagreed with the majority view, stating that the claimant had failed to prove that he had been treated less favorably than other resellers because rebates had been granted

---

203 Id.

204 Ibid., para. 177.

205 The Tribunal did not seriously address the issue of "in like circumstances" beyond saying that in its view, "the 'universe' of firms in like circumstances are those foreign-owned and domestic-owned firms that are in the business of reselling/exporting cigarettes" but that "[o]ther Mexican firms that may also export cigarettes, such as Mexican cigarette producers, are not in like circumstances." See ibid., para. 171.

206 Ibid., para. 176. On the basis of this "evidence", however, the tribunal insisted that "the burden of proof was shifted from the Claimant to the Respondent, with the Respondent then failing to meet its new burden" and that "it is entirely reasonable for the majority of this Tribunal to make an inference based on the Respondent's failure to present evidence on the discrimination issue." Ibid., para. 178.

207 *GAMI*, *supra*, note 177, para. 115.

to him on some occasion(s) and denied on others, and this same policy was followed regarding other resellers.[208] Covarrubias even considered that the evidence relied upon by the majority to establish "a presumption and a *prima facie* case" "is not only limited but null and void, since it proves absolutely nothing with regard to the issue of discrimination"[209] and proceeds thereafter to present a cogent and convincing examination of the specifics of the "evidence" that supports his reasoning.

In any event, in the best case scenario, the majority's decision in the *Feldman* case is highly controversial. The lack of convincing reasons has made the decision an example that should not be followed by other tribunals.

IV. China's practice regarding MFN and national treatment

The BITs signed by China in recent years include both relative standards (NT and MFN treatment) and absolute standards (fair and equitable treatment).[210] For instance, the 1986 China–United Kingdom BIT was the first BIT signed by China that included NT. Its Article 3(3) stipulates that "either Contracting Party shall, to the extent possible, accord treatment in accordance with the stipulations of its laws and regulations to the investments of nationals or companies of the other Contracting Party the same as that accorded to its own nationals or companies." Among all the BITs concluded by China in the 20th century, other than the 1986 China–United Kingdom BIT, only eight of them provided for NT. [211] At that time, the Chinese economy was undeveloped and undergoing significant transformation, and even different types of Chinese domestic enterprises could not enjoy the same standard of treatment. Therefore, according foreign investors "national treatment" would have been extremely difficult and complicated, if not actually impossible, to implement. Since 2002, however, most of China's new and renegotiated BITs have included provisions for full national treatment. Consider the BITs signed by China with Germany and France as examples. The early BITs, signed in 1983 and 1984, respectively, only provided MFN treatment for investors and activities relating to investment, while the 2003 China–Germany BIT and the 2007 China–France BIT include both MFN treatment and NT.

In the newest BITS, the scope of MFN treatment and NT has also been

---

208 *Feldman*, Dissenting Opinion of Jorge Covarrubias Bravo (December 3, 2002), Section 6.
209 Id.
210 In practice, the expressions "relative standards" and "absolute standards" are not used by BITS but only reflect academic usage. In general, the difference between them lies in that relative standards focus on ensuring that each contracting party grants treatment to investments of nationals and companies of the other party on a basis relative to how it treats investments of its own nationals and companies or those of a third country, while absolute standards focus on ensuring that treatment provided by either contracting party is consistent with the requirements of international law.
211 China's contracting partners in these BITs include Japan (1988), Spain (2005), Iceland (1994), Morocco (1995), Macedonia (former Yugoslavia, 1997), Saudi Arabia (1996), the Czech Republic (2005) and the Slovak Republic (2005); see Zhang Caixia, "Review and Reconstruct National Treatment in China-Foreign BITs", *Legal Forum*, 2007, Vol. 1 (in Chinese).

expanded. In the 2003 China–Germany BIT, MFN treatment and NT are to be provided for "investments and activities associated with such investments."[212] For NT, the "activities associated with such investments" are defined in the Protocol to the BIT to include "more particularly, but not exclusively … the management, maintenance, use, enjoyment and disposal of an investment,"[213] whereas those activities for which MFN treatment shall be applicable are nowhere defined. In comparison, the 2004 China–Finland BIT explicitly provides that NT is applicable to "the operation, management, maintenance, use enjoyment, expansion, sale or other disposal of investments that have been made,"[214] whilst MFN treatment is applicable to "the establishment, acquisition, operation, management, maintenance, use, enjoyment, expansion, sale or other disposal of investments."[215] In addition, the 2004 China–Finland BIT and the 2009 China–Switzerland BIT also stipulate that investors have the right to enjoy the more favorable of NT or MFN treatment.[216] The 2005 China–Portugal BIT even provides:

> If the legislation of either Parties or obligations under international law existing at present or established hereafter between the Parties in addition to this Agreement contain a regulation, whether general or specific, entitling investments by investors of the other Party to a treatment more favourable than is provided for by this Agreement, such regulation shall to the extent that it is more favourable prevail over this Agreement.[217]

In the contemporary development of bilateral investment protection, one of the trends is the extension of the application of NT and MFN treatment to the pre-establishment phase of investment.[218] Previously, BITs usually provided that they did not protect the investors' interests in the pre-establishment phase, and the host country could authorize foreign investments, set up the requirements for their establishment, or reserve some industries to domestic investors or those from a third country without violating any obligations to provide NT and MFN treatment.[219] However, most contemporary BITs exclude these rights of the host

---

212 See 2003 China–Germany BIT, Article 3(2) and (3).
213 See ibid., Protocol, para. 4(a).
214 Agreement between the Government of Finland and the Government of the People's Republic of China on the Promotion and Reciprocal Protection of Investment, Article 3(2).
215 Ibid., Article 3(3).
216 Ibid., Article 3(4); Agreement between the Swiss Federal Council and the Government of the People's Republic of China on the Promotion and Reciprocal Protection of Investment, Article 4(3). The North American Free Trade Agreement includes a similar provision.
217 Agreement between the Government of the Republic of Portugal and the Government of the People's Republic of China on the Promotion and Reciprocal Protection of Investment, Article 10(1). On the other hand, Article 5(2) of the 2009 China–ASEAN BIT is noteworthy for its specific exclusion of "any future agreements or arrangements" from inclusion in MFN treatment.
218 For example, Articles 3 and 4 of the 2004 US Model BIT extend NT and MFN treatment, respectively, "with respect to the establishment, acquisition, expansion, management, conduct, operation and sale or other disposition of investments in its territory."
219 This was mainly due to the different levels of economic and technological development of

country, which levels the playing field for foreign investors and domestic investors with regard to market access. In practice, China has extended the application of MFN treatment to the pre-establishment phase,[220] but this is not the case for NT.

To date, about 20 percent of the BITs that China has entered into provide for NT.[221] Of course, a question that may immediately be raised is whether the NT and MFN treatment standards under these BITs could be applied to pre-investment activities.[222]

The 2004 China–Finland BIT explicitly stipulates that national treatment is only applied "with respect to the operation, management, maintenance, use, enjoyment, expansion, sale or other disposal of investments that have been made."[223] At the same time, "[w]ith respect to the establishment, acquisition, operation, management, maintenance, use, enjoyment, expansion, sale or other disposal of investments,"[224] MFN treatment applies. Like the NAFTA Agreement, the China–Finland BIT provides that "each Contracting Party shall accord to investments by the investors of the other Contracting Party the treatment, which, according to the investor is more favorable,"[225] which means that the investors concerned may choose what treatment to receive. In this regard, there would not be any problem, as China has always accorded foreign investors more favorable treatment than its own nationals.[226]

---

individual countries. Compared with those from developed countries, enterprises in developing countries usually have lesser or no international competitiveness. In such a situation, according foreign investment NT for the market access phase may result in their superior status, and domestic industries will not be effectively protected. See Yu Jinsong, "Issues on National Treatment for Foreign Investment of the Market Access Phase in China's Development", *Jurist Review*, Vol. 6, 2004 (in Chinese).

220 Article 3(3) of the 2004 China–Finland BIT and Article 4(3) of the 2009 China–Switzerland BIT are examples of this. Article 5(1) of the 2009 China–ASEAN BIT is even more explicit, extending MFN treatment to "admission, establishment, acquisition, expansion, management, conduct, operation, maintenance, use, liquidation, sale, and other forms of disposal of investments."

221 According to a study of 117 BITs that China had entered into, only 17 provided for NT, whilst the others stipulated fair and equitable treatment as the standard; see Zhang Caixia, "Review and Re-establish the National Treatment System in Sino-Foreign BITs", *Rule of Law Tribune*, 2007, pp. 240–48 (in Chinese).

222 Chinese law has no provisions for pre-investment NT. With the international community paying more and more attention to pre-establishment NT and as China's overseas investment is growing rapidly, it is foreseeable that China will accept pre-investment NT in its BITs in the future.

223 2005 China–Finland BIT, Article 3(2).

224 Ibid., Article 3(3).

225 Ibid., Article 3(4).

226 For example, according to the Circular of the State Council of China on Adjustment of Imported Equipment Taxation Policies, the State Council decided that, starting from 1 January 1998, imported equipment for domestic investment projects and foreign investment projects encouraged by the State should enjoy exemption from tariff and import stage value-added tax within the specified scope. Before January 1, 2007 when the Decision of the State Council on Amending the Interim Regulations of the People's Republic of China on City and Town Land Use Tax entered into force, foreign-invested enterprises had been exempted from the land use tax. They also enjoyed lower income taxation before January 1, 2008, when the Enterprise Income Tax Law entered into force.

As discussed earlier, in China's practice, protection and treatment—MFN treatment and NT—are granted to investors without exceptions. This is in contrast with the NAFTA, Article 1410(1) of which provides: "Nothing in this Part shall be construed to prevent a Party from adopting or maintaining reasonable measures for prudential reasons," even if the effect of such measures (as contrasted with their motive or intent) is discriminatory.[227] The NAFTA exception of prudential measures is apparently confined to financial measures.[228] In China's specific commitments relating to the services sector that were made in the process of it joining the WTO, a similar provision was included.

As it is very difficult, if not impossible, to draw a line between investment and trade in services in many cases, this may cause difficulties in practice. For instance, where a measure is introduced by the Chinese Government pursuant to the prudential principle under the General Agreement on Trade in Services ("GATS"), it may be judged to breach the provisions of BITs relating to fair and equitable treatment, NT, etc. As the WTO dispute resolution mechanisms only permit members to institute complaints, private investors are likely to choose international investment arbitration as a forum to resolve their disputes with the Chinese Government. In these circumstances, it may not be possible for the Chinese Government to use GATS compliance as a defense for not providing fair and equitable treatment or NT as those may be required under the provisions of a BIT.

The 2008 China–New Zealand FTA, as a matter of principle, does not apply to trade in services. Yet it extends its application to government measures that affect the supply of services through commercial presence with respect to the transfer of funds, fair and equitable treatment, compensation, expropriation and subrogation. In such matters, a service supplier may invoke the investor–state dispute settlement mechanism in resolving its differences with the host government.[229]

In any event, NT and MFN treatment have now become standard clauses in China's BITs. The 2006 China–Pakistan FTA follows the model of the 2003 China–Germany BIT, including the limitations with regard to the application of the MFN treatment clause.[230] Article 48(3) of the China–Pakistan FTA modified

227 See, in this regard, *Fireman's Fund Insurance Company v. The United Mexican States*, ICSID Case No. ARB(AF)/02/1, Award (July 17, 2006), para. 162.
228 Olin L. Wethington, the US principal negotiator for financial services under the NAFTA, wrote: "Article 1410(1)(a) ... carves out of the national treatment and other obligations of the financial services chapter a right to take reasonable measures even though discriminatory in application, to protect the safety and soundness of the financial system. This regulatory prerogative to protect the integrity of the financial system is accepted internationally." Olin L. Wethington, *Financial Market Liberalization: The NAFTA Framework*, West Publishing Co., 1994, s. 5.07.
229 2008 China–New Zealand FTA, Article 137. The measures affecting services do not include subsidies provided by a Party or "laws, regulations, policies and procedures of general application governing the procurement by government agencies of goods and services purchased for governmental purposes and not with a view to commercial resale or with a view to use in the production of goods or the supply of services for commercial sale." See Article 137(5) of the China–New Zealand FTA.
230 It also provides that where the laws of either Party or international obligations existing at the conclusion of the FTA or established thereafter between the Parties result in more favorable

the MFN provisions of the China–Germany BIT slightly by providing that MFN treatment shall not encompass the benefit of any treatment, preference or privilege "by virtue of: (a) any other customs union, free trade zone, economic union and any international agreement resulting in such unions, or similar institutions; (b) any international agreement or arrangement relating wholly or mainly to taxation; (c) any arrangements for facilitating small scale trade in border areas." The 2008 China–New Zealand FTA has, however, adopted a much more elaborate standard. In terms of NT, it stipulates that the specific areas should include "management, conduct, operation, maintenance, use, enjoyment or disposal, by the investors" of their investment and associated activities.[231] It also makes like circumstances the condition for according NT.[232]

There are also restraints on the application of NT provisions. These include: (1) existing non-conforming measures; (2) continuation and amendments of non-conforming measures, provided that such amendments do not increase the degree of non-conformity; and (3) a measure that would not fall into the NT obligations under an existing BIT that a party has concluded.[233] This having been stipulated, the parties are under an obligation to remove the non-conforming measures progressively.[234]

The China–New Zealand FTA also explicitly states that dispute resolution procedures under other arrangements do not apply to investors of any party, nor does any differential treatment accorded to third countries "under any free trade agreement or multilateral international agreement."[235] Differential treatment involving fisheries and maritime matters under international agreements may also be considered as exceptions to MFN treatment.[236]

V. Synthesis and conclusions

Investor–state arbitration has become a significant feature of international investment law. Yet the decisions of the tribunals entrusted to deal with investor–state disputes—including those relating to the scope of application of the MFN clause—frequently contradict each other. Such a situation is not conducive to international economic exchanges or to the formation of international economic

---

treatment to the investments of the investors from the other Party than that provided by the FTA, the more favorable treatment should apply. See Article 55 of the China–Pakistan FTA.
231 China–New Zealand FTA, Article 138. The China–Pakistan FTA and BITs that China has entered into recently do not have such detailed provisions.
232 China–New Zealand FTA, Article 138.
233 Ibid., Article 141.
234 The China–New Zealand FTA does not provide specifically what may constitute a non-conforming measure. It instead incorporates the provisions of the WTO Agreement on Trade-Related Investment Measures *mutatis mutandis*. See id.
235 Ibid., Article 139. This exclusion includes "agreements on the liberalization of trade in goods or services or investment, any measures taken as part of a wider process of economic integration or trade liberalization between the parties to such agreements."
236 Ibid., Article 139(5).

law. Improvement of the situation is therefore badly needed. As has been noted by Douglas:

> The decision in *Maffezini* was the first time that a party has been permitted to rely upon an MFN clause to modify the jurisdictional mandate of an international tribunal. Across the hundreds of years of activity of international courts and tribunals leading up to *Maffezini*, there had only been judicial pronouncements against such a device, including the International Court of Justice's judgment in the *Anglo-Iranian Oil Company Case* and the British-Venezuelan Mixed Claims Commission's decision in *Aroa Mines*.[237]

The *Maffezini* decision has triggered so much debate because it is doubtful whether or not such expressions as "all matters" and "all rights" should be interpreted to cover mechanisms for resolving investor–state disputes.[238] The most criticized consequence of the *Maffezini* decision is the potential for treaty-shopping by investors. This problem can be even more serious because, in the words of Arbitrator Stern's dissent in the *Impregilo* case:

> … it appears that in the trend favorable to the use of MFN clause [sic] to expand jurisdiction, the position is not only to import from the third party treaty into the basic treaty the *jurisdictional clause as a whole*, but to import only *such or such aspect of a jurisdictional clause* which appears more favorable, as has been done in the majority Award: in other words there can be a "pick and choose" policy in the implementation of the MFN clause.[239]

Regardless of the consequences of the *Maffezini* decision, the question is whether that tribunal's interpretation is in compliance with rules of international law. As stated by the Special Rapporteur of the International Law Commission on the MFN clause, the "beneficiary State can only claim rights which belong to the subject-matter of the clause,"[240] e.g. like circumstances. Where there are other conditions and restrictions for the application of the MFN clause, they must also be satisfied. In addition, as some commentators have stated, the operation of the MFN clause should not fundamentally subvert "the carefully negotiated balance of [a] BIT."[241]

The solution to the problem of contradictory arbitration awards is to interpret the MFN clause strictly in accordance with VCLT Articles 31 and 32—that is, interpretation in good faith. Tribunals should also keep in mind that in international

---

237 Zachary Douglas, "The MFN Clause in Investment Treaty Arbitration: Treaty Interpretation Off the Rails", *Journal of International Dispute Settlement*, 2010, pp. 1–17, at 5 (references omitted).

238 For instance, in *Berschader*, the Tribunal challenged whether such "not even seemingly clear language … can be considered to have an unambiguous meaning in the context of an MFN clause;" see *Berschader v. The Russian Federation*, SCC Case No. 080/2004, Award (April 21, 2006), para. 184; available at: http://www.italaw.com/documents/BerschaderFinalAward.pdf.

239 *Impregilo*, Concurring and Dissenting Opinion, *supra*, note 71, para. 106.

240 Ustor, *supra*, note 19, Vol. II, p. 170.

241 See Campbell McLachlan, Laurence Shore and Matthew Weiniger, *International Investment Arbitration*, Oxford University Press, Oxford, UK, 2007, p. 254.

negotiations the state parties often take different positions. Yet, once an agreement is reached, it reflects a common position of the contracting parties, each contracting party's previous position notwithstanding. An MFN clause therefore, no matter however worded, reflects the agreement of the contracting parties. Arbitral tribunals should interpret such provisions faithfully. In this regard, the *Maffezini* tribunal failed to do so. When interpreting the MFN clause, it apparently gave weight to the positions of the contracting parties *before* the BIT was reached, stating:

> The Claimant has convincingly explained that at the time of the negotiations of the Agreement, Argentina still sought to require some form of prior exhaustion of local remedies, while Spain supported the policy of a direct right of submission to arbitration, which was reflected in the numerous agreements it negotiated with other countries at that time. The eventual role the treaty envisaged for domestic courts, involving the submission of the dispute to these courts for a period of time, not amounting to the traditional exhaustion of local remedies requirement … coupled with ICSID arbitration, was an obvious compromise reached by the parties. Argentina later abandoned its prior policy, and like Spain and Chile, accepted treaty clauses providing for the direct submission of disputes to arbitration following a period of negotiations.[242]

The very fact that a BIT was a compromise reached by the contracting parties should prohibit a tribunal from interpreting it in accordance with the position of one of the contracting parties at the time of the negotiations. Nor should the fact that the parties have adopted a different policy after the entering into force of a particular BIT entitle a tribunal to give a new meaning to the words of that BIT other than what was agreed when they were negotiated. Precisely in this respect, the *Maffezini* Tribunal misapplied the rules of interpretation stipulated by the VCLT. In fact, even if a BIT or FTA contains ambiguous provisions relating to the application of the MFN clause, tribunals must take caution in extending the clause to dispute resolution for the sake of protecting foreign investments and investors. Unless tribunals interpret the MFN clause in the issue before them strictly in accordance with the rules of international law, it can be expected that affected members of the international community will react strongly.

   The *Maffezini* decision and those following it have already alarmed members of the international community about the potential uncertainty that investment host countries may face. Some countries have begun to take measures to reduce such uncertainty. The third draft text of the Agreement on the Free Trade Area of the Americas ("FTAA") of November 21, 2003 contains such an example. Footnote 13 of that draft of the FTAA reads:

> The Parties note the recent decision of the arbitral tribunal in the Maffezini (Arg.) v. Kingdom of Spain, which found an unusually broad most favored

---

242 *Emilio Agustín Maffezini v. Kingdom of Spain*, ICSID Case No. ARB/97/7, Decision on Jurisdiction (January 25, 2000), para. 57.

nation clause in an Argentina-Spain agreement to encompass international dispute resolution procedures. ... By contrast, the Most-Favored-Nation Article of this Agreement is expressly limited in its scope to matters "with respect to the establishment, acquisition, expansion, management, conduct, operation, and sale or other disposition of investments." The Parties share the understanding and intent that this clause does not encompass international dispute resolution mechanisms ... and therefore could not reasonably lead to a conclusion similar to that of the Maffezini case.[243]

Such statements demonstrate the disapproval by members of the international community of the *Maffezini* decision.[244] In fact, provisions contained in the FTAA are not the only example of this. The 2008 China–New Zealand FTA[245] contains similar provisions. Apparently being aware of the potential impact of the *Maffezini* decision, Article 139 of the China–New Zealand FTA stipulates:

1.   Each Party shall accord to investors, investments and activities associated with such investments by investors of the other Party treatment no less favourable than that accorded, in like circumstances, to the investments and associated activities by the investors of any third country with respect to admission, expansion, management, conduct, operation, maintenance, use, enjoyment and disposal.
2.   For greater certainty, the obligation in this Article does not encompass a requirement to extend to investors of the other Party dispute resolution procedures other than those set out in this Chapter.

Article 4 of the 2011 Japan–Taiwan Investment Arrangement,[246] after stipulating that "Investors of either Side and their investments shall within the Area of the other Side be accorded treatment no less favorable than the treatment accorded in like circumstances to investors of any other countries or regions and to their investments with respect to investment activities," goes on to provide that "[f]or greater certainty," the treatment referred to above "does not include treatment accorded to investors of any other countries or regions and to their investments in regard to dispute settlement mechanisms that are contained in international treaties or agreements." The above position of China and Japan is further reflected in the investment treaty entered into by both countries, together with the Republic of Korea.

243 FTAA—Free Trade Area of the Americas, Draft Agreement, FTAA.TNC/w/133/Rev.3 (November 21, 2003), Chapter XVII Investment, footnote 13, appended to Article 5, Most-Favored-Nation Treatment.
244 For discussion on this issue, also see Yas Banifatemi, "The Emerging Jurisprudence on the Most-Favoured-Nation Treatment in Investment Arbitration", in Andrea Björklund et al. (eds)., *Investment Treaty Law: Current Issues III*, London, BIICL, 2009.
245 The China–New Zealand Free Trade Agreement was signed on April 7, 2008 and entered into force on October 1, 2008.
246 Arrangement between the Association of East Asian Relations and the Interchange Association of the Mutual Cooperation on the Liberalization, Promotion and Protection of Investment, entered into on September 22, 2011.

In the Trilateral Investment Agreement among China, South Korea and Japan, in respect of MFN treatment, it is provided that: "[e]ach Contracting Party shall … accord to investors of another Contracting Party and to their investments treatment no less favorable than that it accords … to investors of the third Contracting Party or of a non-Contracting Party and to their investments …"[247] It then stipulates:

> It is understood that the treatment accorded to investors of the third Contracting Party or any non-Contracting Party and to their investments as referred to in paragraph 1 does not include treatment accorded to investors of the third Contracting Party or any non-Contracting Party and to their investments by provisions concerning the settlement of investment disputes between a Contracting Party and investors of the third Contracting Party or between a Contracting Party and investors of any non-Contracting Party that are provided for in other international agreements.[248]

Taking into consideration the treaty practice of China and Japan, to exclude application of the MFN clause from investor–state dispute settlement is not surprising. It should be pointed out, however, that Japan and South Korea are traditional international investment home countries, whilst China has increased its foreign investment very rapidly in recent years. As extensive application of the MFN clause, at least in theory, favors foreign investors, China, South Korea and Japan would have been expected to have supported a *Maffezini*-like interpretation of the MFN clause. The very fact that these three countries have voted, through treaty practice, against the extension of the MFN clause to dispute settlement shows that they, as well perhaps as East Asian countries as a whole, prefer arbitration tribunals to follow the traditional interpretation of the MFN clause.

While the international community is forming a consensus on certain issues of international law, arbitral tribunals should give more weight to such treaty practices in ascertaining the intent of the contracting parties. Unless the opinions of arbitrators cease to be divergent and the decisions of tribunals become less contradictory, correction and improvement of the situation are no doubt the most important tasks facing the international community.

As countries have reacted strongly to the *Maffezini* decision, it is time to review the situation and for the international community to consider alternatives to improve it. In the first place, it is a well-established practice that consent to arbitration must be given special consideration, which should be distinguished from the general consent or ratification of the treaty in question. In this regard, the ICJ judgment in the case of East Timor is instructive; the Court stated therein that it "considers that the *erga omnes* character of a norm and the rule of consent to jurisdiction are two different things."[249] In that case, the ICJ refused to pass judgment on the rights and obligations *erga omnes*, as such rights and obligations involved

---

247 Trilateral Investment Agreement, *supra*, note 129, Article 4(1).
248 Ibid., Article 4(3).
249 *East Timor (Portugal v. Australia)*, *Judgment, I.C.J. Reports*, 1995, p. 102, para. 29.

another sovereign state that was not a party to the case and that had not consented to the jurisdiction of the Court. For the purpose of re-establishing the authority of investment arbitration tribunals, the international community should consider whether it is desirable to distinguish *erga omnes* norms from the rule of consent to jurisdiction, as pronounced by the ICJ, in interpreting such provisions.

Second, the international community should consider whether tribunals should be encouraged to adopt the position that, unless there is a clearly expressed intent of the contracting parties to a BIT or FTA to the contrary, an MFN clause should not be extended to dispute resolution procedures. In this regard, a recent case—*Koza*—illustrates the awareness of investment tribunals of the concerns and try to deal with such issues with much caution. In that case, the UK-Turkmenistan BIT explicitly authorizes the application of the MFN clause to dispute settlement. The majority of the Tribunal ruled that "it is in the nature of an MFN clause to be used to displace a treaty provision deemed less favourable in favour of another clause, from another treaty, deemed more favourable."[250] An important difference between the *Koza* case and some of the cases discussed previously is that the MFN clause in the *Koza* case specifically refers to the provisions on dispute resolution, which justifies the application of the MFN clause to dispute resolution.

Third, the international community should consider whether investment tribunals should be encouraged to recognize local remedy procedures, such as a waiting period to include negotiations and local court proceedings, as prerequisites for jurisdiction.

In summary, the MFN clause, as one of the oldest principles of international law, has played an important part in international economic exchanges. In the field of investment, however, the contradictory interpretations of MFN clauses contained in BITs have much alarmed the international community. As there exists no institution to correct the mistakes of investment tribunals, and as members of such tribunals have different cultural, educational, legal, and political backgrounds—many of them lacking experience in investment host states, particularly those which are developing countries—the situation of varying interpretations, together with their unhealthy consequences, is most likely to continue. This, to say the least, does not contribute to the flow of direct foreign investment or the strengthening of the legal regime for its protection. It is therefore high time for the international community to emphasize adherence to the well-established international rules in interpreting the MFN clause.

While those who support the extension of the application of the MFN clause apparently intend to ensure protection to foreign investors and therefore, in their view, to promote direct foreign investment, it should be kept in mind that good wishes may not result in good things—the *Tao* says: "some things are increased by being diminished, and others are diminished by being increased."[251] To promote foreign investment by protecting foreign investors and investments, the interna-

---

250   *Garanti Koza LLP v. Turkmenistan*, ICSID Case No. ARB/11/20, Decision on the Objection to Jurisdiction for Lack of Consent, July 3, 2013, para. 54.
251   Ibid., Ch 42.

tional community—especially those countries most concerned—should be open minded and prepared to adjust themselves in understanding and interpreting international obligations. Where strong disapproval of the extensive interpretation of the MFN clause has already appeared, we should nonetheless be strong enough to reconsider what has been done. In this regard, Confucius observed: "The faults of a superior man are like eclipses of the sun and moon. When they occur, all men see them; but, when he rectifies his mistakes, all men look up to him as before."[252]

With regard to NT, the problems are not as serious and complicated in comparison to those relating to MFN treatment. The essential difficulty is again the diversification of interpretations. From the cases discussed, such diversities have most often occurred in interpreting the concepts of "like circumstances" and "less favourable treatment."

In considering whether a foreign investor has been accorded treatment less favorable than that of domestic investors, the foreign investor and the domestic comparator/investor must be in the same circumstances. This should be the case regardless of whether or not the BIT in question contains the words "like circumstances;" otherwise, the comparison may not be relevant. Regarding what may constitute "like circumstances," the *S.D. Myers* Tribunal and the *Pope & Talbot* Tribunal treated competition as the main factor. This analysis is, at least to some extent, in compliance with the GATT/WTO treatment of "like products." As the WTO interpretation of "like products" has the general support of the international community, using competition as an essential factor should be supported. However, investors may compete with each other in many ways. Competition should therefore be limited to those in the same economic or business sector. In doing so, particular attention should be paid to ensure that manufacturers are not compared with service providers, as happened in the *S.D. Myers* case discussed earlier.

The interpretation of "less favourable treatment" seems to be more problematic than that of "like circumstances." Some tribunals started their analysis with an assessment of whether less favorable treatment had been accorded to foreign investors rather than whether the foreign and domestic investors were in like circumstances. As discussed earlier, this approach is not consistent with the principle of judicial/arbitral economy. Still other tribunals, of which the *Feldman* Tribunal is an example, have imported their own notions of administrative law standards as applied in their own countries and considered the ineffective implementation of such law to grant benefits to domestic investors. International investment law, including BITs, should only protect eligible investments from arbitrary or discriminatory measures of host states. Also, where a so-called favorable treatment is the result of violation of the law, it should not be used as a benchmark for comparison. In this regard, the *Feldman* case should serve as a lesson for other tribunals.

In any event, with the newly emerging markets beginning to accord foreign investors and domestic investors the same treatment, which is in line with the

---

252 *Confucian Analects*, Ch 19(21).

practice of the developed countries, it can be expected that there will be more disputes over NT. Against this background, however, DiMascio and Pauwelyn have noted:

> What's apparent, in any event, is that NAFTA tribunals' early enthusiasm for the protection of investor interests has, in more recent cases, been tempered by references to the public interest of host governments. One can only speculate, but this shift seems at least partly a response to outcries by both NAFTA governments and public opinion.[253]

Tribunals should try even harder to give detailed reasons when making decisions. Only by doing so may they contribute to the development of international investment law.

In conclusion, relative standards of treatment have now become an established part of international investment law. Diversified and sometimes contradictory decisions of arbitral tribunals may be a permanent feature of the processes in the ongoing formulation of international investment law. Tribunals are mindful of being cautious in making decisions, as whatever decision is made and the things that are said whilst making those decisions will not only affect the cases before them but will also have an impact on subsequent cases. In addition to giving reasoned decisions, tribunals should disallow any abuse of the processes. The *GAMI* Tribunal strongly pointed out on this matter that "[i]t is not conceivable that a … corporation becomes entitled to the anti-discrimination protections of international law by virtue of the sole fact that a foreigner buys a share of it."[254]

At the same time, however, one should keep in mind that international investment law is there to protect foreign investors and investments from arbitrary and discriminatory government actions. As Mann once said: "It is certainly not always easy to define the circumstances in which lack of equality amounts to unlawful discrimination under international law. But given an inequality which is discriminatory in law, which is arbitrary or constitutes an abuse, no one has attempted to defend it."[255] With this in mind, one can remain optimistic that arbitrary and discriminatory actions will be dealt with more effectively in the future.

---

253 DiMascio and Pauwelyn, *supra*, note 128 p. 79.
254 *GAMI*, *supra*, note 177, para. 115.
255 F. A. Mann, *Studies in International Law*, OUP, 1972, p. 476, cited from A. F. M. Maniruzzaman, "Expropriation of Alien Property and the Principle of Non-discrimination in International Law of Foreign Investment: An Overview", 8 *Journal of Transnational Law & Policy* 58, 1998, p. 68; available at: http://www.academia.edu/586566/Expropriation_of_Alien_Property_and_the_Principle_of_Non-discrimination_in_International_Law_of_Foreign_Investment_An_Overview#.

8   Expropriation

Against the background of world economic integration or globalization, economic cooperation among all countries has become the mainstream trend. Thus, individual countries competing with each other to attract foreign investment has become an important catalyst for economic development. Since the existing capital inflows are far from sufficient to satisfy the needs of most countries, large-scale nationalization or expropriation[1] does not currently constitute a major threat to international investment.[2]

Nevertheless, nationalization and expropriation are still of great concern to private foreign investors,[3] despite their rare occurrence and the fact that the money involved only accounts for a small part of total international investment. Between 1951 and 1975, when nationalization was comparatively more frequent, only 5.4 percent of total international investment was affected. In the mid-1970s, there were around 9750 enterprises established by foreign investors in developing countries and 36,800 in developed countries. During that period, there was an average of 98 nationalizations annually and the enterprises nationalized or expropriated only accounted for 0.9 percent of the total. For investments made by foreign enterprises in developing countries, the capital involved in expropriation

---

1   In the literature of international law and international economic law, nationalization and expropriation are synonymous. However, strictly speaking, nationalization is carried out in the public interest, while expropriation may be for the personal purposes and needs of the ruler. Compared with the latter, the former has a wider scale and larger scope. The two terms are used synonymously in this book.

2   While this is true in general, it is also worth noting that the first decade of the 21st century has seen a new wave of expropriations, especially of investments in the extractive industries and most notably in Latin America and Russia.

3   In addition to confirming that expropriation was among investors' major concerns in making foreign investment decisions in 2009 and 2010, the Multilateral Investment Guarantee Agency ("MIGA") noted that "expropriations and nationalizations in parts of Latin America have spread beyond the extractive industries, into services, public utilities, and manufacturing, thus feeding investors' concerns." See MIGA, *World Investment and Political Risk 2010*, IBDR/World Bank Group, Washington, D.C., 2011, pp. 8 and 19; available at: http://www.miga.org/documents/WIPR10ebook.pdf. In *World Investment and Political Risk 2011* (available at: http://www.miga.org/documents/WIPR11.pdf). MIGA says: "Over the medium term, structural issues related to political risk remain the major preoccupations among foreign investors with operations in developing countries. Of these concerns, two stand out: breach of contractual obligations by the state and expropriatory actions (regulatory takings, creeping expropriation, and outright nationalization)." The report devotes a full chapter to an in-depth study of "Government Takings and Expropriations."

accounted for 18.8 percent. Overall, for the period 1960–1979, MIGA estimates that "15–20 percent of the volume of all U.S. FDI abroad measured in volume terms was nationalized."[4] In 2010, MIGA noted that only 6 percent of respondents to its survey of political risks to international investment reported losses due to expropriation, although it did not report the extent or value of those losses.[5] At the same time, it reported that twice as many respondents considered the risks of expropriation to be "very high" (that is, likely) and more than 50 percent overall considered those risks to be at least "somewhat high."[6]

Historically, nationalization is directly related to colonization. The earliest nationalizations happened in Latin America rather than in the former European colonies in Asia or Africa. In the early 20th century, Latin American countries, including Mexico, expropriated foreign investments. Although some expropriations were deemed to have been carried out for the personal interests of local rulers, it is generally recognized that at least the expropriations in Mexico in 1917 and 1938 were part of its national economic plans and, thus, done in the public interest. Nationalizations carried out in the former Soviet Union and Eastern European countries and by the national governments of newly independent former colonies led to the issue of compensation for nationalization becoming an important one for the international community and international law and has resulted in obviously extremely different opinions. The former Soviet Union, as well as most of the Eastern European countries and the newly independent former colonies or "protectorates" in Asia and Africa, held that the country which carried out nationalization should not undertake the responsibility of compensation, whilst the former suzerain and capital-exporting countries in Western Europe and America emphatically insisted on compensation for nationalization.

Nationalizations in the first half of the 20th century were generally conducted by means of legislation that officially expropriated the assets of foreigners. Almost all such nationalizations were intended to realize the economic development objectives of the host countries by nationalizing the assets of foreigners or transferring the management rights of foreign-invested enterprises to state-owned enterprises or institutions. Regardless of the form taken, the property rights of foreigners were substantially affected. Today, especially in light of the strengthening of economic interdependence within the international community, large-scale nationalization or expropriation no longer constitutes a major threat to international investment, but regulatory, disguised, or creeping expropriation has taken its place. The issues of how to define nationalization and the responsibility of the country concerned for compensation are thus considerably more complicated than in the past. Unfortunately, the international community has as yet failed to establish widely recognized norms applicable to all nationalizations. Not even any consensus has been reached regarding what should be included in any definition of indirect, disguised, or creeping expropriation.

4 MIGA, *WIPR 2011*, *supra*, note 3, p. 30.
5 See MIGA, *WIPR 2010*, *supra*, note 3, p. 23 and Figure 1.15.
6 Ibid., p. 23 and Figure 1.14.

In any case, whatever may be the actual or perceived risks of nationalization, there are still many theoretical and practical issues concerning it which remain unresolved in international investment law. Almost all multilateral and bilateral treaties relating to international investment include provisions regarding nationalization and compensation for nationalization. This is so because, although the overall level of nationalization or expropriation is low, for those foreign investors who are victims of it, it is 100 percent involvement and suffering. International judicial or quasi-judicial practice, as well as the works of scholars, always addresses these issues as well. Therefore, it is of practical significance to address herein the problems with nationalization and compensation for nationalization. This chapter will analyze the preconditions of nationalization, the international norms concerning nationalization, and relevant international judicial and arbitral practice.

I. Expropriation and pertinent conditions

"The right of 'expropriation,' even in its widest sense, is recognized in international law, irrespective of the patrimonial rights involved or of the nationality of the person in whom they are vested. This international recognition has been confirmed on innumerable occasions in diplomatic practice and in the decisions of courts and arbitral commissions, and, more recently, in the declarations of international organizations and conferences."[7] This right of expropriation is considered part of the sovereign rights of all states. The right of a sovereign state to nationalize foreigners' rights, including property rights, within its territory is recognized in many multilateral and bilateral international documents. The most notable ones include the resolutions adopted by the UN General Assembly, including the Charter of Economic Rights and Duties of States. For example, General Assembly Resolution 1803 declares that:

1. The right of peoples and nations to permanent sovereignty over their natural wealth and resources must be exercised in the interest of their national development and of the well-being of the people of the State concerned.
2. The exploration, development and disposition of such resources, as well as the import of the foreign capital required for these purposes, should be in conformity with the rules and conditions which the peoples and nations freely consider to be necessary or desirable with regard to the authorization, restriction or prohibition of such activities.
3. In cases where authorization is granted, the capital imported and the earnings on that capital shall be governed by the terms thereof, by the national legislation in force, and by international law. The profits derived must be shared in the proportions freely agreed upon, in each case, between the investors and the recipient State, due care being taken to ensure that there is no

---

7 F. V. Garcia Amador, "Special Rapporteur's Report on State Responsibility", *Yearbook of the International Law Commission*, 1996, Vol. II, p. 11, para. 41.

impairment, for any reason, of that State's sovereignty over its natural wealth and resources.[8]

The Declaration on the Establishment of a New International Economic Order adopted by the UN General Assembly on May 1, 1974 further acknowledges states' sovereignty over their natural resources.[9]

In short, customary international law recognizes that sovereign states have the power to nationalize or expropriate foreign properties, including foreign investment. Contemporary multilateral treaties and normative documents such as the Energy Charter Treaty, the North American Free Trade Agreement, and the World Bank Guidelines on the Treatment of Foreign Direct Investment all accept that a sovereign state is entitled to nationalize or expropriate assets of foreigners for the public interest. As a matter of fact, even the European Convention on Human Rights and the OECD Draft Convention on the Protection of Foreign Property recognize the right of nationalization by a sovereign state (see Annex Table 1).

Customary international law notwithstanding, contemporary international documents and scholars' writings tend to emphasize the satisfaction of conditions for nationalization or expropriation. Where such conditions are not met, the nationalization or expropriation may be regarded as illegal. For instance, the World Bank Guidelines on the Treatment of Foreign Direct Investment, in dealing with the issue of expropriation, starts with the premise that:

> A State may not expropriate or otherwise take in whole or in part a foreign private investment, ... except where this is done in accordance with applicable legal procedures, in pursuance in good faith of a public purpose, without discrimination on the basis of nationality and against the payment of appropriate compensation.[10]

This shows a change in attitude within the international community on the matter. It is now quite widely accepted that nationalization or expropriation must satisfy the following prerequisites in order to be lawful: (1) the public interest; (2) due process; (3) non-discrimination; and (4) payment of compensation.[11] Among

8 General Assembly Resolution 1803 (XVII) of December 14, 1962, "Permanent Sovereignty Over Natural Resources," recitations 1–3; available at: http://www.ohchr.org/EN/ProfessionalInterest/Pages/NaturalResources.aspx.
9 General Assembly Resolution 3201 (S-VI). "Declaration on the Establishment of a New International Economic Order," UN Doc. A/RES/S-6/3201 (May 1, 1974); available at: http://www.un-documents.net/s6r3201.htm. It called for the creation of a new international economic order based on equity, sovereign equality, interdependence and cooperation of all states, irrespective of their economic and social systems. With globalization ever deepening, however, the international community is no longer interested in a new international economic order.
10 World Bank Guidelines on the Treatment of Foreign Direct Investment, IV Expropriation and Unilateral Alterations or Termination of Contracts, para. 1; full text available at: http://www.italaw.com/documents/WorldBank.pdf.
11 For discussion on this matter, see Rudolf Dolzer and Christoph Schreuer, *Principles of International*

these requirements, non-discrimination was added at a later stage and the one regarding compensation has been especially hotly debated.

In order to ensure the effective and smooth flow of international investment, individual countries always make special arrangements for nationalization and compensation for nationalization when entering into investment treaties. In general, the contracting parties recognize that either party is entitled to nationalize or expropriate domestic or foreign enterprises and assets within its territory. Meanwhile, they always agree that the country conducting nationalization or expropriation should undertake the liability of compensation. Reisman and Sloane consider recent development in investment treaties as moving from the Friendship, Commerce and Navigation treaties ("FCNs") to the "BIT generation," in which more favorable conditions are promised to foreign investments, including an increased recognition of indirect expropriation through measures tantamount to expropriation, as will be discussed later.[12]

Based on the provisions of international treaties and other agreements, it is certain that any nationalization or expropriation of private assets, including foreign investments, carried out by a sovereign state for purposes in the public interest and without discrimination should be deemed to be a legal governmental action. Traditionally, however, judicial and arbitral practices did not emphasize "public interest" as a precondition for expropriation of private properties. For example, in the *Shufeldt Claim*, the arbitral tribunal held that the Guatemalan Government was entitled to enact any law for any reason.[13] In the *Oscar Chinn* case, the Permanent Court of International Justice ("PCIJ"), in considering Belgium's measures in response to the general economic depression which affected the rights and interests of private parties engaging in the transportation business, stated that: "The Belgian Government was the sole judge of this critical situation and of the remedies that it called for—subject of course to its duty of respecting its international obligations."[14] It is understandable that the PCIJ ruled that way, as at that time rules and concepts of international human rights were not well developed. International investment was not sought by all countries, either.

Although the concept of the public interest as a prerequisite for nationalization and expropriation has been included in many international documents, including those of great importance to the development of international law, in practice this

---

Investment Law, Oxford University Press, 2008, pp. 90–92; also see R. Doak Bishop, James Crawford, and W. Michael Reisman, *Foreign Investment Disputes: Cases, Materials and Commentary*, Kluwer Law International, 2005, ch 8.

12 W. Michael Reisman and Robert D. Sloane, "Indirect Expropriation and Its Valuation in the BIT Generation," *British Yearbook of International Law*, Vol. 75, 2004, p. 115, at 118. The more favorable conditions established by BITs include "more significantly and innovatively, an effective *normative* framework: impartial courts, an efficient and legally restrained bureaucracy, and the measure of transparency in decision" (emphasis in original). Ibid. p. 117.

13 See *Shufeldt Claim (U.S. v. Guatemala)* (July 24, 1930), R.I.A.A., Vol. II, 1079–1102, at 1095; available at: http://legal.un.org/riaa/cases/vol_II/1079-1102.pdf.

14 See *Oscar Chinn Case (Britain v. Belgium)*, 1934 P.C.I.J. (ser. A/B) No. 63 (December 12), para. 53; partial text available at: http://www.worldcourts.com/pcij/eng/decisions/1934.12.12_oscar_chinn.htm.

does not always become the focus of debate. In a series of disputes concerning nationalizations in Libya in the 1970s, the United States and the United Kingdom held that nationalization for the purpose of political retaliation was not by nature part of the public interest but could only be deemed to comprise a new explanation for "public interest." Some arbitral tribunals ruled that the nationalizations undertaken by Libya were illegal because they were not based on important political concerns and the action of the administrative agency was arbitrary and discriminatory.[15] Some other arbitral tribunals, however, held distinctly opposite views. For example, in the *LIAMCO* case, the tribunal totally rejected the argument of countries such as the United States and the United Kingdom, holding that:

> … as to the contention that the said measures were politically motivated and not in pursuance of a legitimate public purpose, it is the general opinion in international theory that the public utility principle is not a necessary requisite for the legality of a nationalization. This principle was mentioned by Grotius and other later publicists, but now there is no international authority, from a juridical or any other source, to support its application to nationalization. Motives are indifferent to international law, each state being free to judge for itself what it considers useful or necessary for the public good … the object pursued by it is of no concern to third parties …[16]

As a matter of fact, the above rulings are totally consistent with the stand taken by the European Court of Human Rights, which has held that national legislatures know best the social and economic policy of the related country and that their judgments on the public interest should be respected.[17]

Discrimination is another issue, the core of which is whether it is involved in nationalization. The nub of this issue is whether or not the affected foreign investor is treated the same as a national of the host country and/or whether foreign investors from different countries are treated equally in respect of any nationalization. However, this does not mean that the nationalizing country will violate international law if it provides certain different treatment to investors from different countries or to national investors. Under certain circumstances, in the public interest, a country may only nationalize one sector (instead of all sectors) or one company (but not all the companies). For example, if certain industries of a country, such as the telecommunications system or the steel industry, are controlled by foreign investors, merely nationalizing those enterprises or industries may not be challenged by any foreign government or individual, as these

15 See, for example, *BP Exploration Company (Libya) Ltd. v. Libyan Arab Republic*, Judgment, 53 *I.L.R.* 297, at 317.
16 See *Libyan American Oil Company (LIAMCO) v. Libyan Arab Republic*, Award (April 12, 1977), 62 *I.L.R.* 140.
17 See, for example, *James et al. v. United Kingdom*, Application No. 8793/79, European Court of Human Rights, Judgment of February 21, 1986, para. 46; available at: http://www.human-rights.is/the-human-rights-project/humanrightscasesandmaterials/cases/regionalcases/europeancourtofhumanrights/nr/534.

industries are directly related to the economic lifeline of the country concerned and are easily subject to monopolization by one or a few foreign companies. In addition, sometimes foreign investors may possess properties that are crucial to the related country, such as establishing plants in areas of strategic importance or controlling significant mineral resources.

Most disputes involving discrimination in nationalization arise from the situation that a country has nationalized all investments of the nationals of one given foreign country. The most remarkable examples are the nationalization of all US investments by Cuba in the early 1960s and that of all Dutch investments by Indonesia in the 1950s. In both cases, the local economies were to a large extent under the control of the affected foreign investors. The US Government and investors neither denied their crucial influence on the Cuban economy nor the significance of Cuba's nationalization of US-owned industries and enterprises. They emphasized, however, that even if US interests constituted a threat to the Cuban economy, each individual enterprise did not. Therefore, Cuba's nationalizations should not have targeted all US investors. A similar objection was raised by the Dutch Government against Indonesia's nationalization of Dutch investments. However, based on the above-mentioned exception, the German courts ruled that the nationalization of Dutch assets was legal, even though it was aimed specifically at the Netherlands. The rationale relied on by the German court was that the Netherlands had been ruling Indonesia and controlling its economy, and

> ... the equality concept means only that equals must be treated equally and that different treatment of unequals is admissible ... For the statement to be objective, it is sufficient that the attitude of the former colonial people toward its former colonial master is of course different from that toward other foreigners. Not only were the places of production predominantly in the hands of Netherlanders, for the greater part colonial companies, but these companies dominated the world-wide distribution, beyond the production process, through the Dutch markets.[18]

Of course, this is not to suggest that support should be given to discriminatory nationalization by a country based merely on resentment of foreign colonists. In fact, Indonesia's nationalization of Dutch assets was carried out not only as retaliation, as the German courts observed, but also largely due to concerns of economic development.

The view of the contemporary international community is that no discrimination based totally on race or other factors is acceptable. A recent illustration of this can be found in *Campbell et al. v. Zimbabwe*.[19]

18 See M. Domke, "Indonesian Nationalization Measures before Foreign Courts," 54 *Am. J. Int'l L.* 305 (1960), with a discussion of and excerpts from opinions of the District Court in Bremen and the Hanseatic Court of Appeals in *N.V. Verenigde Deli-Maatschapijen v. Deutsch-Indonesische Tabak-Handelsgesellschaft m.b.H.*

19 *Mike Campbell (Pvt) Ltd. et al. v. Republic of Zimbabwe*, SADC (T) Case No. 02/2007, Judgment (November 28, 2008); available at: http://www.freedomunderlaw.org/wp-content/files/Case_No_2-2007_-_Judgment_28_November_2008.pdf.

As part of its land reform programme, carried out "as a means of correcting colonially inherited land ownership inequities,"[20] the Zimbabwean Parliament enacted in September 2005 an amendment to the Zimbabwean Constitution that authorized the expropriation of certain agricultural lands in Zimbabwe and denied the owners thereof access to the courts to challenge any such expropriations. The claimants, all of whom were white citizens of Zimbabwe, contested the expropriations under terms of the Southern African Development Community ("SADC") Treaty,[21] of which Zimbabwe is a member, and filed an application with the SADC Tribunal claiming unlawful expropriation, lack of due process, racial discrimination, and denial of compensation.

First, the Tribunal found that it had jurisdiction under the SADC Treaty "in respect of any dispute concerning human rights, democracy and the rule of law, which are the very issues raised in the present application."[22] The Tribunal then ruled that: "the Applicants have established that they have been deprived of their agricultural lands without having had the right of access to the courts and the right to a fair hearing, which are essential elements of the rule of law, and we consequently hold that the Respondent has acted in breach of Article 4(c) of the Treaty."[23] Furthermore, after noting that "discrimination of whatever nature is outlawed or prohibited in international law,"[24] as well as under Article 6(2) of the SADC Treaty,[25] and after undertaking a thorough exposition of that principle, the Tribunal found that, although there was "no explicit mention of race, ethnicity or people of a particular origin in Amendment 17,"[26] "its implementation affects white farmers only and consequently constitutes indirect discrimination or *de facto* or substantive inequality"[27] and that Zimbabwe had therefore "violated its obligation under Article 6(2) of the Treaty."[28]

The most important aspect of this ruling is that de facto discrimination may also make a lawful nationalization unlawful. This is very important, because a measure which on its surface is non-discriminatory may be discriminative in its implementation. Unless de facto discrimination is denounced together with de jure discrimination, the provision cannot achieve the intended effect. The Tribunal also implied that where a state act or omission is not arbitrary, for a

---

20 Ibid., p. 16.
21 Treaty of the Southern African Development Community, done at Windhoek, Namibia (August 17, 1992), as amended; available at: http://www.sadc.int/files/9113/5292/9434/SADC_Treaty. pdf.
22 *Campbell et al. v. Zimbabwe*, *supra*, note 19, p. 25.
23 Ibid., p. 41; Article 4(c) of the SADC Treaty, *supra*, note 21, provides: "SADC and its Member States shall act in accordance with the following principles: (c) human rights, democracy and the rule of law …"
24 *Campbell et al. v. Zimbabwe*, ibid., p. 45.
25 Article 6(2) of the SADC Treaty, *supra*, note 21, provides: "SADC and Member States shall not discriminate against any person on grounds of gender, religion, political views, race, ethnic origin, culture, ill health, disability, or such other ground as may be determined by the Summit."
26 *Campbell et al. v. Zimbabwe*, *supra*, note 19, p. 51.
27 Ibid., p. 52.
28 Ibid., p. 53.

legitimately purported object and with compensation paid, nationalization, as a remedy for economic inequalities resulting from colonialism, may be carried out in a discriminatory manner.[29] In the context of the current investment framework of BITs and the fact that decolonization is no longer a threat to the contemporary world, this position should be considered as an exception in expropriation.

In addition to being a ruling made by a tribunal that could not be said to be overly prejudicial towards claims made by "former colonists," the SADC judgment in *Campbell et al. v. Zimbabwe* is also noteworthy in its upholding of the principle of the penetration of international norms into domestic law as a consequence of adherence to international agreements. Even though the judgment did not deal with a claim in international investment law, its appraisal of how international law interacts with and affects national law—and, indeed, of how one type of law (human rights law) may interact with and affect another (the law of expropriation and compensation) has important implications for the future development of the legal issues under consideration here, discrimination perhaps not being the most important of these.[30]

Based on all of the above, it may be said, then, that it is generally accepted within the international community that nationalization or expropriation is a legal action of a sovereign state. However, it is equally true that certain actions – or failures to act – on the part of the state may render a particular expropriation illegal. Most importantly, a state is obliged to carry out any act of expropriation in accordance with international obligations, including those arising from customary law and treaties and its own laws, in particular those relating to procedures.

One of the first cases to distinguish lawful from unlawful expropriations was the *Case Concerning Certain German Interests in Polish Upper Silesia* in 1926.[31] The relevant facts of this case are as follows. In 1915, a German company ("the former German company") established a factory to manufacture sulfate in the Chorzów area of Upper Silesia according to an agreement with the German Government of that time. In 1919, the German Government sold the factory and the land it was located on to another German company ("the second German company"), but

---

29 The Tribunal remarked in *obiter dictum*: "We wish to observe here that if: (a) the criteria adopted by the Respondent in relation to the land reform programme had not been arbitrary but reasonable and objective; (b) fair compensation was paid in respect of the expropriated lands, and (c) the lands expropriated were indeed distributed to poor, landless and other disadvantaged and marginalized individuals or groups, rendering the purpose of the programme legitimate, the differential treatment afforded to the Applicants would not constitute racial discrimination." Ibid., p. 53.

30 Following Zimbabwe's withdrawal from the Tribunal in 2009, the SADC Summit suspended the Tribunal in August 2010, "subject to review of its functions." At the 32nd SADC Summit in Maputo, Mozambique, on August 17, 2012, the SADC Summit resolved that a new Tribunal should be negotiated and that its mandate should be confined to interpretation of the SADC Treaty and Protocols *relating to disputes between Member States*. In other words, a claim such as that considered in *Campbell et al. v. Zimbabwe* may no longer be addressed by the SADC Tribunal.

31 *Case Concerning Certain German Interests in Polish Upper Silesia (Merits)*, Judgment No. 7 (May 25, 1926), *Collection of Judgments, Publications of the Permanent Court of International Justice*, A.W. Sitjhoff, Leyden, 1926; available at: http://www.icj-cij.org/pcij/serie_A/A_07/17_Interets_allemands_en_Haute_Silesie_polonaise_Fond_Arret.pdf.

the former German company was still in charge of its management. According to the Treaty of Versailles, Upper Silesia became Polish territory that same year. In 1922, the Polish Government claimed that the second German company did not have valid ownership of the factory and proceeded to nationalize it. The Chorzów factory was subsequently placed under the management of the Polish Government.

The issue that needed to be resolved by the PCIJ was whether or not the nationalization conducted by Poland breached the Geneva Convention it had concluded with Germany in 1922. According to Article 6 of that Convention, the Polish Government could nationalize industries in Upper Silesia but could not deprive German nationals (natural and juridical persons) of their rights. In 1926, the PCIJ ruled that the nationalization by the Polish Government was "unlawful" on the ground that Poland had violated its international obligation, that is, the Geneva Convention. According to the Court, that Convention had established specific criteria under which expropriations could be carried out. It said: "[I]t is certain that expropriation is only lawful in the cases and under the conditions provided for in Article 7 and the following articles [of the Convention]; apart from these cases, or if these conditions are absent, expropriation is unlawful."[32] In effect, the Court differentiated in this case between "lawful" and "unlawful" nationalizations,[33] and it found that the nationalization of the Chórzow factory by Poland was unlawful.

In subsequent practice, even when they ruled that certain state actions taken in the course of an expropriation were violations of provisions of international agreements to which the relevant state was a party or were otherwise "internationally wrongful acts," both courts and arbitral tribunals were reluctant to label the expropriation itself "illegal." Thus, in *Texaco v. Libya*, for example, the tribunal recognized that "the right of a State to nationalize is unquestionable today"[34] but added that "neither the concept of sovereignty nor the nature of the nationalization measures taken against the plaintiffs provides any legal justification for these measures."[35] Nonetheless, the tribunal made no statement as to whether the nationalization was "legal" or "illegal."

Likewise, in *Biloune et al. v. Ghana*, the tribunal found the expropriation to be contrary to the terms of the agreement between the Ghana Investment Centre and the plaintiffs but did not indicate whether it considered it to be lawful or unlawful under international law.[36] In *CME v. Czech Republic*, the London Tribunal also

---

32 Ibid., p. 21.

33 In the French text of the judgment, these terms are given as "*légitime*" and "*illicite*."

34 *Texaco Overseas Petroleum Company/California Asiatic Oil Co. v. Government of the Libyan Arab Republic*, Award (January 19, 1977) 17 *I.L.M.* 1 (1978), para. 59; available at: http://www.jstor.org/stable/20691828.

35 Ibid., para. 79.

36 *Biloune and Marine Drive Complex Ltd v. Ghana Investments Centre and the Government of Ghana*, ad hoc Tribunal under UNCITRAL Rules, Award on Damages and Costs (June 30, 1990), 95 *ILR* 183, at 209–10.

found the claimant's expropriation claim to be justified[37] and that the expropriation had been carried out through "unlawful acts"[38] and an "[unlawful] situation of coercion,"[39] but did not label the expropriation itself either lawful or unlawful.

This again demonstrates that because nationalization and expropriation are considered part of sovereign rights, unless there are explicit international obligations that have been violated by a state, tribunals would be extremely careful, if not actually reluctant, to conclude that a nationalization is "unlawful." This is so even though international investment is badly sought by every member of the international community.

In recent years, however, there appears to be a new trend in arbitral tribunals' interpretation of the impact of the specific provisions of such international treaties as the Energy Charter Treaty ("ECT") and BITs on the legality of expropriations carried out by states parties to such treaties. Like the PCIJ judgment in the *Case Concerning Certain German Interests in Polish Upper Silesia*, some recent arbitral decisions have labeled expropriations illegal expressly because they breached specific requirements for expropriation contained in the relevant international agreement.

ADC v. Hungary, an ICSID arbitral proceeding carried out under the terms of the Cyprus–Hungary BIT, was the first of these.[40] In this case, the claimants had entered into an agreement in 1995 with Hungary's Air Traffic and Airport Administration ("ATAA") to construct and operate terminal facilities at Budapest's Ferihegy International Airport. In 2001, the Hungarian Government abolished the ATAA, replacing it with two new agencies and, at the same time, unilaterally canceled the claimants' contract for operation of the airport facilities. The claimants subsequently requested arbitration under the BIT, claiming specifically that they had suffered an "illegal expropriation."

Article 4(1) of the Cyprus–Hungary BIT provides that:

> Neither Contracting Party shall take any measures depriving, directly or indirectly, investors of the other Contracting Party of their investments unless the following conditions are complied with:
> (a) The measures are taken in the public interest and under due process of law;
> (b) The measures are not discriminatory;

---

37 *CME Czech Republic B.V. (The Netherlands) v. Czech Republic*; UNCITRAL Partial Award (Merits) (September 13, 2001), para. 591; available at: http://italaw.com/documents/CME-2001PartialAward.pdf. It should be noted that, in a parallel case, carried out in Stockholm, also under UNCITRAL Rules, the tribunal held that no expropriation had occurred. See *CME Czech Republic B.V. (The Netherlands) v. Czech Republic*; UNCITRAL Final Award (March 14, 2003); available at: italaw.com/documents/CME-2003-Final_001.pdf.

38 Ibid., para. 516.

39 Ibid., paras. 518–24.

40 *ADC Affiliate Limited and ADC & ADMC Management Limited v. Republic of Hungary*, ICSID Case No. ARB/03/16, Award (October 2, 2006); available at: http://icsid.worldbank.org/ICSID/FrontSe rvlet?requestType=CasesRH&actionVal=showDoc&docId=DC648_En&caseId=C231.

(c) The measures are accompanied by provision for the payment of just compensation.

Further, Article 3 specifies, in relevant part, that:

1. Each Contracting Party shall ensure fair and equitable treatment to the investment of investors of the other Contracting Party and shall not impair, by unreasonable or discriminatory measure, the operation, management, maintenance, use, enjoyment or disposal thereof by those investors.
2. More particularly, each Contracting Party shall accord to such investment full security and protection which in any case shall not be less than that accorded to investments of investors of any third State.

…

The tribunal ruled that, in its opinion, "this is the clearest possible case of expropriation"[41] and further found that:

… the expropriation of the Claimants' interest constituted a depriving measure under Article 4 of the BIT and was *unlawful* as: (a) the taking was not in the public interest; (b) it did not comply with due process, in particular, the Claimants were denied of "fair and equitable treatment" specified in Article 3(1) of the BIT and the Respondent failed to provide "full security and protection" to the Claimants' investment under Article 3(2) of the BIT; (c) the taking was discriminatory and (d) the taking was not accompanied by the payment of just compensation to the expropriated parties.[42]

It should be noted, however, that ADC—the claimant—lost its contractual property right in its entirety and perpetually, which is distinguishable from other cases in which the claimants did not lose control of their investments. The *ADC* Tribunal's holding is therefore in compliance with the trend of contemporary international investment law.

In another ICSID case, *Siemens v. Argentina*, brought under the provisions of the Germany–Argentina BIT, the tribunal reached a similar conclusion. Article 4(1) and (2) of the BIT provides, in relevant part:

1. Investments of nationals or companies of either Contracting Party shall enjoy full protection and security in the territory of the other Contracting Party.
2. Investments of nationals or companies of either Contracting Party may not, in the territory of the other Contracting Party, be expropriated, nationalized or submitted to other measures having effect equivalent to expropriation

41 Ibid., para. 304.
42 Ibid., para. 476(d) (emphasis added).

or nationalization except for reasons of public utility and shall be compensated in this case. …

The tribunal considered the "public purpose" of the expropriation to be "questionable" and that no compensation had been paid on grounds that were "lacking in justification." It therefore held that "the expropriation did not meet the requirements of Article 4(2) and therefore was *unlawful*."[43]

The tribunal in *Vivendi v. Argentina*,[44] while not expressly finding the expropriation to be "illegal" or "unlawful," nevertheless referred to "unlawful measures of expropriation"[45] and further noted that the France–Argentina BIT, pursuant to which the case was brought to arbitration, "does not purport to establish a *lex specialis* governing the standards of compensation for *wrongful* expropriations" and thereafter applied international standards of compensation for wrongful expropriation to the case.[46]

Kardassopoulos v. Georgia was decided by an ICSID tribunal pursuant to the ECT and the Greece–Georgia BIT in 2010.[47] In 1992, Tramex International, a Panamanian corporation, entered into a joint venture agreement ("JVA") with SakNavtobi, the Georgian state-owned national oil company, to have the "sole, exclusive and uninterrupted" rights to "maintain, operate and use all Oil and Gas Facilities in the Republic of Georgia" and to "deal for the Republic of Georgia in the acquisition, sale and export of Oil and Gas" for "an initial term of 25 years, automatically renewable for a second 25-year term."[48] Tramex was jointly owned and controlled by Mr Ron Fuchs, an Israeli national, and Mr Ioannis Kardassopoulos, a Greek national.

In 1993, after SakNavtobi became a part of the Georgian Ministry of Fuel and Energy, the joint venture (GTI) was granted a 30-year Deed of Concession that allowed it, inter alia, "the sole and exclusive control and possession of the Pipelines [and] all the rights with respect to the Pipelines."[49] That deed further stated that "[t]he Pipelines and all property owned, leased or used by GTI in connection therewith is not subject to expropriation, confiscation, nationalization or the sale or grant of any rights to any persons or entities *whatsoever*."[50] In short, the deed established a complete prohibition of expropriation.[51] Nevertheless, a

---

43 *Siemens A.G. v. Argentine Republic*, ICSID Case No. ARB/02/8, Award (February 6, 2007), para. 273 (emphasis added); available at: http://italaw.com/documents/Siemens-Argentina-Award.pdf.

44 *Compañía de Aguas del Aconquija S.A. and Vivendi Universal S.A. v. Argentine Republic*, ICSID Case No. ARB/97/3, Award (August 20, 2007); available at: http://italaw.com/documents/VivendiAwardEnglish.pdf.

45 Ibid., para. 11.1(iv).

46 Ibid. paras. 8.2.3ff (emphases in original).

47 *Ioannis Kardassopoulos v. Georgia*, ICSID Case No. ARB/05/18, Award (March 3, 2010); available at: http://www.encharter.org/fileadmin/user_upload/Investor-State_Disputes/Award_-_Ioannis_Kardassopoulos_vs_Georgia.pdf.

48 Ibid., paras. 79 and 77, respectively.

49 Ibid., para. 96.

50 Ibid., 102 (emphasis added).

51 In this sense, it bears a striking resemblance to the terms of the Treaty of Versailles, which

series of state actions undermined this agreement, culminating in Decree No. 178 of February 26, 1996, which "cancelled 'all rights (given earlier by the Georgian Government to any of the parties) contradicting the present Decree' [and] brought to an abrupt end Tramex/GTI's rights in Georgia."[52]

After a prolonged, and ultimately futile, series of negotiations over compensation owed to Tramex and its two shareholders as a result of these actions, Mr Kardassopoulos submitted a request for arbitration at the ICSID on August 2, 2005 under the arbitration provisions of the Georgia–Greece BIT and the ECT, alleging that "Georgia unlawfully expropriated [his] interest in GTI and his … interest in Tramex's loan to GTI, contrary to Article 13(1) of the ECT."[53] Article 13(1) of the ECT provides:

> (1) Investments of Investors of a Contracting Party in the Area of any other Contracting Party shall not be nationalized, expropriated or subject to a measure or measures having effect equivalent to nationalization or expropriation (hereinafter referred to as "Expropriation") except where such Expropriation is:
> (a) for a purpose which is in the public interest;
> (b) not discriminatory;
> (c) carried out under due process of law; and
> (d) accompanied by the payment of prompt, adequate and effective compensation.

The tribunal found that "the circumstances of Mr. Kardassopoulos' claim present a classic case of direct expropriation … that this deprivation was not an exercise of the State's bona fide police powers."[54] It further ruled that, although it was "not convinced" that the expropriation violated the public interest or non-discrimination requirements of Article 13(1) ECT,[55] the expropriation could not "by any definition be considered to have been carried out under due process of law"[56] and that "it is uncontroversial on the facts of these cases that no payment was made to Mr. Kardassopoulos by the Georgian Government in compensation for the expropriation of his investment, let alone payment that may be considered *'prompt, adequate and effective.'*"[57] In consequence, the tribunal ultimately ruled that "the expropriation of Mr. Kardassopoulos' investment was *unlawful*, as it violated

---

were interpreted by the PCIJ in 1926 in relation to the expropriation of the Chorzów factory in Upper Silesia, thereby resulting in the so-called *Chorzów* principle of compensation for unlawful expropriation.

52 *Kardassopoulos v. Georgia*, *supra*, note 47, para. 157.

53 Ibid., para. 66. He also alleged unfair and inequitable treatment of his investment, a claim also made, in a separate ICSID filing (ICSID Case No. ARB/07/15) by his partner, Mr Fuchs, who, however, did not allege expropriation. The two cases were subsequently joined and ruled on by the same tribunal.

54 Ibid., para. 387.

55 Ibid., paras. 393 and 394.

56 Ibid., para. 404.

57 Ibid., para. 405 (emphasis in original).

at least one of the prescribed conditions [contained in the ECT] for a lawful expropriation."[58]

Another recent case to follow this trend was *RosInvestCo v. Russia*, concerning the alleged expropriation of RosInvestCo UK's investment in the Russian petroleum giant Yukos by "tax measures directed against Yukos [that] were an unconvincing pretext for an unlawful expropriation."[59] The tribunal, constituted by the Arbitration Institute of the Stockholm Chamber of Commerce, ruled that: "these measures in their totality, including but going beyond application of tax law, can only be understood to have had the aim to deprive Yukos from its assets. Such a taking would only be admissible under Article 5 [of the Russia–UK BIT] if the conditions of that provision are fulfilled."[60] Article 5 of the Russia–UK BIT provides (in relevant part):

> (1) Investments of investors of either Contracting Party shall not be nationalised, expropriated or subjected to measures having effect equivalent to nationalisation or expropriation (hereinafter referred to as "expropriation") in the territory of the other Contracting Party except for a purpose which is in the public interest and is not discriminatory and against the payment, without delay, of adequate and effective compensation.

The tribunal found that no purpose in the public interest had ever "been claimed or shown by Respondent in these proceedings as it does not concede that there was indeed an expropriation;" and "it is clear that Respondent did not offer or pay any compensation to Claimant for the taking." Therefore, the tribunal concluded "that Respondent's measures, seen in their cumulative effect towards Yukos, were an *unlawful expropriation* under Article 5 IPPA."[61] This case in fact also involved indirect expropriation. The tribunal also recognized the cumulative effect of the measures in dispute.

In the most recent case in this vein, *Unglaube v. Costa Rica*,[62] the question of the "lawfulness" of the expropriation centered on the requirement of compensation. The claimants were owners of property in Playa Grande, Costa Rica, which they were in the process of developing for residential construction. Playa Grande is an important nesting site for marine turtles, and the Government of Costa Rica began, as early as 1991, to take measures to create the Las Baulas National Marine Park to protect the nesting habitat, efforts that inevitably affected the

---

58 Ibid., para. 407 (emphasis added).

59 *RosInvestCo UK Ltd. v. Russian Federation*, SCC Case No. ARBV079/2005, IIC 471 (2010), Final Award (September 12, 2010), para. 2, at para. 1 of Claimant's Reply of September 21, 2009); available at: http://opil.ouplaw.com/view/10.1093/law:iic/471-2010.case.1/IIC471(2010)D.pdf.

60 Ibid., para. 630.

61 Ibid., paras. 631–33 (emphasis added); n.b., the acronym IPPA (Investment Promotion & Protection Agreement) is used synonymously with BIT throughout the award.

62 *Marion Unglaube and Reinhard Unglaube v. Republic of Costa Rica*, ICSID Consolidated Cases Nos. ARB/08/1 and ARB/09/20, Award (May 16, 2012); available at: italaw.com/sites/default/files/case-documents/ita1053.pdf.

claimants' property, which was located on or adjacent to the area designated for the park. The claimants alleged that significant portions of their property had been "effectively expropriated" by these measures in violation of the 1998 Costa Rica–Germany BIT.

The tribunal found that a 75-meter by 100-meter strip of land owned by one of the claimants had "been subjected to *de facto* expropriation—in the words of the [Costa Rica–Germany BIT], by 'measure(s) tantamount to expropriation'" as a result of the Cost Rican Government's failure to "make timely arrangements to determine and make payment to Marion Unglaube of the compensation required."[63] In its first declaration, the tribunal did not hold the expropriation to be either "lawful" or "unlawful." However, when addressing the issue of compensation, it was much more straightforward. First of all, it noted that: "there can be no question concerning the right of the government of Costa Rica, pursuant to Article 4(2) of the Treaty, to expropriate the 75-Meter Strip for a bona fide public purpose."[64] But it further observed: "That same Article, however, also establishes, as a necessary condition to the exercise of that right, that the government shall have made provision for the prompt determination and payment of the compensation due."[65] Consequently, it held:

> In the present case, the conduct of the State did not conform to the terms of Article 4(2). Specifically, the violation of the Treaty that rendered Respondent's action *internationally unlawful* (both under the Treaty and under customary international law), was that adequate compensation, meeting the standards of Article 4(2), was <u>not</u>, in fact, paid to Mrs. Unglaube within a reasonable period of time after the State declared its intention to expropriate.[66]

The treatment by the *Unglaube* Tribunal of expropriation by the Costa Rican Government is not unusual, as investment jurisprudence focuses increasingly on the adequacy of compensation for expropriation rather than the legality thereof.

---

63 Ibid., para. 209.

64 Ibid., para. 304 (footnote omitted).

65 Ibid.

66 Ibid., para. 305 (footnote omitted; italics added; underline in original). In another, previous ICSID case involving land expropriations, one referred to by the *Unglaube* Tribunal, the tribunal did not even examine the claimants' claims that the expropriations were not taken in the public interest and under due process of law and were discriminatory, but only the claim that they had not received "just compensation." Instead, the tribunal held that "the conditions enumerated in Article 6 [of the relevant BIT] are cumulative. In other terms, if any of those conditions is violated, there is a breach of Article 6. … [T]he Tribunal concludes that Zimbabwe breached its obligation under Article 6(c) of the BIT to pay just compensation to the Claimants. Accordingly, as stated in paragraph 98 above, the Tribunal does not need to consider whether other provisions of the BIT have been violated." See *Bernardus Henricus Funnekotter and Others v. Republic of Zimbabwe*, ICSID Case No. ARB/05/6, Award (April 22, 2009), paras. 96–98 and 107. Although the *Funnekotter* Tribunal discussed the differences between compensation for "lawful" and "unlawful" expropriation, it never addressed the lawfulness of the subject expropriations head on; see *Funnekotter*, paras. 108–12.

The treaty practice and jurisprudence in international investment have also confirmed the principle that international undertakings, such as bilateral investment treaties and multilateral treaties that include provisions on expropriation, establish *lex specialis* that takes precedence over customary international law. It also supports the idea that in this highly globalized world, with interdependence among all nations as the single most important feature, large-scale nationalization is no longer a threat to foreign investment. Whilst debates may continuously be conducted on what nationalization is lawful and what is unlawful, the international community is more and more seized with the fact and outcomes of indirect expropriation.

II. Indirect expropriation

The distinction between direct and indirect expropriation seems clear enough on the surface. Direct expropriation—or expropriation in its "traditional" sense—is generally considered to involve a formal deprivation of property rights and their transfer to someone else, most often the expropriating state.[67] Indirect expropriation, on the other hand, rarely involves a formal deprivation or transfer of property rights; ownership and title may remain unchanged while the investor has effectively been deprived of his ability to use or control the investment or the investment has been rendered virtually without value.[68] Reisman and Sloane concluded that: "states may accomplish expropriation in ways other than by formal decree; indeed, often in ways that may seek to cloak expropriatory conduct with a veneer of legitimacy. For this reason … expropriation must be analyzed in consequential rather than formal terms."[69]

In practice, however, no tribunal or other organ has clearly defined the necessary elements of indirect expropriation, such as the subjective intentions of host governments and the objective effects of certain measures. Dolzer even stated that: "in any case, the current versions of investment treaties do not in any way illuminate the issue of indirect expropriation; they rather state the problem,

67 See, for example, *Enron Corporation and Ponderosa Assets, L.P. v. Argentina*, ICSID Case No. ARB/01/3, Award (May 22, 2007), para. 243; available at: http://www.italaw.com/documents/ Enron-Award.pdf; *Sempra Energy International v. Argentina*, ICSID Case No. ARB/02/13, Award (September 28, 2007), para. 280; available at: http://icsid.worldbank.org/ICSID/FrontServlet ?requestType=CasesRH&actionVal=showDoc&docId=DC694_En&caseId=C8; Brigitte Stern, "What are the Contours of Indirect Expropriation," LASIL/SLADI *Perspectives—01/09*, 2009, pp. 3–4; available at: http://graduateinstitute.ch/webdav/site/lasil-sladi/shared/Perspectivas/ perspectivas15.pdf.

68 See, for example, *Starrett Housing Corporation, Starrett Systems, Inc., Starrett Housing International, Inc. v. Iran, Bank Oman, Bank Mellat, Bank Markazi*, Iran–United States Claims Tribunal Interlocutory Award No. ITL 32-24-1 (December 19, 1983), 23:5 *I.L.M.* 1090–1145, at p. 1115; *Enron v. Argentina*, ibid., para. 245; *Sempra v. Argentina*, ibid., para. 285; Stern, id.

69 Reisman and Sloane, *supra*, note 12, at 121. Reisman and Sloane also referred to G. C. Christie, "What Constitutes a Taking Under International Law," 38 *BYBIL* 307, 1962, at 310–11, that: (i) "a State may expropriate property, where it interferes with it, even though the State expressly disclaims any such intention," and (ii) "even though a State may not purport to interfere with rights to property, it may, by its actions, render those rights so useless that it will be deemed to have expropriated them." Ibid., at 119–20.

and presumably the rules of general international law are meant to provide solutions."[70] It is noteworthy that, owing to the frequent disputes raised on the ground of indirect expropriation,[71] the bilateral investment treaties concluded by the United States and Canada have in recent years begun to include detailed provisions in this regard, and this now appears to be reflected in BIT practice in general.

A critical issue remains one of definition, especially since the terms "indirect expropriation," "creeping expropriation," "disguised expropriation," "regulatory expropriation" (or "regulatory taking"), and actions "tantamount to expropriation" are frequently employed interchangeably. Over time, however, the latter terms have been generally considered by scholars and tribunals to comprise "types" or sub-categories of the more general term "indirect expropriation."[72] As has been pointed out by Stern:

> … if creeping expropriation and disguised expropriation are certainly two sub categories in the range of measures covered by indirect expropriation, they do not constitute the bulk of the measures that are today under discussion when it comes to indirect expropriation.
>
> In fact, the most heated discussion relates to measures that the Anglo-Saxon doctrine calls regulatory expropriation or regulatory taking.[73]

As recently as 2003, Dolzer identified the issue of indirect expropriation as "the single most important development in state practice" and the definition of expropriation in the context of globalization and regulation for the common good as a dominant issue in international investment law.[74] Addressing the issue in the context of sustainable development, a 2012 "best practices" paper prepared by the International Institute for Sustainable Development put it this way: "The most crucial issue is to determine the clear conditions under which measures of a

70 Rudolf Dolzer, "Indirect Expropriation of Alien Property," *ICSID Review: Foreign Investment Law Journal*, Vol. 1, 1986, p. 56.

71 For example, see *Metalclad Corporation v. Mexico*; *S.D. Myers, Inc. v. Canada*; *Pope & Talbot Inc. v. Canada*; and *Methanex v. United States*.

72 See, for example, Stern, *supra*, note 67; *Tecnicas Medioambientales Tecmed S.A. v. United Mexican States* ("*Tecmed v. Mexico*"), ICSID Case No. ARB (AF)/00/2, Award (May 29, 2003), para. 114. On the other hand, Heiskanen sees a distinct difference between "indirect expropriation' and "*de facto* expropriation," another term frequently employed synonymously. A "*de facto* expropriation" he defines as "expropriation of property that takes place without a formal legislative decree but to the economic benefit of the host State," while he identifies "a loss of property that is directly or proximately attributable to the host State but is effected in a manner that does not economically benefit the host State" as indirect expropriation. See V. Heiskanen, "The Contribution of the Iran–United States Claims Tribunal to the Development of the Doctrine of Indirect Expropriation," *International Law FORUM du droit international*, Vol. 5, No. 3, August 2003, pp. 176–88, at p. 180.

73 Stern, supra, note 67, p. 4.

74 Rudolf Dolzer, "Indirect Expropriations: New Developments?," 11 *NYU Environmental Law Journal* 64, 2002–2003, at pp. 65 and 66.

State may be considered as amounting to an indirect expropriation and, as such, require the State to compensate the investor for the damage caused."[75]

The complexity of determining whether or not indirect expropriation has taken place derives from the fact that every state is expected to take measures for the effective governance of its society. As a result of such measures someone, including foreign investors, may be adversely affected or more adversely affected than others. Where the taking of such measures, that is, laws, regulations, policies, administrative decrees, and other government actions, is considered to fall within the governmental powers which are correctly exercised, no indirect expropriation may be deemed to have occurred.

Clear references to indirect expropriation begin to appear in international normative documents in the latter half of the 20th century (see Annex Table 2 below). One of the earliest of these, the Abs/Shawcross Convention of 1959, makes mention only of "measures … to deprive [nationals of another Party] … directly or indirectly of their property",[76] without more. Soon thereafter, the Harvard Draft Convention of 1961 was much more explicit, providing that:

> A "taking of property" includes not only an outright taking of property but also any such unreasonable interference with the use, enjoyment, or disposal of property as to justify an inference that the owner thereof will not be able to use, enjoy, or dispose of the property within a reasonable period of time after the inception of such interference.[77]

The Organisation for Economic Co-operation and Development ("OECD"), in its Commentary on its 1967 Draft Convention on the Protection of Foreign Property, defined measures of indirect expropriation as those "measures otherwise lawful [which] are applied in such a way as to deprive ultimately the alien of the enjoyment or value of his property, without any specific act being identifiable as outright deprivation."[78] However, it also noted that these must be "measures taken with the *intent* of wrongfully depriving the national concerned of the substance of his rights and *resulting* in such loss."[79]

The above-mentioned documents were, of course, draft texts intended to form the basis for negotiation of multilateral conventions that often failed to materialize. Actual practice in the definition and delimitation of indirect expropriation, especially in the relatively new and rapidly expanding body of BITs, lagged far

---

75 Suzy H. Nikièma, *Best Practices: Indirect Expropriation*, The International Institute for Sustainable Development, Winnipeg, Canada, 2012, p. 1; available at: http://www.iisd.org/publications/pub.aspx?id=1577.

76 Abs/Shawcroft Draft Convention on Investments Abroad (1959), Article III; available at: http://www.unctad.org/sections/dite/iia/docs/Compendium/en/137%20volume%205.pdf.

77 Harvard Draft Convention on International Responsibility for Injuries to Aliens (1961), Article 10(3)(a).

78 OECD Draft Convention on the Protection of Foreign Property (1967), Notes and Comments to Article 3.

79 Ibid. (emphases in original).

behind. Numerous BITs contracted in the 1960s made no mention whatsoever of "indirect expropriation." Those contracted in the 1970s began to use such terms as "deprived, either directly or indirectly," "directly or indirectly nationalize or expropriate," or "other measures which deprive directly or indirectly." Later on, such terms as "measures direct or indirect, tantamount to expropriation," "expropriation, nationalization or similar measures" (or, "measures with similar effect"), or "expropriation, nationalization and any other measure that has an effect tantamount to expropriation or nationalization" began to appear in BITs.[80] Almost always, however, these terms appeared without detailed definition of content or scope, although it was increasingly specified that any such measures were subject to the same conditions as those relating to direct expropriation, that is, they must be undertaken for a public purpose, in a non-discriminatory manner, and with payment of compensation. The United States was perhaps the first to include additional conditions in its BITs, for example that such measures must be accomplished under due process of law and must "not violate any specific provision on contractual stability or any specific provision on expropriation contained in an investment agreement between the national or company concerned and the Party making the expropriations."[81]

It is noteworthy, however, that it was two groups of undeveloped countries— the League of Arab States and the Organization of the Islamic Conference—who first included specific and well-defined limitations on indirect expropriation in real multilateral investment agreements. As such, it is useful to quote them extensively here. Article 9(1) of the Arab League's Unified Agreement for the Investment of Arab Capital reads as follows:

> According to the provisions of this Agreement, the capital of the Arab investor shall not be subject to any specific or general measures, whether permanent or temporary and irrespective of their legal form, which wholly or partially affect any of the assets, reserves or revenues of the investor and which lead to confiscation, compulsory seizure, dispossession, nationalization, liquidation, dissolution, the extortion or elimination of secrets regarding technical ownership or other material rights, the forcible prevention or delay of debt settlement or any other measures leading to the sequestration, freezing or administration of assets, or any other action which infringes the right of ownership itself or prejudices the intrinsic authority of the owner in terms of his control and possession of the investment, his right to administer it, his acquisition of the revenues therefrom or the fulfilment of his rights and the discharge of his obligations.[82]

80 In fact, many similar or identical terms continue to be employed in BITs. For a more complete discussion of the terms used in contemporary BITs, see Nikièma, *supra*, note 75, pp. 5ff.
81 See, for example, Article III of the US–Bangladesh BIT 1989, Article III of the US–Egypt BIT 1992, and Article III of the US–Haiti BIT 1983, among others.
82 Unified Agreement for the Investment of Arab Capital in the Arab States (1980), Article 9(1).

The Islamic Conference's Investment Agreement contained a similar provision:

> The host state shall undertake not to adopt or permit the adoption of any measure—itself or through one of its organs, institutions or local authorities— if such a measure may directly or indirectly affect the ownership of the investor's capital or investment by depriving him totally or partially of his ownership or of all or part of his basic rights or the exercise of his authority on the ownership, possession or utilization of his capital, or of his actual control over the investment, its management, making use out of it, enjoying its utilities, the realization of its benefits or guaranteeing its development and growth.[83]

Both these agreements, however, recognized the right to adopt preventive measures in accordance with a court order as well as the right to carry out expropriation in the public interest, in a non-discriminatory manner, against payment of compensation and in accordance with local law.

The MIGA Convention was the first truly multilateral treaty to adopt a similar approach when it defined "expropriatory measures" as:

> Any legislative action or administrative action or omission attributable to the host government which has the effect of depriving the holder of a guarantee of his ownership or control of, or a substantial benefit from, his investment, with the exception of nondiscriminatory measures of general application which governments normally take for the purpose of regulating economic activity in their territories ...[84]

Although such important subsequent multilateral agreements as the ASEAN Investment Agreement of 1987 and the Energy Charter Treaty of 1991, as well as the World Bank Guidelines on Treatment of Foreign Direct Investment of 1992, resorted to the older practice of prohibiting measures with effects equivalent to expropriation, without more,[85] a crucial change was already occurring in the perception of indirect expropriation on the part of investors, practitioners, and scholars of international investment law. Competition for investment funds brought a nearly complete end to direct expropriation practices by host states, while the multiplication of investment agreements containing provisions for direct investor–state dispute settlement through international arbitration not only expanded investors' rights but raised their awareness of those rights and increased their willingness to exercise them. The inevitable adoption of arbitral awards recognizing indirect expropriations and granting compensation for them inaugurated a new

---

83 Agreement for Promotion, Protection and Guarantee of Investments among the Member States of the Organization of the Islamic Conference (1981), Ch 2, Article 10(1).
84 Convention Establishing the Multilateral Investment Guarantee Agency (1985), Article 11(a)(ii).
85 Although Article 21(5) of the Energy Charter Treaty did establish some special procedural rules to be followed whenever a tax measure is alleged to constitute an expropriation, it did not exclude such measures from the ambit of indirect expropriation.

generation of investment agreements that explicitly affirmed a host state's rights to regulate to protect certain public interests.

The first multilateral agreement to do so was the NAFTA, which specifically excluded "non-discriminatory measure[s] of general application" from being considered "a measure tantamount to an expropriation of a debt security or loan covered by this Chapter solely on the ground that the measure imposes costs on the debtor that cause it to default on the debt"[86] and further affirmed a host state's right to adopt, maintain, and enforce measures intended "to ensure that investment activity in its territory is undertaken in a manner sensitive to environmental concerns."[87] This kind of provision has not come as a surprise, as the world is becoming fully aware of the environmental implications of investment and business activities. In these circumstances, no state can be expected completely to give up regulating environment issues in order to attract foreign investment.

Subsequent practice in the negotiation and adoption of multilateral and bilateral trade and investment agreements contained wording to the effect that "nothing in this agreement shall be construed to prevent a party from adopting or maintaining measures", covering a wide variety of public welfare concerns, including, but not limited to: environmental protection; protection of human, animal or plant life or health; the conservation of exhaustible natural resources; protection of the integrity and stability of its financial system; the pursuit of monetary and related credit policies or exchange rate policies; its own essential security interests; or even the maintenance or restoration of international peace and security.[88]

In addition to such affirmations of states' rights to regulate, some of the most recent investment agreements have included provisions specifically excluding certain measures from the ambit of indirect expropriation. The COMESA Investment Agreement of 2007, for example, contains this provision:

> Consistent with the right of states to regulate and the customary international law principles on police powers, bona fide regulatory measures taken by a Member State that are designed and applied to protect or enhance legitimate public welfare objectives, such as public health, safety and the environment, shall not constitute an indirect expropriation under this Article.[89]

Similar provisions are found in the ASEAN Investment Agreement 2008 and, with some reservations, in the 2004 US Model BIT and 2004 Canada Model Foreign Investment Protection Agreement. These three agreements also have annexes relating to expropriation that, in nearly identical language, provide for

---

86 NAFTA Article 1110(8).

87 NAFTA Article 1114(1).

88 For more detail on the use of such provisions in specific agreements, see Nikièma, *supra*, note 75, pp. 8–9.

89 Investment Agreement for the COMESA Common Investment Area (2007), Article 20(8); available at: http://vi.unctad.org/files/wksp/iiawksp08/docs/wednesday/Exercise%20Materials/invagreecomesa.pdf.

a proportionality test in determining indirect expropriation. The wording contained in the ASEAN Investment Agreement 2008, which is the most exacting, reads as follows:

> The determination of whether an action or series of actions by a Member State, in a specific fact situation, constitutes an expropriation of the type referred to in subparagraph 2(b) [i.e. having an effect equivalent to direct expropriation without formal transfer of title or outright seizure], requires a case-by-case, fact-based inquiry that considers, among other factors:
> (a) the economic impact of the government action, although the fact that an action or series of actions by a Member State has an adverse effect on the economic value of an investment, standing alone, does not establish that such an expropriation has occurred;
> (b) whether the government action breaches the government's prior binding written commitment to the investor whether by contract, licence or other legal document; and
> (c) the character of the government action, including, its objective and whether the action is disproportionate to the public purpose referred to in Article 14(1).[90]

What emerges from this review of treaty practice is that, insofar as indirect expropriation as the result of governmental regulation is concerned, an international consensus is emerging that considers not only the effect of such regulation but the context within which the regulation is adopted. There has been an increasing reaffirmation of a broad compass for states' rights to regulate as well as a new emphasis on proportionality. These newest agreements also emphatically recognize the continuing validity of the conclusion reached by Christie 50 years ago, when he wrote:

> It is evident that the question of what kind of interference short of outright expropriation constitutes a "taking" under international law presents a situation where the common law method of case by case development is pre-eminently the best method, in fact probably the only method, of legal development.[91]

International judicial practice relating, at least in a somewhat incidental way, to cases of indirect expropriation began to appear in the early years of the 20th century. The decision rendered by the Permanent Court of Arbitration in 1922 in the *Norwegian Shipowners' Claims* case[92] is one of the first of these. This case was

---

90 ASEAN Investment Agreement 2008, Annex 2, para. 3.
91 Christie, *supra*, note 69, at 338.
92 *Norwegian Shipowners' Claims, Norway v. United States of America*, Permanent Court of Arbitration, Award (October 13, 1922), *Reports of International Arbitral Awards (R.I.A.A.)*, Vol. XI, pp. 309ff; available at: http://www.haguejusticeportal.net/index.php?id=5185.

the result of certain actions taken by the Government of the United States during World War I "for the purpose of encouraging, developing and creating a naval auxiliary and naval reserve and a merchant marine to meet the requirements of the commerce of the United States with its territories and possessions and with foreign countries."[93] On August 3, 1917, the Fleet Corporation, an agency of the US Government, sent a general order of requisition by telegram to almost all US shipyards expressly requisitioning not only ships and material but also the contracts, plans, detailed specifications, and payments made for uncompleted vessels. In spite of this, the United States maintained throughout the arbitration that there was no requisition of anything except physical property and that the word "contract" in the telegrams only referred to commitments for material. On the other hand, Norway, on behalf of its shipping companies whose uncompleted vessels had been requisitioned, maintained that those companies' contracts for building the vessels had also been requisitioned. The tribunal ruled:

1. That, whatever the intentions may have been, the United States took, both in fact and in law, the contracts under which the ships in question were being or were to be constructed.
2. That in fact the claimants were fully and for ever [sic] deprived of their property and that this amounts to a requisitioning by the exercise of the power of eminent domain within the meaning of American municipal law.[94]

In his seminal article on the topic, Christie also points to the *Case Concerning Certain German Interests in Polish Upper Silesia*[95] as a similar example. In that case, he points out that the PCIJ "ruled that, by seizing the factory and its machinery, the Polish Government also expropriated the patents and contract rights of the management company, even though it did not purport to expropriate these particular items of property."[96]

In contrast to these two cases, the *Oscar Chinn* case[97] is frequently cited as an early example of a case where an alleged "regulatory taking" was found by the tribunal to comprise not expropriation but a legitimate exercise of a state's police powers. In 1929, Oscar Chinn, a British national, established a river transport company on the Katanga River in what was then the Belgian Congo. At the beginning of the Great Depression, the prices of tropical raw materials fell dramatically and the Belgian Government, by decision of June 20, 1931, ordered the state-owned transport company Unatra to lower its rates to a nominal level, with any losses to be reimbursed by the government. Other private transporters, both Belgian and foreign, were excluded from this regime because it was intended to be only a temporary measure.

93 United States Shipping Act of September 1916, as quoted ibid, p. 316.
94 *Norwegian Shipowners' Claims, supra,* note 92, p. 326.
95 *Case Concerning Certain German Interests in Polish Upper Silesia, supra,* note 31.
96 Christie, *supra,* note 69, p. 311.
97 *Oscar Chinn Case, supra,* note 14.

In October 1932, the Belgian Government offered refunds to the private companies. Oscar Chinn, however, sought the protection of the British Government, maintaining that the Belgian Government's creation of a de facto monopoly in favor of Unatra had forced him to go out of business in July 1931. The dispute was submitted to the PCIJ for a ruling on whether the Belgian measure had violated Article 1 of the Convention of Saint-German, which was signed by the two countries in 1919 and guaranteed freedom of trade to their respective nationals in the region.

The Court found, however, that "[f]reedom of trade does not mean the abolition of commercial competition; it presupposes the existence of such competition" and that this includes competition with a state-owned company such as Unatra.[98] It found further that there was no obligation on the part of Belgium, in pursuit of freedom of trade "to guarantee the success of each individual concern" and held that "[s]uch a contention would be inconsistent with the very notion of trade; for there is nothing to prevent a merchant, a ship-owner, a manufacturer or a carrier from operating temporarily at a loss if he believes that by so doing he will be able to keep his business going."[99] This, the Court held, was expressly the purpose of the Belgian measures.

Finally, the British Government asserted that "the measure of June 20th, 1931, by depriving indirectly Mr. Chinn of any prospect of carrying on his business profitably, constituted a breach of the general principles of international law, and in particular of respect for vested rights." The Court, however, said that it was "unable to see in [Mr. Chinn's] original position—which was characterized by the possession of customers and the possibility of making a profit—anything in the nature of a genuine vested right."[100] In this regard, and as a general principle, the Court observed:

> No enterprise—least of all a commercial or transport enterprise, the success of which is dependent on the fluctuating level of prices and rates—can escape from the chances and hazards resulting from general economic conditions. Some industries may be able to make large profits during a period of general prosperity, or else by taking advantage of a treaty of commerce or of an alteration in customs duties; but they are also exposed to the danger of ruin or extinction if circumstances change. Where this is the case, no vested rights are violated by the State.[101]

It seems that international judicial and quasi-judicial practices emphasize the effect of state measures in ascertaining indirect expropriation. With this, there has developed what is known as the "sole effects doctrine."[102] This doctrine requires

---

98 Ibid., para. 82.
99 Ibid., para. 86.
100 Ibid., paras. 88 and 89.
101 Ibid., para. 100.
102 For a complete discussion of the history and development of the sole effects doctrine, see, for example, Dolzer, *supra*, note 74, pp. 79–90; and Ben Mostafa, "The Sole Effects Doctrine, Police

that the only consideration for determining whether or not the impact of state measures on an investment amounts to expropriation is their actual effects on the property allegedly expropriated. However, this doctrine nonetheless may be more conservative than it appears, as it requires that the actual effects be irreversible, permanent and amount to substantial deprivation of property rights. At the very least, they must constitute "unreasonable interference" with such rights. Despite its shortcomings, recent arbitral practices show that it has strong influence in determining issues relating to indirect expropriation.

Another development in the area of indirect expropriation is the huge juris-prudence of the Iran–United States Claims Tribunal, although the views of the international community differ as to its contributions to international investment law.[103] As of mid-2005, the tribunal had issued over 800 awards and decisions—a total of 600 awards (including partial awards and awards on agreed terms), 83 interlocutory and interim awards, and 133 decisions—in resolving almost 3000 cases.[104] Very few of those involved direct expropriation,[105] however, making this the largest body of case law relating to indirect expropriation. With a remark-able degree of consistency, this case law clearly articulated and applied what has become known as the "sole effects doctrine" in determining when indirect expropriation had occurred.[106]

Powers and Indirect Expropriation under International Law," *Australian International Law Journal*, Vol. 15, 2008, pp. 267–96.

103 See, for example, Heiskanen, *supra*, note 72; R. Abtahi, "Indirect expropriations in the jurispru-dence of the Iran–United States Claims Tribunal," *Journal of Law and Conflict Resolution*, Vol. 3, No. 7, 2011, pp. 80–88; D. D. Caron, "The Nature of the Iran–United States Claims Tribunal and the Evolving Structure of International Dispute Resolution," *American Journal of International Law*, Vol. 84, 1990; G. H. Aldrich, "What Constitutes a Compensable Taking of Property? The Decisions of the Iran–United States Claims Tribunal," *American Journal of International Law*, Vol. 88, 1994, pp. 585–610; idem., *The Jurisprudence of the Iran-United States Claims Tribunal: An Analysis of the Decisions of the Tribunal*, OUP U.S.A., 1996; C. S. Gibson and C. R. Drahozal (eds.), *The Iran-U.S. Claims Tribunal at 25: The Cases Everyone Needs to Know for Investor–State & International Arbitration*, OUP U.S.A., 2007.
104 From the publisher's summary of Gibson and Drahozal (eds.), ibid.; available on the OUP web-site at: http://www.oup.com/us/catalog/general/subject/Law/InternationalArbitration/?view =usa&ci=9780195325140.
105 See Heiskanen, *supra*, note 72, p. 179; and Aldrich (1994), *supra*, note 103, p. 587.
106 The notable exception to this consistency was the tribunal's ruling in the *Sea-Land* case (*Sea-Land Service, Inc. v. Islamic Republic of Iran*, Award 135-33-1 (June 22, 1984), 6 *Iran–USCTR* 149), where it held (at p. 166): "A finding of expropriation would require, at the very least, that the Tribunal be satisfied that there was deliberate governmental interference with the conduct of Sea-Land's operation, the effect of which was to deprive Sea-Land of the use and benefit of its investment. Nothing has been demonstrated here which might have amounted to an intentional course of conduct directed against Sea-Land." In addition to dismissing Sea-Land's claim of expropria-tion on this ground, the tribunal also favorably cited *Oscar Chinn* when it held (at p. 163) that the company's alleged "acquired right" to use and benefit from certain port facilities in Iran did not, in its view, constitute "a genuine vested right." Aldrich (1994), ibid., at p. 603, notes that this posi-tion "obtained no support in subsequent Tribunal awards, which generally quoted the relevant language from *Tippetts*."

In one of its earliest decisions, *Starrett Housing*, the tribunal expressed this doctrine in this way:

> … it is recognized in international law that measures taken by a State can interfere with property rights to such an extent that these rights are rendered so useless that they must be deemed to have been expropriated, even though the State does not purport to have expropriated them and the legal title to the property formally remains with the original owner.[107]

Its position in *Tippetts* was stated even more unequivocally when it held:

> A deprivation or taking of property may occur under international law through interference by a state in the use of that property or with the enjoyment of its benefits, even where legal title to the property is not affected.
> …
> [S]uch a conclusion is warranted whenever events demonstrate that the owner was deprived of fundamental rights of ownership and it appears that this deprivation is not merely ephemeral. The intent of a government is less important than the effects of the measures on the owner, and the form of the measure of control or interference is less important than the reality of their impact.[108]

Impregilo v. Argentina[109] also involved claims against, inter alia, alleged expropriation. The tribunal in that case found that "none of [the] measures [taken by the Province of Buenos Aires] amounted to a loss of the concession. Nor could the joint effect of these measures be considered to be a loss of property rights. A loss only occurred when the Province terminated the concession …"[110] It ultimately ruled that "the termination could [not] be regarded as an act of—direct or indirect—expropriation or other appropriation" of the claimant's investment.[111] The *Impregilo* Tribunal, like many others, obviously applied the sole effects doctrine in coming to its decision that there had been no indirect expropriation. Interestingly, in his dissent to this portion of the award, Judge Brower, who has served continuously since 1983 as a judge of the Iran-United States Claims Tribunal, also relied in significant part on that body's jurisprudence but came to a different conclusion, maintaining that "the Award's analysis of Claimant's expropriation claim is deficient in several ways."[112] It was his opinion that: "Applied in succession over a

---

107 *Starrett Housing, supra*, note 68, p. 1115.
108 *Tippetts, Abbett, McCarthy, Stratton v. TAMS-AFFA Consulting Engineers of Iran*, Award No. 141-7-2 (June 29, 1984), 219, at 225–26.
109 *Impregilo S.p.A. v. Argentine Republic*, ICSID Case No. ARB/07/17, Award (June 21, 2011), available at: http://icsid.worldbank.org/ICSID/FrontServlet?requestType=CasesRH&actionVal=showDoc&docId=DC2171_En&caseId=C109.
110 Ibid., para. 272.
111 Ibid., para. 283.
112 *Impregilo v. Argentina*, ICSID Case No. ARB07/17, Consenting and Dissenting Opinion of Judge Charles N. Brower (June 21, 2011), para. 22.

period of years, Argentina's acts left Claimant in possession of shares in an empty corporate shell, which had been deprived of all purpose and value."[113] This is nothing less than a repetition of the Iran–United States Claims Tribunal's formulation of the standard of "substantial deprivation," which is quite understandable taking into account Judge Brower's previous involvement with the work of the Claims Tribunal.

The tribunal in the *Grand River* case[114] rendered a decision that further elucidates the principle of "substantial deprivation." In that case, one of the claimants, Arthur Montour Jr., alleged that "improper enforcement actions by various [US] states … [had] resulted in the expropriation of a substantial portion of the value of his investment" in the distribution of tobacco products in the United States.[115] Beginning with the language of NAFTA Article 1110(1), which the tribunal pointed out "speaks of 'an investment,' not 'an investment or some portion thereof'",[116] it went on to rule:

> The Tribunal has been offered no reason to interpret the language of NAFTA's Article 1110(1) to mean other than it says. An act of expropriation must involve "the investment of an investor," not part of an investment. This is particularly so in these circumstances, involving an investment that remains under the investor's ownership and control and apparently prospered and grew throughout the period for which the Tribunal received evidence. Arthur Montour's expropriation claim fails for failure to establish an expropriation within the scope of Article 1110.[117]

It is noteworthy that many recent investment arbitral tribunals have relied, at least in part, on the Iran–United States Claims Tribunal's jurisprudence, especially on its formulations of the sole effects doctrine, when addressing such allegations. Notable decisions in this regard include *Biloune v. Ghana*,[118] *Metalclad*,[119] *Consortium R.F.C.C. v. Morocco*,[120] *Impregilo v. Pakistan*,[121] *Lauder v. Czech*

113 Ibid., para. 25.
114 *Grand River Enterprises Six Nations Ltd and Others v. United States*, ICSID–UNCITRAL, Award (January 12, 2011) (redacted); available at: http://www.state.gov/documents/organization/156820.pdf.
115 Ibid., para. 146. The tribunal had previously ruled that it had no jurisdiction over the claims of the other claimants.
116 Ibid., para. 147.
117 Ibid., para. 155.
118 See *Biloune et al. v. Ghana*, *supra*, note 36. In that case, the tribunal stated that where state measures were found to have had "the effect of causing the irreparable cessation of work on the project," it constituted "constructive expropriation." Ibid., p. 209.
119 *Metalclad Corporation v. United Mexican States*, ICSID Case No. ARB(AF)/97/1, Award (August 30, 2000). See discussion below.
120 *Consortium R.F.C.C. v. Kingdom of Morocco*, ICSID Case No. ARB/00/6, Award (December 22, 2003) [French original] 20 *ICSID Rev.—FILJ* 391 (2005), in which the tribunal considered that expropriation was characterized by disappearance of title or the right to enjoy the property. See ibid., para. 68 (translated by author).
121 *Impregilo S.p.A. v. Islamic Republic of Pakistan*, ICSID Case No. ARB/03/3, Award on Objections to Jurisdiction (April 22, 2005). The ICSID tribunal in the case noted that "all the key decisions

Republic,[122] *CME Czech Republic v. Czech Republic*,[123] *Alpha Projektholding v. Ukraine*,[124] and *Spyridon Roussalis v. Rumania*.[125]

International judicial, quasi-judicial and arbitration practice confirms that in order to establish direct nationalization and expropriation, an important factor is transfer of a property right from private ownership to public ownership. Unless transfer of ownership occurs, no nationalization or expropriation may be proven. A distinctive feature of indirect expropriation is that the state may disclaim any intent to expropriate and that the stage of the uselessness of property to the foreign investor is reached cumulatively through various acts or omissions. In such cases, the effect and not the intent of government measures is most important in assessing indirect expropriation. For this, Reisman and Sloane concluded: "In some, if not most other, creeping expropriations, however, that intent, though possibly present at some level of the host state's government, will be difficult, if not impossible, to discern."[126] Therefore, the sole effects doctrine should be encouraged to be employed in practice.

relating to indirect expropriation mention the 'interference' of the Host State in the normal exercise, by the investor, of its economic rights. … Moreover, the effect of the measures taken must be of such importance that those measures can be considered as having an effect equivalent to expropriation." Ibid., paras. 278 and 279.

122 *Ronald S. Lauder v. Czech Republic*, UNCITRAL Arbitration, Final Award (September 3, 2001). The *ad hoc* Tribunal in the case stated that "[i]ndirect expropriation or nationalization is a measure that does not involve an overt taking, but that effectively neutralizes the enjoyment of the property" but held that no such measure was taken in that case. Ibid., paras. 200 and 201.

123 *CME Czech Republic B.V. v. Czech Republic*, UNCITRAL Arbitration, Partial Award (September 13, 2001), in which the tribunal noted that "[d]e facto expropriations or indirect expropriations, i.e. measures that do not involve an overt taking but that effectively neutralize the benefit of the property of the foreign owner, are subject to expropriation claims," further held that such "measures" may comprise either action or inactions, and found expropriation to have occurred as a result of actions and inactions that left the claimant with no immediate prospect of restoration of the property rights of which it had been deprived. Ibid., paras. 604 and 607. Note that this and the *Lauder* case, *supra*, note 122, involved the same set of facts; both tribunals defined "indirect expropriation" in essentially the same way; but different conclusions were reached.

124 *Alpha Projektholding GmbH v. Ukraine*, ICSID Case No. ARB/07/16, Award (November 8, 2010). The tribunal, with reference to *Starrett Housing*, held that "even if the 1998 and 1999 JAAs [joint activity agreements] remain nominally in force, Claimant's investment may still have been expropriated if the contracts have been 'rendered useless' by the actions of the Ukraine government" and, as this was clearly the case, that "such deprivation is effectively permanent, and that the deprivation was the result of government action," it ruled that the claimant's rights had been expropriated. Ibid., paras. 408–10.

125 *Spyridon Roussalis v. Romania*, ICSID Case No. ARB/06/1, Award (December 7, 2011), in which the tribunal relied exclusively on the effects of the disputed measures in determining that there had been no expropriation because those measures did not interfere "with Claimant's management and control of his investment" and "did not deprive the investor from [sic] its right to use or enjoy its investment." Ibid., paras. 354 and 355; available at: http://icsid.worldbank.org/ICSID/FrontServlet?requestType=CasesRH&actionVal=showDoc&docId=DC2431_En&caseId=C70.

126 Reisman and Sloane, *supra*, note 12, at 123.

GAMI v. Mexico[127] was a case in which the sole effects doctrine was adopted. In that case, the claimant, GAMI Investments Inc.—a US investment corporation—owned 14.18 percent of the shares of Grupo Azucarero Mexico SA de CV ("GAM"), which was a Mexican holding company whose remaining shareholders were Mexican nationals.[128] GAM owned five sugar mills, which were expropriated by the Mexican Government pursuant to a decree on September 3, 2001. GAM then challenged the constitutionality of the decree in relation to three of its five mills before the Mexican administrative courts, which held the expropriation to be unlawful and ineffective as to the three mills.[129] When the case was heard, the Mexican Government informed the tribunal that compensation for the other two mills was being negotiated.

The uniqueness of the *GAMI* case is that the claimant's share in the local Mexican company—GAM—was not expropriated. Therefore, in making its complaint, the claimant had to argue that it had suffered from the Mexican measures an effect "tantamount to expropriation." In consideration of the case before it, the tribunal referred to the *Starrett Housing*[130] and *Santa Elena* cases.[131] Whilst the tribunal in *Starrett Housing* defined expropriation as rendering rights useless, the ICSID Tribunal in *Santa Elena* held that the effect of an expropriation is "to deprive the owner of title, possession or access to the benefit and economic use" of the property.[132] The *GAMI* Tribunal also reviewed some NAFTA cases, including *S.D. Myers*,[133] in which it was held that "a temporary discriminatory regulation which eliminated the claimant's competitive advantage in a particular market was not expropriatory."[134]

The *GAMI* Tribunal also commented extensively on the *Pope & Talbot* case,[135] which involved Canadian restrictions on exports of softwood lumber to the United States. The *Pope & Talbot* Tribunal considered that for government interference to constitute an expropriation, it must be "sufficiently restrictive" that a conclusion can be drawn that "the property has been 'taken' from its owner."[136] Otherwise, a diminution of profits arising from the restrictions imposed by the host state cannot be regarded as expropriation. Yet, "an impairment of economic value"

---

127 *GAMI Investments, Inc. v. Government of the United Mexican States*, NAFTA Chapter 11 Arbitration under the UNCITRAL Rules, Final Award (November 15, 2004).

128 Ibid., para. 1.

129 Ibid., paras. 18–20.

130 *Supra*, note 68.

131 *Compañia del Desarrollo de Santa Elena v. Republic of Costa Rica*, ICSID Case No. ARB/96/1, Final Award of February 17, 2000; available at: https://icsid.worldbank.org/ICSID/FrontServlet?requestType=CasesRH&actionVal=showDoc&docId=DC539_En&caseId=C152.

132 Ibid., para. 77.

133 *S.D. Myers, Inc. v. Canada*, First Partial Award (November 13, 2000); available at: http://arbitrationlaw.com/files/free_pdfs/SD%20Myers%20v%20Canada%20-%20Partial%20Award.pdf.

134 *GAMI v. Mexico, supra* note 127, para. 124.

135 *Pope & Talbot, Inc. v. Canada*, UNCITRAL, Interim Award (June 26, 2000); available at: italaw.com/sites/default/files/case-documents/ita0674.pdf.

136 Ibid., para. 102.

may be considered as tantamount to expropriation if the degree of impairment is "equivalent" to expropriation.[137] In the view of the *GAMI* Tribunal, however, "[t]he taking of 50 acres of a farm is equally expropriatory whether that is the whole farm or just a fraction. The notion [of expropriation] must be understood as this: *the affected property* must be impaired to such an extent that it must be seen as 'taken.'"[138]

Following the theory it developed, the *GAMI* Tribunal stated that the claimant was "entitled to invoke the protection of Article 1110 if its property rights (the value of its shares in GAM) were taken by conduct in breach of NAFTA."[139] It went on to say that it was "likely that the Expropriation Decree was inconsistent with the *norms* of NAFTA. But Mexican conduct inconsistent with the norms of NAFTA is only a *breach* of NAFTA if it affects interests protected by NAFTA. GAMI's investment in GAM is protected by Article 1110 only if its sharehold-ing was 'taken.'"[140] Yet, as GAM was and remained in the hands of its owners, including the claimant, and as the "Tribunal can only act on the basis of *objective findings justified by evidence* that GAM's value as an enterprise had been destroyed or impaired," the *GAMI* Tribunal decided that the claimant had failed to prove that "its investment was expropriated for the purpose of Article 1110" of NAFTA.[141]

The *GAMI* Decision is very much in line with other arbitral tribunals' decisions on the issue of partial expropriation. For instance, the ICSID tribunal in *Metalclad* considered that expropriation should include "covert or incidental interference with the use of property which has the effect of depriving the owner, in whole or in significant part, of the use or reasonably-to-be expected economic benefit of property even if not necessarily to the obvious benefit of the host State."[142]

Similarly, in *Consortium R.F.C.C. v. Kingdom of Morocco*, the tribunal found: "If it is not necessary that this loss [of property right] is permanent, a temporary measure must have substantial consequences equivalent to a definitive loss. The recovery of title to the property or access to it does not replace the owner in his initial situa-tion, his rights having been substantially reduced by the loss of the profits he could have earned." [143]

The *LG&E v. Argentina*[144] Tribunal also considered that an expropriation must involve "a permanent, severe deprivation" of rights to an investment "or almost complete deprivation of the value" of investment. In that case, the *LG&E*

---

137 Ibid., para. 104.
138 *GAMI v. Mexico, supra*, note 127, para. 126 (emphasis in original).
139 Ibid., para. 129.
140 Id. (emphases in original).
141 Ibid, paras. 132–33 (emphasis in original).
142 *Metalclad v. Mexico, supra*, note 119, para. 104.
143 *Consortium R.F.C.C. v. Kingdom of Morocco, supra*, note 120, para. 68 (translation provided by author).
144 *LG&E Energy Corp., LG&E Capital Corp., LG&E International Inc., v. Argentine Republic*, ICSID Case No. ARB/02/1, Decision on Liability (October 3, 2006), para. 200; available at: http://icsid. worldbank.org/ICSID/FrontServlet?requestType=CasesRH&actionVal=showDoc&docId= DC627_En&caseId=C208. In this case, the tribunal also gave credence to the validity of the "proportionality test" in determining indirect expropriation, even though it does not appear to have relied upon the test in reaching its conclusions; see paras. 189–95.

Tribunal concluded that the circumstances did not constitute an expropriation. In another case—*BG v. Argentina*—the tribunal, after reviewing a number of previous cases, also found there to be no expropriation because it "[did] not find that the measures adopted by Argentina caused a permanent, severe deprivation of BG's rights with regard to its investment."[145]

Based on what can be learned from investment arbitration practice, it is clearly accepted that for a government measure to constitute an expropriation there must be a "taking" caused by the measure. Such measures may include "non-payment, non-reimbursement, cancellation, denial of judicial access, actual practice to exclude, non-conforming treatment, inconsistent legal blocks, and so forth."[146] Where there is no open and overt taking of property, the effect of the government measure complained of must be tantamount to a permanent deprivation of rights or severe and permanent deprivation of enjoyment of such rights. Diminution of economic interests, however, may not constitute expropriation unless the impairment of economic value is tantamount or equivalent to expropriation.[147] Although tribunals have expressed their views in different words, unlike on other issues, the arbitration practice with regard to expropriation and nationalization is quite consistent.

III. Defense of indirect expropriation and conditions

Indirect expropriation relates to the exercise of state powers, which is recognized by customary international law. It is also very often the case that a state measure may have adverse effects on certain economic sectors and individuals. If whenever a state measure has adverse effects on someone, an indirect expropriation is found, the state cannot manage its own affairs. This is so, in particular, because every sovereign state is expected, if not required, to protect health, safety, and morality through legislation and administrative action, and this may require it to regulate business and commercial activities within its territory through such measures as taxation; competition laws; labor laws; and health, safety, and environmental regulations, among others—commonly referred to as police power.

It is true that any such exercise of police powers may have an economic impact on an investment or other property; such impact may even be so great as to remove all benefits of ownership, make a business illegal, or reduce the value of an investment to nothing. In such circumstances, is the state in question responsible? Brownlie noted that state measures "may affect foreign interests considerably without amounting to expropriation."[148] The most extreme expression of the

---

145 *BG Group Plc v. Republic of Argentina*, UNCITRAL Final Award (December 24, 2007), paras. 258–72; available at: italaw.com/sites/default/files/case-documents/ita0081.pdf.

146 Keith Highet's Dissenting Opinion in *Waste Management, Inc. v. United Mexican States*, ICSID Case No. ARB(AF)/98/2, Award (June 2, 2000), quoted from Reisman and Sloane, *supra*, note 12, at p. 123.

147 *Pope & Talbot, Inc. v. Canada*, *supra*, note 135, para. 104.

148 Ian Brownlie, *Public International Law*, 6th ed., Oxford University Press, Oxford, UK, 2003, p. 509.

police powers doctrine states: "A state is not responsible for loss of property or for other economic disadvantage resulting from bona fide general taxation, regulation, forfeiture for crime, or other action of the kind that is commonly accepted as within the police power of states, if it is not discriminatory …"[149] Henckels identified, through her examination of arbitration practice and writings by scholars, three approaches to the issue of whether the exercise of police power constitutes indirect expropriation, namely: (i) the sole effect approach; (ii) treating police powers as an exception from expropriation; and (iii) taking both purpose and effect into account in the assessment.[150]

Recent arbitral decisions upholding the "police powers doctrine," at least in its purest form, are relatively rare. The sole example in the case law of the Iran–United States Claims Tribunal was in *Emanuel Too v. Greater Modesto Insurance Associates*, where the tribunal ruled:

> A state is not responsible for loss of property or for other economic disadvantage resulting from bona fide general taxation or any other action that is commonly accepted as within the police power of States, provided it is not discriminatory and is not designed to cause the alien to abandon the property to the State or to sell it at a distress price.[151]

The decision reached in the NAFTA case *Methanex v. USA*[152] is the one most frequently cited in this regard. Briefly, the case involved a series of measures adopted on grounds of environmental protection by the State of California banning, as of December 31, 2002, the "[sale], offer for sale, supply or offer for supply [of] California gasoline which has been produced with the use of methyl tertiary-butyl ether (MTBE)."[153] Methanex, a Canadian corporation, was, at the time of the dispute, the world's largest producer and supplier of methanol. It claimed that one-third of its methanol production was utilized in the fuel sector, principally for use in the production of MTBE and that it was the largest supplier of methanol to the California marketplace.[154] Methanex alleged that "a substantial portion of its investments, including its share of the California and larger US oxygenate market, were taken by patently discriminatory measures and handed over to the domestic

149 *Restatement of the Law, Third, Foreign Relations Law of the United States*, American Law Institute, Philadelphia, Pennsylvania, 1987, Vol. 1, Section 712, Comment g.
150 Caroline Henckels, "Indirect Expropriation and the Right to Regulate: Revisiting Proportionality Analysis and the Standard of Review in Investor-State Arbitration," *Journal of International Economic Law*, Vol. 15, Issue 1, 2012, pp. 223–35, at 224.
151 *Emanuel Too v. Greater Modesto Insurance Associates*, 23 *Iran-USCTR* 378, para. 26.
152 *Methanex Corporation v. United States of America*, UNCITRAL Final Award on Jurisdiction and Merits (August 3, 2005); available at: http://naftaclaims.com/Disputes/USA/Methanex/Methanex_Final_Award.pdf.
153 California Phase III Reformulated Gasoline Regulations, §2262.6(a)(1), as quoted in *Methanex v. USA*, ibid., Part II, Ch D, para. 19.
154 *Methanex v. USA*, ibid., Part II, Ch D, para. 3.

ethanol industry" and that "such a taking [was] at a minimum tantamount to expropriation."[155]

In reaching its Decision in the case, the tribunal noted:

> [A]s a matter of general international law, a non-discriminatory regulation for a public purpose, which is enacted in accordance with due process and, which affects, inter alios, a foreign investor or investment is not deemed expropriatory and compensable unless specific commitments had been given by the regulating government to the then putative foreign investor contemplating investment that the government would refrain from such regulation.[156]

The tribunal found that "[n]o such commitments were given to Methanex"[157] and concluded that:

> ... the California ban was made for a public purpose, was non-discriminatory and was accomplished with due process. Hence, Methanex's central claim under Article 1110(1) of expropriation under one of the three forms of action in that provision fails. From the standpoint of international law, the California ban was a lawful regulation and not an expropriation.[158]

What is almost always overlooked in discussions of this Award, however, are the paragraphs immediately following this conclusion, beginning with the tribunal's holding that "[n]or has Methanex established that the California ban manifested any of the features associated with expropriation" and its recitation of the observations made in a similar case that "the regulatory action has not deprived the Claimant of control of his company, ... interfered directly in the internal operations ... or displaced the Claimant as the controlling shareholder. The Claimant is free to pursue other continuing lines of business activity."[159] It is obvious that the *Methanex* Tribunal's ruling was affected by the fact that there was no precise promise made by the respondent and that the claimant did not lose control of its invested property.

Another award upholding states' rights to exercise police powers, albeit with some reservations, was delivered in *Saluka v. Czech Republic*.[160] In that case, the arbitration arose out of events following upon the reorganization and privatization of the Czech banking sector. IPB, one of the major Czech banks, was privatized by selling the state's shareholding to a company within the Nomura Holding Group, which in turn transferred them to another Nomura subsidiary, Saluka Investments BV, a company organized under the laws of the Netherlands. In

155 Ibid., Part II, Ch D, para. 28.
156 Ibid., Part IV, Ch D, para. 7.
157 Ibid., Part IV, Ch D, para. 9.
158 Ibid., Part IV, Ch D, para. 15.
159 Ibid., Part IV, Ch D, para. 16.
160 *Saluka Investments B.V. (The Netherlands) v. Czech Republic*, UNCITRAL Partial Award (March 22, 2006); available at: http://www.italaw.com/documents/Saluka-PartialawardFinal.pdf.

June 2000, on the grounds of "mismanagement," the Czech Government put IPB under forced administration and, immediately thereafter, the appointed administrator arranged the sale of IPB to ČSOB, another Czech bank, for a minimal price. Saluka then initiated arbitration proceedings, claiming that the measures taken and attributable to the Czech Republic had deprived it of the value of its investment. The tribunal found this to be the case, and its remarks and reasoning are worthy of extensive quotation in this regard.

It held that: "[i]t is now established in international law that States are not liable to pay compensation to a foreign investor when, in the normal exercise of their regulatory powers, they adopt in a non-discriminatory manner bona fide regulations that are aimed at the general welfare."[161] However, it also noted that "the so-called 'police power exception' is not absolute."[162] The tribunal was of the opinion that "the principle that a State does not commit an expropriation and is thus not liable to pay compensation to a dispossessed alien investor when it adopts general regulations that are 'commonly accepted as within the police power of States' forms part of customary international law today."[163] Furthermore, it observed:

> That being said, international law has yet to identify in a comprehensive and definitive fashion precisely what regulations are considered "permissible" and "commonly accepted" as falling within the police or regulatory power of States and, thus, non-compensable. In other words, it has yet to draw a bright and easily distinguishable line between non-compensable regulations on the one hand and, on the other, measures that have the effect of depriving foreign investors of their investment and are thus unlawful and compensable in international law.
>
> It thus inevitably falls to the adjudicator to determine whether particular conduct by a state "crosses the line" that separates valid regulatory activity from expropriation. Faced with the question of *when, how and at what point an otherwise valid regulation becomes, in fact and effect, an unlawful expropriation*, international tribunals must consider the circumstances in which the question arises. The context within which an impugned measure is adopted and applied is critical to the determination of its validity.
>
> In the present case, the Tribunal finds that the Czech Republic has not "crossed that line" and did not breach Article 5 of the Treaty, since the measures at issue can be justified as permissible regulatory actions.[164]

It is noteworthy that the *Saluka* Tribunal adopted an approach meant to balance the intent of the state in regulating public welfare and the effect on the claimant and that it considered that the determination of whether the measure in question would fall into the category of police power should be decided in accordance with

161 Ibid., para. 255.
162 Ibid., para. 258.
163 Ibid., para. 262.
164 Ibid., paras. 263–65 (emphasis in original).

"commonly accepted" principles under customary international law. Not surprisingly, the *Saluka* Tribunal immediately concluded that customary international law could offer little help in identifying which regulations or measures should be treated as correct exercise of police power and which ones could not. This demonstrates that the intent of the state in adopting certain regulations is easily subject to being questioned. In the end, what matters most is still the effect of the related measure.

The tribunal in *Suez InterAguas v. Argentina*,[165] relying in part on the *Saluka* award, noted that "in evaluating a claim of expropriation it is important to recognize a State's legitimate right to regulate and to exercise its police power in the interests of public welfare and not to confuse measures of that nature with expropriation."[166] The tribunal nonetheless appears to have given the final word to the effect of the exercise of such power in reaching its decision on indirect expropriation by holding:

> In analyzing the measures taken by Argentina to cope with the crisis, the Tribunal finds that they did not constitute a permanent and substantial deprivation of the Claimants' investments. Although they may have negatively affected the profitability of the APSF Concession, they did not take or reduce the property rights of APSF or its investors and did not affect the ability of APSF to hold the Concession and to direct its operations and activities. The Tribunal therefore concludes that such measures did not violate the above quoted BIT articles with respect to direct or indirect expropriation ...[167]

Understandably, the *Suez InterAguas* Tribunal attached much importance to the fact that the claimant was not deprived, substantially and perpetually, of its property. This was confirmed by its comment on the spate of investor–state arbitrations as a result of the measures enacted by the Argentine Government in an effort to deal with the financial crisis it faced in the first years of the 21st century. In its view, the reason why only the *Siemens* Tribunal found that Argentina's measures constituted expropriation was because Siemens had lost its contract with Argentina.[168]

Chemtura v. Canada,[169] a NAFTA case, was decided by an *ad hoc* arbitral tribunal under the UNCITRAL rules at almost the same time as *Suez InterAguas* and shows another view of the interplay between "effect" and "police power." Chemtura, a US corporation, was a manufacturer of lindane, a pesticide used in the treatment of canola seed. In 1998, the Canadian Government took steps to ban the use of lindane on environmental and workers' safety grounds and, in 2002, revoked all

165 *Suez, Sociedad General de Aguas de Barcelona S.A. and InterAguas Servicios Integrales del Agua S.A. v. Argentina*, ICSID Case No. ARB/03/17, Award (July 30, 2010); available at: http://www.italaw.com/documents/SuezInterAguaDecisiononLiability.pdf.
166 Ibid., para. 128.
167 Ibid., para. 129.
168 Ibid., para. 127 (footnotes omitted).
169 *Chemtura Corporation v. Canada*, Ad hoc—UNCITRAL Arbitration Rules Award (August 2, 2010); available at: http://oxia.ouplaw.com/view/10.1093/law:iic/451-2010.case.1/IIC451(2010)D.pdf.

of the claimant's registrations for lindane products.[170] Chemtura alleged that the revocation of its lindane product registrations were "measures tantamount to expropriation" in violation of Article 1110 of NAFTA.[171]

The tribunal undertook an extensive analysis of the standards for determining what measures may be "tantamount to expropriation." With reference to both *Pope & Talbot* and *Metalclad*, it examined especially closely the requirement that, to be so considered, such measures "must amount to a substantial deprivation of the Claimant's investment."[172] It concluded that: "[t]he determination of whether there has been a 'substantial deprivation' is a fact-sensitive exercise to be conducted in the light of the circumstances of each case."[173] By then carrying out such an exercise in the present circumstances, the Tribunal came to the conclusion that "the evidence shows that the measures did not amount to a substantial deprivation of the Claimant's investment."[174]

However, in contradistinction to the *Suez InterAguas* Tribunal, the *Chemtura* Tribunal appears to have given the final word to police power. It said:

> *Irrespective of the existence of a contractual deprivation*, the Tribunal considers in any event that the measures challenged by the Claimant constituted a valid exercise of the Respondent's police powers. … [The government agency concerned] took measures within its mandate, in a non-discriminatory manner, motivated by the increasing awareness of the dangers presented by lindane for human health and the environment. A measure adopted under such circumstances is a valid exercise of the State's police powers and, as a result, does not constitute an expropriation.[175]

Assessment of the risks arising from lindane and like products requires knowledge and data from scientific findings. Measures to be taken must also be based on such scientific findings and the viability of alternative measures. At the same time, where the world is facing the problem of a deteriorating environment, tribunals must take this into account in determining whether or not an environmental measure constitutes indirect expropriation. The *Chemtura* Tribunal's finding is in fact in line with practices of some international and supra-national bodies such as the European Court of Human Rights, in which deference is exhibited toward the decision-makers of states on the grounds that they have better resources and hence know better in assessing what measures should be adopted to meet the needs of their communities.[176]

---

170 See ibid., paras. 6–34.
171 Ibid., paras. 92 and 251.
172 Ibid., paras. 242–49.
173 Ibid., para. 249.
174 Ibid., para. 265.
175 Ibid., para. 266.
176 For discussions on the matter, see David Feldman, "Proportionality and the Human Rights Act 1998," in Eyelyn Ellis (ed.), *The Principle of Proportionality in the Laws of Europe*, Hart, 1999; Howard Yourow, "The Margin of Appreciation Doctrine in the Dynamics of the European Human

In addition, it is clear that there is a constant, perhaps inevitable, dynamic between the exercise of police powers and the effect of that on an investment. Recognition of this dynamic has given rise to the application of the principle of "proportionality" in the determination of indirect expropriation. The "proportionality test" serves as a condition for the state to exercise police power, which is essentially derived from the case law of the European Court of Human Rights. In *Sporrong & Lonnroth v. Sweden*,[177] the Court held that it "must determine whether a fair balance was struck between the demands of the general interest of the community and the requirements of the protection of the individual's fundamental rights." In *James and Others*, the Court endorsed that position and held that: "[n]ot only must a measure depriving a person of his property pursue, on the facts as well as in principle, a legitimate aim 'in the public interest,' but there must also be a reasonable relationship of proportionality between the means employed and the aim sought to be realized" and that "a measure must be both appropriate for achieving its aim and not disproportionate thereto."[178] In general, a tribunal, in assessing the proportionality of a government measure, must also consider if there exists an alternative measure which is not unrealistic or so excessively expensive that it would be impossible to implement it to achieve the same purpose. This point was, however, not analyzed in the above case.

The "proportionality test" was introduced into international investment arbitration by the tribunal in *Tecmed v. Mexico*.[179] In doing so, however, the tribunal appears to have viewed it as the second part of a "two-step test" to determine whether or not measures taken by a state could be considered to constitute indirect expropriation. As such, the tribunal's reasoning is worthy of extensive quotation.

The first criterion in this two-step test, as laid down by the *Tecmed* Tribunal, is clearly the effect of the measures: "To establish whether [a measure] is a measure equivalent to an expropriation … it must be first determined if the Claimant, due to the [measure], was radically deprived of the economical use and enjoyment of its investments, as if the rights related thereto … had ceased to exist."[180] Citing jurisprudence of both the European Court of Human Rights and the Iran–United States Claims Tribunal, the *Tecmed* Tribunal further stated that a measure constituted "indirect *de facto* expropriation" if it had the effect of depriving the property owner, irreversibly and permanently, of his/her property.[181] "Under international

Rights Jurisprudence, 3 *Connecticut Journal of International Law*, 1998, 111; Marc-Andre Eissen, "The Principle of Proportionality in the Case-Law of the European Court of Human Rights," in Ronald St. John Macdonald, Franz Matscher and Herbert Petzold (eds.), *The European System for the Protection of Human Rights*, Kluwer, 1993; and Pieter Van Dijk and Godefridus J. H. van Hoof, *The Theory and Practice of the European Convention on Human Rights*, 3rd ed., Martinus Nijhoff Publishers, 1998.

177 *Sporrong & Lonnroth v. Sweden* (1983) 5 EHRR 35, para. 69.
178 *James and Others* (1986) 8 EHRR 123, para. 50.
179 *Tecmed v. Mexico, supra*, note 72.
180 Ibid., para. 115 (footnote omitted).
181 Ibid., para. 116.

law," said the *Tecmed* Tribunal, "the owner is also deprived of property where the use or enjoyment of benefits related thereto is exacted or interfered with to a similar extent, even where legal ownership over the assets in question is not affected, and so long as the deprivation is not temporary."[182] The intent or purpose of the measure is less important than its effects.[183]

This having been said, the *Tecmed* Tribunal considered, in addition to the effects of the government measures, "whether such actions or measures are proportional to the public interest presumably protected thereby and to the protection legally granted to investments, taking into account that the significance of such impact has a key role upon deciding the proportionality."[184] In fact, the *Tecmed* Tribunal is by far the one that has analyzed in greatest detail the issue of proportionality in investment arbitration by identifying some specific factors, including "community pressure and its consequences" and the "economic impact" of government action leading to indirect expropriation. "These factors must be weighed," stated the tribunal, "when trying to assess the proportionality of the action adopted with respect to the purpose pursued by such measure."[185]

The *Tecmed* Tribunal ultimately found the measures under consideration in that case not to be proportional to the public interest they sought to protect, whilst leading to "the neutralization of the investment's economic and business value and the Claimant's return on investment and profitability expectations upon making the investment,"[186] and it therefore found that they amounted to an expropriation.[187] What the tribunal did establish, however, were some criteria in accordance with which state measures taken under other circumstances might well not be considered to constitute indirect expropriation. Regardless of the outcome of the case, what the *Tecmed* Tribunal did was constructive in the development of international investment law.

The *Tecmed* Tribunal's formulation of the proportionality test has been favorably cited by subsequent tribunals in the *Azurix*[188] and *LG&E*[189] cases, but careful examination of both awards fails to demonstrate that either tribunal made any effective use of the test in determining whether or not the relevant measures were expropriatory. This is not very surprising, as the threshold set by the *Tecmed* Tribunal was not low, according to which a measure may not be considered as expropriatory unless its purpose, effect, and proportionality have met with the requirements. This is so because it is difficult to determine "whether the acts and omissions of the host state (i) were themselves the *causa causans* of the loss of eco-

---

182 Id. (footnotes omitted).
183 Id.
184 Ibid., para. 122.
185 Ibid., para. 133.
186 Ibid., para. 149.
187 Ibid., para. 151.
188 *Azurix Corp v. Argentine Republic*, ICSID Case No. ARB/01/12, Award (July 14, 2006), paras. 311–12; available at: http://icsid.worldbank.org/ICSID/FrontServlet?requestType=CasesRH&actionVal=showDoc&docId=DC507_En&caseId=C5.
189 *LG&E v. Argentina*, *supra*, note 144, paras. 189–95.

nomic value [of the investment to the foreign investor] or (ii) contributed to that loss; or by contrast, (iii) whether the loss should rather be ascribed chiefly to the foreign investor's misjudgments or (iv) to exogenous economic factors independent of the actions (or inactions) of the host state."[190]

In the *Siemens* case,[191] the claimant relied on a legal opinion which stated that "proportionality and reasonableness may play a role in assessing whether the power to expropriate has been exercised properly. But these criteria do not affect the question whether an expropriation exists or not."[192] The tribunal in that case does not appear to have actually addressed this issue. On the other hand, the tribunal in *Fireman's Fund v. Mexico*, while noting that "the proportionality between the means employed and the aim sought to be realized" was one of the factors that may be taken into account "[t]o distinguish between a compensable expropriation and a noncompensable regulation by a host State," citing both *Tecmed* and the European Court of Human Rights, nevertheless expressed the opinion that "it may be questioned whether it is a viable source of interpreting Article 1110 [Expropriation and Compensation]of the NAFTA."[193]

The *Archer Daniels Midland* Tribunal seems to have introduced and applied a significantly different test of proportionality, which it purported to derive from Article 51 of the International Law Commission's Draft Articles on Responsibility of States for Internationally Wrongful Acts.[194] It expressed the opinion that: "[p]roportionality requires not only employing the means appropriate to the aim chosen, but implies an assessment of the appropriateness of the aim itself, considering the structure and content of the breached rule."[195] Therefore, in finding that the relevant measure in that case was not "appropriate to the aim chosen," it found that it "[did] not meet the proportionality requirement for the validity of countermeasures under customary international law."[196]

The decision on liability issued jointly in the cases of *Suez et al. v. Argentina* and *AWG Group v. Argentina* presents an examination of indirect expropriation that gives a degree of importance to each of the three jurisprudential approaches to the issue.[197] First of all, it recalled the essential difficulty in establishing indirect expropriation in this way:

---

190 Reisman and Sloane, *supra*, note 12, p. 130.

191 *Siemens v. Argentina, supra*, note 43.

192 Legal opinion of Professor Christoph Schreuer, cited ibid., para. 238.

193 *Fireman's Fund Insurance Company v. United Mexican States*, ICSID Case No. ARB(AF)/02/01, Award (July 17, 2006), para. 176(j) and footnote 161.

194 See *Archer Daniels Midland Company v. United Mexican States*, ICSID Case No. ARB(AF)/04/05, Award (November 21, 2007) (redacted version), para. 152.

195 Ibid., para. 154.

196 Ibid., paras. 159–60.

197 Suez, Sociedad General de Aguas de Barcelona, Vivendi, and AWG Group were all shareholders in Aguas Argentinas, an Argentine company that held a concession for water distribution and waste water treatment services in the Province of Buenos Aires. Pursuant to alleged acts and omissions by Argentina, the claimants requested ICSID arbitration—Suez and Vivendi under the Argentina–France BIT; Sociedad General de Aguas de Barcelona under the Argentina–Spain BIT; and AWG Group under the Argentina–UK BIT. The first three claimants were

> While determining the existence of a direct expropriation is usually not difficult because of the usually obvious physical manifestations that come with depriving an investor of title and control, identifying an indirect expropriation is often a much more complicated matter which requires an inquiry into whether a regulatory measure has the effect of an expropriation on an investment or is a valid exercise of a State's regulatory power.[198]

In the instant case, the tribunal noted that each of the relevant BITs "specifically refers to the 'effects' of an expropriation measure and thus affirms the importance of evaluating the effects of a measure on the investment in determining whether an expropriation has taken place."[199] It further recalled that "[i]nternational tribunals treat the severity of the economic impact caused by a regulatory measure as an important element in determining if the measure constitutes an expropriation requiring compensation" and that there must be "permanent or lasting results."[200] It therefore held that "in applying the provisions of the three BITs applicable to these cases, this Tribunal will have to determine whether they effected a substantial, permanent deprivation of the Claimants' investments or the enjoyment of those investments' economic benefits."[201] It found that this was not the case and that, therefore, there was no indirect expropriation.[202]

Notwithstanding the findings of the tribunal, its emphasis on the consequential effect of government measures on foreign investment is a correct approach. Unless there is substantial and permanent loss of property, it will be difficult to confirm that expropriation, either direct or indirect, has taken place and even more difficult to determine compensation for such expropriation, albeit the foreign investor in question may still be entitled to compensation for other breaches, if proven.

The *Suez/AWG* Tribunal, however, did not find it sufficient to let the case rest here. It further noted that "in evaluating a claim of expropriation it is important to recognize a State's legitimate right to regulate and to exercise its police power in the interests of public welfare and not to confuse measures of that nature with expropriation."[203] It then went on to deliver a conclusion that, although it does not use the term "proportionality," at least incorporates that concept along with police powers and effects. It said:

> In analyzing the measures taken by Argentina to cope with the crisis, the Tribunal finds that, given the nature of the severe crisis facing the country,

granted ICSID arbitration in ICSID Case No. ARB/03/19 but, owing to specific provisions of the Argentina–UK BIT, AWG Group's case was carried out under UNCITRAL Rules, although administered by the ICSID and arbitrated by the same tribunal. Decisions in the two cases were thus issued jointly; see the Decision on Liability (July 20, 2010), especially paras. 1–4, 17 and 25; available at: http://oxia.ouplaw.com/view/10.1093/law:iic/443-2010.case.1/IIC443(2010)D.pdf.

198 Ibid., para. 132.
199 Ibid., para. 133.
200 Ibid., para. 134.
201 Ibid.
202 Ibid., para. 137.
203 Ibid., para. 139.

those general measures were within the general police powers of the Argentine State, and they did not constitute a permanent and substantial deprivation of the Claimants' investments. Although they may have negatively affected the profitability of the AASA Concession, they did not take or reduce the property rights of AASA or its investors and did not affect the ability of AASA to hold the Concession and to direct its operations and activities. The Tribunal therefore concludes that such measures did not violate the above quoted BIT articles with respect to direct or indirect expropriation; however, that is not to say that they have not violated other treaty commitments.[204]

Thus, in addition to considering the perpetuity of property loss suffered by the foreign investor, the tribunal exhibited a considerable degree of deference to the host state in taking measures to deal with a crisis. This is a reasonable approach given the fact that a hindsight view of the measures taken is always easier than the actual decision-making during crisis. It is also in fact difficult, if not impossible, for a tribunal whose membership is mostly non-national and, above all, may not have the experience of managing a country to be able to make an accurate assessment of such a situation.

In a somewhat similar vein, the tribunal in *El Paso v. Argentina* analyzed the dynamic that exists between the exercise of police powers and their effects, in which neutralization of the use of the investment was considered a necessary condition to qualify the exercise of police powers as a measure of expropriation.[205] In its analysis of whether a general measure would be regarded as unreasonable and therefore disproportionate, the tribunal referred to the following:

> … a regulation in which the interference with the private rights of the investors is disproportionate to the public interest. In other words, proportionality has to exist between the public purpose fostered by the regulation and the interference with the investors' property rights … In other words, discriminatory or disproportionate general regulations have the potential to be considered as expropriatory if there is a sufficient interference with the investor's rights …[206]

Indeed, without sufficient interference, a foreign investor's use of an investment cannot be neutralized. In *El Paso*, the claimant sold its shares, not because it was forced to do so by the respondent but rather because of what was considered by the tribunal to be a general business environment that the claimant faced. In addition, the measure involved was a tax regulation. According to the tribunal, "foreign investments are subject to taxes imposed by the host State and 'the foreign

204 Ibid., para. 140.
205 *El Paso Energy International Company v. Argentina*, ICSID Case No. ARB/03/15, Award (October 27, 2011), para. 233; available at: http://oxia.ouplaw.com/view/10.1093/law:iic/519-2011.case.1/IIC519(2011)D.pdf.
206 Ibid.(para. 243.

investor has neither the right nor any legitimate expectation that the tax regime will not change … during the period of the investment,' even though that may reduce its economic benefits."[207] In fact, even if the tax regulation had a discriminatory effect, it might not be perforce a breach of the obligations under the BIT. In the view of the tribunal, "the standard of the BIT according to which foreign investors are protected against discrimination does not entail the far-reaching consequence that a State cannot treat differently the economic actors in different sectors of the economy, as long as this differential treatment applies equally to national and foreign investors."[208] Surely the tax regulations of any state are subject to frequent changes, and these are, in most cases, unpredictable. Faced with such issues, it was natural for the tribunal to hold that the respondent's measures did not result in expropriation of the claimant's investment.[209]

Clearly, this review of recent arbitral practice reveals that no consensus has yet been achieved on precisely how to determine whether or not and when an indirect expropriation has occurred, although the effect of state measures on the value or control of an investment appears to be the most decisive factor. This is so because where there is no substantial effect on the value or control of an investment, there is no reason for the foreign investors and hence tribunals to interfere with the management by states of their own affairs. In fact, even in cases of substantial effect, the states concerned may still defend their actions by relying on the police power recognized by customary international law. In this regard, as checks and balances, the introduction of the proportionality test is important. The difficulty in practice is that in deciding whether or not a given government measure is in proportion to the objective it aims at achieving, tribunals may not have the means to examine available alternatives for achieving the same result but with less severe effects on foreign investments.

IV. The Chinese practice

As one of the host countries that has attracted the largest amounts of foreign capital, China has always paid particular attention to the issue of expropriation but has essentially limited its understanding of it to the traditional view. For instance, the 1984 China–Norway BIT requires that the expropriation of foreign direct investments be for a public purpose.[210] In addition, it requires the country carrying out the expropriation or nationalization to apply the principle of non-discrimination.[211]

With regard to compensation for expropriation, the China–Norway BIT made some progress from the Chinese Joint Venture Law by providing that:

---

207 Ibid., para. 294 (footnote omitted).
208 Ibid., para. 306.
209 Ibid., paras. 279 and 299.
210 1984 China–Norway BIT, Article 5(1).
211 Ibid.

Compensation shall be made without undue delay and shall be realizable and freely transferable. It shall amount to the value of the investment immediately before the expropriation, and shall include interest until the date of payment.[212]

This, of course, does not meet the requirements of the Hull formula, according to which the host state is required to pay prompt, adequate and effective compensation.[213] Yet considering the fact that Chinese law at that time was quite primitive and that China was solely a recipient of foreign capital,[214] it was an important step in subjecting the country to international norms.

The China–UK BIT brought China closer to the general practice of developed countries. Rather than recognizing expropriation as a right of states, it prescribes that "[i]nvestments ... shall not be expropriated, nationalized or subjected to measures having effect equivalent to expropriation or nationalization" except for a public purpose and with compensation.[215] Expropriation or nationalization conditioned on public purpose and compensation was not a prevailing view among Chinese academics at that time,[216] so including this provision in the China–UK BIT was truly a significant move on the part of China.

The China–UK BIT still adopts the "reasonable compensation" standard in general terms. Yet, immediately thereafter, the reasonable standard is further defined:

Such compensation shall amount to the real value of the investment expropriated immediately before the expropriation or impending expropriation became public knowledge, shall include interest at the normal rate until the

212 Ibid., Article 5(2).
213 The Hull formula was articulated in 1938 by US Secretary of State Cordell Hull in response to the Mexican expropriation of US agricultural and oil interests and became the cardinal principle of US custom in this sphere; see M. Sornarajah, *The International Law on Foreign Investment*, Cambridge University Press, UK, 1994, pp. 229–30.
214 It has only been since 1979 that China has started to receive investments from abroad. Initially, most of its investments were in the areas of construction and catering. There are still restrictions under Chinese law on foreign investments. See "How to invest in prohibited or restricted industries," China Law & Practice, July/August 2012; available at: http://www.chinalawandpractice. com/Article/3058801/How-to-invest-in-prohibited-or-restricted-industries.html.
215 According to the Chinese traditional view, the right to expropriation emanates from the sovereignty of a state; therefore, any condition attached by the Western developed countries to legitimate expropriations is unjustified. However, Article 5 of the China–UK BIT seems to admit that China has given up the right to expropriate foreign investments unless the two conditions are met.
216 In the 1980s, by referring to the Charter of Economic Rights and Duties of States, a state's right to expropriation or nationalization was recognized as an important aspect of its sovereignty over its natural resources; see Wang Tieya, *International Law*, Law Press, Beijing, China, pp. 430–31 (1981). Professor Yao Meizhen held that the concept of a nationalization conditioned on public purpose and compensation was based on the capitalist doctrine of inviolability of private property, which was totally unacceptable theoretically, as the right of nationalization was an attribute of sovereignty; for details, see Yao Meizhen, *International Investment Law*, Wuhan University Press, Wuhan, 1989, p. 379 (in Chinese).

date of payment, shall be made without undue delay, be effectively realizable and be freely transferable.[217]

It should be noted that the prevailing Chinese view on compensation for expropriation at that time was "reasonable compensation." The wording of the China–UK BIT was obviously meant to adopt the Hull formula in effect whilst giving lip-service to the concept of "reasonable compensation" in order to quiet potential internal criticisms.[218] Actually, the adoption of the standard in the BIT surprised many Chinese and foreign scholars, because in other official documents China still refused to recognize the Hull formula as an acceptable standard.[219]

It is also stipulated in the China–UK BIT that: "The national or company affected shall have a right, under the law of the Contracting Party making the expropriation to prompt review, by a judicial or other independent authority of that party, of his or its case and of the valuation of his or its investment in accordance with the principles set out in this paragraph."[220] Judicial review of administrative actions at that time was unheard of in the Chinese legal system.[221] Granting foreign investors such a right in cases of expropriation amounted to inserting "judicial review" into the Chinese legal system.[222] As international treaty provisions have the effect of filling the gap and prevailing over any conflicting provisions of Chinese law, this prescription has served as a tool to move international norms into Chinese domestic law.[223]

---

217 1986 China–UK BIT, Article 5(1).
218 In Chinese culture at that time, any major concession made to foreign countries may have been considered as non-patriotic and a deviation from socialism, and it would have been subject to criticism. This was more so in the mid-1980s, as there were hot debates as to what measures should be considered as reforms and which ones as adopting the techniques of capitalism. The debates ended with Deng Xiaoping's tour in southern China, when he stated that nothing was exclusively patented for capitalism. For discussion of this issue, see Guiguo Wang, *Wang's Business Law of China*, LexisNexis, Hong Kong, 2003.
219 Law on Wholly Foreign-Owned Enterprises, Article 5. Also, it should be noted that at that time China was solely a recipient of foreign direct investment. With its investment in foreign countries growing rapidly after the turn of the century, it is in China's interest to ensure adequate compensation for expropriation.
220 1986 China–UK BIT, Article 5(1).
221 In the Protocol on the Accession to the WTO, China agreed that there shall in all cases be an opportunity for an impartial and independent judicial body to review specified administrative actions. Under the current Chinese legal system, judicial review is only available with respect to concrete administrative actions through the means of administrative litigation. By contrast, based on the doctrine of separation of powers, under the common law, judicial review includes constitutional review of legislation. For a discussion of judicial review in China, see Hu Jinguang, "The Space of Chinese Judicial Review," 14(5) *Henan Social Science*, September 2006, pp. 72–76.
222 It was most probably the first time that a bilateral agreement had had such an important effect on the Chinese legal system.
223 A distinct feature of globalization is that international norms have a direct effect on national legal systems. With China joining the World Trade Organization and international norms moving into the Chinese legal system, impacts on domestic laws and law enforcement mechanisms have become the natural consequences of concluding international agreements. For a discussion of this

A common feature of the BITs that China has entered into lately is making expropriation conditional. Nearly all of these BITs contain the following provisions:

> Neither Contracting Party shall expropriate, nationalize or take other similar measures against the investments of the investors of the other Contracting Party in its territory, unless the measures taken meet the following conditions: (a) for the public interest; (b) under domestic legal procedure [except for the 2003 China-Germany BIT]; (c) without discrimination; and (d) against compensation.[224]

Regarding compensation for expropriation, the 2003 China–Germany BIT stipulates that "such compensation shall be equivalent to the value of the investment immediately before the expropriation is taken or the threatening expropriation has become publicly known, whichever is earlier."[225] In comparison, the 2006 China–Russia BIT, the 2004 China–Finland BIT, the 2005 China–Spain BIT and the 2005 China–Portugal BIT all provide that the compensation "shall be equivalent to the fair market value of the expropriated investment at the time immediately before the expropriation was taken or the impending expropriation became public knowledge, whichever is earlier."[226] This slightly different version may not necessarily lead to arguments that the "value" under the 2003 China–Germany BIT is not the "market value" of the investment in question, even though international arbitration practice does not provide a definite answer.[227]

All the recent BITs concluded by China also contain rules on indirect expropriation in the form of "other legal measures having similar effect,"[228] which is similar to the formulation in the NAFTA Agreement.[229] This, however, offers little help with regard to issues such as the question as to what specific measures may constitute indirect or creeping expropriation. As some commentators have pointed out, "in any case, the wording of the existing investment treaties has

---

issue, see Guiguo Wang, "Globalizing the Rule of Law," 48 *Indian J. Int'l L.*, 2008, pp. 21–44.

224 See, for example, Article 4 of the 2005 China–Portugal BIT, Article 4 of the 2005 China–Spain BIT and Article 4 of the 2004 China–Finland BIT.

225 2003 China–Germany BIT, Article 4(2).

226 2006 China–Russia BIT, Article 4(2); 2004 China–Finland BIT, Article 4(2); 2005 China–Spain BIT, Article 4(2); and 2005 China–Portugal BIT, Article 4(2).

227 The issue relating to compensation is what it should include. For instance, in addition to the investment made, it is questionable whether profits should be part of the market value and, if "yes," whether such profits should be ascertained after deduction of future cash flows or losses. In *CME*, Professor Brownlie obviously held a different view; see Brownlie's Separate Opinion in *CME Czech Republic B.V. v. Czech Republic*, *supra*, note 37.

228 See, for example, 2003 China–Germany BIT, Article 4(2); 2005 China–Portugal BIT, Article 4(1); and 2004 China–Finland BIT, Article 4(1).

229 Article 1100(1) of NAFTA provides that: "No Party may directly or indirectly nationalize or expropriate an investment of an investor of another Party in its territory or take a measure tantamount to nationalization or expropriation of such an investment ('expropriation')."

failed to address the indirect expropriation problem. On the contrary, it brings forward this question, and assumes that general international law can provide the answer."[230] The fact that the United States and Canada not long ago began to stipulate detailed rules in their BITs is seen as a response to such criticism and the situation that more and more disputes in international investment within the NAFTA framework were related to indirect expropriation.[231]

In the Protocol of the China–India BIT signed in 2006, the criteria for indirect expropriation were stipulated in detail, with a balanced emphasis on results and purposes as follows:

> (1) A measure of expropriation includes, apart from direct expropriation or nationalization through formal transfer of title or outright seizure, a measure or series of measures taken intentionally by a Party to create a situation whereby the investment of an investor may be rendered substantially unproductive and incapable of yielding a return without a formal transfer of title or outright seizure.
>
> (2) The determination of whether a measure or a series of measures of a Party in a specific situation, constitute measures as outlined in paragraph 1 above requires a case by case, fact based inquiry that considers, among other factors:
>
> > (i) the economic impact of the measure or a series of measures, although the fact that a measure or series of measures by a Party has an adverse effect on the economic value of an investment, standing alone, does not establish that expropriation or nationalization, has occurred;
> >
> > (ii) the extent to which the measures are discriminatory either in scope or in application with respect to a Party or an investor or an enterprise;
> >
> > (iii) the extent to which the measures or series of measures interfere with distinct, reasonable, investment-backed expectations;
> >
> > (iv) the character and intent of the measures or series of measures, whether they are for *bona fide* public interest purposes or not and whether there is a reasonable nexus between them and the intention to expropriate.
>
> (3) Except in rare circumstances, non-discriminatory regulatory measures adopted by a Contracting Party in pursuit of public interest, including measures pursuant to awards of general application rendered by judicial bodies, do not constitute indirect expropriation or nationalization.[232]

In practice, a measure may include a law, regulation, decree or final court judgment.[233] In particular, a so-called creeping expropriation may involve a variety of

---

230 Dolzer, *supra*, note 74, p. 79.

231 See, for example, *Metalclad Corporation v. Mexico, supra*, note 119; *S.D. Myers, Inc. v. Canada, supra*, note 133; *Pope & Talbot, Inc. v. Canada, supra*, note 135; and *Methanex v. United States, supra*, note 152.

232 Protocol to the Agreement between the Republic of India and the People's Republic of China on Promotion and Protection of Investments, Article III. Ad Article 5.

233 See *The Loewen Group, Inc. and Raymond L. Loewen v. United States of America*, ICSID Case No. ARB(AF)/98/3, Decision on Jurisdiction (January 5, 2001). The tribunal held (at para. 68) that

actions or omissions by the government as a whole. This was eloquently stated by the International Court of Justice in the *Fisheries Jurisdiction* case: "[I]n its ordinary sense the word [measure] is wide enough to cover any act, step or proceeding, and imposes no particular limit on their material content or on the aim pursued thereby."[234]

The importance of treaty provisions on expropriation and compensation is that the question as to what action or omission may constitute expropriation would, via a BIT, be decided by international arbitration tribunals in accordance with the Vienna Convention on the Law of Treaties[235] rather than the domestic law of the contracting parties.[236] It is precisely in this sense that the treaty provisions have taken the power of interpretation away from the national courts.

The FTAs of which China is a party also consistently take the position that expropriation must meet the following conditions.[237] They must be:

(a)   for a public purpose
(b)   in accordance with domestic laws
(c)   carried out in a non-discriminatory manner and
(d)   effected against payment of compensation.

At the same time, the China–New Zealand FTA provides that expropriation must not be contrary to any undertaking that the Party concerned has given.[238] It is noteworthy that in a trilateral agreement with South Korea and Japan entered into in 2012, in addition to public purpose, non-discrimination and compensation, a requirement that any expropriation must be carried out in accordance with "international standard of due process of law" has been made a condition.[239]

Like most other BITs, none of the Chinese BITs has defined the term "expropriation." In practice, when deciding what may constitute an "expropriation," arbitral tribunals sometimes take the following into account:

> the "rule of judicial finality (often described as 'substantive') was thought to be directed to the responsibility of the State for judicial acts." However, it also (at para. 52) distinguished judicial "affirmation of a general principle" from a specific order and deemed only the former to constitute a "measure."

234 *Fisheries Jurisdiction Case (Spain v. Canada)*, 1998 I.C.J. 432, Jurisdiction of the Court, Judgment of December 4, 1998, para. 65.
235 International practice, in particular the dispute resolution practice of the WTO, shows that tribunals are very much prepared to interpret treaties, bilateral or multilateral, according to the Vienna Convention on the Law of Treaties.
236 For standards of determining indirect expropriation, also see L. Yves Fortier and Stephen L. Drymer, "Indirect Expropriation in the Law of International Investment: I Know It When I See It, or Caveat Investors," 19 *ICSID Rev.*, 2004, pp. 293–327.
237 Whilst both of them have adopted the four conditions, Article 49 of the China–Pakistan FTA uses the terms "domestic legal procedure" and Article 145 of the China–New Zealand FTA chooses "applicable domestic law."
238 China–New Zealand FTA, Article 145.
239 Agreement Among the Government of the People's Republic of China, the Government of Republic of Korea and the Government of Japan for the Promotion, Facilitation and Protection of Investment (provisional translation), entered into on May 12, 2012, Article 11.

(a) There must be a taking by the host government or its agency of an investment by a covered investor, which may be either an action or an omission by the host State.[240] In most cases, omission alone may not constitute a measure tantamount to expropriation. The investment expropriated may be in the form of intangible or tangible property.[241]

(b) The taking must be substantial, in the sense that it has effectively deprived the investor of his economic use and enjoyment of the rights to the property or a distinctive part of such property, provided the taking is permanent in nature, which usually involves a transfer of ownership from the investor to another person.[242]

(c) The taking may be de jure or de facto and "direct" or "indirect,"[243] and may involve a single measure or a series of measures the totality of which has the effect of expropriation (often referred to as creeping expropriation).

(d) The taking is outside the ambit of the investor's reasonable "investment-backed-expectations."[244]

In conclusion, nationalization and expropriation by states has been recognized by customary international law as an exercise of sovereignty. As international investment is hotly sought by all states in this age of globalization and the awareness by the international community of human rights, including the property rights of foreign investors, is rapidly growing, large-scale and open nationalization is no longer a major risk to international investment. Instead, indirect and regulatory expropriation has become a major concern of the world. Although consensus on what may constitute an indirect expropriation is forming slowly in practice,

240 See *Draft Articles on Responsibility of States for Internationally Wrongful Acts*, adopted by the International Law Commission at its 53rd session (2001), Article 2; available at: http://legal.un.org/ilc/texts/instruments/english/draft%20articles/9_6_2001.pdf.

241 *Mondev International Ltd. v. United States*, ICSID Case No. ARB(AF)/99/2, Award (October 11, 2002), at 98, available at: http://italaw.com/documents/Mondev-Final.pdf; and also *Methanex v. United States*, *supra*, note 152, at 17.

242 According to the tribunal in the *Tippetts* case, "[a] deprivation or taking of property may occur under international law through interference by a state in the use of that property or the enjoyment of its benefits, even where legal title to that property is not affected;" see *Tippetts*, *supra*, note 108, at 225.

243 Whether a given measure is de jure or de facto expropriatory is insignificant in judging whether or not it constitutes an expropriation or taking of property. Indirect expropriation has also become a common concern of BITs. This is illustrated by Article 1110(1) of the NAFTA, which prescribes that "[n]o Party may directly or indirectly nationalize or expropriate ... or take a measure tantamount to nationalization or expropriation ..." In practice, an indirect expropriation is interpreted as a measure that is equivalent to an expropriation or has the effect of expropriation; see *Pope & Talbot*, *supra*, note 135, at 96 and 104; see also *S.D. Myers*, *supra*, note 133, at 285–86; *Marvin Roy Feldman Karpa v. United Mexican States*, ICSID Case No. ARB(AF)/99/1, Award (December 16, 2002), at 100, available at: http://www.italaw.com/sites/default/files/case-documents/ita0319.pdf.

244 The relevance of investors' expectations to expropriation is that in some businesses, government intervention is expected, in which case a foreign investor may not bring a legitimate complaint for expropriation as a result of an intervention/regulation by the host government.

there is a tendency to make nationalization and expropriation, direct or indirect, unlawful unless they are carried out in satisfaction of certain prerequisites—in particular with payment of compensation—as discussed above. Being a recent active participant as a capital exporter, China's practice in this regard is commensurate with the general trend of the world. Even though no consensus on such matters as determination of direct and indirect expropriation has been reached, insofar as jurisprudence is concerned, investment arbitration tribunals have, compared with other areas, made good progress in unifying the standards. This has obviously benefited from the fact that expropriation is not a new issue and that the international community has been trying hard to attain a shared understanding of the matter, which should be considered as a useful experience for resolving the embarrassment of contradictory decisions by arbitration tribunals in respect of other issues.

ANNEXES

Annex Table 1: Requirements for Nationalization in Multilateral Treaties and Normative Documents

Document Title	Recognition of the Right of Nationalization by a Sovereign State	References to International Law
Draft Havana Charter (1948)	Members have the right to make reasonable provisions as to the ownership of existing and future investment.	---
Universal Declaration of Human Rights (1948)	No one shall be deprived of his property.	---
ICC International Code of Fair Treatment for Foreign Investment (1949)	No expropriation except according to legal procedures and with compensation in accordance with international law. National laws enacting expropriation shall stipulate explicitly the purpose and conditions of expropriation.	Expropriation must be accompanied by fair compensation according to international law.
European Convention on Human Rights (1950)	No one shall be deprived of his possessions except in the public interest and subject to the conditions provided for by law and by the general principles of international law.	Expropriation shall be subject to the general principles of international law.
U.N.G.A. Res. 626 (VII): The Right to Exploit Freely Natural Wealth and Resources (1952)	States have the right freely to use and exploit their natural resources wherever deemed desirable by them for their own progress and economic development.	---
Convention for the Mutual Protection of Property (Köln) (1957)	No expropriation during a term of 30 years after the investment, except in a national emergency or for the public interest.	---

Document Title	Recognition of the Right of Nationalization by a Sovereign State	References to International Law
Abs/Shawcross Convention (1959)	No expropriation except under due process, non-discrimination, the respect of undertakings and compensation. No mention of the public interest.	---
Harvard Draft Convention on International Responsibility of States for Injuries to Aliens (1961)	Taking the property of an alien is wrongful if it is done not for a public purpose, if it is in violation of a treaty or is done without compensation.	---
U.N.G.A. Res. 1803 (XVII): Declaration on Permanent Sovereignty over Natural Resources (1962)	States have the right to nationalization on grounds of the public utility and the security or the national interest, which are recognized as overriding purely private interests.	Appropriate compensation in accordance with the national law of the State carrying out the expropriation and international law.
U.N.G.A. Res. 2158 (XXI): Permanent Sovereignty over Natural Resources (1966)	The right of all countries to secure and increase their share in the administration of enterprises operated by foreign capital and to have a greater share in the advantages and profits derived therefrom on an equitable basis is recognized.	---
OECD Draft Convention on the Protection of Foreign Property (1967)	No measures depriving the foreign national of his property, unless the measures are taken in the public interest, under due process, are not discriminatory and are accompanied by compensation.	---
Agreement on Investment and Free Movement of Arab Capital among Arab Countries (1970)	In case of nationalizations, Arab investors shall be entitled to fair and effective compensation within a reasonable period of time. (Original) No nationalization or expropriation of Arab investments in the sectors earmarked for the same. (1973 Amendment)	---
ICC Guidelines for International Investment (1972)	The government of the host country should respect the recognized principles of international law, in particular fair and equitable treatment, non-discrimination, observance of contractual undertakings and compensation for expropriation.	Respect for the recognized principles of international law.

Document Title	Recognition of the Right of Nationalization by a Sovereign State	References to International Law
U.N.G.A. Res. 3171 (XXVIII): Permanent Sovereignty over Natural Resources (1973)	The application of the principle of nationalization is an expression of a State's sovereignty in order to safeguard its natural resources.	---
U.N.G.A. Res. 3201(S-VI): Declaration on the Establishment of a New International Economic Order (1974)	In order to safeguard its natural resources, each State is entitled to exercise effective control over those resources, including the right to nationalization or transfer of ownership to its nationals.	---
U.N.G.A. Res. 3281(XXIX): Charter of Economic Rights and Duties of States (1974)	Each State has the right to nationalize, expropriate or transfer the ownership of foreign property.	---
Unified Agreement for the Investment of Arab Capital in the Arab States (1980)	Arab investment shall not be subject to expropriation or nationalization. A State shall, however, be permitted to expropriate properties for the public benefit, on a non-discriminatory basis and with the payment of fair compensation.	Conclusions and interpretations derived from the provisions of this Agreement shall be guided by the principles on which it is based and the aims which inspired it, followed by the rules and principles common to the respective legislation of the States members of the League of Arab States and, finally, by the principles recognized in international law.
Agreement for Promotion, Protection and Guarantee of Investments among the Member States of the Organization of the Islamic Conference (1981)	A host country shall not take any measure directly or indirectly affecting the ownership or actual control of the investor's capital. It is permissible to expropriate investments in the public interest in accordance with the law, without discrimination but with the payment of compensation.	---

Document Title	Recognition of the Right of Nationalization by a Sovereign State	References to International Law
ASEAN Agreement for the Promotion and Protection of investments (1987)	Investments of Contracting Parties shall not be subject to expropriation or nationalization except for public use, public purpose or in the public interest and under due process of law, on a non-discriminatory basis and with the payment of adequate compensation.	---
UNCTC Draft Code of Conduct (1990)	States have the right to nationalize or expropriate the assets of a transnational corporation operating in their territory.	In accordance with applicable rules and principles.
Energy Charter Treaty (1991)	Investments of foreign investors shall not be nationalized or expropriated except for a purpose in the public interest; on a non-discriminatory basis; carried out under due process of law; and accompanied by the payment of prompt, adequate and effective compensation.	---
World Bank Guidelines on Treatment of Foreign Direct Investment (1992)	A State may not expropriate a foreign private investment in its territory, except in accordance with applicable legal procedures, in pursuance in good faith of a public purpose, without discrimination on the basis of nationality and against the payment of appropriate compensation.	---
North American Free Trade Agreement (1994)	No Party shall directly or indirectly nationalize or expropriate an investment of an investor of another Party in its territory, except for a public purpose, on a non-discriminatory basis, in accordance with due process of law and upon payment of compensation.	In accordance with international law, including fair and equitable treatment and full protection and security.
Draft Multilateral Agreement on Investment (1998)	A Contracting Party shall not expropriate or nationalize directly or indirectly foreign investment, except for a purpose in the public interest, on a non-discriminatory basis, in accordance with due process of law, and accompanied by payment of prompt, adequate and effective compensation.	---
United States Model Bilateral Investment Treaty (2012)[1]	Neither Party may expropriate or nationalize a covered investment either directly or indirectly through measures equivalent to expropriation or nationalization ("expropriation"),	In accordance with customary international law, including fair and equitable treatment

Document Title	Recognition of the Right of Nationalization by a Sovereign State	References to International Law
	except for a public purpose; in a non-discriminatory manner; on payment of prompt, adequate, and effective compensation; and in accordance with due process of law.	and full protection and security.
China–ASEAN Investment Agreement (2009)	A Party shall not expropriate, nationalize or take other similar measures ("expropriation") against investments of investors of another Party except for a public purpose; in accordance with applicable domestic laws, including legal procedures; carried out in a non-discriminatory manner; and on payment of compensation. However, any expropriations of land may be carried out in accordance with existing domestic laws and regulations of the host State.	---

Source: Original to the author as derived from the texts of the listed treaties and normative documents.

Notes: [1] Although, since 2004, the US Government had not adopted a "model BIT" until 2012, the Office of the United States Trade Representative asserts that: "The United States negotiates BITs on the basis of a model text." It is reasonable, therefore, to conclude that the two most recent BITs concluded by the United States (with Uruguay in 2005 and Rwanda in 2008), which contain identical provisions on expropriation and compensation, reflect the most recent model.

Annex Table 2: Provisions relating to "Indirect Expropriation" in Multilateral Treaties and Normative Documents

Document Title	Provisions on Indirect Expropriation	Definitions, Explications or Official Commentary on Relevant Provisions
Abs/Shawcross Draft Convention on Investments Abroad (1959)	Article III: "No Party shall take any measures against nationals of another Party to deprive them directly or indirectly of their property except under due process of law and provided that such measures are not discriminatory or contrary to undertakings given by that Party and are accompanied by the payment of just and effective compensation …"	---

Document Title	Provisions on Indirect Expropriation	Definitions, Explications or Official Commentary on Relevant Provisions
Harvard Draft Convention on International Responsibility for Injuries to Aliens (1961)	Article 10(3)(a): "A 'taking of property' includes not only an outright taking of property but also any such unreasonable interference with the use, enjoyment, or disposal of property as to justify an inference that the owner thereof will not be able to use, enjoy, or dispose of the property within a reasonable period of time after the inception of such interference."	---
OECD Draft Convention on the Protection of Foreign Property (1967)	Article 3: "No Party shall take any measures depriving, directly or indirectly, of his property a national of another Party" unless the measures are taken in the public interest, under due process, are not discriminatory or contrary to any undertaking given by the Party, and are accompanied by provision for just compensation.	The Notes and Comments to Article 3 read, in relevant part: "3. Taking of Property (a) In the case of <u>direct</u> deprivation ('expropriation' or 'nationalisation') the loss of the property rights concerned is the <u>avowed</u> object of the measure. By using the phrase 'to deprive … directly or <u>indirectly</u> …' in the text of the Article it is, however, intended to bring within its compass <u>any</u> measures taken with the <u>intent</u> of wrongfully depriving the national concerned of the substance of his rights and <u>resulting</u> in such loss … (b) Article 3 deals with <u>deprivation</u> of property. … [I]nterference might amount to <u>indirect</u> deprivation. Whether it does, will depend on its extent and duration. Though it may purport to be temporary, there comes a stage at which there is no immediate prospect that the owner will be able to resume the enjoyment of his property. Thus, in particular, Article 3 is meant to cover 'creeping nationalisation', recently practiced by certain States. Under it, measures otherwise lawful are applied in such a way as to deprive ultimately the alien

Document Title	Provisions on Indirect Expropriation	Definitions, Explications or Official Commentary on Relevant Provisions
		of the enjoyment or value of his property, without any specific act being identifiable as outright deprivation. ... (c) The taking of property, within the meaning of the Article, must result in a <u>loss</u> of title or substance – otherwise a claim will not lie."
Unified Agreement for the Investment of Arab Capital in the Arab States (1980)	Article 9(1): "According to the provisions of this Agreement, the capital of the Arab investor shall not be subject to any specific or general measures, whether permanent or temporary and irrespective of their legal form, which wholly or partially affect any of the assets, reserves or revenues of the investor and which lead to confiscation, compulsory seizure, dispossession, nationalization, liquidation, dissolution, the extortion or elimination of secrets regarding technical ownership or other material rights, the forcible prevention or delay of debt settlement or any other measures leading to the sequestration, freezing or administration of assets, or any other action which infringes the right of ownership itself or prejudices the intrinsic authority of the owner in terms of his control and possession of the investment, his right to administer it, his acquisition of the revenues therefrom or the fulfilment of his rights and the discharge of his obligations." A State shall, however, be permitted to expropriate properties for the public benefit, on a non-discriminatory basis and with the payment of fair compensation.	---

Document Title	Provisions on Indirect Expropriation	Definitions, Explications or Official Commentary on Relevant Provisions
Agreement for Promotion, Protection and Guarantee of Investments among the Member States of the Organization of the Islamic Conference (1981)	Article 10(1): "The host state shall undertake not to adopt or permit the adoption of any measure … if such a measure may directly or indirectly affect the ownership of the investor's capital or investment by depriving him totally or partially of his ownership or of all or part of his basic rights or the exercise of his authority on the ownership, possession or utilization of his capital, or of his actual control over the investment, its management, making use out of it, enjoying its utilities, the realization of its benefits or guaranteeing its development and growth." It is permissible to expropriate investments in the public interest in accordance with the law, without discrimination and the prompt payment of adequate and effective compensation.	---
Convention Establishing the Multilateral Investment Guarantee Agency (1985)	Article 11(a)(ii): "*Expropriation and Similar Measures.* Any legislative action or administrative action or omission attributable to the host government which has the effect of depriving the holder of a guarantee of his ownership or control of, or a substantial benefit from, his investment, with the exception of nondiscriminatory measures of general application which governments normally take for the purpose of regulating economic activity in their territories …"	---
ASEAN Agreement for the Promotion and Protection of Investments (1987)	Article 6(1): "Investments of nationals or companies of any Contracting Party shall not be subject to expropriation, nationalisation or any measure equivalent thereto … except for public use, public purpose, or in the public interest and under due process of law, on a	---

Document Title	Provisions on Indirect Expropriation	Definitions, Explications or Official Commentary on Relevant Provisions
	non-discriminatory basis and with the payment of adequate compensation …"	
Energy Charter Treaty (1991)	Article 13(1): "Investments of Investors of a Contracting Party in the Area of any other Contracting Party shall not be nationalized, expropriated or subjected to a measure or measures having effect equivalent to nationalization or expropriation … except where such Expropriation is: (a) for a purpose which is in the public interest; (b) not discriminatory; (c) carried out under due process of law; and (d) accompanied by the payment of prompt, adequate and effective compensation …"	---
World Bank Guidelines on Treatment of Foreign Direct Investment (1992)	Article IV.1: "A State may not expropriate or otherwise take in whole or in part a foreign private investment in its territory, or take measures which have similar effects, except where this is done in accordance with applicable legal procedures, in pursuance in good faith of a public purpose, without discrimination on the basis of nationality and against the payment of appropriate compensation."	---
North American Free Trade Agreement (1994)	Article 1110 (1): "No Party may directly or indirectly nationalize or expropriate an investment of an investor of another Party in its territory or take a measure tantamount to nationalization or expropriation of such an investment ('expropriation'), except: (a) for a public purpose; (b) on a non-discriminatory basis; (c) in accordance with due process of law and Article 1105(1); and (d) on payment of compensation …"	Article 1110 (8): "For purposes of this Article and or greater certainty, a non-discriminatory measure of general application shall not be considered a measure tantamount to an expropriation of a debt security or loan covered by this Chapter solely on the ground that the measure imposes costs on the debtor that cause it to default on the debt."

Document Title	Provisions on Indirect Expropriation	Definitions, Explications or Official Commentary on Relevant Provisions
Draft Multilateral Agreement on Investment (1998)	Article IV.2.1: "A Contracting Party shall not expropriate or nationalise directly or indirectly an investment in its territory of an investor of another Contracting Party or take any measure or measures having equivalent effect (hereinafter referred to as 'expropriation') except: a) for a purpose which is in the public interest, b) on a non-discriminatory basis, c) in accordance with due process of law, and d) accompanied by payment of prompt, adequate and effective compensation …"	The official Commentary, in Paragraph IV.2.5 notes: "'Creeping expropriation' in general is covered by the words of Article 2: 'measures or measures having equivalent effect'."
United States Model Bilateral Investment Treaty (2012)[1]	Article 6(1): "Neither Party may expropriate or nationalize a covered investment either directly or indirectly through measures equivalent to expropriation or nationalization ('expropriation'), except: (a) for a public purpose; (b) in a non-discriminatory manner; (c) on payment of prompt, adequate, and effective compensation; and (d) in accordance with due process of law and Article 5 [Minimum Standard of Treatment](1) through (3)."	The footnote to Article 6 requires it to be read in conjunction with Annexes A and B. Article 2 of Annex B reads: "An action or a series of actions by a Party cannot constitute an expropriation unless it interferes with a tangible or intangible property right or property interest in an investment." Article 4 thereof clarifies "indirect expropriation" as follows: "…where an action or series of actions by a Party has an effect equivalent to direct expropriation without formal transfer of title or outright seizure. (a) The determination of whether an action or series of actions by a Party, in a specific fact situation, constitutes an indirect expropriation, requires a case-by-case, fact-based inquiry that considers, among other factors: (i) the economic impact of the government action, although the fact that an action or series of actions by a Party has an adverse effect on the economic

Document Title	Provisions on Indirect Expropriation	Definitions, Explications or Official Commentary on Relevant Provisions
		value of an investment, standing alone, does not establish that an indirect expropriation has occurred; (ii) the extent to which the government action interferes with distinct, reasonable investment-backed expectations; and (iii) the character of the government action. (b) Except in rare circumstances, non-discriminatory regulatory actions by a Party that are designed and applied to protect legitimate public welfare objectives, such as public health, safety, and the environment, do not constitute indirect expropriations."
Investment Agreement for the COMESA Common Investment Area (2007)	Article 20(1): "Member States shall not nationalize or expropriate investments in their territory or adopt any other measures tantamount to expropriation of investments except: (a) in the public interest; (b) on a non-discriminatory basis; (c) in accordance with due process of law; and (d) on payment of prompt adequate compensation."	Article 20(8): "Consistent with the right of states to regulate and the customary international law principles on police powers, bona fide regulatory measures taken by a Member State that are designed and applied to protect or enhance legitimate public welfare objectives, such as public health, safety and the environment, shall not constitute an indirect expropriation under this Article."
ASEAN Comprehensive Investment Agreement (2008)	Article 14(1): "A Member State shall not expropriate or nationalise a covered investment either directly or through measures equivalent to expropriation or nationalisation ("expropriation"), except: (a) for a public purpose; (b) in a non-discriminatory manner; (c) on payment of prompt, adequate, and effective compensation; and (d) in accordance with due process of law."	The footnote to Article 14 requires it to be read in conjunction with Annex 2. Article 1 thereof reads: "An action or a series of related actions by a Member State cannot constitute an expropriation unless it interferes with a tangible or intangible property right or property interest in a covered investment." Article 2(b) thereof defines measures equivalent to expropriation as "an action or series of related actions by a

Document Title	Provisions on Indirect Expropriation	Definitions, Explications or Official Commentary on Relevant Provisions
		Member State [that] has an effect equivalent to direct expropriation without formal transfer of title or outright seizure."
China–ASEAN Investment Agreement (2009)	Article 8(1): "A Party shall not expropriate, nationalise or take other similar measures ('expropriation') against investments of investors of another Party, unless the following conditions are met: (a) for a public purpose; (b) in accordance with applicable domestic laws, including legal procedures; (c) carried out in a non-discriminatory manner; and (d) on payment of compensation …"	---

Source: Original to the author as derived from the texts of the listed treaties and normative documents.

Notes:[1] Although, since 2004, the US Government had not adopted a "model BIT" until 2012, the Office of the United States Trade Representative asserts that: "The United States negotiates BITs on the basis of a model text." It is reasonable, therefore, to conclude that the two most recent BITs concluded by the United States (with Uruguay in 2005 and Rwanda in 2008), which contain identical provisions on expropriation and compensation, reflect the most recent model.

9 Compensation for violation of obligations

The principal objective of contemporary international investment law is to provide a normative framework for encouraging the smooth cross-border flow of capital and technology. To achieve this purpose, the normative framework must be mutually beneficial to both the recipient—the host state—and foreign investors. As the worldwide supply of capital is not unlimited, and with all countries competing for what is available, new-generation BITs, in order to attract foreign investment, competitively provide preferential treatment and guarantees to foreign investors, including minimum standards of treatment, fair and equitable treatment, and full protection and security, in addition to the traditional MFN and national treatment. In such circumstances, where a host state breaches its obligations under BITs and customary international law, it will be held liable for the damages caused to foreign investors and will be obligated to pay compensation. This chapter examines the treaty provisions and practices in respect of compensation for breaches of expropriation provisions and, in particular, for non-expropriatory breaches.

I. The basic issues regarding compensation for expropriation

Compensation for nationalization is probably one of the most controversial issues among scholars of international law and international economic law. Capital-exporting and capital-importing countries hold opposing views and, at the same time, no convincing theoretical basis has been established by scholars to address the issue. Taking account of their own interests, most of the capital-exporting countries[1] are in favor of "full and adequate" compensation, which refers to *damnum emergens* and *lucrum cessans* or the market value and predictable profit of the assets at the time of nationalization. In addition, in order to ensure that the owner of the assets can reinvest the compensation in other areas, the question arises whether the country concerned is obliged to convert the compensation into a freely convertible currency or, at least, to allow the investor to do so.

---

1 Although it is difficult to differentiate nowadays between capital-exporting and capital-importing countries, capital mainly flows from developed countries to developing ones. Therefore, the views of these two groups of countries regarding compensation for nationalization diverge considerably.

Regarding full and adequate compensation, it was US Secretary of State Cordell Hull who first proposed this as the standard of compensation, when he dealt with the issue of compensation for nationalization of US investments by Mexico in the early decades of the 20th century. Hull held that Mexico should pay "prompt, adequate and effective" compensation. This is the so-called Hull Formula, which has since been deemed by some to constitute a prerequisite for nationalization. Actually, it can be observed from US official documents that Hull did not deny the legality of the Mexican nationalizations, which in effect amounted to his acceptance of the legality of nationalization in the public interest. Neither did he deem compensation to be a prerequisite for the legality of nationalization, which constitutes a denial of the opposing viewpoint. Unfortunately, after Hull, most Western scholars have placed too much emphasis on his viewpoint of prompt, adequate and effective compensation while ignoring his theoretical contribution of recognizing the right to nationalization and not taking compensation as a prerequisite of lawful nationalization.[2]

Despite the significance of the standard of compensation for nationalization— or precisely because of its significance—the international community has not yet reached consensus in this regard. The fundamental difficulty lies in the extent of compensation. There is great discrepancy among governments, courts, and scholars of the developing and developed countries. Many works of scholars from Western developed countries have tried to clarify the liability for compensation for nationalization from a theoretical perspective.[3] Generally speaking, the issues in dispute mainly involve the principle of compensation, applicable standards, the extent of compensation, and how reasonably to evaluate the assets nationalized.

There are three basic theories on the standard of compensation for nationalization, that is, full compensation, partial compensation and no compensation.[4] Nowadays, as former colonies have already become independent and the wave of large-scale nationalizations has passed, the idea that the nationalizing country shall not undertake any obligation of compensation wins little support. However, it is still controversial whether it should pay full compensation, which is advocated by most of the developed countries. While some courts and arbitral tribunals have accepted the principle of "appropriate compensation" as expressed in UN General Assembly Resolution 1803, the United States and other countries continue to advocate that the nationalizing country should pay "prompt, adequate

---

2 For discussion of the early history of expropriation of the property of aliens and compensation, see Lee A. O'Connor, "The International Law of Expropriation of Foreign-owned Property: The Compensation Requirement and the Role of the Taking State," *Loy. L.A. Int'l & Comp. L.J.*, 1983, Vol. 6, pp. 355–425.

3 See Richard B. Lillich (ed.), *The Valuation of Nationalized Property in International Law*, Vols. I–III, The University Press of Virginia, Charlottesville, 1975.

4 Some commentators regard this division of views as the difference between South and North, noting, for example, that "the decisions of national courts and of academics have been divided according to the development status of the State from which the decision or writer comes;" see Patrick J. Smith, "Determining the Standard Compensation for the Expropriation of Nationalized Assets: Themes for the Future," *Monash University Law Review*, Vol. 23, No. 1, 1997, pp. 159–70, at 166.

and effective compensation." Before emergence of the new generation of BITs, this standard had almost no support from the developing countries. Even scholars from the United States itself were critical of it. Professor Schacter was a representative. He once said:

> Advocates of the Hull formula often characterize it as a traditional rule of international law. The record does not support this. No international juridical or arbitral tribunal, before or after 1938, has declared the "prompt, adequate and effective" payment formula to be generally accepted international law. The leading European scholars, De Visscher, Lauterpacht, Rousseau, have concluded that state practice does not support that standard. The Institute de droit reflected these views in a resolution adopted in 1950 and numerous studies in Europe and the United States have confirmed these conclusions with detailed evidence. I draw attention to the European and American studies to show that the opposition to treating the Hull formula as customary law does not come only from the "third world". Even in the United States where the executive and legislative branches have sought to affirm the Hull formula as accepted law, the courts, including the Supreme Court, have noted the disagreement among states and have declined to find the prompt, adequate and effective standard to be customary law. The restatement of Foreign Relations Law adopted in 1965 by the American Law Institute considered that the formula was qualified by "what is reasonable in the circumstances" and it noted that "less than full value" or "fair market value" was accepted in certain cases. The revised Restatement of 1987 does not consider the Hull formula as internationally accepted law.[5]

The rigid views expressed above, however, are losing support. In the age of globalization, it is difficult, if not dangerous, to assert what is "the view of the developing countries" and what is "the view of the developed countries," as there is no longer a clear division of capital-exporting and capital-importing countries, which by implication refers to developed and developing countries. There is, however, a clear distinction between expropriation in the context of decolonization, which is governed by customary international law, and expropriation within the context of treaties, both multilateral and bilateral. In the latter case, the expropriating state has specific international obligations to carry out expropriation in accordance with the applicable international instrument. Another distinction is that in the latter case there is a contractual relationship between the expropriating state and the foreign investor, whilst there is no such relationship between the parties in the former case.[6] In addition, there is a surging awareness of human rights—property

5 Oscar Schachter, *International Law in Theory and Practice: General Course in Public International Law*, in *Collected Courses of the Hague Academy of International Law*, Vol. 178, Martinus Nijhoff Publishers, Leiden, 1982, pp. 323–24.
6 For discussion of this issue, see A. C. Smutny, "Compensation for Expropriation in the Investment Treaty Context," *Transnational Dispute Management*, Vol. 3, Issue 3, June 2006, pp. 1–12, at 11.

rights being an essential part thereof—and protection of the same. Against this background, any expropriation carried out in the contemporary world must be accompanied by compensation. The remaining question is what principles should be applied for determining the value of the property expropriated.

II. Normative provisions of international instruments

Presently, the multilateral treaties and regional treaties stipulating the principles of nationalization and standards of compensation include the Energy Charter Treaty ("ECT"), the North American Free Trade Agreement ("NAFTA") and the ASEAN Comprehensive Investment Agreement, among others. Under the ECT, investments of investors of a contracting party in the territory of any other contracting party shall not be nationalized, expropriated or subjected to a measure or measures having effect equivalent to nationalization or expropriation except where such expropriation is: (a) for a purpose which is in the public interest; (b) not discriminatory; (c) carried out under due process of law; and (d) accompanied by the payment of prompt, adequate and effective compensation.[7] With regard to the calculation of compensation, it is further provided that "such compensation shall amount to the fair market value of the investment expropriated at the time immediately before the Expropriation or impending Expropriation became known in such a way as to affect the value of the investment …"[8] The nationalizing or expropriating contracting party is obliged to pay the compensation in a freely convertible currency and to pay interest. It is important that the time at which the impending expropriation became publicly known is clearly identified because, logically, once the market is aware of the expropriation or nationalization of certain assets, their market value will decrease. In addition, the ECT also includes detailed provisions regarding the right to appeal and judicial review. As will be discussed later, in case of indirect—creeping—expropriation, it may not be possible to determine when expropriation is publicly known. Consequently, the date for determining compensation may be at issue.

The relevant provisions in the NAFTA are basically consistent with those in the ECT. Apart from including the public interest, non-discrimination and compensation as the requisites for nationalization, the NAFTA further stipulates that nationalization or expropriation shall be in accordance with due process of law as well as international law concerning fair and equitable treatment and full protection and security to foreign investors.[9] Although the NAFTA does not use the wording of prompt, adequate and effective compensation, its provisions require "compensation equivalent to the full market value of the expropriated

---

7 Energy Charter Treaty (Annex 1 to the Final Act of the European Energy Charter Conference), done at Lisbon, Portugal (December 17, 1994), Article 13.1; available at: http://www.encharter. org/fileadmin/user_upload/document/EN.pdf.

8 Id.

9 North American Free Trade Agreement, Article 1110; available at: https://www. nafta-sec-alena.org/Default.aspx?tabid=97&ctl=SectionView&mid=1588&sid=539c5 0ef-51c1-489b-808b-9c20c9872d25&language=en-US#A1110.

investment immediately before the expropriation took place," that the compensation be "paid without delay and [be] fully realizable" and that interest be paid. In effect, these provisions have fully represented the Hull Formula as insisted upon by most developed countries, including the United States.

Although crafted by a multilateral organization made up almost exclusively of developing countries,[10] the ASEAN Comprehensive Investment Agreement, which was drawn up in 2008 and entered into force in early 2012, contains provisions on compensation for expropriation that are nearly identical to those of the ECT and the NAFTA. It establishes the prerequisites for expropriation as being for a public purpose; in a non-discriminatory manner; on payment of prompt, adequate, and effective compensation; and in accordance with due process of law.[11] In addition, such compensation is to be "be equivalent to the fair market value of the expropriated investment immediately before or at the time when the expropriation was publicly announced, or when the expropriation occurred, whichever is applicable" and such fair market value shall "not reflect any change in value because the intended expropriation had become known earlier." Furthermore, it must be paid without delay and be fully realizable and freely transferable.[12]

After reviewing hundreds of bilateral and multilateral treaties concluded between developed and developing countries, the World Bank laid out the most detailed provisions regarding compensation for nationalization among all of these in its Guidelines on the Treatment of Foreign Direct Investment. The Guidelines take due process, the public interest, non-discrimination and appropriate compensation as requisites of nationalization and expropriation. Appropriate compensation therein refers to prompt, adequate and effective compensation.[13] Furthermore, compensation will be deemed "adequate" if it is based on the fair market value of the asset expropriated as such value is determined immediately before the time at which the expropriation occurred or the decision to expropriate the asset became publicly known.[14]

Needless to say, a "fair market value" requires a market as well as someone who is willing to buy the assets concerned, which is not always the case in practice. Therefore, the Guidelines also stipulate that the determination of fair market value will be deemed acceptable if it is calculated on the basis of a method agreed upon by both the host country and the foreign investor or by a tribunal or another body designated by the parties. In the absence of such an agreement, determination of the value by the state involved will be deemed acceptable if it is made in accordance with reasonable criteria related to the market value of the investment.

10 The sole ASEAN member considered to be a developed country is Singapore.
11 See the ASEAN Comprehensive Investment Agreement, Article 14; available at: http://www.thaifta.com/thaifta/Portals/0/acia.pdf.
12 Id.
13 See World Bank Guidelines on the Treatment of Foreign investment, Guideline IV: "Expropriation and Unilateral Alterations or Termination of Contracts;" available at: http://italaw.com/documents/WorldBank.pdf.
14 Id.

Here, "market value" refers to the amount that a buyer would normally pay to a seller after taking into account the nature of the investment, the circumstances in which it would operate in the future and its specific characteristics.[15] Since the host country would take many factors into account when determining the criteria of compensation, and every single factor is directly related to its domestic situation, the discretionary power enjoyed by the host country is obviously considerable.

For determining the fair market value of nationalized or expropriated assets on a "reasonable basis," the Guidelines stipulate different methods to be used under different circumstances. First, for a "going concern" with a proven record of profitability, the value should be calculated on the basis of the discounted cash flow ("DCF") valuation method. Put simply, DCF valuation tries to determine the present value of an expropriated asset based on projections of how much money it would be likely to generate in the future. This normally involves calculating both the likely revenues and associated costs over a specified period (the "forecast period"), as well as a "terminal value" (the value of long-term cash flows after the forecast period). This method necessitates that the enterprise has a comparatively long record of profitability, which can be used as a reliable basis to predict its future profitability. Meanwhile, inflation, operating risks and other factors likely to affect the asset's performance must also be taken into account in determining the appropriate "discount rate" used to determine the present value of the total estimated cash flows. The DCF method's merits notwithstanding, it is considered to be very speculative for determining market value of an investment.[16]

Problems with the application of the DCF valuation method can arise in any of these areas. In *CME v. Czech Republic*,[17] for example, disagreement between the parties arose over the length of the forecast period, the reliability of the cash flow estimates, whether terminal value should be calculated as the end of CME's licensing period or "in perpetuity," the factors that should be considered in calculating the discount rate and the calculations themselves. In short, every factor that enters into the DCF valuation method became an element of contention, and the Tribunal bore the burden of determining each of these for itself and performing its own calculations. In several significant cases,[18] the Iran–United States Claims Tribunal found itself in a similar position and, in the words of Judge Aldrich, "made adjustments to the results of the DCF analysis [presented by the Parties]

---

15 Id.

16 For instance, Smutny commented that the DCF method "requires a lot of assessments about the future—and in some circumstances, those assessments can be difficult to make reliably. ... Where the factors needing to be assessed to use a discounted cash flow valuation are too difficult to discern reliably ... such a measure of valuation should not be used because it leads to a speculative measure." See Smutny, *supra*, note 6, at 5.

17 *CME Czech Republic B.V. (The Netherlands) v. Czech Republic*, UNCITRAL Arbitration Proceedings, Final Award, Stockholm (March 14, 2003); available at: italaw.com/documents/CME-2003-Final_001.pdf.

18 Notably, *Starrett Housing Corp. and Islamic Republic of Iran*, Final Award, 16 *C.T.R.* 112 (1987-III); and *Phillips Petroleum Co. Iran and Islamic Republic of Iran et al.*, Award 425-39-2, 21 *C.T.R.* 79 (1989-I).

and considered all relevant circumstances in reaching a final judgment as to the compensation to which the claimant was entitled."[19]

Second, for an enterprise which is not a proven going concern or which demonstrates a lack of profitability, the Guidelines prescribe that the fair market value should be the liquidation value. In business accounting and appraisal terminology, this term is generally understood to have at least two connotations, that is, the value in a forced liquidation and the value in an orderly liquidation. Obviously, the latter value is more likely to approximate a "fair market value." Because the Guidelines use "liquidation value" as a means of determining "fair market value," it is reasonable to assume that the standard they call for is the amount that might be realized from an assembled or piecemeal disposition of the assets in the second-hand market, assuming a reasonable period of time in which to complete the transaction.

Third, if only part, instead of all, of the enterprise's assets are nationalized or expropriated, the Guidelines state that fair market value shall be the replacement value. In this case, the book value of the assets concerned may also be used, if such value has been recently assessed or has been determined as of the date of the taking and can therefore be deemed to represent a reasonable replacement value. It is important to note that "replacement value" is not the same as "replacement cost." In the latter case, compensation would be equal to the actual cost at the time of the expropriation of acquiring a new, comparable asset. In calculating replacement value, however, the actual cost of a new, comparable asset at the time of the expropriation must be reduced by a "depreciation amount" based on the asset's condition, age and other relevant factors.

In addition, the Guidelines stipulate that regardless of the method employed, a host government, when paying compensation, may also deduct any outstanding taxes and/or fines for his/her illegal acts or debts payable by the foreign investor to the host government.

The Guidelines were drafted in the 1990s, when nationalization or expropriation on a large scale no longer constituted a major threat to international investment. The major concern of the international community at that time was how individual countries, especially the developing countries, could absorb foreign investment. Therefore, the Guidelines mainly deal with improving the investment environment of host countries. Consequently, it is understandable that they take the public interest, non-discrimination and appropriate compensation as prerequisites for nationalization or expropriation.

Since these Guidelines were drafted by the World Bank, which is an authoritative institution and which based them on its own summary of wide international practice, they do largely represent the contemporary trend of opinion within the international community regarding compensation for nationalization or expropriation, even though they lack binding force and thus cannot create any new legal norms. In this sense, at least to a certain degree, the Guidelines should be deemed

19 George H. Aldrich, *The Jurisprudence of the Iran-United States Claims Tribunal*, Clarendon Press, Oxford, UK and Oxford University Press, New York, 1996, p. 266.

to reflect the legal norms recognized by the international community regarding international investment, and they will have substantial impacts on domestic laws related to foreign investment as well as on the conclusion of bilateral or multilateral arrangements on investment.

The aborted Multilateral Agreement on Investment ("MAI") drafted by the OECD almost exactly copied the provisions regarding nationalization contained in the ECT. In addition, many bilateral treaties also include clear and detailed provisions with regard to compensation for nationalization and expropriation. One recent example is the China–ASEAN Investment Agreement,[20] which was concluded in 2009 as part of the Framework Agreement on Comprehensive Economic Cooperation between China and ASEAN and in which all of the participants (except Singapore) are developing countries. It is noteworthy that the relevant provisions of this Agreement are essentially consistent with those of the ECT, the NAFTA, the MAI, and the World Bank Guidelines. They provide that:

> A Party shall not expropriate, nationalise or take other similar measures ("expropriation") against investments of investors of another Party, unless the following conditions are met: (a) for a public purpose; (b) in accordance with applicable domestic laws, including legal procedures; (c) carried out in a non-discriminatory manner; and (d) on payment of compensation …[21]

Such compensation "shall amount to the fair market value of the expropriated investment at the time when expropriation was publicly announced or when expropriation occurred, whichever is earlier, and it shall be freely transferable in freely usable currencies …"[22] In addition, it must be "settled and paid without unreasonable delay" and "shall include interest at the prevailing commercial interest rate from the date of expropriation until the date of payment."[23]

While the Agreement notably avoids use of the term "due process of law," the phrase it does employ ("in accordance with applicable domestic laws, including legal procedures") recognizes the same principle while taking into consideration the disparate legal systems employed by its signatories. Although no reference is made to international law in the context of expropriation, the previous Article 7, entitled "Treatment of Investment," refers to the familiar standards of "fair and equitable treatment" and "full protection and security" while, moreover, giving those terms a more precise meaning (in Article 7.2.(a) and (b), respectively) than they are accorded in any similar agreement.

Similarly, although the Agreement did not use the term "prompt, adequate and effective compensation," its provisions give practical effect to that principle

---

20 See Agreement on Investment of the Framework Agreement on Comprehensive Economic Cooperation between the People's Republic of China and the Association of Southeast Asian Nations, done at Bangkok, Thailand (August 15, 2009), entered into force January 1, 2010; available at: http://fta.mofcom.gov.cn/inforimages/200908/20090817113007764.pdf.
21 Ibid., Article 8.1.
22 Ibid., Article 8.2.
23 Ibid., Article 8.3.

by requiring compensation "without unreasonable delay" (prompt), at "the fair market value" (adequate) and "freely transferable in freely usable currencies … [with] … interest" (effective).

The China–New Zealand Free Trade Agreement[24] adopted a similar approach. Like many other FTAs, the China–New Zealand FTA also contains a chapter on investment. Regarding compensation for expropriation, Article 145 stipulates:

> The compensation referred to above shall be equivalent to the fair market value of the expropriated investment immediately before the expropriation measures were taken. The fair market value shall not reflect any change in value due to the expropriation becoming publicly known earlier.

As a practical matter, the China–New Zealand FTA also adopted the Hull Formula. It provides that compensation "shall be paid without delay and shall be effectively realizable and freely transferable."[25]

In fact, fair market value for compensation for expropriation has become a treaty standard for China in recent years. In the 2012 Trilateral Agreement on Investment between China, Korea and Japan,[26] for instance, Article 11 provides that in case of expropriation, the "compensation shall be equivalent to the fair market value of the expropriated investments at the time when the expropriation was publicly announced" or occurred. It further requires compensation to be paid without delay, be effectively realizable and freely transferable and "be freely convertible, at the market exchange rate prevailing on the date of expropriation, into the currency of the Contracting Party of the investors concerned, and into freely usable currencies."[27]

Thus it is clear that through international treaty practices, which constitute the major source of international law and international economic law, fair market value has been accepted by more and more countries as the standard of compensation for expropriation. This is so for several reasons. In the first place, in this highly globalized world, foreign investment has become an inseparable and indispensable part of every economy and, as a consequence, countries compete for this scarce resource—capital. Second, in order to attract foreign investment, every country has to make a commitment not to conduct arbitrary nationalizations and must provide fair compensation for those that it may deem necessary. Third, contemporary foreign investment is different from that of the colonial era and is invited by the host country at its own initiative, while the latter was made unilaterally by the colonialists. The remaining issue is how in practice arbitration

24 The China–New Zealand Free Trade Agreement came into force on October 1, 2008; text available at: http://www.chinafta.govt.nz/1-The-agreement/2-Text-of-the-agreement/index.php.

25 Ibid., Article 145(2).

26 Agreement among the Government of China, Korea and Japan for the Promotion, Facilitation and Protection of Investment, entered into on May 13, 2012; available at: http://www.bilaterals.org/IMG/pdf/20120513001-3.pdf.

27 Ibid., Article 11.

tribunals and other bodies apply such norms, which is of the utmost importance for foreign investors as well as the host states.

III. International judicial and arbitral practice

The above-mentioned international legal documents show that it is generally accepted within the international community that a sovereign state has the right to nationalize or expropriate foreign assets within its jurisdiction. Most of the international treaties and international documents with normative effect have provided that nationalization or expropriation shall be conducted in the public interest and without discrimination. Even though it may be argued otherwise, it is quite generally accepted that a lawful expropriation must be for the public interest, non-discriminatory and with compensation.

As regards standards of compensation, in 1977, in the case of *Texaco v. Libya*, the sole Arbitrator, Professor René-Jean Dupuy, declared that "appropriate" compensation as proposed by UN General Assembly Resolution 1803 represented the principle of compensation for expropriation in contemporary customary international law.[28] He emphasized that UN General Assembly Resolution 1803 had been widely supported by both developing and developed countries.[29] In 1980, in *Banco Nacional de Cuba v. Chase Manhattan Bank*, the US Court of Appeals for the Second Circuit, by referring to related works on compensation for nationalization, ruled that: "[i]t may well be the consensus of nations that full compensation need not be paid 'in all circumstances', … and that requiring an expropriating state to pay 'appropriate compensation,' even considering the lack of precise definition of that term, would come closest to reflecting what international law requires."[30]

In 1982, the tribunal that dealt with the dispute between Kuwait and the American Independent Oil Company held in its award that the "appropriate compensation standard" in UN General Assembly Resolution 1803 had been generally recognized as reflecting law binding on all states.[31] It also stated that "the determination of the amount of an award of 'appropriate' compensation is better carried out by means of an enquiry into all the circumstances relevant to the particular concrete case, than through abstract theoretical discussion."[32] In reviewing the case, the tribunal placed much emphasis on the legitimate and reasonable expectations of both parties and confirmed that when entering into such a long-term contract, especially one that involves an important investment project, both parties must have fully considered their own economic interests and weighed up rights and obligations as well as chances and risks. Therefore, such an

---

28 See *Texaco Overseas Petroleum Company/California Asiatic Oil Co. v. Government of the Libyan Arab Republic*, Award of January 19, 1977, 17 *ILM* 1 (1978), at paras. 81–87.

29 Ibid., paras. 84 and 86.

30 See *Banco Nacional de Cuba v. Chase Manhattan Bank*, 658 F. 2d 875 (2nd Cir,. 1981), at 967, para. 88 (footnotes omitted); available at: http://openjurist.org/658/f2d/875/banco-nacional-de-cuba-v-chase-manhattan-bank.

31 See *American Independent Oil Company v. Kuwait*, 21 *ILM* 976 (1982), at 979.

32 Ibid., para. 144.

investment agreement should fully represent the considerations of both parties in the above-mentioned aspects. The standard of "prompt, adequate and effective compensation" was not addressed by the tribunal.

The series of awards made by the Iran–United States Claims Tribunal is particularly instructive as to international arbitral practice regarding compensation for nationalization or expropriation. The first case of nationalization dealt with by the Tribunal was *American International Group, Inc. v. Iran.*[33] The claimant, an insurance company, claimed compensation for all its losses, including the book value of related assets and prospective profits, which meant that the valuation of the nationalized assets should be based on its existence as a going concern. Iran, however, insisted that the value of the assets should be based solely on their book value. The Tribunal rejected the Iranian view and ruled that the losses suffered by the claimant should be calculated according to the market value of the assets concerned but that the possible influence of the changed circumstances after the nationalization in Iran should also be taken into account. Needless to say, the loss of profits could not be very high by using this method. However, the Tribunal also maintained the position that the losses should be determined according to their market value. Judge Mosk, who entered a separate concurring opinion in the case, however, considered that the award was a compromise. The compensation awarded by the Tribunal was around one-fourth of the amount claimed by the claimant.[34] It is noteworthy that the award was based on customary international law instead of on the Treaty of Amity between Iran and the United States.

The Tribunal held that the criterion for compensation should be market value, regardless of the legality of the nationalization. It is not clear why the Tribunal did not adopt Iran's book value assertion nor on what basis the compromise, as maintained by Judge Mosk, was reached, although certainly the effect of not using the book value method avoided unjust enrichment of Iran. After all, where an enterprise has operated successfully for a number of years, it can hardly be said that its value is limited to what is on the account books. In this regard, the Tribunal's ruling would seem to be based on good reasons, notwithstanding that it did not set out any grounds to support its position under customary international law. Elsewhere, the Iran–United States Claims Tribunal held that compensation for legal nationalization should not include prospective profits.[35]

INA Corporation v. Iran was also a case involving the nationalization of an insurance company.[36] The Tribunal understood this case as being typical of a situation in which the host country legally carried out a systematic expropriation of an

---

33 *American International Group, Inc. et al. v. Islamic Republic of Iran et al.*, Award No. 93-2-3 (December 19, 1983), reprinted in 4 *Iran–U.S.C.T.R.* 96.

34 Of course, the proportion of the amount of compensation in an arbitral award to that claimed by the claimant cannot fully reflect whether or not any arbitral Tribunal has adopted the standard of full compensation because, in general, claimants will request the highest possible compensation.

35 See, for example, *Amoco Iran Oil Co. v. Islamic Republic of Iran et al.*, Interlocutory Award No. ITL 12-55-2 (December 30, 1982), reprinted in 1 *Iran–U.S.C.T.R.* 493.

36 *INA Corporation v. Government of the Islamic Republic of Iran*, Award No. 184-161-1 (August 13, 1985), reprinted in 8 *Iran–U.S.C.T.R.* 373.

entire industry that it deemed crucial for its economic development. According to the Tribunal, the relevant law governing nationalizations of this kind had changed hugely by the time of its award. It stated:

> In the event of such large-scale nationalizations of a lawful character, international law has undergone a gradual reappraisal, the effect of which may be to undermine the doctrinal value of any "full" or "adequate" (when used as identical to the "full") compensation standard as proposed in this case.
>
> However, the Tribunal is of the opinion that in a case such as the present, involving an investment of a rather small amount shortly before the nationalization, international law admits compensation in an amount equal to the fair market value of the investment.[37]

The *INA* award employed a somewhat special approach in referring to both the size of the investment and the length of the company's operating period before the nationalization as a factor to determine which standard of compensation should be applied.[38] It is at least controversial whether the scale of the company concerned should affect the standard of compensation, and the length of the operating period before nationalization should only be used as a reference to calculate prospective profits. It is submitted that regardless of the size of the company, where an enterprise is expropriated—that is, its property has been taken away—the applicable standard for compensation should be the same.

A frequently significant issue is whether legal nationalization allows any right to compensation for prospective profits or *lucrum cessans*. The *INA* Tribunal considered that there was a "'*lex specialis*', in the form of the Treaty of Amity, which in principle prevails over general rules."[39] Therefore, there was no need to differentiate, in the *INA* case, among businesses with different lengths of operation. Actually, since the Tribunal based its determination of compensation on the Iran–United States Treaty of Amity (*lex specialis*) rather than on customary international law, its application of general international norms (*lex generalis*) in respect of compensation for expropriation is rendered somewhat less relevant.

In his separate opinion in the *INA* case, Judge Lagergren indicated that Sir Hersch Lauterpacht had suggested in *Oppenheim's International Law* (1955), which the latter had edited, that partial compensation for the nationalization of alien property is probably enough if the nationalization was conducted for the long-term economic development objectives of the nationalizing country. Judge Lagergren held that the standard of compensation applied by UN General Assembly Resolution 1803 (XVII) (the Declaration on Permanent Sovereignty over Natural Resources) was "capacity restoration," and that:

> … an application of current principles of international law, as encapsulated in the "appropriate compensation" formula, would in a case of lawful large-scale nationalizations in a state undergoing a process of radical economic

37　Ibid., p. 378.
38　See ibid.
39　Ibid.

restructuring normally require the "fair market value" standard to be discounted in taking account of "all circumstances". However, such discounting may, of course, never be such as to bring the compensation below a point which would lead to "unjust enrichment" of the expropriating state. It might also be added that the discounting often will be greater in a situation where the investor has enjoyed the profits of his capital outlay over a long period of time, but less, or none, in the case of a recent investor, such as INA.[40]

It should be noted that even though Judge Lagergren was in favor of the standard set by UN General Assembly Resolution 1803 (XVII), he put forward a proviso that no matter how fair market value might be discounted, there should be no unjust enrichment of the expropriating state—a principle that should be supported. The practice further shows that some regional international courts and domestic courts are in favor of the view that when a state has nationalized private assets for the sake of economic development it may not pay full or adequate compensation. In the *James* case, the European Court of Human Rights ("ECHR") stated:

> Clearly, compensation terms are material to the assessment whether the contested legislation respects a fair balance between the various interests at stake and, notably, whether it does not impose a disproportionate burden on the applicants. The Court further accepts the Commission's conclusion as to the standard of compensation: the taking of property without payment of an amount reasonably related to its value would normally constitute a disproportionate interference which could not be considered justifiable under Article 1 (P1-1). Article 1 (P1-1) does not, however, guarantee a right to full compensation in all circumstances. Legitimate objectives of 'public interest', such as pursued in measures of economic reform or measures designed to achieve greater social justice, may call for less than reimbursement of the full market value. Furthermore, the Court's power of review is limited to ascertaining whether the choice of compensation terms falls outside the State's wide margin of appreciation in this domain.[41]

Decisions of the ECHR are often referred to in investment arbitration, in particular with regard to compensation. It is submitted that where legislation dealing with matters of wide social issues has adverse effects on foreign investors, a higher standard of proportionality should be applied to foreign investors than to nationals. The reason is that nationals, as permanent residents of the country should be able to benefit, at least in theory, from such social reforms, etc., whilst foreign investors may not remain in the country permanently and therefore cannot be assumed to be able to enjoy the results of such social reforms like the nationals do. In another case—*Lithgow*—the ECHR took the position that:

40 Ibid., p. 390.
41 See *James et al. v. United Kingdom*, Application No. 8793/79, European Court of Human Rights, Judgment of February 21, 1986, para. 54 (citations omitted); available at: http://www.human-rights.is/the-human-rights-project/humanrightscasesandmaterials/cases/regionalcases/europeancourtofhumanrights/nr/534.

A decision to enact nationalization legislation will commonly involve consideration of various issues on which opinions within a democratic society may reasonably differ widely. Because of their direct knowledge of their society and its needs and resources, the national authorities are in principle better placed than the international judge to appreciate what measures are appropriate in this area and consequently the margin of appreciation available to them should be a wide one. It would, in the Court's view, be artificial in this respect to divorce the decision as to the compensation terms from the actual decision to nationalize, since the factors influencing the latter will of necessity also influence the former. Accordingly, the Court's power of review in the present case is limited to ascertaining whether the decisions regarding compensation fell outside the United Kingdom's wide margin of appreciation; it will respect the legislature's judgment in this connection unless that judgment was manifestly without reasonable foundation.[42]

The ECHR's decision in *Lithgow* exhibited its tradition of deference toward national authorities. Apparently, the Court made democratically elected government a prerequisite for its deference. It then follows that in practice the legislature's action is less subjective to review by the Court than administrative decisions.[43] The basis for respecting decisions of the national authorities is that such authorities have "direct knowledge of their society and its needs and resources." Whilst this approach may also apply to determination of compensation in the context of the *Lithgow* case, it may not be applicable in case of expropriation—direct or indirect—under BITs and other international instruments because in such circumstances the expropriating state has international obligations to observe.

Insofar as international judicial practice regarding compensation for unlawful nationalization is concerned, the most frequently quoted case that has been considered as an authority on compensation for both illegal expropriation and internationally wrongful non-expropriation breaches is the *Chorzów Factory* case.[44] First, it should be pointed out that according to the judgment issued by the PCIJ in the earlier *Case Concerning Certain German Interests in Polish Upper Silesia* in 1926,[45] the nationalization of the Chorzów factory was illegal.

After the judgment of 1926, Poland and Germany conducted negotiations in regard to the status of the Chorzów factory. Because the negotiations failed, Germany initiated another proceeding on indemnity. In the documents submitted by Germany to the PCIJ, there was a list of indemnity claims, but loss of profits was not included. In fact, even the claims related to the loss suffered as a

---

42 *Lithgow v. United Kingdom*, 8 EHRR 329 (1986), at 373.

43 For discussion of this issue, see Caroline Henckels, "Indirect Expropriation and the Right to Regulate: Revisiting Proportionality Analysis and the Standard of Review in Investor–State Arbitration," *Journal of International Economic Law*, 2012, Vol. 15, No. 1, pp. 223–55.

44 *Case Concerning the Factory at Chorzów*, PCIJ Reports, Vol. A (1928), No. 17.

45 *Case Concerning Certain German Interests in Polish Upper Silesia (Merits)*, Judgment No. 7 (May 25, 1926), *Collection of Judgments, Publications of the Permanent Court of International Justice*, A.W. Sijthoff, Leyden, 1926; available at: http://www.icj-cij.org/pcij/serie_A/A_07/17_Interets_allemands_en_Haute_Silesie_polonaise_Fond_Arret.pdf.

result of Poland's prohibitions on exportation of the factory's products to some countries were rejected by the Court. In its judgment on indemnity, made in 1928, it stated:

> The action of Poland which the Court has judged to be contrary to the Geneva Convention is not an expropriation – to render which lawful only the payment of fair compensation would have been wanting; it is a seizure of property, rights and interests which could not be expropriated even against compensation … It follows that the compensation due to the German Government is not necessarily limited to the value of the undertaking at the moment of dispossession, plus interest to the day of payment. This limitation would only be admissible if the Polish Government had had the right to expropriate, and if its wrongful act consisted merely in not having paid to the two Companies the just price of what was expropriated; in the present case, such a limitation might result in placing Germany and the interests protected by the Geneva Convention, on behalf of which interests the German Government is acting, in a situation more unfavorable than that in which Germany and these interests would have been if Poland had respected the said Convention.[46]

Regarding unlawful expropriation, the PCIJ stated in that case that "it is a principle of international law, and even a general conception of law, that any breach of an engagement involves an obligation to make reparation."[47] As will be discussed later, this principle announced by the PCIJ has been favorably regarded by investment tribunals in their decisions regarding compensation for breach of obligations other than that relating to expropriation. Also based on the above principle, if restitution in kind is impossible, the compensation paid shall be equal to the value that restitution in kind would bear. In addition, if the injured party has sustained losses which would not be covered by restitution in kind or compensation in place of that, damages must be paid. This is the principle of compensation for internationally illegal acts.

In more recent practice, tribunals have frequently referred to the decision of the PCIJ as the "Chorzów principle" whenever they have found it necessary to compensate a claimant for damages suffered as the result of unlawful acts of a state. A rather remarkable application of this principle was that of the ICSID tribunal in *AMCO Asia v. Indonesia*.[48]

This case concerned the construction and subsequent management of a hotel in Jakarta, Indonesia. An Indonesian company began construction of a hotel in 1964 but stopped in 1965 due to a lack of funds. By order of the Indonesian Government, the company was reorganized under the new name of P.T. Wisma

---

46 *Case Concerning the Factory at Chorzów, supra*, note 44, paras. 123 and 124.
47 Ibid., para. 73.
48 *AMCO Asia Corp. et al. v. Indonesia*, ICSID Case No. ARB/81/1; Award on the Merits (November 21, 1984), 24 *ILM* 1022 (1985) (excerpts); *Ad hoc* Committee Decision on the Application for Annulment (May 16, 1986), 25 *ILM* 1439 (1986); and Award of June 5, 1990 and Decision on Supplemental Decisions and Rectification of October 17, 1990, 5 *Int'l Arb. Rep.* 11, at Sec. D (November 1990).

and placed under the control of a cooperative established under Indonesian law for the welfare of active and retired Indonesian Army personnel. In 1968, P.T. Wisma found a US investor, AMCO, to complete the construction of the hotel and undertake its management for a limited period of time. AMCO was successful in obtaining an investment license from the Indonesian Government to perform the profit-sharing agreement and formed, as required, an Indonesian company, P.T. AMCO, to do so. The hotel construction was completed substantially as planned, but a dispute arose over AMCO's performance of the management portion of the Agreement.

Because P.T. AMCO and P.T. Wisma could not resolve the dispute, P.T. Wisma sought to discontinue AMCO's involvement in the arrangement in 1980 and, according to testimony in the case, enlisted forces of the Indonesian military to take over control and ownership of the hotel from the US company and persuaded the Indonesian Foreign Investment Board to revoke P.T. AMCO's investment license. Both actions were then approved by an Indonesian court in an action brought by P.T. Wisma, and the Court's decision was finally affirmed by the Indonesian Appellate Court.

AMCO then filed for ICSID arbitration against the Indonesian Government, claiming expropriation, breach of contract and unjust enrichment. The tribunal found that there had been no expropriation or taking.[49] It did conclude, however, that the takeover of the hotel by Indonesian police and military forces constituted an "internationally wrongful act"[50] and that "the revocation [of the investment license] was unlawful in respect of the procedure that resulted in it."[51] The tribunal, referring to Indonesian law, other municipal codes of law, the Chorzów principle and other arbitral awards, ruled that "the full compensation of prejudice, by awarding to the injured party the *damnum emergens* and *lucrum cessans* is a principle common to the main systems of municipal law, and therefore, a general principal of law which may be considered as a source of international law"[52] and consequently awarded "in the present case, damages calculated to fully compensate the prejudice suffered by the Claimants."[53]

Indonesia started procedures to annul the award and, because the annulment Committee found that the tribunal had failed to state the reasons for its findings on several substantive issues, it was duly annulled. The annulment, however, applied to the award, not to the tribunal's finding that the takeover of the hotel by the Indonesian army and police was an internationally wrongful act. Consequently, when AMCO resubmitted the case to ICSID in 1987, the second tribunal found that it was *res judicata* that Indonesia had an obligation to compensate AMCO for damages caused by the unlawful intervention of the army and police[54] and by the failure to provide due process in the procedures leading to revocation of AMCO's

---

49 *AMCO Asia v. Indonesia*, Award on the Merits, ibid., para. 163.
50 Ibid., para. 172.
51 Ibid., para. 203.
52 Ibid., paras. 266–67.
53 Ibid., para. 268.
54 *AMCO Asia v. Indonesia*, Award of June 5, 1990, *supra*, note 48, para. 75.

investment license.[55] Once again, in determining the standard of compensation for these damages, the second tribunal referred to the *Chorzów Factory* case and others in reaching the conclusion that the measure of compensation ought to be such as to approximate as closely as possible in monetary terms to the principle of *restitutio in integrum*.[56]

AMCO Asia v. Indonesia was different from most of the investment arbitration cases today. There was no BIT involved in the case. As a result, the tribunal applied, in addition to Indonesian law, the "international law principle pacta sunt servanda and the doctrine of respect for acquired rights." Naturally, even though expropriation was determined not to exist, the Chorzów principle was nonetheless relied upon to establish the standard of compensation for damages caused an investor by unlawful acts of the host state—Indonesia.[57] In a way, the ruling of *AMCO* Tribunal has the effect of confirming the Chorzów principle as part of customary international law. Subsequent adoption of the Chorzów principle by later investment arbitration tribunals exhibits that there exists a standard in customary international law for full reparation—*damnum emergens* and *lucrum cessans*—for internationally wrongful acts, including unlawful expropriation.

In both *Biloune et al. v. Ghana*[58] and *CME v. Czech Republic*,[59] the tribunals found that expropriations had occurred but did not expressly indicate whether they were legal or illegal. In *Biloune*, the tribunal found that the expropriation was contrary to the terms of an agreement to which both the claimant and the respondent were parties. It ruled that:

> The standard for compensation in cases of expropriation is restoration of the claimant to the position he would have enjoyed but for the expropriation. This principle of customary international law is stated in many recent awards of international arbitral tribunals. … This standard is also reflected in hundreds of bilateral investment treaties. The respondents in this case have not challenged this principle, and indeed have explicitly "recognize[d] that there exists a generally accepted principle of international law that prompt, adequate and effective compensation be paid in case of expropriation."[60]

---

55 Ibid., para. 70.
56 Ibid., paras. 183–85.
57 A nearly identical position was taken by the tribunal in *MTD Equity Sdn. Bhd. and MTD Chile S.A. v. Chile*, ICSID Case No. ARB/01/7, Award (May 25, 2004), when it ruled that "[t]he issue in this case is not of expropriation but unfair treatment by the State" (para. 214) and determined the compensation due the Claimants on the basis of the Chorzów principle (para. 238).
58 *Biloune and Marine Drive Complex Ltd. v. Ghana Investments Centre and the Government of Ghana*, Ad hoc Tribunal under UNCITRAL Rules, Award on Damages and Costs (June 30, 1990), 95 I.L.R. 183, at 209–10.
59 *CME Czech Republic B.V. (The Netherlands) v. Czech Republic*, UNCITRAL Partial Award (Merits) (September 13, 2001), para. 591; available at: http://italaw.com/documents/CME-2001PartialAward.pdf. It should be noted that, in a parallel case, carried out in London, also under UNCITRAL Rules, the tribunal held that no expropriation had occurred; see *Ronald S Lauder v. Czech Republic*, UNCITRAL Final Award (September 3, 2001); available at: http://www.italaw.com/sites/default/files/case-documents/ita0451.pdf.
60 *Biloune et al. v. Ghana*, *supra*, note 58, p. 211.

In *CME v. Czech Republic*,[61] the claimant alleged that the host state—in the person of the Czech Republic's Media Council—had breached its obligations by having destroyed the value of its investment in a television broadcasting license and operation. The Stockholm Tribunal found that expropriation had occurred as the result of "unlawful acts" attributable to the host state and held that "[a] fortiori unlawful measures of deprivation must be remedied by just compensation."[62] It relied upon the *Chorzów* dictum of reparation in ruling that "the Respondent is obligated to compensate the Claimant by payment of a sum corresponding to the value which a restitution in kind would bear."[63]

Occidental v. Ecuador[64] is also a recent case that involved both expropriatory and non-expropriatory breaches. In that case, the claimants were awarded an amount of US$1,769,625,000 for damages suffered—apparently the highest-ever amount in ICSID history. As will be discussed later, having found that the termination measure—the *Caducidad* Decree—was not a proportionate response to the claimant's breaches of contract, the tribunal then stated that it had "no hesitation in finding that, in the particular circumstances ... the taking by the Respondent of the Claimants' investment by means of this administrative sanction [*Caducidad* Decree] was a measure 'tantamount to expropriation'."[65] In reaching its decision, the *Occidental* Tribunal relied on the decision in *Metalclad v. Mexico*[66] that:

> Thus, expropriation under NAFTA includes not only open, deliberate and acknowledged takings of property, such as outright seizure or formal or obligatory transfer of title in favour of the host State, but also covert or incidental interference with the use of property which has the effect of depriving the owner, in whole or in significant part, of the use or reasonably-to-be-expected economic benefit of property even if not necessarily to the obvious benefit of the host State.[67]

With regard to compensation under the BIT, that is, the "full market value" of the investment, the *Occidental* Tribunal adopted the definition proposed by one of the expert witnesses as follows:

> Measurement of fair market value in a context such as at hand here properly entails consideration of *market* outcomes. Specifically, the fair market value today of a stream of net revenues (i.e., gross revenues minus attendant costs) that can be earned from operation of a multi-year project such as OEPC's development of Block 15 entails assessment of the amount that a willing

---

61 *CME v. Czech Republic*, UNCITRAL Partial Award (September 13, 2001), *supra*, note 59.
62 Ibid., para. 615.
63 Ibid., paras. 616–18.
64 *Occidental Petroleum Corporation and Occidental Exploration and Production Company v. Republic of Ecuador*, ICSID Case No. ARB/06/11, Award (October 5, 2012).
65 Ibid., para. 455.
66 *Metalclad Corporation v. United Mexican States*, ICSID Case No. ARB(AF)/97/1, Award (August 30, 2000).
67 Ibid., para. 103.

buyer would reasonably be expected to have to pay a willing seller to induce the seller to give up its rights to those net revenues. Here, Occidental is in the position of a seller in the sense that we seek measurement of the amount Occidental would reasonably have been willing to accept to be voluntarily bought out of the instant contract and associated income-generating opportunities, as opposed to having had that contract and those opportunities involuntarily terminated by Ecuador.[68]

The above cases demonstrate that in modern investment arbitration, the lawfulness or unlawfulness of expropriation is no longer the crucial issue, as each one of them involved breaches by the respondent state of either a contract—in *Biloune et al. v. Ghana*—or a BIT—in the other two cases. As the tribunals in each case found that the respondents had breached their contractual or treaty obligations, the respondents were held liable for the losses suffered by the claimants. In these circumstances, the unlawfulness of the acts was not determinative of the amount to be paid as compensation. In this regard, the *Biloune* Tribunal relied on customary international law to secure support for its decision. The *CME* Tribunal, although the claimant in the case contended that the respondent had breached the Netherlands–Czech BIT, also referred to the *Chorzów* dictum. The *Occidental* Tribunal's analysis indicated that compensation should include *damnum emergens* and *lucrum cessans*, again a reflection of the *Chorzów* dictum.

These cases, although very selective, clearly show a trend in arbitral practice regarding compensation for expropriation, that is, that whether under customary international law or in accordance with BITs or even national law, fair market value has been recognized as the standard to restitute losses suffered by foreign investors. This is easily understandable, because most modern BITs and multilateral agreements stipulate fair market value as the standard of compensation for expropriation. At the same time, where a foreign investor has not entered as a colonialist but has been invited to invest in a country which later on expropriates—directly or indirectly—its property, naturally the foreign investor should not suffer a loss by being paid a compensation less than the fair market value of his investment. If he does, others may be deterred from investing in that country. The combination of treaty and judicial practices in establishing fair market value as the compensation standard has also had an impact on the determination of compensation for non-expropriatory breaches.

IV. The power of tribunals in cases of non-expropriatory breaches

Modern BITs and FTAs all contain provisions in respect of minimum standards, fair and equitable treatment and full protection and security. Some also have a so-called umbrella clause. Unlike in the case of expropriation and nationalization, BITs and FTAs in general do not provide explicitly the forms and standards

---

68 *Occidental v. Ecuador*, Award, *supra*, note 64, para. 707.

of compensation in cases where breaches of the above provisions take place. In practice, as discussed earlier, many investment tribunals regard the decision of the PCIJ in the *Chorzów Factory* case as a statement of international law principles relating to compensation for wrongful acts. In that case, the PCIJ ruled:

> The essential principle contained in the actual notion of an illegal act—a principle which seems to be established by international practice and in particular by the decisions of arbitral tribunals—is that reparation must, as far as possible, wipe out all the consequence of the illegal act and reestablish the situation which would, in all probability, have existed if that act had not been committed. Restitution in kind or, if this is not possible, payment of a sum corresponding to the value which a restitution in kind would bear; the award, if need be, of damages for loss sustained which would not be covered by restitution in kind or payment in place of it—such are the principles which should serve to determine the amount of compensation for an act contrary to international law.[69]

The significance of the pronouncement by the PCIJ in the *Chorzów Factory* case is that it has established the principle of compensation. It has not, however, settled nor could it have been able to settle such issues as (1) in the absence of treaty provisions, whether tribunals have the discretion to choose a method of compensation or (2) what categories of compensation may be awarded, just to name a few. Such issues are thus left to arbitral tribunals to decide in practice.

In *S.D. Myers v. Canada*,[70] the tribunal stated that the ILC Articles on Responsibilities of States for Internationally Wrongful Acts, which were under consideration at that time, referred to the *Chorzów Factory* case and that the parties to the dispute did not argue against applying the principle derived from that case.[71] Therefore, the tribunal adopted the Chorzów *dictum* as a guiding principle of customary international law.

The *S.D. Myers* Tribunal also considered the NAFTA provisions on compensation concerning expropriation (fair market value) as guiding principles. The difficulty in applying these principles is that they only relate to lawful expropriation, whilst other breaches are unlawful acts on the part of host states. Having apparently realized this difficulty, the tribunal concluded:

> By not identifying any particular methodology for the assessment of compensation in cases not involving expropriation, the Tribunal considers that the drafters of the NAFTA intended to leave it open to tribunals to determine a measure of compensation appropriate to the specific circumstances of the case, taking into account the principles of both international law and the provisions of the NAFTA. In some non-expropriation cases a tribunal might

69 *Case Concerning the Factory at Chorzów, supra*, note 44, p. 47.
70 *S.D. Myers, Inc. v. Government of Canada*, an Arbitration under the UNCITRAL Arbitration Rules, First Partial Award (November 13, 2000); available at: http://www.naftaclaims.com/Disputes/Canada/SDMyers/SDMyersMeritsAward.pdf.
71 Ibid., paras. 312–13.

think it appropriate to adopt the "fair market value" standard; in other cases it might not.[72]

The tribunal's conclusion was based on Article 1131 of the NAFTA, which authorizes tribunals dealing with investment disputes to decide "*in accordance with [the NAFTA] and applicable international law*," and Article 1135 of the NAFTA, which authorizes tribunals "to award only … *monetary damages and any applicable interest or restitution of property*."[73] Presumably, in the view of the *S.D. Myers* Tribunal, "applicable international law" should include customary international law concerning compensation, namely, the *Chorzów* dictum, according to which fair market value could be considered as the standard of compensation for expropriation.

The tribunal should at least have explained why it considered that the fair market value standard should be adopted for non-expropriatory breaches. Its statement that the tribunal should have the liberty to assess the damages suffered by a foreign investor and hence the compensation for breach of obligations on the part of host state was not convincing. Even in the Second Partial Award in the case, the tribunal still kept saying that it should exercise "its own judgement where judgemental decisions are required to be made."[74] One could ask: where a tribunal is permitted to take such liberty in deciding its own power, what checks and balances are available in investment arbitration? After all, absolute power will lead to absolute corruption. To say the least, the *S.D. Myers* Tribunal owed an explanation to the international community in addition to the disputing parties.

In *Feldman v. Mexico*,[75] in which the respondent was found to have violated Article 1102 of the NAFTA (national treatment), on the matter concerning the quantum of damages the tribunal observed that the NAFTA "provides no further guidance as to the proper measure of damages or compensation for situations" of treaty breaches other than expropriation[76] and that the "fair market value" standard could only be applied to situations of expropriation. Nevertheless, the tribunal considered that "the amount of loss or damage that is adequately connected to the breach" should be awarded to the claimant. It further stated: "In the absence of discrimination that also constitutes indirect expropriation or is tantamount to expropriation, a claimant would not be entitled to the full market value of the investment."[77] Apparently, in ascertaining the quantum of damages, the *Feldman* Tribunal exercised "considerable discretion in fashioning what they believed to be reasonable approaches to damages consistent with the requirements of NAFTA."[78] This decision of the *Feldman* Tribunal has been followed by a number

72 Ibid., para. 309.
73 Ibid., para. 304 (emphasis in original).
74 *S.D. Myers, Inc. v. Canada*, Second Partial Award (October 21, 2002); available at: http://italaw.com/sites/default/files/case-documents/ita0752.pdf, para. 175.
75 *Marvin Feldman v. Mexico*, ICSID Case No. ARB(AF)/99/1, Award (December 16, 2002); available at: https://icsid.worldbank.org/ICSID/FrontServlet?requestType=CasesRH&actionVal=showDoc&docId=DC587_En&caseId=C175.
76 Ibid., para. 194.
77 Id.
78 Ibid., para. 197.

of subsequent investment arbitration tribunals. As in the *S.D. Myers* case, the *Feldman* Tribunal indeed exercised "considerable discretion" in determining compensation. For instance, it even did not explain why a non-discriminatory government measure would disqualify the claimant from the entitlement to receive full compensation, even where the dispute involved tax refunds.

The *SPP (Middle East) Ltd. v. Egypt*[79] case is another, but much earlier, case in which the tribunal exercised discretion in determining compensation. In that case, agreements for developing a tourist village—the Pyramids Oasis project—were entered into between the claimant and an entity of Egypt on September 23, 1974. Due to subsequent opposition to the project, which was attacked on both legal and environmental grounds, the Egyptian Government issued several Decrees which led to its cancellation.

The agreements between the parties did not provide specifically for the applicable law. The parties, after having fully debated the issue, came to the conclusion that "in view of the circumstances of the case the relevant domestic law is that of Egypt."[80] This was, in fact, not surprising. Albeit this arbitration was between an investor and a host state—Egypt—the dispute did not arise from a breach of any BIT. Instead, it concerned a breach of contract. In many cases, host states require foreign investment projects to be governed by domestic law.[81] In relation to calculating damages, the *SPP* Tribunal decided to apply Article 221 of the Egyptian Civil Code.[82]

The Egyptian law permits compensation for loss suffered plus interest, provided that the claimant has taken measures to avoid failure to perform its contract

---

79 *Southern Pacific Properties (Middle East) Ltd. v. Egypt*, ICC *ad hoc* Arbitration, Award No. 3493 (February 16, 1983); (hereinafter "SPP ICC Award"), an abstract of the unpublished award available at Pieter Sanders, (ed), *Yearbook Commercial Arbitration 1984* – Volume IX, Kluwer Law International, 1984, pp. 111–123. After the ICC award was rendered, the Respondent appealed the ICC award to the French *Cour d'Appel*, which annulled the ICC award on the ground that the Respondent was not a party to the agreement and therefore was not bound by the arbitration clause contained therein. The Claimants then referred the decision of the *Cour d'Appel* to the *Cour de Cassation (Pouvoi M' 84/17/274)*, requesting to set aside the decision, which request was rejected by the *Cour de Cmatlon* on 1 January 6, 1987. Then the Claimants instituted arbitration proceedings in the ICSID whose tribunal rendered an award on 20 May 1992: *Southern Pacific Properties (Middle East) Limited v. Arab Republic of Egypt*, ICSID Case No. ARB/84/3, award, 20 May 1992 (hereinafter "SPP ICSID Award"), available at: https://icsid.worldbank.org/ICSID/FrontServlet?requestType=CasesRH&actionVal=showDoc&docId=DC671_En&caseId=C135.

80 *SPP IIC Award, supra*, note 12, para. 49.

81 For instance, Chinese law requires all foreign-invested projects to be governed by Chinese law. For a discussion of China's practice in this respect, see Guiguo Wang, *Wang's Business Law of China* (4th ed.), LexisNexis, ch 8.

82 *SPP v. Egypt, supra*, note 12, para. 62. Article 221 of the Egyptian Civil Code provides: "The judge will fix the amount of damages, if it has not been fixed in the contract or by law. The amount of damages includes losses suffered by the creditor and profits of which he has been deprived, provided that they are normal results of the failure to perform the obligation or of delay in such performance. These losses shall be considered to be a normal result, if the creditor is not able to avoid them by making a reasonable effort. When, however, the obligation arises from contract, a debtor who has not been guilty of fraud or gross negligence will not be held liable for damages greater than those which could normally have been foreseen at the time of entering into the contract."

obligations and there is no fraud or negligence on its part. The question then was whether the Egyptian Government's action or omission involved bad faith or negligence. The tribunal considered that there was no evidence to demonstrate that Egypt's actions, in particular the issuance of the Decrees, were capricious. Thus the Egyptian Civil Code could be applied.

The claimant maintained that it should be compensated for (1) money invested, (2) value of the investment at the time of cancellation of the project, and (3) loss of opportunity. It also suggested using the DCF method to measure damages, an approach which was rejected by the tribunal on the grounds that "the risk factor [was] much higher than [had] been assumed in the projections,"[83] including the uncertainty of the political situation, tax elements and possible incompletion of the project. The tribunal then decided that it was "more appropriate to take the amount of the claimant's actual investment and add to that an incremental factor representing the increase in the value of the investment over its actual cost. Taking into account all the various factors placed before us, we have come to the conclusion that a fair sum to award would be $12.5 million."[84] This compensation must be considered in light of the claimaint's initial investment of US$5,062,657 which is compared with the committed amount of US$ 2,040,000 plus loans to the joint venture to be provided by the Claimant.[85] From an investment point of view, this decision indicates that in the short span of four years (1974–1978), SPP's initial invested capital made a gain of more than 140 percent. The respondent was also ordered to pay interest at the rate of 5 percent per annum from the date of the request for arbitration. Although the DCF method was not adopted, the rate of investment return for SPP was still quite high.

In this case, the Tribunal did not adopt the DCF method in calculating the compensation due to the Claimant. There are apparently multi-reasons. In the first place, according to the applicable Egyptian law, unless there has been guity of fraud or gross negligence on the part of the debtor—the Egyptian government in the case—the amount of damages should include losses suffered by the creditor—the SPP—and profits which it has been deprived.[86] In the view of the Tribunal, the contract breach by the Egyptian government was "neither fraudulent nor grossly negligent".[87] Secondly, the Tribunal believed that the risk factor was much higher than had been assumed in the projection by the Claimant, i.e., a much higher discount rate that should be applied.[88] Thirdly, the "project was a unique one in a very sensitive area from an environmental and political point of view." As such, even the Egyptian government could not give full guarantees.[89] All these factors lead to a lot of uncertainty to the project. Therefore, it is understandable that the Tribunal declined to adopt the DCF approach. It should be noted that the ICSID

---

83 Id.
84 Ibid., para. 64.
85 *SPP ICSID Award, supra*, note 12, para. 118
86 *SPP ICC Award, supra*, note 12, para. 62.
87 Id.
88 Ibid., para. 65.
89 Id.

Tribunal of the case also declined to aopt the DCF approach on grounds that at the time the project was cancelled only six percent of the total lots had been sold, which could not generate a reliable data for DCF calculation.[90] The second limb of the Tribunal's rejection of the DCF method was that it would provide *lucrum cessans* for illegal transactions.[91] This is one of the few cases where the DCF method was analyzed and the reasons for not applying it were explained by both the ICC and ICSID Tribunals. Such an approach is conducive for establishing a stable legal framework for foreign investment and should therefore be encouraged.

V. Fair market value as the standard of compensation for non-expropriatory breaches

Fair market value ("FMV") is often adopted in BITs as the standard of compensation for expropriations. Whilst BITs seldom stipulate any standard in respect of compensation for breaches by host states of their international obligations other than expropriation, a number of tribunals have adopted the FMV standard in practice. For instance, as mentioned earlier, in *CME v. Czech Republic*,[92] the tribunal, in its Partial Award, found that the respondent had breached its obligations relating to expropriation. In the Final Award, the tribunal found the respondent to have breached, in addition to the expropriation provisions of the relevant BIT, those regarding fair and equitable treatment, protection against unreasonable or discriminatory measures and full protection and security in conformity with international law.[93] It then employed the FMV standard in assessing compensation for all breaches.

In commenting on the respondent's contention that the fair market value would amount to more than just compensation, the *CME* Tribunal stated that it "did not adjudicate the compensation of the 'fair market value' on theoretical grounds … but on the basis of the 'fair market value' reflecting the facts and circumstances at the given point of time."[94] For the tribunal, the point of time for determining FMV was the date of the consummation of the respondent's breach of its obligations.[95] The tribunal also considered FMV to be an equivalent of "just compensation" that represented the "genuine value" of the investment.[96]

The *CME* Tribunal actually adopted the standard of compensation relating to expropriation to determine compensation in case of non-expropriation breaches.[97]

---

90 *SPP ICSID Award, supra*, note 12, para. 188.
91 Ibid., para. 190.
92 *CME v. Czech Republic*, Partial Award, *supra*, note 59.
93 *CME v. Czech Republic*, Final Award, *supra*, note 17, para. 52.
94 Ibid., para. 493.
95 Ibid., para. 492.
96 In that case, the BIT prohibited the contracting parties from taking expropriatory measures unless in compliance with specified conditions, inter alia, that the "measures are accompanied by provision for the payment of just compensation. Such compensation shall represent the genuine value of the investment affected." Ibid., para. 496.
97 In doing so, the tribunal also adopted the Hull Formula— prompt, adequate and effective com-

In reaching its decision, the tribunal also stated that the respondent "did not contest Claimant's seeking relief through monetary compensation by payment of the 'fair market value' of the investment" during the proceedings of the first phase of the arbitration, which led to the Partial Award.[98] As the tribunal had determined that the Partial Award would be binding on the parties, the objection made by the respondent in relation to adoption of the FMV standard could not stand.

The disputing parties in the *CME* case agreed to use the DCF method to quantify the compensation. The tribunal analyzed in detail the DCF valuations submitted by the parties and concluded that they were not plausible.[99] In particular, the tribunal considered the US$200 million difference between the estimates of the disputing parties to be largely driven by the expectations of the experts retained by them. It then adopted a more conservative approach in evaluating the claimant's investment.[100] Having considered that the DCF valuations submitted by the disputing parties contained "a rather high element of uncertainty and speculation,"[101] the tribunal ultimately came up with its own DCF calculation based on a recent arm's-length purchase offer for the company.

This case illustrates to what extent calculation by "experts" employing the DCF method of compensation may fluctuate. As the disputing parties' own calculations of damage were considered to be unreliable, the tribunal's decision to come up with its own assessment based on an arm's-length offer was a reasonable choice, the danger that it might be regarded as a comprise of the two extreme assertions notwithstanding.

In *CMS v. Argentina*,[102] the claimant was a US company which had made an investment in the Argentine gas transportation sector. It brought claims against Argentina for, inter alia, alleged breaches of the BIT between Argentina and the United States due to cancellation of a tariff adjustment arrangement and other Argentine measures. Such alleged breaches included those relating to wrongful expropriation, fair and equitable treatment, arbitrary and discriminatory measures, the umbrella clause and free transfer of funds.

The *CMS* Tribunal found that there had been no expropriation of the investment[103] nor any arbitrary and discriminatory behavior on the part of the Argentine

---

pensation—as a reflection of "just compensation" that represented the genuine value of the claimant's investment; ibid., para. 497.

98 Ibid., para. 495.

99 Ibid., para. 595.

100 Id.

101 Ibid., para. 604.

102 *CMS Gas Transmission Company v. Republic of Argentina*, ICSID Case No. ARB/01/8, Award (May 12, 2005).

103 The tribunal stated that "the investor is in control of the investment, the Government does not manage the day-to-day operation of the company, and the investor has full ownership and control of the investment." Therefore, no expropriation had taken place; ibid., paras. 263–64.

Government.[104] Yet Argentina was found to have breached the fair and equitable treatment provision[105] and the umbrella clause.[106]

The tribunal, however, considered that there were three main standards of reparation in international law, namely, restitution, compensation and satisfaction.[107] Having recognized that it was a common problem that BITs did not contain standards of compensation other than that relating to expropriation, the tribunal held that "the cumulative nature of the breaches discussed here is best dealt with by resorting to the standard of fair market value."[108] Its reasoning was that although the FMV standard is most prominently relied upon in cases of expropriation, its application to other breaches is not excluded. In its view, where the effects of other breaches result in "important long-term losses," the FMV standard should be applied.[109] In analyzing the principles of compensation, as has been done in many other cases, the *CMS* Tribunal also referred to the PCIJ's judgment in *Chorzów Factory* for guidance.[110] This was so because in the view of the tribunal what the claimant suffered were long-term or permanent losses.

With regard to the method of assessing compensation, the *CMS* Tribunal considered that "[c]ompensation is designed to cover any 'financially assessable damage including loss of profits insofar as it is established'."[111] In its view, where restitution is not possible or will not be made, compensation is called for. The tribunal then proposed four ways to determine the value of property:

> (1) The "asset value" or the "replacement cost" approach which evaluates the assets on the basis of their "break-up" or their replacement cost; (2) the 'comparable transaction' approach which reviews comparable transactions in similar circumstances; (3) the "option" approach which studies the alternative uses which could be made of the assets in question, and their costs and benefits; (4) the "discounted cash flow" ("DCF") approach under which the valuation of the assets is arrived at by determining the present value of future predicted cash flows discounted at a rate which reflects various categories of risk and uncertainty.[112]

The *CMS* Tribunal, after some analysis, concluded that no method other than the DCF method was appropriate[113] and that it had "no hesitation in endorsing it."[114] The reason, stated the tribunal, was that the DCF method had been "universally adopted, including by numerous arbitral tribunals, as an appropriate method for

---

104 Ibid., para. 295.
105 Ibid., paras. 275 and 281. The tribunal also held the view that fair and equitable treatment was inseparable from stability and predictability; ibid., para. 275.
106 Ibid., para. 303.
107 Ibid., para. 399.
108 Ibid., para. 410.
109 Id.
110 Ibid., para. 400.
111 Ibid., para. 401.
112 Ibid., para. 403.
113 For the discussions by the tribunal to exclude the use of other methods, see ibid., paras. 411–15.
114 Ibid., para. 416.

valuing business assets."[115] No matter which method is adopted, what is most important is that the evidence and data must be readily available so that a rational and realistic decision can be made.

In the *CMS* case, the tribunal found that the respondent had violated BIT provisions on both expropriation and other treatment. It was therefore understandable that the tribunal decided to adopt the FMV as the standard for compensation, as the Argentina–United States BIT, like many others, does not provide the standard of compensation for non-expropriatory breaches. In that case, the claimant was a going concern and it had been operating in Argentina for a number of years. Its profit-making prospects could be assessed on the basis of its past record. In such circumstances, to use the DCF method to calculate the FMV was acceptable. In this regard, the tribunal recognized the potential uncertainty that use of the DCF method might introduce and reminded itself to be cautious in employing it. These factors have reasonably justified the tribunal's decision relating to making use of the FMV standard and the DCF method for calculating it.

Azurix v. Argentina[116] is another case in which no expropriation was established but where the tribunal applied the expropriation standard of compensation— FMV—to compensation for other treaty breaches. In that case, the claimant, Azurix, was a US company incorporated in the State of Delaware which had secured a concession for water treatment and disposal in the Argentine Province of Buenos Aires. It claimed that Buenos Aires had failed to safely transfer the concession, apply the proper tariff regime and complete some work for the investor, [117] all of which actions were attributable to Argentina. The claimant alleged that the effects of the above failures constituted an expropriation of its investment and a breach of the provisions on fair and equitable treatment, non-discrimination, and full protection and security required by the Argentina–United States BIT.[118] The tribunal found that the conduct of the Province of Buenos Aires had constituted "arbitrary actions without base on the Law [sic] or the Concession Agreement and [had] impaired the operation of Azurix's investment."[119] It also determined that Argentina had breached its obligations in respect of the fair and equitable treatment[120] and full protection and security standards.[121]

Regarding compensation, the *Azurix* Tribunal first referred to the Argentina–United States BIT's requirements relating to expropriation[122] and then discussed some NAFTA cases, including *Feldman*, in respect of a tribunal's discretion in

---

115 Id.

116 *Azurix Corp. v. Argentine Republic*, ICSID Case No. ARB/01/12, Award (July 14, 2006).

117 Ibid., paras. 69–75.

118 Ibid., para. 43.

119 Ibid., para. 393.

120 Ibid., para. 377.

121 Ibid., para. 408. The Tribunal considered that there was an interrelationship between fair and equitable treatment and full protection and security. It further stated that "full protection and security was understood to go beyond protection and security ensured by the police. It is not only a matter of physical security; the stability afforded by a secure investment environment is as important from an investor's point of view." Id.

122 Ibid., para. 419.

employing compensation standards.[123] It also quoted the passage of the *CMS* award on adopting the FMV standard.[124] In the end, the *Azurix* Tribunal concluded that "a compensation based on the fair market value of the Concession would be appropriate, particularly since the Province has taken it over."[125] At the same time, the tribunal adopted the definition of FMV as provided in the American Society of Appraisers' *International Glossary of Business Valuation Terms.*[126] As in the *CMS* case, because the respondent was found to have committed both expropriatory and non-expropriatory breaches, adoption of the FMV as the standard of compensation would be the least controversial option and naturally became the tribunal's choice.

Enron v. Argentina[127] is another case where no expropriation was found[128] but where the tribunal upheld the claim that the respondent had violated its obligations relating to fair and equitable treatment[129] and the umbrella clause.[130] In matters of compensation, the tribunal adopted the FMV as the standard for compensation.[131] In its view, FMV was "indeed the applicable Treaty guideline for measuring damages in cases of expropriation."[132] Yet what the tribunal faced was not expropriation but compensation for violation of fair and equitable treatment and the umbrella clause. The tribunal justified its application of the FMV standard to the situation by stating:

> On occasions, the line separating indirect expropriation from the breach of fair and equitable treatment can be rather thin and in those circumstances the standard of compensation can also be similar on one or the other side of the line. Given the cumulative nature of the breaches that have resulted in a finding of liability, the Tribunal believes that in this case it is appropriate to apply the fair market value to the determination of compensation.[133]

123 Ibid., para. 421.
124 Ibid., para. 420.
125 Ibid., para. 424.
126 The *International Glossary of Business Valuation Terms* (available at: http://www.aicpa.org/ InterestAreas/ForensicAndValuation/Resources/Standards/DownloadableDocuments/ International_Glossary_of_BV_Terms.pdf) defines FMV as "the price, expressed in terms of cash equivalents, at which property would change hands between a hypothetical willing and able buyer and a hypothetical [willing] and able seller, acting at arm's length in an open and unrestricted market, when neither is under compulsion to buy or sell and when both have reasonable knowledge of the relevant facts."
127 *Enron Corp. and Ponderosa Assets LP v. Argentine Republic*, ICSID Case No. ARB/01/3, Award (May 22, 2007).
128 Ibid., paras. 244 and 246.
129 Ibid., para. 268.
130 Ibid., para. 277.
131 Ibid., para. 379.
132 Ibid., para. 362. Regarding FMV, the tribunal stated that "[t]he notion of 'fair market value' is generally understood as the price at which property would change hands between a hypothetical willing and able buyer and a hypothetical willing and able seller, absent compulsion to buy or sell, and having the parties reasonable knowledge of the facts [sic], all of it in an open and unrestricted market." Ibid., para. 361.
133 Ibid., para. 263.

It may be true that in some cases it is difficult to distinguish breach of fair and equitable treatment from indirect expropriation, in particular creeping expropriation or measures tantamount to expropriation in which the accretion of various events lead to ultimate deprivation of the property rights of a foreign investor. Yet, there is at least one essential feature of expropriation, and that is the taking of property or property rights. In breach of fair and equitable treatment provisions, a foreign investor's property right or control of an investment may be seriously and adversely affected but the foreign investor is still in control of its investment. In other words, the essential difference between expropriation, including indirect expropriation, and breach of fair and equitable treatment provisions is the "taking" of property. It is a pity that the *Enron* Tribunal, in order to apply the FMV standard, did not try to distinguish indirect expropriation from breach of fair and equitable treatment provisions.

Like many others, the *Enron* Tribunal also considered the *Chorzów* dictum to be the guiding principle in quantifying damages. To undo the material harm, the tribunal decided to adopt the DCF model to measure the amount of compensation. In its view, the company in which the claimant had made its investment was a "going concern," and it held that since the "DCF [method] reflects the companies' capacity to generate positive returns in the future, it appears as the appropriate method" for the case.[134] In addition, the tribunal considered the DCF method to be

> … a sound tool used internationally to value companies, albeit that it is to be used with caution as it can give rise to speculation. It has also been constantly used by tribunals in establishing the fair market value of assets to determine compensation of breaches of international law.[135]

By adopting the DCF method, the tribunal excluded the methods of book value, unjust enrichment and market capitalization suggested by the respondent and its expert.[136] It said that book value was "by definition valid for accounting purposes,"[137] the unjust enrichment method only computed "damages by looking at the extent of unfair enrichment by the Government"[138] and market capitalization in an illiquid market like the one in the instant case "might provide distorted valuation indications."[139] Enron– the claimant—was a "going concern," and its profit-making capability could be assessed with a degree of certainty. In these circumstances, the adoption of the DCF method for calculating the FMV was justifiable. Also it was a sound comment by the *Enron* Tribunal that "unjust enrichment" was a concern, in most cases, in relation to the host state and not so much to the claimant. In addition, the tribunal expressed the view that the DCF method should be used with caution so that it would not give rise to speculation. From

134 Ibid., para. 385.
135 Id.
136 Ibid., para. 381.
137 Ibid., para. 382.
138 Id.
139 Ibid., para. 383.

the above, it was quite clear that the *Enron* Tribunal's decision was presented with reasons, which is very important in investment arbitration.

In *Occidental v. Ecuador*,[140] the dispute concerned the termination (*"Caducidad"*) of a participation contract between Occidental Exploration and Production Company ("OEPC") and Empresa Estatal Petróleos del Ecuador ("PetroEcuador"). OEPC started to provide services to the oil and gas sector of Ecuador in 1985. In 1993, Ecuador amended its Hydrocarbons Law ("HCL") to permit foreign participation in oil exploration and production. On 21 May 1999, OEPC and Ecuador, through PetroEcuador, entered into a participation contract according to which OEPC "had the right to develop and to exploit"[141] an area of an oil field known as Block 15 covering approximately 200,000 hectares. The amount of OEPC's participation was determined on the basis of an equation. By the end of 2005, OEPC's participation was approximately 70 percent of the oil produced from Block 15, which, after payment of expenses, taxes and other assessments, accounted for about 30 percent of total net profits.[142]

The participation contract provided, inter alia, that any transfer or assignment to third parties of the "rights" thereunder "must have the authorization of" the Ecuadorian Government—the ministry in charge.[143] OEPC, however, entered into a so-called Farmout Agreement with Alberta Energy Corporation Ltd ("AEC") on 19 October 2000 under which AEC acquired 40 percent of OEPC's economic interest in Block 15. OEPC and AEC also signed a Joint Operating Agreement according to which a two-person (one from each party) management committee was established which had the "power and duty to authorize and supervise Joint Operations that are necessary or desirable to fulfill the Participating Agreements and properly explore and exploit the Agreement Area in accordance with this Agreement and in a manner appropriate in the circumstances."[144] In other words, by signing the Farmout Agreement and Joint Operating Agreement, OEPC had effectively transferred 40 percent of its interest and rights to AEC without the approval of the Government of Ecuador.

Ecuador learned about OEPC's transfer of part of its economic interest in Block 15 through an audit report in 2004. After several rounds of exchanges of communications between the Attorney General and Minister of Energy of Ecuador and with mounting pressure from the Congress as well as the local community, the Minister of Energy issued a *Caducidad* Decree on May 15, 2006.[145] The *Caducidad* Decree terminated OEPC's participation contract with immediate effect and ordered the latter to "turn over to PetroEcuador all its assets relating to Block 15."[146] The claimants alleged that Ecuador had breached its obligations

---

140 *Occidental v. Ecuador*, Award, *supra*, note 64.
141 Ibid., para. 115.
142 Ibid., para. 117.
143 Ibid., para. 119.
144 Ibid., para. 136.
145 Ibid., para. 199.
146 Id.

under the Ecuador–United States BIT relating to fair and equitable treatment, minimum standard of treatment and expropriation.

The *Occidental* Tribunal first considered the transfer of the 40 percent interest by OEPC under the Farmout Agreement to AEC to be a violation of the participation contract and the HCL by stating:

> ... by virtue of having "ownership" over "all the rights and interests in and under the Participating Agreements", albeit to the extent of its 40% respective Participating Interest, the parties intended that AEC acquire such ownership as a result of a transfer of such rights and interests effected by the Joint Operating Agreement.[147]

The *Occidental* Tribunal also opined that the prohibition mentioned above was not limited to total transfer or assignment of interest but that it applied to a partial transfer as well.[148] Therefore, the 40 percent transfer by OEPC of its interest in Block 15 to AEC was not permitted unless it received the prior authorization of the Ecuadorian Government. According to the Joint Operating Agreement, AEC had the right to veto all acts of significance,[149] which, the tribunal stated, "demonstrate[d] incontrovertibly that the Joint Operating Agreement conferred to AEC real and specific managerial and voting rights,"[150] OEPC's holding the legal title over Block 15 notwithstanding. Thus, the tribunal determined that "OEPC, by failing to secure the required ministerial authorization, breached ... the Participation Contract and was guilty of an actionable violation of ... the HCL."[151] The tribunal also ruled that OEPC was negligent in its failure to secure the required authorization and that it could not rely on legitimate expectations as a defense.[152]

Since OEPC, through its negligence, had violated the participation contract and the HCL, the next issue was to determine whether the issuance of the *Caducidad* by the Minister of Energy was proportionate. It was agreed by both the claimant and the respondent that the minister had the discretion to issue the *Caducidad*.[153] In its assessment of whether the declaration of the *Caducidad* was proportionate, the tribunal stated:

> It can be accepted that some punishment or other step may well have been justified, or at the very least defensible. ... But the overriding principle of proportionality requires that any such administrative goal must be balanced against the Claimants' own interests and against the true nature and effect of the conduct being censured. ... the price paid by the Claimants – total loss of an investment worth many hundreds of millions of dollars – was out

147 Ibid., para. 304.
148 Ibid., para. 305.
149 Ibid., para. 315.
150 Ibid., para. 317.
151 Ibid., para. 381.
152 Ibid., para. 383.
153 Ibid., para. 424.

of proportion to the wrongdoing alleged against OEPC, and similarly out of proportion to the importance and effectiveness of the "deterrence message" which the respondent might have wished to send to the wider oil and gas community.[154]

The *Occidental* Tribunal also suggested alternatives that the respondent could have adopted as punishment other than the *Caducidad,* including a claim for damages from OEPC and renegotiation of a more favorable contract with it.[155] Then the tribunal concluded that Ecuador's issuance of the *Caducidad* constituted a violation of Ecuadorian law, customary international law and the provisions of the Ecuador–United States BIT relating to fair and equitable treatment and minimum standard of treatment.[156]

The next question was compensation, in which an important issue was whether OEPC should be entitled to 100 percent of the loss that resulted from the *Caducidad* Decree or only 60 percent—after deduction of the transfer of the 40 percent interest to AEC—as was contended by the respondent. The determinative factor was the validity of the assignment that Occidental sought to accomplish with the Farmout Agreement and the Joint Operating Agreement, which, it had already been decided, were unlawful. On the matter of the validity of the assignment, the tribunal found that according to the HCL and the Civil Code of Ecuador, as well as the judicial practice of the Ecuadorian Supreme Court:

> … where the law itself clearly states that the contract is deemed to be unexecuted, and therefore has no life, there is no requirement for judicial confirmation. Similarly … the law itself has deemed that an unauthorised assignment has no validity whatsoever, and therefore has no life. The logical consequence of this provision is that no further action is required to invalidate an unauthorised assignment.[157]

The effect of this finding was that because the Farmout Agreement and Joint Operating Agreement were invalid *ab initio* and no judicial intervention to declare the invalidity of the transaction was needed, the claimant would be entitled to 100 percent of the loss suffered from the *Caducidad* Decree. Professor Brigitte Stern, in her Dissenting Opinion said, however, that "in my understanding … a judge has to intervene to declare absolute nullity and … that it is mandatory for a judge to declare the nullity of an act considered to be null by law."[158] In her view, to

154 Ibid., para. 450.
155 Ibid., paras. 431–32.
156 Ibid., para. 452.
157 Ibid., para. 628. The tribunal also stated that it is "clear that a null act produces no legal effects, even before a judicial declaration is obtained. As such, an agreement to assign without authorization produces no actual assignment and a judicial declaration does not reverse the assignment—a valid assignment never occurred." Ibid., para. 632.
158 *Occidental Petroleum Corporation and Occidental Exploration and Production Company v. Republic of Ecuador,* ICSID Case No. ARB/06/11, Dissenting Opinion of Professor Brigitte Stern, para. 85.

award the claimant 100 percent of the loss would not be acceptable because "in the absence of *caducidad*, OEPC could not have claimed the rights to 40% of the oil back. Why could it claim these 40% with *caducidad*?"[159]

In the end, the *Occidental* Tribunal adopted the FMV standard to determine compensation for the respondent's violations of its obligations relating to fair and equitable treatment and minimum standard of treatment as well as for expropriation of the claimant's investment.[160] For the measurement of the FMV, the tribunal decided to use the DCF model.

Among the items it considered important in applying the DCF model,[161] the *Occidental* Tribunal considered the determination of volume and production most important. It then analyzed the expert reports submitted by both parties relating to various aspects of Block 15 that might contribute to the production and potential economic benefit to the claimant and made adjustments. In accordance with international law, in particular Articles 31 and 39 of the ILC Articles on Responsibilities of States for Internationally Wrongful Acts, before deciding the amount to be awarded to the claimant the Tribunal conducted an analysis of the claimant's contribution to the injury it had suffered.[162] In its discussion, the tribunal emphasized that in order to constitute contributory negligence, any act of the claimant must be "material and significant."[163] As the tribunal found that the claimant had "acted negligently and committed an unlawful act,"[164] it reduced the compensation for damages to the claimant by 25 percent.[165]

---

159 Ibid., para. 35. Professor Stern also commented that an investment "requires a contribution: it is uncontested that OEPC has contributed only for 60% of the value of the investment, 40% of that value ... having been paid by AEC/Andes. How would it be possible to grant damages pertaining to rights that no longer belong to OEPC, without disregarding the basic rules that confer jurisdiction on ICSID tribunals?" ibid., para. 138. In this regard, she considered the new holder of the 40% interest of Block 15 to be Andes, a Chinese entity, for which the tribunal lacked jurisdiction *ratione personae* insofar as nationality was concerned; ibid., para. 137.

160 *Occidental v. Ecuador, supra*, Award, note 64, para. 707.

161 For the DCF calculation, the tribunal adopted the following steps of analysis: (a) determination of the size of the reservoir (projection of the number of barrels that are in the field); (b) creation of a production profile (to establish the number of barrels that could be economically produced each year); (c) assignment of risk adjustment factors ("RAFs") to the reserves (to reflect the risk that certain categories of reserves might not produce the amount of oil projected); (d) application of a price forecast (multiplication of the number of barrels in the production profile by a projected price of oil and subtraction of the costs to produce those barrels); and (e) application of a discount rate (to reflect, among other things, the time value of money and business and country risks). Ibid., para. 709.

162 For details of the tribunal's discussion in this regard, see ibid., paras. 664–85.

163 Ibid., para. 670.

164 Ibid., para. 679. The tribunal considered that the claimants' fault "prevented the Respondent from exercising, in a formal way, its sovereign right to vet and approve AEC as the transferee of those rights and, even more importantly ... to vet any other unknown investor to which AEC could eventually transfer its rights." Id.

165 Ibid., para. 825. Professor Stern also dissented on the amount by which the damages awarded to the claimant should be reduced as a result of its own contributory negligence. Citing several other cases, she believed a 50% reduction would be more appropriate. See the Dissenting Opinion of Professor Brigitte Stern, *supra*, note 153, paras. 7–8.

There are several issues in the *Occidental* case that require further discussion. In the first place, according to the participation contract between the claimant and PetroEcuador, when the claimant wished to transfer the whole or part of its interest in the contract, including forming a consortium, it had to satisfy two conditions—prior consent of PetroEcuador and approval of the responsible ministry of the Ecuadorian Government. The participation contract further provided that any integration of such consortium or association, presumably including the Farmout Agreement and Joint Operation Agreement, without authorization of the responsible ministry "shall constitute legal grounds for declaring the termination" of the participation contract.[166] Strictly speaking, Ecuador was entitled to terminate the contract, because the claimant had failed to secure approval of the responsible Ecuadorian ministry. It was irrelevant that Ecuador might or would have approved it, had the claimant submitted the Farmout and Joint Operation Agreements for approval. The fact was that the claimant did not seek approval from the Ecuadorian Government and that constituted grounds for termination of the contract. There might be political and other considerations on Ecuador's part, yet, so long as Ecuador followed the stipulated procedures to terminate the contract, whether or not the ministry had the discretion to terminate the contract and whether the Ecuadorian Government's measure was in compliance with the principle of proportionality should not have been considerations of the tribunal. The claimant's failure to secure approval could not be rectified by an argument that the transfer was not valid *ab initio* under the laws of Ecuador.

Another questionable decision of the *Occidental* Tribunal was its award of damages to the claimant for the 40 percent interest it had transferred to AEC under the Farmout Agreement. Where the claimant had been paid for transferring 40 percent of its interest to another party, there could not be any possibility for the claimant to suffer any loss in relation to that portion of interest. In these circumstances, the tribunal's decision constituted double benefits for the claimant and was an incorrect decision.

VI. Actual losses suffered and benefits denied as benchmark

Full reparation may be adopted as the standard of compensation in cases where restitution proves to be an impossibility. *LG&E v. Argentina*[167] is one case that illustrates this. This case concerned three US companies with investments in gas distribution in Argentina. The claimants alleged that Argentina had breached its obligations under the Argentina–United States BIT in relation to wrongful expropriation, breaches of the fair and equitable treatment and minimum standard of treatment provisions, the prohibition against discriminatory and arbitrary

---

166 *Occidental v. Ecuador*, *supra*, note 64, para. 119, in which the tribunal quoted the relevant provisions of the participation contract.
167 *LG&E Energy Corp., LG&E Capital Corp., and LG&E International, Inc. v. Argentine Republic*, ICSID Case No. ARB/02/1, Decision on Liability (October 3, 2006).

measures, and the umbrella clause.[168] These claims were based on the measures taken by Argentina during its economic crisis that took place at the turn of this century.[169] The tribunal dismissed the claims of wrongful expropriation and the taking of arbitrary measures.[170] It did, however, determine that Argentina was liable for breach of the provisions concerning fair and equitable treatment, no less favorable treatment than that to be accorded under international law (minimum standard of treatment) and adoption of discriminatory measures.[171] Because the tribunal agreed with the respondent on its necessity defense, it awarded the claimant no compensation for damages it suffered from the above breaches during the period of the state of necessity between December 1, 2001 and April 26, 2003.[172]

Yet, for other periods, the respondent was held liable for its wrongful actions. As to damages suffered by the claimants,[173] the *LG&E* Tribunal considered reparation to be the most important consequence of violation of international obligations. It considered that "to make reparation for the injury caused by" an act or omission of state is "well established in international law."[174] It at the same time recognized that "questions are particularly thorny when it comes to defining the standard and measure of compensation applicable for treaty breaches other than expropriation."[175] This is so because "[t]here are no express provisions in the Treaty addressing these issues and pre-existing guidance in arbitral jurisprudence is very limited."[176] Unlike some other tribunals, the *LG&E* Tribunal considered that in establishing the standard of compensation it should have "recourse to the principles governing reparation under international law and the few precedents in investment treaty arbitration."[177] Apparently, the international law principle the tribunal had in mind included the guidance provided in the *Chorzów Factory* judgment and codified in Article 31 of the ILC Articles on Responsibilities of States for Internationally Wrongful Acts. Because the claimant requested reparation in the form of compensation, the tribunal turned its attention to the methods and measurement thereof. It did not accept the claimant's proposal of FMV nor the respondent's recommendation of using the DCF method. In its view, "FMV is … [a] measure of compensation in cases of expropriation" and, therefore, "its application does not extend similarly to other treaty standards."[178] It should be pointed out that the reason the tribunal did not consider the FMV standard to be appropriate

---

168 Ibid., para. 72.
169 The material facts of this case are similar to those of a number of other cases involving Argentina as respondent, including *CMS v. Argentina*, which was discussed earlier.
170 *LG&E v. Argentina*, Decision on Liability, *supra*, note 162, para. 267.
171 Id.
172 Id.
173 For damages, the tribunal issued a separate award; see *LG&E Energy Corp., LG&E Capital Corp., and LG&E International, Inc. v. Argentine Republic*, ICSID Case No. ARB/02/1, Award (July 25, 2007).
174 Ibid., para. 29.
175 Ibid., para. 30.
176 Id.
177 Id.
178 Ibid., para. 37.

was that it rejected the claimant's claim of indirect expropriation on the basis that Argentina's measures:

> ... did not deprive the investors of the right to enjoy their investment ... the true interests at stake here are the investments' asset base, the value of which has rebounded since the economic crisis of December 2001 and 2002 ... the effect of the Argentine State's actions has not been permanent on the value of the Claimants' shares, and Claimants' investment has not ceased to exist.[179]

This decision is instrumental for determination of compensation for non-expropriatory breaches. As the claimants did not suffer from expropriation or a measure tantamount to expropriation or any permanent loss of the value of their investment, the *LG&E* Tribunal awarded the claimants compensation to offset their actual losses. In these circumstances, the tribunal's decision not to apply the FMV standard is quite reasonable.

In measuring the claimant's losses, the *LG&E* Tribunal considered that it was necessary to distinguish "accrued losses" from "lost future profits."[180] In its view, whilst accrued losses "have commonly been awarded by tribunals," lost future profits "have only been awarded when '*an anticipated income stream has attained sufficient attributes to be considered legally protected interests of sufficient certainty to be compensable*'."[181] In calculating the amount of compensation, the tribunal awarded the investors full reparation that could "[wipe] out the consequences of Argentina's breach of the Treaty protections."[182] It stated:

> Compensation is to be measured by the actual loss incurred by the Claimants as a result of Argentina's wrongful acts. This loss corresponds to the amount of dividends that Claimants would have received *but for* Argentina's breaches. The method to quantify compensation should account for the principles stated by the Tribunal and at the same time assures that the Claimants are "fully" compensated for the damage incurred as a result of Argentina's breaches.[183]

Ultimately, what the investors were awarded included dividends plus interest. The *LG&E* case is distinguishable from others. In the first place, there was no permanent loss suffered by the claimants and therefore there was no taking or expropriation. Second, as there was no expropriation, the tribunal considered it was inappropriate to employ the FMV standard in assessing the loss. Yet the claimants were awarded compensation to cover both dividends otherwise due and interest. Even though the tribunal did not use the DCF method in calculating the loss, the award of dividends plus interest is also quite close to the market worth of the property. This illustrates that FMV is most often the yardstick for compensation even in cases of non-expropriatory breaches.

179 Ibid., para. 35, citing paras. 198–200 of the Decision on Liability.
180 Ibid., para. 51.
181 Id. (emphasis in original).
182 Ibid., para. 58.
183 Id.

The *Chevron v. Ecuador (I)* case[184] is also instructive in terms of compensation for losses. The claimant had, through its subsidiary Texaco Petroleum Company, engaged in seven cases in the Ecuadorian courts for 13 years without any result and asserted that the respondent had breached its obligations under Article II(7) of the Ecuador–United States BIT, which provides: "Each Party shall provide effective means of asserting claims and enforcing rights with respect to investment, investment agreements, and investment authorizations." It should be noted that most BITs do not contain such provisions. The *Chevron* Tribunal considered that such provisions significantly overlap with similar provisions on denial of justice under customary international law.[185]

Like the *Duke Energy v. Ecuador*[186] Tribunal, the *Chevron* Tribunal viewed the purpose of Article II(7), by setting out an "effective means" standard, as intended to "implement and form part of the more general guarantee against denial of justice."[187] Regarding the nature of the provision, the tribunal stated that it is "a *lex specialis*" and not a "restatement of the law on denial of justice."[188] As such, it is distinctive from denial of justice and at the same time involves a "less-demanding test"[189] that is easier to be satisfied than that for denial of justice. The difference is that, for denial of justice, an element of bad faith must be established, whilst Article II(7) of the Ecuador–United States BIT does not require the same. In such circumstances, the tribunal found that Ecuador had an obligation to maintain a legal system that could "provide foreign investors with means of enforcing legitimate rights within a reasonable amount of time."[190]

Yet, to have a system or means is one thing, but its effectiveness is another. The tribunal held that neither the complexity of the cases concerning Chevron nor the respondent's behavior justified the delay and, in consequence, the respondent was held to have violated Article II(7).[191] With this finding, the tribunal did not examine whether the respondent's acts had also violated other provisions, such as those relating to fair and equitable treatment, full protection and security and restraining from taking arbitrary or discriminatory actions, as was further alleged by the claimant.[192] This could be considered as an exercise by the tribunal of judicial economy.

Clearly, what the *Chevron* Tribunal did was to retry the cases before the Ecuadorian courts. The question is whether the tribunal was authorized by the BIT to perform its functions in such a way. In fact, the tribunal not only retried the cases but also assessed the damages as if it were a court of Ecuador.

---

184 *Chevron v. Ecuador (I)*, UNCITRAL, PCA Case No. 34877, Partial Award on the Merits (March 30, 2010).
185 Ibid., para. 242.
186 *Duke Energy Electroquil Partners & Electroquil S.A. v. Republic of Ecuador*, ICSID Case No. ARB/04/19, Award (August 18, 2008).
187 *Chevron v. Ecuador (I)*, *supra*, note 179, para. 242.
188 Id.
189 Ibid., para. 244.
190 Ibid., para. 250.
191 Ibid., para. 254.
192 Ibid., para. 12.

Regarding the assessment of damages, the *Chevron* Tribunal said the starting point should be what the Ecuadorian court would do[193] and that it (the tribunal) should be "guided by the principle that the Claimants must be made whole."[194] In other words, the claimant should be entitled to an amount of compensation equivalent to its rights under the contracts. In accordance with this principle, the tribunal awarded the claimant close to US$7 million[195] but left the final amount to the experts to work out[196] because the effect of domestic tax laws must be taken into account. It should be pointed out that although the tribunal's decision was based on the Ecuador–United States BIT, insofar as the claimant is concerned, what it received was the amount that the Ecuadorian courts, in the view of the tribunal, would have granted. One may wonder if and to what extent the *Chevron* Tribunal's assessed amount of compensation can reliably match what would have been awarded by the Ecuadorian court.

The *Chevron* case has triggered several questions, the first of which is whether the BIT intends to impose an obligation on the contracting parties to improve their existing judicial system so that foreign investors would be provided with an effective means for enforcing their rights. Obviously the tribunal considered that each contracting party had an obligation to ensure that foreign investors were provided with "means of enforcing legitimate rights within a reasonable amount of time" and that whether or not the time required to enforce rights was reasonable should be determined "against an objective, international standard."[197] This having been said, there is no such thing as an internationally recognized "objective" standard in respect of decision-making by national judicial bodies. Such matters have to be decided by all relevant factors, the complexity of the case and the backlog of the courts being examples. In the end, the tribunal still used its own judgment without referring to any specific examples of an objective international standard.

Second, the tribunal relied heavily on its findings of the Ecuadorian courts' inaction for prolonged periods of time and their "apparent unwillingness" to "allow the cases to proceed."[198] This, in a sense, demonstrates that, at least in the minds of the tribunal, there was bad faith on the part of the host state. Although, by relying on Article II(7), such bad faith did not need to be proven, there was, in fact, plenty of evidence that the Ecuadorian courts did not actively proceed with the cases—thereby exhibiting bad faith. In these circumstances, it was quite easy for the tribunal to reach its decision of "unreasonableness." The difference is that the unreasonableness is a judgment of the tribunal, whilst bad faith must be proved in accordance with international law.

The third question is whether the backlog of court cases could have been a good defense. The tribunal considered that court congestion "must be temporary and

193 Ibid., para. 546.
194 Ibid., para. 551.
195 Ibid., para. 550.
196 Ibid., para. 552.
197 Ibid., paras. 250 and 263.
198 Ibid., paras. 256 and 262.

must be promptly and effectively addressed."[199] This decision is in sharp contrast with that in the *White Industries* case,[200] in which the backlog of cases was considered a good defense. In comparison, the *White Industries* Tribunal's decision on this matter is more workable, as it is easy to say that a state must resolve the problem of court congestion but very difficult to do so, as to address the issue does not mean to resolve it. Lastly, unlike the *White Industries* Tribunal, the *Chevron* Tribunal did not deal with the issue as to whether or not, before entering the Ecuadorian market, Chevron had been aware of the behavior of the local courts. If the answer is "yes," then the claimant must be responsible, at least to a certain extent, for its own decision.

In *S.D. Myers*, the tribunal adopted the common law tort standard in assessing damages. The tribunal first stated that "damages may only be awarded to the extent that there is a sufficient causal link between the breach of a specific NAFTA provision and the loss sustained by the investor."[201] The tribunal considered that "[t]he inquiry in this case is more akin to ascertaining damages for a tort or delict. The damages recoverable are those that will put the innocent party into the position it would have been in had the interim measure not been passed."[202] As that was the case, one of the most important issues was whether the harm caused was too remote. At the same time, the concept of foreseeability in the law of contracts would not be applicable in the law of torts but, rather, "[r]emoteness is the key."[203] Since the *S.D. Myers* Tribunal adopted the tort standard, the economic losses suffered by the claimant which were caused by the Respondent's measures should be compensated and would not be confined to "those that appear on the balance sheet of its investment."[204] The tribunal in the end considered the loss of net income to be the standard for compensation, provided that such loss was neither speculative nor too remote.[205]

With the compensation standard decided, the remaining question was whether the claimant's claim for compensation for lost opportunities, in particular with regard to the lost use of money, could stand. The tribunal did not support that claim, stating that "[t]o be compensated for the value of the lost use of money by a payment of interest that reflects what the market considered to be the value of money at the time is appropriate. To allow [the Claimant] a return based on what it might have done with the money would be to recognise claims that are speculative and too remote."[206] The tribunal was not convinced by the alternatives for

---

199 Ibid, para. 264.
200 *White Industries Australia Limited v. Republic of India*, UNCITRAL Case, Final Award (November 30, 2011).
201 *S.D. Myers*, Second Partial Award, *supra*, note 74, para. 140.
202 Ibid., para. 159.
203 Id.
204 Ibid., para. 122.
205 Ibid., para. 173.
206 Ibid., para. 161.

use of money proposed by the claimant and stated that it was not clear what the claimant "would have done with the money if it were to have been earned."[207]

Regarding loss of future profits, the *S.D. Myers* Tribunal considered that "a claimant who has succeeded on liability must establish the quantum of his claims to the relevant standard of proof."[208] That is, on the one hand, the claimed sum should not be speculative or too remote and, on the other hand, fairness must be done to the claimant.[209] As the *S.D. Myers* case involved not only development of a new business but also a new business in a foreign country, the issue of "first-mover advantage" had to be taken into account. The respondent asserted that the market was price sensitive, which left little room for other factors to affect the market. Nevertheless, the tribunal decided that the claimant had a first-mover advantage. Yet it said further that:

> … considering the totality of the evidence, the Tribunal concludes that, although not inconsequential, it has not been shown to be as substantial as claimed by [the Claimant]. Further, insofar as [the Claimant] did have a first-mover advantage, the Tribunal concludes that, while it was eroded by the closure, the extent of that erosion is incapable of precise assessment on the evidence before the Tribunal.[210]

Thus, the *S.D. Myers* Tribunal believed that because the market was highly price sensitive, what first-mover advantage the claimant could take was that of under-cutting the prices of its competitors. It also considered goodwill as a factor in determining first-mover advantages. Most probably *S.D. Myers* is the first investor–state arbitration case in which the tort standard was applied for determining compensation. On the whole, the decision of the tribunal was balanced with a careful analysis of reasons. Whilst the case provides an alternative for grounds of compensation, precaution should be taken when using the book value for determining compensation, as it may lead to unjust enrichment of the host state. Depending on the nature of the investment, sometimes a foreign investor may have incurred a great deal of expenditure before "making" its investment. In such circumstances, adoption of book value as the basis for compensation is not appropriate.

Lemire v. Ukraine[211] was also concerned with non-expropriatory breaches, in regard to which the tribunal adopted a "but for" approach regarding compensation for damages. The claimant, a citizen of the United States, made an investment as a majority shareholder, via CJSC "Mirakom Ukraina", in CJSC "Radiocompany Gala" ("Gala"), a closed joint stock company incorporated under the laws of Ukraine. Gala was licensed to broadcast, as a music radio station, on various frequencies in Ukraine. Owing to disputes over the operation of his radio station and difficulties in obtaining approval for extension of the license, the claimant brought

207 Ibid., para. 162.
208 Ibid., para. 173.
209 Id.
210 Ibid., para. 185.
211 *Joseph Charles Lemire v. Ukraine*, ICSID Case No. ARB/06/18, Decision on Jurisdiction and Liability (January 14, 2010); Award (March 28, 2011).

the case to arbitration at the ICSID by alleging that the respondent had violated its obligations of minimum standard of treatment and fair and equitable treatment under the United States–Ukraine BIT. Having ascertained that there was no distinction between the minimum standard of treatment and fair and equitable treatment,[212] the tribunal criticized the respondent's practice of issuing licenses as being "without transparency or publicity and without meeting the requirements of or following the procedures established" in Ukraine, which constituted a violation of the fair and equitable standard under the BIT.[213] In the tribunal's view, the Ukrainian practice relating to licenses lacked transparency and was carried out "with total disregard of the process of law and without any possibility of judicial review" and so must be considered arbitrary on the basis of the "Saluka test" of "*manifestly violat[ing] the requirements of consistency, transparency, even-handedness and non-discrimination*"[214] and "*shock[ing], or at least surprise[ing], a sense of juridical propriety,*"[215] as that test had been applied in the decisions of previous tribunals.

Regarding compensation for violation of the fair and equitable treatment obligations, the *Lemire* Tribunal, referring to the ILC Articles on Responsibilities of States for Internationally Wrongful Acts, acknowledged that the very purpose of compensation was to eliminate all the negative consequences of the respondent's wrongful acts.[216] Regarding the amount to be determined as compensation, the tribunal departed from the FMV standard and adopted a "but for" approach— the damage being the "difference between a real 'as is' value of Gala Radio – what the investor now actually owns – and a hypothetical 'but for' value – what the investor would have owned if the host State had respected the BIT."[217]

At the same time, the tribunal recognized that the broadcasting business is subject to strict regulation in every country. That being the case, there are always interactions between regulators and those being regulated, which requires that in reconstructing the "but for" hypothetical one must not only consider what is required from the host state under the BIT but also what is expected from the investor.

In any event, the tribunal concluded, "based on the available evidence, that Claimant has indeed suffered a loss, resulting from Gala Radio's curtailed growth, and consequent loss of value, and that the proximate cause of the loss were [sic] the wrongful actions of Respondent."[218] The tribunal, however, did not support the claimant's prayer for lost opportunities and confined its loss to actual damages.[219]

---

212 Ibid., para. 251.
213 Ibid., paras. 417–18.
214 *Saluka Investments B.V. v. Czech Republic PCA*, UNCITRAL, Partial Award of March 17, 2006, para. 307, as quoted ibid., para. 418 (emphasis in original).
215 *Tecnicas Medioambientales Tecmed S.A. v. United Mexican States*, ICSID Case No. ARB (AF)/00/2, Award of May 29, 2003, para. 154; and *Loewen Group, Inc. and Raymond L. Loewen v. United States of America*, ICSID No. ARB(AF)98/3, Award of June 26, 2003, para. 131; as quoted id. (emphasis in original).
216 *Lemire v. Ukraine, supra*, note 211, para. 151.
217 Ibid., para. 244.
218 Ibid., para. 247.
219 Ibid., para. 252.

In relation to measurement of the appropriate compensation, the *Lemire* Tribunal found that Gala Radio was not an institutionalized enterprise nor could the environment in which it was operating ensure its evolution to that status. Based on this assessment, the tribunal, in its evaluation, treated the claimant's business as an example of family-owned small-to-medium businesses which would not be entitled to "residual value beyond the one that reflects lost value,"[220] even though it considered this approach to be very conservative. Using the DCF model, in the end the tribunal awarded the claimant an amount of US$8,717,850 as compensation for losses suffered.[221]

The tribunal's analysis of the nature of the investment as one which is subject to strict regulation in every country is sound. It also mentioned that as a family-owned business the claimant was not entitled to residual value. This is not convincing, as whether an entity is entitled to residual value should depend on its potential, not so much on its size or form of ownership. Yet, for calculating compensation, the tribunal adopted the most unreliable DCF method, which is contrary to its comment on the lack of residual value of the claimant's investment. In its view, the claimant was not entitled to any compensation beyond lost value; yet, by using the DCF method, how could the tribunal ensure that the compensation would not be beyond such value?

In *Feldman*, in the absence of a finding of expropriation of the investment,[222] the tribunal nonetheless determined that Mexico had violated its obligations of national treatment under the NAFTA.[223] Regarding compensation for damages arising from the violation of national treatment, however, the tribunal opined that the "NAFTA provides no further guidance as to the proper measure of damages or compensation for situations that do not fall under Article 1110 (expropriation)"[224] and that the FMV standard was only applicable in cases of expropriation. The tribunal therefore concluded that for a breach of national treatment obligations, "what is owed by the responding Party is the amount of loss or damage that is adequately connected to the breach. ... Thus, if loss or damage is the requirement for the submission of a claim, it arguably follows that the Tribunal may direct compensation in the amount of the loss or damage."[225] Again, the tribunal adopted implicitly the *Chorzów* dictum on compensation.

The *Feldman* Tribunal further observed "at the outset that the appropriate measure and amount of damages is only generally and cursorily discussed by

220 Ibid., para. 270.
221 Ibid., para. 296.
222 See *Feldman v. Mexico, supra*, note 75, in which the tribunal stated (at para. 112) that "not all government regulatory activity that makes it difficult or impossible for an investor to carry out a particular business, change in the law or change in the application of existing laws that makes it uneconomical to continue a particular business, is an expropriation under Article 1110. Governments, in their exercise of regulatory power, frequently change their laws and regulations in response to changing economic circumstances or changing political, economic or social considerations."
223 Ibid., para. 187.
224 Ibid., para. 194.
225 Id.

the Parties."[226] In general, the tribunal considered three categories of damages, namely, loss of profits, going concern value and loss of tax rebates.[227] It asked the claimant to prove item by item its losses and verified the evidence he submitted. Nonetheless, the tribunal found itself still limited by "the amount of evidence" submitted by the disputing parties. For instance, with regard to the alleged lost profits, the tribunal said that "[e]ven if the Claimant asks ... for lost profits for one month ... the claim does not specify its amount with regard to that particular month and, in any case, has not convinced the Tribunal with respect to both existence and extent."[228] It further stated that "even had there been greater specificity on the part of the Claimant, the Tribunal is not convinced on the basis of the evidence in the record that CEMSA's operations would have been profitable, should CEMSA have received the IEPS rebates during the relevant time in the proper amounts."[229] In the end, the tribunal awarded the claimant the actual loss that resulted from the respondent's non-payment of export tax rebates plus simple interest.[230] It did not consider that the "going concern value" should be applied in the case, as it did not involve expropriation.[231]

Clearly, the *Feldman* decision was well reasoned. This is particularly important when the international documents in question provide no standards or methods for assessing damages. The tribunal's reasoning for not applying the "going concern value" was also well considered, as the claimant was not a viable business in any event. In fact, the *Feldman* Tribunal, in its analysis, also made references to the decisions in the *S.D. Myers* and *Pope & Talbot*[232] cases.

Unlike the *S.D. Myers* Tribunal, in the *Pope & Talbot* case the tribunal did not go through the process of rationalizing the method for determining compensation for violation of Article 1105 of the NAFTA.[233] The *Pope & Talbot* Tribunal, however, rejected the claimant's claim for damages in respect of management time. It stated that "the evidence revealed that the management who were involved in matters covered by the present claim were paid annual salaries that did not vary in respect of the issues or matters to which each of them devoted his or her working time."[234]

226 Ibid., para. 189.
227 Ibid., paras. 198–202.
228 Ibid., para. 199.
229 Ibid., para. 200.
230 Ibid., para. 205.
231 Ibid., para. 198. In addition, the tribunal did not believe that the claimant was a viable business and was convinced that the claimant "could not have made a profit regardless of whether SHCP provided the IEPS rebates." These factors have obviously influenced the decision-making of the tribunal not to employ the "going concern value." See ibid., para. 201.
232 *Pope & Talbot, Inc. v. Government of Canada*, UNCITRAL, Award in Respect of Damages (May 31, 2002).
233 The claimant alleged the respondent to have breached Article 1105 of the NAFTA, which provides, inter alia: "Each Party shall accord to investments of investors of another Party treatment in accordance with international law, including fair and equitable treatment and full protection and security." It also requires Contracting Parties to ensure non-discriminatory treatment to investments from the other Party in its territory.
234 *Pope & Talbot, Inc. v. Canada*, *supra*, note 227, para. 82.

With regard to the claimant's lost profits for the short period of time in which its mills were shut down by the respondent, the tribunal said that "the investment suffered no loss of profits from the shutdown because it was always able to meet the needs of its customers on a timely basis."[235] In the end, the tribunal only awarded compensation for out-of-pocket expenses incurred by the claimant in defending itself against the respondent's violation.[236]

This is a very interesting case. It is, of course, difficult to prove loss relating to management time, even though those in management must have devoted time on matters relating to the claim. The thorny issue in the case is about lost profits, as the government measure did not affect the claimant's ability to meet the demand of clients. As a matter of policy,[237] the host state should be subject to some consequences for its violation of treaty obligations. Yet the claimant could not prove what loss of profit it had suffered. An unfortunate effect of the *Pope & Talbot* decision is that it is unlikely to serve as a deterrent to host states' violations of treaty obligations. Yet, the function of investment arbitration is to ensure that treaty violations that cause actual damages to investors have consequences. As there is no provable damage, it is difficult for investment arbitral tribunals to impose penalties for the simple/formal violation of an obligation. Where there are other damages, such as moral damages, that can be proved, the tribunal should not be prevented from awarding compensation for such damages.

Occidental v. Ecuador[238] is another case which involved denial of benefits. The history of the investment in this case is the same as that in the *Occidental v. Ecuador* case decided by the ICSID, which was discussed earlier. In this case, the claimant alleged that Ecuador's failure to pay certain value-added tax ("VAT") reimbursements constituted a breach of its obligations under the Ecuador–United States BIT relating to fair and equitable treatment, national treatment and the prohibition of arbitrary or discriminatory measures, as well as expropriation.[239] The tribunal determined that the respondent "did not adopt measures that could be considered as amounting to direct or indirect expropriation. In fact, there has been no deprivation of the use or reasonably expected economic benefit of the investment, let alone measures affecting a significant part of the investment."[240]

The tribunal was not persuaded by the claimant's argument that Ecuador had impaired its management and other rights, stating that the claimant "continues to

---

235 Ibid., para. 84.

236 Ibid., para. 85.

237 When commenting on compensation for expropriation, Reisman and Sloane observed: "[T]he distinction between *damnum emergens* and *lucrum cessans*, for all its anachronism, serves a useful policy purpose insofar as it permits international tribunals to penalize egregious expropriations and, hopefully, to deter them in the future." W. Michael Reisman and Robert D. Sloane, "Indirect Expropriation and its Valuation in the BIT Generation," *British Yearbook of International Law*, Vol. 75, 2004, pp. 115–50, at 137.

238 *Occidental Exploration and Production Corporation v. Ecuador*, final award in the matter of an UNCITRAL arbitration (London Court of International Arbitration Administered Case No. UN 3467) (July 1, 2004) [hereinafter the "VAT Award"].

239 Ibid., para. 36.

240 Ibid., para. 89.

exercise all these rights [management, operation, maintenance, use, enjoyment, acquisition, expansion or disposal of the investment] in a manner which is fully compatible with the rights to property."[241] Yet the tribunal found Ecuador's actions to be arbitrary, at least to some extent, and thus that the claimant's "rights under the Contract and Treaty have not been fully safeguarded."[242] The tribunal also found that Ecuador had violated its national treatment obligations under the BIT, even though the discrimination was without intent on the part of the respondent.[243]

Based on the above findings, the *Occidental* VAT Tribunal considered that there were four situations in which the claimant's rights had been affected and damage had ensued. They were (1) the amount of VAT refunded which the respondent had required the claimant to return, (2) the amount of VAT refund which the claimant had requested but which was denied by the respondent, (3) the amount of VAT which had been paid by the claimant but for which it had not requested a refund, and (4) the VAT not yet due or paid.

With regard to the first three situations, the tribunal held that the claimant was entitled to the VAT refunds, including for the amount for which no refund had been requested, "again because no alternative mechanism was included in the Contract."[244] In awarding, after adjustments, an amount of US$71,533,649 as compensation, the tribunal announced that the amount was for Ecuador's breaches of treaty obligations.[245] In pronouncing the award, the tribunal explicitly ordered the claimant not to make double recovery through other channels. As for the fourth situation, the tribunal refused to award any payment of VAT refunds not yet due or paid. It relied on the rulings in the *SPP*, *Amoco*[246] and *Chorzów Factory* cases for its decision that it could not award on "contingent and undeterminate damage[s]."[247]

Apparently the *Occidental* VAT case was quite straightforward. The tribunal's findings and decisions were not outrageous, either. The tribunal was also conscious of the potential political sensitivity of its decision in the host state, as it encouraged the parties to explore, in addition to a refund, other forms of compensation.[248] Unfortunately, the tribunal's decision triggered considerable public anger in Ecuador, which, as discussed earlier, eventually led to the termination of the claimant's contract for exploration and production of oil in Ecuador.

In conclusion, the actual loss suffered and denial of benefits are two sides of the same coin. As demonstrated by *LG&E* and *Lemire*, regardless of whether a given case involves losses or denial of benefits, the "but for" standard may be applied as a measurement of damages. The *S.D. Myers* Tribunal adopted the principles of tort law in assessing the loss alleged by the claimant. All these and other cases show that in the end, the "but for" standard is the key in assessing whether loss or denial of

241 Ibid., para. 161.
242 Ibid., paras. 162 and 166.
243 Ibid., para. 177.
244 Ibid., para. 205.
245 Ibid., paras. 207–208.
246 *Amoco International Finance Corp. v. Iran*, 12 *Iran–US CTR* 170 (1986), at 238.
247 *Occidental v. Ecuador*, VAT Award, *supra*, note 233, para. 210.
248 Ibid., para. 214.

benefits has occurred. As illustrated by *Feldman*, *Pope & Talbot* and *Occidental*, the "but for" standard is especially useful in determining damages relating to taxation, such as tax refunds, for example. To compensate a foreign investor for what actual losses it has suffered or benefits it has been denied, plus interest, is equitable in nature. In some cases, *Pope & Talbot* being an example, however, where the host state's actions or omissions are clearly in violation of its treaty obligations, the claimant may not be able to prove certain losses—loss of profits—at least not immediately. For instance, potential clients, upon learning about certain government measures against the foreign investor, may have gone to other suppliers of products or services, even though the demands of existing clientele may continue to be satisfied. In such circumstances, tribunals should consider whether any loss of opportunities has been suffered by the foreign investor. Otherwise, the host state may not have to bear any liabilities for its violations, which is not conducive for formulating a sound legal system for international investment.

VII. Compensation for moral damages

Moral damages may not be a common phenomenon in international investment. Yet, where an investment is subjected to severe and wrongful actions by the host state and, in particular, the foreign investor's safety is in danger, this may involve mental suffering, duress and defamation, which may all give rise to moral damages. In such cases, how should the foreign investor be compensated? The *Diallo* case, recently decided by the International Court of Justice,[249] is one such case. Mr Ahmadou Sadio Diallo is a businessman of Guinean nationality who had resided in the Democratic of Republic of Congo ("DRC") for more than 30 years before the dispute arose. Guinea, as Mr Diallo's home country, complained that the DRC unjustly imprisoned Mr Diallo; despoiled his sizable investments, businesses, movable and immovable property and bank accounts; and then expelled him.[250] Guinea further alleged that the expulsion of Mr Diallo came at a time when he "was pursuing recovery of substantial debts owed to his businesses [Africom-Zaire and Africontainers-Zaire] by the [Congolese] State and by oil companies established in its territory and of which the State is a shareholder."[251] This case, however, was not based on a BIT. The plaintiff state—Guinea—relied on the principles of international law regarding treatment of aliens and their property. It is therefore, to a large extent, a case of human rights concern, notwithstanding its involvement with investments. Among the damages sought, non-material injury or mental and moral damages were pleaded by Guinea.

The ICJ first considered that non-material injury to a person was "cognizable under international law" and might take "various forms," including mental suffering, injury to a person's feelings, humiliation, shame, degradation, loss of social

249 *Republic of Guinea v. Democratic Republic of the Congo*, ICJ, Judgment (June 19, 2012); available at: http://www.icj-cij.org/docket/files/103/17044.pdf.
250 Ibid., para. 1.
251 Id.

position or injury to a person's credit or reputation.[252] It further stated that "non-material injury can be established even without specific evidence."[253] Apparently, when making this statement, the Court had in mind the specific suffering of Mr Diallo—having been "arrested without being informed of the reasons for his arrest and without being given the possibility to seek a remedy" and being "made the object of accusations that were not substantiated."[254] These, together with some other facts, prompted the Court to conclude that the "DRC's wrongful conduct caused Mr Diallo significant psychological suffering and loss of reputation."[255]

Regarding quantification of compensation for non-material damages, the ICJ adopted the principle of equity. It also cited practices of international arbitration and regional human rights courts, in particular the decision of the ECHR in *Al-Jedda v. United Kingdom*, in respect of assessment of non-material damages:

> Its guiding principle is equity, which above all involves flexibility and an objective consideration of what is just, fair and reasonable in all the circumstances of the case, including not only the position of the applicant but the overall context in which the breach occurred.[256]

Nonetheless, even though the Court pointed out that the fact that Mr Diallo had been detained and then expelled from the DRC whilst attempting to recover debts owed to his companies by, inter alia, the DRC and DRC-owned companies aggravated the situation of non-material injury, it only awarded US$85,000 as damages.

The value of the ICJ judgment of the *Diallo* case is obviously not significant. The significance of the case however cannot be underestimated. After all it was the first time that the World Court issued a judgment on moral damages in an investment case. The principle pronounced by the ICJ will be followed by other tribunals regarding compensation for non-material injuries.

Desert Line Projects[257] is most probably the first ICSID case that awarded a substantial amount for moral damages. In that case, the claimant was a construction company organized under the laws of the Sultanate of Oman which was engaged by Yemen to build asphalt roads. During the course of construction, there were a number of interruptions of work caused by local tribal groups and others. In early to middle 2004, when the works were completed and the claimant requested payment of amounts due, the parties had disputes which led to an arbitral award in favor of the claimant. The claimant then raised complaints about some clerical and calculation mistakes in the award.[258] Thereafter, an altercation took place

---

252 Ibid., para. 18.
253 Ibid., para. 21.
254 Id.
255 Id.
256 Ibid., para. 24.
257 *Desert Line Projects LLC v. Republic of Yemen*, ICSID Case No. ARB/05/17, Award (January 29, 2008).
258 Ibid., para. 32.

between the claimant's personnel and the Yemeni Army, which resulted in a four-day arrest of three of the claimant's personnel.[259] On September 22, 2004, the respondent applied to a local court for annulment of the arbitral award. On December 22, 2004, the claimant resorted to local court procedures to oppose the respondent's annulment request. On the same day, the claimant and the respondent reached a settlement agreement.[260] Soon after the local court approved the settlement agreement and the Central Bank of Yemen made payment to the claimant in accordance with the settlement agreement and the release of two bank guarantees issued by the claimant in favor of Yemen, the claimant started to challenge the validity of the settlement agreement. Ultimately, the claimant informed Yemen of its intent to bring the dispute to arbitration at the ICSID.[261]

The claimant requested that the settlement agreement be rescinded[262] and that the ICSID tribunal order the respondent to pay compensation for (a) the claimant's outstanding rights under the contracts or, alternatively, (b) the amount awarded in the Yemeni arbitration.[263] The claimant's argument relating to rescinding the settlement agreement was that it had entered into the agreement under duress. As mentioned in the award, the claimant's assertions involved a series of violations of substantive provisions of the Yemen–Oman BIT.[264] With a finding that the settlement agreement was signed under duress, the tribunal concluded that the entering into force of the agreement "contravened the respondent's obligations" in respect of fair and equitable treatment under Article 3 of the BIT.[265] Therefore, the claimant should be entitled to compensation, for which, in the view of the tribunal, "the Yemeni Arbitral Award should constitute the bench-mark for the reparation" due to the claimant.[266]

Regarding moral damages, the claimant's allegations included (1) that its "executives suffered the stress and anxiety of being harassed, threatened and detained" by both the respondent and armed tribes; (2) that there was a significant injury to its credit and reputation, as well as a loss of prestige; and (3) that there had been intimidation of the claimant's executives.[267] The tribunal determined:

> Even if investment treaties primarily aim at protecting property and economic values, they do not exclude, as such, that a party may, in exceptional circumstances, ask for compensation for moral damages. It is generally accepted in most legal systems that moral damages may also be recovered besides pure economic damages. There are indeed no reasons to exclude them.[268]

259 Ibid., para. 33.
260 Ibid., para. 43.
261 Ibid., para. 48.
262 Ibid., para. 146.
263 Ibid., para. 232.
264 Ibid., para. 148.
265 Ibid., para. 194.
266 Ibid., para. 253.
267 Ibid., para. 286.
268 Ibid., para. 289.

At the same time, it acknowledged the difficulties, if not impossibilities, in quantifying moral damages.[269] It then relied on the decision in the *Lusitania* case, in which the tribunal considered non-material or moral damages to be "very real, and the mere fact that they are difficult to measure or estimate by monetary standards makes them none the less real and affords no reason why the injured person should not be compensated."[270] Also, in the tribunal's view, moral damages should be available to both natural and legal persons, as the latter may suffer from an injury to reputation. As the tribunal considered the respondent's acts to be "malicious and … therefore constitutive of a fault-based liability" as well as substantial, it awarded the claimant an amount of US$1 million as compensation for moral damages.[271] In reaching its conclusion of substantial injury, the detention of the executives, harassment of personnel and harmful effects on the claimant were taken into account.

Desert Line is a very rare case in which the foreign investor was subject to physical threat. If such behavior of the host state can go without being punished, the system created for attracting foreign investment will be regarded as useless and meaningless. It is therefore understandable that the *Desert Line* Tribunal emphasized, in its analysis, the role played by duress in concluding the settlement agreement between the claimant and the respondent. As the tribunal stated, compensation for moral damages exists in most, if not all, legal systems. To apply a principle that is generally recognized by civilized societies to investment relations is a natural choice in the case. This having been said, the principle relating to moral damages, as exhibited by the *Lemire* case, should be applied restrictively.

The *Lemire* Tribunal, after examining the approach of the *Desert Line* Tribunal, concluded that "as a general rule, moral damages are not available to a party injured by the wrongful acts of a State."[272] It opined that the exceptional circumstances in which moral damages may be awarded included physical threat and illegal detention. It stated that "deterioration of health, stress, anxiety, other mental suffering such as humiliation, shame and degradation, or loss of reputation, credit and social position," and the cause of the suffering and its effects must be "grave or substantial."[273] In essence, the *Lemire* Tribunal's decision was not contrary to that of *Desert Line*. It only refined the position of the latter. Also, because the claimant in the *Lemire* case had already been awarded a significant amount of economic compensation, the tribunal refused to also award it moral damages.[274] Thus, to read the *Desert Line* and *Lemire* decisions together, guided by the principle pronounced by the ICJ in *Diallo* case, a conclusion can be drawn that compensation for moral damages is permissible under international investment law but should be restricted to cases involving physical and mental damages.

---

269 Id.
270 See *United States v. Germany*, November 1923, VII RIAA 32, at p. 42, quoted in *Desert Line Projects*, ibid., para. 289.
271 *Desert Line Projects*, ibid., para. 290.
272 *Lemire v. Ukraine*, Award, *supra*, note 206, para. 333.
273 Id.
274 Ibid., para. 344.

VIII. Conclusions and alternatives

Compensation is the most important aspect of investment dispute resolution. No matter for what reasons the disputing parties have engaged in arbitration or judicial proceedings, in the end, whatever compensation the party having suffered losses may get is the measurement of the fairness, justice and reasonableness of the system through which foreign investment is made and of whether the system is conducive to encouraging cross-border investment. Generally speaking, compensation may be divided into that given for either expropriatory or for non-expropriatory actions of a host state that cause damages to foreign investors. This section will conduct a summary discussion on the practice relating to the determination of compensation in both cases. That discussion is followed by suggestions for alternatives to improve current practice.

A. FMV as the standard for expropriatory measures

Practice illustrates that in cases where expropriation—direct or indirect expropriation notwithstanding—is found, tribunals have been consistent in awarding compensation according to the market value or FMV of the investment.[275]

Whether a given conduct or regulation is a direct or indirect expropriation, a measure tantamount to expropriation or constitutes a creeping expropriation is not material, at least insofar as compensation is concerned. Further, more recent arbitral practice, which has shown an increase in the number of expropriations found "illegal" or to constitute "internationally unlawful acts," has also shown a significant degree of consistency in choosing the standard of compensation. An example of this practice can be found in *ADC v. Hungary*. As a result, whether a given conduct or regulation is a direct or indirect expropriation, a measure tantamount to expropriation or constitutes a creeping expropriation is not material, at least insofar as compensation is concerned.

On the issue of compensation, after finding the expropriation carried out by the respondent to constitute an internationally wrongful act, the *ADC* Tribunal said that it was "subject to the customary international law standard as set out in *Chorzów Factory*"[276] because the "BIT only stipulates the standard of compensation that is payable in the case of a lawful expropriation, and these cannot be used to determine the issue of damages payable in the case of an unlawful expropriation."[277] Nevertheless, as the Cyprus–Hungary BIT made a reference to just compensation, which amount must correspond to the market value of

---

275 For a comparative study of state practices relating to compensation for indirect expropriation, see Matthew C. Porterfield, "State Practice and the (Purported) Obligation under Customary International Law to Provide Compensation for Regulatory Expropriations," *N.C.J. Int'l L. & Com. Reg.*, Vol. 37, 2012, pp. 160–97.

276 *ADC Affiliate Limited and ADC & ADMC Management Limited v. Republic of Hungary*, ICSID Case No. ARB/03/16, Award (September 26, 2006), para. 480.

277 Ibid., para. 481.

the expropriated investment at the moment of expropriation, after reviewing international practices the tribunal decided to adopt the market value standard which would be calculated by the DCF method.[278] *Siemens v. Argentina*,[279] *Vivendi v. Argentina*,[280] and *Kardassopoulos v. Greece*[281] also found that the standard of compensation for expropriation stipulated in the relevant agreements applied only to lawful expropriation and that a different standard—on the basis of customary international law as best represented by the *Chorzów* dictum—must be applied in cases of illegal expropriation. Having found illegal expropriation, these tribunals unanimously adopted the FMV method in assessing damages, the same method that is stipulated in BITs and FTAs as the standard of compensation in relation to lawful expropriation.

Insofar as the compensation standard is concerned, it is evident that tribunals unanimously regard the principle of reparation pronounced by the PCIJ in the *Chorzów Factory* case as a reflection of customary international law. As a result, the FMV standard has been adopted by more and more tribunals for compensating losses resulting from unlawful or illegal expropriations.

Another aspect of compensation in cases of expropriation is the method of calculation, on which debates are likely to continue,[282] despite the fact that the DCF method has been employed in many cases.

These practices exhibit that despite the lack of treaty stipulations on compensation for unlawful expropriation, decisions of arbitration tribunals are quite consistent, which is not only helpful for establishing commonly accepted international norms for such cases but also provides guidance for the determination of compensation for non-expropriatory breaches. As large-scale and direct expropriation is unlikely to be an immediate concern of the international community in the foreseeable future, the traditional distinction of compensation for lawful and unlawful expropriation may not be emphasized.

B. Varied standards adopted for non-expropriatory breaches

Facing the issue of compensation for non-expropriatory breaches, arbitral tribunals have consistently asserted the right, in accordance with the applicable BITs and other international instruments, to exercise discretion in determining the standard thereof. Decisions of tribunals in this regard are, consequently, far from consistent. Some have applied the FMV standard; the *CME*, *CMS* and *Azurix* cases

---

278 Ibid., paras. 501–502.
279 *Siemens A.G. v. Argentine Republic*, ICSID Case No. ARB/02/8, Award (February 6, 2006).
280 *Compañía de Aguas del Aconquija S.A. and Vivendi Universal S.A. v. Argentine Republic*, ICSID Case No. ARB/97/3, Award (August 20, 2007).
281 *Ioannis Kardassopoulos v. Republic of Georgia*, ICSID Case No. ARB/05/18, Award (March 3, 2010).
282 Concerning the choice of the method for calculating compensation, one commentator has noted that: "The 'South' looks to book value as what has been spent but not recovered, while, conversely, the 'North' argues that the DCF value represents the economic measure of the market value and thus equals the opportunity cost of the taken asset." See Thomas R. Stauffer, "Valuation of Assets in International Takings," *Energy Law Journal*, Vol. 17, pp. 459–88, at 462.

are examples. Other tribunals, such as those in the *LG&E* and *S.D. Myers* cases, refused to adopt the FMV standard because they considered it "not a logical, appropriate or practicable measure of the compensation to be awarded."[283] The *Feldman* and *Occidental* tribunals awarded the foreign investors compensation in accordance with the benefits they had been denied—the "but for" formula. Still others applied the norms of customary international law in assessing damages; *Nykomb v. Latvia*[284] is a case in point.

In that case, the claimant, Nykomb Synergetics Technology Holding AB, was a joint stock company incorporated under the laws of Sweden which had acquired 100 percent of the shares of Windau, a company organized under the laws of Latvia. The dispute concerned the delivery price under purchase contracts entered into between Windau and Latvenergo, a state-owned enterprise of Latvia whose functions include carrying out government policies in the economic sector. Nykomb brought claims against the host state for violation of its obligations under the ECT relating to fair and equitable treatment and the minimum standard of treatment, the prohibition against unreasonable or discriminatory measures, and expropriation.[285] The essence of the claims was that Latvenergo failed to pay a double tariff for electricity produced by Windau, the responsibility for which was attributed to Latvia. The tribunal found the respondent to have violated its treaty obligations and therefore ruled that it must "be liable for the losses or damages incurred" by the claimant.[286] Indeed, the tribunal considered "the damage or loss caused by the non-payment of the double tariff is the same. Thus, in order to establish liability for the republic it is strictly speaking sufficient to find that one of the relevant provisions has been violated."[287]

On the matter of compensation, the *Nykomb* Tribunal said that the principles of compensation set out in Article 13(1) of the ECT were for "the special case" of nationalization or expropriation, or for measures tantamount to expropriation. The tribunal, however, did not find Latvenergo's refusal to make payments to constitute nationalization or expropriation. It thus decided that the treaty standard of compensation for expropriation was not applicable to other violations.[288] In the tribunal's view, compensation for violation of "obligations under Article 10 of the Treaty must primarily find its solution in accordance with established principles of customary international law," which, it further stated, had "authoritatively been restated in the International Law Commission's Draft Articles on State Responsibility,"[289] Article 35 of which permits restitution as means of compensation. The tribunal, however, after "taking into regard the requirements under applicable customary international law of causation, foreseeability and the

---

283 *S.D. Myers*, First Partial Award, *supra*, note 70, para. 309.
284 *Nykomb Synergetics Technology Holding AB v. Latvia*, Stockholm Chamber of Commerce, Award (December 16, 2003).
285 Ibid., Section 1.2.3.3.
286 Ibid., Section 4.3.4.1.
287 Ibid., Section 4.3.2.3.
288 Ibid., Section 5.1.1.
289 Ibid., Section 5.1.3.

reasonableness of the result," ruled on monetary compensation.[290] The difficulty in obtaining a precise amount of the double-tariff treatment to which the claimant was entitled but was not paid might have been the reason the tribunal chose not to award restitution. It was nonetheless a pity that the tribunal did not take the opportunity to provide a more thorough discussion of its reasoning after having entered into the issue.

C. Alternatives for improvement

In view of the issues raised by the practice discussed above—inconsistent arbitral decisions, a failure to agree on both standards for and methods of calculating compensation, and a lack of generally agreed principles for compensating non-expropriatory breaches of investment agreements, among others—there is clearly room for improvement in investment arbitration. The following are some suggestions for such improvement.

Restitution: Under Article 35 of the ILC Articles on Responsibilities of States for Internationally Wrongful Acts, a state that commits a wrongful act, which certainly includes a breach of a BIT, has an obligation to make restitution. As these Articles are regarded as representing customary international law, such obligation to make restitution exists even without the assistance of BITs and other international instruments. In investment arbitration, however, restitution has seldom been awarded as a form of compensation. For instance, in *Amco Asia v. Indonesia*, the tribunal refused to touch on the issue of non-monetary relief, stating: "It is obvious that this tribunal cannot substitute itself for the Indonesian Government in order to cancel the revocation and restore the license; such actions are not even claimed, and it is more than doubtful that this kind of *restitution in integrum* could be ordered against a sovereign State."[291] It is true that a tribunal cannot substitute itself for the host state. Yet, in an appropriate case such as *Amco*, the tribunal could make restitution an option for both the respondent and claimant. By doing so, it may offer an opportunity for the disputing parties to continue their cooperation.

Goetz v. Burundi[292] is one of the very few cases in which restitution was awarded. The case involved a Belgian investor with an investment in the production of silver, gold, and other precious metals through a local company in Burundi. The dispute arose from Burundi's revocation of a certificate held by the claimant, which entitled it to some tax advantages. The host state was alleged to have breached its obligations relating to non-discrimination and expropriation under the Belgium–Burundi BIT. The tribunal considered Burundi's revocation of the certificate to be a measure tantamount to expropriation, although no discrimination was established, and decided to give Burundi an option in order to put an end to the contested measure. The tribunal said that Burundi could carry out the award "either by the repeal of the ministerial ruling [revocation of the certificate]

---

290 Ibid., Section 5.2.b.8.
291 *Amco Asia v. Indonesia*, Award, *supra*, note 48, para. 202.
292 *Antoine Goetz and Others v. Burundi*, ICSID Case No. ARB/95/3, Award (February 10, 1999).

... followed by the restoration of the certificate of free export company, or even by the restoration of the certificate of free export company without preliminary abrogation of [the] ministerial ruling."[293] The tribunal further stated that both choices were "within the competence of the sovereign decision of the Burundi Government."[294] Thus, the respondent was given an opportunity to rectify its wrongful act by restitution, in which case the foreign investment could continue to operate. The claimant was not disadvantaged, either, since after all its interest was the investment and not just receiving a monetary award and then seeking other opportunities.

In any event, the cases in which tribunals award non-monetary relief are very few for multiple reasons. In the first place, international law in this area imposes strict conditions. The ILC Articles on Responsibilities of States for Internationally Wrongful Acts, which are recognized as representing contemporary customary international law, require that restitution be awarded only if it is not "materially impossible" and if it "does not involve a burden out of all proportion to the benefit deriving from restitution instead of compensation."[295] The question is what may constitute a material impossibility. Would the respondent's indication that it would not enforce the arbitral decision be adequate? Indeed, where a respondent refuses to enforce an order of restitution or any other non-monetary relief, what are the means available for the foreign investor to enforce the award? The balancing of the benefits of restitution and compensation is an even more challenging task for tribunals. Such difficulties were also anticipated in the drafting of the ILC Articles on Responsibilities of States for Internationally Wrongful Acts. On this matter, Professor Crawford said, "Even where restitution is made, it may be insufficient to ensure full reparation. The role of compensation is to fill in any gaps so as to ensure full reparation for damage suffered."[296]

Insofar as ICSID arbitration is concerned, the difficulty of enforcing a non-monetary relief may also be intrinsic to the Convention itself. Article 54(1) of the ICSID Convention provides, that: "Each Contracting State shall recognize an award rendered pursuant to this Convention as binding and enforce the *pecuniary obligations* imposed by the award within its territories as if it were a final judgment of a court in that State" (emphasis added). By relying on these provisions, a losing respondent may be able to make a good defense for not enforcing a non-monetary relief such as restitution.

Difficulties in deciding on and enforcing an award of restitution notwithstanding, in appropriate cases tribunals should explore restitution as an alternative to pecuniary compensation. As discussed earlier, restitution may turn out to be a win-win situation for both the foreign investor and the host state. Regarding the potential difficulty in enforcement, it is evident that foreign investors often have

---

293 Ibid., para. 134.
294 Ibid., para. 136.
295 ILC Articles on Responsibilities of States for Internationally Wrongful Acts, Article 35; available at: http://legal.un.org/ilc/texts/instruments/english/draft%20articles/9_6_2001.pdf.
296 See James Crawford, *The International Law Commission's Articles on State Responsibility*, Cambridge University Press, Cambridge, UK, 2002, at 218.

significant difficulties in enforcing awards for monetary compensation, as will be discussed in Chapter 10 of this book.

Injunctive relief: Among the non-monetary relief that may be offered as a means of compensation, injunctions, although very rarely used or even sought, may serve as an option. In *Enron v. Argentina*,[297] the tribunal's power to order injunctive relief was challenged.[298] The tribunal stated that its examination of "the powers of international courts and tribunals to order measures concerning performance or injunction and of the ample practice that is available in this respect, leaves this tribunal in no doubt about the fact that these powers are indeed available."[299] Because the respondent was found to have violated its obligations on fair and equitable treatment and in relation to the umbrella clause, the tribunal arguably could have, in addition to pecuniary compensation, awarded injunctive relief. Yet it chose not to do so. Whether or not the tribunal's decision was made in anticipation of the challenges likely to be made by the respondent is not known. In any event, to retain the availability of injunctive relief as an option for compensation is very important, because in certain cases where a foreign investor is still interested in maintaining its investment, pecuniary damages may not do it justice.

Better reasons required: As in other aspects of arbitration, some tribunals have more thoroughly explained their reasoning than have others in determining compensation. As decisions on compensation for non-expropriatory breaches are mostly made, due to lack of specifications in treaties, at the discretion of the tribunals, it would be helpful and carry more persuasive force if tribunals would give more extensive and adequate reasons. Unfortunately, not every tribunal fully explains the reasons behind their decisions. For instance, in the *Nykomb* case, while facing a number of allegations of the claimant, the tribunal decided to examine only whether or not the respondent had violated Article 10(1) of the ECT relating to "unreasonable or discriminatory measures." It simply stated that although the respondent's actions might qualify as a violation of various treaty provisions, it considered it sufficient to find just one such violation because "the damage or loss caused … is the same."[300] From the point of view of judicial economy, there is no problem with that decision. The tribunal should, however, have more thoroughly explained its reasons.

The *Nykomb* Tribunal took a similar approach in its decision on whether or not the respondent's measures were discriminatory. It simply said that two other entities and the claimant were in the same business and that:

297 *Enron Corp. and Ponderosa Assets LP v. Argentine Republic*, ICSID Case No. ARB/01/3, Decision on Jurisdiction (January 14, 2004).
298 Ibid., para. 76. In the view of the respondent, the tribunal's power was confined to making a declaration to satisfy the claimant or determining the amount of compensation if breaches of the Treaty were found.
299 Ibid., para. 79. At the merits stage of the arbitration proceedings, Argentina's tax measures were not found to be tantamount to measures of expropriation—neither direct nor indirect expropriation—and the tribunal awarded the claimant only pecuniary damages.
300 *Nykomb v. Latvia, supra*, note 279, para. 4.3.2.3.

> ... little if anything has been documented by the Respondent to show the criteria or methodology used in fixing the multiplier or to what extent Latvenergo is authorized to apply multipliers other than those documented in this arbitration. On the other hand, all of the information available to the Tribunal suggests that the three companies are comparable, and subject to the same laws and regulations.[301]

A little more explanation would make a difference. Yet the *Nykomb* Tribunal did not do so. Such information includes, for instance, the products, size and number of employees of entities concerned.

In practice, when no adequate reasons are given, the decisions of tribunals may be challenged by one party or the other. Where cases involve ICSID arbitration, inadequately reasoned decisions may be challenged in accordance with Article 52(1)(e) of the Convention.[302] Therefore, from either a legal or other point of view, a better reasoned decision is preferred.

Moral damages: A few tribunals have awarded moral damages to claimants in investment-related cases. Moral damages are often related to damages to the reputation or status of natural or legal persons. Legal persons, in fact, are becoming increasingly vulnerable to the adverse impact of government actions and omissions on their reputations in the sophisticated computerized world, with wide use of Internet technology enabling information to travel at the speed of light around the world. Any rumor or comment, intended or unintended, may tremendously affect a company, product or management. For instance, where a host state investigates a foreign-invested enterprise for violations of local laws and detains its key managers, the news will be known to the whole world without delay. Upon learning that the foreign investment is in trouble, those who may be interested in entering into transactions with the business would naturally give a second thought to such a decision, meaning a loss of business opportunities for the foreign investment. At the same time, where the product of a foreign investment is under investigation for health or environmental reasons, or even subject to an antidumping investigation, regardless of the end result, the reputation and/or market share may be badly affected.

Therefore, where a host state imposes any measures or makes any statement that may have an impact on the status and reputation of a foreign investment, it must be liable for what is said or done. As the general principle of compensation is to put the foreign investor in the position that it would have been in had there been no breaches by the host state of its international obligations, moral damages resulting from such breaches should be as fully compensated as monetary damages. Caution, however should be taken in awarding moral damages, which can be very speculative and possibly even immeasurable.

One commentator has suggested that "[f]ault ... seems to play the role of a

---

301 Id.
302 For a discussion of this matter, see Markham Ball, "Assessing Damages in Claims by Investors Against States," 16 *ICSID Review: Foreign Investment Law Journal* 408, 2001, at 428.

gatekeeper, which, when present, permits the arbitrators to be more generous in awarding a higher amount of compensation in general and that for moral damage in particular."[303] Fault, or the intention to damage the reputation of either an individual or a legal person may be difficult to prove in many circumstances, in antidumping and subsidies investigations or environment and tax-related investigations, for example. Hence, if fault is made the prerequisite for awarding compensation for moral damages, many cases will fail the test. Yet it should be used for assessing a higher amount of compensation.

The FMV standard and the DCF method: Even though BITs and FTAs do not stipulate standards for compensation for damages suffered from treaty breaches other than expropriation, no one would argue that states party to BITs and FTAs bear no liability for such violations. In fact, no state has ever contended that no compensation should be paid for such breaches.[304] The question then arises as to why no provisions are incorporated into BITs and FTAs to regulate compensation for damages arising from non-expropriatory breaches. There are undoubtedly multiple reasons for this, including the relatively short history of awarding such damages, the uncertainty of contracting parties about the issue and/or the acquiescence or silent consent to arbitral tribunals' exercise of discretionary power, among others. The very fact that the international community has not reacted— as it has done in regard to arbitral decisions in the cases relating to the expansive interpretation of the MFN clause—to the decisions of arbitral tribunals to award compensation based on either FMV or actual loss or benefits denied confirms the general acceptance of such awards, notwithstanding the inconsistency of outcomes. This situation renders the jurisprudence, comprised mainly of arbitral decisions, very important for the development of this area of law. Faced with this important task of formulating international investment law, tribunals should act with great caution and state clearly the reasons behind their decisions.

Related to the FMV standard is the calculation of the compensation—how to determine the total amount that reflects the FMV. As discussed earlier, investment tribunals have in practice adopted various methods to calculate compensation for damages, including book value, the value of an arm's-length offer, the amount of denied benefits and DCF, among which the DCF method is the most controversial.

Wälde offered a cogent explanation for the development of the use of the DCF method to determine compensation in international investment arbitration. In his view:

> … the *damnun emergens/lucrum cessans* combination needs to be seen as arising in a time when valuation was mainly backwards/historic and based on

303 B. Sabahi, "Moral Damages in International Investment Law: Some Preliminary Thoughts in the Aftermath of Desert Line v. Yemen," *Transnational Dispute Management*, Vol. 9, Issue 1, January 2012, pp. 252–64, at 260.

304 For a discussion of this matter, see Campbell McLachlan, Laurence Shore, and Matthew Weniger, *International Investment Arbitration: Substantive Principles*, Oxford University Press, 2007, p. 315.

the accounting value of individual items of property. That did not represent market value properly as the combination of all items—the package value—and the ability to make profits was not taken into account. The *lucrum cessans* add-on was therefore meant, at least until payment of a judgment, to compensate for the short-comings of a purely historic and cost-based focus on individual property items.[305]

The DCF method seems to be able to take into account the capability of profit-making by the foreign investor. However, as it deals with the future, and nobody can accurately predict—not to mention accurately assess—what may happen in the future, the DCF value may not be reliable even in a mature market situation. As one group of commentators noted:

> When active and reasonably efficient markets do exist, uncertainty for investors leads to wide spreads between bids and offers and to large fluctuations in prices, sometimes from hour to hour. In the face of high uncertainty and very volatile markets, even free market prices do not provide a good basis for long-term commitments and investor's interest may tend to dry up.[306]

At the same time, however, as Reisman and Sloane point out, treaty provisions on compensation should "be construed to deter not reward" breaches by host states of their international obligations.[307] Among the different methods of calculation of compensation for damages, although DCF value may not be precise or accurate, it serves to compensate foreign investors adequately, while at the same time it may serve to deter or at least not to encourage non-expropriatory breaches, which in turn will help stabilize the international investment system. This having been said, it is submitted that caution should be taken in adopting the DCF method. For instance, in assessing the future values, detailed itemized accounting of future earnings should be based on reliable data. Tribunals should explain their calculations of the totality of compensation, as the impreciseness of the quantum of compensation has often been subject to criticisms.[308] Caution in use of the DCF method is also called for by scholars because of the risk it presents

---

305 Thomas W. Wälde, "Remedies and Compensation in International Investment Law," Report for the ILA Committee on International Law of Foreign Investment (First Draft), July 2005, published at *Transnational Dispute Management*, Vol. 2, Issue 5, November 2005, at 60–61.

306 Edith Penrose, George Joffé, and Paul Stevens, "Nationalisation of Foreign-owned Property for a Public Purpose: An Economic Perspective on Appropriate Compensation," *The Modern Law Review*, Vol. 55, 1992, pp. 351–67, at 364.

307 Reisman and Sloane, *supra*, note 232, at 148.

308 Some consider that "many arbitral tribunals seem to arrive at quantum figures in an imprecise manner even where the parties have presented detailed submissions accompanied by expert analyses, exacting calculations, alternative formulae and valuations;" see Abby Cohen Smutny, "Some Observations on the Principles Relating to Compensation in the Investment Treaty Context," *ICSID Review—Foreign Investment Law Journal*, Vol. 22, No. 1 (2007), pp. 1–23, at 22.

of "over"-compensating the foreign investor, particularly in the valuation of long-term contracts or concessions.[309]

In conclusion, international treaty practices and arbitral decisions demonstrate that market value or fair market value has become the norm for compensation in cases of both legal and illegal expropriation—direct and indirect expropriation as well as measures tantamount to expropriation. This consensus of the international community has also served as guidance for the establishment of standards of compensation for damages arising from non-expropriatory breaches. Faced with the issue of compensation for breaches other than expropriation, tribunals have been cautious in choosing applicable methods for calculating damages, variously using such methods as book value, the value of a recent arm's-length offer, the amount of denied benefits and DCF value, as seemed most appropriate to the case at hand. Despite the criticisms in respect of the DCF method, it may help stabilize the contemporary investment system by discouraging breaches by host states. Although arbitral decisions in this regard are not and should not be expected to be consistent, it appears that the international community has accepted the current state of compensation determinations in investment arbitration. It is evident that as the jurisprudence in this area continues to be enriched, the international community will be able to reach some consensus on the standards of compensation in the not-too-distant future.

309 Wälde was particularly critical of this potential, maintaining that: "… *lucrum cessans* can tempt an unwary tribunal to first order pay out [sic] of market value calculated in a historic, cost-based way and then again the value of future income expected long into the future. That means the investor in effect obtains twice (or possibly even three times) compensation: The value based on historic costs (that should in average be equal to the going concern/market value), the going concern/market value based on future income and, if the future income is not discounted by the risk factor, a third measure of the value. The investor can invest the costs into one new project without risk and the now, after compensation payment, risk-free future income value into a second new project which pays him twice the value and frees him of the risk. The slope towards multiple recovery is therefore particularly slippery when long-term contracts are in dispute." Ibid., p. 61 (footnote and cross-reference omitted).

10 State responsibility and enforcement of obligations

Foreign investments are subject to the laws and regulations of host countries and therefore involve the actions and omissions of those states. It is widely recognized that foreign investments make important contributions to the economy of host countries. As that is the case, bilateral investment treaties ("BITs") and free trade agreement ("FTAs") are entered into to regulate the conduct of host countries for the main purpose of protecting foreign investments and investors.[1] In other words, the international investment law regime must have the effect of limiting "the sovereign right of a state to subject foreign investors to its domestic administrative legal system."[2] Where a state has entered into a BIT or FTA, it is expected to perform its obligations arising therefrom. If a state refuses to enforce, or violates, its obligations under a BIT or FTA or a principle of customary international law, it must bear the consequences. For this purpose, the determination of whether an action or omission is attributable to the state is essential.

International law has made important progress in this area with the adoption by the United Nations International Law Commission in 2001 of the Draft Articles on Responsibility of States for Internationally Wrongful Acts ("ILC Articles"). Investment arbitration tribunals have also on numerous occasions decided on the imputability of acts or omissions of entities which are considered to be agencies or instrumentalities of states. That jurisprudence, together with the customary international law rules which are mainly reflected in the ILC Articles, forms an important legal source for determining the obligations of host states.

Traditionally, host states, as sovereigns, enjoy immunity in international law. Since the middle of the last century, however, some developed countries have adopted a doctrine of restricted sovereign immunity,[3] which has had a significant

---

1 For a discussion of this issue, see Asha Kaushal, "Revisiting History: How the Past Matters for the Present Backlash Against the Foreign Investment Regime," *Harvard International Law Journal*, Vol. 50, No. 2, Summer 2009.

2 Rudolf Dolzer, "The Impact of International Investment Treaties on Domestic Administrative Law," 37 *N.Y.U. J. Int'L L. & Pol.* 953, 2005.

3 Various writers and jurists refer to "sovereign immunity" as a "theory" or a "doctrine," sometimes using those as interchangeable terms. It seems clear to this author that "sovereign immunity" is neither a "theory" nor a "fact" but that it is rather a jurisprudential doctrine applied by national and international courts in specific circumstances. As we shall see later, sovereign immunity was

impact on the jurisdiction of national courts in respect of actions and omissions of foreign countries, including investment host states. With the introduction of the doctrine of restricted sovereign immunity, national courts have gained the power to exercise jurisdiction over certain acts of other states.

Any policy relating to sovereign immunity, in particular to changes in policy, has always been closely linked to international investment. Take, for example, the situation where a host state has breached treaty obligations that it has entered into but refuses to bear the consequences by paying compensation after an arbitration award is made against it. What options does the winning party—a foreign investor—have to enforce the award? It may, of course, request its home country to provide diplomatic protection.[4] It may also resort to a national court to enforce the award. In the latter case, whether the host state has immunity from jurisdiction and, even more importantly, whether it has immunity from execution are issues of major importance to foreign investors and, hence, to international investment law. In most countries where the doctrine of restricted sovereign immunity is followed, a distinction is still made between immunity from jurisdiction and immunity from execution. That being the case, when considering the enforcement of state obligations one must take into account not only treaty provisions and practices of investment arbitrations but also national laws and the practices of national courts.

This chapter will first examine the international law rules and their implementation, if any, relating to state responsibility. As sovereign immunity still presents difficulties for the enforcement of treaty obligations, a brief survey of the international efforts to codify international law in this area will be offered, which will be followed by a discussion of state practices in regard to sovereign immunity. Particular attention will be paid to the practices relating to sovereign immunity from jurisdiction and sovereign immunity from execution. Last, but not the least, the Chinese perspective on sovereign immunity will be considered.

originally conceived as being "absolute," i.e. all acts of a sovereign were considered to be immune from the jurisdiction of national courts. Later on, some states began to speak of exceptions to or limitations on sovereign immunity. Such a position is variously referred to as "the restrictive theory/doctrine of sovereign immunity" or "the theory/doctrine of restrictive sovereign immunity," as opposed to (most often) "the theory/doctrine of absolute sovereign immunity." In the interests of precision—from the legal, grammatical and aesthetic (symmetry) perspectives—the term used throughout this work will be "the doctrine of restricted sovereign immunity."

4 This option was effectively explained by the Permanent Court of International Justice ("PCIJ") in the *Mavrommatis Palestine Concessions Case*: "It is an elementary principle of international law that a State is entitled to protect its subjects, when injured by acts contrary to international law committed by another State, from whom they have been unable to obtain satisfaction through the ordinary channels. By taking up the case of one of its subjects and by resorting to diplomatic action or international judicial proceedings on his behalf, a State is in reality asserting its own rights—its right to ensure, in the person of its subjects, respect for the rules of international law." See the *Mavrommatis Palestine Concessions Case* (1924) PCIJ Rep Series A, No. 2, 12 (August 30, 1924).

I. Attribution of state responsibility

As in other circumstances, in respect of investment law a host state is responsible for its acts and omissions in accordance with its international obligations under both customary international law and treaties to which it is a party. Such treaties may include BITs and FTAs. Where a host state is in breach of its obligations, it must bear the consequences. This has been long recognized as a principle of international law. For instance, according to *Oppenheim's International Law*:

> In international law, … a state bears responsibility for its conduct in breach of its international obligations. Such responsibility attaches to a state by virtue of its position as an international person. The sovereignty of the state affords it no basis for denying that responsibility. Failure to comply with an international obligation constitutes an international wrong by the state giving rise to international responsibility of that state from which flow certain legal consequences, both for that state … and for others. … The most usual consequence of an international wrong is to enable the injured state to avail itself of the measures and procedures available to it in accordance with international law to compel the delinquent state to fulfill its obligations, or to obtain from that state reparation for the failure.[5]

A host state's responsibility is not affected by the immunity that it may enjoy in the courts of other countries. In practice, investment tribunals seek assistance in reaching their decisions not only from the BITs and FTAs in question but also from customary international law, in particular the ILC Articles. It is generally agreed that these ILC Articles represent, if not precisely customary international law itself, at least the widely accepted views of the international community on the matter.[6] For instance, in *Cargill, Incorporated v. Mexico*, the tribunal considered

---

5 Robert Jennings and Arthur Watts (eds.), *Oppenheim's International Law* (9th ed.), Oxford University Press, UK, 2008, at 500–501.
6 See, for example, Kaj Hobér, *State Responsibility and Investment Arbitration*, Report for the June 2005 Stockholm Conference on Investment Arbitration and the Energy Charter Treaty, 2005, pp. 5–7; Abby Cohen Smutny, "State Responsibility and Attribution: When Is a State Responsible for the Acts of State Enterprises? *Emilio Agustin Maffezini v. Kingdom of Spain*," in T. Weiler (ed.), *International Investment Law and Arbitration: Leading Cases from the ICSID, NAFTA, Bilateral Treaties and Customary International Law*, Cameron May, 2005, at 28. There are also commentators who caution the reliance on the ILC Articles; see, for example, David D. Caron, "The ILC Articles on State Responsibility: The Paradoxical Relationship between Form and Authority," 96 *AJIL* 857–873, 2002. Caron states that "the arbitrators and other decision makers to whom the articles are addressed (particularly the former) may give too much authority (and therefore influence) to the articles" (at 858) and that "they are not part of a treaty, and … it is inappropriate to approach them as if they were" (at 868). He states further that "recognizing that the ILC articles are not themselves a source of law is critical because, as I see it, arbitrators can otherwise defer too easily and uncritically to them," citing the practice of the Iran–United States Claims Tribunal (at 867).

that the ILC Articles "in part are a codification of custom and in part manifest a progressive development of international law."[7]

Even those who may not agree on the authoritativeness of the ILC Articles as a whole do not question that they at least in certain parts represent contemporary customary international law. In his Concurring Opinion in *Archer Daniels Midland v. Mexico*, Arthur Rovine stated:

> Whether and to what extent the ILC Articles, and the Commentaries thereto, constitute accurate restatements of customary international law, and to what extent they represent progressive development of international law, is hardly a matter on which there is general agreement. But for purposes of the instant case, … in my judgment an authoritative indication of customary international law on at least one matter, i.e., countermeasures, may be found at Article 49 of the ILC's Articles, and the Commentary thereto, as well as other Articles and Commentaries relevant to countermeasures.[8]

It is now common for tribunals to refer to the ILC Articles as statements of international law. The *LG&E* case is an example, in which the tribunal stated that it "recognizes that satisfaction of the state of necessity standard as it exists in international law (reflected in Article 25 of the ILC's Draft Articles on State Responsibility) supports the Tribunal's conclusion."[9] Also, in *CMS v. Argentina*, the tribunal stated that it "considers that Article 25 of the Articles on State Responsibility adequately reflect[s] the state of customary international law on the question of necessity."[10] Whilst the *ad hoc* Committee annulled part of the *CMS* Tribunal's award, including the way in which the tribunal applied Article 25 of the ILC Articles, it did not challenge the tribunal's view that the ILC Articles represent customary international law. In this regard, it stated:

> If … state of necessity in customary international law goes to the issue of responsibility, it would be a secondary rule of international law – and this was the position taken by the ILC. In this case, the Tribunal would have been under an obligation to consider first whether there had been any breach of the BIT and whether such a breach was excluded by Article XI. Only if it concluded that there was conduct not in conformity with the Treaty would it

7 *Cargill, Incorporated v. United Mexican States*, ICSID Case No. ARB(AF)/05/2, Award (September 18, 2009), para. 381.
8 See *Archer Daniels Midland Company and Tate & Lyle Ingredients Americas, Inc. v. United Mexican States*, ICSID Case No. ARB(AF)/04/5, Concurring Opinion of Arthur W. Rovine, "Issues of Independent Investor Rights, Diplomatic Protection and Countermeasures" (September 20, 2007).
9 See *LG&E Energy Corp., LG&E Capital Corp., and LG&E International, Inc. v. Argentine Republic*, ICSID Case No. ARB/02/1, Decision on Liability (October 3, 2006), para. 245.
10 See *CMS Gas Transmission Company v. Republic of Argentina*, ICSID CASE No. ARB/01/8, Award (May 12, 2005), para. 315.

have had to consider whether Argentina's responsibility could be precluded in whole or in part under customary international law.[11]

Recognition of the authority of the ILC Articles is also found in other fields of international investment law, such as interpretation of the most-favored-nation clause.[12]

According to the ILC Articles, a state must be responsible for the acts and omissions of its organs—"state organs." Such state organs may include any instrumentality that "exercises legislative, executive, judicial or any other functions."[13] Emphasis is laid on the function of such organs and not their position or characterization by the national laws and within the domestic legal system. At the same time, a state organ may be an individual or a legal person.[14] In practice, it is essential whether an entity can be classified as an organ of the state to which it belongs. In determining whether a given institution or entity is a state organ, however, blind reliance on national law may lead to abuse of the system. This was also in the minds of the drafters of the ILC Articles, as reflected in the words of James Crawford, former director of the Lauterpacht Centre for International Law:

> Where the law of a State characterizes an entity as an organ, no difficulty will arise. On the other hand, it is not sufficient to refer to internal law for the status of State organs. In some systems the status and functions of various entities are determined not only by law but also by practice, and reference exclusively to internal law would be misleading. The internal law of a State may not classify, exhaustively or at all, which entities have the status of "organs." In such cases, while the powers of an entity and its relation to other bodies under internal law will be relevant to its classification as an "organ," internal law will not itself perform the task of classification. Even if it does so, the term "organ" used in internal law may have a special meaning, and not the very broad meaning it has under Article 4 … Accordingly, a State cannot avoid responsibility for the conduct of a body which does in truth act as one of its organs merely by denying it that status under its own law.[15]

To prevent states from avoiding their responsibilities by availing of their own national laws, Article 5 of the ILC Articles provides that where a person or entity

---

11 See *CMS Gas Transmission Company v. Republic of Argentina*, ICSID Case No. ARB/01/8, Decision of the *ad hoc* Committee (September 25, 2007), para. 134.

12 Almost all tribunals that have interpreted the MFN clause have regarded the ILC's Draft Articles on Most-Favoured-Nation Treatment (1978) as customary international law. The most recent example is the *Daimler Financial Services* case, in which the tribunal discussed in length the nature and application of the Draft Articles on MFN Treatment; see *Daimler Financial Services AG v. Argentine Republic*, ICSID Case No. ARB/05/1, Award (August 22, 2012).

13 Article 4(1) of the ILC Articles.

14 Article 4(2) of the ILC Articles.

15 James Crawford, *International Law Commission's Articles on State Responsibility—Introduction, Text and Commentaries*, Cambridge University Press, UK, 2002, at 98.

is not "an organ of the State ... but which is empowered by the law of that State to exercise elements of the governmental authority," its act "shall be considered an act of the State under international law." In such circumstances, the person or entity would be considered to be an organ of the state *de facto*, provided that it had not acted beyond its authority. The ILC Articles further attribute to a state the "conduct of a person or group of persons" insofar as the conduct is carried out "on the instructions of, or under the direction or control of, that State."[16] Based on the above-mentioned provisions of the ILC Articles, it is clear that where an entity or individual is a statutory body, its or his/her conduct is automatically attributed to the state concerned. In other circumstances, whether the act or omission can be attributed to the state depends on the conditions to be satisfied. The *Vivendi* case, decided by an ICSID tribunal, confirmed this view. The tribunal in that case stated:

> Under international law, ... it is well established that actions of a political subdivision of [a] federal state ... are attributable to the central government. It is equally clear that the internal constitutional structure of a country cannot alter these obligations. Finally, the Special Rapporteur of the International Law Commission, in discussing the proposed Commentary that confirms the attribution of conduct of political subdivisions to the federal State, has referred to the "established principle" that a federal state "cannot rely on the federal or decentralized character of its constitution to limit the scope of its international responsibilities."[17]

As the circumstances in that case did "not amount to a breach by the Argentine Republic of the BIT based on actions of the Province," Argentina was not held liable. This conclusion was also based on the fact that "the Claimants have never argued that the Province violated a legal duty to revise the Concession Contract" and that "there is ample evidence in the record that federal officials of the Argentine Republic played a constructive role in the renegotiation process involving Tucumán officials and representatives of CGE."[18] In other words, had Tucumán Province breached the BIT in question or international law, Argentina would have been held liable.

In international investment, it is often the case that a foreign investor enters into a contract with an entity of the host state which may be state-owned. In such cases, when the local entity breaches the contract with the foreign investor, it may claim that the breach was caused by an action or omission of the host state government and thereby attempt to avoid liability. The question is whether, in addition to the

---

16 Article 8 of the ILC Articles.
17 *Compania de Aguas del Aconquija S.A. and Compagnie Générale des Eaux (Vivendi Universal) v. Argentine Republic*, ICSID Case No. ARB/97/3, Award (November 21, 2000), para. 49.
18 Ibid., para. 82.

local entity, the host state can be held liable for such actions or omissions. The *Himpurna* case is illustrative of such situations.[19]

The *Himpurna* case involved a US entity that had entered into a contract with PLN, an entirely state-owned power company of Indonesia, to build a power project within the country. PLN argued that it was independent of the Indonesian Government and could not be held liable "in circumstances where the Contract 'was suspended by government action binding on the parties.'"[20] The tribunal, however, having examined PLN's enabling legislation, legal status and operational history, ruled that PLN was not separate from the Indonesian Government on the basis of "the relationship between PLN and the Government of Indonesia, *de jure* and *de facto*, and … the implications of the fact that the Contract itself expressly contemplated the effects of Governmental action."[21] The tribunal's decision was based on three grounds, namely, "PLN's *de jure* subservience to the Government," "the contractual allocation of the risk of Governmental action" and "PLN's *de facto* subservience to the Government."[22] In the end, the tribunal concluded that "PLN cannot avoid liability by invoking state actions because the GOI [Government of Indonesia] and PLN cannot, in light of the legal framework which has given legal life to PLN and under which it operates, be characterized as separate."[23]

In *SPP v. Arab Republic of Egypt*, an ICC arbitration, in relation to the issue of jurisdiction, the claimant contended that the Government of Egypt had become a party to an agreement including an arbitration clause. The respondent did not deny that its Minister of Tourism had signed the agreement. It nevertheless contended that it was not a party to the contract because the signature of the Minister of Tourism had no contractual significance. In its view, the Minister's signature:

> … was to be ascribed either to the fact that the Minister was Chairman of the Assembly of EGOTH [the Egyptian General Organization for Tourism and Hotels] and was signing in that capacity to indicate on behalf of the "share-holder" approval of EGOTH entering into that Agreement; or to supervisory powers that he possessed in an administrative capacity. … In either event, … the signature did no more than perfect the obligation of EGOTH.[24]

The tribunal in that case did not agree with the respondent. It stated that:

> … although structured in the form of separate agreements, … the transaction as a whole is to be viewed as a unified contractual scheme. … Irrespective of specific rights and obligations based upon each individual party, … the

19 *Himpurna California Energy Ltd. v. Republic of Indonesia*, *ad hoc* arbitration under UNCITRAL rules, Final Award (May 4, 1999).
20 Ibid., para. 84.
21 Ibid., para. 86.
22 Ibid., paras. 36–42.
23 Ibid., para. 89.
24 *SPP (Middle East) Ltd. v. Egypt*, ICC Case No. 3493, Award (February 16, 1983), para. 33.

three parties were to be involved throughout the venture; the Government, EGOTH and the foreign investor.[25]

The *SPP* case, however, is distinguishable from the other cases discussed earlier. Because the Minister had signed the agreement, it was unnecessary for the tribunal to determine whether EGOTH was in fact an organ of the state or an organ whose conduct is carried out "on the instructions of, or under the direction or control of, that State."[26] What is reflected as a common feature in international investment is that whenever an arbitration proceeding has been instituted against it, the host state, almost without exception, will argue that it is not a party to the underlying contract complained of.

In *Noble Ventures Inc. v. Romania*,[27] the complainant was a corporation from Maryland, USA, whose business activity consisted primarily of business consulting services for steel companies in Eastern Europe. It entered into an agreement with the Romanian State Ownership Fund ("SOF"), which was a Romanian institution of public interest. One of the issues involved was whether the acts of SOF could be attributed to Romania. The tribunal stated that in international investment dispute resolution there is always a question whether a given action or omission of natural persons may be attributed to a state. It further said that as the BIT does not provide a solution to the issue, it had to rely on general international law as a supplement. In this regard, the tribunal considered the ILC Articles to be "widely regarded as a codification of customary international law."[28] In particular, "Art. 4 2001 ILC Draft lays down the well-established rule that the conduct of any state organ, being understood as including any person or entity which has that status in accordance with the internal law of the State, shall be considered an act of that State under international law."[29] Nevertheless, as SOF and its successor the Authority for Privatization and Management of State Property ("APAPS") were "legal entities separate from the Respondent," they should not be regarded as de jure organs of Romania.

The tribunal then went on to state that an entity that is "not a *de jure* organ but which is empowered by the law of that State to exercise elements of governmental authority" may also act on behalf of the state. It considered that this principle, as articulated in Article 5 of the ILC Articles, "is equally well established in customary international law."[30] As SOF and APAPS were "at all relevant times acting on the basis of Romanian law which defined their competence,"[31] "no relevant legal distinction is to be drawn between SOF/APAPS, on the one hand, and a government ministry, on the other hand, when the one or the other acted as the

---

25 Ibid., para. 41.
26 See Article 8 of the ILC Articles.
27 *Noble Ventures, Inc. v. Romania*, ICSID Case No. ARB/01/11, Award (October 12, 2005).
28 Ibid., para. 69.
29 Id.
30 Ibid., para. 70.
31 Id.

empowered public institution under the Privatization Law."[32] The tribunal also considered the issue of *ultra vires* and concluded that both SOF and APAPS acted within their competence stipulated by law. Therefore, the acts of both institutions were attributed to the State of Romania.[33]

In *Bayindir v. Pakistan*,[34] the tribunal seems to have adopted a more restrictive stand. On the one hand, it recognized that "NHA [the National Highway Authority] is generally empowered to exercise elements of governmental authority"[35] and, on the other hand, it stated that the existence of such powers was "not sufficient in itself to bring the case within Article 5"[36] of the ILC Articles. In its view, the attribution also requires "that the instrumentality acted in a sovereign capacity in that particular instance."[37] Apparently, the tribunal accepted the view that even though an organ may be empowered to exercise governmental functions its conduct should not be attributed to the state when it is acting in a private capacity. On this basis, the tribunal concluded that it was "not persuaded on the balance of the evidence presented to it that in undertaking the actions which are alleged to be in breach of the Treaty, the NHA was acting in the exercise of elements of the governmental authority."[38] Being that was the case, the NHA's acts were not attributed to Pakistan.

Where an act is carried out by persons or entities not empowered by law to perform government functions, it is more difficult to attribute their acts to the state. This was illustrated in the *Tradex Hellas*[39] case, in which the claimant was a party to a joint venture. The claimant contended that the occupation by villagers of a farm owned by the joint venture was tantamount to expropriation and should be attributed to the host state. The tribunal found the claimant's evidence to be insufficient and rejected its claim. What should be noted is the statement by the tribunal when rejecting the claim that "even if the villagers felt encouraged to such occupations by [Albania's action and government officials' speech], that would not be a sufficient basis to attribute such occupations to the State of Albania"[40] unless more persuasive evidence was available. In support of its view, the tribunal cited the decision in the *Amco Asia* case, in which "a much more direct and active

---

32 Ibid., para. 79.

33 In the *F-W Oil Interests* case, the tribunal held a similar view that "it is theoretically possible that the enterprise's conduct (acts or omissions) may engage the responsibility of the State either as an organ of the State; or as a body exercising elements of the governmental authority of the State; or as a body which is in fact acting on the instructions of the State, or under its direction or control." See *F-W Oil Interests, Inc. v. Republic of Trinidad & Tobago*, ICSID Case No. ARB/01/14, Award (March 3, 2006), para. 203.

34 *Bayindir Insaat Turizm Ticaret Ve Sanayi A.S. v. Islamic Republic of Pakistan*, ICSID Case No. ARB/03/29, Award (August 27, 2009).

35 Ibid., para. 121.

36 Ibid., para. 122.

37 Id. The tribunal cited the Commentary to the ILC Articles to support its position. The Commentary made a distinction between *jure imperii* and *jure gestionii*.

38 Ibid., para. 123.

39 *Tradex Hellas S.A. v. Republic of Albania*, ICSID Case No. ARB/94/2, Award (April 29, 1999).

40 Ibid., para. 165.

involvement by the state in a private taking by army and police"[41] was considered not to constitute sufficient evidence to attribute private acts to the state.

The *Maffezini*[42] case is most probably the only case in which attribution of acts and omissions of individuals and entities to the state, by applying the structural and functional tests, was analyzed in detail. The entity whose conduct was alleged to be attributable to Spain—the host state—was a state-owned company, Sociedad para el Desarrollo Industrial de Galicia ("SODIGA"). It was contended by the claimant that SODIGA was "not only owned by several State entities, but it is also under the control of the State and operated as an arm of the State for the purposes of the economic development of the region of Galicia."[43] Accordingly, argued the claimant, the actions and omissions of SODIGA should be attributed to Spain.

The tribunal in *Maffezini* was faced with two questions, i.e. whether or not SODIGA was a state entity and, regardless of the answer to the first question, whether the actions and omissions complained of by the claimant were imputable to Spain. As there was no difficulty in determining that SODIGA was a state entity, the tribunal concentrated on the second question. It first cited Article 7 of the 1996 version of the ILC Articles, which read:

> The conduct of an organ of an entity which is not part of the formal structure of the State or of a territorial governmental entity, but which is empowered by the internal law of that State to exercise elements of the governmental authority, shall be considered as an act of the State under international law, provided the organ was acting in such capacity in the case in question.[44]

The tribunal then commented that "a State will not necessarily escape responsibility for wrongful acts or omissions by hiding behind a private corporate veil."[45] It then introduced the structural test and the functional test for assessing whether an action or omission of an entity can be attributed to the state. In its view, "a private corporation operating for profit while discharging essentially governmental functions delegated to it by the State could, under the functional test, be considered as an organ of the State and thus engage the State's international responsibility for wrongful acts."[46] In determining whether a private or state entity carries out certain government functions, should only the nature of the conduct be taken into account?

The *Maffezini* Tribunal took a holistic view of the matter. In doing so, it first

---

41 Id. See, also, *Amco Asia Corporation, Pan American Development Limited, PT Amco Indonesia v. Republic of Indonesia*, ICSID Case No. ARB/81/1, Award on the Merits (November 21, 1984), 24 *ILM* 1022 (1985) (excerpts).

42 *Emilio Agustin Maffezini v. Kingdom of Spain*, ICSID Case No. ARB/97/7, Decision on Jurisdiction (January 25, 2000).

43 Ibid., para. 72.

44 Albeit with slightly different wording, this is now Article 5 of the ILC Articles.

45 *Maffezini, supra*, note 42, para. 78.

46 Ibid., para. 80.

analyzed the government intent and process for establishing SODIGA. As the
entity's duties included inducement of foreign investment, provision of subsidies,
etc., the tribunal considered that "these objectives and functions are by their very
nature typically governmental tasks."[47] As such, they cannot be carried out by
private institutions and are not *jure gestionis*. Regarding this matter, the tribunal
made it clear that so long as an entity, its being a private company notwithstanding, is delegated with government functions and carries out such tasks in such a
way, the government concerned cannot escape responsibilities arising from the
entity's actions.

According to the *Maffezini* Tribunal, a claimant need only establish a prima
facie case that an entity is carrying out activities on behalf of the state at the jurisdictional stage. Whether the actions and omissions of the entity can be attributed
to the state may be decided at the merits stage. That was exactly what happened
in *Maffezini*. In its award,[48] the tribunal considered SODIGA's provision of information and advice on compliance in respect of environmental requirements to be
commercial in nature. By the transfer of funds to the joint venture from Maffezini's
personal account, another claim made by the claimant, an employee of SODIGA
helped effectuate the transaction through a private bank. This employee sought
approval from the president of SODIGA but not from Maffezini. The tribunal
ruled that the fact "that Mr. Soto Baños failed to consult with Mr. Maffezini, but
sought and obtained authorization to act from the president of SODIGA, compels the conclusion that Mr. Soto Baños' action, whether within the terms of the
mandate or *ultra vires*, is attributable to SODIGA."[49] The tribunal's reasoning was
that since SODIGA was an entity of Spain this action was therefore imputable
to the state. Spain was also under a treaty obligation to protect foreign investors
fairly and equitably.

Apparently, the tribunal's position was also influenced by the way the transfer
of funds was conducted, i.e. that is there was no contract signed either before or
after the transaction. The private banks' conduct also led the tribunal to conclude that these banks recognized "SODIGA's orders and instructions" as public
functions.[50]

As the above cases illustrate, it is difficult to attribute actions and omissions of
entities other than state organs to the state. Yet, in practice, a host state may still
be liable despite the fact that it may not be a party to the contract with the foreign
investor that is alleged to have been breached. This is so because a breach of
contract may, at the same time, constitute a violation of treaty obligations, including national treatment, fair and equitable treatment, full protection and security,
the umbrella clause, etc. In such cases, the host state's responsibility arises from
treaty obligations and general international law. A case in point is *Wena Hotels Ltd.*

47 Ibid., para. 86.
48 *Emilio Agustin Maffezini v. Kingdom of Spain*, ICSID Case No. ARB/97/7, Award (November 13, 2000).
49 Ibid., para. 76.
50 Ibid., paras. 75 and 78.

v. Egypt,[51] in which Wena Hotels and the Egyptian Hotels Company ("EHC"), a company wholly-owned by Egypt, entered into an agreement for the development and operation of two hotels in Egypt. The claimant attributed EHC's actions, including seizure of the hotels, to Egypt. The tribunal considered that "even if Egypt did not instigate or participate in the seizure of the two hotels, ... there is sufficient evidence to find that Egypt was aware of EHC's intentions and took no actions to prevent the seizures or to immediately restore Wena's control over the hotels."[52] Based on this finding, Egypt was held to have violated, inter alia, the obligations relating to fair and equitable treatment and full protection and security as stipulated in the BIT between Egypt and Great Britain.[53] The reason underpinning the *Wena Hotels* Tribunal's decision was that Egypt's failure to provide protection was in breach of the BIT; it constituted a violation of the treaty, which was independent of the contractual breach by EHC, as alleged by the claimant.

The tribunal in the *Salini v. Morocco*[54] case took a similar approach. In that case, Salini Costruttori S.p.A., an Italian company, entered into a contract with the Société Nationale des Autoroutes du Maroc ("ADM"), a limited company mainly controlled (89%) by the Government of Morocco, for building, managing and operating highways and other roads in accordance with a government lease. Pursuant to a dispute relating to payment for construction work, Salini brought an arbitration request to the ICSID. As respondent, Morocco challenged the jurisdiction of the tribunal by arguing that it was not a party to the contract between ADM and Salini.

It was not disputed that ADM was an entity with separate personality from the respondent, notwithstanding that its main object was to "accomplish tasks that are under State control."[55] The tribunal considered ADM to be a "State company, acting in the name of the Kingdom of Morocco."[56] It then stated that its jurisdiction depended on the existence of an investment under the BIT between Italy and Morocco. It further stated that the Morocco–Italy BIT "compels the State to respect the jurisdiction offer in relation to violations of the Bilateral Treaty and any breach of a contract that binds the State directly. The jurisdiction offer ... does not, however, extend to breaches of a contract to which any entity other than the State is a named party."[57] Although the tribunal agreed that it would not have jurisdiction on the basis of a pure breach of contract, it emphasized that "the Arbitral Tribunal retains jurisdiction in relation to breaches of contract that would constitute, at the same time, a violation of the Bilateral Treaty by the

---

51 *Wena Hotels Ltd. v. Arab Republic of Egypt*, ICSID Case No. ARB/98/4, Award (December 8, 2000).
52 Ibid., para. 85.
53 Ibid., para. 95.
54 *Salini Costruttori S.p.A. and Italstrade S.p.A. v. Kingdom of Morocco*, ICSID Case No ARB/00/4, Decision on Jurisdiction (July 23, 2001).
55 Ibid., para. 33.
56 Ibid., para. 34.
57 Ibid., para. 61.

State."[58] In other words, where a contract breach is at the same time a breach of the BIT, an investment arbitration tribunal has jurisdiction.

In what circumstances then may a contract breach constitute a treaty breach? One possibility could be that a contract breach by a private party is caused by the action or omission of the state or its organ. Another possibility may be that where a state is, in addition to being a party to the BIT, a party to a contract with a foreign investor, the breach by the state of a contract may also constitute a breach of the BIT in question.

The *SGS v. Pakistan*[59] case is apparently the first ICSID case that involved such a situation. The claimant was a Swiss company, which signed a contract with Pakistan for the provision of pre-shipment inspection services. Subsequently, a dispute was triggered because of Pakistan's termination of the contract. Whilst the contract provided dispute resolution procedures and both parties did avail themselves of such procedures, SGS requested the ICSID to arbitrate in accordance with the BIT between Switzerland and Pakistan. The claimant argued, inter alia, that Pakistan had violated the umbrella clause of the BIT.

The issue facing the tribunal was whether, under the umbrella clause contained in the BIT,[60] a breach of contract could be elevated to a violation of the BIT. In other words, the tribunal needed to decide whether Pakistan had breached the BIT with Switzerland by having breached, as alleged by the claimant, its contract. The tribunal ruled that "under general international law, a violation of a contract entered into by a State with an investor of another State, is not, by itself, a violation of international law."[61] It pointed out, however that this was not to say "that States may not agree with each other in a BIT that henceforth, all breaches of each State's contracts with investors of the other State are forthwith converted into and [shall] be treated as breaches of the BIT."[62] This was in line with the tribunal's belief that a treaty interpreter should give effect to the object and purpose of the provisions of the treaty under consideration.[63] Because the claimant did not submit clear and persuasive evidence to prove the intent of both contracting parties and because Pakistan denied such an intent in the BIT, the tribunal ruled that the BIT, in particular the umbrella clause, did not permit the elevation of a contract breach to a treaty breach in this particular instance.

Even beyond the debate on the scope of application of the umbrella clause, the determination of state responsibility is important. Yet the purpose of ascertaining for what a state should be responsible is to make the state liable for its

---

58 Ibid., para. 62.
59 *SGS Société Générale de Surveillance S.A. v. Islamic Republic of Pakistan*, ICSID Case No. ARB/01/13, Decision on Objections to Jurisdiction (August 6, 2003).
60 Article 11, the umbrella clause, of the Switzerland–Pakistan BIT provided: "Either Contracting Party shall constantly guarantee the observance of the commitments it has entered into with respect to the investments of the investors of the other Contracting Party." Similar provisions can be found in many modern BITs and FTAs.
61 *SGS v. Pakistan, supra*, note 59, para. 167.
62 Ibid., para. 173.
63 For discussion of this issue, see ibid., para. 165.

wrongdoings. To this end, the ICSID Convention has its own system for enforcing investment arbitration awards. Article 53(1) of the Convention provides:

> The award shall be binding on the parties and shall not be subject to any appeal or to any other remedy except those provided for in this Convention. Each party shall abide by and comply with the terms of the award except to the extent that enforcement shall have been stayed pursuant to the relevant provisions of this Convention.

Regarding the above provisions, Schreuer commented:

> This responsibility for compliance would not rest on any role of the host State as party to the proceedings or as award debtor. Rather, it would arise from its role as designating and approving authority under Art. 25(1) and (3), from the obligation of Art. 54 to recognize and enforce awards, and generally from the principle of good faith.[64]

The question then arises as to what shall be the result if a host state refuses to enforce an arbitration award despite its international obligations. In such situations, the affected party has to resort to national courts for enforcement of either ICSID arbitral awards or those of other arbitration bodies. In such circumstances, foreign investors must consider attempting to enforce such awards in those national courts in countries where the losing host states have properties. Yet, in order to enforce an award against a host state in a foreign country, state immunity in relation to the jurisdiction of national courts and the execution of awards, including attachment of property may become hurdles. Unless these problems are resolved satisfactorily, international investment cannot be promoted and encouraged. These circumstances indicate that changes in respect of the traditional view toward sovereign immunity are needed.

II. Efforts to codify the principle of sovereign immunity

Traditionally, the principle of sovereign immunity, which is derived from the principle of independent and equal sovereignty of all states, "generally means that one State is not under the jurisdiction of another. As for judicial jurisdiction, one State shall not be challenged in the domestic court of another State and its property shall not be seized or executed."[65] The basic effect of this legal principle is that every sovereign state in the international community is obligated to respect the sovereignty of other states and not to exercise jurisdiction over the acts of other states. Charles Cheney Hyde, the eminent jurist and scholar of international law,

64 Christoph H. Schreuer, *The ICSID Convention: A Commentary*, (2nd ed.), Cambridge University Press, UK, 2009, p. 1101.
65 See Ni Zhengyu, "On the Theory and Practice of State Immunity," *Chinese Yearbook of International Law*, Chinese Society of International Law, Beijing, 1982, pp. 3ff.

said that a state is not subject to the jurisdiction of another state and, without its consent, no lawsuit against it can be brought in the court of another state.[66] As a fundamental principle of international law, the doctrine of sovereign immunity began to gain prominence in the international community in the 19th century.

One of the first attempts to establish an international codification of the rules on sovereign immunity was the Draft International Regulations on the Jurisdiction of Courts in Proceedings against Foreign States, Sovereigns or Heads of States, adopted by the *Institut de Droit International* at Hamburg in 1891.[67] These Draft Regulations expressly rendered acts of state (*actes de souveraineté*) immune from the jurisdiction of national courts.[68] Even though at that time absolute sovereign immunity was the main trend, the Draft Regulations itemized numerous exceptions to sovereign immunity, most importantly:

1. when the State, sovereign or Head of State has waived immunity, either expressly or tacitly (by either bringing a suit or participating in one without challenging the jurisdiction of the court)[69] and
2. when a court proceeding relates to a commercial or industrial establishment or a railway operated on the territory of the State of the forum.[70]

Another step was taken by the *Institut de Droit International* in 1954. Noting that since 1891 "new questions have arisen that require a solution" ("*nouvelles questions se sont posées qui appellent une solution*"), it offered some clarifications of the Draft Regulations by adopting a Resolution on the Immunity of Foreign States from Jurisdiction and Forced Execution.[71] The new Resolution made a clear distinction between acts of public power (*actes de puissance publique*) and other acts. Acts of public power were deemed to be immune from the jurisdiction of national courts unless the foreign state had waived such immunity.[72] A state could waive immunity either expressly or tacitly, but such waiver must "in every case be certain" ("*elle doit être en tous cas certaine*"). A tacit waiver was deemed to have been made whenever a state deposited a "substantive submission" before a court, as well as when it initiated or participated in any court action.[73] Any suit that "relates

---

66 See Chen Tiqiang, "State Sovereign Immunity and International Law: Comment on the Hukuang Railway Bonds Case," *Chinese Yearbook of International Law*, Chinese Society of International Law, Beijing, 1982, pp. 32ff.

67 *Projet de règlement international sur la compétence des tribunaux dans les procès contre les Etats, souverains ou chefs d'Etat étrangers, Session de Hambourg* (September 11, 1891); available at: http://www.idi-iil.org/idiF/resolutionsF/1891_ham_01_fr.pdf (in French).

68 Ibid., Article 5.

69 Ibid., Article 4(4).

70 Ibid., Article 4(3).

71 *L'immunité de juridiction et d'exécution forcées des Etats étrangers, Session d'Aix-en-Provence* (April 30, 1954); available at: http://www.idi-iil.org/idiF/resolutionsF/1954_aix_02_fr.pdf (in French).

72 Ibid., Articles 1–2.

73 Ibid., Article 2 (in relevant part): "*Un Etat peut renoncer à se prévaloir de son immunité. La renonciation peut être expresse ou tacite; elle doit être en tous cas certaine. Elle résulte du dépôt par l'Etat de conclusions au fond. L'Etat demandeur, intervenant, ou tiers opposant devant un tribunal étranger, est censé accepter la compétence de ce tribunal.*"

to an act which is not one of public power" could be heard by a national court, and the determination of whether or not an act was one of public power was to be determined by its status under local law (*lex fori*).[74] It should be noted that this Resolution came two years after the Tate Letter was issued by a representative of the US Department of State, expressing a new policy of the United States on sovereign immunity according to which the doctrine of restricted sovereign immunity would be followed in that country.[75] Taking into account the practice of the Western countries as indicated in the Tate Letter and this Resolution, it appears that after World War II, Western countries were in general prepared to accept the doctrine of restricted sovereign immunity.

In 1991, the *Institut de Droit International* further amended its rules on sovereign immunity with the adoption of the Resolution on Contemporary Problems Concerning the Immunity of States in Relation to Questions of Jurisdiction and Enforcement. This Resolution was adopted with the express purpose of "limiting the immunity, while maintaining the protection of essential States interests [sic],"[76] and it firmly established the *Institut*'s support of the doctrine of restricted sovereign immunity and, in particular, the commercial exception to such immunity. Most importantly, national courts are specifically declared competent in the following instances:

- "in respect of proceedings relating to a commercial transaction to which a foreign State (or its agent) is a party"[77]
- "in respect of proceedings concerning legal disputes arising from relationships of a private law character to which a foreign State (or its agent) is a party"[78] and
- "in respect of proceedings concerning contracts of employment and contracts for professional services to which a foreign State (or its agent) is a party."[79]

A distinction between sovereign immunity from jurisdiction and sovereign immunity from enforcement was also confirmed by Article 4 of the Resolution. Essentially, the only property owned by a state, its agencies or subdivisions that is subject to constraint or seizure is "property allocated or earmarked by the State for the satisfaction of the claim in question" or "property of the State within the

---

74 Ibid., Article 3: "*Les tribunaux d'un Etat peuvent connaître des actions contre un Etat étranger et les personnes morales visées à l'article premier, toutes les fois que le litige a trait à un acte qui n'est pas de puissance publique. La question de savoir si un acte n'est pas de puissance publique relève de la lex fori.*"

75 For discussion of this matter, see Section III of this chapter.

76 *Contemporary Problems Concerning the Immunity of States in Relation to Questions of Jurisdiction and Enforcement, Session of Basel* (September 2, 1991), Preamble, second recital; available at: http://www.idi-iil.org/idiE/resolutionsE/1991_bal_03_en.PDF.

77 Ibid., Article 1.2.a.

78 Ibid., Article 1.2.b.

79 Ibid., Article 1.2.c.

territory of the forum State which is in use or intended for use for commercial purposes."[80]

In any event, the invocation of sovereign immunity from jurisdiction or enforcement was precluded if a state has consented to such jurisdiction or enforcement, either by international agreement, a written contract, a declaration relating to the specific case, or voluntary submission in the form of initiation of or intervention in proceedings.[81] A clear distinction was also made between consent to jurisdiction and consent to enforcement "for which separate and explicit consent is required."[82]

The International Law Association of the United States also attempted to promote an international codification of the rules of sovereign immunity. It began its work in the latter years of the 1970s and initially offered the text of a Draft Convention on State Immunity for consideration by governments and the UN's International Law Commission.[83] The Draft Convention was intended to apply to the government of a foreign state, any other state organs, agencies lacking legal personality distinct from the state and the constituent units of a federal state.[84] As might be expected, the Convention excluded immunity from national jurisdiction when the cause of action arose out of "[a] commercial activity carried on by the foreign State; or … [a]n obligation of the foreign State arising out of a contract."[85] Sovereign immunity could also be waived either expressly or by implication under the terms of the Draft Convention. Article VIII.A of the Draft Convention excluded from immunity from attachment, execution or enforcement any state-owned property in the forum state for which the foreign state had waived such immunity or any property which "is in use for the purposes of commercial activity or was in use for the commercial activity upon which the claim is based." "Commercial activity," according to the definitions in Article 1.C of the Draft Convention, was to "be determined by reference to the nature of the act, rather than by reference to its purpose."

A formal move by the international community to establish general principles of sovereign immunity was made with the questionnaire submitted to Members of the League of Nations in 1927 by the Committee of Experts for the Progressive Codification of International Law relating to the competence of national courts in regard to foreign states. The results led the Committee of Experts to report to the Council in June 1928 that the subject was "sufficiently ripe for codification." The League of Nations Assembly, however, in September of that year reserved

---

80 See ibid., Article 4.3.a and 4.3.b, and Article 4.4.

81 Ibid., Article 5.1.

82 Ibid., Article 5.2.

83 International Law Association, *Draft Convention on State Immunity*, adopted at the 60th Conference of the ILA, Montreal, Canada (August 29–September 4, 1982), 22 *ILM* 287, 1983.

84 Ibid., Article I.B. The Article further states: "An agency or instrumentality of a foreign State which possess[es] legal personality distinct from the State shall be treated as a foreign State only for acts or omissions performed in the exercise of sovereign authority, i.e. *jure imperii*."

85 Ibid., Article III.B.

the matter "with a view to subsequent conferences."[86] For a number of reasons (among them the fact that the Committee of Experts did not meet again after 1928 and the general disarray in the organization in the 1930s), the League of Nations never readdressed this issue.[87]

It was to be another 45 years before the international community considered the matter again. The United Nations included sovereign immunity in the work programme of the International Law Commission ("ILC") in 1977. Dr Sompong Sucharitkul, Special Rapporteur for the topic, submitted his initial report in 1979,[88] which was essentially an exploration of the nature of the subject matter, a survey of some historical and contemporary state practice and jurisprudence relating to sovereign immunity, and an outline of issues to be addressed in any relevant international convention. Two points raised by Dr Sucharitkul are particularly relevant to the present discussion:

(i) he appears to have assumed that the restrictive approach to sovereign immunity was normative or desirable and that certain exceptions to sovereign immunity were to be recognized[89] and

(ii) he held that there was a distinct difference between immunity from jurisdiction and immunity from attachment or enforcement, and that the latter was more "absolute" than the former.[90]

Among the "possible exceptions to the general rule of State immunity" listed by Dr Sucharitkul were included those related to commercial activities, contracts of employment and arbitration.[91] When the ILC accepted this Report, it noted that "the exceptions identified in the preliminary report were merely noted as possible limitations, without any assessment or evaluation of their significance in State practice."[92] Nevertheless, when the first draft of the proposed UN Convention was

---

86 See "General Introduction" to the Reports and Draft Conventions of the Harvard Research in International Law, 26 *AJIL Supp.* 1, 1932, at 2.

87 In response to the League's initiative, the Law School of Harvard University established "a research in International Law for the purpose of preparing a draft international convention on each of the subjects selected by the [League for codification]." This resulted in 1932 in the Harvard Draft Convention on the Competence of Courts in Regard to Foreign States. See *Draft Convention on Competence of Courts in Regard to Foreign States*, Harvard Research in International Law, Philip C. Jessup, Reporter, 26 *AJIL Supp.* 451, 1932.

88 *Preliminary report on jurisdictional immunities of States and their property, by Mr Sompong Sucharitkul, Special Rapporteur*, UN Doc. No. A/CN.4/323, in *Yearbook of the International Law Commission*, 1979, Vol. II (Part One), pp. 227–44.

89 In para. 68, ibid., he stated: "There are areas of activity where State immunity is applicable and others where the rule of State immunity does not apply."

90 At para. 67, ibid., he noted: "Consent to the exercise of local jurisdiction is not consent to execution of judgment. Waiver of jurisdictional immunity does not constitute or automatically entail waiver of immunity from execution. A separate waiver will be needed at the time satisfaction of judgment is sought." Further, at para. 85, he observed: "Whereas execution is possible, it can only be levied against certain types of State property in commercial use."

91 See ibid., paras. 68–81.

92 International Law Commission, "Jurisdictional Immunities of States and their Property,"

adopted by the ILC in 1991 and reported to the General Assembly, it contained eight of the nine exceptions listed by Dr Sucharitkul,[93] including the definition of "commercial transaction."

The Draft Articles further recognized only express waivers of sovereign immunity by means of "international agreement; a written contract; or a declaration before the court or by a written communication in a specific proceeding" "with regard to the matter or case."[94] It did not address implicit waivers but addressed in Draft Article 8 the "[e]ffect of participation in a proceeding before a court," in which it provided that a state's initiation of a proceeding or its intervention in a proceeding relating to the merits, unless it lacked the possibility of having "acquired knowledge of facts on which a claim to immunity can be based until after it took such a step," would exclude the possibility of such state invoking immunity from jurisdiction.

The distinction between immunity from jurisdiction and immunity from enforcement was outlined in Article 18, which established quite restrictive terms for limiting the latter; i.e. the property to be attached must be "allocated or earmarked property for the satisfaction of the claim which is the object of that proceeding; or … specifically in use or intended for use by the State for other than government noncommercial purposes and is in the territory of the State of the forum and has a connection with the claim which is the object of the proceeding or with the agency or instrumentality against which the proceeding was directed."[95] Furthermore, "[c]onsent to the exercise of jurisdiction under article 7 shall not imply consent to the taking of measures of constraint under paragraph 1, for which separate consent shall be necessary."[96]

This may appear to be an insignificant achievement. Yet, considering the non-homogeneous nature of the United Nations and the fact that the doctrine of restricted sovereign immunity was still relatively new, what had been done was quite a major step in forming some consensus within the international community on the matter. It also paved the way for the adoption of the United Nations Convention on Jurisdictional Immunities of States and Their Property 13 years later.[97]

The provisions of the UN Convention on Jurisdictional Immunity of States and

"Summary," on the website of the UN; available at: http://untreaty.un.org/ilc/summaries/4_1.htm.

93 See, *Draft Articles on Jurisdictional Immunities of States and Their Property, 1991*, text adopted by the Commission at its 43rd session, in 1991, and submitted to the General Assembly as a part of the Commission's report covering the work of that session, Articles 10–17; available at: http://legal.un.org/ilc/texts/instruments/english/draft%20articles/4_1_1991.pdf. Only the exception covering fiscal and customs liabilities in Dr Sucharitkul's Report was omitted, and no additional exceptions were included.

94 Ibid., Article 7.

95 Ibid., Article 18.1(b) and (c).

96 Ibid., Article 18.2.

97 United Nations Convention on Jurisdictional Immunities of States and Their Property, UN resolution 59/38 of December 2, 2004; available at: http://legal.un.org/ilc/texts/instruments/english/conventions/4_1_2004.pdf.

Their Property closely followed those of the Draft Articles of 1991. For example, the text of the Convention's Article 10.1, establishing the "commercial exception" to sovereign immunity, as well as its definition of "commercial transaction" in Article 2.1(c), is identical with the wording of the Draft Articles as cited above.[98] Even the treatment of the effect of commercial transactions undertaken by certain state-owned enterprises on the exercise of sovereign immunity is effectively the same, although the structure of the wording in the Convention's Article 10.2 has been somewhat altered from the Draft Articles' prototype.

On the other hand, the alteration of just a few words in the text of Article 2.2 has introduced a complete reversal in the way in which the "purpose" of a transaction is to be considered in determining its "commercial character" between what was proposed in the Draft Articles and what was adopted in the Convention. Both documents state that:

> In determining whether a contract or transaction is a "commercial transaction" under paragraph 1 (c), reference should be made primarily to the nature of the contract or transaction, but its purpose should also be taken into account if, … that purpose is relevant to determining the non-commercial character of the contract or transaction.

The crucial difference lies in the wording that appears following the "if" in each document. In the Draft Articles, those words were: "in the practice of the State which is a party to it [i.e. the transaction]." In the Convention, the wording has become: "in the practice of the State of the forum." With these words, the Convention has apparently overturned the Draft Articles' acknowledgment of the concerns of those States that might be willing to accept some restrictions on sovereign immunity in the case of "commercial" transactions so long as the purpose of the state for entering into the transaction was to be taken into account, favoring instead the position of those states that maintain a fully restrictive approach to sovereign immunity in this regard.

The Convention's provisions on waivers of immunity are identical to those of the Draft Articles.[99] On the other hand, its provisions on "measures of constraint" against state-owned property are both more and less restrictive than those contained in the Draft Articles. First of all, the Convention makes a distinction, not found in the Draft Articles, between pre- and post-judgment measures. In the former case,[100] it severely limits the scope of state-owned property that is subject to constraint; in the latter case, it expands it by allowing measures of constraint/ enforcement against "property that has *a connection with the entity against which the proceeding was directed,*"[101] not just that property which "has *a connection with the claim*

---

98 See ibid., Articles 10.1 and 2.1(c).
99 See the UN Convention on State Immunity, *supra*, note 97, Articles 7 and 8.
100 See ibid., Article 18.
101 Ibid., Article 19(c) (emphasis added).

which is the object of the proceeding or with the agency or instrumentality against which the proceeding was directed."

It is therefore clear that the 2004 Convention presented a set of compromise provisions on sovereign immunity that both the ILC and the UN General Assembly expected would be acceptable to the international community as a whole. It appears, however, that this assessment was overenthusiastic. So far, this expectation has proven illusory. As at February 17, 2014, the Convention had 28 signatories (amongst which were the United Kingdom, Russia, and China, all without stated reservations) and 15 parties.[102] The Convention, which requires the accession, acceptance or ratification of 30 countries before coming into effect is still not in force.

The sole multinational treaty dealing with sovereign immunity in force today is the European Convention on State Immunity,[103] drawn up by a committee of experts and opened for signature by member states of the Council of Europe on May 16, 1972. Although it entered into force on June 11, 1976, it did so with the minimum number of three ratifications. As of February 17, 2014, it still had fewer parties than the UN Convention—only eight of the Council's 47 member states: Austria; Belgium; Cyprus; Germany; Luxembourg; the Netherlands; Macedonia and the United Kingdom.[104]

The European Convention on State Immunity has several unique characteristics. First of all, it makes no effort to include countries outside Europe. The Explanatory Report on the Convention points out that:

> [The Convention] operates only between the Contracting States on the basis of the special confidence subsisting among the Members of the Council of Europe. The Convention confers no rights on non-Contracting States; in particular, it leaves open all questions as to the exercise of jurisdiction against non-Contracting States in Contracting States, and vice versa.[105]

Second, the Convention applies only to the jurisdiction of national courts; it does not address issues related to proceedings that may be conducted by the administrative authorities of member states.

---

102 Note that Kazakhstan, Latvia, Saudi Arabia, and Spain have become Parties to the Convention without having signed it. The United States has never signed or otherwise accepted the Convention. See "Status of the United Nations Convention on Jurisdictional Immunities of States and Their Property;" available at: http://treaties.un.org/pages/ViewDetails.aspx?src= TREATY&mtdsg_no=III-13&chapter=3&lang=en.

103 European Convention on State Immunity, Basel (May 16, 1972); available at: http://conventions.coe.int/Treaty/en/Treaties/Html/074.htm.

104 See European Convention on State Immunity, "Status Report;" available at: http://conventions.coe.int/Treaty/Commun/ChercheSig.asp?NT=074&CM=&DF=&CL=ENG.

105 Explanatory Report on the European Convention on State Immunity, Council of Europe Doc. ETS No. 074; available at: http://conventions.coe.int/Treaty/en/Reports/Html/074.htm. Also, Article 37 does make provision for states not members of the Council of Europe to accede to the Convention, but only by unanimous vote of the members casting a vote. Even then, if a state that has already acceded to the Convention objects to the accession of a particular non-member state, the Convention shall not apply to relations between those two states.

Third, the Convention expressly applies only to member states themselves. Article 28 provides that the constituent states of a federal state do not have sovereign immunity unless that state specifically declares that its constituent states may invoke the provisions of the Convention. Article 27 provides that the Convention does not apply to legal entities which are distinct from a member state and are capable of suing or being sued, even if they carry out public functions. However, it does provide that "the courts may not entertain proceedings in respect of acts performed by the entity in the exercise of sovereign authority (*acta jure imperii*)."

The Convention contains, in Article 23, an express prohibition of "execution or preventive measures" against the property of a member state by another member state "except where and to the extent that the [former] state has expressly consented thereto in writing in any particular case." Instead, what the Convention requires is that parties must give effect to judgments rendered against them in those cases where the Convention's provisions do not permit them to claim immunity. Nevertheless, the requirement to give effect to judgments is subject to numerous provisos, including that a state need not do so if "it would be manifestly contrary to public policy in that State to do so."[106] In addition, when a state does not give effect to a judgment, Article 21 leaves the final word on whether or not such failure is in accordance with the provisions of the Convention "to the competent court of that State."

Among those cases where a state may not claim immunity from jurisdiction are included those that concern that state's relationship with private persons with whom it participates "in a company, association or other legal entity having its seat, registered office or principal place of business on the territory of the State of the forum"[107] or that relate to the activity of "an office, agency or other establishment [which it has on the territory of the State of the forum and] through which it engages, in the same manner as a private person, in an industrial, commercial or financial activity."[108] Further, among the Convention's "optional provisions" is one that permits a forum State to enforce a judgment against property of another State used exclusively in connection with "an industrial or commercial activity, in which the State is engaged in the same manner as a private person" if both concerned states have made a declaration specifically accepting those optional provisions.[109] The Convention also contains the familiar provisions on waivers of immunity, both explicit and as the effect of instituting or intervening in proceedings or taking any step in a court proceeding related to the merits.

What can be gleaned from this survey of normative documents and the sole multinational treaty in force on the subject of state immunity is that there still exists no consensus within the international community in this regard, which may be considered as unfortunate but understandable. In general, legal scholars and

---

106 European Convention on State Immunity, *supra*, note 103, Article 20.2.a. But see Article 20 in its entirety.
107 Ibid., Article 6.
108 Ibid., Article 7.
109 See, ibid., Articles 24–26, especially Article 26.

practitioners of the developed countries have shown a fairly uniform acceptance of the doctrine of restricted sovereign immunity, including, inter alia, commercial exceptions. With the developing countries, in particular such newly emerging economies as China and India, increasing their outbound investments in other countries, it is likely that the doctrine of restricted sovereign immunity will be accepted by more countries and scholars in the future. Yet, for the time being, matters relating to sovereign immunity, determination of commercial exceptions, etc. still have to be left to the decisions of national courts.

III. Evolution of national laws regarding sovereign immunity

With the increase in international exchanges, especially economic exchanges, and more government involvement in commercial activities, national courts have no choice but to interpret customary international law. States also feel pressure to enact laws to deal with the matter of sovereign immunity. This development has resulted in the divergence of the doctrines of absolute sovereign immunity and restricted sovereign immunity in theory and practice.

A. Absolute sovereign immunity

The major issue involved in the principle of sovereign immunity is jurisdiction, i.e. whether or not one state has jurisdiction over acts performed by another state within its territory when that act directly affects the former, as well as whether or not property owned by a sovereign state which is located in another state can be seized or subject to execution by domestic courts of the latter. This principle was first applied to visiting foreign leaders, warships, diplomats abroad, etc. Since these carry out their mandates on behalf of a sovereign state, foreign states were not to exercise jurisdiction over them. The application of this principle was later extended to any person or institution that carried out a mandate as representative of a state, as well as to property owned by a state, regardless of the nature of the activity concerned. This is the so-called doctrine of absolute sovereign immunity.

Up until the 1950s, the doctrine of absolute sovereign immunity was supported by the developed countries, including the United Kingdom and the United States. This was established by the US Supreme Court in the *Exchange* case as early as 1812.[110] In this case, a US national brought a suit requesting the US District Court for the District of Pennsylvania to seize the French warship *Exchange*, owned by Napoleon, which had entered into US territorial waters. The plaintiff alleged that the ship concerned had been a merchant ship owned by him but was confiscated by Napoleon to be used as a warship. The US Attorney for the District of Pennsylvania filed a "suggestion" with the Court to the effect that:

> … inasmuch as there exists between the United States of America and Napoleon, Emperor of France and King of Italy, & c., a state of peace and

---

110 See *Schooner Exchange v. McFaddon*, 11 U.S. (7 Cranch) 116 (1812).

amity, the public vessels of his said Imperial and Royal Majesty, conforming to the law of nations and laws of the said United States, may freely enter the ports and harbors of the said United States and at pleasure depart therefrom without seizure, arrest, detention or molestation.[111]

The district court held that "a public armed vessel of a foreign sovereign in amity with our government is not subject to the ordinary judicial tribunals of the country so far as regards the question of title by which such sovereign claims to hold the vessel."[112] In effect, both the US District Attorney and the district judge asserted the existence of a principle of sovereign immunity from jurisdiction.

After the Circuit Court of Appeals reversed the holding of the district court, the US District Attorney appealed the reversal to the Supreme Court. As noted in the syllabus of the Supreme Court decision:

> This being a cause in which the sovereign right claimed by Napoleon, the reigning emperor of the French, and the political relations between the United States and France were involved, it was, upon the suggestion of the Attorney General, ordered to a hearing in preference to other causes which stood before it on the docket.[113]

Chief Justice Marshall, writing the Opinion of the Court, held that:

> The jurisdiction of the nation within its own territory is necessarily exclusive and absolute. It is susceptible of no limitation not imposed by itself. Any restriction upon it, deriving validity from an external source, would imply a diminution of its sovereignty to the extent of the restriction, and an invest-ment of that sovereignty to the same extent in that power which could impose such restriction.
>
> …
>
> The world being composed of distinct sovereignties, possessing equal rights and equal independence, whose mutual benefit is promoted by intercourse with each other, and by an interchange of those good offices which humanity dictates and its wants require, all sovereigns have consented to a relaxation in practice, in cases under certain peculiar circumstances, of that absolute and complete jurisdiction within their respective territories which sovereignty confers.[114]

Chief Justice Marshall further indicated that "[a] nation would justly be con-sidered as violating its faith, although that faith might not be expressly plighted, which should suddenly and without previous notice, exercise its territorial powers

111 Ibid., at 118.
112 Ibid., at 120.
113 Ibid., at 116.
114 Ibid., at 137.

in a manner not consonant to the usages and received obligations of the civilized world."[115] This shows that sovereign immunity had already become a customary rule, at least among the Western nations of the international community, even if a particular state had not expressly accepted it. He further noted that:

> One sovereign being in no respect amenable to another; and being bound by obligations of the highest character not to degrade the dignity of his nation, by placing himself or its sovereign rights within the jurisdiction of another … This perfect equality and absolute independence of sovereigns, and this common interest impelling them to mutual intercourse, and an interchange of good offices with each other, has given rise to a class of cases in which every sovereign is understood to wa[i]ve the exercise of a part of that complete exclusive territorial jurisdiction, which has been stated to be the attribute of every nation.[116]

Obviously, in Chief Justice Marshall's view, the immunity granted by one state within its territory to another state is based on the equality of sovereign states, with reciprocity as its precondition. Is this kind of sovereign immunity an exception to the inherited exclusive jurisdiction of the state concerned, or is it a principle of customary international law? As can be seen from the above discussion, in Marshall's view, it was both.

It is important to note, as Bankas points out in his careful consideration of this case: "There was no *lex scripta*, i.e., written law, on the question of state immunity to guide Chief Justice Marshall when the Schooner Exchange case was brought before him."[117] Nor, as Bankas also notes, was there any *lex non scripta*, i.e. scholarly literature, on the subject. However, "in order to keep himself within the confines of reasonableness, [Chief Justice Marshall] threw his efforts behind the authority of the writings of the past … specifically on the philosophical writings of Vattel, coupled with the inherited precepts of the social contract, cleverly adumbrated by Hobbes and Rousseau."[118]

At the outset of his Opinion, Chief Justice Marshall wrote: "In exploring an unbeaten path with few if any aids from precedents or written law, the Court has found it necessary to rely much on general principles and on a train of reasoning founded on cases in some degree analogous to this."[119] In so doing, he repeatedly employed such terms as "common usage," "common opinion," "received obligations" and "the unanimous consent of nations." His use of these terms is consonant with what Roberts refers to as "traditional custom" as a source of international law.[120] At the same time, however, he also consistently made use of these terms

---

115 Id.

116 Id.

117 Ernest K. Bankas, *The Sovereign Immunity Controversy in International Law: Private Suits Against Sovereign States in Domestic Courts*, Springer Verlag, Heidelberg/Berlin, 2005, p. 15 (footnote omitted).

118 Id. Footnotes omitted, but see, especially, note 8.

119 *Schooner Exchange, supra*, note 110, at 136.

120 Anthea Elizabeth Roberts, "Traditional and Modern Approaches to Customary International

in reference to "the civilized world" and "civilized nations," by which it is fair to infer he meant almost exclusively the United States and the nations of Europe, so that his use of these terms reflects what D'Amato called "special customary international law," including rules limited to countries of a certain region.[121] This understanding is reinforced by the legal practices already underway on the part of the United Kingdom in its dealings with the sovereign states of the Indian sub-continent and those of the United States, Great Britain and other Western powers in enforcing extraterritoriality in China, Japan, Korea, and Thailand.

Nonetheless, it is fair to say that Chief Justice Marshall gave us the first extensive jurisprudential statement of the modern doctrine of sovereign immunity, a doctrine that, in one form or another, has been adopted by all nations[122] and that continues to influence international scholarship and practice.[123]

In 1926, the US Supreme Court reaffirmed the principle of absolute sovereign immunity in the *Pesaro* case,[124] this time involving a merchant ship of the Italian Government employed for commercial activities. In this instance, the US Supreme Court ruled that the ship was owned by Italy and thus was not within its jurisdiction.[125] The Court's decision reaffirmed that at that time it recognized no "commercial exception" to sovereign immunity. According to the Court, although the Italian ship was engaged in commercial activity, its purpose was to preserve and promote the economic interests of the Italian people. Owing to its performance of public acts, the Court refused to exercise jurisdiction over it. Undoubtedly, the United States took the same position as the United Kingdom, refusing to recognize the doctrine of restricted sovereign immunity that had been adopted by European countries. The US Supreme Court specifically stated that the *Pesaro* conducted activity in its public capacity because Italy itself maintained the doctrine of restricted sovereign immunity. It is understandable that, in order to maintain the equality of international intercourse and treatment, the US Supreme Court had carefully chosen the rationale and wording employed in the judgment so as not to give people an impression that it had bent to the will of the Italian Government.

Law: A Reconciliation," 95 *AJIL* 757, 2001. "Traditional custom," she writes, "results from general and consistent practice followed by states from a sense of legal obligation. It focuses primarily on state practice in the form of interstate interaction and acquiescence." Ibid., at 758; footnote omitted.

121 See Anthony D'Amato, "The Concept of Special Custom in International Law," 63 *AJIL* 211, 1969.

122 Although some nations have since adopted the doctrine of restricted sovereign immunity, this author has not been able to uncover a single national or court formulation of a "doctrine of no sovereign immunity." Lauterpacht argued that the jurisdictional immunity of sovereign States is not a principle of international law, which, in his view, derives instead out of consideration of the dignity of foreign States and reciprocity; see Hersch Lauterpacht, "The Problem of Jurisdictional Immunities of Foreign States," 28 *Brit. Y.B. Int'l L.* 220, 1951.

123 See, for example, Harvard Research in International Law, "Competence of Courts in Regard to Foreign States" 26 *AJIL Supp.* 455, 1932, at 527.

124 See *Berizzi Brothers v. Pesaro*, 271 U.S. 562 (1926).

125 Ibid., at 576.

After World War II, governments became more involved in economic activities. Some of them even owned merchant fleets and trading companies. Consequently, countries such as the United States and the United Kingdom became aware that adhering to the principle of absolute sovereign immunity would result in disadvantages for their domestic companies and nationals doing business with foreign state-owned enterprises. After the 1940s, they began to consider adopting the doctrine of restricted sovereign immunity. For example, in 1943, a vessel owned by Peru was seized by the United States. In its ruling on whether the ship could be considered immune from its jurisdiction, the US Supreme Court held that the statement made by the US State Department suggesting that the ship should enjoy immunity should "be given full force and effect by this court."[126] Although the US President and State Department have the power to make decisions regarding foreign affairs, this was the very first time in US legal history that a court clearly expressed its willingness to accept the opinion of the State Department and use it as its final ruling on jurisdiction.[127]

In 1945, the US Supreme Court reconfirmed this viewpoint in *Republic of Mexico v. Hoffman*, affirming that "[i]t is ... not for the courts to deny an immunity which our government has seen fit to allow, or to allow an immunity on new grounds which the government has not seen fit to recognize."[128] This changed attitude of the US Supreme Court to sovereign immunity, whereby it essentially refused to rule on the issue but accepted the authority of the executive branch of government to determine its limits, paved the way for the United States to adopt the doctrine of restricted sovereign immunity.

B. Restricted sovereign immunity

After the *Pesaro* case and *Ex parte Republic of Peru*, the US Government's preference for a doctrine of restricted sovereign immunity became increasingly evident. In 1952, the Department of State's Acting Legal Advisor, Jack B. Tate, wrote to the Acting Attorney General, Philip B. Perlman,[129] alleging that there existed two concepts of sovereign immunity, the absolute theory of sovereign immunity and the restrictive theory of sovereign immunity, and supporting the latter:

> According to the newer or restrictive theory of sovereign immunity, the immunity of the sovereign is recognized with regard to sovereign or public acts of a State (*jure imperii*), but not with respect to private acts (*jure gestionis*).
> ...

---

126 See, *Ex parte Republic of Peru*, 318 U.S. 578 (1943).

127 Although, as was seen earlier, a US District Attorney did intervene in the seminal *Exchange* case and the US Supreme Court granted *certiorari* to the appeal, at least partly, at the request of the US Attorney General. See *supra*, notes 110ff and accompanying text.

128 *Republic of Mexico v. Hoffman*, 324 U.S. 30 (1945), at 35.

129 For the full text of the Tate Letter, see H. J. Steiner and D. F. Vagte (eds.), *Transnational Legal Problems: Materials and Texts* (3rd ed.), Foundation Press, New York, 1986, pp. 705–707.

The newer or restrictive theory of sovereign immunity has always been supported by the courts of Belgium and Italy. It was adopted in turn by the courts of Egypt and of Switzerland. In addition, the courts of France, Austria, and Greece, which were traditionally supporters of the classical theory, reversed their position in the 20's [sic] to embrace the restrictive theory. Rumania, Peru, and possibly Denmark also appear to follow this theory.

. . .

The Department feels that the widespread and increasing practice on the part of governments of engaging in commercial activities makes necessary a practice which will enable persons doing business with them to have their rights determined in the courts. For these reasons it will hereafter be the Department's policy to follow the restrictive theory of sovereign immunity in the consideration of requests of foreign governments for a grant of sovereign immunity.[130]

Tate specifically indicated that the US Government itself was subject to the jurisdiction of its domestic courts and would not claim immunity for US vessels. His real intent, however, was to remove the application of sovereign immunity to commercial activities by state-owned enterprises. He admitted that "[t]he reasons which obviously motivate State trading countries in adhering to the theory with increasing rigidity are most persuasive that the United States should change its policy."[131]

The doctrine of restricted sovereign immunity is intended to protect private property interests, which is the fundamental concern of Western countries. In accordance with this doctrine, where a state does not deem the act of a foreign state to be a typical exercise of state sovereignty it may put the foreign state in an equal position with an individual person, enterprise or company.

In fact, the major distinction between the doctrines of absolute sovereign immunity and restricted sovereign immunity lies in the different extent and scope of immunity granted to foreign sovereignties. Even under the former, a foreign government or its representatives should not do whatever they want in a foreign country or refuse to implement the agreements it has signed in regard to commercial activities. Moreover, although some European countries had already exercised jurisdiction over acts of state done in another state's private capacity, there was no consensus on the distinction between acts done in the private capacity and those done in the public capacity. This was true not only among different countries but also among different courts within a single country. As one scholar has pointed out, the state's purchase of army boots which was deemed by French and US courts to be an act done in the public capacity might be taken as a private act by an Italian court; operating railways was considered a public act in some countries but was considered a private act by the Belgian Supreme Court; and,

130 Ibid.
131 Ibid.

whilst one French court thought it was a private act for a state to purchase goods and resell them to its nationals, another one might take an opposite view.[132]

The core of the doctrine of restricted sovereign immunity lies in the principle that the decision whether or not to grant immunity from local jurisdiction depends on the nature of the relevant matter or act instead of that of the actor. This has fundamentally changed the basis of the traditional doctrine of sovereign immunity, which recognized in a sovereign the capacity both of sovereignty and of a private entity. Under the doctrine of restricted sovereign immunity, a sovereign only enjoys immunity for acts performed in its public capacity—which are thereby defined as acts of state—but not private acts or commercial activity. In accordance with the logic of the doctrine of restricted sovereign immunity, in the above-mentioned *Pesaro* case, where the ship was used by Italy for commercial purposes, it would not have been entitled to enjoy any immunity from the jurisdiction of US courts due to the commercial or private nature of the activity involved.

The fundamental questions raised by this doctrine, which depends on the nature instead of the purpose of an act, include how to tell what are private acts and what are public acts, or what acts constitute commercial activity. For example, is it a commercial act for a government to borrow foreign funds to build up a military harbour? In terms of the nature of the transaction, it involves a loan contract between a lender and a borrower. Without taking the purpose of the loan or the nature of the borrower into account, there would be no difference between this and commercial loans made to private entities. If the purpose of the loan and the nature of the borrower are taken into account, on the other hand, this is clearly a transaction with governmental characteristics that would have been considered in the 18th and 19th centuries to be an act of state. In the contemporary world, moreover, matters may be further complicated by a transaction whereby a private entity borrows foreign funds to develop a military harbour on behalf of the government of a sovereign state. In developing the harbour, could the private entity be considered to be acting as "an organ of the State"? If so, how should the loan transaction be characterized?[133]

C. Laws on sovereign immunity

Since World War II, Western developed countries have gone further in advocating the doctrine of restricted sovereign immunity. Following the initiative of

---

132 See Ni Zhengyu, *supra*, note 65, at 9. See, also, Lauterpacht, *supra*, note 122, at 222–24.

133 Lauterpacht, ibid., commented on another aspect of the problem of distinguishing the "nature" of an act that, on the face of it appears to be a "commercial" transaction. He said (at 225): "To what extent is it true to say that contracts made by the state for the purchase of shoes for the army, or of a warship, or of munitions, or of foodstuff necessary for the maintenance of the national economy, are not immune from the jurisdiction for the reason that they are contracts and that an individual can make a contract? For can it not be said that these particular contracts can be made by a state only, and not by individuals? Individuals do not purchase shoes for their armies; they do not buy warships for the use of the state; they are not, as such, responsible for the management of the national economy."

the United States, major developed countries have successively enacted laws on sovereign immunity with the doctrine of restricted sovereign immunity as their theoretical basis. In 1976, the United States took the lead in this regard by passing the Foreign Sovereign Immunities Act ("FSIA").[134] It was followed by the United Kingdom in 1978, Singapore in 1979, Pakistan and South Africa in 1981, and Canada in 1982.

In principle, the US FSIA does grant foreign states immunity from local juris-diction.[135] However, there are many exceptions to such immunity, including:

1.   when a foreign government explicitly waives its right to sovereign immunity, notwithstanding any withdrawal of the waiver
2.   when commercial activity is carried on in the United States, an act is per-formed in the United States in connection with a commercial activity else-where or an act performed in connection with a commercial activity of a foreign state elsewhere has a direct effect in the United States
3.   in regard to property located in the United States that is related to commer-cial activities that are carried on inside or outside the United States by foreign states or state organs
4.   when a suit is brought to enforce a maritime lien against a vessel of a foreign state and such maritime lien is based upon a commercial activity of the for-eign state or
5.   when a counterclaim arises from a suit brought or participated in by a foreign state in a US court.[136]

In 1988, the FSIA was amended to include an arbitration exception. Under these provisions, foreign states enjoy no immunity in actions to enforce arbitration agreements or to confirm arbitration awards if: (a) the arbitration takes place or is intended to take place in the United States; (b) the agreement or award is or may be governed by a treaty or other international agreement calling for the recogni-tion and enforcement of arbitral awards that is in force for the United States; (c) the underlying claim, were it not for the arbitration agreement, could have been brought in the United States under the provisions of the FSIA; or (d) the foreign state has waived immunity within the terms of the FSIA waiver exception men-tioned above.[137]

Obviously, the totality of the above exceptions in the US FSIA go far beyond US case law or even the terms of the Tate Letter. By virtue of the FSIA, the issue of sovereign immunity once again became subject to determination by US courts. In other words, it was up to the courts, instead of the testimony or sug-gestion of the Department of State, to determine whether a foreign state should enjoy sovereign immunity based on the nature, but not the purpose, of related

---

134   See US Foreign Sovereign Immunities Act of 1976, 90 Stat. 2891–98.
135   Ibid., Section 1604.
136   Ibid., Section 1605(1)–(5).
137   Ibid., Section 1605(6).

activity. In consequence, not only the commercial activities performed by foreign governments or their organs within the United States but also activities performed outside the United States that are deemed by a US court to have a direct effect in the United States cannot enjoy any immunity. The US FSIA not only takes the explicit waiver of a foreign state as the basis to exercise jurisdiction but also allows US courts to construe such a waiver in accordance with the acts of a foreign state, i.e. an implicit waiver. This means that domestic US courts are entitled not only to judge which activities carried on by a foreign state are commercial in nature but also to construe whether an implicit waiver was made by the state involved so as to exercise jurisdiction over them.

The first case with significant impact after enactment of the US FSIA was *Texas Trading v. Nigeria*, regarding the performance of a letter of credit.[138] In the early 1970s, Nigeria began to import large amounts of cement. It entered into 109 contracts with foreign suppliers, among which four were signed with companies registered in New York. These four companies, who were not industrial corporations but "trading companies," were obliged to provide 10,000 million metric tons of cement. In accordance with the contracts, Nigeria applied for two banks in New York and Hamburg to establish irrevocable letters of credit. The suppliers committed to provide 20,000 metric tons of cement every month with delivery to Lagos harbour. The suppliers were obligated to give the shipping documents to the above banks once the cargo was shipped in Spain. The banks were to make payment in cash after checking the accuracy of the documents.

In 1975, due to poor planning on the part of Nigeria, about 400 ships, mostly ships carrying cement, clogged Lagos harbour, and cargoes could not be unloaded. On August 18, 1975, the Nigerian Government instructed the issuing banks in New York and Hamburg not to make further payments under the letters of credit. It also promulgated a decree prohibiting entry into Lagos port to any ship that had not secured approval to do so two months in advance of its arrival and imposing criminal penalties for unauthorized entry. Consequently, foreign suppliers had to negotiate with the Nigerian Government to deal with the problem. However, the four New York trading companies failed to settle with Nigeria and thus brought suit against the Nigerian Government and its Central Bank in US federal court.

Based on the principle of sovereign immunity in international law, Nigeria claimed that a US court should not deal with a suit against the Nigerian Government and its Central Bank. The US Second Circuit Court of Appeals held that, in accordance with the US FSIA, Nigeria's purchase of cement and establishment of letters of credit were commercial activities and, thus, did not enjoy sovereign immunity in US courts. The purpose of the purchase was not important, no matter whether it was for civilian use or military use.

This case further reflects the power enjoyed by US courts to determine whether the acts of a foreign state constitute commercial activity. The Court of Appeals clearly indicated that the key to its jurisdiction was whether the act involved was of a commercial character. However, since the 1976 FSIA gives a very broad

---

138 See *Texas Trading & Milling Corp. et al. v. Federal Republic of Nigeria et al.*, 647 F.2d 300.

definition of "commercial activities,"[139] it is up to the courts to differentiate commercial activity and governmental activity.

In determining the character of the activities of the Nigerian Government, the Court of Appeals relied on the FSIA's legislative history, precedents of US courts and principles of modern international law and came to the conclusion that Nigeria's acts of contracting and purchasing cement were commercial activities. In fact, the Court of Appeals mainly based its conclusion on the legislative history of the FSIA. According to the statement made by Monroe Leigh, Chief of the Foreign Litigation Section of the Civil Division of the US Department of Justice at the time the Act was under consideration, "if a government enters into a contract to purchase goods and services, that is considered a commercial activity. It avails itself of the ordinary contract machinery. It bargains and negotiates. It accepts an offer. It enters into a written contract and the contract is to be performed."[140]

The judgment further stated that since Nigeria's acts in dispute were commercial activities, the US court would have jurisdiction over them as long as the plaintiffs could prove they were carried on within or in connection with the United States. It was stipulated in the contracts signed by the Nigerian Government and the foreign suppliers that the suppliers should collect their payments through certain banks in New York on the basis of Nigeria's letters of credit. Therefore, Nigeria's acts were directly connected with the United States. In accordance with the judgment, as long as one disputing party was a US company or a foreign company doing business in the United States, there would be a direct connection with the United States.

In its decision in *Republic of Argentina v. Weltover*, delivered in 1992,[141] the US Supreme Court further clarified both the basis on which acts of state should be considered commercial acts and what constitutes a direct connection of such acts with the United States. In 1982, the Republic of Argentina, through its Central Bank, issued government bonds to be repaid upon maturity in US dollars in London, Frankfurt, Zurich or New York. In 1986, when the bonds began to mature, Argentina lacked the foreign exchange necessary to pay them off and offered bondholders substitute financial instruments instead. Weltover and two other bondholders refused the offer and demanded payment in US dollars in New York. When Argentina did not pay, the bondholders filed suit in US District Court, relying on the US FSIA for jurisdiction. Argentina objected to the jurisdiction, but its objection was dismissed by the District Court, a decision later upheld by the Court of Appeals. Argentina then appealed to the US Supreme Court, which granted *certiorari* and heard the appeal. In the words of Justice Scalia, the

139 The US Foreign Sovereign Immunities Act of 1976, Section 1603(d) reads: "A 'commercial activity' means either a regular course of commercial conduct or a particular commercial transaction or act. The commercial character of an activity shall be determined by reference to the nature of the course of conduct or particular transaction or act, rather than by reference to its purpose."

140 See, Hearings on H.R. 11315 Before the Subcommittee on Administrative Law and Governmental Relations of the House Committee on the Judiciary, 94th Cong., 2d Sess. 51 (1976).

141 *Republic of Argentina et al. v. Weltover, Inc. et al.*, 504 U.S. 607 (1992); available at: http://supreme. justia.com/cases/federal/us/504/607/case.html.

case required the Court "to decide whether the Republic of Argentina's default on certain bonds issued as part of a plan to stabilize its currency was an act taken 'in connection with a commercial activity' that had a 'direct effect in the United States' so as to subject Argentina to suit in an American court under the Foreign Sovereign Immunities Act of 1976."[142]

Regarding the term "commercial," the Court acknowledged that the FSIA fails clearly to define it. However, it noted that the Act "largely codifies the so-called 'restrictive' theory of foreign sovereign immunity first endorsed by the State Department in 1952. The meaning of 'commercial' is the meaning generally attached to that term under the restrictive theory at the time the statute was enacted."[143] In that context, it held:

> … the commercial character of an act is to be determined by reference to its "nature" rather than its "purpose," [and therefore] the question is not whether the foreign government is acting with a profit motive or instead with the aim of fulfilling uniquely sovereign objectives. Rather, the issue is whether the particular actions that the foreign state performs (whatever the motive behind them) are the type of actions by which a private party engages in "trade and traffic or commerce, …"[144]

As for the specific acts considered in the case, the Court upheld previous rulings that they were commercial in nature because "there is nothing about the issuance of these [bonds] (except perhaps its purpose) that is not analogous to a private commercial transaction."[145]

On the question as to whether or not Argentina's acts had a direct effect in the United States, it affirmed the holding of the Court of Appeals that an effect does not have to be either "substantial" or "foreseeable" to be considered "direct" but rather that "an effect is 'direct' if it follows 'as an immediate consequence of the defendant's … activity.'"[146] Because New York was the place where Argentina's contractual obligations were to be performed, but were not, the Court held that these acts "necessarily had a 'direct effect' in the United States."[147]

From the above cases, although they cannot be used as a comprehensive construction of the FSIA, it is quite evident that US courts are prepared to interpret the commercial exceptions to the exercise of sovereign immunity broadly. As the United States is today the strongest power in the world, its court practice, like its practice of legislation, has immediate effects on courts of other countries.

The United Kingdom's approach to sovereign immunity is similar to that of the United States. Before the 1950s, the doctrine of absolute sovereign immunity was basically adhered to in UK cases. For example, in an 1851 case handled by

142 Ibid., at 609.
143 Ibid., at 612–13.
144 Ibid., at 614.
145 Ibid., at 614–15.
146 Ibid., at 617–18.
147 Ibid., at 619.

the Queen's Bench involving the Queen of Portugal, it was clearly stated that "to cite a foreign potentate in a municipal court, for any complaint against him in his public capacity, is contrary to the law of nations, and an insult which he is entitled to resent."[148] However, after the 1950s, there was an obvious change in attitude towards sovereign immunity in the United Kingdom. In 1977, *Trendtex Trading Corp. v. Central Bank of Nigeria*, another case involving cement purchasing contracts, the British Court of Appeal ruled that the defendant should not enjoy immunity.[149] It held that the Central Bank was not an arm of the State of Nigeria and, even if it were, international law gave it no immunity from jurisdiction in regard to its commercial activities, of which its issuance of the letter of credit in dispute was a clear example.

The UK State Immunity Act ("SIA") came into force in 1978. It adopted the doctrine of restricted sovereign immunity, differentiating the acts carried out by a state in its public capacity from those carried out in its private capacity and granting only the former sovereign immunity. Generally speaking, the SIA adopted almost all the principles and provisions contained in the US FSIA. Like the US FSIA, it provides that a state is immune from the jurisdiction of the domestic courts except as provided in the law. It also stipulates various exceptions to this general immunity from jurisdiction, including voluntary waiver of sovereign immunity, commercial activities and transactions conducted by a foreign state, judgments on property used for commercial purposes, enforcement of arbitration awards, admiralty proceedings relating to ships and cargoes, etc.

The interpretation of "voluntary waiver of sovereign immunity" by a UK court was reflected in *Svenska Petroleum Exploration AB v. Lithuania*.[150] Svenska Petroleum Exploration AB ("Svenska"), a petroleum exploration and refinement company, entered into an agreement with the Lithuanian Government and Gargzdai State Oil Geology Enterprise to establish a joint venture to exploit Lithuanian oil reserves in April 1993. Under the dispute settlement clause in Article 9 of the agreement, the contracting parties could submit any dispute to the Court of the Republic of Lithuania or to independent arbitration in Denmark. Article 35 provided that the Lithuanian Government and Gargzdai State Oil Geology Enterprise waived all rights to sovereign immunity and the agreement would be governed by the laws of Lithuania. Svenska and Gargzdai State Oil Geology Enterprise signed the agreement as the contracting parties. Technically, the arbitration clause was only binding for the two contracting parties. However, the Lithuanian Government also signed and approved the agreement, which also contained a rubric providing that "The Government of the Republic of Lithuania hereby approves the above agreement and acknowledges itself to be legally and contractually bound as if the Government were a signatory to the Agreement."

In 2000, a dispute arose because Svenska did not receive the consideration expected under the agreement, and Svenska submitted this dispute for arbitration

---

148 See *De Haber v. The Queen of Portugal* (1851) 17 QB 171, at 196.
149 See *Trendtex Trading Corp. v. Central Bank of Nigeria* [1977] QB 529.
150 *Svenska Petroleum Exploration AB v. Lithuania (No. 2)* (2006) EWCA Civ 1529.

in Demark in accordance with the arbitration agreement. The arbitral tribunal made its Final award in December 2003, ruling that the Lithuanian Government and AB Geonafta (the former Gargzdai State Oil Geology Enterprise) had breached their contractual obligations and were liable to pay damages. Consequently, Svenska requested the UK court to enforce the award in accordance with Section 101 of the UK Arbitration Act 1996. However, Lithuania argued that it was not a party to the arbitral agreement and requested the Court to annul the order to enforce the Final award.

The Court of Appeal held that a state can sign a contract in an administrative capacity merely to indicate its approval of its terms and without itself undertaking obligations of any kind to the contracting parties. However, in the present instance, the Government's intention in signing the agreement appeared to be clearly stated in the rubric, which was not only to "approve" the agreement but also to acknowledge itself to be "legally and contractually bound as if it were a signatory to the Agreement." The Court held that the arbitral tribunal thus had jurisdiction over the dispute. Moreover, if a state has agreed to submit a dispute for arbitration, it should be bound by related proceedings to enforce the arbitral award. Both the arbitral proceedings and the enforcement proceedings are "proceedings ...which relate to the arbitration" under Article 9(1) of the SIA. Therefore, the Lithuanian Government was not entitled to request sovereign immunity regarding the enforcement proceedings in the UK court.

Of course, there are differences between the UK SIA and the US FSIA. For example, in the UK SIA, commercial transactions are concretely defined as:

> ... any contract for the supply of goods or services; any loan or other transaction for the provision of finance and any guarantee or indemnity in respect of any such transaction or of any other financial obligation; and any other transaction or activity (whether of a commercial, industrial, financial, professional or other similar character) into which a State enters or in which it engages otherwise than in the exercise of sovereign authority.[151]

Following in the footsteps of the United States and the United Kingdom, Canada enacted its own State Immunity Act in 1982.[152] The Canadian Act is almost an exact copy of the US FSIA. On the one hand, it grants wide sovereign immunity and, on the other hand, it stipulates numerous exceptions to the immunity, including the following:

1. when an explicit waiver of jurisdictional immunity has been made by a foreign sovereign state
2. when an explicit or implicit waiver of immunity to forfeiture, enforcement, arrest, etc. has been made by a foreign sovereign state and

---

151 After the passing of the UK State Immunity Act, UK courts reviewed a series of cases regarding sovereign immunity; see G. Delaume, "The State Immunity Act of the United Kingdom," 73 *AJIL* 185, 1979.
152 See State Immunity Act, RSC 1985, c S-18.

3. when commercial activities or transactions whose nature is commercial are
    conducted by a foreign sovereign state.

Canada's move was not at all surprising. In the first place, its laws are deeply
rooted in the UK common law system. Second, it always has very close economic
and other relations with the United States. As such, to adopt a policy and law corresponding to their counterparts in the United States and the United Kingdom
is a natural choice. What is a little surprising is that some developing countries
have also adopted the doctrine of restricted sovereign immunity. These include
Singapore in 1979 and Pakistan and South Africa in 1981.[153]

The developments discussed above indicate that in an age of global legalism[154]
against the background of economic globalization, it has become necessary to
recognize some legitimate restraints on the exercise of sovereignty insofar as certain aspects of international investment law are concerned. After all, the primary
purpose of the international investment law regime is to protect foreign investors
and not the host states. As such, the international investment law regime must
have the effect, intended or unintended, of limiting "the sovereign right of a State
to subject foreign investors to its domestic administrative legal system."[155] At
the same time, even for those states that have adopted the doctrine of restricted
sovereign immunity, there exists a distinction between immunity from jurisdiction and immunity from execution. Whilst their national courts are prepared to
exercise jurisdiction on the basis of a commercial transaction or activity, they are
in general more prudent, however, in applying the commercial exception in cases
of execution or attachment of property.

IV. National practices relating to execution of investment awards

Investor–state arbitration involves a sovereign state. For purposes of conducting
such arbitration and the subsequent enforcement of arbitral awards, the issue of
sovereign immunity must be taken into consideration. In general, where a state
consents to arbitration, that act at least implies a waiver of sovereign immunity.[156]
The importance of waiving sovereign immunity lies in the fact that where an arbitral award is made in favor of a foreign investor and where the losing foreign state

---

153 See Burkhard Hess, "The International Law Commission's Draft Convention on the Jurisdictional
     Immunities of States and Their Property," 4 *EJIL* 269–82, 1993, at 269, n. 3.
154 Global legalism is the view that a world government is not a practicable approach to global
     collective action problems but that these are nonetheless susceptible to legal solutions. For
     more discussion of global legalism, see Eric Posner, *The Rise of Global Legalism*, Max Weber
     Lecture Series No. 2008/04; also, idem., *The Perils of Global Legalism*, University of Chicago
     Press, 2011.
155 Dolzer, *supra*, note 2.
156 W. Michael Reisman et al., *International Commercial Arbitration: Cases, Materials and Notes on the
     Resolution of International Business Disputes*, Foundation Press, 1997, p. 1286.

refuses to give effect to the award,[157] the foreign investor has to resort to national courts for redress.

Where a national court is requested to enforce an arbitral award and considers that it has jurisdiction, another question still remains. That is, whether the losing state has immunity from enforcement over particular assets seized to execute the arbitral award. On this issue, neither customary international law nor the practice of investment arbitration is necessarily very clear. In *MINE v. Guinea*, one of the very few cases involving the issue of sovereign immunity in respect of enforcement of arbitral awards, the *ad hoc* Committee stated that:

> State immunity may well afford a legal defense to forcible execution, but it provides neither argument nor excuse for failing to comply with an award. In fact, the issue of State immunity from forcible execution of an award will typically arise if the State party refuses to comply with its treaty obligations. Noncompliance by a State constitutes a violation by that State of its international obligations and will attract its own sanctions. The Committee refers in this connection among other things to Article 27 and 64 of the [ICSID] Convention, and to the consequences which such a violation would have for such a State's reputation with private and public sources of international finance.[158]

Article 27 of the ICSID Convention requires states to refrain from diplomatic protection unless the other contracting party has failed to perform its obligations arising from the Convention. In today's highly globalized world, it can hardly be expected that a state would resort to diplomatic protection to enforce an investment arbitral award made in favor of one of its nationals, especially since only strong powers have the means to exercise diplomatic protection. Article 64 of the ICSID Convention refers to the resolution of disputes between contracting parties through the International Court of Justice ("ICJ"), which can hardly be considered a "sanction."

The ICSID Convention in fact has a self-enforcing system. Article 54(1) of the Convention provides: "Each Contracting State shall recognize an award rendered pursuant to this Convention as binding and enforce the pecuniary obligations imposed by that award within its territories as if it were a final judgment of a court in that State." Under Article 54(1), Contracting states have an obligation

---

157 On this matter, one writer has commented that "[t]hough most respondents have indeed paid the awards rendered against them, States have not inevitably done so: Liberia, Senegal, Congo, and Kazakhstan have each failed to pay awards, and their successful invocations of sovereign immunity defences illustrate the difficulties that even victorious investors face vis-à-vis recalcitrant States." See, Andrea K. Bjorklund, "State Immunity and the Enforcement of Investor-State Arbitral Awards," in Christina Binder et al. (eds.), *International Investment Law for the 21st Century: Essays in Honour of Christoph Schreuer*, Oxford University Press, 2009, pp. 302ff.

158 *Maritime International Nominees Establishment (MINE) v. Republic of Guinea*, ICSID Case No. ARB/84/4, Interim Order No. 1 on Guinea's Application for Stay of Enforcement of the Award (August 12, 1988), 4 *ICSID Rep.* 115/6.

to recognize ICSID arbitral awards as final judgments of their own countries' courts. Yet this obligation only relates to the pecuniary obligations of such awards. Regarding this provision, Schreuer has remarked:

> The Convention's drafting history shows that domestic authorities charged with recognition and enforcement have no discretion to review the award once its authenticity has been established. Not even the ordre public (public policy) of the forum may furnish a ground for refusal. The finality of awards would also exclude any examination of their compliance with international public policy or international law in general.[159]

In a way, the system established by Article 54 of the ICSID Convention is more forceful than that contained in the 1958 New York Convention, which provides certain exceptions, including public policy ("*ordre public*"). In connection with the execution of awards, however, the ICSID system is not as self-governing. Article 54(3) of the ICSID Convention provides that "[e]xecution of the award shall be governed by the laws concerning the execution of judgments in force in the State in whose territories such execution is sought." Thus, in enforcing an ICSID arbitral award, whether particular assets of the losing host state may be seized or attached to satisfy the award is left to national courts. If, according to the laws and policies of the enforcing forum, certain such assets are entitled to immunity from execution, the ICSID arbitral award cannot be actually enforced. This is confirmed by Article 55 of the ICSID Convention, which provides that "[n]othing in Article 54 shall be construed as derogating from the law in force in any Contracting State relating to immunity of that State or of any foreign state from execution."

In other words, in cases where the losing foreign countries refuse to enforce arbitral awards, the fate of claimants seeking redress from the ICSID will depend on the sovereign immunity laws of the forum. Furthermore, unless the laws of the forum state dictate otherwise, "submission of a dispute to ICSID arbitration cannot be interpreted as a waiver of immunity from execution."[160] This is also an issue for enforcement of awards made by tribunals of other arbitral bodies and *ad hoc* tribunals.[161]

What then is the actual system relating to award execution in the practice of

---

159 Schreuer, *supra*, note 64, at 1129.

160 Claudia Annaker and Robert T. Greig, "State Immunity and Arbitration," *ICC International Court of Arbitration Bulletin*, Vol. 15, No. 2, Fall 2004, pp. 70–78, at 77–78; available at: http://www.cgsh.com/news/pubdetail.aspx?pub=95.

161 Professor van den Berg considered the two-tiered waiver of immunity illogical and said: "If a State agrees to arbitration, it must be deemed to have accepted all its consequences, including compliance with an unfavourable award. If in the latter case it does not carry out the award, the State's assets, like assets of a private person, should be capable of execution. In other words, waiver of immunity from jurisdiction should imply waiver of immunity from execution. This rule is nothing other than an application of the principle of *pacta sunt servanda*." See Albert Jan van den Berg, "Recent Enforcement Problems Under the New York and ICSID Conventions," 5 *Arb. Int'l* 2, 1989, p. 12.

the international community? This section will examine the practice of the United States, Great Britain and France, which are important players in the field.[162]

A. The US practice

As discussed earlier, the United States adopted the doctrine of restricted sovereign immunity and enacted the FSIA in 1976, Section 1609 of which provides that the property of a foreign state located in the United States is "immune from attachment, arrest and execution" unless it falls into one of the exceptions stipulated in the FSIA.[163] In this regard, Section 1610(a) of the FSIA provides:

> The property in the United States of a foreign state, as defined in section 1603(a) of this chapter, used for a commercial activity in the United States, shall not be immune from attachment in aid of execution, or from execution ... , if –
> (1) the foreign state has waived its immunity from attachment in aid of execution or from execution either explicitly or by implication, notwithstanding any withdrawal of the waiver the foreign state may purport to effect except in accordance with the terms of the waiver, or
> (2) the property is or was used for the commercial activity upon which the claim is based.

In addition to the property of sovereign states, the FSIA in Section 1610(b) further stipulates that "any property in the United States of an agency or instrumentality of a foreign state engaged in commercial activity in the United States shall not be immune from attachment in aid of execution, or from execution." According to the FSIA, therefore, where any property of a state is used for a commercial purpose that is the basis of a claim, it may be subject to seizure and attachment to satisfy claims against an arbitral award. Other property of a state that is located in the United States and is "used for" a commercial purpose but which is not the basis of the claim may also be subject to seizure or attachment, provided immunity from execution is waived by the state. In comparison, the exceptions to the immunity from attachment of state agencies and instrumentalities are broader; where an agency or instrumentality is "engaged in" commercial activity in the United States, any of its property which is the basis for the underlying claim will not have sovereign immunity from execution. In addition, if it has waived such immunity, any of its property may be attached or executed. Not only is the phrase "engaged in" adopted here interpreted as denoting a broader concept than that of

---

162 For a more general survey of recent European practice in this regard, see August Reinisch, "European Court Practice Concerning State Immunity from Enforcement measures," *EJIL*, Vol.17, No. 4, 2006, pp. 803–36. See also Mag. Eva Wiesinger, "State Immunity from Enforcement Measures," July 2006; available at: http://intlaw.univie.ac.at/fileadmin/user_upload/int_beziehungen/Internetpubl/wiesinger.pdf.

163 28 U.S.C. § 1609, 74Id. § 1610(a).

"used for" to be discussed later, but the property in this case need not be involved in the act upon which the claim is based.

Soon after the enactment of the FSIA, its Section 1610 was tested in the *Birch Shipping* case,[164] in which the plaintiff Birch Shipping petitioned to enforce an arbitral award against Tanzania arising from a commercial contract between them. The District Court of the District of Columbia stated that Section 1610 set forth "a two-step analysis" for determining the immunity of property not the basis for the underlying claim, i.e. (1) there had been a waiver by the foreign state of immunity from attachment and (2) the property was used for a commercial purpose.[165]

The property that the plaintiff wanted to attach was a checking account of the Embassy of Tanzania in the United States, which was used for maintaining the Embassy, including paying employee salaries and purchasing goods and services incident to the Embassy's operation. The District Court stated that "the fact that goods or services to be procured through a contract are to be used for a public purpose is irrelevant; it is the essentially commercial nature of an activity or transaction that is critical."[166] Apparently, the Tanzanian Embassy's admission of the commercial nature of the checking account contributed to the Court's belief that in such cases the best solution is to have separate accounts for funds used for public purposes and those used for "commercial activity." Because the Embassy used the account for both public and commercial purposes, the Court decided not to quash the writ of garnishment.[167]

The *LETCO* case[168] is often cited in relation to the enforcement of an ICSID award. In that case, the Court found that the defendant Liberia's waiver of immunity from jurisdiction for enforcement of an ICSID arbitral award had no impact on execution of the award under Section 1610(a) of the FSIA. Its finding was based on Article 54 of the ICSID Convention as discussed earlier.[169] The Court found the ways through which the defendant (Liberia) had collected the taxes and fees irrelevant, because it considered the use of the funds essential. The reasoning behind this decision is that the funds were used as "public funds" and were "not property used for commercial activities."[170] What is important here is that the Court ruled that some funds in a bank account used for commercial activity did not necessarily defeat the account's entitlement to immunity. Instead, it held, in a ruling which was nearly the exact opposite of that in the *Birch Shipping* case:

> Indeed, a diplomatic mission would undergo a severe hardship if a civil judgment creditor were permitted to freeze bank accounts used for the purposes

---

164 *Birch Shipping Corp. v. Embassy of United Republic of Tanzania*, 507 F. Supp. 311 (D.C. Or. 1980).

165 Ibid., p. 312.

166 Id.

167 Ibid., p. 313.

168 For the decision on jurisdiction for the enforcement of the arbitral award, see *Liberian Eastern Timber Corp. v. Republic of Liberia*, 650 F. Supp. 73 (S.D.N.Y. 1986); for the decision relating to execution of the award, see *Liberian Eastern Timber Corp. v. Republic of Liberia*, 659 F. Supp. 606 (DD.C. 1987).

169 Ibid., 659 F. Supp. 606 (DD.C. 1987).

170 Id.

of a diplomatic mission for an indefinite period of time until exhaustive discovery had taken place to determine the precise portion of the bank account used for commercial activities. Such a scenario would practically gut one of the purposes behind immunity: to afford deference to the governmental affairs of foreign states. In addition, requiring diplomats to segregate funds of a public character from commercial activity funds to avoid the risk of attachment is not the solution. Courts, let alone diplomats, have difficulty determining whether funds are public or commercial in nature.[171]

In *Connecticut Bank of Commerce v. Republic of Congo*,[172] the Fifth Circuit Court of Appeals also emphasized that in determining whether immunity from execution should be availed, "[w]hat matters … is what the property is 'used for,' not how it was generated or produced."[173] In the view of the Court, where a property is used for commercial activity, even if it is purchased with public funds such as tax revenues, immunity should not be permitted. By the same reasoning, a property that is purchased with funds generated from commercial activity but which is used for public purposes should be granted immunity from attachment and execution.

As for the meaning of "used for," the Fifth Circuit Court of Appeals adopted the dictionary definition of the phrase "to use" and said that the property is "used for" means "to put the property in the service of the commercial activity [or] to carry out the activity by means of the property."[174] In this regard, the Court also compared "used for a commercial activity" of Section 1610 of the FSIA with "in connection with" a commercial activity of Section 1605 in respect of exceptions to immunity from jurisdiction. It considered that the difference denotes that Section 1605 allows broader exceptions (commercial activities), whilst Section 1610 should be interpreted restrictively. Its reasoning was based, inter alia, on the legislative history and views of the international community at the time of enactment of the FSIA. It stated that at that time "the international community viewed execution against a foreign state's property as a greater affront to its sovereignty than merely permitting jurisdiction over the merits of an action."[175]

Walker International Holdings Ltd. v. Republic of Congo[176] also concerned interpretation of Section 1610 of the FSIA. The property involved in the case was intangible. In that case, the Republic of Congo and Sadelmi Cogepi S.p.A., an Italian

---

171 Ibid., at 610 (footnote omitted).
172 *Connecticut Bank of Commerce v. Republic of Congo*, US Court of Appeals, Fifth Circuit, 309 F.3d 240 (2002); available at: http://scholar.google.com.hk/scholar_case?case= 11878922430991882048&q=Connecticut+Bank+of+Commerce+v.+Republic+of+Congo &hl=en&as_sdt=2,5&as_vis=1.
173 Ibid., at 251.
174 Ibid., at 255.
175 Ibid., at 256.
176 *Walker International Holdings Ltd., Plaintiff-Appellant, v. Republic of Congo; Caisse Congolaise D'amortissement, Defendants-Appellees, and Murphy Exploration & Production Company International, Garnishee-Appellee*, United States Court of Appeals, Fifth Circuit, 395 F.3rd 229 (2004); available at: http://scholar. google.com.hk/scholar_case?case=396225869849875673&q=walker+international+holdings+ v.+Republic+of+Congo&hl=en&as_sdt=2,5&as_vis=1.

company, entered into a contract for the construction of electric infrastructure in Congo, which subsequently defaulted on the payment. Walker International Holdings purchased the debt from Sadelmi and, in accordance with the contract between Sadelmi and Congo, brought the dispute to arbitration at the ICC, which issued an award in favor of Walker.

Walker then filed a garnishment action in US District Court against Murphy Exploration & Production Company to secure some funds that it suspected Murphy owed to Congo. Upon the District Court granting the motions, Murphy paid Congo the funds and produced surety bonds of equivalent amount, which would be paid to Walker upon a final judgment in the latter's favor. Congo and Murphy appealed on grounds of immunity from execution.

The Court of Appeals pointed out that to avail a Section 1610 exception a three-step analysis was required, namely, waiver of immunity, property in the United States, and property used for a commercial activity. Regarding whether Congo had waived its immunity from attachment, its contract with Sadelmi provided that: "Congo hereby irrevocably renounces to claim any immunity during any procedure relating to any arbitration decision handed down by an Arbitration Court." The Fifth Circuit Court of Appeals considered the phrase "any immunity" to have satisfied the requirement of waiver.[177]

As the property involved in the case was intangible, the question remained as to how to determine its situs or whether it was a property located in the United States, as required by the FSIA. The Court, by referring to its previous decisions in *Af-Cap Inc. v. Republic of Congo*[178] and *Tabacalera Severiano Jorge, S.A. v. Standard Cigar Co.*,[179] stated that "courts consistently hold that the situs of debtor obligation is the situs of the debtor."[180] This is an important ruling, as in practice very often a property involved may be intangible in nature.

The contribution of the Fifth Circuit Court of Appeals in respect of determining what a property is being "used for" is also significant. The question in the *Walker* case was whether reimbursement by Congo to Murphy for administrative and transactional costs would meet the requirement of "used for" a commercial activity. The Court stated:

> Even if there were evidence that the ROC [Congo] paid Murphy for commercial services under this provision, Walker's argument still fails. Murphy was merely able to deduct certain expenses from the amount it owed the ROC; there was no commercial activity separate from the transaction that

177 Ibid., at 234.
178 *Af-Cap Inc. v. Republic of Congo*, 383 F. 3d 361 (5th Cir. 2004); available at: http://scholar.google.com.hk/scholar_case?case=38150208394893945925&q=walker+international+holdings+v.+Republic+of+Congo&hl=en&as_sdt=2,5&as_vis=1.
179 *Tabacalera Severiano Jorge, S.A. v. Standard Cigar Co.*, 392 F. 2nd 706 (5th Cir. 1968); available at: http://scholar.google.com.hk/scholar_case?case=6796942084903281044&q=walker+international+holdings+v.+Republic+of+Congo&hl=en&as_sdt=2,5&as_vis=1.
180 *Walker International Holdings Ltd. v. Republic of Congo, supra*, note 176, at 235.

generated the property in the first place. In addition, contextually and holistically, minor reimbursements would not reach this standard.[181]

The "minor reimbursements" were mentioned in relation to the decision in the *Af-Cap* case, in which "at least fifty percent of the proceeds had been used for commercial activity." As the reimbursement in the *Walker* case would not be "anywhere near fifty percent," the Court concluded that the property was not used for a commercial activity.[182]

The above cases clearly indicate that US courts are quite prepared to enforce investment awards via any of the exceptions to immunity under the FSIA. In order to seize or attach the property of a host state or its agency or instrumentality, it must first be evident that there exists a waiver of immunity from the execution of the arbitral award. Thereafter, it must be proved that the property in question is used for a commercial activity and is in the United States. Although the commercial exception is applicable to both a state and its agencies or instrumentalities, when it is applied to a state, in determining whether or not an act is commercial, the exception has been interpreted narrowly. A conclusion can therefore be drawn that even in a country like the United States that has laws restricting sovereign immunity and whose courts are prepared to exercise jurisdiction over foreign states, it is still difficult to execute an investment arbitral award.

B. The UK practice

Like the United States, the United Kingdom enacted its SIA in the late 1970s. Regarding their provisions on immunity from execution, the SIA and the FSIA are parallels. The SIA also focuses on the "use" of property by providing, inter alia, "the property of a State shall not be subject to any process for the enforcement of a judgment or arbitration award or, in an action in rem, for its arrest, detention or sale."[183] However, it then continues to stipulate that "Subsection (2) (b) above does not prevent the issue of any process in respect of property which is for the time being in use or intended for use for commercial purposes."[184] The phrasing "for the time being" and being "in use or intended for use for a commercial purpose" makes it clear that the mere connection or relationship between a property and commercial activity may not make the property subject to execution. At the same time, the SIA provides that a "State is not immune as respects proceedings relating to: (a) a commercial transaction entered into by the State."[185] Thus, in this respect, the SIA also parallels the FSIA.

In the UK practice, waivers stipulated in contracts have been confirmed by the courts as having satisfied the requirements of the SIA.[186] As to determination of

181 Ibid., at 236.
182 Id.
183 The State Immunity Act 1978 of Great Britain, c. 33. Section 13, Subsection 2(b).
184 Ibid., Subsection 4.
185 Ibid., Section 3.
186 For instance, in *Sabah v. Pakistan*, the Court considered a guarantee issued by Pakistan as showing

property "for the time being in use or intended for use for commercial purposes," the UK courts have also adopted an approach similar to that of the US courts. In *Alcom Ltd. v. Republic of Colombia & Others*,[187] the question was whether a bank account of the Colombian Embassy was subject to attachment. The Ambassador of Colombia issued a certificate stating that the account was for the day-to-day operation of his Embassy. The House of Lords (in charge of the case) stated that because "the bank account was earmarked by the foreign state solely (save for *de minimis* exception) for being drawn on to settle liabilities incurred in commercial transactions, as for example by issuing documentary credits in payment of the price of goods sold to the state, it cannot, in my view, be sensibly brought within the crucial words of the exception for which section 13(4) provides."[188] As the account in question was held by the Embassy of a foreign state, it was easier to prove that it was for public purposes. Nevertheless, it is understood that once a statement is issued by a foreign state in respect of the use of the property, a party petitioning to attach the property has the burden to prove otherwise.[189]

The UK courts have also considered several cases relating to the determination of whether an agency or instrumentality is part of the state and its property is subject to attachment. A most recent case is *La Générale des Carrières et des Mines (Appellant) v. F.G. Hemisphere Associates LLC (Respondent)*,[190] in which Hemisphere had purchased two international arbitration awards against the Democratic Republic of Congo (DR Congo) and tried to enforce the awards against the assets of La Générale des Carrières et des Mines ("Gécamines"), a state-owned company of DR Congo.

The core issue in the case was if Gécamines should be regarded as an entity separate from DR Congo. Lord Mance referred to Lord Goff of Chieveley's observation in *Kuwait Airways Corp v. Iraqi Airways Co*[191] that there existed a "possible contrast under the 1978 Act between the exemption from immunity of states as respects any commercial transaction entered into by the state and the (potentially more limited) immunity granted to entities distinct from the executive organs of the state as respects acts done in the exercise of sovereign authority."[192] Lord Mance then moved on to find Gécamines not to be an arm of Congo. He said:

    its consent to jurisdiction, which guarantee provided that Pakistan "waives any right of immunity which it or any of its assets … may in the future have in any jurisdiction;" see, *Sabah v. Pakistan* [2003] Lloyd's Rep. 571.

187 *Alcom Ltd. v. Republic of Colombia & Others* [1984] A.C. 580.

188 Ibid., at 604, *per* Lord Diplock.

189 Commentators believe that the burden to disprove the public nature of such property is severe. See Judith Gill, Stephen Jagusch and Anthony Sinclair, "Enforcement of Arbitral Awards against Sovereigns—Experience in the Courts of England and Wales," in R. Doak Bishop (ed.), *Enforcement of Arbitral Awards against Sovereigns*, JurisNet, LLC, 2009, 273ff, at 305.

190 *La Générale des Carrières et des Mines (Appellant) v. F.G. Hemisphere Associates LLC (Respondent)* [2012] UKPC 27, Privy Council Appeal No. 0061 of 2011, *per* Lord Mance (July 17, 2012).

191 *Kuwait Airways Corp v. Iraqi Airways Co* [1995] 1 WLR 1147, 1158E–1160F.

192 *La Générale des Carrières et des Mines v. F.G. Hemisphere Associates LLC, supra*, note 190, p. 9.

> There is no doubt that Gécamines had responsibility for operations in a sector of vital importance to the national economy of the DRC, but that may be said of many state-owned corporations in centrally planned or dirigist economies. … There is no doubt that Gécamines' assets originated in the State, but there is nothing surprising or significant about that. Once it acquired them, they became its assets, albeit that dispositions and acquisitions were liable to veto by State authorities. Those in day-to-day charge of Gécamines' affairs were vulnerable to having any important decisions which they took reviewed and vetoed by other State authorities. But that does not mean that Gécamines had no real existence as a separate entity.[193]

From this ruling, it seems that insofar as an entity maintains an actual status separate from its state, it should not be treated as an instrumentality of the state.[194] This is close to the definition of the ILC Articles on state instrumentality and investment arbitration practice. With the functional test in mind, having been satisfied that Gécamines had substantial assets and business and separate accounts and that the "Revenue went from time to time to the lengths of enforcing tax claims by execution against Gécamines' assets,"[195] the Lords concluded that Gécamines "was not in any sense by reason of its functions or activities a core department"[196] of its state. In fact, the House of Lords considered that even if Gécamines had performed some government functions in the past that would not affect its status as an entity separate from the state.

The UK approach toward the execution of investment arbitral awards further illustrates the difficulties that foreign investors may face in enforcing their property rights. Even though the United Kingdom may not be considered as economically very strong, it is still regarded as the birth place of common law. Members of the Commonwealth still follow the practice of the United Kingdom in their enforcement of laws. Thus, the UK approach can represent the views of a good number of countries, which implies difficulties in executing investment arbitral awards in those countries.

C. The French practice

France has a reputation of being an arbitration friendly country. As such, it does not have many legal hurdles in respect of the recognition and enforcement of arbitral awards.[197] Like the United States and Great Britain, France has

---

193 Ibid., at 29.
194 In the judgment delivered by Lord Mance, it was stated that the function of the instrumentality remains an important aspect for ascertaining the juridical personality of an entity. Ibid., at 13.
195 Ibid., at 38.
196 Id.
197 For discussion of this and related issues, see Sara Francois-Poncet, Brenda Horrigan and Lara Karam, "Enforcement of Arbitral Awards against Sovereign States or State Entities—France," in Bishop (ed.), *supra*, note 189, 355ff. See also Reinisch, *supra*, note 162, who argues that "French

adopted the doctrine of restricted sovereign immunity and also makes a distinction between immunity from jurisdiction and immunity from execution. Yet the French courts are "reluctant to permit measures of execution absent the foreign sovereign's consent."[198] The same applies to entities considered to be agencies and instrumentalities of states.

In the *SNPC* case,[199] one of the issues to be decided by the Paris Court of Appeal was whether or not SNPC (Société Nationale des Pétroles du Congo) was an instrumentality of the Republic of Congo rather than a mere state-owned industrial and commercial company. SNPC was a state-owned company established by a Congolese law, and its Board of directors consisted mainly of representatives of various state departments who were appointed through a decree of the Congolese Cabinet. In addition, the operation of the company was under the strict control of a Ministry to "ensure the application of the government's policies, laws, and regulations, to approve investment programs and supervise their execution, to supervise the allocation of profits and personnel policy governed by the collective bargaining agreement on hydrocarbons, and even the acquisition of participating interests and the creation of subsidiaries, agencies, or branch offices."[200] With these functional characteristics, the French court considered that SNPC did not have any "functional independence," de jure or de facto, from Congo. What was even more important was that SNPC's "accounting [did] not clearly indicate the nature and value of any commercial activity as distinct from its public service function."[201] Therefore, SNPC was not regarded as being a state-owned company but, rather, to be an instrumentality of the State of Congo.

Like its counterparts in the United States and Great Britain, the Paris Court of Appeal also paid special attention to the overall functional elements of an entity in ascertaining its nature. As mentioned earlier, French courts are reluctant to interpret broadly the exceptions to immunity from execution. In the view of the Paris Court of Appeal, in ordinary circumstances the governmental supervision and control over a company and the mixed functions of public policy and commercial activities of a company would not automatically disqualify the company as an independent legal person. Yet the Court indicated that Congo "has reserved to itself not only control over SNPC but also a real power of direction and approval constituting true interference which deprives of all substance the autonomy of SNPC."[202] Thus, it established that genuine independence or autonomy is a

courts have tended until very recently to regard enforcement immunity as absolute" (p. 807) and dates the change to a "more restrictive approach" to the 1980s (at note 23).

198 Francois-Poncet, Horrigan and Karam, ibid., at 358.

199 *Société Nationale des Pétroles du Congo v. S. A. Walker International Holdings Ltd*, Paris Court of Appeals, 8ième Chamber, Section B, Decision of July 3, 2003. Discussion of this case is based on a translation of the French original, for which see Emmanuel Gaillard and Jennifer Younan (eds.), *State Entities in International Arbitration*, IAI Series on International Arbitration No. 4, Juris Publishing, Huntington, NY, 2008, Annex 5, at 487.

200 Id.

201 Id.

202 Id.

general test to distinguish a commercial entity from an agency or instrumentality of a state, either de jure or de facto.

To a large extent, this position is similar to that maintained by the United States and the United Kingdom. It should be noted that in the US case of *Walker International Holdings v. Congo* discussed above, Walker also claimed that SNPC was an alter ego of Congo. The US Fifth Circuit Court of Appeals, however, stated that even though SNPC was an alter ego, agency or instrumentality of Congo, in order to attach its assets, Section 1610(b) of the US FSIA would apply and, since Congo's property could not be attached, its alter ego's or SNPC's property could not be subject to attachment.[203] The US Court's ruling was based on its determination that SNPC's property was not used for commercial activities. Thus, it would not have made any difference whether or not SNPC were an agency or instrumentality of Congo. In this respect, the French Court's decision appears to be inconsistent with the US Court's judgment in its application of the standards for determining sovereign immunity. If anything, the French Court appears to have applied an even more restrictive doctrine than did the US Court.

Central Bank of Iraq v. Hochtief AG[204] concerned whether or not the Central Bank of Iraq ("CBI") should be considered to be an instrumentality of the State of Iraq. In that case, CBI, as a central bank, had conducted both private commercial transactions and missions and prerogatives as a public authority. As CBI had its own assets, debtors, budget and accounting, the Paris Court of Appeal ruled that it had separate personality despite the tight control exercised by Iraq over the bank's management and even over its profits. This decision, however, is not surprising, because central banks always enjoy a special privilege under French law.[205]

From the above brief survey of the cases decided by courts in the United States, the United Kingdom and France, it should be noted that these countries' laws and law enforcement are very much like each other. The policy to restrain sovereign immunity is shared by the courts of these countries in scope and extent. For instance, they all grant broader exceptions, the commercial exception in particular, and restrictively interpret the exceptions in relation to enforcement or execution of judgments and arbitral awards. The practice of these countries, combined with their political influence, shows that the international community is still not completely ready to enforce investment arbitral awards against the will of the host states. One of the reasons for this is perhaps that, in the contemporary world, almost every country invests in other countries and hence may become the defendant in a foreign court for enforcement of an investment award. Fearing such circumstance, every country is extremely prudent in executing judgments against the property of foreign states. This having been said, national practices

---

203 *Walker International Holdings Ltd. v. Republic of Congo, supra*, note 176, para. 43.

204 *Central Bank of Iraq v. Hochtief Aktiengesellschaft*, Paris Court of Appeals, 8ieme Chamber, Section B, Decision of September 1, 2005. The discussion of this case is based on a translation of the French original, for which see Gaillard and Younan (eds.), *supra*, note 199, at 547.

205 See Francois-Poncet, Horrigan and Karam, *supra*, note 197, at 363–64. According to Article L. 153-1 of the French Monetary and Financial Code, assets and credit notes of central banks are not subject to seizure; id.

do appear to be moving closer to possible enforcement of investment awards by so doing.

V. The Chinese perspective

China's modern attitude toward sovereign immunity and acts of state can be inferred from its relations with other countries. For instance, on April 23, 1958, China concluded a Treaty of Trade and Navigation with the former Soviet Union. Article 4 of the Annex to that Treaty stipulated:

> The trade delegation shall enjoy all the immunities to which a sovereign State is entitled and which relate also to foreign trade, with the following exceptions only, to which the Parties agree:
> (a) Disputes regarding foreign commercial contracts concluded or guaranteed under Article 3 by the trade delegation in the territory of the receiving State shall, in the absence of a reservation regarding arbitration or any other jurisdiction, be subject to the competence of the courts of the said State. No interim court orders for the provision of the security may be made;
> (b) Final judicial decisions against the trade delegation in the afore-mentioned disputes which have become legally valid may be enforced by execution, such execution may be levied only on the goods and claims outstanding to the credit of the trade delegation.[206]

This provision reveals that in the view of the Chinese Government at that time, commercial activities could be excluded from sovereign immunities but that such exclusion must be agreed upon by the parties concerned. In *Jackson v. People's Republic of China et al.* (the *Huguang Railway Bonds* case),[207] after the US District Court for the Northern District of Alabama delivered a default judgment against the Chinese Government in 1981, the Chinese Embassy in Washington, D.C. issued a memorandum to the US State Department which stated that as a sovereign state China was entitled to enjoy judicial immunity and would accept no suit against it filed in a foreign court nor any judgment against it delivered by any foreign court.

Later, the Chinese Government restated its position as follows:

> Sovereign immunity is an important principle of international law. It is based on the principle of sovereign equality of all States as affirmed by the Charter of the United Nations. As a sovereign State, China incontestably enjoys judicial immunity. It is in utter violation of the principle of international law of sovereign equality of all States and the UN Charter that a district court of the United States should exercise jurisdiction over a suit against a sovereign

---

206　The Annex was reprinted in *Materials on Jurisdictional Immunities of States and Their Property*, U.N. Legal Series, 1982, UN Doc. ST/LEG/SER.B/20, at 135–36.

207　*Jackson v. People's Republic of China et al.* (the *Huguang Railway Bonds* case), 794 F.2d 1490 (1986).

State as a defendant, make a judgment by default and even threaten to exe-cute the judgment. The Chinese Government firmly rejects this practice of imposing US domestic law on China to the detriment of China's sovereignty and national dignity. Should the US side, in defiance of international law, execute the above-mentioned judgment and attach China's property in the United States, the Chinese Government reserves the right to take measures accordingly.[208]

The Chinese position towards sovereign immunity is determined by its economic and political powers and its influence at the international level. It also reflects its experience in the past. As the US State Department stated in the *Huguang Railway Bonds* case, "China's adherence to this principle [absolute sovereign immunity] results, in part, from its adverse experience with extraterritorial laws and jurisdic-tion of western powers [within China] in the 19th and 20th centuries."[209] From China's perspective, the doctrine of restricted sovereign immunity has not yet become a rule of international law because only a small number of nations—which by and large do not include developing countries—have adopted it.[210] China believes that the doctrine of restricted sovereign immunity will do more harm than good to the developing countries.

Chinese practice on sovereign immunity is, however, very limited. The most well known case is *FG Hemisphere v. Democratic Republic of Congo*, decided by the Court in Hong Kong. This case most probably best reflects China's current posi-tion on sovereign immunity. The case arose from FG Hemisphere's attempt to enforce two ICC arbitral awards against the Democratic Republic of the Congo. The arbitrations related to financing of US$37 million that FG Hemisphere's predecessor provided to DR Congo in the 1980s. In 2008, FG Hemisphere com-menced proceedings seeking enforcement in Hong Kong by intercepting certain "entry fees" payable by China Railways to DR Congo. The money was part of an infrastructure project involving an umbrella cooperation agreement entered into by the Chinese and the Congolese Governments. A basic question in this case was whether Hong Kong adopts a doctrine of absolute or of restricted sovereign immunity. The Court of First Instance declined to enforce the two ICC arbitral awards.[211] FG Hemisphere appealed, and the Court of Appeal held that the doc-trine of restricted sovereign immunity applied in Hong Kong, that the relevant acts to be considered were *acta jure gestionis*, and that, therefore, DR Congo could not assert immunity from suit.[212] The majority of the judges upheld the doctrine

---

208 See, Aide Memoire by Chinese Minister of Foreign Affairs Wu Xueqian to US Secretary of State George Shultz on February 2, 1983.

209 *Huguang Railway Bonds* case, *supra*, note 207, at para. 25.

210 Ibid. China forwarded its view while defending the case by raising the plea of absolute sovereign immunity.

211 *FG Hemisphere v. Democratic Republic of Congo* [2009] 1 H.K.L.R.D. 410 (CACV Nos. 373 of 2008 and 43 of 2009).

212 *FG Hemisphere v. Democratic Republic of Congo* [2010] 2 H.K.L.R.D. 66 (FACV Nos. 5, 6 & 7 of 2010).

of restricted sovereign immunity in terms of both jurisdictional and enforcement immunity. They held that even though China continues to follow the absolute doctrine, its failure to impose this doctrine on Hong Kong through legislation justified a finding that the common law's restrictive doctrine continued to apply in Hong Kong.

The Court of Final Appeal decided the case by a 3:2 majority on June 8, 2011. It firstly upheld the principle that the law on sovereign immunity was "an act of State" under Article 19 of the Basic Law of Hong Kong. It then went on to note that it is the province of the Executive to determine how states are to treat others and that such a determination must be adhered to by the entire territory over which the Executive exercises jurisdiction. Permitting otherwise "would embarrass and prejudice the State in its conduct of foreign affairs."[213] Since "China has consistently adhered to the doctrine that a state and its property enjoy absolute immunity from jurisdiction and from execution,"[214] Hong Kong must also adhere to this doctrine. In effect, the Hong Kong Court adopted the principle adhered to by US courts in the middle of the 20th century, prior to adoption of the US FSIA, whereby the courts abdicate their responsibility or power to determine their own jurisdiction in cases involving foreign states in deference to the opinion of the executive branch of government.

In addition, the Court of Final Appeal pointed out that it had a duty to refer the interpretation of Basic Law Articles 13 and 19 to the Standing Committee of the National People's Congress ("SCNPC") because it was that body's responsibility to interpret these provisions, which concern affairs falling within the responsibility of the Central Government or the Central-Regional relationship.[215] Having previously proclaimed that state immunity is unquestionably related to foreign affairs, the majority concluded that they are "bound to respect and act in conformity" with the decisions of the Central Government regarding the treatment of foreign states.[216] On August 24, 2011, the SCNPC Draft Interpretation of the Law on State Immunity in Hong Kong was put to a vote and passed unanimously. An SCNPC official explained that: (i) this is not only a legal issue but also a policy issue; (ii) Hong Kong must "apply and give effect to the rules or policies on state immunity" that Beijing has determined to adopt; (iii) Hong Kong courts "have no jurisdiction over State acts involving foreign affairs," and "no jurisdiction over the act of the Central Government in determining the rules or policies on state immunity;" and (iv) it would violate the Basic Law if the courts in Hong Kong were to apply or give effect to "inconsistent" rules.[217] Following the SCNPC Interpretation, the Court of

---

213 *Democratic Republic of Congo v. FG Hemisphere Assocs. L.L.C.* [2011] HKCFA 41, para. 269.
214 Ibid., at para. 260.
215 Ibid., at para. 339. Article 13 establishes that the Central Government has exclusive control over Hong Kong's foreign affairs; Article 19(3) removes from the Hong Kong courts jurisdiction "over acts of state such as defence and foreign affairs."
216 Ibid., at para. 324.
217 See "Mr LI Fei explains the SCNPC Interpretation: State Immunity Principle Applies to Hong Kong," *Wenweipo* (August 25, 2011) (in Chinese); available at: http://paper.wenweipo.com/2011/08/25/HK1108250010.htm.

Final Appeal went on to confirm its preliminary judgment on September 8, 2011, thereby affirming its lack of autonomy from the executive branch of government in such matters.[218]

Another important issue raised in this case concerns the "waiver of immunity," in particular whether or not DR Congo had waived its immunity from execution in Hong Kong. FG Hemisphere insisted that DR Congo had made an implicit waiver of its sovereign immunity defense by agreeing to the arbitration provisions in the credit agreement. At first instance and on appeal, all judges rejected FG Hemisphere's alternative argument that DR Congo had waived the right to claim immunity by agreeing to ICC arbitration. They held that there had been no waiver of adjudicative immunity but merely a limited waiver of immunity with regard to the supervisory jurisdiction.[219] The Court of Final Appeal held that any waiver of immunity must be explicit in order to be effective; a state waives immunity "by voluntarily submitting to the exercise of jurisdiction by the courts of the forum State over the waiving State's governmental entities or property."[220] That is, a waiver must be explicit and occur after the dispute has arisen.

What a private business may learn from the *FG Hemisphere v. DR Congo* case is that in concluding contracts with sovereign states or state-owned enterprises, it is advisable to have sovereign immunity waiver clauses carefully considered and drafted to ensure that such clauses are sufficiently broad to cover waiver of immunity from jurisdiction/suit as well as execution/enforcement. This may then enable the foreign investor to enforce an arbitral award even in a country that supports the doctrine of absolute sovereign immunity.

From the above limited exposure, it is certain that to a large extent, the Chinese position in relation to sovereign immunity reflects the view of the developing countries. The reason for the developing countries' preference for the doctrine of absolute sovereign immunity is protection of their national interests. In theory, according to the doctrine of restricted sovereign immunity, courts of every country may adjudicate cases involving a foreign government or state for disputes in connection with a commercial transaction or activity. In practice, however, courts of the developing countries may not have an opportunity to exercise jurisdiction over such cases. Even in cases where courts of the developing countries are requested to exercise such jurisdiction, they may not be capable of having their judgments enforced. The difficulty in ascertaining the relevant rules of international law, all of which have obviously been strongly influenced by the developed countries, is yet another reason for the hesitation of the developing countries to adhere to the doctrine of restricted sovereign immunity.

The Chinese position on sovereign immunity, including the Hong Kong court decisions in *FG Hemisphere v. DR Congo*, will inevitably have significant impacts on its efforts to attract foreign direct investment. As discussed elsewhere in this book, China has agreed to investor–state arbitration in all the BITs and FTAs

---

218 *Democratic Republic of Congo v. FG Hemisphere Assocs. L.L.C.*, [2011] HKCFA 66 (September 8, 2011).
219 *FG Hemisphere v. Democratic Republic of Congo*, *supra*, note 211, at para. 171.
220 *Democratic Republic of Congo v. FG Hemisphere Assocs. L.L.C.*, *supra*, note 213, at para. 377.

it has entered into recently. This is likely to be construed as consent to waiver of immunity from jurisdiction. With Chinese entities making more and more investments overseas, however, it would be in China's interest to consider adopting the doctrine of restricted sovereign immunity. This would also be in line with China's foreign policy as reflected in its signing of the UN Convention on Jurisdictional Immunities of States and Their Property. In fact, in the *FG Hemisphere v. DR Congo* case, the Court of First Instance of Hong Kong stated that it was "at a loss on how the stance stated in the letter [from the Chinese Ministry of Foreign Affairs] is to be reconciled (if at all) with the signing of the Convention,"[221] as according to Article 18 of the Vienna Convention on Treaties (which China has signed), a state that has signed a treaty is "obliged to refrain from acts which would defeat the object and purpose of a treaty." Therefore, the adoption by China of the doctrine of restricted sovereign immunity would not only be in its long-term interest relating to Chinese entities investing overseas but would also bring its practice into compliance with its stated policy.

In conclusion, in accordance with well established international law, states are bound by treaty obligations that they have assumed and principles of customary international law.[222] This principle of *pacta sunt servanda* is of absolute importance to international investment law. In international investment, particularly investment disputes, a sovereign state is often involved, so sovereign immunity is frequently an issue. As the *SPP* Tribunal noted 30 years ago: "Sovereign immunity has been frequently invoked by states with a view to getting rid, either of the obligation to arbitrate, or of the duty to execute the award."[223]

The international community's view on this issue has evolved, although slowly, over the last few decades. Whilst some countries still maintain the doctrine of absolute sovereign immunity, more and more countries are accepting restrictions on the exercise of sovereign powers. The fact that investor–state arbitration has become a common provision in all contemporary BITs and FTAs is evidence of the development. At the same time, insofar as enforcement of investment arbitral awards is concerned, even those countries which insist on restricted sovereign immunity still show a reluctance to execute such awards through attachment of the property of foreign states. The trend is, however, that where cases are clear, national courts are prepared to enforce investment awards by executing judgments against the property of foreign states.

---

221 *FG v. Congo*, Miscellaneous Proceedings No. 928 of 2008, para. 81.
222 For instance, in *SPP (Middle East) Ltd. v. Egypt*, the tribunal stated that the "principle of *pacta sunt servanda* is generally acknowledged in international law and it is difficult to see any reason why it should not apply here. A sovereign State must be sovereign enough to make a binding promise both under international law and municipal law." See *SPP (Middle East) Ltd. v. Egypt, supra*, note 24, para. 54.
223 Id.

11 Conclusions and alternatives

Foreign direct investment ("FDI") is an important feature of globalization and hence is significant for the economic development of all countries. International investment law, which relates to and regulates FDI, should be able to promote and encourage it among all countries in the world. The fast growing number of bilateral investment treaties ("BITs") and free trade agreements ("FTAs") that offer protection and preferential treatment to foreign investments and investors evidences the trend. As in other aspects of human society, obligations and rights stipulated in BITs and FTAs are closely linked with each other. In other words, where a person or a group of persons has a given right, another person or group of persons must have a corresponding obligation. Under international investment law, it is the host states which apparently assume the bulk of the obligations, whilst foreign investors are entitled to the corresponding rights. For instance, where a host state is obliged not to treat foreign investments and investors arbitrarily or not to expropriate foreign investments without compensation, a foreign investor is entitled to be treated accordingly and, if it is not, it may claim that the host state in question has breached its international obligations.

Where then is the balance between the rights and obligations of foreign investors and host states? To begin with, the obligations assumed by one contracting party toward investments and investors from the other contracting party through a BIT or FTA are reciprocal in nature. Therefore, they are accompanied by the rights offered by both (or all) contracting parties to investments and investors from the other(s). At the same time, where a foreign investor enjoys its rights, it must satisfy certain conditions and assume certain obligations. There is thus a balance between rights and obligations, even though international investment law may appear to be primarily oriented towards investment/investor protection.

In fact, international investment law, by its very nature, should be primarily oriented towards investment/investor protection. It is of the utmost importance to stress that this apparent orientation towards investment/investor protection is not meant to create an imbalance between rights and obligations, because very often an arbitral decision is criticized for being too pro-foreign investment/investor. The balanced rights and obligations approach can be testified to by the practice of international investor–state dispute settlement. The determination of qualified investors and investments, the ascertainment of consent, obligations to accord foreign investors and their investments fair and equitable treatment, etc. are all examples of this. This chapter, taking into account that specific conclusions and alternative measures have been made in the relevant chapters of this book, will offer some general comments on the most important issues relating to investment, as well as some alternatives for improving the contemporary system.

The value of every system lies in its effectiveness in practice. The same is true with the legal system relating to international investment—international investment law, which is comprised of BITs, the investment chapters of FTAs and multilateral treaties, customary international law and, sometimes, the domestic law of the host states. The effectiveness of international investment law, like the law governing other sectors of any society, depends on the behavior of its enforcement bodies. Therefore, its investment/investor-protection-oriented nature notwithstanding, whether international investment law can achieve its object and purpose is subject to how tribunals perform their functions. As discussed previously, tribunals often contradict each other in their legal analysis, even where the material facts and treaty provisions are similar or even the same.

The *CME*[1] and *Lauder*[2] are cases in point and serve to illustrate the extent to which tribunals may contradict each other. The claimants in both cases lodged similar allegations against the respondent—the Czech Republic—for violation of treaty obligations, including fair and equitable treatment, full protection and security, minimum international standards, the prohibition of expropriation without compensation, etc. The material facts of the two cases and the relevant provisions of the two BITs—the Netherlands–Czech Republic BIT in the *CME* case and the United States–Czech Republic BIT in the *Lauder* case—are almost identical. Any differences in the allegations made by the claimants in the two cases reflect the differences in the wording of the relevant BIT. (There may be some question about the wording "and" or "or" in Article II.2(b) of the United States–Czech Republic BIT.) Despite such similarities in the two cases, however, the tribunals came to totally contradictory decisions: the *CME* Tribunal only reached majority decisions, whilst the dissenting arbitrator's view in that case was totally in line with that of the *Lauder* Tribunal.

What is especially difficult to understand is that the two tribunals reached differing conclusions even in ascertaining the relevant evidence. For instance, with the same evidence before them, the majority of the *CME* Tribunal saw coercion in the actions taken by the Czech Republic's Media Council in 1996,[3] and it referred to coercion numerous times in the award and also made frequent use of some form of the phrase "forced" in references to the effect on the Claimant of Media

---

1 *CME Czech Republic B.V. (The Netherlands) v. Czech Republic*, UNCITRAL, Partial Award (September 13, 2001); available at: italaw.com/sites/default/files/case-documents/ita0178.pdf; Final Award (March 14, 2003); available at: http://italaw.com/documents/CME-2003-Final_001.pdf.

2 *Ronald S. Lauder v. Czech Republic*, UNCITRAL, Final Award (September 3, 2001); available at: italaw.com/sites/default/files/case-documents/ita0451.pdf.

3 See *CME*, Partial Award, *supra*, note 1, para. 601, for example: "The basic breach by the Council of the Respondent's obligation not to deprive the Claimant of its investment was the coerced amendment of the MOA in 1996."

Council actions. The dissenting arbitrator on the tribunal, however, maintained: "General talkings [sic] and allegations, as well as very indirect reproductions of alleged coercion cannot replace the evidence necessary to be brought in arbitration proceedings to prove such allegations."[4] The *Lauder* Tribunal, on the other hand, not only failed to find any such coercion, but even failed to use any form of the word (except in a definition of "expropriation" contained in para. 200 of its award).

The *CME* Tribunal's majority also found collusion between the Media Council and Dr Železný, a Czech national who had at one time been a principal in ČNTS, the investment allegedly affected by the Media Council's actions.[5] On the other hand, neither the *Lauder* Tribunal nor the dissenting arbitrator on the *CME* Tribunal saw evidence supporting collusion and, in fact, never even used the word in any form.

The opinion of the majority of the *CME* Tribunal, then, was that there was both coercion and collusion, an opinion best expressed when it said that "the clear intention of the [Media Council's] 1996 actions was to deprive the foreign investor of the exclusive use of the Licence under the MOA and the clear intention of the 1999 actions and inactions was [to] collude with the foreign investor's Czech business partner to deprive the foreign investor of its investment."[6] The *Lauder* Tribunal, like the dissenting Arbitrator on the *CME* Tribunal, however, saw the evidence as supporting the Respondent's assertion that the Media Council had acted in accordance with its responsibilities on the basis of reasonable concerns. None of these arbitrators saw evidence of either coercion or collusion.

Obviously, if a state agency engaged in coercion and colluded with a third party to deprive a foreign investor of its investment, that would be a serious violation of treaty obligations, including fair and equitable treatment and full protection and security, as the *CME* Tribunal found. At the same time, if the state agency acted in accordance with its responsibilities on the basis of reasonable concerns and did so in a non-discriminatory manner, and if some of the actions complained of could not even effectively be attributed to the state agency, both propositions which were upheld by the *Lauder* Tribunal and the dissenting *CME* Arbitrator, violations of fair and equitable treatment and/or full protection and security would be unlikely to be found.

In essence, both Lauder, a US citizen who controlled the investment, and CME complained of six distinct acts which they attributed to the Media Council and, therefore, the Czech Republic.[7] It suffices to say that the majority of the

---

4 *CME*, Dissenting Opinion of the Arbitrator JUDr Jaroslav Hándl against the Partial Arbitration Award (September 3, 2001), 1st paragraph of §V; available at: italaw.com/sites/default/files/case-documents/ita0179.pdf.

5 See *CME*, Partial Award, *supra*, note 1, para. 555: "The March 15, 1999 letter, a regulatory letter of the broadcasting regulator, was fabricated in collusion between Dr. Železný and the Media Council behind the back of ČNTS (TV NOVA) to give CET 21 a tool to undermine the legal foundation of CME's investment."

6 Ibid., para. 612.

7 See ibid., paras. 166–70; and *Lauder*, Final Award, *supra*, note 2, paras. 196, 214, and 237.

CME Tribunal and both the dissenting arbitrator on that tribunal and the *Lauder* Tribunal again took diametrically contradictory positions on each action, which constituted the underpinning of their respective findings—for the majority of the *CME* Tribunal, there were violations of fair and equitable treatment and full protection and security, whilst for the dissenting *CME* arbitrator and the *Lauder* Tribunal there were no such breaches.

If anything, what is shared by the *CME* and *Lauder* tribunals is that neither of them offered much elucidation of the jurisprudence of "fair and equitable treatment" or associated legal principles in international investment law, unless one finds the *CME* Tribunal's majority conclusion that a state agency's coercion of a foreign investor to consent to changes in the legal form of its investment and its collusion with a third party to enable the third party to "vitiate" the foreign investment are considered noteworthy.

What is perhaps most remarkable about the two cases is that of six arbitrators, only two (the majority of one tribunal) found both coercion and collusion and also interpreted both the terms of the relevant BIT and the dictates of international law[8] as requiring attribution of the eventual harm and damages suffered by the claimant to actions of the state agency that had been taken several years before the harm and damage occurred and had been "consented" to (or at least not protested) by the claimant at the time those actions occurred, even though the "proximate cause" of the harm and damage were those of a third, non-state party. Meanwhile, the other four arbitrators (the entirety of one tribunal plus the dissenting arbitrator on the other) saw no coercion or collusion; viewed certain actions complained of as either legitimate exercises of "police powers" or as measures not attributable to the state agency; and (having not found coercion) were of the opinion that the claimants' failure to protest the actions at the time they occurred, and even to cooperate in carrying them out (rather analogous to a failure to challenge the jurisdiction of an arbitral tribunal before entering into an argument of the merits of a case), meant that they could not now complain of them in the arbitration.

Similar findings, although not to the same degree, have also occurred with regard to determination of qualified investors and investments, application of the MFN clause to dispute resolution procedures in relevant BITs and the interpretation of provisions relating to expropriation and compensation. It may be argued that there is nothing wrong for different tribunals to reach different decisions, for after all what appear to be similar facts and treaty provisions may be subject to varied interpretations and truth may not always be on the side of the majority. In addition, in international investment arbitration, no tribunal is bound by earlier decisions of other arbitral tribunals since none of them has precedential effect. All the above possible arguments notwithstanding, for a system to be effective, the laws and rules must be interpreted with some consistency and the bodies that enforce those rules must win respect and trust from the society of which they form a part.

---

8 In this regard, see *CME*, Partial Award, *supra*, note 1, paras. 580–85.

For a rule-enforcement body like an investment arbitration tribunal properly to carry out its most important function—interpreting treaties—it is essential that the members thereof exercise their powers within the limits defined by the consent of the parties. For instance, regarding the interpretation of the scope of the MFN clause, the most severe criticism concerns the innovative way in which some tribunals have applied the MFN clause to the dispute resolution mechanisms of the BITs. This might have been done within the overall spirit of BITs, since it does serve to give broader protection to investors' interests. However, the question is whether it is also in compliance with the requirements of the rules relating to treaty interpretation as reflected in the Vienna Convention on the Law of Treaties ("VCLT"). Those tribunals which have not expanded application of the MFN clause to investor–state dispute settlement have indicated, either implicitly or expressly, that their refusal to adopt an expansive interpretation was based on the good faith interpretation of the BITs. This has provided support for critiques that the expansive interpretation does not reflect the intent of the contracting parties. Treaty practices subsequent to the expansive interpretation of MFN clauses have further reinforced such criticisms. Unfortunately, however, there is no system to curb or discourage such expansive interpretation.[9] It seems, however, that recently tribunals have demonstrated more restraint in interpreting the MFN clause.[10]

While there is an annulment mechanism within the ICSID system, it cannot resolve problems of either the inconsistency of different arbitral decisions or the incorrect application of law. In the first place, several of the annulment decisions have been subject to criticisms because some *ad hoc* annulment Committees have

9 For instance, in *Impregilo*, the *ad hoc* annulment Committee noted that there were two extreme positions on the issue of whether or not the MFN clause could be applied to dispute resolution procedures: "[O]ne supports the application of the MFN clause to dispute resolution mechanisms as a means of access to ICSID jurisdiction, the other considers that the MFN clause cannot be given effect for jurisdictional purposes." See *Impregilo S.p.A. v. Argentine Republic*, ICSID Case No. ARB/07/17, Decision on Annulment (January 24, 2014), para. 136. The *Impregilo ad hoc* annulment Committee also noted Professor Zachary Douglas' conclusion that "the MFN clause does not extend to jurisdictional matters" (ibid., para. 138, citing Zachary Douglas, "The MFN Clause in Investment Arbitration: Treaty Interpretation Off the Rails", *Journal of International Dispute Settlement*, Vol. 2, No. 1, 2011, pp. 97–98) and that the tribunal was seriously divided on the issue. Yet, it rightly held that to decide whether the tribunal (the majority view) had manifestly exceeded its powers by extending the MFN clause to dispute mechanisms was not its task, because "[t]he analysis required to reach a conclusion other than the majority's would imply a new and complex analysis of the issues at stake, a review that is far from the responsibility of this Committee according to Article 52 [of the ICSID Convention]." Ibid, para. 140.
10 For instance, in *Kılıç v. Turkmenistan*, the claimant, a Turkish construction company with investments in Turkmenistan, sought, through operation of the MFN clause in the Turkey–Turkmenistan BIT, to invoke the dispute resolution provisions in the Switzerland–Turkmenistan BIT, which does not require local remedy procedures. The tribunal distinguished substantive rights and procedural rights under the Turkey–Turkmenistan BIT and held that the BIT both "textually and contextually suggested limitation [of] the scope of application of Article II.2's MFN treatment of investments to the *substantive rights* provided" therein. See *Kılıç İnşaat İthalat İhracat Sanayi ve Ticaret Anonim Şirketi v. Turkmenistan*, ICSID Case No. ARB/10/1, Award (July 2, 2013), paras. 7.3.1 and 7.4.1 (emphasis in original).

been considered to have exceeded the limits of their mandate. Differently from appeal bodies, an ICSID *ad hoc* annulment Committee is only authorized to annul an arbitral award on any of the grounds listed in Article 52(1) of the ICSID Convention. As such, where a tribunal has identified the right law (some tribunals prefer the phrasing "the right rule"), e.g. the relevant BIT or the clause or provision thereof and applied it, the resulting award cannot be annulled regardless of whether the application of that law/rule is correct or incorrect, expansive, or unexpansive. Second, the annulment decisions have proven to be by no means more consistent than those of arbitral tribunals. Taking into account the above, it is unrealistic to expect that the ICSID annulment mechanism can be a solution to the difficulties that the international community is facing.

One may wonder whether investment tribunals and *ad hoc* annulment Committees perceive their functions correctly, as they claim that they have performed their treaty interpretation functions strictly in accordance with the VCLT but have given contradictory decisions. In this regard, the New Haven School of Jurisprudence's approach should be considered. An often asked question of those familiar with the New Haven School of Jurisprudence is "who are you"? This question is very important, because those in different positions are bound to look at the same issue from different angles and, in fact, even the same person may consider the same issue differently in accordance with the changing positions he/she serves. For instance, a lawyer representing a party would take up a legal issue differently from the judge or arbitrator hearing the case. By the same token, a scholar's analysis may vary sharply from that of both the lawyer and the judge or arbitrator. How then should an investment tribunal or *ad hoc* annulment Committee perform its duties?

Professor Reisman, who helped found the New Haven School of Jurisprudence and to elevate it to a new height, encourages making a distinction between rule-makers and rule-appliers in their decision-makings. For Reisman, rule-appliers, such as judges and arbitrators, should "approach the issues before them through the prism of rules"—the textual-rule-based mode; rule-makers, on the other hand, should "approach the issues before them through the prism of policy and context"—the policy-context-based mode.[11] In other words, judges and arbitrators have an obligation to follow what the rule stipulates or to interpret such rules faithfully and in accordance with the relevant rules of interpretation. In the case of investor–state dispute resolution, according to the New Haven School of Jurisprudence, arbitrators must exercise their interpretive powers within the parameters of the rules and may not intrude into the policy area, something which is reserved for the rule-makers.

To be specific, under the textual-rule-based mode, "great emphasis is placed on [the] origin and the validity of the rules … [T]he principles of interpretation of texts and other verbal communications which lay claim to some authority are

11 W. Michael Reisman, *The Quest for World Order and Human Dignity in the Twenty-First Century: Constitutive Process and Individual Commitment*, General Course on Public International Law, Hague Academy of International Law, Martinus Nijhoff Publishers (2012), Chapter VI, pp. 145–65.

virtual articles of faith." Where the rule or text proves unclear, the rule-appliers must not "break out of the text into the domain of policy." The most they can do is to resort to "the records of the process that produced the text."[12] In applying the textual rule-based mode, the applier must do the following:

(a) explore the facts, including the precipitating events, within their larger factual context, and assemble a provisional factual picture
(b) explore the prescriptions invoked by the parties
(c) make a determination of the facts
(d) specify the prescriptions deemed relevant to those facts
(e) formulate the substance of the decision
(f) determine, as distinct from the preceding phase, the content and mode of promulgation of the decisions
(g) enforce the decision
(h) review the decision for its conformity to the procedural and substantive standards of the relevant application process.[13]

With regard to the rule-makers, their decision-making should follow the policy context-based mode. That means that in making policy decisions—what law or rule is to be adopted—the question to be addressed is "what ought to be goal values of the community," including clarification of the community policy—that is, identification of the goal value, examination of the effectiveness of the existing arrangements for achieving the goal value, "the extent to which existing arrangements are likely to achieve the policies in various imagined futures and, if the prognosis is that the policies are unlikely to be secured, the invention of alternative inventions that are more likely to realize the policies."[14] Thus, in policy-making, the rule-makers need to explore the community values and examine if the law or rule to be adopted would be in conformity with the interests of the community. Likewise, rule-makers must also frequently check to verify if the existing law still reflects the value goals of the community and, if the answer is negative, they have an obligation to change it.

In comparing the above teachings of the New Haven School of Jurisprudence with the practice of investment tribunals, it is not difficult to discern that in every pair of the contradictory decisions, very often one tribunal (or sometimes the majority of a tribunal) functioned as a rule-maker rather than as a rule-applier. The same is true with regard to those tribunals which have interpreted treaty provisions expansively. In doing so, tribunals usually refer to the preamble of a treaty, because the wording of treaty preambles is often vague, and thus adaptable to various interpretations.

In order to win the trust of the users of investment law, tribunals and *ad hoc* annulment Committees should redefine their role by adopting the "textual-rule-based

12 Id.
13 Ibid., pp. 151–52.
14 Ibid., p. 147.

mode," as promoted by the New Haven School of Jurisprudence, when interpreting treaty provisions. By doing so, the purpose and object of BITs and FTAs in protecting foreign investments and investors are better served. As discussed earlier, the protection offered under international law does not come without conditions and limits. Unless the true intent of the parties is given effect, host states may have to take counter-measures by negotiating new treaties or modifying the existing ones, neither of which is conducive to the positive development of international investment law.

With globalization ever deepening in scope and depth, new issues in respect of investment are bound to emerge. As a result, arbitration tribunals and *ad hoc* annulment Committees are unavoidably involved with such novel developments, which require more sophisticated knowledge and experience. For instance, in *Kılıç v. Turkmenistan*,[15] the first stage of the arbitration involved determination of the authenticity of the multi-version BIT between Turkey and Turkmenistan. According to the authentic English version of the BIT, it was *"DONE at Ashgabat on the day of May 2, 1992 in two authentic copies in Russian and English,"* whilst under the authentic Russian version, the BIT was *"Executed on May 2, 1992 in two authentic copies in Turkish, Turkmen, English and Russian languages.."*[16] The English version is a translation from the Russian version. The disputing parties disagreed over which texts should be considered official and how they should be translated.

It was undisputed that, although the Russian version mentioned authentic copies in the Turkish and Turkmen languages, the respondent could not produce any signed copy in those languages. The Tribunal concluded that there had been no signed copy of the BIT in any languages other than English and Russian. Another issue in the case was the accuracy of the English translation of Article VII.2 of the BIT from the Russian, which provides that where an investor cannot have its dispute with the host state settled within six months, it may submit the dispute to international arbitration, "provided that, if the investor concerned has brought the dispute before the courts of justice of the Party that is a party to the dispute and a final award has not been rendered within one year." The question was whether the word "if" should be in the text. Consequently, if it does stay, the local remedy becomes optional and if not, it is compulsory.[17] As the claimant did not go through the local court procedures, this translation became very important to the outcome of the case.

The tribunal then requested the disputing parties to submit translations of the English version from the Russian language. As the claimant did not provide a translation itself and both parties objected to the tribunal retaining an

---

15 *Kılıç İnşaat İthalat İhracat Sanayi ve Ticaret Anonim Şirketi v. Turkmenistan*, ICSID Case No. ARB/10/1, Decision on Article VII.2 of the Turkey–Turkmenistan BIT (May 7, 2012) [hereinafter "*Kılıç* Decision on Article VII.2"]. The tribunal rendered an award dismissing the application for arbitration on July 2, 2013, in which the tribunal copied word for word its substantive analysis of the decision on Article VII.2. See *Kılıç İnşaat İthalat İhracat Sanayi ve Ticaret Anonim Şirketi v. Turkmenistan*, ICSID Case No. ARB/10/1, Award (July 2, 2013).

16 Ibid., paras. 2.8 and 2.9 (emphasis in original).

17 See ibid., paras. 9.1, 9.3 and, especially, 9.7.

independent translator, the tribunal relied on the translation provided by the respondent-appointed translator[18] and decided to accept the English translation that had removed the word "if" from the English language text of the BIT.[19] As a result, the claimant was held to have an obligation to submit its dispute to the local court before resort to international arbitration.

It is amazing that, in interpreting a BIT, the translators played such a crucial part.[20] What one may not feel comfortable with is that the revised translation was done well after the BIT came into effect—indeed, well after commencement of the arbitration and only three days before the oral hearing. Also, as the revised translation has only been accepted by the *Kılıç* Tribunal, subsequent tribunals are not bound to accept the translation as an official version of the BIT. If they adopt different translations, there will be many more problems.

Another recent case that also requires attention is *Electrabel v. Hungary*.[21] In that case, whether EU law or the ECT should prevail in case of inconsistency between the two was at issue. The tribunal surprisingly concluded that: "from whatever perspective the relationship between the ECT and EU law is examined, the Tribunal concludes that EU law would prevail over the ECT in case of any material inconsistency."[22] This is clearly a mistake on the part of the tribunal. With such decisions, it will be very difficult for international investment tribunals to win the confidence of the disputing parties and the investment community at large.

It was indeed very unfortunate, to say the least, that the *Electrabel* Tribunal made such obvious mistakes. Yet it is not alone. The *Sanum* Tribunal did no better. In the *Sanum* case,[23] the claimant was incorporated under the laws of the Macao Special Administrative Region ("SAR") and made an investment in the gaming business in the Lao Republic—the respondent. One of the issues involved was whether the BIT between the People's Republic of China and Laos should apply to the disputes between the claimant and respondent. The *Sanum* Tribunal refused to give effect to Article 8 of the Joint Declaration between China and Portugal and Article 138 of the Basic Law of Macao SAR (the two Articles are worded identically) that:

> Subject to the principle that foreign affairs are the responsibility of the Central People's Government, the Macao [SAR] may on its own, using

---

18 According to the translator, "the correct meaning (or sense) of the Russian text is conveyed properly by a translation which removes the word 'if' from the second line of sub-paragraph (c). This is because the inclusion of the word 'if' in the Russian text, while part of the correct syntax required in Russian to create the conditional, does not operate to create a second or separate conditional, as the original translation into English ... provided." Ibid., para. 8.9.

19 Ibid., para. 8.22.

20 The tribunal admitted that the reason for requiring an English translation of the Russian text was that it was unable to "construe properly the Russian text. Had the Tribunal been composed of Russian speakers, such a translation may not have been required." Ibid., para. 8.2.

21 *Electrabel S.A. v. Republic of Hungary*, ICSID Case No. ARB/07/19, Decision on Jurisdiction, Applicable Law and Liability (November 30, 2012).

22 Ibid., para. 4.192.

23 *Sanum Investments Limited v. Government of the Lao People's Democratic Republic*, UNCITRAL Arbitration, Award on Jurisdiction (December 13, 2013).

the name "Macao, China", maintain and develop relations and conclude and implement agreements with states, regions and relevant international or regional organizations in the appropriate fields, such as the economy, trade, finance, shipping, communications, tourism, culture, science and technology and sports. [...]

The application to the Macao [SAR] of international agreements to which the [PRC] is a member or becomes a party shall be decided by the Central People's Government, in accordance with the circumstances and needs of the [SAR], and after seeking the views of the government of the [SAR].

The *Sanum* Tribunal held that "the Basic Law of the Macao SAR in and of itself, as an internal law, cannot be considered as legally capable of modifying the international rule ... It is well known that 'the binding character of treaties is determined by international law, which on this point takes precedence over internal law.'"[24] Certainly, no internal or national law may modify international law. The internal or national law may, however, define the scope of application of international law on its territory. What the *Sanum* Tribunal did gives the impression that it was determined not to recognize the constitutional status of the Macao SAR—that is, that under the policy of "one country two systems," which has the endorsement of the Constitution of China, Macao has a limited capacity directly to enter into international agreements, which, at least by implication, excludes the application of the BITs concluded by the Central Government of China. In fact, the *Sanum* Tribunal was aware that a BIT between Macao and Laos existed in parallel with the BIT between China and Laos. Yet it decided that because there was no formal procedure to inform Laos that its BIT with China would not apply to the Macao SAR and that the China–Laos BIT itself does not exclude its applicability to the Macao SAR, that BIT should apply to the Macao SAR.[25] To be sure, the *Sanum* Tribunal was well informed of the political environment in which the Macao Basic Law was formulated. Yet it still reached such a decision. Instead, it should have asked why a Macao SAR–Laos BIT exists if the China–Laos BIT equally applies to the Macao SAR.

On another issue—state succession—the *Sanum* Tribunal, considering whether the China–Laos BIT should apply to the Macao SAR under customary international law, stated:

It is well known that it is the PRC's contention that no transfer of sovereignty took place in December 1999, since it merely "resumed" its exercise of sovereignty over Macao, as it did over Hong Kong. The Tribunal wants to put it beyond doubt that its approach does not contradict this position of the PRC when it applies the rules on State succession.[26]

---

24 Ibid., para. 257.
25 Ibid., paras. 268–71.
26 Ibid., para. 237.

The tribunal then immediately quoted Mushkat's comments about Hong Kong in support of its position.[27] Both Mushkat and the *Sanum* Tribunal, however, have failed to understand that China's non-recognition of the hand-overs of Hong Kong and Macao as state succession reflects its position that the old treaties in respect of Hong Kong and Macao were unequal and therefore should not be recognized. The *Sanum* Tribunal's ruling is therefore obviously contrary to China's official position, although the tribunal claimed that it was not. In any event, the *Sanum* Tribunal failed to explain why its position on the rules on state succession was not contradictory with the official position of China.

Clearly the *Sanum* Tribunal's interpretation was contrary to the constitutional arrangement of China and the intent of the People's Republic of China insofar as the China–Laos BIT is concerned. An error of this kind is no less disturbing than that in the *Electrabel* case. Taken together, the two cases show the extent to which investment tribunals exercise their so-called discretion in their decision-making. Unless they return to their role of arbitrators, decisions of this kind will do more harm than good to the development of international investment law.

Another issue facing the international community is of the recent proliferation of requests for annulment of investment awards. It is now very often the case that the losing party regards it as its duty to initiate an annulment proceeding and does so by listing all the grounds for annulment contained in Article 52(1) of the ICSID Convention as their own reasons for the application for annulment. The proliferation of applications for annulment has alarmed the investment circle because, at least in a number of cases, the procedure appears to have been used solely to delay enforcement of ICSID arbitral awards. It has also threatened the finality of arbitral awards.

To deal with the situation, Schreuer has suggested the introduction of a security system, according to which "security could be given e.g. in the form of a bank guarantee. This would not just be a condition for a stay of enforcement under Arbitration Rule 54. (A guarantee of this kind has sometimes been required by ad hoc committees.) What I am suggesting is that the security would be a condition for the institution of annulment proceedings."[28] Under Schreuer's proposed scheme, where an application for annulment is successful, the security would be returned. Where the application is not successful, the security would be used for enforcing the arbitral award.[29]

---

27 The *Sanum* Tribunal (at para. 237) quoted Mushkat to the effect that "there is little doubt that the 'transition' [of Hong Kong] on 1 July 1997 largely comports with the definition of 'state succession'—as 'the replacement of one state by another in the responsibility for the international relations of territory'—and that the issues raised as a result of this event are generally covered within the branch of international law which 'deals with the legal consequences of change of sovereignty over territory;'" Roda Mushkat, "Hong Kong and Succession of Treaties," 46 *ICLQ*(1), 1997, pp. 181–201.

28 Christoph Schreuer, "Why Still ICSID?" *Transnational Dispute Management*, Vol. 9, Issue 3, April 2012, pp. 1–7, at p. 6.

29 Ibid., p. 7.

In Schreuer's view, this proposed scheme could be put in place merely by modifying ICSID's Arbitration Rules, without amending the ICSID Convention.[30] To be sure, revision of the Arbitration Rules requires only the consent of the Administrative Council, and the adoption of such an amendment is relatively easier than amendment of the ICSID Convention.[31] Nevertheless, as the proposed amendment would involve the rights of the contracting parties, strong resistance to such an initiative could be expected. The question is then whether a better choice is to focus on fixing the annulment procedures.

Compared with the total number of arbitration cases dealt with under the auspices of the ICSID, applications for annulment only arise in a small percentage. Also, even if the annulment procedures are fixed, those cases handled by other institutions cannot benefit. The most important and urgent issue in investment law is the inconsistency of arbitral and *ad hoc* annulment Committee decisions and the lack of mechanisms to correct the mistakes of tribunal decisions, including those discussed in this book. Taking into account the diversification of membership of the tribunals and *ad hoc* annulment committees, which comprise individuals of varying cultural and legal backgrounds, differing and contradictory decisions are likely to remain the trend in the foreseeable future.

One of the ways to resolve this issue would be the establishment of a control system. Take the WTO, for example. Before the WTO was established, there was little consistency among the decisions reached by GATT panels. With an Appellate Body in place, the jurisprudence of the multilateral trade organization has been developing steadily and consistently. As a result, the number of cases is also declining. To resolve the issue of inconsistency of investment arbitration decisions, creation of an appeal authority is needed, although it may take a long time, if it is at all possible, for the international community to reach an agreement on such a mechanism. Even if this is the case, the move is still worth recommending. As the WTO Appellate Body has functioned so efficiently and gained worldwide confidence and respect, why should not the international community consider expanding its powers and functions to include investment appeal cases?

There are certain advantages to making use of the WTO's Appellate Body to hear investment appeal cases. As all members of the Appellate Body are elected through a stringent process, they at the least carry more authority than do ICSID *ad hoc* annulment Committees. At the same time, use of the WTO Appellate Body would help rectify the shortcomings of the ICSID annulment system.[32]

---

30 Ibid.
31 The Administrative Council is empowered to amend the Arbitration Rules by a two-thirds majority of its membership pursuant to Article 6 of the ICSID Convention, whilst Article 66(1) of the ICSID Convention requires approval of all the contracting parties for any amendment of the Convention.
32 Some scholars have suggested establishing a permanent body for investment disputes. Schreuer, for instance, has said: "A mechanism of this kind would require the establishment of a central and permanent or semi-permanent body that is charged with the task of giving preliminary rulings. This would leave Article 53 of the ICSID Convention untouched. A preliminary rulings facility could be established either by ICSID's Administrative Council or through a separate treaty. It would not require an amendment of the Convention." See Schreuer, *supra*, note 28, p. 8.

Currently, services and investments overlap with each other and an increasing number of BITs and FTAs regulate both subjects without making a distinction between them. As such, investment arbitration tribunals often find it necessary to refer to WTO decisions. If the WTO Appellate Body were entrusted to hear investment-related appeals, that would help make its analysis and reasoning on services convergent with that on investment. In the end, both international trade in services and foreign direct investment would be encouraged.

Enforcement of arbitral awards is another thorny issue requiring a solution. As discussed earlier, the losing host states understandably try all means not to enforce the awards that are not in their favor. Although the ICSID has its own recognition and enforcement system, which depends to a large extent on the willingness of the host states, there is no mechanism to force a losing state to implement an arbitral award. As for the awards made by other arbitration bodies which have no self-contained enforcement mechanisms, their enforcement may be accomplished, arguably, through the operation of the 1958 New York Convention on the Recognition and Enforcement of Foreign Arbitral Awards. In practice, however, attempts to seize the property of a losing state to enforce an investment arbitral award is very difficult, if it is possible at all. In the end, the winning party has to rely on the goodwill of the losing host state. Compared with the retaliation mechanisms under the WTO—although these are not entirely satisfactory, either—the enforcement mechanism relating to investment arbitration requires much improvement.

As discussed elsewhere, the international community should consider creating a system where the interests of both investors and host states can be better protected.[33] For instance, WTO members might be encouraged to have their FTAs and BITs stipulate that arbitration awards in investment disputes may be appealed to the Appellate Body of the WTO for review. Once the Appellate Body has made a ruling, that ruling could be enforced by the host state, failing which, the member that is the home country of the investor could be entitled to substitute for the investor and to request retaliation in accordance with the WTO process—that is, cross-retaliation between trade and investment.

Above all, no matter how good a system may be on paper, its effectiveness still depends on the quality of those who operate it—in the case of international investment law, arbitrators and *ad hoc* annulment Committee members. No serious challenge has been made so far with regard to the ethical standards of the arbitrators who make up investment tribunals. It therefore can be assumed that mistakes that may have been made by tribunals relate to other aspects of arbitration, including knowledge of the subject matter, arbitration skills and experience, and understanding of the culture and political and legal systems of the host states. Where a tribunal, or the majority of a tribunal, lacks any of these elements, the

---

33 For a fuller discussion of this issue, see Guiguo Wang, "Radiating Impact of WTO on Its Members' Legal System: The Chinese Perspective," *Collected Courses of The Hague Academy of International Law*, Vol. 349, Martinus Nijhoff Publishers, 2010, pp. 525–35.

award rendered may reflect such shortcomings, although not all of them may result in serious mistakes that require rectification.

The lack of the required knowledge, experience, and cultural understanding on the part of arbitrators is due to the current practice that arbitrators grow by themselves. To cope with this situation, it is submitted that education programs should be organized by arbitration institutions, such as the ICSID, which could be in the form of seminars, workshops, and even degree programs. Currently, conferences are held not infrequently, but they are mostly intended for the purposes of business promotion, and the exchange of experiences becomes secondary. The seminars, workshops or other programs suggested here should be aimed at educating the participants and sharing practical arbitration experiences, especially lessons learned. With continuous efforts in educating existing and future arbitrators, together with the possibility of introducing other alternatives discussed above, it can be hoped that international investment law will achieve its objectives.

Index